# Pride's Purge

# Pride's Purge

## Politics in the Puritan Revolution

DAVID UNDERDOWN

London
**GEORGE ALLEN & UNWIN**
Boston           Sydney

**George Allen & Unwin (Publishers) Ltd,
40 Museum Street, London WC1A 1LU, UK**

George Allen & Unwin (Publishers) Ltd,
Park Lane, Hemel Hempstead, Herts HP2 4TE, UK

Allen & Unwin, Inc.,
Fifty Cross Street, Winchester, Mass. 01890, USA

George Allen & Unwin Australia Pty Ltd,
8 Napier Street, North Sydney, NSW 2060, Australia


First published in 1971 by Oxford University Press.
First paperback edition, 1985.

---

**British Library Cataloguing in Publication Data**

Underdown, David
    Pride's Purge: politics in the Puritan Revolution.
1. Great Britain – Politics and government – 1642–1649
I. Title
942.06′2        DA415
ISBN 0-04-822045-0

---

**Library of Congress Cataloging in Publication Data**

Underdown, David.
    Pride's Purge.
Includes bibliographical references and index.
1. Great Britain – Politics and government – 1642–1649.
I. Title.
DA415.U5  1985       941.06′2       85-1218
ISBN 0-04-822045-0 (pbk.: alk. paper)

---

Printed in Great Britain by
The Blackmore Press, Shaftesbury, Dorset.

TO

MEBBA

# ACKNOWLEDGEMENTS

By the time his book is finished any author must be aware, if he was not already, that scholarship is a co-operative, not an individual or competitive undertaking. In the course of writing this book I have received countless favours from institutions, colleagues, and friends on both sides of the Atlantic, which can never be adequately acknowledged.

The book would not have been written without summer grants from the University of Virginia, Brown University, and the American Philosophical Society. The generosity of the John Simon Guggenheim Memorial Foundation made possible a year's respite from teaching, during which a large part of the research was undertaken. Owners of manuscripts have been unfailingly kind in giving access to their collections and permission to quote from them: I wish to thank the Duke of Northumberland, the Duke of Portland, the Marquess of Bath, Lt.-Col. John Chandos-Pole, and Major Ralph B. Verney. Librarians and archivists gave unsparingly of their time and professional knowledge: in Great Britain, the staffs of the British Museum, the Public Record Office, the House of Lords Record Office, the Institute of Historical Research, the Historical Manuscripts Commission, the Guildhall Library (London), the Bodleian Library, the John Rylands Library, Chetham's Library, the Birmingham Public Library, and the Essex and Somerset County Record Offices; in the United States, those of the Folger Library (Washington), and the university libraries of Brown, Harvard, Virginia, and Yale. The help of many individual scholars is acknowledged in later pages. Special thanks are due to Alan Everitt and J. T. Cliffe for patiently answering tedious questions about the counties for which they are the recognized authorities; to D. H. Pennington, Caroline Robbins, Violet Rowe, P. T. Underdown, and C. M. Williams for material on particular M.P.s; to B. Duke Henning for so generously providing information about Restoration M.P.s, and (with Thomas G. Barnes) for expanding an investigation of seventeenth-century J.P.s to include the Civil War period. At various stages of my work Nelson Baird and John Thelin were conscientious and uncomplaining research assistants.

Burr Litchfield, J. R. MacCormack, Valerie Pearl, and Blair Worden all read parts of the book in manuscript and made many helpful suggestions. I also wish to thank Mr. Worden for so freely making available to me the results of his work on the Rump and its members. My more general debts to these and other scholars will be evident in the pages that follow; the stimulus I have received from the work of J. H. Hexter, Christopher Hill, and H. R. Trevor-Roper cannot, however, pass without mention. How far I have mis-understood or misapplied their ideas, and how far I have profited from their immense contributions to seventeenth-century studies, the reader will be able to judge. The dedication of this book is an all too insufficient expression of my gratitude to one who has given far more towards its completion than she, or anyone but myself, can possibly realize.

*Providence, Rhode Island*
*June 1970*

## NOTES

Throughout this book quotations have been modernized for both spelling and punctuation.

Dates, except when otherwise stated, are old style, with the year regarded as beginning on January 1.

# CONTENTS

# ABBREVIATIONS

| | |
|---|---|
| *Agr. Hist. Rev.* | *Agricultural History Review.* |
| *Baillie* | David Laing, ed., *Letters and Journals of Robert Baillie* (Edinburgh, 1841–2). |
| *B.I.H.R.* | *Bulletin of the Institute of Historical Research.* |
| B.M. | British Museum (sometimes in square brackets = Brit. Mus. pressmark for a printed item). |
| Bodl. | Bodleian (Library, Oxford). |
| *Cal. C. Comp.* | M. A. E. Green, ed., *Calendar of the Proceedings of the Committee for Compounding* (London, 1889–92). |
| *Cal. S.P. Dom.* | *Calendar of State Papers, Domestic.* |
| *C.J.* | *Journals of the House of Commons.* |
| *D.N.B.* | *Dictionary of National Biography.* |
| *Econ. H.R.* | *Economic History Review.* |
| *E.H.R.* | *English Historical Review.* |
| Firth and Rait, *A. and O.* | C. H. Firth and R. S. Rait, eds., *Acts and Ordinances of the Interregnum* (London, 1911). |
| *H.L.Q.* | *Huntington Library Quarterly.* |
| H.M.C. | Historical Manuscripts Commission. |
| *Hutchinson* | C. H. Firth, ed., *Memoirs of the Life of Colonel Hutchinson . . . by his Widow, Lucy* (London, 1906). |
| *J.B.S.* | *Journal of British Studies.* |
| *Jour. Eccl. Hist.* | *Journal of Ecclesiastical History.* |
| *L.J.* | *Journals of the House of Lords.* |
| *Ludlow's Memoirs* | C. H. Firth, ed., *Memoirs of Edmund Ludlow* (Oxford, 1894). |
| *Merc. Elen.* | *Mercurius Elencticus.* |
| *Milit.* | *Militaris.* |
| *Prag.* | *Pragmaticus.* |
| *Milton State Papers* | John Nickolls, ed., *Original Letters and Papers of State . . . among the Political Collections of Mr. John Milton* (London, 1743). |
| *N. & Q.* | *Notes and Queries.* |
| *Old Parl. Hist.* | *The Parliamentary or Constitutional History of England*, 2nd edn. (London, 1761–3). |
| P.R.O. | Public Record Office. |
| *Rel. Baxt.* | Matthew Sylvester, ed., *Reliquiae Baxterianae* (London, 1696). |
| R.O. | Record Office. |
| R.S. | Record Society. |
| S.P. | State Papers. |
| *Thurloe's S.P.* | Thomas Birch, ed., *Collection of the State Papers of John Thurloe* (London, 1742). |
| *T.R.H.S.* | *Transactions of the Royal Historical Society.* |
| *V.C.H.* | *Victoria County History.* |

# PREFACE

Reappraisal of the politics of the English Revolution has continued apace since this book was published in 1971. The book's principal focus is of course on the period 1647–49. The years immediately preceding these have now been closely examined in Mark Kishlansky's *The Rise of the New Model Army* (1979), the years immediately following in Blair Worden's *The Rump Parliament* (1974), with Austin Woolrych's *Commonwealth to Protectorate* (1982) providing a valuable continuation on the Barebones Parliament. Other aspects of Interregnum politics have also received attention and two in particular have been strikingly illuminated. Our understanding of the revolution's radical 'left' has been transformed as a result of several books by Christopher Hill, notably *The World Turned Upside Down* (1972); that of provincial localism by John Morrill's *The Revolt of the Provinces* (1976) and by a stream of important county studies by Morrill, Anthony Fletcher, Clive Holmes, and several more.

If these and other valuable recent works on the period had been available when *Pride's Purge* was being written, it would undoubtedly have been a better book. But to take full account of them would certainly require the writing of a completely different one, reflecting the enhanced understanding of the revolution that the insights of these historians have made possible. That task being beyond my present abilities, the only changes made in this edition involve the correction of a small number of misprints and obviously erroneous statements. In any case, the basic conception of politics in the later 1640s that I present in the book does not, in my view, require substantial revision. I still stand by my interpretation of the complex interaction between the parliamentary factions, the Army, London, and both radicals and conservatives in the provincial communities. I am still persuaded that the split between the 'middle group' (or whatever else we choose to call that amorphous entity) and the 'Independents' was a crucial element in the realignment that made possible both the Purge and the execution of Charles I. And I still believe that the almost immediate admission of so many conformist moderates to the Rump was a major reason for the Commonwealth's subsequent failure to implement the goals of the more committed revolutionaries.

A few words should perhaps be said, however, about the various categories I used in classifying supporters and opponents of the Purge (see below, Chapter VIII). In the course of some generously constructive comments on my employment of these categories, Dr. Worden suggests that my definition of 'revolutionary' is probably too broad, leading to the inclusion of some M.P.s whose outlook was little different from that of the 'conformists'. I suspect that he is right, yet I can still see no satisfactory alternative to the objective criteria – regicide or early dissent from the 4 December vote – that I have used to establish the former category. Anything else would require a series of subjective decisions about often little-known individuals, a procedure that undermined some earlier attempts at such analysis.

More recently, in a painstaking analysis of the proceedings of the High Court of Justice ('The Numbers of the English Regicides', *History*, lxvii, 1982, pp. 195–216), A. W. McIntosh has pointed out that the conventional definition of 'regicide', which I like most other historians adopted, is too narrow. Besides the fifty-nine (forty-three of them M.P.s) who signed the warrant for the King's execution, another ten (seven of them M.P.s) were present at the reading of the sentence, signified their assent by standing, and just as much as the signers, were regarded as regicides both then and in 1660. Although I am not fully convinced that the ten failed to sign only as a result of accident or forgetfulness, the rest of McIntosh's argument is persuasive, and I accept that there were indeed sixty-nine, not fifty-nine regicides. However, of the seven new M.P. regicides thus provided, six are already classed as revolutionaries in this book on other evidence – and 'revolutionary' is the operative category for the purpose of analyzing Pride's Purge. The one exception is William Heveningham, classed below as a 'conformist' but who on the basis of this (and other evidence in Dr. Worden's book) I should now regard as a revolutionary if I was revising the statistics.

I am grateful to countless students and colleagues – some of them named in this Preface, but there are many others – for their friendly comments on and criticisms of this book, both in conversation and in print. Even more than in 1971 I am impressed by how much historical scholarship is a collaborative as well as an individual enterprise; one of its greatest rewards is the creative stimulus that an author receives from this dialogue. I hope that this reissue of *Pride's Purge* will contribute to the continuing discussion and reinterpretation, by students and specialists alike, of the politics of the English Revolution.

*Providence, Rhode Island*
*November 1984*

# Pride's Purge

# INTRODUCTION

PRIDE'S PURGE is one of those venerable historical incidents known, as the old phrase has it, to every schoolboy. At the end of the Civil War, according to the familiar version, the victorious Parliamentarians split, as successful revolutionary movements are notoriously liable to do, into their moderate and extremist wings. The moderates, or Presbyterians, vainly tried to halt the revolution in midcourse by an abortive compromise with King Charles I. They thus incurred the wrath of the extremists, the Independents, who were determined to destroy both monarch and monarchy. To achieve their aims the Independents, with the Army behind them, had to expel their enemies from the seat of power, the House of Commons. And so on 6 December 1648 Colonel Thomas Pride, commanding a strong force of soldiers, stood outside the House and arrested or turned away the majority of the members (Presbyterians) trying to get in. The purged Parliament, or Rump, composed solely of a hand-ful of revolutionary Independents, could now proceed with the execution of the King, the abolition of the monarchy and House of Lords, and the establishment of a Puritan Commonwealth.[1]

On the surface, Pride's Purge looks satisfyingly straightforward. But the simplicity, as so often proves to be the case in history, is deceptive. When subjected to closer examination, the Purge be-comes an event that is both more complex in itself and more sur-rounded by interesting historical questions than the proverbial schoolboy would suppose. The traditional account of the Purge's antecedents has already been fatally undermined. It used to be thought that the conflict of Independents and Presbyterians was foreshadowed during the war by a similar, and related, division in Parliament into a war party and a peace party. That the political divisions of the Long Parliament were too complicated to be explained by such a simple dualism was first clearly shown by J. H. Hexter, who discovered that in 1643 there was a third faction, the 'middle group' headed by the great John Pym, standing between the parties on the two extremes. Hexter also drew attention to the

---

[1] For a convenient summary of the old orthodoxy see J. H. Hexter, *Reappraisals in History* (London, 1961), pp. 163-4.

bewildering absence of correlation between the terms 'Presbyterian' and 'Independent' and the actual religious positions of the members of each group, and coined the term 'Presbyterian Independents' to account for some of those responsible for this confusion.[2]

Since Hexter's pioneering efforts, historians have become accustomed to the idea that there was in the seventeenth century no such thing as a two-party system. Parties, it is clear, were at best vague, ephemeral, and transitory, loose associations of individuals or groups who might temporarily co-operate on some of the major issues of the day, but might equally well be divided quite differently on others. Mary Frear Keeler, David Brunton, and Donald Pennington have analysed the membership of the Commons in a way that owes more to the structural analysis of Sir Lewis Namier than to the classical Whig narrative of S. R. Gardiner and G. M. Trevelyan. Valerie Pearl has established that the middle group did not die with Pym, but survived into the post-war years. Alan Everitt has shown that national party lines bore little resemblance to the political divisions and conflicts within a county community, even one as close to Westminster as Kent.[3]

In certain respects, of course, the old historical structure still stands. Colonel Pride did purge Parliament, the King was executed, the Commonwealth was established. However much sophisticated modern scholars may blur its outlines, there was a revolution in England, and the events of December 1648 and January 1649 mark its greatest climax. But it is now possible to rewrite the history of that revolution in the light of the changes in historical thinking just described. Such an attempt is the main purpose of this book. It will be found that at the level of national politics Pride's Purge was not the straightforward outcome of the familiar party division of Presbyterians and Independents. Nor can the revolution be understood exclusively, or even mainly, in terms of parliamentary politics. To grasp its meaning it is necessary to explore the relationship between politics at the national and the grass-roots levels, between

---

[2] J. H. Hexter, *The Reign of King Pym* (Cambridge, Mass., 1941); Hexter, 'The Problem of the Presbyterian Independents', *Amer. Hist. Rev.* xliv (1938-9), 29-49, reprinted in *Reappraisals*, pp. 163-84.

[3] Mary F. Keeler, *The Long Parliament, 1640-1641* (American Phil. Soc. Memoirs, xxxvi, Philadelphia, 1954); D. Brunton and D. H. Pennington, *Members of the Long Parliament* (London, 1954); Valerie Pearl, 'Oliver St. John and the "middle group" in the Long Parliament', *E.H.R.* lxxxi (1966), 490-519, and 'The "Royal Independents" in the English Civil War', *T.R.H.S.* 5th Ser. xviii (1968), 69-96; Alan Everitt, *The Community of Kent and the Great Rebellion* (Leicester, 1966).

the revolution at Westminster and the revolution in the counties and boroughs, and between the State and the local communities.

The revolution we are talking about was a political revolution; but it is also, for good reasons, familiar to us as the Puritan Revolution. Most of the articulate Englishmen of the governing class, members of the 'political nation', who supported Parliament in the Civil War, were indeed Puritans of one sort or another. But they were rarely either simply Puritans or simply politicians; they were both. There was, in other words, a fundamental dualism in the parliamentarian cause. Most of its adherents were at one and the same time Puritan idealists (and thus, if carried away by enthusiasm, potential revolutionaries),[4] and practical conservatives, who saw the war merely as a means of redressing certain constitutional grievances. Many of the leading Independents in Parliament shared the same political assumptions as the Presbyterians (to adopt the familiar terminology). Far from being the architects of a revolution, these 'middle group' Independents strove desperately to avert one, and the survival of the Independent party, hazy and indefinite as it may have been, was indeed the best guarantee that revolution would not occur.[5] The revolution, we shall find, became inevitable only when the Independents split, and the party collapsed, in the spring and summer of 1648.

The behaviour of the conservatives in Parliament in 1648, whether Presbyterians or middle-group Independents, reflected the pressure to which they were subjected from outside; the desperate demands from the City of London, from the counties, for peace, settlement, and a return to the old ways. This desperation was all the greater because the war had unleashed the 'many-headed multitude', had released forces that threatened the very survival of the comfortable, gentry-dominated social order. For even if the Independents were not collectively revolutionary, there was a revolutionary minority in Parliament, and an equally determined minority in the Army, in the towns, and in the countryside, which saw the crisis of 1648 as the dawn of a new day, the great climactic struggle for the New Jerusalem. Many would define this new order in religious terms, as the completion of the Godly

---

[4] For a stimulating recent discussion of the revolutionary implications of Puritanism see Michael Walzer, *The Revolution of the Saints* (Cambridge, Mass., 1965), see esp. pp. 262–3 for this point.

[5] For the aims of the 'middle-group' Independents see the two articles by Valerie Pearl cited above, n. 3.

Reformation, the rule of the Saints; some more realistically as the establishment of a freer, more equitable political order. The relationship between the revolutionaries in Parliament and in the nation at large will be another of the major themes of this book.

In view of the limitations of the surviving historical evidence, however, much of our attention will necessarily be directed to the revolutionaries in Parliament. As a group they have never been clearly identified. One reason for this is that historians have assumed that the Independent party survived down to Pride's Purge and even afterwards, that this party was responsible for the revolution, and that all members of the Rump were by definition Independents: all, as we shall see, false assumptions. These alleged Independents have been examined, but without any serious effort to distinguish between Rumpers who were committed supporters of the revolution and those who merely climbed on the band-wagon after the event. No serious effort has been made to isolate and analyse the revolutionaries as a group, either before or after Pride's Purge. The historians who have given the matter the closest attention have therefore been able to conclude that the Independents, or Rumpers (the terms being for them almost interchangeable) were virtually indistinguishable in social composition from the Parliamentarians as a whole, thus throwing doubt upon the hypothesis that there may have been social causes behind the revolution.[6] If the real revolutionaries are isolated, however (and an attempt to do so is made in this book), it will be found that there were in fact some significant differences between them and the more conservative majority. For óne thing, many of them display a fiercer, more intense Puritan zeal, though not necessarily of the Independent or sectarian variety. But the revolutionaries also seem to have been drawn in a marked degree from families which were insecure ('declining gentry', in a famous phrase), or from outside the traditional political establishment (*nouveaux riches*, lesser gentry, families of obscure and usually urban origins). Whether this discovery makes it plausible to argue that their revolutionary behaviour

---

[6] This remains my chief criticism of George Yule, *The Independents in the English Civil War* (Cambridge, 1958), and of Brunton and Pennington, *Long Parliament*, ch. iii ('The Rump'). Brunton and Pennington, to be sure, recognize that 'the proportion of old parliamentary families' in the House was reduced by the Purge (p. 52). But the main thrust of their argument is to stress the similarities between Rumpers and other M.P.s. For discussion of this and related points see David Underdown, 'The Independents Reconsidered', *J.B.S.* iii (1964), 57–84; Yule, 'Independents and Revolutionaries', ibid. vii (1968), 11–32; and Underdown, 'The Independents Again', ibid. viii (1968), 83–93.

represented the typical aspirations of the groups from which they were drawn is another question that will be discussed in this book.

There was, then, a revolution in 1648-9. But perhaps it was not a real revolution, just a *coup d'état*? It is certainly true that once in power the revolutionaries were oddly half-hearted about implementing the rest of their programme. It is as though the Jacobins in the French Revolution, having ousted the Girondins and set up the Committee of Public Safety, immediately begin to display the caution of the Thermidorian reaction—without an intervening Thermidor. The explanation of this paradox lies in the nature of Pride's Purge and the events that immediately followed it. Revolutionaries they may have been, but the men of December 1648 still retained strong vestiges of their constitutional past. They were held back by some of their leaders (Oliver Cromwell, for example) who were not revolutionaries by conviction, and therefore repeatedly hesitated and faltered. Furthermore, all but the most thorough-going of them wished to mask the brutal reality that their regime rested ultimately on the sword, wished to broaden the base of their support, and to regain some shreds of constitutional legitimacy. As soon therefore as the crucial step had been taken and the King was dead, they made it as easy as possible for all those who were not their open, irreconcilable opponents to return to the fold and take their seats in the Rump and the other institutions of government. Having admitted the moderates, the extremists were hedged in by them. They still had their programme: a Church settlement (disestablishment, abolition of tithes); a constitutional settlement (parliamentary reform, redistribution, law reform); but the moderates were able to sidetrack or talk them to death. To achieve the reaction a Thermidor was unnecessary; the revolutionaries engineered it themselves by their tactics in the late winter and spring of 1649.

It would be both tempting and easy to push the familiar French parallel still further. But this book does not purport to be a complete history of the Interregnum. Its purpose is more limited: to return to the immediate subject of the Purge, to explore in detail the set of historical circumstances that provoked it, and to suggest some of the consequences that stemmed from its peculiar nature. This brief outline of a few of the problems involved may be enough to suggest that the exercise is worth while. With Pride's Purge, as with so many apparently simple and familiar phenomena, it is unwise to stop short at the remembrance of what every schoolboy knows.

B

# *Part One · Prologue*

## I

## PURITANISM AND REFORMATION

WHEN Colonel Thomas Pride stood at the top of the stairs leading to the House of Commons on that December morning in 1648, he was directing the first scene of a revolution which within a few weeks turned England into a republic. He was also, in the rough and unreflective way typical of the military man, providing his answer to the question of what the civil wars of the previous half-dozen years had been about. The parliamentarian party which had gone to war against the King in 1642 was in essence a coalition, and, like most coalitions, one united less by positive than by negative aims. It was united by dislike of the Crown's allegedly arbitrary, illegal government and violations of 'Liberty and Property', of the court's extravagance and frivolity, of Arminian innovation in the Church, and of a vaguely sensed yet passionately feared popish design to destroy English religious and political independence. But on positive aims there was disagreement, dispute that was bound to fracture the victorious coalition when the war was won. Broadly, and with much oversimplification, two general positions can be observed. That of the majority of the parliamentarian gentry was that the war was fought for limited goals, mainly political and constitutional, but also including a further moderate reformation of the Church, leaving the essential framework of government and society intact. That of the minority for whom Pride was the obedient agent was that it was fought for a total and complete reconstruction of Church and State, in the interests of 'Godly Reformation' and (for some) social justice, to achieve which all measures, even revolution, were justified.

The presence of these two contradictory elements, one moderate and reformist, the other radical and revolutionary, accounts for most of our difficulties when we try to grasp the central meaning of the Puritan Revolution. Few of its original leaders were revolutionaries; some, like the witty, erratic Henry Marten, with his mistresses and his cheerful spells in a debtors' prison, were not even Puritans. But Marten and his amusing friends were, of course, the exceptions. Most of the active Parliamentarians *were* Puritans—religious idealists who strained towards the Godly Reformation that had been so nearly accomplished in the reign of the much admired (often for reasons that would have horrified her) Queen Elizabeth. Many had grown to manhood in the 1620s—that bitter decade whose haunting impact on the young men who lived through it resembles the 30s of our own century—nursing still their memories of the years in which England stood humiliatingly aside through the blunders and ill will of its kings and statesmen, while good and evil, Christ and Antichrist, Geneva and Rome, were ranged against each other in the great climactic struggle of the Thirty Years War.[1] They were Puritans with one half of their minds. But with the other they were also conservative country gentlemen, conditioned by the old-boy network of the Universities and the Inns of Court, reverencing Parliament, the Common Law and its new bible, Coke's *Institutes*, and firmly attached to that stable system of interlocking hierarchies of which they themselves formed the summit. The two elements are present in varying proportions in most of the parliamentarian leaders. In some, for example the almost 'Jacobin' revolutionary Henry Ireton, who married Cromwell's daughter and helped to direct the revolution, one element, the Puritan idealist, is usually uppermost. In some, as in the pedantic, conservative antiquarian Sir Simonds D'Ewes—D'Ewes who during the war opposed the fortification of a town threatened by royalist troops because it would be illegal[2]—it is the other. Yet again the two conflicting forces may produce the baffling contradictions and hesitations of an Oliver Cromwell. In all of them the precise line of action taken at any given time was the resultant between these underlying forces, as individual temperament was acted upon by changing circumstances—by the war, by the danger from the King or the

---

[1] The 'generation of the 1620s' is admirably described by Hugh Trevor-Roper, *Religion, the Reformation and Social Change* (London, 1967), pp. 246-7.

[2] Hexter, *Reign of King Pym*, p. 8.

Scots, by the fear or hope of social and political revolution threatening from the Army rank-and-file, the emerging democratic Levellers, or the more extreme Puritan sects like the Baptists and Fifth Monarchy Men.

Looking back, people usually agreed that the Civil War was not originally fought over doctrine. 'Religion', said Oliver Cromwell in an often-quoted phrase, 'was not the thing at first contested for.' For many the war was essentially defensive, against the aggressive designs of the King's malignant councillors. 'It was not for a service-book, or for abolishing episcopacy, this war was made', thought Nathaniel Fiennes, as fervent a Puritan as any, '. . . it was indeed a war made to destroy the Parliament of England.'[3] John Lambert was unable to decide 'whether the militia, negative voice, or delinquency, were the first occasion of the quarrel'. But no matter which, he argued, it arose from 'all the united prerogatives and exorbitances of an old monarchy, and the defence of the people to reduce it to its just limits'. [4] When that stout republican Edmund Ludlow argued with Cromwell before the Protector's Council in 1656 he had fewer doubts about the real origins of the struggle. 'What is it that you would have?' Cromwell asked him in exasperation, '. . . What can you desire more than you have?' Ludlow had no difficulty in telling him: 'That which we fought for, . . . that the nation might be governed by its own consent.'[5] For all these men, of varying points of view, the immediate cause of the war was the dispute over the King's militia powers, its most important goal the limitation of monarchical prerogative.

'Religion was not the thing at first contested for'; yet Cromwell added his well-known sequel: 'but God brought it to that issue at last.' We cannot leave Puritanism out of the Puritan Revolution. It was a seventeenth-century commonplace that religion and politics were ultimately inseparable. 'Every prayer is a stratagem, most sermons mere plots against the state', a Commonwealth journalist remarked. The point was sadly familiar to Charles I. 'If the pulpits teach not obedience . . . the king will have

[3] [Nathaniel Fiennes], *Vindiciae Veritatis, Or an Answer to a Discourse intituled, Truth it's Manifest* (1654: B.M. pressmark E. 811, 2), p. 33. The authorship of the pamphlet is discussed by Pearl, *T.R.H.S.* 5th Ser. xviii (1968), 93 n., with the suggestion that Lord Say may have collaborated with his son.

[4] Speech, 9 Feb. 1659: J. T. Rutt, ed., *Diary of Thomas Burton, Esq.* (London, 1828), iii. 186.

[5] *Ludlow's Memoirs*, ii. 11. Cf. his answers to Harrison, ibid., pp. 7-8.

but small comfort of the militia', he told the Queen in 1646.[6] Forms
of government and society had their natural equivalents in Church
polity: 'No Bishop, no King', his own father had said. It was an
exaggeration, for many who voted down bishops had no thought
of voting down monarchy, resisted doing so in 1648 at the price of
their own political destruction, and welcomed it back with outward
enthusiasm in 1660. Yet the general point still stands, especially
when applied to the more radical Puritan sects. 'They seek to shake
off all obedience to lawful authority', a royalist divine warned his
flock of the Anabaptists in 1642.[7] For those few who denied the
rarely questioned belief in a universal Church coexistent with
society, religion was a matter of choice, a choice symbolized by the
baptism of adults who could make up their own minds, rather than
of infants automatically received into a universal Church to which
all by definition belonged. And if men could choose in so supremely
important a matter as salvation, in what could they not choose?
The majority of 'Church-type' Puritans had no thought of pursuing
such dangerous, subversive doctrine—but even for them Puritanism
meant active commitment, the fulfilment of the priesthood of all
believers, the duty of the elect minority, the Saints in the Puritan
sense of the word, to change the world in the name of Godly
Reformation. To this extent, then, the Parliamentarians were something new: a party committed to change by political as well as
religious activism.[8] Even the moderates like Sir William Waller
and D'Ewes, who preferred limited episcopacy or a tightly disciplined presbytery, therefore shared in the heady excitement of 1640
and 1641 when the 'Revolution of the Saints' seemed just round
the corner.

Although Puritans were to be found among all sorts and conditions of men, the appeal of their ideas was stronger in the middle
ranks of society than at either end. Ever since its birth in the dissatisfaction of a righteously Protestant minority at the politic com-
promises of the Elizabethan Settlement, the Puritan movement had
depended heavily on two groups of lay supporters: a minority of
the nobility and gentry, and a much larger number (important

[6] Marchamont Nedham, *Case of the Commonwealth of England Stated* (1650: [B.M.] E.
600, 7), p. 63. Charles I to Henrietta Maria, 30 Nov. 1646: John Bruce, ed., *Charles I in
1646* (Camden Soc. lxiii, 1856), p. 79.

[7] Bruno Ryves, in Zachary Grey, *Impartial Examination of the Third Volume of Mr.
Daniel Neal's History of the Puritans* (London, 1737), App., p. 13.

[8] See Walzer, *Revolution of the Saints*, esp. ch. vii.

collectively rather than as individuals) of what seventeenth-century Englishmen often called 'the middling sort of people', especially in London and in the clothing towns and villages.[9] We need not question the sincerity of their leaders' Puritan convictions, but as members of a governing class they were inevitably more open to the restraining force of constitutionalism than their less exalted followers. For these inferiors, especially as the enthusiasm generated by conflict began to take hold, it was another story. Richard Baxter conceded that 'the public safety and liberty wrought very much with most, especially with the nobility and gentry', but rightly observed that it was 'principally the differences about religious matters that filled up the Parliament's armies, and put the resolution and valour into their soldiers'. Most of the peers and gentry, he notes, were for the King, except in the Home Counties and East Anglia, where Charles I and his forces never penetrated: 'And could he have got footing there, it's like that it would have been there as it was in other places.' Parliament's support, on the other hand, came from 'the smaller part (as some thought) of the gentry in most of the counties, and the greatest part of the tradesmen and freeholders, and the middle sort of men; especially in those corporations and counties which depend on clothing and such manufactures'.[10]

Baxter was not the only one to observe a connection between the 'middle sort' and the Puritan-parliamentarian cause. His point about the clothworkers was a familiar commonplace, and had been noted in the previous century by Lord Burghley, who thought them much less willing 'to be quietly governed than the husbandmen'. People in the clothing districts, an anonymous writer noted in 1648, 'being poor and populous are naturally mutinous and bold, . . . so that the clothiers through the whole kingdom were rebels by their trade'.[11] Baxter's contemporaries were unanimously of the opinion that, taking the nation as a whole, there were social differences between the two sides. They do not say that the war was fought between a feudal aristocracy and a bourgeoisie, between backward

[9] Patrick Collinson, *The Elizabethan Puritan Movement* (London, 1967), pp. 22, 50-4, 77, 84-8; Christopher Hill, *Society and Puritanism in Pre-Revolutionary England* (London, 1964), esp. pp. 133-5.

[10] *Rel. Baxt.* i. 30-1. See also ibid., p. 18. Baxter advances some intelligent reasons for the division, though in the end he begs the question.

[11] H.M.C., *Twelfth Report*, App. IX (Beaufort MSS.), p. 23. Burghley is quoted in F. J. Fisher, 'Commercial Trends and Policy in Sixteenth-Century England', *Econ. H.R.* x (1940), 111.

conservative landlords and improving capitalist ones, between aristocracy and gentry, between gentry and yeomanry, or between any such convenient sets of abstractions. But they do say, which accords with the observable facts of the situation, that the majority of the gentry and aristocracy, with their dependants among the lower ranks of society, tended to be for the King, and that Parliament's strength rested on its appeal to the 'middle sort', the craftsmen and small merchants in the towns, the yeomanry and substantial freeholders in the countryside, led by a minority of the aristocracy and gentry, in proportions varying according to local circumstance. The Royalists Clarendon and Sir Philip Warwick agree that over most of the country the larger towns, especially the ports, were parliamentarian, the rural areas under gentry control, including the smaller inland towns, royalist. In Nottinghamshire, according to Lucy Hutchinson, 'all the nobility and gentry, and their dependants, were generally for the king'.[12] John Corbet, chaplain to the Gloucester garrison, notes how in his county 'some gleanings of the gentry' took up arms for Parliament, but for the most part 'the yeomen, farmers, clothiers, and the whole middle rank of the people were the only active men'. There were three reasons for this, Corbet thought: Puritanism first of all, certainly; secondly the dislike of royal financial and economic policy by 'a generation of men truly laborious, jealous of their properties, whose principal aim is liberty and plenty'; and thirdly the tendency of the craftsman to ask questions, to apply the lessons of his technical education, to form his own conclusions by the light of his own natural reason. 'Thus we have found', Corbet continues, 'that the common people addicted to the King's service have come out of blind Wales, and other dark corners of the land; but the more knowing are apt to contradict and question.'[13] Enlightened Londoners had a significant contempt for submissive rustic provincials. In an anonymous pamphlet of 1648 one of them put it even more plainly than Corbet, in the course of an attack on a royalist judge's absolutist theories:

[12] Edward, Earl of Clarendon, *History of the Rebellion*, ed. W. Dunn Macray (Oxford, 1888), Bk. V, § 385; Bk. VI, §§ 261, 271; see also Christopher Hill, *Puritanism and Revolution* (London, 1958), pp. 204-6 for further refs. Sir Philip Warwick, *Memoirs of the Reign of King Charles I* (Edinburgh, 1813), pp. 239-40. *Hutchinson*, pp. 92-4.

[13] John Corbet, *A True and Impartial History of the Military Government of the City of Gloucester*, in Sir W. Scott, ed., *A Collection of Scarce and Valuable Tracts . . . Selected from . . . Libraries; particularly that of the late Lord Somers*, 2nd edn. (London, 1809-15), v. 303-4, 307. Cf. also *Vindication of Richard Atkyns*, in Peter Young and Norman Tucker, eds., *Military Memoirs: The Civil War* (London, 1967), p. 7.

'Well might he preach these doctrines to his simple countrymen of Wales, bred in the mountains, . . . whose understandings were never burdened with the weight of an argument of the principles of nature, justice and reason; . . . but alas, the sun is too much up in England, especially in London, that we should be caught with such silly and chaffy notions as these.'[14]

Baxter, Corbet, and their like were realistic enough to know that they were an embattled minority, and all the more determined for that. Below the 'middling sort', the great mass of the peasants and the urban poor were scarcely touched by the great issues of either politics or religion. 'The poor ploughmen understood but little of these matters', Baxter complains, though he also notes that it took little to 'stir up their discontent when money was demanded'.[15] Another Puritan minister, Ralph Josselin in Essex, wept over the apathy of his flock, their unseemly preference for wrestling-matches over Parliament's officially proclaimed days of fasting and humiliation, their stinginess when called on to contribute to their defending armies, or even, worst of all, to Josselin's own mainten-ance.[16] In the 'dark corners of the land', in the still half-feudal North, in Wales and the Welsh Border counties—Herefordshire was described by its leading Puritan, Sir Robert Harley, as 'the most clownish county of England'[17]—and in far-off Cornwall, tenants did as they were told and obediently followed their land-lords in support of Church and King, with never a thought of Godly Reformation. Baxter's strongest recollection of his youth was of how his very moderate father, who 'never scrupled Common-Prayer or ceremonies, nor spake against bishops', was made 'the derision of the vulgar rabble, under the odious name of a Puritan'.[18]

But although the 'vulgar rabble' might be unregenerate, there were enough who were not so, among the middling sort, to give the servants of Parliament their joyful zest for doing the Lord's work. Yeomen and craftsmen, inspired by the cumulative effects of being for generations a people apart, persecuted yet elect of God, charged

[14] *Salus Populi Solus Rex* (17 Oct. 1648: [B.M.] E. 467, 39), p. 12. Cf. also Christopher Hill, *Intellectual Origins of the English Revolution* (Oxford, 1965), esp. pp. 65-9.

[15] *Rel. Baxt.* i. 17.

[16] E. Hockliffe, ed., *Diary of the Rev. Ralph Josselin, 1616-1683* (Camden Soc., 3rd Ser. xv, 1908), pp. 19-20, 22, 32, 56-7.

[17] Keeler, *Long Parliament*, p. 50. Cf. also Wallace Notestein, *English Folk* (London, 1938), pp. 288-93.

[18] *Rel. Baxt.* i. 2-3.

with the duty of the Saints to change for the better a world dominated by the reprobate majority—these were the men who ran Parliament's local administration, weeding out untrustworthy clergy and officials, extorting men, money, and materials from an often sullen, recalcitrant, neutralist population. With Star Chamber censorship removed, repressive bishops and ecclesiastical courts abolished, preaching ministers no longer silenced, it is not surprising that intoxicating millenarian dreams affected many who might a few years earlier have thought of taking refuge in New England. 'This hath been a heavenly day', exulted one sober citizen from Northampton after hearing Stephen Marshall and Cornelius Burges preach the opening sermons to the Long Parliament in November 1640, hearing them deliver 'glorious things with extraordinary zeal and fervour'.[19]

Even more important, as Baxter says, it was this spirit that 'filled up the Parliament's armies', especially after the reorganization of the winter of 1644-5 which produced the New Model Army, and got rid of cautious aristocratic generals like the Earls of Essex and Manchester. As sectarian enthusiasm spread in its ranks, the Army became a meeting-place for common men of like opinions, a forum hitherto denied to all but the governing class. It could produce preaching captains and colonels, could inspire an unlettered tinker to dream of holy war and Armageddon, of a pilgrim's journey to the Eternal City, and to enter pulpits hitherto denied to all but the educated and the ordained. There were the Army chaplains like John Saltmarsh, Thomas Collier, and the great Hugh Peter to inspire their men to fervent belief in the righteousness of their crusade, to encourage and formulate their half-articulate desires for political and social as well as religious reformation.[20] The war itself was a great inspirational experience, furnishing the blood of countless martyrs to the cause, the necessary fertilization of the seeds of the Church. So it was for the men of Puritan Taunton, sustaining themselves through heroic siege during the long winter of 1644-5, and acquiring the reputation that gave their town for years afterwards the spirit of an English La Rochelle.[21] It was all very

[19] H.M.C., *Ninth Report*, App. II (Pyne-Woodforde MSS.), p. 409. See also S. R. Gardiner, *History of England . . . 1603-1642* (London, 1883-4), ix. 237.

[20] Leo F. Solt, *Saints in Arms* (Stanford, Calif., 1959), pp. 9-21, 90 ff.

[21] The Army chaplains contributed to the spread of Puritan fervour in the regions in which they served. Thomas Collier, for example, helped to establish Baptist congregations in the Taunton area: Thomas Edwards, *Gangraena*, Pt. III (Dec. 1646: [B.M.] E. 368, 5), pp. 41, 52-3. See also G. F. Nuttall, 'The Baptist Western Association 1653-1658', *Journ. Eccl. Hist.* xi (1960), 213-18.

disturbing to men like Baxter, who rejected 'Church democracy' as well as its inevitable accompaniment, 'State democracy'; or his neighbour Thomas Hall at King's Norton, who wanted the nailer to 'keep to his hammer, the husbandman his plough', and argued that 'God hath set every calling its bounds. . . . Superiors must govern; inferiors obey and be governed; ministers must study and preach; people must hear and obey.'[22] But for those less hidebound by convention it was the intoxicating dawn of a new and better day, in which neither the King nor Parliament itself could stand against the Saints' duty to press on towards the New Jerusalem. Nothing better expresses the exultation, the expectancy, than Baxter's picture of Captain Thomas Harrison, the former lawyer's clerk who was the son of no one more eminent than a prosperous Midland butcher, gazing at the fleeing Cavaliers through the dust of a blazing July day at Langport in 1645. As the royalist line broke, Baxter, standing near by, heard him 'with a loud voice break forth into the praises of God with fluent expressions, as if he had been in a rapture'.[23]

\* \* \*

Harrison's brand of heady millenarian excitement was far less common in Parliament than in the Army. For most of the nation's governors, as Baxter reminds us, legal and constitutional issues came first. Furthermore, though seventeenth-century M.P.s might be inspired by the moral earnestness of Calvinism, they were also human beings. As the dour Scots emissary Robert Baillie noted, there were plenty of 'worldly profane men' in Parliament[24]— though Baillie was inclined to label as worldly and profane anyone who disagreed with him, especially if they put Erastianism above Kirk theocracy. The overwhelming majority of the members who remained at Westminster after 1642 were Puritans in the broad, undifferentiated moral sense used by Baxter.[25] They took religion seriously, disliked sabbath-breaking, stage plays, church-ales, and long hair, wished to purge the Church of England of the 'popish' innovations introduced by the Arminians, and to have no more of episcopacy as practised in the 1630s. They were not necessarily opposed to bishops in principle—staunch Puritans like John Crewe,

[22] *Rel. Baxt.* i. 50-1, 53; Thomas Hall, *The Pulpit Guarded with XVII Arguments* (1651: [B.M.] E. 628, 4), p. 23.

[23] *Rel. Baxt.* i. 54.

[24] *Baillie*, ii. 336.

[25] Hexter, *Reappraisals*, p. 177; Yule, *The Independents*, pp. 32-3.

Sir Simonds D'Ewes, and William Prynne would all have preferred primitive episcopacy—but by 1643 the case for episcopacy had gone by default, for the choice was between Laudian bishops and none at all.[26] The question of what form of Church polity would replace it could safely be postponed, as Pym, correctly foreseeing the divisive nature of the issue, long succeeded in doing. There is a certain appropriateness in the fact that the first ordinance on a religious matter passed by Parliament after the outbreak of war dealt not with one of the larger issues of polity or doctrine, but with the prohibition of Prynne's pet aversion, stage plays.[27] The final abolition of episcopacy, and the settlement that would replace it, were not yet matters of urgency.

But the Long Parliament was in the end divided by the religious dispute of Presbyterians and Independents. Although argument had long raged in the Assembly (seventeenth-century clergy thrived on controversy), it was not until 1645 and 1646 that the question of the Church settlement came to dominate proceedings in Parliament. When this occurred, the adoption of the Directory to replace the Book of Common Prayer, the establishment of a system of classical presbyteries, new laws for the ordination of ministers, the suppression of heresy and blasphemy, and for excommunication procedures, all raised crucial issues that were political as well as religious. Both of the main groups, however, included men of widely varying opinions. There were Presbyterians by conviction, men like Edmund Prideaux, who argued for a thoroughgoing Scottish system, giving ministers and elders full powers of excommunication;[28] and there were Presbyterians by adoption, like D'Ewes and the others who would have preferred primitive episcopacy. There were tolerant Erastians like Selden, and intolerant ones like Prynne, united only in bitterly denouncing the *jure divino* claims of the Presbyterian ministers, as once they had the similar doctrines of Laudian bishops.[29] There were vindictively intolerant Presbyterians, like Sir Samuel Luke, rigorously suppressing sectaries in his garrison of Newport Pagnell, accusing them of practising free love and the destruction of 'Magistracy or

---

[26] For the religious preferences of these three see Pearl, *T.R.H.S.* 5th Ser. xviii (1968), 84; Yule, *The Independents*, p. 32; and William M. Lamont, *Marginal Prynne, 1600-1669* (London, 1963), pp. 15-21, 41, 58-63.

[27] S. R. Gardiner, *History of the Great Civil War* (London, 1886-91), i. 17.

[28] B.M. Harl. MS. 166 (D'Ewes Journal), fol. 204. See also *Baillie*, ii. 237.

[29] See Lamont, *Prynne*, ch. vii, esp. p. 165.

government', and fearing the imminent arrival of Sodom and Gomorrah, if he was not allowed to 'free the town of them'.[30] There were tolerant Presbyterians like Sir John Holland, married to a Roman Catholic (he prudently kept her abroad, out of harm's way), who in 1645, in a speech in favour of an Erastian Presbyterian solution, spoke also against persecution of tender consciences.[31] There were men in between, like Sir Robert Harley, second to none in his old-fashioned antipapal iconoclasm, 'very zealous for the settling of Church government, . . . earnest for Presbytery', as his son recollected, but also notably tolerant of Puritan diversity.[32]

The Independents were marked by equally striking differences of tone and opinion. Most of the zealots, like Harrison and John Carew, came into the Commons as Recruiters, but they had a handful of predecessors, grouped around young Sir Harry Vane. Nobody knew exactly what the Vanists stood for, perhaps not even Sir Harry himself. Baxter rightly says that his ideas were 'so cloudily formed and expressed, that few could understand them', but at least they included 'universal liberty of conscience', and the total abolition of any kind of authority by magistrates and ministers.[33] There were also moderate Independents, like Cromwell's friend Henry Lawrence, who, even if a Baptist in religion, could still attack 'spiritual Levellers', holders of 'extravagant opinions', who rejected established ordinances of worship.[34] And there were Independents, sincere and dedicated ones like Nathaniel Fiennes, who saw clearly that the things uniting Presbyterians and Independents, as Protestants and Puritans, were far more important than those dividing them. To Fiennes, indeed, the whole argument between them was 'inconsiderable', a matter of 'mere human policy', not to be compared with the issues of real importance confronted by men of the Reformation era: 'they played for the kernel itself, we for the shell of Religion.'[35] The issue was not toleration, for Independents could

---

[30] H. G. Tibbutt, ed., *The Letter Books, 1644-45, of Sir Samuel Luke* (London, 1963), pp. 43, 49, 56-7, 77, 197, 226; Sir Henry Ellis, ed., *Original Letters Illustrative of English History* (London, 1826-46), 3rd Ser. iv. 261-6.

[31] Bodl. MS., Tanner 321 (Holland, Speeches 1640-7), fol. 11v. For Lady Holland, see Keeler, *Long Parliament*, p. 219.

[32] Notestein, *English Folk*, pp. 275-7; Geoffrey F. Nuttall, *The Welsh Saints, 1640-1660* (Cardiff, 1957), pp. 3-9; Keeler, *Long Parliament*, p. 203. Edward Harley's comment is from Welbeck MSS., B.M. Loan 29/88, no. 73.

[33] *Rel. Baxt.* i. 74-5. See also Yule, *The Independents*, p. 43.

[34] Henry Lawrence, *A Plea for the Vse of Gospell Ordinances* (5 Feb. 1651/52: [B.M.] E. 654, 2), esp. Epistle Dedicatory, and pp. 1-2.

[35] [Fiennes], *Vindiciae Veritatis*, pp. 24, 35, 126-8.

be just as intolerant as Presbyterians, as their brethren of Massachusetts had shown. 'Many of them had in their hearts, according to their pattern in New England (though it was not policy for the present to profess it) to make themselves the only Sarah or Mistress', one of their enemies noted in 1649.[36] Nor was it the existence of a national Church, for the Independents (though not their Baptist and other sectarian offshoots) believed in that too. It was in fact the less dramatic choice between centralized and decentralized Presbyterianism. 'They can endure a Presbytery as well as any government else', Marchamont Nedham sneered, 'so it be of their own setting up.'[37] The question, as Fiennes put it, was whether the synodal and classical organizations 'should have a power coercive over a particular Congregation, walking in Church fellowship, being organical and complete in themselves'. Sir James Harrington, another Independent, had an answer for that, too: the whole issue could be settled by giving the synod coercive powers, but only after each question had been submitted to a democratic vote of the component congregations.[38]

The line separating religious Presbyterians from Independents was often tantalizingly vague and indefinite. It was easy for many sincere and honest Puritans who had no fixed opinions on questions of Church polity to straddle it, or to cross from one side to the other. The term 'Presbyterian Independent' has recently come under attack, and there may be some dangers in introducing it with a slightly different meaning. But there is no better description for men like Sir James Harrington—upholders of non-separating Independency, with each congregation organized on disciplined Presbyterian lines, yet without the tight centralization of classes and synods possessing absolute authority. 'Congregational Presbytery' the system was sometimes called. There were, as we shall see, a good many M.P.s for whom the term 'Presbyterian Independent' in this revised sense is appropriate.[39]

[36] R. Bacon, *The Labyrinth the Kingdom's In* (1649: [B.M.] E. 541, 26), p. 32.

[37] *Merc. Prag.*, no. 4 (5-12 Oct. 1647: [B.M.] E. 410, 19). For a good discussion of this issue see Yule, *The Independents*, pp. 11-12.

[38] [Fiennes], *Vindiciae Veritatis*, p. 122; [Sir James Harrington], *Noah's Dove* (London, 1645), sig. Zzzzz.

[39] Hexter's 'Problem of the Presbyterian Independents' (above, p. 2, n. 2) broke new ground by showing that Long Parliament religious and political categories did not coincide. In 'Presbyterians, Independents and Puritans', *Past and Present*, no. 47 (May 1970), 135, Hexter reproves me for misconstruing his definition of political Independent. But the passage he quotes does not affect my argument, as it refers to *religious* Independents. In Hexter's

Among the clergy the occupational diseases of controversy and denominationalism were naturally more common than among the laity. Yet their biographies, too, reveal time after time men who fit Baxter's description of his Worcestershire brethren in the 1650s: 'men of no faction, nor siding with any party, but owning that which was good in all.'[40] There must have been many like Robert Armitage, of whom it was said, 'It could never be discerned what Judgment he was of: whether Presbyterian, Congregational, or Episcopal.' What are we to make of Thomas Hardcastle, member of a Baptist church, although apparently never rebaptized, licensed as a Presbyterian in 1672, but pastor of Broadmead Baptist church in Bristol two years later? Or John Wilson, vicar of Backford in Cheshire from 1656 to 1662, who said: 'I never was one of [the Congregational men], nor intend to be', yet was licensed for both Presbyterian and Independent congregations in 1672?[41] Or the great Stephen Marshall, denounced by both sides as a trimmer for trying to steer a middle course? In that 'bustling year', 1646, when Adam Martindale noted the growing rivalry of Presbyterians and Independents in Lancashire, he also observed the difference between the rigid 'Scottish' Presbyterians, and the more moderate ones who could acknowledge the piety of the Independents, and try to conciliate them.[42]

If the clergy are bafflingly elusive, obstinately refusing to conform to a Presbyterian-Independent dualism, the laity are no less so. Time and again we find men of differing views on Church polity working and worshipping together in peace and harmony. The friendships and associations of John Harington, elected as recruiter M.P. for Somerset in 1646, provide a striking illustration. Harington was deeply pious, deeply Puritan, a typical representative of the 'country' as against the court, preferring retirement at Kelston and the performance of his duties as landowner and J.P. to the ambitious court career which his father, the witty translator of

original article, 'Independent' is usually (not quite consistently) a political term, Independent (no quotation marks) a religious one. The test for 'Independent' is Rump membership: *Reappraisals*, p. 165. This is clearly a 'contrafactual assumption' for the religious sense of the term, but not for the political one. Yule (*The Independents*, pp. 35-6) reads Hexter as I do. Reviewing Yule in *Am. Hist. Rev.* lxiv (1959), 362-3, Hexter did not reject this reading, nor Yule's own equation of Rumper with political Independent.

[40] *Rel. Baxt.* i. 97.

[41] A. G. Matthews, *Calamy Revised* (Oxford, 1934), pp. 15, 247, 536; the book abounds with many more examples.

[42] R. Parkinson, ed., *Life of Adam Martindale* (Chetham Soc., iv, 1845), pp. 61-4.

*Orlando*, had mapped out for him. As deputy *custos rotulorum* and chairman of Quarter Sessions in the threatening days before the war, he read charges to his fellow Somerset J.P.s which fully expound the religious duties of 'Christian Justices'. Harington was a Presbyterian all right, writing busily in favour of their doctrines, and no sooner elected to the Commons than he was drafting the Bill for the Ordination of Ministers, in August 1646. He was especially severe in support of the ordinance against heresy, unorthodox opinions being, as he said in a speech on 15 September, 'as a gangrene or cancer'. Yet he was also a firm Erastian, telling his constituents that 'the Parliament is to follow the advice of the synod no farther than [they] see good cause so to do'.[43] From all this one might expect a vindictive partisanship similar to that of Harington's friend Prynne. Yet Harington managed to remain on good terms with the political and religious radicals in Somerset,[44] and his London friends were by no means limited to men of Presbyterian opinions. To be sure, he could enjoy a sermon by his friend Cornelius Burges, or weep at the eloquence of Jonathan Devereux. Yet he could also dine with Sir William Brereton and Cornelius Holland, both political Independents, and pray for the healing of partisan differences. Most strikingly, Harington was by 1650, and perhaps earlier (his diary has been mutilated, and from September 1647 to May 1650 the pages are missing) one of a prayer-circle at Lincoln's Inn which included his Erastian Presbyterian friend Samuel Browne, the latter's allegedly Independent kinsman Oliver St. John, and a number of other M.P.s. And the pastor of this little congregation was none other than James Ussher, Archbishop of Armagh.[45] Ussher, author of the scheme for modified episcopacy, which if adopted might have preserved the unity of the Church of England, had been installed as preacher at Lincoln's Inn in 1647 on the initiative of St. John and Browne.[46] Harington was at this time already under Browne's wing (Browne helped him write his speeches), and a regular supper guest at St. John's. That the Archbishop was attracting great crowds to Lincoln's Inn chapel during

[43] Ian Grimble, *The Harington Family* (London, 1957), pp. 179–80; Thomas G. Barnes, *Somerset, 1625–1640* (Cambridge, Mass., 1961), pp. 34–5, 71; B.M. Add. MS. 10114 (Harington's Diary), fols. 16, 17ᵛ, 18ᵛ. Yule (*The Independents*, pp. 62, 101) unaccountably attributes this diary to Sir James Harrington, who could not have been more different.

[44] He had been elected with their help, as I hope to show in a forthcoming study of Somerset politics after the Civil War.

[45] B.M. Add. MS. 10114, fols. 17, 20, 22ᵛ, 26, 27–33.

[46] *C.J.* v. 393.

the interval when Harington's diary is silent is evident from a letter of Sir Ralph Assheton in September 1648. Assheton was then trying to secure rooms closer to Lincoln's Inn so that he could arrive early enough to avoid being shut out when the chapel was full, as it invariably was when Ussher preached.[47]

To find, at the height of the Puritan Revolution, people labelled as both Presbyterians and Independents seeking out the ministry of an Anglican Archbishop, albeit a conspicuously moderate one, demonstrates once again the fragile borderline separating the denominations. St. John, it has been convincingly shown, was at heart not an Independent, but a man of 'orthodox Calvinist-inclined views which were as compatible with low-church Anglicanism as with classical Independency or Presbyterianism', giving temporary support to either for pragmatic reasons, through force of political circumstances.[48] For him, as for Browne, Harington, and Assheton, Ussher was a godly man, with the root of true religion in his preaching; that was enough. Their association suggests that Baxter was right when he observed that most people he knew were 'against the *ius divinum* of lay elders, and for the moderate primitive episcopacy'.[49] In the same way the more partisan Prynne, aiming like his friend Harington at a reformation of society through Christian magistracy, could be a thoroughpaced Presbyterian in 1641 only because moderate episcopacy was a non-starter, turning towards Erastianism a few years later in revulsion against the Presbyterian clergy's *jure divino* claims.[50]

Throughout the 1650s, when revolution had come and gone, there were many who continued to affirm that, as the Welsh evangelist Walter Cradock put it, Presbyterianism and Independency were 'not two religions: but one religion to a godly, honest heart'.[51] The Puritan Lord Wharton appointed Presbyterians and Independents to his livings with fine impartiality.[52] The Kent Presbyterians John Boys and Henry Oxinden met 'very comfortably and profitably' in regular services with the Independent John

[47] Assheton to B. Driver, 12 Sept. 1648: Chetham's Library, Manchester, MS. A 3, 90 (Assheton's Letter Book, 1648).

[48] Pearl, *E.H.R.* lxxxi (1966), 500-1; Pearl, *T.R.H.S.* 5th Ser. xviii (1968), 79-81.

[49] *Rel. Baxt.* i. 146, quoted in Yule, *The Independents*, p. 31.

[50] Lamont, *Prynne*, chs. iii, vii.

[51] Quoted in Nuttall, *Welsh Saints*, pp. 16-17.

[52] G. F. Trevallyn Jones, 'The Composition and Leadership of the Presbyterian Party in the Convention', *E.H.R.* lxxix (1964), 311. See also G. F. T. Jones, *Saw-Pit Wharton* (Sydney, 1967), pp. 87, 106, 186.

C

Dixwell, under the joint ministry of the Presbyterian Nicholas
Thorogood and the Independent John Barton, in a way that shows
no serious concern with doctrinal differences.[53] Nathaniel Fiennes
was not the only one to feel that the names Presbyterian and
Independent were invented by the Devil 'to cast a ball of contention and division in all companies, stirring animosities and ill
affections in them'. But, reflected Fiennes, even the Devil could
not prevent the mutual co-operation of honest, reasonable men:

It might be truly said of many reverend and godly men amongst them
in those times, both ministers and Christian brethren, that notwithstanding such a difference, they prayed together, fasted together, had
the same gracious presence of God with them in their praying, . . . and
took so little notice of these differences of opinion in things of this inferior
nature, as that notwithstanding they were of one heart and one soul,
walking together in love as brethren.[54]

There were, then, Saints in the Puritan sense, among people of
all shades of theological opinion, and this fund of fellowship, the
common aim of working for Godly Reformation through a Christian
magistracy, was for many at least as important as the minor differences of tone, of rhetoric, or theological temperature, and the
peripheral arguments over Church polity which separated Presbyterians from Independents. The differences between both of these
'Church-type' positions and that of the Baptists were obviously
more fundamental, yet the example of Henry Lawrence shows that
it was possible to be a Baptist and still be a man of moderation. As
we are dealing with human beings, we encounter contradictions,
hesitations, frequent unwillingness to push arguments to their
logical conclusions, to accept what fanatics on both sides self-
righteously defined as the only valid line. Obviously many people
changed with the times, discovered that they could swallow what
a few years before they would have shuddered at, discovered that
previously held opinions were left behind by events and made
irrelevant, and were swung by the war and the revolutionary

[53] Edmund Calamy, *A Continuation of the Account of the Ministers . . . who were Ejected
or Silenced after the Restoration* (London, 1727), p. 536. Boys was clearly a religious Presbyterian, regularly named to committees for establishing the classical system and a patron of
the younger Calamy after the Restoration: G. J. Gray, 'Diary of Jeffrey Boys of Gray's Inn,
1671', *N. & Q.* clix (1930), 452. For the religion of the other two see Everitt, *Community
of Kent*, p. 121, and Yule, *The Independents*, p. 94. Thorogood had been the Earl of Warwick's
chaplain and refused the Engagement: Calamy, *Continuation*, p. 536. For Barton see Yule,
*The Independents*, p. 140.
[54] [Fiennes], *Vindiciae Veritatis*, p. 146.

enthusiasm it generated either forward into militant enthusiasm or backward into conservatism. In 1640, when the Long Parliament met, there were no open Presbyterians in the Commons; by 1645 a majority of the House were Presbyterians, of one sort or another. In 1640, with the exception of Vane, there were no Independents; by 1645 they were a significant number. By the end of the war Baptists are beginning to appear out of the sectarian underworld; later, after 1648, millenarian enthusiasm produces a handful of Fifth Monarchy Men. Each surge of the revolutionary tide, in other words, opened up new choices. It is thus possible to find men like Sir Gilbert Pickering, who travelled through the whole range of beliefs from Presbyterianism to Anabaptism, John Hutchinson, converted to Baptist opinions towards the end of the war, or even Bulstrode Whitelocke, who joined an Independent congregation in 1650, when courting a rich widow who happened to be a member.[55] People changed, and all the related controversies were far too complicated to be compressed into a simple Presbyterian-Independent dualism.

Religion was not the determining, nor perhaps even the most important, issue in the split in the parliamentarian movement that produced Pride's Purge and the revolution of 1648-9. Yet it cannot be doubted that it was of very great importance indeed. The men who led Parliament into war in 1642, and the overwhelming majority of their committed or reluctant gentry supporters, were moderate reformers in both Church and State. In the end, in 1648, they were pushed aside by a handful of revolutionaries; a small handful in Parliament, though supported by a much larger number of lesser men in the Army and the country at large. Some of the revolutionaries in Parliament, those from whom the main initiative came, and a larger proportion, perhaps most, of their supporters, were motivated not so much by any sharply distinguished theology as by a Puritan determination to achieve the reformation of society fiercer than that exhibited by the original leadership. For them, at least, Puritan idealism would triumph over constitutional conservatism. For them a reform movement would become a revolutionary one.

[55] D.N.B. ('Pickering'), citing John Walker, Sufferings of the Clergy. Hutchinson, pp. 242-3. For Whitelocke, see Underdown, J.B.S. viii (1968), 89 and n.

# II

## THE CIVIL WAR AND THE COMMUNITIES

PURITAN idealism: constitutional conservatism; Presbyterianism:
Independency; the antitheses discussed in the previous chapter are
obviously basic to the revolutionary situation of 1648-9. Yet in
some respects they are misleading, as they imply the existence of
a national political consciousness to which these concepts can be
referred. It is true that Pride's Purge cannot be understood except
through national politics—the party politics which developed in the
Long Parliament during and after the Civil War. But it is a mistake
to regard parliamentary politics in isolation, whether in the 1640s
or any other period. Man may be by nature a political animal, but
this does not necessarily make him a parliamentary animal. It is
vital to enter the context of the time. And in that context the real
starting-point for any discussion of the revolution must be the
communities in which Englishmen lived, the counties and boroughs.

For both the country gentlemen who provided the leadership of
the parliamentary side in the Civil War, and for the merchant
oligarchies who governed the towns, it still required an effort to
think in national terms. England in one sense remained a confederation of overlapping communities, politically united only on
the unusual occasions when the representatives of these communities
were summoned together in Parliament. A national consensus
might be faintly visible, as it was beginning to be in the Parliaments
of Elizabeth's reign, and was more obviously in the 1620s, but
before 1640 the political horizon of the average Englishman,
whether rural or urban, was largely confined to his county or his
town. The Civil War, and the unprecedented duration and regularity of sessions of the Long Parliament, created a new situation,
yet the old attitudes persisted. A parliament-man was the representative of his community, sent by his 'country' to do his duty
as their spokesman, not an obedient member of a political party
organized on national lines. Within his county community he lived,

married, brought up his children, and died; within that community he bought and sold, improved or neglected his estates, and dealt with his tenants; within that community he hawked and hunted, wined and dined, enjoyed the amity or enmity of his neighbours; and within that community he did his duty as a J.P. and in the multiplying commissions of local government, finding the focus of county politics at the meetings of shire court, quarter sessions, and assizes. Until the Civil War disrupted it, there was in each county a recognizable and relatively stable governing hierarchy: a handful of noble or greater gentry families who monopolized the most prestigious positions as Lord Lieutenant or his deputy, as knight of the shire and as *custos rotulorum*; a larger number, perhaps twenty or thirty, of 'county' gentry families who served as sheriffs and J.P.s (the most exalted and experienced being of the Quorum) went occasionally to Parliament, more often for borough seats than for the shire, and had an influence that was of county-wide, though scarcely of national extent; and a still larger number (several hundred in each of the larger counties) of local, lesser, 'parochial' gentry, who rarely aspired to the dignity of a J.P., but did much of the essential work at the lower level as collectors and commissioners, under-sheriffs, members of grand juries, and the like.[1]

Much of the original enthusiasm of the Long Parliament was generated by localist resistance to the centralizing pressures of 'Thorough' government in the 1630s. On this the country gentlemen were at one, as they were in their dislike of the excessive powers of bishops who offended their political prejudices as well as their Puritan anti-popishness. In 1640 the local communities were united against the court; hence the virtual unanimity of their representatives in tearing down the fabric of conciliar rule during the first session of the Long Parliament. But then, with the Grand Remonstrance and the dispute over the militia, the nation split, and the county communities with it.[2] The split was accompanied, it need hardly be said, by agonizing efforts to avert it. All over England in the winter of 1642-3 there were efforts to stave off the war, abortive neutrality compacts to keep it away from the county's borders. Some, like Sir Ferdinando Gorges, professed themselves 'fearful

---

[1] See J. E. Neale, *The Elizabethan House of Commons* (London, 1950), ch. i; Barnes, *Somerset*, chs. i–ii; William B. Willcox, *Gloucestershire: a Study in Local Government, 1590–1640* (New Haven, Conn., 1940), chs. iii–iv; Everitt, *Community of Kent*, pp. 33–45.

[2] For reasons which led many former 'country' opponents of the court to support the King see Christopher Hill, *The Century of Revolution* (Edinburgh, 1961), pp. 124-6.

to side with either party, as not able to judge of so transcendent a difference'. Others, like Sir William Courtenay, felt that peace was essential for economic reasons, for without it trade would collapse, rich and poor be ruined, and in the inevitably ensuing disorders 'greater oppression will certainly follow on men of the best ranks'.[3] Some were neutral for less worthy motives. Christopher Guise in Gloucestershire stayed out of it in reaction to his grandfather's Puritanism, which, Guise tells us, produced 'abundance of zeal in himself and very profound hypocrisy in most of his'. Carried to extremes this might lead to the unabashed cynicism of a Howell Gwynne, whose motto was 'Heigh god, heigh devil, I will be for the strongest side'.[4] But even men of integrity, men later famous for their service to the Parliament—Fairfaxes in Yorkshire, Brownes and Trenchards in Dorset—entered neutrality agreements in vain attempts to shut out the war. And when war came there were many who, like Sir John Holland, avoided service in Parliament's local Committees because of the 'relations of blood and obligations of friendship' which tied them to their communities and made them unwilling to sequester friends and neighbours.[5]

Second only in importance to this neutralist undercurrent was the continuing strength of provincialism. Many were the counties where committees resisted the use of their forces outside their own borders, or where officers complied only reluctantly, as Edmund Ludlow did when he grudgingly took his men into Hampshire to join the siege of Basing House; 'it not being properly my work', Ludlow complained, 'who was raised by and for the county of Wilts'. Even the nationally oriented radicals in Kent resisted subordination to the South-Eastern Association. When arguments for submerging county independence were compelling enough, however, it was the regional rather than the national relationship that was preferred. Thus the counties of East Anglia made no difficulty

<hr/>

[3] Gorges to Fairfax, 1 June 1646: Robert Bell, ed., *Memorials of the Civil War: comprising the Correspondence of the Fairfax Family* (London, 1849), i. 299. Courtenay to Sir Richard and Francis Buller, 5 Aug. 1641 and Nov. 1642: R. N. Worth, ed., *The Buller Papers* ([Plymouth], 1895), pp. 48, 85, and cf. also p. 91.

[4] G. Davies, ed., *Autobiography of Thomas Raymond and Memoirs of the Family of Guise of Elmore, Gloucestershire* (Camden Soc., 3rd Ser. xxviii, 1917), pp. 113, 115, 124; A. H. Dodd, *Studies in Stuart Wales* (Cardiff, 1952), p. 133.

[5] Bertram Schofield, ed., *The Knyvett Letters, 1620-1644* (Norfolk Record Soc., xx, 1949), p. 38, n. For the whole subject of neutralism see Brian Manning, 'Neutrals and Neutralism in the English Civil War, 1642-1646' (Oxford D.Phil. thesis, 1957), esp. ch. i, and pp. 134-5.

about joining forces in the Eastern Association, but a great deal of difficulty when the army of that Association was taken out of their control and incorporated in the New Model.[6]

In the end, though, parochial or neutralist by inclination as they may have been, Englishmen of the governing class did divide in a civil war. For most people, religion and politics naturally provided the conscious motivation when they took sides. But as we have seen, social class also had something to do with it. Some of the reasons for the association between parliamentary Puritanism and the 'middling sort' have been discussed in the previous chapter. There were equally good reasons why gentlemen who had opposed the centralization and innovation of the 1630s might in the end find themselves in arms for the King. To question royal authority was to open the door to an attack on all forms of authority, including that of the gentry over their manors and parishes. In many of the gentry, John Corbet regretfully noted, 'there appeared an hatred of the commons, and a strong disposition to the ends of tyranny'. Edmund Ludlow agreed: 'How many of the nobility and gentry were contented to serve [the King's] arbitrary designs, if they might have leave to insult over such as were of a lower order.'[7] Fear of the underprivileged was the inspiration of peers like the Earl of Derby, who noted in his semi-feudal Lancashire domain how 'the baser sort thought it a fine thing to set against the great ones'.[8] Such attitudes could also be used for propaganda purposes, as when the Parliamentarians gleefully jumped on the unguarded remarks allegedly made by the royalist Lord Poulett in the Market Place at Wells in 1642: 'It was not fit for any yeoman to have allowed him of his labours any more than the poor moiety of £10 a year; and when the power should be totally on their side, they shall be compelled to live at that low allowance.'[9]

An impressionistic survey of the English counties confirms the existence of a predominantly royalist gentry opposed by a minority

---

[6] *Ludlow's Memoirs*, i. 105; Everitt, *Community of Kent*, p. 149; Alan Everitt, ed., *Suffolk and the Great Rebellion* (Suffolk Records Soc., iii, 1960), pp. 28-34.

[7] Corbet, in *Somers Tracts*, v. 307; *Ludlow's Memoirs*, i. 96.

[8] Quoted in B. G. Blackwood, 'Social and Religious Aspects of the History of Lancashire 1635-1655' (Oxford B.Litt. thesis, 1956), p. 132. Derby's feelings were amply reciprocated by the Puritan gentry; cf. John Moore to Lenthall, 24 Apr. 1647: H.M.C., *Tenth Report*, App. IV (Stewart MSS.), pp. 81-2; Hill, *Puritanism and Revolution*, pp. 204-5.

[9] Quoted in A. R. Bayley, *The Great Civil War in Dorset, 1642-1660* (Taunton, 1910), p. 55. According to the same source, Poulett narrowly escaped being lynched by the by-standers.

of gentry and a larger number of yeomen and craftsmen. The West Country was not overwhelmingly royalist—even in notoriously royalist Cornwall the gentry were surprisingly evenly divided— but the most solid parliamentarian strength lay in Exeter, Plymouth, and the other ports.[10] In Dorset and Somerset most of the leading gentry were royalist, leaving only a minority to carry on the work of government when the counties were under Parliamentary control, though again with a substantial body of support from the ports and clothing towns like Taunton.[11] Nottingham exhibits the same pattern: the nobility and greater gentry mainly royalist, opposed, as Lucy Hutchinson observes, by some of the lesser gentry like the Hutchinsons and Iretons, and a collection of yeomen and townsmen.[12] Lancashire was divided more on geographical lines, with a largely Catholic, royalist north and south-west, a predominantly Puritan, parliamentarian south-east, but again a clear urban-rural division, towns like Liverpool, Warrington, and Manchester being largely Puritan. A complicating factor here was the feudal power of the Stanleys, which may have tempted more than one gentry family into jealous opposition.[13] The great exception to this general rule of gentry Royalism is the south-east. In Puritan East Anglia, in counties within the orbit of London, such as Buckinghamshire, the royalist gentry were in a marked minority, though there is Baxter to remind us that this may reflect the harsh realities of military power. And in nominally parliamentarian Kent, the great mass of the gentry, whether county or parochial, were always vaguely royalist at heart.[14]

But though in most counties the bulk of the established leadership was royalist, and thus excluded from power by the end of the Civil War, there always remained a significant minority of gentry of the same type who were willing and able to execute the commands of Parliament. The Civil War did not at first, therefore, involve any basic change in the structure of the county communities. Those who were named to Parliament's original County Com-

[10] Mary Coate, *Cornwall in the Great Civil War and Interregnum* (Oxford, 1933), pp. 32-9. However, I think Miss Coate underestimates the predominance of Royalism among the leading Cornish gentry; it was the lesser gentry who were more evenly divided.

[11] Bayley, *Civil War in Dorset*, pp. 1-2. See also Manning, 'Neutrals and Neutralism', pp. 105-12.

[12] Alfred C. Wood, *Nottinghamshire in the Civil War* (Oxford, 1937), pp. 33-5.

[13] Blackwood, 'Lancashire, 1635-1655', *passim*.

[14] Everitt, *Community of Kent*, chs. vi, vii; Everitt, ed., *Suffolk and the Rebellion*, pp. 11-16; A. M. Johnson, 'Buckinghamshire, 1640 to 1660: a Study in County Politics' (Univ. of Wales, Swansea, M.A. thesis, 1963), ch. ii.

mittees (set up in 1643 to execute Parliament's military and sequestration ordinances), or who took over when their counties were recovered from the King's armies, might or might not be more fervent Puritans, more ardent constitutionalists, than their Cavalier opponents, but they were men of the same class, of the same education and experience, in the long run equally anxious to heal the breach caused by the war. Harleys in Herefordshire, Stephenses in Gloucestershire, Horners in Somerset, might have been besieged in or ejected from their homes, might even seem to their enemies menacing and irreconcilable firebrands. But they were not revolutionaries. They might envisage a further modest dose of Godly Reformation, but not a radical one; they might prefer to see local power in the hands of men of their own side, but not the promotion of upstarts from the lower ranks of county society; in particular, they would bitterly oppose any reduction of county independence, any attempted merging of their county community into the larger national one. They were, above all else, country gentlemen.

\*     \*     \*

Obviously no English county could come through the Civil War with the composition of its power élite completely unaltered. The nature and extent of the change-over, however, varied considerably from place to place, and no simple formula can account for the variations. The variations range from the remarkable stability of East Anglia, the rapid transfer of power in Kent and Somerset, the belated change-over in Herefordshire, and the violent fluctuations in Lincolnshire. Nevertheless, through the variations some common patterns can be observed. Stability, the retention of local power by members of the old county establishment, was the rule in counties with a relatively wide political base (in which power had been shared among a score or more substantial families, rather than monopolized by one or two), and where Puritanism had deep roots among the gentry. Instability, a struggle for power often leading to a loss of control by the old county families, was more likely in counties hitherto dominated by one or two great aristocratic houses or where Puritanism was not deeply rooted. The quite different histories of the neighbouring midland shires of Northampton and Leicester demonstrate the operation of the first factor. In Northamptonshire there was no overwhelmingly dominant noble house, but county power rested in the hands of a fairly large number of

solid gentry families: the result was stability, few difficulties for the
County Committee, and no significant change of leadership.
Leicestershire, on the other hand, was more feudal, with a larger
gulf between the three dominant families (Grey, Hastings, and
Manners) and the lesser or parochial gentry, with few county
gentry in between. The faction fights for control of the county
between the Hastings and their lesser rivals had been notorious
ever since Elizabethan times, and had little to do with Puritanism
or national politics. The Hastings were by tradition Puritan, the
Elizabethan Earl of Huntingdon having been one of the greatest
of the Puritan laity, yet they were royalist in the Civil War. The
Greys, the Hastings's more recent rivals, were also Puritans, but
parliamentarian. They too bickered incessantly with their gentry
allies (Stamford and Sir Arthur Haselrig came to blows); such
private feuds soon split the County Committee irrevocably.[15] The
importance of the second factor, gentry Puritanism, is evident in the
contrast between Kent and Suffolk. In both power was widely distributed between the leading families of the county community,
and we might thus expect them to display a common stability. We
certainly find it in Puritan Suffolk, but we find the reverse in Kent,
where the general lukewarmness of the gentry to Puritanism and
the parliamentary cause permitted the rise of, and eventual seizure
of power by, one of the most violent and radical of the local Puritan
machines, and the disruption of the county community.

It is, indeed, Kent that provides the best example of this disruption. In 1642 the overwhelming majority of the Kent gentry
were moderates, neutrals by inclination, who put the unity of the
county ahead of partisanship. Their outlook was well expressed by
Sir Edward Dering, who said 'a composing third way was my wish
and my prayer'.[16] Dering and his friends, Sir Roger Twysden and Sir
Thomas Peyton, were conservative Kentishmen rather than
extreme Royalists, but they found themselves forced out of Parliament, out of local office, and into sequestration, by the pressure
of events. Even men like Sir Norton Knatchbull, Sir Edward
Partheriche, and Sir Humphrey Tufton, who in the end stayed with
Parliament, hesitated over the Covenant, and would obviously have

[15] For much of this paragraph I am indebted to conversation with Alan Everitt, and to his
*Local Community and the Great Rebellion* (Hist. Assoc. pamphlet, G. 70, 1969), pp. 10–22.
For the conflict in the Leicestershire Committee see also B.M. Harl. MS. 166 (D'Ewes
Journal, 1644–5), fol. 212; and Add. MS. 31116 (Whitaker's Diary), fols. 155$^v$, 211–17.

[16] Everitt, *Community of Kent*, p. 120. My constant debt to this brilliant study is obvious.

preferred neutrality. There was in Kent little Puritan zeal outside the towns and cloth-trade villages. In a county potentially neutralist, but nominally parliamentarian by strategic necessity, the problem therefore was to find men willing to govern the county and harness it for war, who were also Parliamentarians by conviction. The men who took over the core of the County Committee, driving out most of the leaders of the old system, were a miscellaneous lot—members of declining families like Sir Thomas Walsingham, Puritan zealots like Sir William Springate, recent arrivals in the county like Augustine Garland and John Dixwell, violent political radicals like Thomas Blount, quarrelsome and maladjusted individuals like Sir Michael Livesey and the embittered ex-courtier Sir Anthony Weldon. By the end of 1643 they were already well entrenched in the County Committee; the half-hearted moderates were retreating into inactivity, and to replace them were emerging the lesser men, the parochial gentry. Lacking strong natural authority at home, they looked, inevitably, to Westminster. Weldon and his allies thus became the agents of centralization and of the subordination of the county community to the nation.[17]

Somerset's military history during the Civil War is very different from that of Kent—the county was in royalist hands for almost two years from the summer of 1643—but its social and political structure was not dissimilar. As in Kent, there was no single great noble family, but local power was shared by a stable establishment of a score or so of reputable families—Portmans, Phelipses, Poulets, Pophams, and their like.[18] As Somerset was a frontier county, contested by armies of both sides, there was none of the compelling military necessity that made the Kentish gentry into outward Parliamentarians. The Somerset gentry were able to follow their own inclinations, and the inclinations of a majority were royalist. Of the major families, only the Horners, Pophams, and rather halfheartedly the Luttrells, stayed with Parliament; the rest were excluded, when the county was recovered, from the circle of governors. The Luttrells were inactive (the head of the family, Thomas, died in 1644, leaving sons too young for leadership), the Pophams (old Sir Francis, who also died in 1644, and his sons Alexander and Edward) absorbed in national politics and military affairs. Into the vacuum of local power moved the formidable figure

---

[17] Ibid. 126, 145, 147-52, 218.
[18] Barnes, *Somerset*, ch. ii.

of Colonel John Pyne of Curry Mallet, a man similar in many ways
to Kent's Weldon, in personality and political methods, though of
different origins. He came of a gentry family of moderate wealth,
on the fringe of the county establishment, a family with its own
history of turbulent opposition to the Crown.[19] By the end of the
Civil War John Pyne had already emerged as the leader of the local
war party. Allied with the few violent gentry Puritans, like Sir
Thomas Wroth of North Petherton,[20] with the ambitious lawyer
Roger Hill of Poundsford, M.P. for Bridport (Pyne himself sat in
Parliament for another Dorset borough, Poole), and with that stout
Puritan hero Robert Blake of Bridgwater, by 1645 Pyne led a
faction which was ready to take over the County Committee and the
other institutions of local government. In the process it would,
inevitably, spell the end of the influence of the surviving parliamentarian families of the old establishment. Sir John Horner,
sheriff at the close of the war, tried to fight the new men. He won
a parliamentary seat for his son George, but lost his influence in the
Committee. John Harington more sensibly came to terms with
them, but he too was not an active committeeman.[21]

As in Weldon's Kent, the men who came to the front in Somerset
in 1645 and 1646 were from outside the traditional establishment.
The handful of prominent men allied with Pyne—the Pophams,
Wroth, the lawyers Roger Hill and Lislebone Long—were generally
kept out of the county by military or parliamentary duties; and
several even of Pyne's allies in Parliament (Blake, George Serle,
and John Palmer) came of mercantile or obscure origins. After the
county was recovered from the Royalists in 1645 the Committee's
real work was done by Pyne and his obedient henchmen, men 'of
mean quality', as their enemies rightly described them. They
included a few gentry of the second rank—John Preston of Cricket
St. Thomas, his cousin Henry Bonner of Combe St. Nicholas, and
Edward Ceely of Creech St. Michael—and a larger number of small
parochial gentry and men of recent mercantile origins. Richard
Trevillian's family had been at Midelney since before the Dissolution, but his father was a yeoman. Christopher Pittard lived at
Martock, a village where the observant Richard Symonds noted in

---

[19] His uncle, Hugh Pyne, had been deputy *custos rotulorum* twenty years earlier, until
removed for violent words against Buckingham, and even the King, at the Ilchester sessions
in 1626, words which led to a charge of treason against him: Barnes, *Somerset*, pp. 34, 70.

[20] Ibid., pp. 15-16 and n.

[21] For the county election see David Underdown, 'Party management in the recruiter
elections, 1645-1648', *E.H.R.* lxxxiii (1968), 241 and references there given.

1644 that there were no resident gentry. Thomas English of Pud-
dimore Milton and Henry Minterne of Chiselborough came of
families that were both minor and recent arrivals in the county.
Nicholas Sandys of South Petherton and Jonathon Pitts of Curry
Rivel were both sons of merchants; Robert Morgan, Mayor of
Wells in 1642–3, one of the type of lesser urban gentry, an attorney
with interests in the malting business; Matthew Clift a Bath draper.
Apart from the M.P.s, only Henry Henley of Leigh, the Committee's defeated candidate in the county election in December
1645, represented solid county position in the new regime after the
end of that year. It is not strange that even a loyal Parliamentarian
like Sir Edward Hungerford thought the Somerset Committee 'very
hard to the gentry'.[22]

The committees of many other counties were little better. There
were, to be sure, a few in which moderate Puritans from the old
establishments managed to hang on to positions of power. The
Harleys did so in Herefordshire, the Onslows in Surrey.[23] Dorset,
in spite of its predominantly royalist gentry, remained firmly in the
grip of the minority of leading families who were parliamentarian,
its Committee being run by M.P.s like John Browne, William
Sydenham, John Bingham, Thomas Erle, and the powerful
Trenchards. At least one of their colleagues, however, John Fitzjames of Leweston, stayed in the Committee only to avoid loss of
local influence, not because he approved of their doings. 'If Committees continue, what do you think will become of the Country?'
he asked rhetorically in September 1646, with a hearty prayer for
their dissolution.[24] In more stable Puritan Suffolk, old gentry
families like the Barnardistons also retained control, but even there
complaints about the 'mean men' on the Committee, yeomen,
mariners, tanners, woollen-drapers, 'men that have neither good
blood nor breeding in them', were occasionally heard.[25]

[22] John Rose to Mrs. Norwood, 29 Aug. 1646: H.M.C., *Bath*, iv. 279; I am grateful to
the Secretary of the Historical Manuscripts Commission, Mr. Roger Ellis, for permitting
me to read this volume while still in proof. The above account of the members of the Somerset
Committee is based on my forthcoming study of Civil War Somerset. The comment on
their quality is in *Articles of Treason . . . committed by John Pine of Curry-Mallet* (2 Mar.
1648/49: B.M., 669 f. 13, 94), p. 4.

[23] For an attack on the Onslows' domination see George Wither, *Justitiarius Justificatus.
The Justice Justified* (13 Apr. 1646: [B.M.] E. 506, 30), pp. 2–13.

[24] Fitzjames to ——, 16 Sept. 1646: Fitzjames Letter-book, i (Duke of Northumberland
MSS., 547, B.M. Film 330), fol. 44ᵛ. For the general character of the Dorset Committee
see C. H. Mayo, ed., *Minute Book of the Dorset Standing Committee* (Exeter, 1902), *passim*.

[25] G. Carter to D'Ewes, 20 May 1645: B.M. Harl. MS. 387 (D'Ewes Corr.), fol. 30.

With these partial exceptions, in county after county a phenomenon similar to that in Kent and Somerset can be observed. By
the end of the war the old leadership is being pushed aside by
energetic new men from lower down the social scale, lesser gentry
and townsmen, often of radical Puritan inclinations, aiming at
power as well as reformation. In Essex both the County Committee
and its divisional offshoots were taken over, as the old gentry were
forced out, or withdrew out of resentment at religious radicalism,
high taxation, and centralization. By 1646 the divisional committee
at Romford was completely under the control of the merchant
Joachim Matthews, who had bought an estate in the county only
in 1642, and John Fenning, a man of minor urban gentry origins,
allied with the local Independents.[26] In Buckinghamshire the old
community lost control early in the war, its leaders being either
Royalists like the Verneys and Packingtons, or diverted into affairs
outside the county, as M.P.s or Army officers, like Hampden, Sir
Peter Temple, Richard Ingoldsby, and the Drakes of Amersham.
Thomas Tyrrel was one of the few who remained to lead the opposition, but he, like the Horners in Somerset, could play only an
obstructive role. A few of the major gentry, young George Fleetwood for instance, co-operated, but the Committee's real leaders
came from the lesser gentry: Edmund West, Simon Mayne, and
above all Thomas Scot of Little Marlow, an insignificant attorney
who rose to power through his treasurership of the Committee from
1644 to 1646. All were men of Independent leanings. By the end of
1645 they were also all M.P.s, but their allies who took over the day-
to-day business of the Committee were of similar or inferior origins:
Mayne's half-brother Henry Beke, Christopher Eggleston, William
Russell, John Deverell, and the townsman (allegedly a butcher)
Christopher Henn of Aylesbury.[27]

The effort to unseat the old establishment in Sussex can be
observed as early as 1644, when a local petition charged Sir Thomas
Parker and Sir Thomas Pelham with lukewarmness to the parliamentary cause. The details are obscure, but it appears that a Committee faction led by the Chichester upstart William Cawley and
his friend Stephen Humphrey, the Committee's treasurer, in
alliance with the more firmly entrenched Herbert Morley, was out

---

[26] B. W. Quintrell, 'The Divisional Committee for Southern Essex during the Civil Wars'
(Manchester M.A. thesis, 1962), pp. 33-7, 142-5, 150-2, 163-8.
[27] A. M. Johnson, 'Buckinghamshire', ch. iii.

to take over from the old county families. The Earl of Northumberland was soon accusing the Committee of employing 'men of so base a condition as renders them unworthy of such trust', and of 'unnecessary oppression and insolent behaviour' towards men of property.[28] In the Isle of Wight, according to Sir John Oglander, it was a similar story. The Committee was run by 'Ringwood of Newport, the pedlar; Maynard, the apothecary; Matthews, the baker; Wavell and Legge, farmers, and poor Baxter of Hurst Castle'. These, Oglander concludes, probably with some exaggeration of their obscurity, took over from such men as Sir John Leigh and Sir Henry Worsley, the former D.L.s and J.P.s, and 'ruled the whole Island'.[29] Further west, although prominent men like the Bampfields and Sir John Northcote were still active in the Devon Committee as late as 1648, one of the members admitted that most of his really active colleagues were merchants.[30]

The midland and northern counties display a similar trend. Sir William Brereton's allies in the Staffordshire Committee were for the most part men of lesser gentry stamp.[31] In Warwickshire the Committee was under the control of the radical M.P. William Purefoy and his supporters before the end of the war. In October 1645 they were using their power over the county militia against the gentry candidates in the shire election, Sir John Burgoyne and Thomas Boughton; unsuccessfully, as it turned out.[32] In Nottinghamshire, too, the pattern is familiar. The only aristocratic or upper gentry members of the Committee, the Pierreponts, Francis Thornhaugh, and John Hutchinson, were all involved in national or military affairs, and control was exercised locally by lesser gentry, or lawyers and merchants from Nottingham town.[33] The old system in Yorkshire had long since been shattered with the eclipse of

---

[28] Northumberland to Sussex D.L.s, 14 Aug. 1645: B.M. Add. MS. 33058 (Pelham MSS.), fol. 71. The conflict was largely fought out in a struggle between the Standing Committee and the Sub-Committee of Accounts: H.M.C., *Portland*, i. 314; B.M. Add. MS. 31116 (Whitaker's Diary), fol. 167; there are many references to the dispute in the papers of the Committee of Accounts, P.R.O., S.P. 252-7. See also Charles Thomas-Stanford, *Sussex in the Great Civil War and the Interregnum* (London, 1910), p. 161.

[29] Francis Bamford, ed., *A Royalist's Notebook: the Commonplace Book of Sir John Oglander* (London, 1936), pp. 110-11.

[30] H.M.C., *Portland*, i. 484. Justinian Peard to Richard Hill, 17 Nov. 1648: B.M. Add. MS. 5494 (Seq. Co. Papers), fol. 99.

[31] D. H. Pennington and I. A. Roots, eds., *The Committee at Stafford, 1643-1645* (Manchester, 1957), Intro., pp. xxii-xxiii, lxxiv-lxxxii.

[32] *Scottish Dove*, nos. 108, 109 (7-12 Nov. and 12-19 Nov. 1645: [B.M.] E. 309, 5, 24).

[33] Wood, *Notts. in the Civil War*, esp. p. 130.

families like the Wentworths and Saviles, who had dominated, or
fought, the Council of the North. The Fairfaxes were clearly at the
summit, but in 1646 Lord Fairfax was too old, and his son the
General too indifferent and too often absent to be effective. The
men who really governed Yorkshire after the war included some
of standing, like the Darleys, Sir Thomas Mauleverer, Sir John
Bourchier, Christopher Ledger, and Sir Edward Rhodes, but also
upstarts like the M.P.s Thomas Stockdale, John Wastell, and
Francis Thorpe, and the treasurer for the North Riding, Ralph
Rymer.[34] At least the Yorkshire Committees were made up of local
men. In Cumberland, on the other hand, an enemy of Richard
Barwis and the ruling group charged that they had set up 'a committee of strange men', upstarts and outsiders, 'to subdue the
gentry and to set beggars on horseback'. A royalist petition echoed
the complaint, summarizing the general character of committeemen: 'the tail of the gentry . . . men of ruinous fortunes and despic-
able estates.'[35]

The question arises to what extent the new men who took over
so many counties at the end of the Civil War represented the aspirations of their class. There can be little doubt that in fact they did
not; that, as in most revolutions, the revolutionaries were an activist
minority, and that the majority of the lesser gentry and yeomanry
would have been content to be left alone under the old system in
which the greater gentry exercised the real power. Somerset provides a convenient case-study. A brief description of what little is
known of the religious sympathies of Pyne's allies and subordinates
reveals that this was not only a minority, but a radically Puritan one.
Pyne himself was a Presbyterian elder and probably a fairly eclectic
Puritan. But his letters share the vocabulary, the rhetoric of enthusiasts, and show his sympathy for their aspirations. His minister at
Curry Mallet, John Baker, was a political radical but a Presbyterian,
though Pyne may have had an Anabaptist chaplain at Poole in
1645.[36] In the Barebones Parliament he voted with the radicals
against tithes, and in 1659 the local Quakers found him 'very
loving and friendly'. Pittard, Trevillian, and Ceely were also

---

[34] *The Countrey Committees laid open* (5 June 1649: [B.M.] E. 558, 11).

[35] Isaac Tullie, *Narrative of the Siege of Carlisle in 1644 and 1645*, ed. S. Jefferson (Carlisle,
1840), pp. 1, 3. Petition quoted in Bayley, *Civil War in Dorset*, p. 352.

[36] Edwards, *Gangraena*, Pt. I (26 Feb. 1645/6: [B.M.] E. 323, 2), p. [51]. Yule, *The
Independents*, p. 146, regards Baker as an Independent; but he signed the 'Attestation' in
1648, and was licensed as a Presbyterian in 1672: Matthews, *Calamy Revised*, pp. 23, 557.

regarded as friends by the Quakers, and most of Pyne's other allies were at least tolerant towards them, Wroth and Bonner being the only exceptions—and Bonner had an Independent minister at Combe St. Nicholas in 1654.[37] Several of the Committee's lesser officials, including Pyne's secretary, Jasper Batt, became Quakers, while their Marshal, David Barret, was one of the leading Baptists in the county. Edward Curll, sequestrator of Catsash Hundred, was an enthusiastic Puritan, and it may not be coincidental that in 1649 the inhabitants of Batcombe, where he was a prominent resident, were refusing to pay tithes. John Barker of High Ham, who commanded the Committee troop in 1646, was later an officer in Henry Marten's regiment of Levellers, and an extreme, committed Commonwealthsman.[38] Thomas Edwards was not the only observer who by 1646 was noting the spread of sectarian opinions in Somerset. A visitor to Bath in September of that year found 'the pulpit to be the hottest bath in town, for it one day sweats Independency and Presbytery the next', with the more radical preacher proclaiming 'Christ a King, and every new-moulded congregation his Kingdom'.[39] The connection between radical politics and religion was taken as a matter of course. 'A sword and a trowel are not incompatible for building of churches as well as fortifying of towns', Roger Hill told Pyne in February 1647.[40]

In spite of this marked infusion of radical Puritans, the Pyne regime did not succeed in making any great change in the parochial composition of the county. The Presbyterian classical organization was in operation by 1648, and only a handful of Independents held Somerset livings.[41] More serious than the new regime's religious aspirations was the blustering misgovernment for which Pyne soon became notorious, and which was as unpopular with the yeomanry and freeholders as it was with the gentry. The Committee quickly became the scapegoat for all the by-products of military government

---

[37] Norman Penney, ed., 'Extracts from State Papers relating to Friends', *Journal of Friends Hist. Soc.*, Supplements 8-11 (1910-13), pp. 107-8; Yule, *The Independents*, p. 146.

[38] *Cal. C. Comp.*, pp. 137, 179; *Cal. S.P. Dom., 1659-60*, pp. 238-9, 319; P.R.O., Asz. 24/21 (W. Circuit Order-book), fol. 146ᵛ; Army Committee order, 16 Feb. 1648/9: Worcester College, Clarke MS. lxxii.

[39] Edwards, *Gangraena*, Pt. I, pp. [49-50, 117-18]; Pt. III, pp. 41, 52-3, 107; C. Paman to W. Sancroft, 29 Sept. 1646: Bodl. MS. Rawl. D. 945, fol. 34. See also *Scottish Dove*, no. 144 (22-31 July 1646: [B.M.] E. 346, 10).

[40] [Hill to Pyne, Feb. 1647]: Somerset R.O., Hippisley MS., DD/HI/10.

[41] William A. Shaw, *History of the English Church during the Civil Wars and under the Commonwealth* (London, 1900), ii. 413-22; Yule, *The Independents*, p. 146.

D

—high taxes, quartering, mutinous outbursts by unpaid and ill-disciplined forces—even when they were not directly responsible for them. In 1646 there was a revival of the Clubmen in Somerset, under the same leader, Humphrey Willis, who in the previous year had helped to turn them into useful auxiliaries of the New Model in the campaign around Bristol. This time the Club outbreaks were directed against the Committee, and caused serious concern at the time of the county election in July 1646, for one of Pyne's principal enemies, the rich landowning clothier William Strode of Barrington, had long since seen the Clubmen's potential value, and was very popular among them. The smouldering opposition of the peasantry, expressed in riotous attacks on isolated bands of soldiers, or violent disturbances like one at Bridgwater in November, in which several people were killed, show that the Committee cannot be viewed merely as the mouthpiece of the lesser gentry and freeholders in a simple class struggle.[42] It was, like its counterparts in so many other counties, the weapon of a militant minority.

From the later months of 1645 on into 1647 a chorus of voices demanded reform. The Presbyterian newspaper, *The Scottish Dove*, was particularly lavish in its accounts of Committee oppression, corruption, and interference with elections. People with special grievances against them, like Clement Walker in Somerset and Lilburne's old enemy Colonel Edward King in Lincolnshire, added their complaints.[43] It is not surprising, therefore, that there were recurrent moves in Parliament to abolish the Committees, and return county government to the traditional authorities, the J.P.s. As early as 1644 the Earl of Manchester thought that the Committees' misbehaviour could be restrained only if men of higher status were employed. John Wylde, speaking for his colleagues at Haberdashers' Hall, admitted the inferior rank of the committee-men, but pointed out unkindly that Parliament had only used them 'when they saw the remissness of others of better quality'.[44] By

---

[42] Again the reader is asked to await my study of Civil War Somerset politics for documentation of this paragraph.

[43] Clement Walker, *Mystery of the Two Juntoes* (1648), in Francis Maseres, ed., *Select Tracts Relating to the Civil Wars* (London, 1815), i. 338; Edward King, *A Discovery of the Arbitrary, Tyranicall, and illegall Actions of some of the Committee of the County of Lincoln* (1 Feb. 1646/7: [B.M.] E. 373, 3). See also [Bruno Ryves], *Mercurius Rusticus . . . Angliae Ruina* (12 Nov. 1647: [B.M.] E. 414, 5). *Scottish Dove* accounts are frequent between nos. 108 (7-12 Nov. 1645: [B.M.] E. 309, 5), and 160 (11-18 Nov. 1646: [B.M.] E. 362, 14).

[44] Wylde to Manchester, 3 Apr. 1644: P.R.O., S.P. 20/1 (Seq. Co. Order-book, 1643-5), fols. 129-30.

1646, things having gone from bad to worse, Manchester's colleagues in the Lords appointed a committee to prepare an ordinance
for abolition. In June the Commons took up the matter, referring
to one of their own committees the question of how to restrain the
'oppressions and illegalities' prevailing in the counties. The Lords
duly passed their abolition Bill, but the issue had now become one
of the principal bones of contention between Presbyterians and
Independents, and the Bill ran into opposition in the Commons. In
February 1647 the Lords were still complaining that nothing had
been done, that the Committees' abuses were still widespread, and
that 'great disorders have been occasioned, by the continuance of
them', singling out Somerset for special mention.[45]

\*          \*          \*

The gentry's dislike of seeing local government fall into the hands
of a minority of militant Puritans, often of lower-class origins, was
not the only reason for the conservative reaction of 1646–7. Military
and Committee rule meant subordination to Westminster, and the
destruction of the comfortable independence of the county communities. The whole pressure of military government, and the disorderly excesses of unpaid soldiers, combined to produce a general
longing for a return to normality and stability. To the effects of war,
high taxation, and the breakdown of the old machinery of local
government were added the burdens of quartering undisciplined
soldiers, often months without pay, and all the more inclined to
savage, drunken, outbursts. There were violent clashes between
men of Ireton's regiment and local inhabitants in Hampshire in
August 1646.[46] In the summer of the same year the western counties
suffered badly from the men of Massey's brigade, who added
organized highway robbery and murder to the customary pastimes
of unemployed soldiers. Later in the same year there were similar
complaints about the behaviour of troops on their way to Ireland.[47]
Nor was this confined to the West Country. There were mutinies
at Chester, Nantwich, Wolverhampton, and St. Albans; at Bury
St. Edmunds soldiers imprisoned two local M.P.s, Sir William

[45] *L.J.* viii. 287, 474; *C.J.* iv. 583; v. 85; Bulstrode Whitelocke, *Memorials of the English
Affairs* (Oxford, 1853), ii. 34, 53, 92.
[46] *Moderate Intelligencer*, no. 76 (13–20 Aug. 1646: [B.M.] E. 350, 21).
[47] *C.J.* iv. 638, 640; *Moderate Intelligencer*, no. 75 (6–13 Aug. 1646: [B.M.] E. 350, 6);
B.M. Add. MS. 10114 (Harington's Diary), fol. 17; Bodl. MS. Dep. C. 167 (Nalson Papers,
xiv), fol. 309; Thos. Pigott to Sir P. Perceval, 18 Sept. 1646: H.M.C., *Egmont*, i. 318.

Spring and Maurice Barrowe, while Sir John Curzon and other local committeemen suffered the same indignity at Derby. At York in November 1646 mutineers broke into the Lord Mayor's bedroom, using 'opprobrious speeches', and awoke their commander, Col. Sydenham Pointz, with shouts of 'Money, money, money'.[48] In a country wracked by plague, food shortages, and high prices, and with violent demonstrations against the excise a regular occurrence, something like a complete breakdown of law and order, with all the accompanying dangers to life and property, threatened parts of England in 1646. Long before the end of the war the Earl of Berkshire had been convinced that the soldiers on both sides were interested only in making their fortunes from the plunder of noblemen's estates.[49] Now sectarian enthusiasm added to the danger. When a petition from Hertfordshire and Buckinghamshire against tithes was presented to the Commons in May 1646, there were M.P.s who said that if this kind of thing was countenanced, 'in the next place we might expect a petition that no tenants should pay rents to the landlords'.[50]

Conditions were more stable in the towns, at least until 1648. The towns, to be sure, had their share of the violence of mutineers, and there were several serious conflicts of authority between corporations and the military. At Exeter a long argument began in 1646. Soldiers were alleged to have obstructed the constables, to have imprisoned citizens illegally, and to have engaged in unlicensed preaching. When the town magistrates tried to put a stop to it by reading the Ordinance against unlicensed preaching, the Deputy-Governor protested and said that his men would continue the practice. And when the magistrates sent a letter of protest to Parliament it was intercepted and opened by the officers.[51] There were, too, repeated demonstrations against the excise, particularly violent by the Norwich butchers, which led Thomas Atkin, M.P. for the town, to convey several stern warnings to the corporation.[52] But urban government was on the whole less disrupted by the war than

[48] *Mercurius Civicus*, no. 165 (23–30 July 1646: [B.M.] E. 346, 6); *Perfect Account*, 7–14 Aug. 1646, 13–20 Nov. 1646: ([B.M.] E. 513, 3; E. 362, 23); James Hall, ed., *Memorials of the Civil War in Cheshire . . . by Thomas Malbon* (Record Soc. Lancs. and Cheshire, xix, 1889), pp. 208–10.

[49] Berkshire to Earl of Bath, 6 June 1645: H.M.C., *Fourth Report*, Appendix (de la Warr MSS.), p. 309. [50] B.M. Add. MS. 31116 (Whitaker's Diary), fol. 268.

[51] Edwards, *Gangraena*, Pt. III, pp. 42–5.

[52] B.M. Add. MS. 19399 (Turner MSS.), fol. 26; 22620 (Norwich Collections), fols. 45, 54, 56.

that of the counties. The current of neutralism among the town oligarchies, their sturdy efforts to protect the interests of their towns against the warring armies, their skill in avoiding outright commitment to one side or the other, meant that there were fewer opportunities for new men to move into a vacuum of leadership in the way they did in the counties. Even in such places as Bedford, High Wycombe, and Wells, where there was a marked swing to the left after 1647, the corporations showed remarkable stability until then.[53] Furthermore, the towns resemble the more stable counties like Norfolk and Suffolk in that, as we should expect, more of the leaders were Puritan, and Puritanism was more widely diffused among the population generally, so that there was less pressure for change from an embattled minority. Although in a larger town such as Bristol the rich men of the old oligarchy might be royalist, Sir Edward Hungerford was probably not far wrong when he said in 1642 that the rest of the citizens were parliamentarian by about three to one.[54] Although Lucy Hutchinson thought that less than a quarter of the inhabitants of Nottingham were active Puritans, this was enough to provide leadership, for 'the ordinary civil sort of people coldly adhered to the better', even if at heart they obviously preferred neutrality.[55]

When, therefore, royalist mayors and aldermen were removed during or after the Civil War, it was easier in towns than it was in many counties for stability to be preserved. The old oligarchies might be broadened by the inclusion of men slightly less wealthy than their predecessors, but there might be no substantial change in the real character of the government. This was obviously the case at Newcastle upon Tyne, where Marlays, Coles, and Liddells were removed, but where their successors were near enough to the 'Inner Ring' to be easily and quickly absorbed.[56] Similarly at Bristol, where the purge of 1645-6 removed the royalist aldermen, and brought the city more firmly under control from Westminster through the election of Edmund Prideaux as Recorder, but where the newcomers were also men not far from the old centre of power.

---

[53] For the subsequent 'swing to the left' in these places see below, pp. 320, 322-4.

[54] Hungerford and others to Speaker, 26 Nov. 1642: H.M.C., *Fifth Report*, Appendix (House of Lords MSS.), p. 58.

[55] *Hutchinson*, p. 105; cf. also p. 130. Hutchinson's regiment was chiefly composed of townsmen: ibid., pp. 110-11.

[56] Roger Howell, *Newcastle upon Tyne and the Puritan Revolution* (Oxford, 1967), pp. 162-3, and ch. v.

Thomas Edwards, always on the look-out for sinister Independent infiltration, thought that no one had any chance of civic employment in Bristol who did not follow 'the New Light and New Way', but the evidence does not support him.[57] Nor is there any sign of marked political or religious change in towns like Dorchester or Gloucester; in the former the corporation appointed the highly Presbyterian Stanley Gower to Holy Trinity, when the patriarch John White died in 1648; in the latter the corporation seem to have been notably biased against Independents in 1646.[58] There were, indeed, places where local feelings ran high before 1648. At Colchester the grocer John Langley, who with another strong Puritan, Henry Barrington, had organized mob violence against Royalists in 1642, was elected mayor in 1646, after a period of 'unhappy jars and differences' which the Recorder, Sir Harbottle Grimston, thought brought 'great reproach and scandal' to the town.[59] And at Ipswich the corporation beat off only with difficulty, and after temporarily surrendering to pressure from the commonalty, an effort to democratize the system of election to the corporation, during the autumn of 1647.[60] But on the whole the evidence supports the anonymous author who thought that although there were 'nests of Sectaries' in many towns, their influence was weakened by the tendency of the more active ones to leave and serve in the Army or as government officials, leaving their towns in more conservative, though outwardly Puritan, hands.[61] The return of demobilized enthusiasts was soon to change the situation.

There was, however, one urban centre where the threat of popular upheaval was even in 1646-7 something more than a distant possibility: London. The capital obviously demands separate consideration. London had had its first, and moderate revolution in 1641-2, when the parliamentary Puritans, acting through the Common Council, got rid of Lord Mayor Gurney and his equally

---

[57] Edwards, *Gangraena*, Pt. I, p. [92]; John Latimer, *Annals of Bristol in the Seventeenth Century* (Bristol, 1900), pp. 207-14.

[58] C. H. Mayo, ed., *Municipal Records of the Borough of Dorchester* (Exeter, 1908), esp. pp. 603-5; John Corbet, *Vindication of the Magistrates and Ministers of the City of Gloucester* (13 May 1646: [B.M.] E. 337, 15).

[59] George Rickword, 'Members of Parliament for Colchester, 1603-1683', *Essex Review*, v (1896), 203-7; H.M.C., *Verulam*, pp. 203-5.

[60] Nathaniel Bacon, *Annals of Ipswich*, ed. W. H. Richardson (Ipswich, 1884), Preface, pp. ii, v.

[61] *Certaine Considerations touching the Present Factions* (Oct. 1648: [B.M.] E. 466, 3), p. 2.

royalist aldermen, installed Isaac Penington as Lord Mayor, and gradually brought the Court of Aldermen into line. In the process they built up something like an organized political party, working through demonstrations, petitions, and mass meetings, and using churches, ward organizations, and tavern clubs to promote their ideas. Once again there was a broadening of the oligarchy, with men who were substantial merchants, but not the big men of the Levant or East India Companies, taking their place at the head of London's government. But although the radicals could increase the powers of the more democratic Common Hall, and could work through the Militia Committee, there was no revolutionary change in the government of the City. When Sir John Wollaston succeeded Penington as Lord Mayor in 1643, there began a long period of moderate government in the capital, government by men of solid wealth even if they were not the millionaires who had run the City before 1642.[62] In terms of the national political nomenclature of 1646-7, some of the aldermen, like Andrewes, Foot, and Fowke, were Independents; others, like Bunce, Cullum, and Langham, Presbyterians; yet others, like Gibbs and Wollaston, trimmed their course to the prevailing wind. None, however, could be regarded as violent revolutionaries.

Yet below them, among the journeymen, the craftsmen, the 'middling sort', the ferment was at work. In July 1646 there appeared *A Remonstrance of Many Thousand Citizens*, the first manifesto of what in the following year came to be called the Leveller party. We are not here concerned with the circumstances which impelled John Lilburne into national prominence. What is important is that in the summer he and his highly vocal friends were claiming (and the known extent of Leveller support a few months later makes the claim not implausible) to be the spokesmen for a mass movement whose roots were among the weavers, the printers, the journeymen of the City companies. In their conflict with the big merchants who dominated the companies and the corporation the prospects of such men had been improved only imperceptibly by the recent changes. In September 1646 some of them tried unsuccessfully to claim their rights as citizens at the election of the Lord Mayor, and there was a disturbance at the Guildhall. With Lilburne to voice

---

[62] Valerie Pearl, *London and the Outbreak of the Puritan Revolution* (Oxford, 1961), pp. 132-59, 230-4, 240-7, 273-5, 280-4. See also ibid., App. II for biographical information.

their aspirations in *London's Liberty in Chains*, it was clear that what the men of property on both sides had always feared might be the outcome of civil war had in fact occurred—the 'many-headed multitude' were on the scene and demanding their birthright.[63] To the alarming spread of sectarian Puritanism, with all its democratic implications, in the Army, was now added the spectre of urban radicalism. The Levellers, too, came to democratic politics by way of sectarian (mainly Anabaptist) Puritanism, and voiced the same demands for the ending of tithes, the separation of Church and State, the toleration of all opinions; but they quickly translated this into a politics that was secular and rational, deducing the sovereignty of the people from natural reason rather than Biblical exegesis, and adding their own muddled but effective version of the popular historical myth of the Norman Yoke. Whatever their modifications in detail (it is arguable, for instance, that the Levellers still wished to preserve the connection between power and property by excluding servants and wage-earners from the franchise), the psychology of the Leveller movement was democratic, and the men of property, even the radicals among them, took fright. There could be no doubt about the meaning of the popular Leveller cliché, echoing down the years to be repeated by a grizzled veteran on the scaffold in 1685: 'None comes into the world with a saddle on his back, neither any booted and spurred to ride him.'[64] In such language lay the threat of political as well as religious upheaval. In both country and town the war had generated a revolutionary minority.

[63] H. N. Brailsford, *The Levellers and the English Revolution*, ed. Christopher Hill (London, 1961), ch. vii.

[64] Ibid. p. 624. I am not entirely convinced by the argument of C. B. Macpherson, *The Political Theory of Possessive Individualism* (Oxford, 1962), pp. 107–59, that the Levellers were less democratic than they seemed. It seems apparent that they spoke with two voices. See the criticism of Macpherson by J. C. Davis, 'The Levellers and Democracy', *Past and Present*, no. 40 (July 1968), 174–80.

# III

## PRESBYTERIANS AND INDEPENDENTS

WHILE revolutionary minorities were taking over in some English counties, confronting old establishments in others, and emerging from the shadows as Levellers in London and the Army, the focus of national politics, Parliament itself, was beginning to divide into something resembling political parties. Or, stated more accurately, *some* Members of Parliament were doing so. The parties of the Long Parliament, though their conflict is directly relevant to the revolution of 1648-9, were far less clear-cut than they appear at first sight. Indeed, few words have caused more difficulties for historians than 'party'. The fact that Presbyterian and Independent 'parties' are so prominent in 1645-8 makes it hard to escape from the essentially two-party view of the situation both in the Long Parliament and the country espoused by the great Victorian S. R. Gardiner. Conditioned by the experience of the past century, the modern reader, British or American, naturally expects the analysis of W. S. Gilbert's sentry to be regularly repeated. When he looks into history and finds Whigs and Tories, Presbyterians and Independents, he feels himself on safely familiar ground. The division of a revolutionary party into its moderate and extremist components—Girondists and Jacobins, Mensheviks and Bolsheviks—is equally familiar and comforting for those who like their history to follow a predictable pattern. Since the publication of J. H. Hexter's *Reign of King Pym*, however, it is obvious that this simple dualism does not fit the Long Parliament. Independents and Presbyterians, or the war and peace parties as their Civil War predecessors were called, occupied only the extremes; between them lay that small but influential clique, led at first by John Pym and after his death by Oliver St. John, which Hexter labelled the 'middle group'.[1] Civil War parties, furthermore, bore only the vaguest resemblance to the monolithic leviathans of modern times. They were at

---

[1] Hexter, *Reign of King Pym*; Pearl, 'Oliver St. John and the "Middle Group" in the Long Parliament', *E.H.R.* lxxxi (1966), 490-519.

best loose, amorphous, and transient, with neither discipline nor organization; vaguely identifiable goups of men who happened for a time to think alike on one or ·more of the major issues of the day.

Even after the introduction of the middle group into the picture, the temptation still remains to think of these parties as excessively all-embracing.[2] The fact is that the majority of members of the Long Parliament cannot be regularly associated with any of them, did not think of themselves as party men, and indeed regarded the whole concept of party as factious and reprehensible. Because they were caught up in a crisis that aroused intense passions, and because they were Puritan idealists with important religious and political goals, more of them were compelled to take sides than would normally have wished to do so; but if they took sides, it would still be on the merits of the issues, not through a consistent subscription to a party formula. Then, and for more than a century afterwards, organized partisanship was by definition to be deplored: 'the ignominious term of a Party, men that drive their own interests', a pamphleteer defined it in 1647.[3] The Army's impeachment of the eleven Presbyterian leaders in 1647 included the charge that by manipulated elections and other improper methods they had attempted to 'make a faction' in the House.[4] That lively pamphleteer and intense partisan Clement Walker struck a popular note when he professed to speak for 'the honest middle men of the House (whose consciences will not let them join in any faction to rend the Commonwealth in sunder)' and deplored 'those badges of factions, and terms of distinctions and separations . . . Presbyterians and Independents'.[5]

These protests make it clear that by the end of the war parties were indeed appearing. Yet it is important not to put the cart before the horse, not to become entangled in the superficialities of party until we have appreciated the political context in which those parties arose. If we cannot start with the parties, where can we

[2] See, for example, Yule, *The Independents*; Yule, 'Independents and Revolutionaries', *J.B.S.* vii (1968), 11-32; Brunton and Pennington, *Members of the Long Parliament*, esp. pp. 38-9; and my criticisms in 'The Independents Reconsidered', *J.B.S.* iii (1964), 57-84; and 'The Independents Again', ibid. viii (1968), 83-93.

[3] [Tom Tell-Troth], *Works of Darkness brought to Light* (23 July 1647: [B.M.] E. 399, 36), p. 8.

[4] Bell, *Memorials*, ii. 381.

[5] Clement Walker, *Mystery of the Two Juntoes*, quoted in Underdown, 'Independents Reconsidered', *J.B.S.* iii (1964), 64-5.

start? Fortunately, if we are willing to make use of analogies from other periods of English history, in which the structure of politics has been more searchingly examined, we may obtain some guidance. Sir Lewis Namier's brilliant analysis of the English establishment of the eighteenth century obviously cannot be uncritically imported into the Puritan Revolution without anachronism. For one thing, Namier, as he himself often warned, was writing about a politics in which there were no compelling issues of principle, in which therefore the motive force of personal ambition could freely operate within the network of interest-groups and connections. This is obviously a long way from the passionate clash of ideals in the 1640s. Yet applied with due caution, the Namierite analysis does provide some valuable insights into the Long Parliament. Readers of Namier will recall the familiar division of M.P.s into three main categories: the court-treasury group of office-holders; the professional politicians, competing for places, and grouped in a variety of antagonistic factions; and the great mass of independent country gentry, without ambition for office, meeting issues on their merits, giving their support to any ministry which could carry on the government with efficiency and reasonable trustworthiness, but reserving their right to disagree if it went too far in violating their principles or their pocket-books.[6] To them, without doing violence to Namier, we can add a fourth: the clients of great noblemen. All four categories can be observed in the Long Parliament, and it is through their interaction that the party system, in its limited and often confusing way, operated.

In spite of efforts to restrict the already dwindling interest of the aristocracy in the lower House,[7] the clients and dependants of great noblemen are there. Some were entirely without political ambition, like Hugh Potter, who told his employer, the Earl of Northumberland, that he had no other aim 'than to live and die in your service'. Others played a more active role, like the Earl's legal adviser and secretary Robert Scawen, the hard-working chairman of the Army committee.[8] Some who had been elected with aristocratic help

---

[6] Sir Lewis Namier, 'Monarchy and the Party System', in *Crossroads of Power* (London, 1962), pp. 220-34.

[7] Keeler, *Long Parliament*, p. 9; Underdown, 'Party management', *E.H.R.* lxxxiii (1968), 242-3.

[8] H.M.C., *Third Report*, Appendix (Northumberland MSS.), pp. 86-9. There are many references to both Potter and Scawen in the Northumberland MSS., B.M. Films 286-7, 384, 398.

became independent when their patrons died or were disgraced. Henry Lucas owed his election for Cambridge University to his employer, the Earl of Holland, who was Chancellor, but must have been on his own after Holland wildly broke loose from his always hesitant support for Parliament in 1648. Walter Kyrle and Sir John Meyrick, both clients of the Earl of Essex, were similarly detached after Essex's death in 1646.[9] Meyrick's father had served Essex's father; there was a parallel relationship between Sir John Temple and the Sidneys. Temple's father, the Ramist philosopher, was a client of the great Elizabethan Sir Philip; Sir John himself served the Earl of Leicester, Sidney's nephew. At heart a neutral, Leicester had briefly joined Charles I at Oxford before retiring to Penshurst later in the war; but his two sons, Philip Lord Lisle and Algernon Sidney, remained active Parliamentarians. Until December 1648 Temple generally followed their line, rather than the Earl's.[10]

The men with the greatest personal followings in the Commons were Ferdinando, Lord Fairfax and the Earl of Pembroke. Old Lord Fairfax (a Scottish peer) sat in the Commons for Yorkshire until his death in March 1648; his sons-in-law Sir Thomas Widdrington, Sir William Constable, and Henry Arthington represented Berwick, Knaresborough, and Pontefract respectively; and his son Thomas, the General, narrowly missed at Cirencester early in 1647, when a double return was deadlocked in the Committee of Privileges. His nephew by marriage James Chaloner and the latter's brother Thomas came in as Recruiters for Aldborough and Richmond, and his clients Thomas Stockdale and William White took the other Knaresborough and Pontefract seats.[11] As for Pembroke, he had in the House three sons, his secretary Michael Oldisworth, another client William Stephens (Recruiter

---

[9] Kyrle was steward of Essex's Herefordshire estates, and served the Earl's royalist sister, the Marchioness of Hertford, when she inherited them: Welbeck MSS., Harley Papers, v (B.M. Loan, 29/175); B.M. Add. MS. 11047 (Scudamore MSS.), fol. 141; H.M.C., *Bath*, iv. 242. Meyrick's military career had been largely under Essex's command, and his father had been one of the Essex party in the 1590s: Keeler, *Long Parliament*, pp. 272–3; Dodd, *Stuart Wales*, p. 56.

[10] R. W. Blencowe, ed., *Sydney Papers* (London, 1825), pp. 181–6, 212, 240, 245–6; Arthur Collins, ed., *Letters and Memorials . . . transcribed from the Originals at Penshurst Place* (London, 1746), ii. 691; H.M.C., *De L'Isle*, vi, *passim*, esp. pp. 416, 439, 578; H.M.C., *Egmont*, i, *passim*, esp. p. 359.

[11] Bell, *Memorials*, i, *passim*. See also Underdown, 'Party management', *E.H.R.* lxxxiii (1968), 245–6. The Fairfax interest was less successful at Scarborough in 1645, however: G. C. F. Forster, 'Parliamentary Election Scandals in Stuart Yorkshire', *Trans. Yorks. Dialect Soc.* xi (1963), 28–31. I am indebted to the author for this reference.

for Newport, Isle of Wight), and two older courtiers, Sir Robert Pye and Sir Benjamin Rudyard, both men of some reputation in their own right, but also closely connected with the Herberts.[12]

The ties of clientage and kinship affected other M.P.s besides those dependent on members of the peerage. John Dove, the local brewer and alderman who sat for Salisbury, was nicknamed 'Sir John Evelyn's pigeon' because of his dependence on his patron.[13] The correspondence of Sir William Brereton, commander of the parliamentary forces in the west Midlands, reveals how less prominent M.P.s could serve the interests of more powerful ones: John Swynfen and William Ashhurst, two very active members, were agents both to Brereton's army and to him personally.[14] Herbert Morley of Glynde, a prominent Sussex member, led his brother-in-law John Fagge and his cousins Herbert and William Hay.[15] Sir Arthur Haselrig exercised similar influence over his son-in-law George Fenwick, and possibly over Edward Apsley, Fenwick's brother-in-law, who was also related to Haselrig's deceased first wife.[16] The influence of a man like William Purefoy over his son-in-law Godfrey Bosvile, the interlocking ties of kinship which bound together Binghams, Sydenhams, Brownes, and Trenchards in Dorset, and all the other family connections which produce the genealogical tangle of an English Parliament, might often compete with, or cut across political lines.

Besides the clients of great men, the office-holders or civil servants are there. We cannot call them 'King's Friends', for those that were had defected to Oxford. But there remained at Westminster plenty of men whose determination to hang on to office might tempt them to trim their sails to the political wind. In a crisis as passionate as that of the 1640s there were many who put principles above

[12] For Stephens's dependence on Pembroke see H.M.C., *Sixth Report*, Appendix (House of Lords MSS.), p. 68; and *C.J.* v. 98. Pye was one of the fourth Earl's executors: *Cal. S.P. Dom.*, *1652-3*, p. 47. Rudyard had sat in six earlier Parliaments under Herbert patronage: Keeler, *Long Parliament*, p. 329.

[13] M. Nicholas to Sir Edward Nicholas, 8 Feb. 1649: G. F. Warner, ed., *The Nicholas Papers* (Camden Soc., 1886-1920), i. 108.

[14] See Brereton's Letter-books in B.M. Add. MSS. 11331-3 (Apr.-May 1645, Oct. 1645-Jan. 1646); and in Birmingham Public Library (Apr.-May 1646).

[15] Yule, *The Independents*, pp. 96, 101, though the author is totally confused about the relationships.

[16] Keeler, *Long Parliament*, p. 213; Yule, *The Independents*, p. 97; *D.N.B.* ('Fenwick'); J. and J. A. Venn, *Alumni Cantabrigienses*, Pt. I: *To 1751* (Cambridge, 1922-7), i. 36. But cf. Hexter, *Reign of King Pym*, p. 73, for a caution against too much emphasis on family connections.

self-interest, and thus do not behave in the predictable way of Namier's placemen. Clement Walker espoused the cause of the independent back-benchers, but he was also an Usher of the Exchequer, and though he had inherited the office and held it for life, his vocal opposition to the Army radicals led inevitably to his dismissal in 1650.[17] Nor did office deter Walter Long (Chief Register in Chancery), Anthony Nicoll (Receiver of the Duchy of Cornwall, Master of the Armoury), and William Wheeler (Remembrancer of the Exchequer, Clerk of First Fruits and Tenths) from standing out against those in power—though Wheeler was still enjoying his offices in 1652, in spite of seclusion and temporary imprisonment at Pride's Purge.[18] There were also many office-holders who were solid landowners in their own right, and more likely to behave as such than as obedient servants of an administration. Sir John Curzon might be Receiver-General of the Duchy of Lancaster, but he was also a former sheriff of Derbyshire, a J.P., and a Deputy-Lieutenant. Sir John Fenwick, Master of the Stead and of Tutbury Race, was not likely to be influenced solely by his possession of office—Fenwick who was worth £6,000 a year and bred, his nephew says, 'the best horses ever was in England for coursing'—though he may have been by his enormous wartime losses, having had '£15,000 worth of horse flesh gone by the Scots Army in one morning'.[19] And though the Mastership of the Mint may have been more important to Sir Robert Harley, his dominant position in Herefordshire, and his deep-rooted Puritanism, make it absurd to categorize him as a mere office-holder.[20]

But though we cannot explain the internal politics of the Long Parliament, any more than the larger conflict of the Civil War, in the simple terms of a struggle between ins and outs, a fair proportion of M.P.s suggest by their behaviour that they were placemen first and politicians second. One well-founded instance is Daniel Blagrave, elected for Reading in June 1648. He came of a reputable local gentry family, but he was a younger son, embarked on a legal career, and became Recorder of Reading in 1645 after establishing sound parliamentarian credentials as Treasurer to the Berkshire County Committee. By the time of his election he held the office of

[17] For Walker's office, see *D.N.B.* ('Walker'), and *The Case between Clement Walker Esq. and Humphrey Edwards, Truely Stated* (July 1650: B.M., 669 f. 15, 38).
[18] *Cal. S.P. Dom., 1651–2*, p. 160.
[19] H.M.C., *Tenth Report*, App. IV (Stewart MSS.), pp. 108-11.
[20] G. E. Aylmer, *The King's Servants* (London, 1961), pp. 373-9.

Exigenter in the Court of Common Pleas, and in the following year acquired the more lucrative one of a Mastership in Chancery.[21] Blagrave's preoccupation with office is attested by something better than the charges of malicious royalist pamphleteers.[22] He was related to the wife of Elias Ashmole the astrologer, and between 1650 and 1652 he deluged Ashmole with requests for horoscopes to determine his chances of advancement. 'Whether Mr. Daniel Blagrave shall have the office of recording conveyances he hopes for', Ashmole asked of the stars in November 1650, with later inquiries about 'the place at Goldsmiths Hall', and the Register's place in Chancery. 'He must bribe', Ashmole pronounced on one of these occasions, advice which may not have been rejected as unthinkable, for Blagrave had been accused of precisely this offence when his election was in dispute in 1648. Blagrave may have been a Puritan revolutionary by conviction, as well as an office-seeker by profession, yet it is interesting that in 1650 he could denounce the 'godly-pretending party' at Reading as nothing more than a 'malicious rabble'.[23]

Few M.P.s provide such unassailable testimony to their place-seeking proclivities as Blagrave, but there is strong circumstantial evidence for a good many others. Two well-known examples are the former courtier-monopolists, Cornelius Holland and Sir Henry Mildmay, both so universally distrusted that it is impossible to disregard the allegations that they were chiefly motivated by personal greed. Holland, son of a minor household official, had risen on the coat-tails of the elder Vane, taking in such offices as Comptroller to

[21] *D.N.B.* ('Blagrave'); E. A. Smith, 'The Stuart and Early Hanoverian Periods', in A. Aspinall *et al.*, *Parliament through Seven Centuries: Reading and its M.P.s* (London, 1962), pp. 54–6; John Rylands Library, Manchester, Pink MS. 297/259. Previous difficulties about Blagrave's legal training (e.g. Brunton and Pennington, *Members of the Long Parliament*, p. 34) are easily solved on the assumption that he was the D.B., 5th son of Alexander B. of Southcoate, admitted to Inner Temple 1637, called to bar 1648: *Students Admitted to the Inner Temple, 1547–1660* (London, 1877), p. 292. The record gives the county of origin as Derbyshire, obviously in error: the Blagraves were of Southcotes, Berks.

[22] For example, *The Mystery of the Good Old Cause Briefly Unfolded* (1660), p. 12, in J. C. Hotten, ed., *Sarcastic Notices of the Long Parliament* (London, 1863). The tendency of partisan writers, from Clement Walker to Clarendon, to ascribe selfish motives to their enemies must always be allowed for.

[23] H.M.C., *Eleventh Report*, App. VII (Reading Corp. MSS.), p. 218; *Merc. Prag.*, no. 20 (8–15 Aug. 1648: [B.M.] E. 458, 24); C. H. Josten, ed., *Elias Ashmole (1617–1692): his Autobiographical and Historical Notes, his Correspondence, and other Contemporary Sources Relating to his Life and Work* (Oxford, 1966), ii. 556, 594–6, 617. The editor is incorrect in identifying Blagrave's father as Anthony B. of Bulmarsh (ii. 472, n.); there is no doubt that he was the son of Alexander of Southcotes (see n. 21, above).

the Prince of Wales, Clerk of the Green Cloth, Revenue Commissioner, Paymaster to the King's children, and Warden of the Tower
Mint. Inside the zealous Independent that was Holland's exterior
there undoubtedly lurked the ambitious careerist that was the
reality.[24] Mildmay, scion of a great landowning clan whose fortunes
had been founded by office, was Master of the Jewel House. Always
on the lookout for profit, he is variously described by modern historians as a timeserver, a 'rapacious scoundrel', and a man guilty of
'notorious peculation'.[25] Less well known is the reluctant regicide
John Downes. A 'poor, ordinary, mean man', Downes described himself in his defence in 1660, of origins so poor and ordinary that they
still defy detection. Somehow Downes found his way to the Inner
Temple, bought the post of Auditor to the Duchy of Cornwall,
worth £550 a year, and was elected M.P. for Arundel in 1641. The
sale of Crown lands after the Civil War threatened his livelihood,
so Downes had good reason to stay in Parliament, in which until
1649 he was inconspicuous, to secure himself. Security came his
way in 1649, when he received £3,000 compensation for loss of
office.[26]

Possible additions to the office-holding category are the two Six
Clerks in Chancery, Lenthall's friend Nicholas Love, and Henry
Smith, who always followed the lead of his more distinguished
father-in-law, Cornelius Holland.[27] Others are Humphrey Salway,
less active as a politician than his enthusiastically Puritan son
Richard, but who came of an Exchequer family, and held the post
of King's Remembrancer, and Richard Edwards, whose family had
a similar tradition of Chancery employment.[28] We know little
about such people's motives. But we know a good deal about

[24] For his Independency, see Tibbutt, ed., *Luke Letter Books*, pp. 56, 197, 226, 492.

[25] C. V. Wedgwood, *The Trial of Charles I* (London, 1964), p. 100; Brunton and Pennington, *Members of the Long Parliament*, p. 126; Yule, *The Independents*, p. 109. However,
Aylmer, *King's Servants*, pp. 353-4, 382, 384-5, defends Mildmay's consistency, in religion
at least.

[26] *Cobbett's Complete Collection of State Trials* (London, 1809-28), v. 1214; *Students adm.
to Inner Temple*, p. 267. List of offices held by M.P.s, 1646: Bodl. MS. Dep. C. 166 (Nalson
Papers, xiv), fol. 217; Keeler, *Long Parliament*, pp. 157-8; *C.J.* vi. 261; *Cal. S.P. Dom.,
1649-50*, p. 233.

[27] Brunton and Pennington, *Members of the Long Parliament*, p. 32; *Mystery of the Good
Old Cause*, pp. 26-7; *D.N.B.* ('Henry Smith').

[28] *Collectanea Topographica et Genealogica*, vi (1840), 290-1; Brunton and Pennington,
*Members of the Long Parliament*, p. 31. The Edwards family had acquired a couple of
Bedfordshire manors by 1659, but at least one of these was bought in the year of Richard's
death, 1657: *V.C.H., Bedfordshire*, ii. 244, 262.

another office-holder, Bulstrode Whitelocke, because he wrote his memoirs. Successful lawyer, son of a prominent judge, and prosperous Buckinghamshire landowner, Whitelocke obviously cannot be regarded as an office-holder and nothing more; but after 1648 he is a convincing candidate for inclusion in the category. Until then Whitelocke had been busy with his legal practice, skilfully threading his way between the parliamentary factions, and acquiring only a few minor dignities such as the High Stewardship of Greenwich. But in March 1648 he became one of the Commissioners of the Great Seal, a post which brought him £1,540 during his first year of tenure, as well as great power and dignity at the summit of the legal profession. Confronted with changes of government the conscience of Bulstrode Whitelocke invariably wrestled with the self-interest of the Commissioner of the Great Seal, and equally invariably, Whitelocke's conscience lost. One significant exception proves the rule: he lost the Seal in 1655 for opposing Cromwell's Chancery reform proposals, but this time lawyers' fees were at stake. And though he lost the Seal, Whitelocke stayed in the Protector's government as a member of the Treasury commission. There were always sound and sensible pragmatic reasons for accepting Pride's Purge, the King's execution and the establishment of the Protectorate; only when he supported the Committee of Safety against his old friends in the Rump in the autumn of 1659 did Whitelocke go too far. This was once too often, and when the politicians returned Thomas Scot vindictively threatened to have him hanged with the Great Seal about his neck.[29] If the office-holder's motto is 'Never resign', then Whitelocke was certainly in that category from March 1648.

The office-holders are there; so too are the independent country gentry. 'Public spirited men', Lucy Hutchinson calls them, who 'stood up in the parliament and the army, declaring against these factions and the ambition of the grandees of both.' In a later passage she mentions those who were of no faction, 'but looked upon themselves as called out to manage a public trust for their country'.[30] The independent gentry not only existed, they had too their

---

[29] Whitelocke, *Memorials*, esp. ii. 472, 475, 519, 523-4; iv. 367-8, 384; Bodl. MS. Dep. C. 166 (Nalson Papers, xiv), fol. 223; B.M. Add. MS. 37344 (Whitelocke's Annals), fol. 278. In this, the MS. version, Whitelocke often uses the first person singular for the impersonal pronoun that is found in the printed *Memorials*. In other ways, too, the MS. version is much more revealing. See also Underdown, *J.B.S.* iii (1964), 70-1.

[30] *Hutchinson*, pp. 256, 268.

E

self-appointed spokesman, Clement Walker, loudly addressing 'the
honest middle men of the House', pitching his whole appeal to the
non-partisan majority. The argument between Presbyterians and
Independents, Walker argued, was totally artificial, contrived by
the 'Juntoes' of both sides to conceal a tacit log-rolling agreement
to divide up the available patronage among themselves. 'The controversy between the two Juntoes', Walker declared, was 'no more
than whose slaves we shall be.' He was not the last frustrated M.P.
to discover an identity of interests between government and
opposition, a conspiracy of the front benches against the back.
The Junto leaders, Walker recognized, had immense advantages
through their mastery of procedure and tactics; the remedy was to
restore the independent members' initiative by creating a third
party out of the 'middle and disengaged men' to hold the balance
between the other two: ingenious, but self-defeating, for would
not the leaders of the new party rapidly acquire the same occupational characteristics as the old? Furthermore, as it suited Walker
not to recognize, there already was a third party, a 'middle group',
in the House, whose leadership he affected not to distinguish
from that of the Independents. With all its limitations, Walker's
outlook does help to define the existence of the non-party country
gentry as a political force. And his profession to be their mouthpiece was not, in spite of his ferocious conservatism and his own
status as an office-holder, a mere pose. Although more muted
than his attacks on the Independent Junto, his criticisms of the
Presbyterians are severe enough to include charges of intending
to found their own power on an army of their own, formed out
of the 'lewd supernumeraries' they kept on foot in 1647-8 on
the dishonest pretext that they were preparing to send them to
Ireland.[31]

The independent gentry as a general phenomenon can be
detected, but it is more difficult to identify them as individuals,
especially in view of their tendency to appear as supporters of one
faction or the other, or of both in turn, on particular issues. It is
tempting to conclude that any M.P. who cannot be consistently
associated with one of the parties must be in the independent
category. But the argument from silence is dangerous, for on the
one hand there were then, as always, men who trimmed or changed
sides, and others who were not so much independent as totally

[31] Walker, *Mystery of the Two Juntoes*, in Maseres, *Tracts*, i. 333-52.

inactive. It is, for instance, useless to put such a man as the elder Sir Francis Knollys, who was 90 at the time of his election and can have tottered into the House only on the rarest of occasions, in any category at all; yet he remained a member until his death towards the end of 1647.[32] But even though most of the independent gentry can only be so classified on negative evidence, some others express either in words or actions attitudes typical of the breed. Not all of them found it possible to maintain their independence in the highly partisan atmosphere of 1645-8, and their protestations of independent virtue must sometimes be taken with a grain of salt. On his wife's showing, John Hutchinson was by instinct always one of the country interest; she repeatedly stresses his avoidance of faction, local or national. Hutchinson was certainly no ambitious place-seeker, preferring to live quietly at Owthorpe and do his duty as a Christian magistrate. 'He was above the ambition of vain titles', Lucy assures us, '. . . well contented with the even ground of a gentleman.' But even if Hutchinson always acted according to his conscience, and 'never was any man's sectary, either in religious or civil matters', his Puritan zeal eventually pushed him into the arms of the radicals. For all that, he was no obedient party hack, and it is clear from his wife's dutiful biography that he did not regard politics primarily in party terms.[33]

Less passionately Puritan gentlemen than John Hutchinson were correspondingly less exposed to the danger of involvement. We must be content with three examples. Perhaps the best is Sir Roger Burgoyne, whose correspondence with his exiled friend Sir Ralph Verney is that of a man independent of (and totally disenchanted with) all factions: 'From them all, Libera nos', he prayed in May 1648. 'I have been taken for a country fellow, but never a courtier', he assured Verney in the same letter. Ambitious placemen and party leaders were his regular targets. 'Your servant happily may come to the honour of being one of their court cryers', he observed when Oliver St. John and his legal friends had themselves elevated to the bench in October of that year, but 'in the meantime I will be as merry as I can without it.'[34] The Somerset Presbyterian John

[32] Keeler, *Long Parliament*, pp. 243-4.

[33] *Hutchinson*, esp. pp. 28, 56-7, 239. It might be noted that Hutchinson had been tempted during a time of financial difficulty in his youth, and was providentially saved from buying an office in Star Chamber only by its abolition.

[34] Burgoyne to Verney, 4 May and 12 Oct. 1648: Verney MSS., B.M. Film 636, 8. I am grateful to Major Ralph B. Verney for permission to quote from the Verney MSS.

Harington can be our second example. Harington's earlier career, his preference for virtuous 'country' independence above the corrupting attractions of the court, his ability to remain on good terms with both conservatives and radicals in his county, and his eclecticism in his choice of London friends, all mark him out as a probable independent. A reading of his diary for 1646–7 confirms this impression. On the rare occasions when Harington uses the terms Presbyterian and Independent in the political sense he does so with equal distaste, and when he uses the word 'we', as he frequently does, it is in the sense of the whole House.[35] For a third example we can take the scholarly Sussex iron-master, Samuel Gott. After a period of pious contemplation in the leisure provided by his enforced exclusion from politics, in 1650 Gott published his *Essay of the True Happines of Man*.[36] The whole book breathes an air of sensible moderation, a preference for the golden mean. Like so many of the country gentry whose lineage was more exalted than that claimed by his own *arriviste* credentials, Gott preferred a country retirement and modest seclusion to the dangers and exhilarations of national politics: 'the best condition of life, is between a Constable and a Justice of Peace', and 'it is no small happiness to live comfortably within doors, and to entertain ourselves with our own thoughts'.

Attitudes like these inevitably carried with them the temptations of trying to steer a middle course even in the greater conflict between King and Parliament. The strength of neutralism in 1642 has already been described. And the motive in all the attempted neutrality compacts was the same as that which prevented men later from discarding their independence in favour of Independent or Presbyterian partisanship: to preserve the ordered fabric of society, the integrity of the county and national communities. In 1642 Sir Henry Worsley, an appropriate neighbour in the Isle of Wight for that familiar mouthpiece of the country gentry, Sir John Oglander, tried to resign his seat in Parliament, 'by reason of some scruples that he hath in his conscience', which led him to 'great dispute with himself'.[37] Indecision of this kind could lead to association with moves hostile to Parliament. Henry Oxinden of Deane was agonizingly unable to make up his mind in 1642, and

[35] B.M. Add. MS. 10114 (Harington's Diary), fols. 24ᵛ–25ᵛ. See also above, pp. 19–21.
[36] 10 June 1650: [B.M.] E. 1407. See esp. Preface, and pp. 50, 55–6, 78.
[37] Petition of Sir H. Worsley, 1642: B.M. Add. MS. 46501 (Worsley MSS.), no. 18.

though he conformed to Parliament and was elected to the Commons three years later, in 1648 he was still putting his county ahead of his parliamentarian loyalties by supporting, admittedly rather equivocally, the Kent petition that preceded the outbreak of the second Civil War.[38] He was not the only one who found it hard to take sides either in 1648 or earlier. Sir Hugh Owen and his brother Arthur in Pembrokeshire were typical of many of the Welsh gentry in their uncertain behaviour in 1648, and Sir Hugh ('as much as is understood of him a Royalist') had been accused of an earlier defection to Oxford.[39] George Horner, John Harington's fellow knight of the shire for Somerset, was accused of being 'a known neuter, if not worse', who had lived quietly at his father's house at Mells during royalist occupation, when he was first elected in 1645.[40] For most of these men, the explanation for their hesitations lies not so much in their being especially untrustworthy or unreliable, as in their preference for an uncommitted independence, in which the tight bonds of neighbourliness and kinship that bound together the local establishments, counted for more than support for party policies.

The innate localism of the country gentry is one of their most obvious characteristics. Another is their equally strong dislike of placemen; hence the support given by many to the Self-Denying Ordinance, and the recurrent efforts to enumerate and control the number of office-holders. A committee of the Commons appointed on 16 March 1646 collected a great deal of valuable information about them, and was revived in 1648 under the chairmanship of John Bulkeley, who in the previous year had also been chairman of another committee for receiving complaints of corruption against M.P.s. Suspicions that placemen appointed by Parliament might oppose a settlement with the King out of fear that his return would lead to their dismissal were commonly expressed, and were behind the unsuccessful introduction of a Bill in the Lords in July 1648 prohibiting members of either House from holding any office of profit that they had not held before the war. Such an office-holder was to resign immediately, 'lest, fearing that by a settlement of a lasting peace he might lose his place, he may be swayed to fit his

---

[38] Everitt, *Community of Kent*, pp. 108-9 and n., 244.

[39] Dodd, *Stuart Wales*, pp. 123, 141, 153-4; Arthur L. Leach, *History of the Civil War (1642-1649) in Pembrokeshire and on its Borders* (London, 1937), pp. 220-1; W. R. Williams, *Parliamentary History of the Principality of Wales* (Brecknock, 1895), p. 161.

[40] *Scottish Dove*, no. 119 (21-9 Jan. 1645/6: [B.M.] E. 319, 17).

vote to his private interest rather than the public'.[41] An anonymous country gentleman took the same line when the Treaty of Newport was being arranged: 'I, for my part, envy not those gentlemen
that enjoy great offices by the favour of the House, being, I thank
God, contented with my own estate, and desire nothing of others.'
In view of the general belief that placemen were 'enemies to peace',
he proposed 'that no such gentlemen may be employed as commissioners in this Treaty'.[42] Such virtuous suspicions are echoed by
successive generations of country gentlemen down the centuries.

Among the Boscawens, Norths, and Hungerfords, and many
more of the M.P.s whose names read like a record of the great
county families of England, we can therefore find the men of whom
the Burgoynes and Haringtons are typical, at the opposite pole from
professional office-holders like Cornelius Holland and Mildmay.
But as in the parliaments of the eighteenth century, so in the Long
Parliament there was another part of the political spectrum,
occupied by men who might or might not be in office, might or
might not be clients of greater men, but who were above all else
politicians, striving to promote definite policies or interests, and for
this purpose combining sometimes with each other, sometimes with
groups of placemen or independent gentry. As the war progressed,
as issues arose which produced violent partisanship, as the heads of
families or interest-groups died or were disgraced, the ties of kinship and connection became less likely to determine the behaviour
of M.P.s, though there were always some who continued to be
affected by them. And when the negative character of Parliament's
original unity was revealed there developed the conflicting factions,
the rudimentary parties of the Long Parliament.

*       *       *

Most of the parliamentarian gentry, in or outside of Parliament,
would have agreed with Nathaniel Fiennes when he said that the

[41] H.M.C., *Seventh Report*, Appendix (House of Lords MSS.), p. 36; *L.J.* x. 372, 375. The
information collected by the 1646 committee is in the Nalson Papers in Bodl. MSS. Dep. C.
157, fol. 54; 165, fol. 388; 166, fols. 215-25; 167, fols. 327-8, 340, 361, 490; 168, fol. 334;
and Bodl. MS., Tanner 59, fols. 491-503, 665, 683, 728; printed in part in Henry Cary,
ed., *Memorials of the Great Civil War* (London, 1842), i. 149; H.M.C., *Portland*, i. 412-13;
and Francis Peck, ed., *Desiderata Curiosa* 2nd edn. (London, 1779), p. 366. See also *C.J.* v.
220-1, 563, 619.
[42] *The Parliamentary or Constitutional History of England* 2nd edn. (London, 1761-3),
xvii. 435-6—henceforth cited as *Old Parl. Hist.* For similar expressions of this attitude
cf. ibid. xviii, 87, 291.

war was essentially defensive, to restore the balance of the constitution in Church and State. Pursuing this argument, Fiennes pointed out the essential difference between the aims of his respectable colleagues, 'fighting to maintain the laws and true religion', and that of the few (Presbyterians as well as political radicals) who were 'fighting against law to overthrow one government thereby established, and set up another'.[43] Far removed from Fiennes in his party connections, John Maynard made the same point in the debate on the Vote of No Addresses in January 1648: 'I will fight to maintain a law, but never to get a [new] law.'[44] But there were from the outset a few, Puritan zealots like Vane, doctrinaire republicans like Henry Marten, who were indeed out to overthrow one government and set up another. Their emergence into positions of power and influence through the harsh pressure of war drove many to question their own former acquiescence in resistance to the King, and to seek peace and reconciliation on the most lenient terms possible. Such a one was Denzil Holles, a 'fiery spirit' and determined seeker after victory at the outset of the war, who turned against it after seeing the cowardly behaviour of his men at the siege of Sherborne.[45] But it was not only contempt for the common soldiers that made Holles a leader of the 'peace party'. The war, he observed, had undone the ordered harmony of society, had threatened the natural hierarchy. The opening words of his memoirs, written in temporary exile in the winter of 1647-8, proclaim Holles's recognition of the connection between war policy and the threat of social revolution, the fulfilment of the 'great evil, that servants should ride on horses', a situation in which 'the meanest of men, the basest and vilest of the nation, . . . have got the power into their hands; trampled upon the crown; baffled and misused the Parliament; violated the Laws; destroyed, or suppressed the nobility and gentry'.[46] Peace-party backbenchers shared their leader's fears of the results of an appeal to the people. 'My own endeavours here have been for peace', Sir John Potts confided to D'Ewes on the eve of the war; '. . . whensoever necessity shall

---

[43] *Vindiciae Veritatis*, p. 35, and cf. the whole argument from p. 33.

[44] David Underdown, ed., 'The Parliamentary Diary of John Boys, 1647-8', *B.I.H.R.* xxxix (1966), 155.

[45] Hexter, *Reign of King Pym*, p. 9. A more charitable explanation is Holles's revulsion from bloodshed after his experiences at Brentford: Gardiner, *Civil War*, i. 66, 71.

[46] *Memoirs of Denzil, Lord Holles*, in Maseres, *Tracts*, i. 191.

enforce us to make use of the multitude I do not promise myself safety.'[47]

The original division in the Long Parliament was, then, between a peace party and a war party. The peace party wanted settlement with the King on almost any terms, even if it meant abandoning the Grand Remonstrance and the Nineteen Propositions, abandoning the Root-and-Branch reformation of the Church (though they would prevent the restoration of Laudian episcopacy), forgetting the militia question and the Parliament's grasp at executive power by nomination of the King's councillors. In so far as it was necessary to fight the war at all they wanted it done with extreme caution and under safe, aristocratic generals like the Earls of Denbigh, Manchester, and their party leader Essex. Always on the look-out for negotiation, they wished to do nothing to make peace difficult, or to release the forces of militant radicalism, and had no interest in fighting energetically to establish a strong bargaining position. Essentially the peace party's position rested on a willingness to trust the King, a belief that the measures of 1641 could be sustained without inflicting on him a total military defeat, and without the additional safeguards demanded by more tough-minded members. Through all the shocks to their faith provided by repeated disclosures of Charles I's duplicity in such war party windfalls as the Naseby letters, they clung to this touching belief in the King's integrity. 'Mr. Speaker, I cannot yet depart from my principles, principles of peace and reconciliation', declaimed Sir John Holland after his faith had been fortified by a spell as a commissioner with the King at Holmby in 1647. People who distrusted Charles, Holland thought, ought to go and attend him as he had done, and would then be convinced that he was a prince 'under whose government we may yet be happy'.[48] Negotiate, negotiate, even in conditions of military weakness in which the results would be virtual surrender: such was the policy of the peace party.

But as Henry Marten frequently pointed out, 'There is another and a more natural way to peace and to the ending of a war than by agreement, namely by conquest.'[49] A dictated peace following the unconditional surrender of the King: such was the policy of the

---

[47] Potts to D'Ewes, 19 Aug. 1642: B.M. Harl. MS. 386 (D'Ewes Corr.), fol. 233.

[48] Bodl. MS., Tanner 321 (Holland's Speeches), fols. 24–5.

[49] Henry Marten, *The Independency of England Endeavoured to be Maintained* (11 Jan. 1647/8: [B.M.] E. 422, 16), p. 15.

war party. This would permit not only the total elimination of monarchical power, perhaps even of monarchy itself (though Marten was alone in going as far as that in 1643, and was suspended from the House for it), but also a total reconstruction of the government, including that of the Church (though as we have seen, there was no agreement on what would replace episcopacy). In order to achieve this, the revolutionary minority would wage war by the most ruthlessly effective methods, getting rid of the half-hearted aristocrats under whose command the Parliament's armies fumbled and failed in the first two years of the war. If this meant promoting and encouraging the radical Puritans of the lower class, arming and organizing them, and stirring them up with the millenarian preaching of the Army chaplains and mechanic preachers, and if this led to the spread of dangerous, subversive opinions, this was a price that they were willing to pay. But although the war party looked forward to peace (a dictated one), the pursuit of total victory became, as is the way with hawks, an end in itself, and the denial of negotiations a substitute for policy.

By the winter of 1644-5 it was clear that the division between war and peace parties went far beyond the actual conduct of the war. Clarendon, who as Sir Edward Hyde was one of Charles's commissioners at the Treaty of Uxbridge, had his earlier Oxford-formed impressions of the situation confirmed in meetings with the more moderate of the parliamentary commissioners. In Parliament, he was told,

> There were many who desired to have peace, without any alteration in the government, so they might be sure of indemnity and security for what was past; . . . but that there was another party that would have no peace upon what conditions soever, who did resolve to change the whole frame of the government in State as well as Church, which made a great party in the army: and all those of the Parliament who desired to remove the earl of Essex from being general of the army, and to make another general, were of that party.[50]

Clarendon, like many outsiders, over-simplified the situation, for not all of those who wanted a more vigorous conduct of the war and the replacement of Essex were dedicated to the radical aims of war-party leaders like Marten, Haselrig, and the younger Vane. But

[50] Clarendon, *History*, Bk. VIII, § 241. Cf. Osmund Airy, ed., *Burnet's 'History of My Own Time'* (Oxford, 1897-1900), i. 64.

on the basic division between the two groups of extreme partisans in Parliament Clarendon was right.[51]

Besides the war and peace factions, however, the party spectrum also included a crucially important 'middle group' of experienced politicians, whose leadership and balancing functions were in importance out of all proportion to their numbers. Brilliantly led by John Pym, and after his death by Oliver St. John,[52] the middle group had clear political aims, and above all the parliamentary expertise, the grasp of tactics and procedure, to establish them as the common policy. The middle group wanted peace, but it was not to be a peace of surrender. The settlement of 1641 was to be buttressed by the additional safeguards demanded in 1642—control of the militia power, and of the nomination of the King's councillors. The middle group were ready to negotiate, but they saw the connection between negotiation and the military situation, saw that only a vigorous conduct of the war could persuade Charles I to an acceptable peace. The war, they hoped, need not be protracted by insisting on impossible terms; but in the meantime it was essential to close ranks in both Parliament and Army, conduct the war with the maximum efficiency, and harness diplomacy to military power by adding to their forces those of the Scots. Thus, while working with the peace party to head off attacks on Essex, Pym also worked with the war party for improved military preparations, and for the Scots alliance. That alliance, indeed, was chiefly the work of the war party Vane and the middle group St. John. But although the middle group might agree with the war party on the conduct of the war, they did not share their radical political and religious aims, indeed their view of the society which would follow the war was essentially conservative. A strict settlement with the King, preserving the goals of 1641-2, yes, but no tinkering with the traditional fabric of society. Nathaniel Fiennes, who was one of them, summarizes the underlying philosophy of the middle group. Denying that they intended 'a total alteration of the government from a mixed monarchy, duly bounded as this is, into something else', Fiennes continues:

As we hate tyranny in one, so we do factions in a few equals, and as

[51] See Hexter, *Reign of King Pym*, esp. pp. 54–9, for the early history of the war and peace parties.

[52] It will be evident that I follow Valerie Pearl, *E.H.R.* lxxxi (1966), 490–519, rather than the alternative argument put forward by Lotte Glow, 'Political Affiliations in the House of Commons after Pym's Death', *B.I.H.R.* xxxviii (1965), 48–70, that the middle group disintegrated after Pym's death.

much, or more, confusion in the many-headed multitude. We resolve therefore to keep the three estates co-ordinate equally to poise and balance each other. . . . We need not, we will not, to gain a peace, be without a King, no nor without this King: only he himself hath brought this necessity upon us, not to trust him with that power whereby he may do us and himself hurt.[53]

As for religious aims, the middle group had none more specific than those dictated by the undifferentiated moral Puritanism of the majority of members. Fiennes and his father Lord Say, the party's *eminence grise*, were both Independents, but this did not prevent their allying with Erastian Presbyterians like Samuel Browne, and supporters of moderate episcopacy like St. John, Crewe, and Pierrepont. They had been willing to make vaguely Presbyterian promises to the Scots, but they made certain that whatever was established would be no more than a 'lame Erastian presbytery' by allying themselves with the other Erastians and the religious Independents in the House. By July 1644 Robert Baillie was lamenting to his friends in Scotland: 'The politic part in the Parliament is the stronger, who are resolute to conclude nothing in the matters of religion that may grieve the sectaries, whom they count necessa[ry?] for the time.'[54]

Such were the main political factions of the Long Parliament. What was the relationship between these parties and the rest of the House of Commons in this middle period of the war? It is clear that none of the parties—the Vane-Haselrig war party, the St. John–Fiennes middle group, and the Essex-Holles peace party—accounted for more than a fraction, and that together they were less than half, of the active membership of the Commons. Each of the three had about thirty identifiable adherents, in a House whose active membership before the recruiting of vacant seats began in August 1645 was just under 200. As most of the office-holding element can also be identified with one or other of the parties, this leaves over 100 of the independent gentry.[55] Many occasional

---

[53] *Vindiciae Veritatis*, p. 6. For the middle group's aims see also Pearl, 'Royal Independents', *T.R.H.S.* 5th Ser. xviii (1968), 69–96.                                    [54] *Baillie*, ii. 211.

[55] Holles, who had good reason to magnify the opposition, says that there were about fifty war-party members in 1645: Maseres, *Tracts*, i. 214. Hexter's analysis of the middle group suggests a minimum of thirty-six for that party, with a larger number attached in a 'loose confederation': Hexter, *Reign of King Pym*, p. 70. My own view is that both these estimates are too large. The largest monthly average of divisions during the war was 170: Vernon F. Snow, 'Attendance Trends and Absenteeism in the Long Parliament', *H.L.Q.* xviii (1954–5), 304. But the total number of members who were at least intermittently active was somewhat greater than this.

middle-group adherents were probably independent gentry, whose support for middle-group positions did not alter their uncommitted non-party status. It would be natural to expect the country gentry on the backbenches to be more often on the middle-group side, since this was after all the one that reflected the consensus position. Country gentlemen who were solid Puritans but not denominational zealots, who stood fast by the terms set forth in the Nineteen Propositions but wanted peace and stability, would find in the middle-group programme the nearest approximation to their needs. They might differ on the details, but more often than not they would support the realistic, practical combination of war and negotiation represented by Pym, St. John, and their allies. Furthermore, the middle group's grasp of political tactics was also likely to keep them in touch with the aspirations of the country gentry whose support would provide their majority. Individual members might shift from support for a peace proposal to support for a war measure, yet on any given issue the middle-group position was likely to be nearest to the consensus.

But there are two ways of looking at the loose, unstable political situation in Parliament in the first two years of the Civil War. If we examine the members in one way they divide into war, peace, and middle groups, with a shifting mass of country gentry behind them. If we look at them in another, especially as the religious issue begins to emerge in 1644, they divide into Independents, Presbyterians, Erastians, and moderate episcopalians. Although none of the handful of Independents were also members of the peace party, and the upholders of moderate episcopacy are rarely found in the war party, none of the religious groups bears any absolute correspondence with the political ones. There are Presbyterians in the war party—John Gurdon, Edmund Prideaux, Zouch Tate; in the middle group—William Ashhurst, Sir John Clotworthy, Sir Robert Harley; and in the peace party—Sir Robert Pye, Sir John Trevor, Lawrence Whitaker. There are Erastians in the peace party—D'Ewes, Selden, Sir John Holland; in the middle group—Oliver St. John, Samuel Browne, Sir John Evelyn, Bulstrode Whitelocke; and almost certainly in the war party, though it is harder to identify them. The moderate episcopalians, usually outwardly Presbyterian by 1644, are more heavily represented in the peace party, but the presence of John Crewe, John Glyn, Richard Knightley, and William Pierrepont in the middle group demon-

strates that it was possible to reconcile a desire for primitive episcopacy with support for resolute prosecution of the war. On a political
issue such as the conduct of the war or the presentation of peace
terms to the King, therefore, the members of the House of Commons would divide in one way; on religious issues the same
members would divide in quite another.

It is therefore not surprising to find particular groups of men
whose religious aims were quite dissimilar co-operating in politics
in the manner that Nathaniel Fiennes fondly recollected. In the
same way it is no surprise to find men whose political aims were
profoundly different co-operating in religious matters. Oliver
Cromwell was a religious Independent; he was also a man of the
middle group, whose instinctive conservatism was far different
from the urgent radicalism of a Sir Henry Vane. Yet, as Baxter
noted, Cromwell and Vane were strong allies in religion, and this
could carry over across the borderline separating spiritual from
political issues. 'The Vanists in the House, and Cromwell in the
Army', Baxter tells us, 'joined together, outwitted and over-reached
the rest, and carried on the interest of the sectaries in special, while
they drew the religious party [i.e. the broad mass of undifferentiated
Puritans] along as for the interest of godliness in the general.'[56] Two
things in particular helped to cement the alliance between the
Independents, the war party, and the middle group: the behaviour
of the Scots, and the bitter struggle over the formation of the New
Model Army. Out of these two issues came the great transformation, the reversal of alliances in 1644, in which the Presbyterian and
Independent parties were born.

\* \* \*

The Scots, it will be recalled, had been called in by Vane and St.
John, by the war party and the middle group, and against the
opposition of the peace party, in order to win the war. But as the
rosy dawn of Marston Moor was succeeded by the defeats and dis-
appointments of the late summer and autumn of 1644—by Lostwithiel and the second battle of Newbury—it became evident that
the Scots were interested in something other than winning the war
for an English Parliament. For them the purpose of the alliance was
to promote the establishment of a theocratic Presbytery in England.
To this they were committed by both principle and expediency, to

[56] *Rel. Baxt.* i. 47.

protect their kirk from either a repeat performance of the Laudian
intervention against which they had rebelled in 1637, or infection
from the dangerous heresies which flourished in England during
what Baillie called the 'long anarchy' in which there was no ecclesiastical establishment.[57] Hence the disagreements and rivalries between the officers, such as those between Crawford and Cromwell,
which disfigured the alliance and made co-operation difficult during
the year 1644. The Scots were little concerned with the constitutional issues which were uppermost for most of their English
allies; if Presbytery could be established by a deal with the King,
restoring him to his full executive powers and sacrificing the programme of 1641, they would have no objection.

This divergence of aims between the English and the Scots
quickly became connected with the intensifying antipathy between
the war and peace parties. Although the prospect of total defeat had
receded, after Lostwithiel and Newbury it was also evident that
Parliament was unlikely to win a quick victory under half-hearted
aristocratic generals. If Essex was discredited by Lostwithiel,
Manchester was no less so by Newbury. The trouble, as Cromwell
rightly said in the course of his quarrel with Manchester, was that
the peers and their peace-party friends did not really want to win:
Manchester was not alone in his 'unwillingness to have this war
prosecuted into a full victory'.[58] For Essex and his like peace was
necessary to avoid a total alteration of the constitution and the sub-
version of the social order; for the Scots it was necessary to avoid
a victory for the Independents and the sects. It was not difficult to
see that these two statements might refer to different aspects of one
and the same thing. The peace party, which had opposed the Scots
alliance as being likely to prolong the war when it was first negotiated,
thus began to turn to the Scots in the autumn of 1644 as counters to
Cromwell and Vane, to the sects and the radicals.

The peace-party alliance with the Scots lies behind the bitter
debates during the winter of 1644-5 over the Self-Denying Ordinance and the New Model Army. It became a striking reality in the
desperate discussion at Essex House on the night of 3 December
1644, when the Earl met with Holles, other leaders of the peace
party, and the Scots commissioners to plan the impeachment of

---

[57] H. R. Trevor-Roper, 'Scotland and the Puritan Revolution', in H. E. Bell and R. L.
Ollard, eds., *Historical Essays, 1600-1750* (London, 1963), pp. 84-96.
[58] Quoted in Ivan Roots, *The Great Rebellion, 1642-1660* (London, 1966), p. 92.

Oliver Cromwell. The plot came to nothing—the lawyers Whitelocke and Maynard wisely stressed the political as well as the legal
difficulties—but its very existence, and the names of the participants, shows how closely the Scots and the peace party were now
working together.[59] By the time the next round of peace negotiations began at Uxbridge at the end of January, the new alignment
was public knowledge. On 3 February the radical John Pyne warned
his allies in Somerset: 'I doubt there is some sour Scottish ale
a-brewing.' The Scots, he told his friends, had 'withdrawn their
intimateness' from the middle group and war-party-dominated
Committee of Both Kingdoms, and instead had 'joined themselves
in a seeming confederacy and compliance' with the Holles-
Stapleton faction. 'What is the design, is not yet discerned', Pyne
continued, ''Tis hoped that 'tis only done to advance the Presby-
terial government with us.' However, he was suspicious that there
was more to it than that. Between the lines of Pyne's letter can be
detected the fear of a Scots and peace party sell-out to the King:
'The consideration of this horrible thing, if true, causeth a trepida-
tion in my thoughts and spirit.'[60]

The letter fell into royalist hands, and the cat was out of the bag.
Communicated from Oxford to the parliamentary commissioners
negotiating at Uxbridge, the violence of Pyne's language reinforced
the strong belief of Holles and his friends that peace was an urgent
necessity. Essex ('I hope to see him and his accomplices laid aside',
Pyne had said) received copies from his royalist brother-in-law
Hertford and from Prince Rupert, and steps were soon being taken
to bring Pyne to book. Early in April he was summoned to answer
for himself in the Commons and although no action appears to have
been taken against him, he was now marked down as a passionate
adherent of the extremists.[61] Coming as it did at the time of the
peace party's efforts to secure a compromise at Uxbridge, and
the war party and middle group's promotion of the New Model,
the Pyne affair dramatically illustrates both the nature of the new
alignment and the passions it aroused.

The Self-Denying Ordinance and the New Model cemented the

---

[59] Gardiner, *Civil War*, ii. 25–7.

[60] Pyne to Edward Popham, 3 Feb. 1644/5: *Mercurius Aulicus*, 23 Feb.–2 Mar. 1644/5
([B.M.] E. 273, 13).

[61] Clarendon, *History*, Bk. VIII, §§ 240–1; Essex to Rupert, 28 Feb. 1644/5: Eliot War-
burton, *Memoirs of Prince Rupert and the Cavaliers* (London, 1849), iii. 62; *C.J.* iv. 97,
100.

close ties between the war party and the middle group. As the New Model was from the first an army dominated by the Independents, and as the Scottish ties of the peace party necessarily made them press more urgently for a Presbyterian establishment, it is not surprising that the process which broadened the two extreme groups became, in the eyes of many contemporaries, a conflict of Presbyterians and Independents, particularly as the debates on Church government began more and more to occupy the time of Parliament after the spring of 1645. Although the two terms came only gradually into general usage in the course of the year 1645, and although both remained loose confederations of groups rather than close-knit parties, with most of the really independent gentry only tenuously attached to either, it is now possible, with all these reservations, to speak of the Presbyterian and Independent parties. Throughout the year the pressure of events continued to solidify them—the Savile affair, for example, in which the defecting royalist peer Lord Savile accused Holles and Whitelocke of backstairs intrigues with the Royalists during the Uxbridge negotiations. Lord Say, it is worth noting, was suspected of having put up Savile to make the accusation, while two of the most active promoters of the subsequent investigation were St. John and Samuel Browne, both obviously determined to destroy Holles.[62]

The resumption of elections after August 1645, when the Commons set out to 'recruit' the House, and fill the places of the deceased or the expelled Royalists, also helped to harden party lines. 'Many will break out in factions about elections', Whitelocke rightly foresaw when the first writs were debated.[63] Although most of the by-elections held in the three years after September 1645 were of the traditional kind—personal, family, local contests, with little direct bearing on national politics—in at least a few of them the Presbyterian-Independent conflict was crucial. When the first elections were held the most obvious attempt at management came from the middle group and the centre, out to recruit reliable Parliamentarians, but not partisan politicians: hence the irresistibly 'centre' complexion of the committee of managers which accompanied John Ashe and Anthony Nicoll into the western counties in the autumn of 1645. But the radicals were also learning electioneering tech-

---

[62] Whitelocke, *Memorials*, i. 457–81, esp. pp. 466, 469, 470–1, 476.
[63] Quoted in Underdown, 'Party management', *E.H.R.* lxxxiii (1968), 238–9. See this article in general for the hardening of party lines during the elections.

niques. It was widely believed that Hugh Peter and other Army preachers were their election agents. Even if this was true, however, the efforts of Peter and his like were no more than peripheral, for in Edmund Prideaux, chairman of the Committee of the West, Postmaster-General, and Commissioner of the Great Seal (with all the control of election tactics through the timing of writs that this entailed), the Independents had an election manager of both energy and ability. In 1646 the Presbyterians belatedly learned to play the same game. They struck back at, and eventually removed, Prideaux's control of the Seal, and then, through Anthony Nicoll in Cornwall and the Committee for South Wales, adopted the methods that had been used against them in 1645 and 1646. They also tightened up their organization in the House. By 1647 they had in Walter Long a recognizable party Whip. Long, his enemies charged, used to 'place himself near the door of the House', where he could persuade departing supporters to stay for impending divisions. Like his modern counterpart, Long was 'very inquisitive' about the movements of his back-benchers when they left the House, and when a vote was imminent he would 'speedily run out of the House himself to call and drive them in again'.[64]

\* \* \*

Neither the Independents nor the Presbyterians, in spite of this gradual acquisition of party characteristics, were homogeneous entities. Both were loose coalitions of groups, shading off into the grey mass of the uncommitted, who might support one or other occasionally on the merits of particular issues. The main component of the Presbyterians was the older peace party led by Denzil Holles, and typified by such men as D'Ewes and Sir John Holland. These had been joined, by the end of 1644, by some of Pym's old middle group—his nephew Anthony Nicoll, Sir Philip Stapleton, Sir John Clotworthy, and the Recorder of London, John Glyn, were the most notable. Others drifted over during 1645 or even later: Sir Walter Erle, for example, was not consistently identified with the Presbyterians until 1646.[65] The Self-Denying Ordinance

[64] 'A Particular Charge of Impeachment' (1647), in Bell, *Memorials*, ii. 383. It is doubtful if modern Whips would approve of Long's frequent resort to physical violence against members on the other side: see Whitaker's diary, 8 Jan. 1645/6: B.M. Add. MS. 31116, fol. 253.

[65] Glow, *B.I.H.R.* xxxviii (1965), 61; Pearl, *E.H.R.* lxxxi (1966), 493 n., 494 n., 508, 513 n.

F

brought in discontented former generals like Sir William Waller (hitherto a war-party man), and after their election as Recruiters, Major-Generals Richard Browne and Edward Massey, together with other discarded officers like Lionel Copley. With these naturally coalesced all the enemies of the Army, all supporters of a soft peace with the King; some of them crypto-Royalists, who were, a 1648 observer thought, naturally 'of the Presbyterian persuasion, as it is most favourable to Monarchy'.[66]

There were a good many men in the House whose sympathies were pretty clearly with the King. Northumberland's servant Hugh Potter, suspended for a time in 1645-6, managed to convince the House that his attendance on the Queen at York had been merely incidental to his supervision of the Earl's estates. Potter might well be thought a typical peace-party adherent, hoping that God would 'incline the hearts of both parties to prevent the utter ruin of these kingdoms'. But he went further than this, retaining close friendships with men at Charles I's court, a 'true heart' who was still assuring Secretary Nicholas of his service in 1647.[67] In that same year the Army accused a score or more of members of having flirted with Oxford during the war, including Inchiquin's agent Sir Philip Perceval, the two Hereford members, Hoskins and Edmund Weaver, and some others.[68] Allowance must be made for the Army's motives—they were out to remove as many of their opponents from the House as they could—but there is no doubt that many such people had royalist, or at least neutralist leanings. The same might have been said of at least a dozen others. Samuel Terrick, denounced as 'a neuter at best' by Sir William Brereton when he was elected, had been with the Royalists at Lichfield during the siege, and was a friend of the royalist astrologer Ashmole.[69] The Lancastrian John Holcroft was alleged to have sent to Oxford for a pardon, and to have applied to Parliament Sir Walter Raleigh's description of the Athenian tyrants; naturally he denied it all.[70] George

---

[66] *Certaine Considerations touching the Present Factions* (Oct. 1648: [B.M.] E. 466, 3), p. 2. Cf. *Ludlow*, i. 135-6, 146-7.

[67] Potter to Earl, 21 Feb. 1644/5: Northumberland MS. PI/3/p, B.M. Film 387; N. Oudart to Nicholas, 18 Feb. and 4 Mar. 1647: *Nicholas Papers*, i. 76, 81.    [68] See below, p. 82.

[69] Brunton and Pennington, *Members of the Long Parliament*, p. 24; Josten, ed., *Ashmole*, ii. 355-6, 423, 541, 642.

[70] H.M.C., *Tenth Report*, App. IV (Stewart MSS.), p. 101. See also J. Brownbill, ed., *Calendar of . . . Papers of the Moore Family* (Record Soc. Lancs. and Cheshire, lxvii, 1913), pp. 167-8; and G. Ormerod, ed., *Tracts relating to Military Proceedings in Lancashire* (Chetham Soc. ii, 1844), p. 33.

Evelyn evidently shared the inactive Royalism of his diarist brother; Sir John Fenwick, Sir William Uvedale, and Walter Kyrle were all suspected, probably correctly, of the same.[71] Men of this stamp can scarcely be regarded as reliable members of a unified faction.

If the Presbyterian party was merely a loose alliance of different groups, even more so was the Independent party. Its original nucleus, the war party, contained men of very different attitudes and aims. There was the small handful of until 1648 still covert republicans led by Henry Marten. There was the slightly larger handful of religious zealots of either Independent or sectarian hue, led by young Sir Harry Vane. These received a marked accession of strength when the recruiter elections brought in men like the Cornish Baptist John Carew, the flamboyant Colonel Harrison, and Vane's later ally Richard Salway, the former London apprentice whose father Humphrey sat for Worcestershire. There were the men whose religious principles, keenly Independent as they often were, took second place to their desire for political reform—men like Sir Arthur Haselrig, Edmund Ludlow, and John Pyne: the group later to be described as the Commonwealthsmen. But the total number of these radicals of various description was certainly not more than seventy or eighty. Assuming an average attendance of two-thirds of this number, this is not enough to explain how the Independents were able to withstand, and frequently outvote, the Presbyterians and moderates, in divisions which in 1646 several times attracted over 250 members.[72] The conclusion is inescapable that the Independents were able to attract considerable support from the uncommitted and the members in the middle.

The fact is that one major component of the Independent alliance between 1645 and 1648 was the middle group. So consistently did St. John and his friends co-operate with the radicals that they were frequently labelled as Independents by their enemies, and it is indeed permissible to regard the middle group as part of the Independent party during these years. Actually men like William Pierrepont, the Wiltshire Sir John Evelyn, John Crewe, and Lord Say with all his sons and connections, had little in common with the political or religious radicals as far as ultimate aims were

[71] E. S. de Beer, ed., *Diary of John Evelyn* (Oxford, 1955), i, Intro., pp. 6-7; C. H. Firth, ed., *The Clarke Papers* (Camden Soc., 1891-1901), ii. 158; B.M. Add. MS. 10114 (Harington's Diary), fol. 21; Add. MS. 31116 (Whitaker's Diary), fol. 286; Bell, *Memorials*, ii. 381; Bodl. MS. Dep. C. 166 (Nalson Papers, xiv), fol. 208 (abstract in H.M.C., *Portland*, i. 352); *C.J.* iv. 588.     [72] Snow, *H.L.Q.* xviii (1954-5), 303-4.

concerned.[73] But on immediate objectives they could work together: to get rid of the Scots, to frustrate an intolerantly Presbyterian religious settlement, to keep the Army in being until Charles I had been forced to accept their political goal—the constitution of 1641, fortified by additional checks against the prerogative. A combination of able leadership with a realistic, moderate programme thus enabled the Independents to appeal successfully to a large proportion of the non-partisan centre. The Independent party of 1645-8 was therefore essentially an alliance between the middle group and the radicals, with firm ties with the Army leadership, especially in the person of Oliver Cromwell, whose relations with St. John were close indeed.[74]

This brief analysis of the Presbyterian and Independent parties is of course highly over-simplified. To see how politics actually worked, how men threaded their way from group to group, the best way is to look closely at the path followed by an individual. The time-serving lawyer Bulstrode Whitelocke is not the best example of either body of opinion; nevertheless he was not yet the placeman he afterwards became, and his memoirs are revealing. By temperament a man of extreme caution, Whitelocke had generally worked with the middle group in the early years of the war.[75] By the summer of 1644 he was moving closer to the peace party, joining with Holles and other new recruits from the middle group, such as Stapleton and Clotworthy, in a desperate attempt to protect Essex and make peace as a necessary pre-condition for the reconquest of Ireland.[76] When Holles and Whitelocke went to Oxford to begin the preliminaries to the Uxbridge treaty, frightened by now open radicalism in both Parliament and Army, they argued 'that it was absolutely necessary the king should put an end to the war by a treaty: a new party of hot men was springing up, that were plainly for changing the government'.[77] Both then and later at Uxbridge, Whitelocke was unmistakably an apostle of peace (Pyne's letter identified him as one of the malignantly pro-Scottish group) and the result was the series of contacts which led to his involvement in the Savile accusation.

In spite of the severity with which Samuel Browne pressed the

---

[73] Pearl, *T.R.H.S.* 5th Ser. xviii (1968), 73-96.

[74] See Pearl, *E.H.R.* lxxxi (1966), 503, 516.

[75] Glow, *B.I.H.R.* xxxviii (1965), 48; Pearl, *E.H.R.* lxxxi (1966), 494 n., 518.

[76] There is a very revealing letter, 9 Aug. 1644, from Stapleton, Clotworthy, and Robert Reynolds to Holles and Whitelocke on this theme: Whitelocke Papers (Longleat), ix, fol. 27.

[77] Airy, ed., *Burnet*, i. 64.

charges against him, Whitelocke escaped from the Savile affair with nothing worse than a severe case of fright. For a time this shared experience of common danger cemented his friendship with Holles, who for a long time after the episode used to call Whitelocke brother. When there was talk of a revival of the accusation, Holles defiantly confided, 'Let them do their worst, we will not care a fig for them.' Until the spring of 1647 Whitelocke outwardly remained on good terms with his Presbyterian friends, but he then backed away from their dangerous plan to disband the Army. At this time, he says, 'I took the more opportunity of following my practice, and waiving my often private meetings and consultations with them, and took occasion to have the more converse with Cromwell and that party.' In fact, Whitelocke had for months been mending his fences with the radicals and the middle group, who obviously sensed his vulnerability, his willingness to be courted in return for oblivion of Savile's charges. By September 1645 he was already dining regularly with St. John, Browne, Vane, Haselrig, and 'other grandees of that party', as Whitelocke describes them, and when he was ill St. John sent him a gift of venison. With a foot in both camps, Whitelocke could complacently reflect how good it was to be 'esteemed by all parties, and believed (as it was truly of me) that you follow your own conscience and no faction'. Throughout this period, in fact, Whitelocke was a target for the attentions of both sides, and his experience demonstrates how it was possible for an active politician to survive, for however unworthy motives, without being a party man. Only when he disgracefully abandoned Holles in the summer of 1647, at the time of the impeachment of the Eleven Members, can Whitelocke be said to have thrown in his lot decisively with the Independents.[78]

\* \* \*

What then were the issues between Presbyterians and Independents when the war ended in 1646, and Charles I made his way to Newcastle and Scottish custody? Many of them were of course tactical, attempts by one group to improve its position as against the other, effects rather than causes of the party strife. Thus the Commons in 1646 spent a good deal of time deciding whether or when to permit the series of by-elections in royalist Cornwall,

---

[78] For Whitelocke's behaviour in this period, see his *Memorials*, i. 516–91; ii. 1–178; and the much more revealing Annals: B.M. Add. MS. 37344, fols. 1–89.

which might transform the balance of the House, to go forward. In the autumn there was a long and bitter struggle over the control of the Great Seal, important not only for the electoral influence which the Commissioners could exercise through their control of the writs, but also for their powers of approving and nominating J.P.s, through whom the shires could be controlled when the County Committees were done away with.[79] They spent a good deal of time on the dismantling of garrisons, and the disbandment of local and auxiliary forces outside the New Model, for example Massey's unpaid and indisciplined men in the western counties— all important means of promoting or controlling local power. But the fundamental issue was the future settlement of the kingdom, the terms to be offered to the King, the terms on which the Scots could be got rid of, the timing of the return to normal methods of government in the counties, and the nature of the religious settlement.

The Independents—the radical-middle-group alliance—were strong enough to ensure that the terms to be offered to the King did not involve any surrender of the essential principles for which the war had been fought. The Propositions of Newcastle, sent to Charles in July, included the vital demands: the militia for twenty years, severity towards Papists and delinquents, restriction of the King's prerogative to select his own councillors by the disqualification of Royalists. They were strong enough to obtain votes for dispensing with the Scottish Army in May 1646, though not to prevent the payment of generous compensation as the price of their departure a few months later.[80] By the end of January 1647 the King was in the hands of the English commissioners at Newcastle, and the Scots were leaving. The Church settlement was more complicated, cutting as it did across party lines. Hard-line war-party men, political Independents, like Prideaux and Purefoy, were also rigid Presbyterians in religion, and could combine with religious Presbyterians from other groups or from none, and indeed with Erastians who wanted a national Church to avoid the indiscipline and social dangers that went with sectarian toleration, to achieve some kind of Presbyterian settlement. At the same time, the Erastian majority, which again included men of all political groups

---

[79] Underdown, *E.H.R.* lxxxiii (1968), 253, 256-7, 260, for these matters.
[80] Gardiner, *Civil War*, ii. 481-2, 519. For the Newcastle Propositions, see S. R. Gardiner, ed., *Constitutional Documents of the Puritan Revolution*, 3rd edn. (Oxford, 1906), pp. 290-306.

as well as a large proportion of the uncommitted gentry, could ensure that it would be that anathema to Baillie and his compatriots, a 'lame Erastian Presbytery'. In April 1646 the Presbyterian clergy of the Assembly were voted guilty of breach of privilege when they had the temerity to question Parliament's recent vote for the appointment of lay commissioners to determine ecclesiastical offences, on the grounds that it conflicted with the foundation of Presbytery *jure divino*. A committee of three came from the Commons to the Assembly to rub in the lesson, and their names demonstrate the leading part taken by the middle group in defining this Erastian position: Sir John Evelyn of Wiltshire, Nathaniel Fiennes, and Samuel Browne. 'You are not to make use of the public character the Houses have put upon you, to contradict to their votes', Fiennes warned the embarrassed divines.[81] The point was well taken outside the Assembly. When the parishioners of St. Dunstans in the West met for the election of elders a few months later, they wisely followed the lead of their betters. 'After some debate under what form . . . they should proceed, whether according to *Ius Divinum*, or by authority of Parliament, they thought fit to waive the first as yet unresolved, and to take for rule the Ordinance of Parliament.'[82]

The divine right of Presbytery, important as it might be to members of the Assembly and elders of London parishes, was for all that only peripheral to the now deepening political conflict. In that conflict, the survival of the Independent party, and above all the role of the middle group, were the critical factors. As long as the middle group held together, as long as it retained its ties with the Army grandees, so long could the potentially revolutionary threat posed by the radicals and their militant allies among the junior officers and the other ranks, together with the sectarian congregations, be contained. So long was it possible to envisage a settlement which, while fulfilling the aims for which Parliament had gone to war, fell short of revolution. So long in fact could the tension between the two sides of the parliamentarian movement—its radical religious idealism and its conservative constitutionalism—be resolved. But should anything happen to disturb the alliance the Independent party would be destroyed. The Army and the radicals would be out of control, and the result would be revolution.

[81] A. F. Mitchell and J. Struthers, eds., *Minutes of the Westminster Assembly of Divines* (Edinburgh, 1874), pp. 225, 448–56; *C.J.* iv. 506, 511, 518. See also Gardiner, *Civil War*, ii. 468–9. [82] *Moderate Intelligencer*, no. 74 (30 July–6 Aug. 1646: [B.M.] E. 349, 12).

# IV

## THE COLLAPSE OF THE INDEPENDENT PARTY

IN 1647 came the first great test of the Independent party; the middle-group-radical alliance survived it. In 1648 came the second; the alliance, and with it the Independent party, collapsed, bringing revolution in its wake. Revolution, to be sure, did not seem far away in the first of the two great crises. In the summer of 1647 all the forces making for tension in the uneasy, unsettled, war-ravaged nation converged explosively. The spread of sectarian and revolutionary opinions in and outside the Army convinced conservative Parliamentarians that it was time to act against them before it was too late. In city and in county dislike of high taxes and quartering combined with Presbyterian fear of military radicalism to produce a move to disband the Army and achieve a settlement that would restore Charles I with Scots connivance. On the other side, the soldiers' grievances were inflamed by Leveller agitation, the County Committees grew more repressive as they feared for their survival, and the Independent politicians strove to keep the Army on foot until Charles I had been brought to heel. The Army itself began to act as a directly political force, with a sweeping programme of constitutional reform expressing the demands of the officers, and in some respects those of the men. Even if, like Cromwell, they had doubts about the propriety of acting against constitutional authority, the officers found themselves pushed into a militant posture in order to preserve the unity of the Army, and keep control of their more angry rank and file. The Army created for the defence of Parliament found that its purposes could be achieved only by forcing Parliament to reform itself. Some, though not all, of the Army's friends in Parliament came to the same conclusion. But neither officers nor radical M.P.s were ready for revolution. They might strike at their opponents' leaders by impeachment, but they were not ready for a full-scale purge.

The Presbyterian scheme to disband the Army reflected the

swelling feeling in the counties against committees and military rule. Committeemen, declared William Strode, one of Pyne's bitterest enemies in Somerset, were 'all rogues', their survival dependent on the Army; 'the country will rise and knock them all in head, as soon as their guard is gone'.[1] In Lincolnshire Col. Edward King repeatedly denounced the Committee in his charges to the Grand Jury, appealing to traditionalist county sentiment, as well as to prejudice against 'Anabaptists, Brownists, Separatists, Antinomians and Heretics'. By April 1647 his obstruction had brought the collection of assessments to a standstill.[2] Later in the year members of the Westmorland Committee were attacked by rioting countrymen and imprisoned for a few days, along with one of Lord Wharton's Puritan clerics, at Kendal.[3] Such incidents were not exceptional.

Even more unpopular than the committees were the costly, everpresent soldiers. Herefordshire complained of the 'heathenish' troopers on their way to Ireland, and the continuing misbehaviour of the locally based Col. John Birch and his men, which led to bloodshed and loss of life at Longtown, when countrymen resisted quartering. But in Hereford the Committee, dominated by the moderate Harleys, was still in touch with county opinion.[4] In more divided Somerset the Irish-bound levies were so much hated that by May 1647 some of the local authorities were conniving at assaults on them by bands of Clubmen. Another of the recurrent petitions from the Grand Jury brought no relief, so the High Sheriff, Richard Cole, summoned the able-bodied men of his neighbourhood to a rendezvous on Dolebury Warren, to assist in apprehending the marauding soldiers. Unrest continued throughout the West during the summer. There were the now familiar mutinies by unpaid soldiers—in Dorset they imprisoned some of the County Committee—and rumours reached John Harington in London that a full-scale insurrection was in progress in Somerset and

---

[1] Information of Col. Thos. Galloppe, 22 Mar. 1647/8: H.M.C., *Portland*, i. 448. Strode's outburst had occurred more than a year earlier, about Feb. 1647.

[2] Lincs. Co. Co. to M.P.s, 2 Apr. 1647: Bodl. MS., Tanner 59, fol. 39. See also ibid., fols. 551, 585-8, 668; Bodl. MS. Dep. C. 167 (Nalson Papers, xiv), fols. 409-15; and Edward King, *A Discovery of the Arbitrary, Tyrannicall, and Illegall Actions of some of the Committee of the County of Lincoln* (1 Feb. 1646/7: [B.M.] E. 373, 3).

[3] Henry Massey to Wharton, 18 Oct. 1647: Bodl. MS., Rawlinson Letters 52 (Wharton Corr.), fol. 96.

[4] H.M.C., *Portland*, iii. 148-58; viii. 5; Welbeck MSS., Harley Papers, v (B.M. Loan, 29/175); ibid., Papers Concerning Col. Birch (29/15); John and T. W. Webb, eds., *Military Memoir of Colonel John Birch* (Camden Soc., N.S. vii, 1873), p. 233.

Dorset.[5] Nor was this confined to the West Country. The Leicester-shire Committee suffered the same indignity as their counterparts in Dorset; at Chester the Deputy Lieutenants were the victims; and at York soldiers again besieged the Committee 'in extraordinary multitudes', demanding their arrears. The blame, of course, rested on a Parliament that was unwilling to pay the men; but local opinion, frightened by the outbreaks, ignored this. Some of the soldiers, conscripts many of whom had served the other side, were as frightening to Puritan zealots as they were to the gentry. At Worcester in June 1647 they went Morris-dancing through the streets, hailing the shocked citizens with cries of 'roundhead dogs, roundhead whores, gospel whores'.[6]

Out of the turmoil came the Presbyterian counter-attack. How-ever intractable the political division between Parliament and King, settlement and a return to stable government were essential to both: 'for otherwise', Sir Henry Cholmley feared, 'clubs and clouted shoes will . . . be too hard for them'. Without a settlement, the royalist Dr. Bruno Ryves warned a few months later, 'a general insurrection against the wealthier sort' was inevitable.[7] Renewed petitions against tithes, an organized petitioning campaign in favour of the Army, and an important Leveller one which demanded law reform and redress of other social grievances—'mutinous stuff', the diarist Lawrence Whitaker contemptuously dismissed it—showed that the danger to stability was not confined to the Army.[8] The moderates responded with a propaganda offensive of their own, which in February and March 1647 produced petitions from Suffolk, Essex, and other eastern counties, calling for immediate disbandment, so that the nation might not be 'eaten up, enslaved, and destroyed' by the Army. The Presbyterian-dominated City of London, its

---

[5] H.M.C., *Egmont*, i. 318, 403, 408; Sir W. C. and Sir C. E. Trevelyan, eds., *Trevelyan Papers*, iii (Camden Soc., cv, 1872), 257; H.M.C., *Sixth Report*, Appendix (House of Lords MSS.), p. 173; *L.J.* ix. 172; Cary, *Memorials*, i. 295-7; B.M. Add. MS. 10114 (Harington's Diary), fol. 25. See also Bodl. MS., Tanner 58, fol. 448, for a mutiny at Plymouth in August.

[6] Cary, *Memorials*, i. 277-82; Yorks. and Leics. Committees to Speaker, 28 May and 3 July 1647: Bodl. MS., Tanner 58, fols. 113, 329; S. Moore to N. Lechmere, 1 July 1647: ibid., fol. 305.

[7] Cary, *Memorials*, i. 293; *Mercurius Rusticus* (12 Nov. 1647: [B.M.] E. 414, 5), p. 2.

[8] *The Husbandmans Plea against Tithes, Or two Petitions presented unto the House of Commons* (25 May 1647: [B.M.] E. 389, 2); B.M. Add. MS. 31116 (Whitaker's Diary), fol. 304ᵛ. See also Gardiner, *Civil War*, iii. 72-5; Brailsford, *The Levellers*, pp. 132-3. Holles's friends on the Wiltshire Committee asked for his authority to suppress one such petition, a printed copy of one in general circulation: Thistlethwaite *et al.* to Holles, 27 Mar. 1647: Bodl. MS., Tanner 58, fol. 14.

wealthy oligarchy fearing the spread of the Leveller infection, added its voice to the campaign.[9]

Presbyterian firebrands were already boasting of their determination to get rid of the Army. 'We will destroy them all', said William Strode, '. . . Sir Thomas Fairfax will be deceived, for part of his army will join with us, and besides the Scots are very honest men and will come to assist us.'[10] Wild as his words were, Strode correctly outlined the Presbyterians' tactics. After systematically reducing local garrisons in a way the Taunton lawyer Roger Hill thought would bring down many 'dangers and calamities' on the godly party, the Commons voted to send the main force of the Army to Ireland and disband the rest. When the soldiers protested, Holles and his friends embarked on the course of action which led directly to the summer crisis, and ultimately to the revolution itself. On 29 March they voted the promoters of opposition in the Army 'enemies of the State and disturbers of the public peace'.[11] In April they authorized the Common Council to remodel the London militia. Soon they were laying the foundations of a force to support the Londoners, creating a Committee of Safety, empowering the Committee on Irish affairs to raise troops, and appealing to discontented 'Reformadoes' who had served under Presbyterian generals like Massey in the war to join deserters from the New Model in enlisting in their ranks.[12] Over-optimistic as these preparations may seem, with the Scots threatening in the north they posed the threat of renewed civil war.

Against these dangers the Army closed ranks, giving the revolutionaries an institutional base far more potent than that hitherto provided by the radical fringe of the Independents in Parliament. In the meetings of the officers with the parliamentary commissioners sent to Saffron Walden in March and April a clearly defined political consciousness was born, a consciousness which through the pen of the cold, clear-minded theoretician Henry Ireton was soon outlining,

[9] Gardiner, *Civil War*, iii. 29, 34–5. Further 'heady petitions . . . tending to disturbance' were circulated in Essex during the ensuing months: *Josselin's Diary*, p. 43.

[10] H.M.C., *Portland*, i. 447–8.

[11] [Hill to Pyne], 23 Feb. 1646/7: Somerset R.O., Hippisley MS. DD/HI/10; Gardiner, *Civil War*, iii. 44.

[12] Ibid. 67–8, 112–15. One who responded was Massey's old friend, Col. John Fitzjames of Leweston, whose correspondence with fellow officers was resumed in Apr. 1647, and who came to London in the summer to serve under his old commander. Fitzjames to Col. Cooke and Q.M.G. Wood, 12 Apr. 1647: Fitzjames Letter-book, i (Northumberland MS. 547, B.M. Film 330), fol. 91. See also Letter-book, ii. fols. 1–3.

in petitions, vindications, and declarations, a distinct political programme. Beginning with limited, specifically military grievances,
by 14 June the officers could produce a *Representation from the Army*
in which they claimed to speak for the people of England.[13] In this
document they advanced the programme that was to be repeated
with variations in the *Heads of the Proposals*, and on many other
occasions down to Pride's Purge. A purge (which Ireton thought
could be performed by Parliament itself) of corrupt and delinquent
M.P.s; a dissolution followed by new elections for future Parliaments of regular but limited duration; affirmation of the right to
petition; government by law; religious toleration: the officers had
not yet come to a republican solution, and still expected to achieve
their objectives constitutionally. But in defining the programme,
the Army had gone far beyond the limited goals of the majority of
their employers in Parliament.

However, the officers were not in full control of the Army in the
spring of 1647. Inspired by bitter resentment at the governing
Presbyterian oligarchy, by sectarian zeal, and by the dawning
flickerings of democratic feeling, the soldiers were now pushing
them from behind. The convergence of these feelings was danger-
ously evident in a report from Suffolk in April, where the troopers
were using 'most bitter language' against the tyrannical Stapleton-
Holles clique, and threatening never to disband 'till we have cut all
the [Presbyterian] priests' throats'. 'Lilburne's books', the reporter
of this noted, 'are quoted by them as statute-law.'[14] The March
petition for arrears and indemnity, the election of Agitators to represent the regiments at the end of April, and the mutinies a month
later against the now imminent disbandment, mark the stages of this
growing radicalizing of the rank and file. By this time the officers
and soldiers had come together sufficiently for the discussions in
mid May to enable them to return a united answer to Parliament's
commissioners, and to display their solidarity in the rendezvous at
Newmarket and Triploe Heath in early June.[15] This solidarity in
turn was institutionalized by the creation of an Army Council to
chart the Army's future course of action.

[13] Gardiner, *Civil War*, iii. 115-19. A. S. P. Woodhouse, ed., *Puritanism and Liberty*,
2nd edn. (London, 1950), Intro., pp. [20]-[25].

[14] H.M.C., *Portland*, iii. 156. See also *C.J.* v. 154. Ralph Josselin in April and May 1647
records constant fear and dislike of the soldiers quartered in his village, and the violence
of their language: *Josselin's Diary*, pp. 42-3.

[15] Gardiner, *Civil War*, iii. 39-41, 59-60, 82-3, 99-100, 108-9.

The unity was more apparent than real; a product of the need, recognized by Cromwell and Ireton, to present a united front against disbandment, and of the grandees' determination not to permit the Leveller-influenced soldiers to get out of hand. The generals' tactics are clearly shown in their handling of the Holmby affair. Whatever the truth about Cromwell's part in Joyce's seizure of the King may be, it is difficult to believe that the original idea came from him; more probably Joyce was acting on behalf of the radical junior officers and Agitators.[16] But Cromwell and Ireton quickly accepted the *fait accompli*, and made no effort to reverse it. Charles was now in the Army's power, and the opportunities of binding him to an advantageous settlement on their own terms, avoiding the danger of a Presbyterian-Scottish betrayal, could be exploited. Hence the complicated negotiations between Cromwell and the King, which aroused acute suspicion in the Army and among the Levellers during the summer and autumn of 1647. Hence, too, the *Heads of the Proposals*, in which the programme outlined in the 14 June *Representation* was offered to the King, with the addition of provisions for a redistribution of constituencies, more clearly defined powers for the Council, appointment of officials and control of the militia power by Parliament for ten years. The proposals for constituency reform would be attractive to the lesser gentry and yeomanry, but for the Army rank and file there was no word of a broadened franchise or Leveller democracy.[17]

Another result of the Army's decision to take the initiative was the first attempt at a limited purge of the Commons. On 16 June the Army presented charges of impeachment against eleven of the most prominent Presbyterian leaders, Holles and Stapleton heading the list. The main charge, levelled at all eleven, was that they had promoted the recent Presbyterian design against the Army, to restore Charles I with the aid of the Scots, and to foment a new war by raising forces in London. In addition, Sir John Clotworthy, Anthony Nicoll, and John Glyn were charged with flagrant corruption, Glyn and Sir William Lewis with sinister favouritism for Welsh Royalists, Edward Harley with being responsible for bringing the soldiers' March petition to the attention of the Commons,

---

[16] For discussions of the Holmby affair see Gardiner, *Civil War*, iii. 86-94; Wilbur C. Abbott, ed., *Writings and Speeches of Oliver Cromwell* (Cambridge, Mass., 1937-47), i. 452-7; and Roots, *Great Rebellion*, p. 109.

[17] See Gardiner, *Civil War*, ch. lii, for all this.

Nicoll with improper election management in Cornwall, and Walter Long with having acted as party Whip.[18] A successful impeachment would deprive the Presbyterian party of its effective leaders. At the same time the Army's friends ferreted out information of past delinquency, or suspicious flirtations with the King, on the part of about thirty other M.P.s. The Independents' Irish lobby, headed by the Sidneys and Sir John Temple, were going after the newly elected Sir Philip Perceval, Lord Inchiquin's agent, as early as 2 June, and a committee was set up under John Corbet to consider this and other accusations of delinquency. On 5 July the Commons voted to exclude members who had at any time sued for pardon of the King, as well as those who had been in arms; a vote that Fairfax's secretary Rushworth thought would 'produce a good effect' by getting rid of such men as Sir Samuel Rolle and Sir John Bampfield, and 'near thirty more'. On 15 July a number of such cases were referred to Corbet's committee. Even if still technically members of the House, those accused were effectively silenced.[19]

The impeached Eleven Members by now had withdrawn from the Commons. They did not take the charges lying down, however, but under the leadership of the forthright, pugnacious Holles, demanded immediate opportunity of defending themselves. Five distinguished lawyers, including the formidable Prynne, were appointed as their counsel. At the same time they prepared a vigorous printed defence in which Prynne's hand can be detected. They also attempted to line up support from the middle group, the trimmers, and the uncommitted. Bulstrode Whitelocke was so terrified of being asked to defend Holles that he fled to his house in the country, and on his return stayed in his chamber at the Temple, 'a kind of prisoner, not opening the door to any, to avoid meeting with Mr. Holles, or his party'.[20] But on the 20th the Eleven Members temporarily abandoned the struggle, being given leave to go abroad and to postpone final presentation of their defence for six months.

Cromwell and Ireton, hopeful of obtaining the King's consent to the *Heads of the Proposals*, were still firmly against anything

---

[18] Bell, *Memorials*, ii. 367–83. See also *Old Parl. Hist.* xv. 470–3; xvi. 70–92.

[19] *C.J.* v. 195, 233, 244–5; Rushworth to Lord Fairfax, 13 July 1647: Bell, *Memorials*, i. 367–8; H.M.C., *Egmont*, i. 411, 423–31.

[20] Whitelocke, *Memorials*, ii. 162–79. The unprinted Annals, from which the quotation above is taken, are as usual more revealing: B.M. Add. MS. 37344, fols. 97–8ᵛ. *The Full Vindication and Answer of the XI. Accused Members* (15 July 1647: [B.M.] E. 398, 17); also printed in *Old Parl. Hist.* xvi. 116–59. See also Gardiner, *Civil War*, iii. 129, 156–7.

resembling a military coup. 'That which you have by force', Cromwell told the Agitators, when they demanded an immediate march on London to get rid of the Eleven Members and destroy the threatening combination of apprentices and Reformadoes, 'I look upon it as nothing.' Violence was only to be used if 'we cannot get what is for the good of the kingdom without force'. Cromwell still hoped to see 'a reformed and purged Parliament', but the purge would have to be an inside job, undertaken freely and constitutionally by Parliament itself.[21] When on the 22nd the Commons voted to restore the London militia to its former Independent hands, it appeared for a brief moment that Parliament might indeed be tractable. But mob violence took control. A shouting crowd of apprentices burst into Parliament and forced first Lords and then Commons to repeal the Militia ordinance, and to invite the King to London. The City was in arms; counter-revolution was at hand. On the morning after the riot, Ludlow, Haselrig, and some of the other Independent leaders decided to secede from Parliament, to seek the Army's protection.[22] By the time the Commons reassembled on the 30th, fifty-eight members, including the Speaker, had taken refuge with the Army; another sixteen or twenty quickly signified their approval of the action, by subscribing the *Engagement* of 4 August to this effect.[23] For a week the Presbyterians held out. They voted back the Eleven Members, elected new Speakers (Henry Pelham and the crypto-Royalist Lord Willoughby), and prepared to resist. But then came the Army, welcomed by friendly Southwark, entering the City in triumph on 6 August; on the same day the seceding Independents resumed their places in Parliament, under the old Speakers.[24] The Eleven Members departed once more; some, like Holles and Massey, into temporary exile, one, Sir Philip Stapleton, to a grave at Calais.

\*     \*     \*

Through all these turbulent months the Independent alliance held together, its unity repeatedly proclaimed by the appearance

[21] Ibid. 155; Abbott, *Cromwell*, i. 481, 483.

[22] Gardiner, *Civil War*, iii. 166-9. See also Rushworth's account in Bell, *Memorials*, i. 379-84; and *Ludlow's Memoirs*, i. 161-2.

[23] Lists of those seceding or signing the *Engagement* are in *L.J.* ix. 385; John Rushworth, ed., *Historical Collections* 2nd edn. (London, 1721-2), vii. 755 (slight variations); *Old Parl. Hist.* xvi. 243-4; and H.M.C., *Egmont*, i. 440 (numerous variations). See also Yule, *The Independents*, p. 69 and n.          [29] For all this see Gardiner, *Civil War*, iii. 169-70, 174-6.

of the middle-group Evelyn and the radical Haselrig as tellers in divisions. The middle group was at one with the radicals in resisting disbandment, in voting to receive military or radical petitions, in opposing Presbyterian proposals to negotiate with the King, and in adopting a generally conciliatory posture towards the Army. The crucial point was that there should be no disbandment before a settlement with the King; a premature agreement would put power into his and the Scots hands.[25] They were, to be sure, not anxious to push matters to extremes, and were always quick to scent an opportunity for conciliating the parliamentary factions. Thus Bulkeley and Samuel Browne were members of a committee appointed on 30 June to pursue an accommodation.[26] In the crisis, however, as their principles of resisting surrender to the King and the Scots demanded, most of them sided with the Army. St. John, Say and his sons John and Nathaniel, Pierrepont, and Evelyn all either fled to the Army at the end of July or signed the 4 August *Engagement*. A few others, John Boys for example, stayed at Westminster and later argued for the legality of Parliament's proceedings during the Speakers' absence.[27] But in spite of a few defections, the middle group kept in step with the rest of the Independents on the main issues of supporting the Army and preventing a sell-out to the King.

When the Speakers returned to Westminster there was another chance of a settlement on the middle group's terms. Apart from a handful of actual or potential republicans, all groups agreed that a permanent settlement was impossible without the King.[28] While the King was in the hands of the Army at Hampton Court the middle-group leaders joined the generals in an attempt to persuade

[25] See for example the divisions of 17 and 19 Feb.; 5 Mar.; 4, 20, and 25 May; 2, 3 (2 votes), 8, 16 (2 votes), and 21 June; 17 and 21 July: *C.J.* v. 90-253. These and other divisions indicate that Boys, Bulkeley, and Sir Richard Onslow were either regular or occasional supporters of the middle group at this time. See also Underdown, *B.I.H.R.* xxxix (1966), 143-4, for Boys and the middle group. [Fiennes], *Vindiciae Veritatis*, esp. p. 26, gives the middle group's attitude to disbandment.　　　　　　　　　　　　　　　[26] *C.J.* v. 228.

[27] Several members who both earlier and later can be associated with the middle group (e.g. Ashhurst, Sir Gilbert Gerard, Knightley, and Swynfen) seem to have defected more regularly to the Presbyterians at this time. However, some others (the Ashe family triumvirate, for instance) stayed at Westminster during the crisis but continued to vote against the Presbyterians. See *C.J.* v. 262-6. The behaviour of middle-group supporters in 1647 obviously demands further study.

[28] The republicans' maximum strength must have been thirty-four, the number voting against negotiations on 22 Sept. The next day they could muster only twenty-three: *C.J.* v. 312, 314.

him to accept the *Heads of the Proposals*. They had at one and the
same time to control both Parliament and Army. The first they
could do by persuasion and tactical skill, but also by paralysing the
Presbyterians through the continued exclusion of their leaders:
hence the consistency with which their adherents, especially
Evelyn, supported strong measures against the Eleven Members
and the impeached Lords.[29] To do the second they had to dissuade
the officers from the unconstitutional courses, including a wholesale purge, which Cromwell was said to have contemplated in his
mood of impatience after the July–August crisis.[30] Finally they had
to preserve close collaboration with the Army leaders at every stage
of their negotiations with the King.

There is ample evidence for the continued vitality of the middle
group, the 'grandees' as their enemies labelled them, in September
1647. The Levellers Wildman and Lilburne could discern a
'Cabinet Council' of the grandees, which included Cromwell,
Ireton, Vane, St. John, Say, Nathaniel Fiennes, Evelyn, and Pierrepont. These, Lilburne told his fellow prisoner Sir Lewis Dyve,
'now steer the affairs of the whole kingdom'.[31] On 22 September, at
the urging of this powerful combination and against the opposition
of Marten and the radicals, the Commons went into committee 'to
take into consideration the whole matter concerning the King',
with the middle-group lawyer John Boys as chairman.[32] The breach
between the grandees and the extreme radicals, the 'root and
branch men' as one observer called them, was now in the open, with
each 'snapping' at the others, and the republican Thomas Scot
denouncing 'underhand treaties' with the King.[33] On 20 October
Cromwell made a three-hour speech in defence of monarchy; he
and his parliamentary allies were obviously working desperately to

---

[29] For example, *C.J.* v. 295-6.

[30] *Sundry Reasons Inducing Major Robert Huntingdon to Lay Down his Commission* (1648),
in Maseres, *Tracts*, ii. 402. For other references to Cromwell's discussion of a purge at
about this time see *Ludlow's Memoirs*, i. 148; Airy, ed., *Burnet*, i. 77; *Short Memorials of
Thomas, Lord Fairfax*, in Maseres, *Tracts*, ii. 446; and C. H. Firth, ed., *Stuart Tracts*
(London, 1903), p. 358. See also Abbott, *Cromwell*, i. 462, 496; and Gardiner, *Civil War*,
iii. 182–3 and nn., for discussion of the date of this episode.

[31] John Lawmind [Wildman], *Putney Projects* (30 Dec. 1647: [B.M.] E. 421, 19), sig. F3;
H. G. Tibbutt, ed., *Letter-Book of Sir Lewis Dyve* (Beds. Hist. Record Soc. xxxviii, 1958),
pp. 57, 89.

[32] Gardiner, *Civil War*, iii. 200–2; Abbott, *Cromwell*, i. 507; *C.J.* v. 312; *Clarke Papers*,
i. 230–1, n.

[33] W. Smith to Sir R. Leveson, 27 Sept. 1647: H.M.C., *Fifth Report*, Appendix (Sutherland MSS.), p. 173.

G

frustrate both Presbyterian rigidity on a Church settlement and republican opposition to any settlement at all.[34] Between the lines of the *Journals* the political moves can be hazily discerned, and they show the tactical skill of the middle-group Independents in managing committees and conferences with the Lords. On 26 October, for instance, a conference over the propositions to be sent to the King was managed by three of their henchmen (Boys, Bulkeley, and Swynfen), with the addition of the more radical Independent John Lisle. Four days later Boys and Swynfen were joined in a similar conference with another middle-group man, Richard Knightley, and this time with several other radicals.[35] Meanwhile, outside the House, Lord Say was busily co-ordinating policy with the generals at Putney, in an atmosphere of great secrecy.[36]

Say's appearance at Putney was no doubt related to a more celebrated series of discussions in the village church there during these same October days. The Army Council were debating the Leveller *Agreement of the People*, the clearest statement that had yet appeared of the left-wing reform programme. Besides revealing the warmth and passion of the Levellers' attachment to liberty, the Putney debates also demonstrated (as had indeed been obvious in the pamphlet outbursts of the past two months) the soldiers' deep suspicions of Ireton and Cromwell for their part in the recent middle-group approach to the King. The debates show that Ireton, the Levellers' most effective critic, might go a long way towards a radical constitutional reform, but that he was no social revolutionary. Democracy, he argued, setting a now familiar precedent, led inevitably to communism. To the Leveller claim that the vote was a basic natural right, Ireton retorted that on the same grounds 'you must deny all property too', for 'by the same right of nature [any man] hath the same equal right in any goods he sees'. You wish to give poor men the vote, Ireton concluded: 'Why may not those men vote against all property?'[37]

[34] Gardiner, *Civil War*, iii. 217. The question of a time-limit for the Presbyterian establishment produced an interesting example of middle-group disunity. What began as collaboration between Cromwell and Evelyn ended as a disagreement over tactics: *C.J.* v. 332.

[35] *C.J.* v. 343-6. With negotiations beginning again, people like Swynfen and Knightley were, I think, now resuming their co-operation with the middle group.

[36] *Merc. Elen.*, no. 2 (5-12 Nov. 1647: [B.M.] E. 414, 4). The royalist author's assertion that Say was trying to prevent an agreement between Charles I and the Army is clearly wrong, but the passage is useful evidence for Say's actual movements.

[37] See Woodhouse, *Puritanism and Liberty*, pp. 1-124, for the most accessible account of the debates, and pp. 422-55 for related documents.

The Levellers were beaten; the *Agreement of the People* was shelved. On 8 November the Council voted to send the Agitators back to their units, and when, a week later, some of the regiments defiantly came on parade with copies of the *Agreement* in their hats, Cromwell quelled the mutiny, and had one of the ring-leaders shot on the spot.[38] Yet although Cromwell had temporarily repulsed 'this drive at a levelling and parity',[39] the threat of another Leveller eruption haunted both Army leaders and Parliamentarians of all political hues during the year that followed. To the moderates, the Levellers were a further reason for coming to terms with the King. For Cromwell and Ireton, the Levellers might provide a reason for going further than they intended in the direction of political revolution, to preserve the unity of the Army.[40] Too conservative a posture might permit the violent men in the ranks to get out of hand; political revolution might be the necessary price that would have to be paid to avoid social revolution.

While they argued with the Levellers at Putney, Cromwell and Ireton were still aiming, in common with the middle-group grandees, at a restoration of Charles I on the terms of the *Heads of the Proposals*. But by the time of the Corkbush Field mutiny the basis for any such settlement had been destroyed by the King's escape from the Army's custody and his decision to rely on the Scots. On the evening of 11 November he left Hampton Court for the Isle of Wight, and one more chance of an agreed restoration by the Army-middle-group combination had vanished. The King's flight led on all sides to a hardening of positions. On 27 November the Commons followed the Lords in voting that Four Bills should be presented to Charles as pre-conditions to negotiations, with demands for the militia for twenty years, annulment of past declarations against Parliament, revocation of royal grants of honours, and acceptance of Parliament's right to adjourn to any place of its own choice. Once again the middle group played a prominent role. The final drafting committee for the Bills included St. John, Browne, and Boys, while Evelyn and Knightley were among the tellers in several crucial divisions before their

[38] Ibid. pp. 454–5; Gardiner, *Civil War*, iii. 253–5.

[39] Cromwell, Speech, 23 Nov. 1647: Boys's Diary, *B.I.H.R.* xxxix (1966), 152–3.

[40] Sir John Berkeley rightly observed that Cromwell's apparent inconsistencies could usually be explained by his determination to prevent a split in the Army: Abbott, *Cromwell*, i. 465.

adoption.[41] But the Four Bills possessed only academic interest, for Charles was now bent on his ultimate folly, the alliance with the Scots. Although John Bulkeley, one of the commissioners sent to the Isle of Wight with the Bills, told Boys that there were tears in the King's eyes when he gave his answer, they must have been crocodile ones. Scornfully secure in his Scottish alliance, Charles had replied, when an additional proposition for the abolition of bishops, deans, and chapters was read, 'And all pastors, curates, and the congregations committed to their charge'.[42]

With the King's rejection of the Four Bills, St. John and the middle-group grandees had to face a new situation. Obviously a permanent settlement on anything except the terms of virtual surrender advocated by crypto-Royalists and some Presbyterians would have to be indefinitely postponed. Postponed, it should be stressed, not abandoned: in the long run the middle group, still aiming at something like the constitution of 1641, would have no alternative to another approach to the King. In the meantime it was vital to preserve party unity. Hence the Vote of No Addresses on 3 January 1648 and the hiatus in negotiations that followed. The Vote itself was the work of radicals, proposed by the militant Sir Arthur Haselrig and seconded by Sir Thomas Wroth in an outrageously republican speech. But men of the middle group were also behind it. Pierrepont spoke for it in debate, Sir John Evelyn was one of the tellers, while Nathaniel Fiennes was mainly responsible for drafting the declaration in its defence which soon followed. Yet there were disturbing signs that the generals were leaving themselves room for manœuvre in case their radical rank and file would not swallow another round of talks. 'True', said Cromwell, 'we declared our intentions for monarchy, and they still are so, unless necessity enforce an alteration.' If they did not stand firm against the King, he added with equal menace, 'the honest people may take such courses as nature dictates to them'. Ireton spoke in similar terms, adding that as the King had broken his contract with the people, they could now 'settle the Kingdom without him'.[43] On the other side, some of the middle

---

[41] *C.J.* v. 370-1. For the debate see Boys's Diary, *B.I.H.R.* xxxix (1966), 153. The size of the minority is probably to be explained, as Gardiner suggests (*Civil War*, iii. 264, n.), as a coalition of republicans with Presbyterians who regarded the terms as too harsh.

[42] Boys's Diary, *B.I.H.R.* xxxix (1966), 154.

[43] *C.J.* v. 415-16; Boys's Diary, *B.I.H.R.* xxxix (1966), 155-7; Clement Walker, *Relations and Observations . . . upon the Parliament Begun A.D. 1640: the History of Independency* (London, 1648-9), i. 71-3.

group were unhappy about the severe language of Fiennes's Declaration. Boys wanted to water down the conclusion that the King could no longer be trusted by adding 'until his heart changes, and he comply with his Parliament'. Bulkeley voted against it altogether.[44]

For some time after the Vote the middle-group leaders marked time. They strengthened their hold on the government of the country by adding Nathaniel Fiennes and Evelyn to the Committee of Both Kingdoms, which, shorn of its Scots, now became the Derby House Committee. In spite of their antipathy to the Scots, they did not want a war, and did their best to avoid one by sending four commissioners to Edinburgh to negotiate. Two of them, Ashhurst and Robert Goodwin, were of middle-group outlook but Presbyterian in religion, a third, John Birch, Presbyterian in both religion and politics (though firm enough to warn Sir William Waller against 'an evil-grounded peace'), and only one, Brian Stapleton, an outright radical. Once in Scotland, the commissioners tried to delay the war by exploiting Scottish divisions, directed, an observer noted, 'by their private combination with the Lord Say, Mr. Pierrepont, Sir [sic] Oliver St. John and others, with whom they held joint correspondence and from them received continual instructions'.[45] In England there were rumours that Cromwell and St. John contemplated a deposition of Charles I and his replacement by the Prince of Wales.[46] Perhaps with this in mind, Cromwell was now courting Marten, Ludlow, and other open republicans. During a meeting with the grandees at about this time, Ludlow found them irritatingly elusive about their intentions: 'monarchical, aristocratical or democratical government . . . might be good in themselves, or for us, according as providence should direct us.'[47] Such vagueness may

---

[44] C.J. v. 455, 461-2; Boys's Diary, B.I.H.R. xxxix (1966), 160-1; Text of Declaration in Old Parl. Hist. xvii. 2-24. Fiennes's authorship is discussed by Pearl, T.R.H.S. 5th Ser. xviii (1968), 90, n.

[45] Thomas Reade's Relation: C. H. Firth, ed., 'Narratives illustrating the Duke of Hamilton's Expedition to England in 1648', Scottish Hist. Soc., Miscellany, ii (1904), 295-6; Birch to E. Harley, 3 July 1648: Welbeck MSS., Harley Papers (B.M. Loan, 29/73). Nathaniel Fiennes was also nominated to the Edinburgh mission, but his name was not put to a vote, presumably at his own request: C.J. v. 442. Ashhurst was allegedly persuaded to accept the assignment by Say and Cromwell, the latter arranging for him to be voted £1,000 for his war losses: Westminster Projects, or the mysterie of Darby House discovered (23 Mar. 1647/8: [B.M.] E. 433, 15), p. 6; see also L.J. x. 11, and Merc. Prag. no. 3 (11-18 Apr. 1648: [B.M.] E. 435, 42).    [46] Gardiner, Civil War, iii. 294-5, 326-7.

[47] Ibid. 296; Abbott, Cromwell, i. 580; Ludlow's Memoirs, i. 183-6, and nn. There can be no doubt that by 'those called the grandees of the house and army' Ludlow means the middle-group leaders.

have been a way of papering over the cracks now threatening the
Independent party's existence. The civilian leaders were in fact
about to make yet another effort to come to terms with Charles I.

*     *     *

The arguments for such a settlement were overwhelming to men
who, like Say and St. John, thought of the purpose of the war in
limited terms. On the one side was the Army, steadily more implac-
able against the King, more revolutionary in its intentions, more
threatened by Leveller disaffection. On the other was the growing
evidence of disorder in the countryside, and of the passionate desire
of the gentry—royalist, neutral, and moderate parliamentarian
alike—for a final settlement that would protect the old settled order
of society. The evidence of both a dangerous level of social discontent and of the alienation of the country gentry and yeomanry
from the Parliament was clear. Social and political grievances combined to foreshadow a counter-revolutionary explosion. Prices were
high after the war and a succession of bad harvests; 1647 was the
worst, 1648 was to be almost as bad. Ralph Josselin noted it as
'a sad, dear time for poor people' in his Essex parish in February
1648: 'money almost out of the country'. By April wheat was
approaching famine prices; it had reached 64s. a quarter in Wiltshire
by midsummer.[48] Wiltshire had been in a state of hungry disorder
since the previous winter, with miserable unemployment among the
weavers, complaints of the engrossing of grain by maltsters (with
the connivance of interested J.P.s, some injudicious petitioners
complained), and food riots at Warminster and Melksham. On
New Year's Eve 1647 a gang of demonstrators attacked the soldiers
and excisemen at Chippenham, and were said to have expected help
from surrounding counties. Disorder was never far from the surface in seventeenth-century England, but in an area with recent
memories of the Club outbreaks, and not much longer ones of
the violence of 1629–31, there was obviously cause for alarm. 'I

---

[48] *Josselin's Diary*, pp. 46, 49; B. H. Cunnington, ed., *Records of the County of Wilts.*
(Devizes, 1932), p. 208. From the recurrent complaints about the wet summer and autumn
of 1648 one would imagine it to have been even worse than 1647. However, wheat prices (and
grain prices generally) fell slightly in the harvest year 1648, though they were still disastrously
high: Joan Thirsk, ed., *Agrarian History of England and Wales*, iv: *1500–1640* (Cambridge,
1967), Appendix, Tables vi, vii. According to W. G. Hoskins, 'Harvest Fluctuations and
English Economic History', *Agr. Hist. Rev.* xvi (1968), p. 19, there was a slight fall in the
price of bread in London in 1648; but at 8½d. a quartern loaf it was still extremely dear.

believe you will have much trouble with the poor people', one Wiltshire J.P. warned another early in July.[49]

Government could always be blamed for the decay of trade, for
shortages, high prices, and heavy taxes. A Puritan minority, suppressing popular festivals in the interest of Godly Reformation
(and civic order, it might be added), was an unusually easy target
for all forms of discontent, particularly when, in such a county as
Weldon's Kent, it was represented by a notoriously oppressive
local regime. The Canterbury riot at Christmas 1647, beginning as
a football match ('we know not that the season of the weather gave
any invitation to it', the Kent Committee commented sarcastically),
quickly became a sprawling, drunken attack on both Puritan magistrates and ministers. After a few hours, the intrusion of the country
gentry and their dependants turned it into a real, though abortive
rebellion against the Committee, a short-lived preview of the following summer's turmoil.[50] A few months later the anniversary of
Charles I's accession (27 March) provided another natural outlet
for anti-Puritan, anti-Parliament demonstrations. At Norwich the
mayor permitted bonfires and feasting. When summoned to answer
for himself before Parliament he refused to go, and organized a
petition on his behalf. On 24 April a crowd of his supporters got
out of hand, and seized the headquarters of the Norfolk Committee.
The house was also the county magazine, and when troops arrived
to suppress the disturbance it blew up, killing at least 100 people.
The Puritan members of the corporation took advantage of the
soldiers' presence to elect a new mayor, expel a couple of 'royalist'
aldermen, and make known their dislike of 'popular elections',
which experience showed them to be 'continually disquiet, factious,
and perilous'.[51] There were outbreaks in London, too, that same
April; a bloody riot after the attempted suppression of a Sunday
tip-cat game in Moorfields; for a time, indeed, the whole City
was in the rioters' hands. A disciplined force of New Model troops
restored order, but did not add to their popularity; a few months
earlier it had been observed that 'all the miseries of the City, decay

[49] Cunnington, ed., *Wilts. Records*, pp. 181-3, 200, 208; H.M.C., *Various Collections*, i
(Wilts. Quarter Sessions MSS.), 115-17; Letter from Windsor, 5 Jan. 1647/8: *A Declaration
Concerning His Majesties Royall Person* (6 Jan. 1647/8: [B.M.] E. 422, 6).

[50] Everitt, *Community of Kent*, pp. 231-5; Boys's Diary, *B.I.H.R.* xxxix (1966), 159-60.

[51] Cary, *Memorials*, i. 399-403; *C.J.* v. 534-5, 546; *A True Relation of the Late Great
Mutiny which was in the City and County of Norwich* (3 May 1648: [B.M.] E. 438, 6); News-
letter, 29 Apr. 1648: Somerset R.O., Phelips MS. DD/PH/28, fol. 96; R. W. Ketton-
Cremer, *Norfolk Assembly* (London, 1957), pp. 131-50.

of trade, scarcity and dearness of provisions, not bringing in of bullion, and all other causes of poverty are imputed to the Army'.[52]

There was growing turmoil in other parts of the country as winter passed into spring. A hurling match between the men of Devon and Cornwall was suspected of being a pretext for action against the Army.[53] At Blandford in neighbouring Dorset troops had to be used to quell a riot when the County Committee tried to arrest a royalist minister, and Pyne's Somerset clique were faced with endemic resistance to their authority, particularly when they tried to collect taxes. At Bath the local riff-raff defiantly held bull-baitings outside the walls, parading 'with a drum before their dogs in affront of authority'. With the war over, large numbers of 'malignants and Cavaliers' were now resorting to the spa, and there was further trouble when Captain Henry Chapman, an ebullient local Royalist, led a riot in defence of another disaffected cleric. The scandalized Recorder, William Prynne, tried to put a stop to it, but had no authority because the riot took place outside the walls, in the county—and he had just been removed, at Pyne's instigation, from the Commission of the Peace.[54] At Exeter there was another head-on collision between the civic authorities and the military when Sir Hardress Waller came to quarter 600 troops. The mayor refused to assign them quarters, suggesting that there were 'Taverns, Inns and Alehouses sufficient for their entertainment', and threatened to ring the market bell to raise the citizens against them. Samuel Clarke, one of the city's M.P.s, took a leading part, with some wild speeches against the Army. Waller found such hostility that he was surprised the western counties were not 'all in one flame', and commented bitterly on the neutralist or Cavalier spirit of most of the committeemen; it was easy to mistake localism for malignancy.[55]

[52] William Clarke to Lt.-Col. Rede, 25 Jan. 1647/8: B.M., Stowe MS. 189, fol. 39. See Gardiner, *Civil War*, iii. 340-1, for the April riots.

[53] Letter to Lanerick, 28 Mar. 1648: S. R. Gardiner, ed., *The Hamilton Papers* (Camden Soc., N.S. xxvii, 1880), p. 171.

[54] *Merc. Prag.*, no. 2 (4-11 Apr. 1648: [B.M.] E. 435, 12); *Perfect Weekly Account*, no. 9 (3-10 May 1648: [B.M.] E. 441, 22). For repercussions of the Bath episode see *C.J.* v. 548, and Prynne, *Irenarchus Redivivus* (13 July 1648: [B.M.] E. 452, 23), esp. pp. 43-4.

[55] *Old Parl. Hist.* xvii. 159-67; H.M.C., *Exeter*, p. 212; *L.J.* x. 269-72; Bodl. MS., Tanner 57, fols. 124-9; Mary Coate, 'Exeter in the Civil War and Interregnum', *Devon and Cornwall Notes and Queries*, xviii (1934-5), 350. Cf. Cromwell's warning to Fairfax on 9 May: Abbott, *Cromwell*, i. 606.

It is against this background that the petitions which confirmed the middle group's desire for settlement, and which in the end precipitated the second Civil War, must be seen. There had been an earlier campaign in the spring of 1647. Even after the Independents' success in the summer sporadic petitions, expressing the hostility of the counties to military occupation, continued to be presented. The Somerset Quarter Sessions produced one of their regular complaints about the 'heavy pressures and burdens by free quartering of soldiers' in October 1647.[56] After the Vote of No Addresses the radicals in turn mounted a systematic campaign to show that public opinion was on their side. 'Framed at Westminster', Marchamont Nedham charged, probably correctly, the petitions were sent into the counties and circulated by leaders of the radicals' local organizations: William Purefoy in Warwickshire, Sir Arthur Haselrig in the North, Sir Henry Mildmay in Essex, Pyne in Somerset, Thomas Scot and Simon Mayne in Buckinghamshire. Mildmay ran into difficulties. According to Nedham, he got a packed Grand Jury to adopt the petition, but at a general meeting of freeholders at Romford there was strong opposition, headed by his cousin Carew Mildmay. In spite of speeches by the committeemen and by the Army chaplains Dell and Hugh Peter, the meeting broke up without adopting the petition, and Mildmay had to abandon his intention of attempting the same tactics at Chelmsford and Colchester.[57] In Buckinghamshire, where the freeholders were notoriously radical, Scot and Mayne were more successful, claiming 5,000 signatures. Their petition was presented to the House by one of the committeemen, Christopher Eggleston, and the two M.P.s celebrated the occasion by supping with the accompanying delegation.[58] And in Somerset Pyne and his cohorts made their usual thorough preparations. It was easy to get Puritan Taunton to lead the way with a petition of its own, thanking the Commons for the recent votes, and calling on them to 'go on effectually

[56] E. H. Bates Harbin, ed., *Quarter Sessions Records for the County of Somerset*, iii: *Commonwealth* (Somerset Record Soc. xxviii, 1912), Intro., p. xxix.

[57] *Merc. Prag.*, no. 25 (29 Feb.–7 Mar. 1647/8: [B.M.] E. 431, 5). Carew Mildmay later recalled having successfully obstructed a similar Essex petition in the latter part of 1648, but may possibly have confused the two incidents: H.M.C., *Seventh Report*, Appendix (Mildmay MSS.), p. 596.

[58] *C.J.* v. 488; *The Humble Petition and Representation of many inhabitants of the County of Buckingham* (15 Mar. 1647/8: [B.M.] E. 432, 12); *Kingdomes Weekly Intelligencer*, no. 251 (7–14 Mar. 1647/8: [B.M.] E. 432, 6); *Merc. Elen.*, no. 16 (8–15 Mar. 1647/8: [B.M.] E. 432, 11).

and vigorously to prosecute the settlement of Religion among us'.[59]
A county petition was then circulated. It commented approvingly
on the Vote of No Addresses, drew Parliament's attention to the
prevailing high prices and scarcities, complained of the continued
presence in local offices of persons ill-affected to Parliament, and
asked above all that the county might be freed from all 'Malignants,
Neutrals, and Apostates' (which, as Clement Walker acidly translated it, meant all 'Presbyterians and moderate men'). According
to the hostile Walker, the petition got nowhere in the eastern division of the county, but in west Somerset, the real centre of Pyne's
power, signatures were obtained by threats of sequestration. At the
March assizes a carefully packed Grand Jury, composed of 'schismatics and sequestrators', in Walker's words, then adopted the
petition, and had it presented to Parliament by the judge, the radical
Serjeant John Wylde. The whole episode shows the careful
management of which a local Puritan machine was capable, and
the machine's value as the mouthpiece of a national party: Walker's
charge that the jury was packed was certainly correct.[60]

These were the efforts of a revolutionary minority. More representative of gentry opinion were the petitions presented in retaliation a few weeks later by the ring of south-eastern counties from
Essex to Hampshire which touched off, or accompanied, the second
Civil War. That these overwhelming demonstrations of opposition
to military government and centralization came from the richest,
most populous counties of England, all within the orbit of London,
from a region hitherto mainly parliamentarian in its loyalties,
strikingly shows the extent of the alienation of the moderate 'political nation' from the Army in the spring of 1648. The first of them,
from Essex, is particularly important, as the knowledge of its pre-

---

[59] *C.J.* v. 460; *The Humble Petition and Grateful Acknowledgement of the Town of Taunton*
(17 Feb. 1647/8: [B.M.] E. 427, 21). Having thus prepared the ground, Taunton quickly
followed this up with another petition asking for a new charter and other favours: *C.J.* v. 497.

[60] *C.J.* v. 534; H.M.C., *Portland*, i. 448; *Perfect Diurnall*, no. 247 (17-24 Apr. 1648:
[B.M.] E. 522, 20), which prints the names of the Grand Jury; Walker, *Independency*, i.
91-2. 'Mercurius Pragmaticus' [Nedham], *A Plea for the King, and Kingdome* (27 Nov.
1648: [B.M.] E. 474, 2), p. 5. That the jury was packed is evident from a study of the Freeholders' Book of the High Sheriff, John Preston: Somerset R.O., Hippisley MS. DD/HI/9.
The book contains many insertions and additions of men who were not included in the lists
originally submitted by the constables. Almost all these additions are men known to have
been connected with Pyne's organization; and they, with a few of the original entries who
were men of known radical sympathies, account for fourteen of the nineteen members of the
Grand Jury. Against the name of one of them in the Freeholders' Book stands the marginal
note 'Mr. Pyne'.

paration may have helped to influence Say and his friends in the latter part of March. Mildmay's failure to carry the Essex freeholders on behalf of the Vote of No Addresses evidently convinced the local moderates that the time was ripe for a countermove, to harness the tide of opinion in favour of a final settlement. At Chelmsford Assizes on 22 March the Grand Jury adopted a petition calling for what was soon to become the familiar programme of the moderates: a 'personal treaty' with Charles I, and the ending of quartering and high taxation by disbandment of the Army. The Earl of Warwick, the county's leading magnate, suggested a compromise, no doubt afraid that the royalist language of the petition would produce a countermove by the radicals at Westminster. But it is also possible that he knew something of the middle group's intentions, that a new approach to the King was in the wind, for he proposed that the petition should be suspended for ten days, during which time, he thought, agreement between King and Parliament might in fact be reached.[61]

A compromise to forestall the Scots invasion, to satisfy the national mood for settlement, and to avoid the threatened disorders, was certainly in the air. Cromwell, for one, was involved in it. He was at Farnham in Surrey on 28 March, on business connected with his son's marriage, but also, rumour had it, conferring with Robert Hammond, Governor of the Isle of Wight, about the new overtures.[62] But the scheme was far more the work of the civilian grandees, and particularly of Lord Say. 'Old Subtlety' disappeared from London about the middle of March, and was soon said to be in the Isle of Wight, trying to bring the King to reason.[63] In the last week of March the other middle-group leaders—Say's son Nathaniel, St. John, Pierrepont, and Sir John Evelyn—also left London, and met with Say at Wallingford, where Evelyn's brother Arthur was Governor. On the 31st the two Evelyns, with Pierrepont and St. John, rode over to Phillis Court, a few miles away, to dine with the politic Whitelocke. Unfortunately the memorialist was too politic to record what was said, but according to a correspondent

[61] *The Petition and Desires of . . . the County of Essex* (4 Apr. 1648: [B.M.] E. 434, 22). See also *Hamilton Papers*, p. 171. Radical opinion was that Warwick himself helped to promote the petition: *Westminster Projects*, no. 5 (6 June 1648: [B.M.] E. 446, 5).

[62] Gardiner, *Civil War*, iii. 338–9; Abbott, *Cromwell*, i. 590–1.

[63] Letter of intelligence, 23 Mar. 1647/8: Bodl. MS., Clarendon 31, fol. 7. Hyde's minute to this letter reads: 'This is also confirmed by other relations.' The rumours were repeated a week later: ibid., fol. 42. Say was absent from the House of Lords between 6 Mar. and 20 Apr.: *L.J.* x. 98–211.

of the Earl of Lanark, they 'concluded it necessary to entertain a treaty with his Majesty, thereby (if possible) to disengage him from the Scottish interest'. Ashburnham, as usual, was involved in it on the royalist side, and the Earl of Southampton was to have been the intermediary with the King.[64] On returning to London, Say lobbied busily among members of all factions, trying to line up support for the negotiation. The King's agreement was apparently pressed by the threat of deposition in favour of the Duke of York: hence the urgent motive for York's escape from the hands of Parliament on 21 April.[65]

When in the previous September the Independent grandees had begun their approach to the King, they had the generals on their side. But now circumstances were totally different: a war was imminent. Fighting had already begun in South Wales, with the revolt of Poyer's disaffected supernumeraries, before the end of March.[66] At last, on 25 April, news reached Westminster that the die had been cast in Edinburgh: the Scots were to raise an army for war. The result was the final breach between the middle-group leaders and their radical allies in and outside the Army. In the scripture-laden hysteria of a Windsor prayer-meeting the officers sought God, confessed their errors in the recent 'politic' negotiations with the King, and resolved that after the now inevitable war they would bring Charles Stuart, 'that man of blood', to final account.[67] The Army was out of hand; Cromwell and Ireton could no longer control it even if they wished.

A great turning-point had been reached. The middle-group moderates could preserve their alliance with the radicals and the Army only at the cost of their long-sought settlement; they could pursue settlement only at the cost of the alliance. Impressed, it can

[64] Letter to Lanerick, 4 Apr. 1648: *Hamilton Papers*, p. 174; B.M. Add. MS. 37344 (Whitelocke's Annals), fol. 142ᵛ; *Merc. Elen.*, no. 22 (19–26 Apr. 1648: [B.M.] E. 437, 10). See also Gardiner, *Civil War*, iii. 339 and n.

[65] Letter of intelligence, 6 Apr. 1648: Bodl. MS., Clarendon 31, fol. 43; Gardiner, *Civil War*, iii. 342–4. It may not be fanciful to connect with these overtures the incident which led to the temporary banning of the newspaper *The Moderate Intelligencer*. On 8 May the paper carried the motto 'Dieu nous donne les Parlyaments briefe, Rois de vie longue'. John Dillingham, the paper's editor, had for a long time been connected with Oliver St. John: Pearl, *E.H.R.* lxxxi (1966), 506, n. That he was believed to retain middle-group associations in 1648 is apparent from the rumour (quickly retracted) that in July Lord Say, Wharton, and Cromwell met in his house at Barnet to discuss possible use of the Army against the City: *Merc. Prag.*, nos. 17, 18 (18–25 July, 25 July–1 Aug. 1648: [B.M.] E. 454, 4; E. 456, 7). For the 8 May issue and its consequences see Brailsford, *The Levellers*, pp. 402–3; and Joseph Frank, *Beginnings of the English Newspaper* (Cambridge, Mass., 1961), pp. 152–3.

[66] Gardiner, *Civil War*, iii. 325, 357–8.

[67] William Allen, *A Faithful Memorial* (1659), in *Somers Tracts*, vi. 500–1.

only be supposed, by the dual threat of revolution and counter-revolution, Say and his friends chose the second alternative. In doing so, reluctantly but inevitably, they lined up with the Presbyterians in a reversal of alliances more sweeping than any since the winter of 1644-5. After a great debate on 28 April, the Commons declared that they would not alter 'the fundamental Government of the Kingdom, by King, Lords, and Commons'. Pierrepont and even the wavering radical Vane voted among the majority of 165, though the size of the minority, 99, suggests that some hitherto middle-group supporters, presumably Army men, joined the radicals in opposition.[68] The Hampton Court propositions were brought out of cold storage for a debate on 'the Settlement of the Peace of the Kingdom', and the Vote of No Addresses temporarily suspended so that members could propose whatever terms for a restoration of the King they thought fit. The middle-group leaders had made their choice. The Independent party, as it had existed since 1645, was dead. And when that happened, as we have already seen, no longer could Army radicalism be controlled and revolution avoided.

\*     \*     \*

By now the counties were exploding. The Essex petition had been enthusiastically subscribed (20,000 signatures, its friends claimed), and Warwick could not play for time for ever. The Commons prohibited a meeting at Stratford on 4 May that was to send it in procession, but could not prevent its presentation to Parliament by a delegation said to number over 2,000. London's sympathies were plain enough: the Essex men were cheered through the streets and welcomed by the church bells. With further disorders threatening, Warwick used his authority as Lord Lieutenant to call out the Essex trained bands, until the Commons ordered him to desist; no doubt they feared the disaffection of the freeholders in the militia.[69] Surrey too was stirring. A petition similar to that from Essex calling for a personal treaty was widely circulated, and was adopted at a great meeting of freeholders at Dorking on 8 May. Further signatures were systematically collected, 500 copies printed, constables were told to obtain subscriptions in their hundreds, and the petitioners

---

[68] *C.J.* v. 547; Gardiner, *Civil War*, iii. 362. The large numbers in the division are partly explained by the presence of members who had come up for the call of the House on the 24th.

[69] *C.J.* v. 547, 551, 563; *L.J.* x. 243-4; F. F. Bennitt, ed., 'Diary of Isabella, Wife of Sir Roger Twysden', *Archaeologia Cantiana*, li (1939-40), 124; William Bray, ed., *Diary and Correspondence of John Evelyn* (Bohn edn., London, 1859), iii. 12.

summoned to meet again at Putney on the 16th. Alarmed, the
Commons sent Sir Richard Onslow, who still dominated the
County Committee, and other Surrey M.P.s to put a stop to it.
George Evelyn refused to go, but William Owfield, the member for
Gatton, played his part: 'at the *Fox* at Chipstead he feasted the
country people', a royalist newspaper reported, 'and dissuaded
them from petitioning'. When the 16th came, in spite of Onslow
and Owfield, a great throng of Surrey men assembled on Putney
Heath and marched to Westminster. Neither the petition's inflam-
matory royalist tone, nor the tumultuous manner of the delegation, pleased the Commons. The petitioners were kept waiting for
several hours in and around Westminster Hall, some of them being
plied with drink and Cavalier slogans by the bystanders. Insults
were hurled at the Parliament's guards, and in the end several
people were killed when the troops cleared the hall.[70] The first
blood had been shed in the Army's conflict with the county communities, otherwise known as the second Civil War.

In Kent, as in Essex and Surrey, the May demonstrations were
compounded of many different elements: excise and assessments,
petty tyranny by county committees, violation of the traditional
rights of the county through government from Westminster. Once
again can be felt a widespread yearning for the good old days,
for a return to the old government of J.P.s and locally controlled
militias, even at the cost of some crucial elements in the programme
for which Parliament had gone to war. In Kent the explosion was
precipitated by the trial of the Canterbury rebels arrested in the
Christmas troubles. Weldon had failed to persuade the Commons
to let him try them by martial law, and when Serjeants Wylde and
Cresheld came down to the May assizes even a carefully chosen
Grand Jury would not convict. Flushed with success, the Kent
moderates drew up a petition in much the same terms as those from
Essex and Surrey, calling for a personal treaty and disbandment.
Weldon vainly tried to suppress it, but it was received with even

---

[70] *The Humble Petition of . . . the County of Surrey* (16 May 1648: [B.M.] E. 442, 17).
There are many accounts of the violence in tracts under B.M. pressmark E. 443. On the
events surrounding the petition see also *C.J.* v. 561-2, 565-6; *L.J.* x. 260-1; *Old Parl.
Hist.* xvii. 139-41, 169-85; H.M.C., *Portland*, i. 453; Cary, *Memorials*, i. 425; Whitelocke,
*Memorials*, i. 314; Twysden Diary, *Archae. Cant.* li. 124; *Merc. Elen.*, no. 26 (17-24 May
1648: [B.M.] E. 443, 45); Boys's Diary, *B.I.H.R.* xxxix (1966), 164; and *Evelyn* (Bohn
edn.), iii. 18, 20. Sir Roger Burgoyne blamed the petitioners for their provocative behaviour,
but agreed that the soldiers were glad to find a pretext for the confrontation: Burgoyne to
Sir R. Verney, 18 May 1648: Verney MSS., B.M. Film 636, 9.

greater enthusiasm than in Surrey, with even a majority of Weldon's committeemen among the overwhelming number of gentry subscriptions. Weldon—and Parliament—took fright, began military preparations, and provoked corresponding measures on the other side. And so the Kent petition began a county-wide rebellion, the first major campaign of the second Civil War, the final confrontation between the conservative localists of the county community and a centralizing Puritan minority.[71] For all its exaggerations, gentlemen in many other counties would have recognized their own situation in the picture drawn by one of the rebels in Kent:

On the one side you have a whole County, represented by all the Knights, Gentlemen, and Yeomen thereof . . . in a word such a general and public unanimity and concurrence as was never yet seen or heard of in one county. . . . On the other side, you have about six or seven, or a few more, busy pragmatical Committee-men, having neither honour nor honesty, patronizing the Separatists and Sectaries of the County, by them alone had in veneration.[72]

With the military events of the second Civil War—the failure of the Kent rising, the mutiny of the fleet, the eruption in Essex (which began with the imprisonment of the County Committee by the rebels), and the fighting with the Scots—we are not immediately concerned. It is, though, important to note that these were not isolated occurrences, but merely the tips of the iceberg of submerged gentry discontent. Other petitions calling for a personal treaty followed the ones that produced the rising. One from Sussex early in June was presented by a delegation that included sons of two local M.P.s, Sir Thomas Parker and Thomas Middleton. A few weeks later Middleton himself was implicated in a rising at Horsham, after carefully alienating his estate as a precaution against possible sequestration.[73] Another petition, from Hampshire, identified Puritan doctrinaires ('those that think they have monopolized all truth'), greedy office-holders ('that ought to make audit for the many thousands received for the public'), and power-seeking republicans ('that had a design by taking away Monarchical Government, of making themselves

---

[71] For the preceding, Everitt, *Community of Kent*, pp. 236-47.

[72] *Letter from a Gentleman in Kent* (26 June 1648: [B.M.] E. 449, 34), pp. 12-13.

[73] *C.J.* v. 591, 614-15, 640; *L.J.* x. 315; *Cal. C. Comp.*, p. 2233; *Perfect Occurrences*, no. 76 (9-16 June 1648: [B.M.] E. 522, 40). See also Thomas-Stanford, *Sussex in the Civil War*, pp. 197-202.

high and mighty'), as the three main obstacles to settlement.[74] The Somerset Committee complained that local juries 'would have condemned all those that act for the Parliament', after one of their troopers was sentenced for killing a Royalist who obstructed the collection of assessments.[75] Localist sentiment continued to obstruct Parliament's military moves. When the Eastern Association was reconstituted at Cambridge during the summer, several M.P.s from the region frustrated a scheme, put forward by Mildmay and the radicals, to make the Association committee subordinate to Fairfax.[76] Yarmouth was openly disaffected, protesting vigorously when Fairfax tried to put in troops to protect the town against the rebellious fleet; in the end the Derby House Committee counter-manded his order out of fear of disturbances.[77] From all sides came pleas for settlement of county militias in local hands; from the moderate Devon Committee, from the Shropshire M.P. Robert Clive, from the more radical John Moyle in Cornwall. Moyle regarded the regular forces as 'military Janizaries', in many cases 'unsound and heterodox in points of religion . . . mere Infidels and perfect Atheists'. Only if the militia was settled in the hands of the local gentry could the country be freed of 'that insupportable burden, under which it groans by reason of the soldiers'.[78] Parliament was indeed in the process of settling a new militia, but it was done on a piecemeal basis during the summer, and no general ordinance for the whole country was completed. The County Committees in many cases therefore retained their old powers.[79]

The summer's violence confirmed the middle group's conviction that a settlement with the King was vital, even if it meant the final breach between them and the Army. Their leaders' parliamentary skill is once again demonstrated, in highly unpromising circumstances, in preparing the sort of treaty they wanted. They had to circumvent not only the radicals, who wanted no treaty at all, but also the Presbyterians, who wanted one, but with no safeguards,

[74] *The Declaration; Together with the Petition and Remonstrance of the . . . County of Hampshire* (14 June 1648: [B.M.] E. 447, 18).

[75] Somerset Co. Co. to Speakers, 9 June 1648: abstract in H.M.C., *Portland*, i. 457; in full in Grey, *Impartial Examination, III*, Appendix, p. 65.

[76] J. Eldred and W. Harlakenden to Mildmay, 22 Aug. 1648: H.M.C., *Seventh Report*, Appendix (House of Lords MSS.), p. 47.

[77] Whitelocke, *Memorials*, ii. 367; H.M.C., *Ninth Report*, App. I (Yarmouth Corporation MSS.), pp. 313-14.

[78] Moyle to F. Buller, 1 June 1648: *Buller Papers*, pp. 108-9; H.M.C., *Portland*, i. 484.

[79] *C.J.* v. 550-683, *passim*; *L.J.* x. 276-393, *passim*; Firth and Rait, *A. and O.* i. 1136-7, 1141.

and now had most of the cards in their hands. The middle group
still had important assets. They had, for one thing, regained the
support of several of their former adherents who had temporarily
defected to the Presbyterians in 1647; men like Sir Gilbert Gerard,
William Ashhurst, Richard Knightley, and John Swynfen.[80] But
as the Presbyterian strength revived in the summer of 1648 the
middle group found it increasingly difficult to control the Commons.
There were warning signs as early as 24 May. On that day, in
response to a request from the City, the Commons again voted to
resume treating with the King, though (evidently at middle-group
instigation) they also demanded that all declarations against Parliament be first annulled, and 'religion and the militia' settled, without as yet specifying how. The size of the majority—169 to 86—
was ominous.[81] The renewal of civil war sent more and more of the
radical and middle-group members away to their counties to
organize the defence, and the Presbyterians, aided by the City's
constant pressure for a personal treaty, were back in force. At the
beginning of May men of the middle group were still controlling
vital committees: Boys, for example, presided over one drafting
a new militia ordinance when Bulkeley had to withdraw through
illness. But on the 25th the news from Kent sent him hurrying into
the county.[82] On 3 June the long-slumbering impeachment of the
Eleven Members was dropped, and within a few days they were
given permission to resume their seats.[83] Thus, even while the fighting intensified in the provinces, more lenient propositions were
advanced as preliminaries for the Treaty.

The initiative came, significantly, from London. The City, its
governing oligarchy not only fearing revolution, but also desperately
trying to repair the interruption of trade caused by the second Civil
War, pressed strongly for talks. By the beginning of June the aldermen who had been arrested with the Eleven Members were
released, and with Recorder Glyn resumed their places in the City
government. On the 22nd a committee was appointed to draw up

[80] See above, nn. 27, 35, 45. Sir Edmund Verney, in a letter from Paris on 9 Aug. 1648
N.S., noted the return of these and other M.P.s to the 'Independent party': Verney MSS.,
B.M. Film 636, 9. See also *Westminster Projects* (Mar. 1648: [B.M.] E. 433, 15), p. 7; *Old
Parl. Hist.* xvii. 384, 394–5; and *L.J.* x. 386.

[81] *C.J.* v. 572; Gardiner, *Civil War*, iii. 378–9. The middle-group position is suggested
by the presence of Vane among the majority. Although usually more radical, he was at this
time generally co-operating with them: *Clarke Papers*, ii. 17.

[82] *C.J.* v. 558–9; *Cal. S.P. Dom., 1648–9*, p. 79.

[83] *C.J.* v. 583–90.

H

a petition calling for a Personal Treaty; it was approved by Common Council on the 27th and presented at Westminster the same day. An engagement in support of the Treaty was quickly circulated among the leading citizens and enthusiastically subscribed.[84] By this time the two Houses had agreed that besides the annulment of declarations the King would have to concede a Presbyterian settlement for three years and the militia power for ten as preconditions for the Treaty—the former a significant addition, the latter a significant retreat from the terms of the previous winter's Four Bills. They also set up a joint committee to consider the terms of the Treaty; its Commons members included the Wiltshire Evelyn, Crew, Pierrepont, Swynfen, Sir Gilbert Gerard, Sir Richard Onslow, and perhaps two others (Sir Robert Harley and Sir Walter Erle) who might sometimes support the middle-group line, but also three radicals and nine highly pacific Presbyterians.[85] The Lords' representatives being equally pacific (Say was not a member), the Presbyterians dominated the joint committee, and opened the door to negotiations considerably further than the middle group wanted to go, proposing that the Vote of No Addresses be repealed (the Commons agreed to this on 30 June), and that even the lenient preconditions be dropped. This the Commons, at middle-group advice (Evelyn was a teller for the majority), for a time refused to do, but the Presbyterians stood out still for unconditional negotiations. On 5 July the Lords went further and endorsed another London petition urging that the King be brought to London 'in honour, freedom and safety' for the opening of the talks, which would thus be held in the heart of the smouldering feeling against Army and Parliament, in as favourable an atmosphere for him as possible.[86]

Not surprisingly, the middle group retreated into one of their periodic bouts of reappraisal. Early in July Pierrepont called on Whitelocke and took him to dine with Evelyn at Chelsea, where they had 'much discourse together . . . about the public affairs'. Lord Say, for his part, had opposed the start of negotiations on such excessively mild terms, though he told the Duke of Richmond privately that he was not against negotiations as such.[87] In the end, after a well-reasoned speech by Swynfen at a conference had failed

---

[84] *L.J.* x. 347-50; Guildhall, Common Council Journal, xl (1641-9), fols. 281-2ᵛ. See also R. R. Sharpe, *London and the Kingdom* (London, 1894-5), ii. 282-4.

[85] *L.J.* x. 307-9; *C.J.* v. 614.  [86] *L.J.* x. 353-4, 361-4, 367, 371; *C.J.* v. 617, 622.

[87] B.M. Add. MS. 37344 (Whitelocke's Annals), fols. 163-4; Walker, *Independency*, i. 111. Walker characteristically regards Say's attitude as proof of his duplicity.

to sway the Lords, most of them accepted a compromise. On 28 July the Commons voted 71 to 64 to abandon their insistence on the preconditions, in return for the Lords agreeing that the treaty should be in the Isle of Wight, where Charles would be less able to mobilize public opinion than in London.[88]

In spite of their only partial success in laying the groundwork of the Treaty, the middle-group position in the summer was clear and consistent, and can be quickly summarized. It involved, first of all, a tough line towards the Scots and their English allies. No record survives of the debate of 20 July, when the Commons voted that all who invited the Scots into the kingdom were rebels and traitors, but the general outlook of the middle group shows that they must have endorsed it with enthusiasm. Swynfen helped to draft an answer to a petition which gave the House another opportunity to label the Scots 'enemies to this kingdom'.[89] And when on 18 August the Lords suggested that Scots representatives should be invited to the forthcoming treaty, 'the faction', as Marchamont Nedham often described the middle group, replied with bitter objections. The message was an affront to the Commons, Boys declared, and Nathaniel Fiennes predictably agreed that 'the Scots were in no case to be treated as friends'.[90] Firmness towards the Scots accorded with the middle-group's own prejudices; it also carried with it the hope that the Independent alliance might yet be repaired, if the moderate officers could keep the Army in line once the passions of war had begun to subside. First among those moderate officers was undoubtedly Cromwell, who on 1 September was still writing to St. John with affection, and closing his letter with greetings to Pierrepont, Evelyn, 'and the rest of our good friends'.[91]

Yet the middle-group's determination to initiate a treaty made any real restoration of the alliance impossible. They would prefer negotiations in which Charles was tied to prior conditions, negotiations, as Swynfen told the Lords on 20 July, with a 'foundation of

[88]  *L.J.* x. 386-7, 402-3; *C.J.* v. 649-50. Evelyn was as usual a teller, and Samuel Browne took the compromise to the Lords, but Swynfen's opposition shows that religious Presbyterians on the fringe of the middle group still insisted on the preconditions in order to get at least a limited Presbyterian establishment. They thus joined radicals like John Weaver, Scot, and Blakiston, who also insisted on the preconditions, but in the hope of making negotiations impossible: *Merc. Prag.*, no. 18 (25 July–1 Aug. 1648: [B.M.] E. 456, 7).

[89]  *Old Parl. Hist.* xvii. 393-5.

[90]  *Merc. Prag.*, no. 21 (15–22 Aug. 1648: [B.M.] E. 460, 21).

[91]  Abbott, *Cromwell*, i. 644-5.

security first laid', in which they could not be forced into disastrous concessions by the turmoil of the war or the manipulation of public opinion. As Fiennes put it, they wanted 'a safe, well-grounded peace', but not one 'which is neither safe, well grounded, nor likely therefore to continue'.[92] The tactics, in other words, were those of Pym in 1643: war, in order to negotiate, not negotiations in order to avoid war, of which the outcome would be probable surrender. But neither did they regard war as a substitute for policy. 'God forbid', said Say in the Lords after Preston, 'that any man should take advantage of this victory to break off the treaty.'[93] So determined were they to prevent the erection of unnecessary barriers to negotiation that in spite of their resolute opposition to the presence of an independent Scottish delegation they agreed to the issue of safe-conducts for Scots invited by the King as his advisers. When on 19 August the radicals tried to prevent this, Pierrepont and Evelyn carried the day against them.[94]

By 1 September the commissioners to treat with the King in the Isle of Wight had been chosen and their instructions approved. The middle group was well represented. Say and four Presbyterian peers (Northumberland, Pembroke, Salisbury, and Middlesex) were chosen by the Lords. Of the ten Commoners, four (Pierrepont, Crewe, Samuel Browne, and Bulkeley) were clearly middle group; a fifth, Vane, while more radical, had voted with them for negotiations on several occasions in 1648; a sixth, Sir John Potts, though a peace-party man who had managed to be absent during the 1647 crisis, was also a strong opponent of the Scots;[95] and a seventh, Glyn, although one of the impeached Eleven Members in 1647, had been prominent in the middle group in 1643 and 1644.[96] The remaining three, Holles, Lord Wenman, and Sir Harbottle Grimston, were all peace-party men, 'Presbyterians', anxious for

[92] *L.J.* x. 386; [Fiennes], *Vindiciae Veritatis*, p. 5.

[93] Walker, *Independency*, ii. 11.

[94] *Merc. Prag.*, no. 21 (15–22 Aug. 1648: [B.M.] E. 460, 21). The middle group may also have been behind the choice of the trimming old courtier Sir John Hippisley to join Bulkeley and the Earl of Middlesex as commissioners to make preliminary arrangements for the Treaty. Hippisley was a compromise choice after the House had been unable to accept either the crypto-Royalist Thomas Povey or the radical Sir James Harrington. See *Old Parl. Hist.* xvii. 357–8; and *C.J.* v. 660.

[95] Potts to D'Ewes, 2 Sept. 1642: B.M. Harl. MS. 386 (D'Ewes Corr.), fol. 234; Evelyn to Potts, 18 Oct. 1648: Cary, *Memorials*, ii. 36–7. See also *C.J.* v. 248, 330.

[96] Hexter, *Reign of King Pym*, pp. 38–43; Pearl, *E.H.R.* lxxxi (1966), 494, n. Glow, however, thinks he had already swung over to the peace party by 1644: *B.I.H.R.* xxxviii (1965), 61.

settlement on almost any terms, but they were surrounded by a strong element of the middle group.

The middle group knew what they wanted: to tie the King's hands by a surrender of the militia power, preferably for twenty years; to subject his choice of ministers to parliamentary approval, with Royalists disqualified; and to obtain a clear-cut abolition of episcopacy and the establishment of a Presbyterian system for at least three years. Few of them were enthusiastic about Presbyterianism, and some were willing to toy with alternatives at Newport (Pierrepont, for example), but as a matter of hard political reality they needed it to get the Treaty through the House. Above all, they wanted a final settlement, a restoration of legality. The middle group knew what they wanted, but two problems they were unable to solve. First, how, on the evidence of his past behaviour, could Charles I be trusted to observe any agreement, even one hedging him about with the most careful conditions, once restored to Whitehall and able to appeal to his royalist supporters and to the neutral and disillusioned, tired of argument, tired of war, tired of high taxation, tired of the Army and the County Committees? Secondly, even if agreement could be reached with the King, how could it be made acceptable to an Army fired with furious anger after the unnecessary blood-letting of 1648, inspired by the loftiest Puritan idealism, and seeing political compromise as a repetition of the sins of the previous winter? The middle group had chosen not to ride the tiger; no longer was there an Independent party to restrain the radicals. It would be but a 'Mock-Treaty', the King decided as early as 2 August.[97] He at least had no illusions. Neither had the Army.

[97] Charles I to W. Hopkins, 2 Aug. 1648: C. W. Firebrace, *Honest Harry: being the Biography of Sir Henry Firebrace* (London, 1932), p. 330. Besides Firebrace's own narrative of events at Newport, this work contains in App. B–G a very useful collection, drawn from various sources, of the King's secret correspondence in 1648.

# *Part Two · Revolution*

## V

### THE TREATY OF NEWPORT

THE sullen autumn presaged the outcome. Englishmen, stoical about their climate as they were and are, long remembered 1648's disastrous rains. In 1692, another bad year, John Evelyn thought 'the like had not been known since . . . 1648, when Colchester was besieged'. From May to mid September Sir John Oglander noted 'scarce three dry days together'. In Yorkshire there were great floods, ruining both haymaking and harvest.[1] Against this gloomy background, three distinct but inseparable lines of action converged inexorably: at Newport, the negotiations between the King and the parliamentary commissioners; at Westminster, the manœuvres of the political factions; and at St. Albans and later Windsor, the forging of the unity necessary before the Army could interrupt the Treaty and impose their own solution. Behind them all, incomparably more difficult to evaluate, was the struggle for the half-articulate mass of the country at large.

The gentry yearned for peace and settlement, and their hopes were fastened on the Treaty. Royalist and parliamentarian alike, they would accept a final settlement on almost any terms that would mend the fractured unity of the social order, restore the ancient government by King, Lords, and Commons, and give back to the county communities the independence lost to the institutions of centralization, Parliament and its County Committees. In war-torn Lancashire, Sir Ralph Assheton of Whalley Abbey reflected bitterly on the misgovernment of soldiers and committee-

---

[1] De Beer, ed., *Evelyn*, v. 112; Bamford, ed., *Oglander*, pp. 121-2; D. Parsons, ed., *Diary of Sir Henry Slingsby* (London, 1836), p. 185.

men. He told his steward to let the half-ruined mansion to 'some very old widow or two . . . that are not capable of their insolency and oppressions'. But there was a gleam of hope. 'It may be', he continued, 'you may see occasion to return again at spring, by which time by God's blessing, we may see a happy issue of this distemper, for praised be God there is a hopeful beginning of the Treaty.'[2]

The gentry yearned for peace. Yet there were many for whom the old order meant something far removed from the comfortable, privileged stability of Assheton and his like. Even among the gentry, and more obviously among the freeholders and townsmen, there was still enough passion for Puritan reform, for social reform, for political reform, for retribution against the authors of the second Civil War, to drive the radical leaders in Army and Parliament onward to revolution. Fired by the vindictive enthusiasm of the summer's war, borne up by the conviction that the hand of God had been visible at Preston and Colchester, the Puritan militants awaited expectantly the coming of their new Zion. God's people need not fear their enemies, one such zealot enthused from Tavistock: 'We are all fixed and ready, with many thousand well-affected in these parts, to act what God shall put us upon, for his glory and the people's freedom.'[3] The combination of religious fervour and democratic politics strikes the authentic Leveller note of 1648. The mobilization of this kind of sentiment through petitions from Army regiments, counties, and boroughs forms one more continuous theme of the months before the Purge. Lacking the kind of rudimentary political organization the radicals possessed through the Army and the County Committees, the moderates could mount no retaliatory propaganda campaign. All they could do was press on with the Treaty, and hope that the nation could be reunited before the radicals had settled their course of action.

The outcome was certainly far from inevitable. Although a few single-minded revolutionaries were willing from the first to adopt any available means of disrupting the Treaty, they had to overcome the reluctance of colleagues who were conservative country gentlemen as well as Puritan reformers to use the sword against lawful

---

[2] Assheton to B. Driver, 19 Sept. 1648: Chetham's Library, MS. A3, 90.

[3] *Packets of Letters*, no. 35 (14 Nov. 1648: [B.M.] E. 472, 9). Cf. the Dartmouth skipper's story that there were in Devon 100,000 (*sic*) men ready to support the Army at an hour's notice. John Winthrop to John Winthrop Jr., 3 Feb. 1648/9: *Winthrop Papers* (Mass. Hist. Soc., 1929-47), v. 312.

authority. Even more, they had to decide, if it was necessary to purge the backsliding moderates, the kind of purge they wanted.

Early in September the Army leaders and their parliamentary allies began to discuss the situation. Colchester had fallen, the war was over; but the opening of the Treaty was imminent. Sometime before the 6th, 'by the advice of some friends', Ludlow went down to Colchester to talk to Fairfax. The General was his maddeningly indecisive self. Ludlow urged that the Treaty was designed to 'betray the cause', and that it was vital for the Army 'to prevent the ruin of themselves and the nation'. Fairfax did not argue, but would only say that he would 'use the power he had, to maintain the cause of the public'. Fuming, Ludlow went to Ireton, and their conversation demonstrates both the agreement of the officers with the parliamentary radicals on aims, and their profound disagreement over tactics and timing. 'We both agreed that it was necessary for the army to interpose', Ludlow recalls, '. . . but differed about the time; he being of opinion that it was best to permit the King and the Parliament to make an agreement, . . . whereby the people becoming sensible of their own danger, would willingly join to oppose them.' Ludlow, on the other hand, thought it vital to act *before* the Treaty was completed, fearing that a reunited King and Parliament would bid for popularity by disbanding the army, 'under pretence of lessening their taxes', thus presenting the military opposition as selfish 'disturbers of the public peace'.[4] Ludlow's arguments carried conviction, but Ludlow, after all, could not purge Parliament. Ireton could, but he was not yet ready.

Before Ireton could be ready the intense feeling in the Army for drastic action had to be communicated to the more cautious officers and to the country at large. The revolutionary minority in the country also had to be given time to bring pressure on Parliament to break off the Treaty. Hence the petitioning campaign which began in September and continued throughout the autumn. How much official inspiration for this there was it is hard to say. In the Army, obviously, a good deal; outside it, there was at least the spontaneous recognition by 'violent party' supporters that this was the moment to speak out. Ireton could thus afford to delay in the hope that the petitions might persuade the Parliament to draw back from the Treaty; if they did not, then at least a climate of opinion favourable to more drastic courses was being prepared.

[4] *Ludlow's Memoirs*, i. 203-5.

The Levellers, not surprisingly, were in the van. On 11 September their *Humble Petition of Thousands of Well-affected Persons* was presented to Parliament, calling for implementation of the *Agreement of the People*, and for abolition of the veto power of King and Lords. Two days later, after the Commons had ignored the petition, a crowd of Levellers appeared at the door of the House with another one repeating these demands. There was a disturbance, and the demonstrators were heard to say 'that they knew no use of a King or Lords any longer; and that such distinctions were the devices of men, God having made all alike'. There were men in the House who, without accepting the democratic implications of such language, recognized its political value. Scot, Blakiston, and John Weaver came out to encourage the demonstrators, and Brian Stapleton remarked 'that the House must yield to them, or else it might be too hot to hold such as opposed it'. The moderate majority were not deterred, however; for them the episode merely showed, as Sir Roger Burgoyne remarked, 'what we are to look for from such a kind of men . . . if the Treaty should not proceed'.[5]

On 15 September, amid the incessant rain, the parliamentary commissioners arrived in the Isle of Wight to open the negotiations.[6] The first of the county petitions against the Treaty was adopted the very next day, in Leicestershire. It had been circulated by the Committee and the sequestrators, and may well have been inspired by the Earl of Stamford's radical son, Lord Grey, the county's leading extremist. Compared with later petitions, it was relatively restrained, calling only for a suspension of the Treaty pending investigation of Charles I's conduct. The conclusion, however, was more threatening: that since God had put 'the main principal enemies into your hands . . . impartial and personal justice may be speedily administered'.[7] This could mean Hamilton and the instigators of the second Civil War; it could also mean the King.

---

[5] *Old. Parl. Hist.* xvii. 462; Whitelocke, *Memorials*, ii. 402; Burgoyne to Sir R. Verney, 14 Sept. 1648: Verney MSS., B.M. Film 636, 9. See also Gardiner, *Civil War*, iii. 471-2; and Brailsford, *The Levellers*, pp. 350-4. The 11 Sept. petition is printed in W. Haller and G. Davies, eds., *The Leveller Tracts, 1647-1653* (New York, 1944), pp. 147-55.

[6] *The Kings Majesties Speech Delivered to the Commissioners* (21 Sept. 1648: [B.M.] E. 464, 28). Glyn, who had been on circuit in Gloucestershire, arrived a few days later: *Perfect Occurrences*, no. 90 (15-22 Sept. 1648: [B.M.] E. 526, 7).

[7] H.M.C., *Portland*, i. 497; Petition of James Smith: H.M.C., *Seventh Report*, Appendix (House of Lords MSS.), p. 121. The petition was presented to the Commons on 2 Oct.: *C.J.* vi. 41.

Similar petitions were soon being prepared—a Leveller one in Oxfordshire, and three in Newcastle, Yorkshire, and Somerset, which were presented to the Commons on 10 October. Of these three, the Somerset one was the most violent. With Serjeant John Wylde again presiding, it had been adopted at Taunton Assizes on 22 September, and as with the same county's petition of the previous March there is no doubt that its chief promoter was the irascible local dictator, Colonel John Pyne. And again the Grand Jury had been carefully handpicked, packed with an overwhelming majority of Pyne's obedient, radical henchmen. The Somerset men rejected the Treaty absolutely as the 'ruin of God's people', declared that Charles could not be trusted to keep any engagement, and called in the plainest language for him to be brought to trial: 'that justice be executed upon all delinquents, from the highest to the lowest, without exception'. In case of any doubts about its meaning, Pyne is said to have openly declared 'that the King's life should be taken from him'.[8]

Though the Army was marking time in September while the petitions were being prepared, this was not the case with supporters of the Treaty in the Commons. On 26 September there was a call of the House which produced a large attendance.[9] As always, a full House benefited the moderates, bringing up from the country the non-party backwoodsmen, innately conservative and profoundly hostile to the Army. But the proponents of the Treaty could rely on more than disorganized numbers. Correspondence between the commissioners in the island and their friends at Westminster reveals a concerted effort, on one side to force the King to concessions, and on the other to prevent the more rigid Presbyterians, with radical encouragement, from insisting on impossible terms. Sir Harbottle Grimston urged old Sir Robert Harley to see that his friends attended regularly and frustrated any outright rejection of the King's answers. The highly pacific Francis Drake promised Sir John Potts to further 'a good reception of all that is done by

---

[8] *Old Parl. Hist.* xviii. 31-2; *C.J.* vi. 49; *Perfect Diurnall*, no. 270 (25 Sept.-2 Oct. 1648: [B.M.] E. 526, 11); *Articles of Treason . . . committed by John Pine* (B.M., 669 f. 13, 94). No list of the members of this Somerset Grand Jury has survived. However, there is in John Preston's papers an undated list of persons 'warned for the Grand Jury' that clearly does not match any other jury during Preston's shrievalty, and must therefore relate to this one: Somerset R.O., DD/HI/9. Once again the prospective jurors are drawn mainly from the additions to the Freeholders' Book, and those identifiable are almost entirely members of Pyne's radical clique. See above, p. 94, n. 60.

[9] There were, even so, 162 absentees: *C.J.* vi. 34.

you'. John Crewe at Newport and John Swynfen, like Crewe a middle-group supporter but also a key man among the hard-line Presbyterians, exchanged many letters on similar lines. 'We shall use our utmost endeavours here', wrote Crewe, 'to bring the King nearer the Houses, and you will do good service at London in persuading the House to come nearer the King. . . . No man knows what will become of religion and the Parliament if we have not peace.'[10]

Although progress at Newport was slow, and full agreement still far away, the two sides were inching painfully towards each other. On 9 October Charles made a major concession—parliamentary control of the militia for twenty years[11]—and the commissioners' hopes rose accordingly. With the possible exception of Sir Henry Vane, they were united in a passionate anxiety for the successful conclusion of the Treaty. But the religious stumbling-block remained. Inspired, his enemies unkindly said, by a promise of the Lord Treasurership for himself and other lucrative places for his kinsmen and clients, Lord Say went down on his knees and tear-fully implored the King to swallow the unpalatable Presbyterian establishment, which he too disliked. The alternative to agreement, as Say correctly foresaw, was Army rule, and the destruction of both monarchy and peerage.[12] Bulkeley, Holles, and Grimston also urged the King to comply, the two last-named warning him not to listen to Vane's tempting promises of better terms from the Army, includ-ing toleration for episcopacy and the Common Prayer.[13] Vane, as his enemies charged, may have been insincere in these offers, merely trying to prolong the Treaty until the Army was ready to move. But his frequent support for moderate proposals during the previous year, his subsequent opposition to the Purge, and the language of Cromwell's letter to Robert Hammond on 6 November,

[10] Grimston to Harley, 21 Oct. 1648: H.M.C., *Portland*, iii. 165; Drake to Potts, 26 Sept.: Bodl. MS., Tanner 57, fol. 313; Crewe to Swynfen, 6 Nov.: *Cal. S.P. Dom., 1648-9*, p. 319. For earlier correspondence between Crewe and Swynfen, see ibid., pp. 296-309.

[11] Sir Edward Walker, *Perfect Copies of all the Votes, Letters, Proposals and Answers . . . in the Treaty Held at Newport* (London, 1705), p. 53.

[12] Clarendon, *History*, Bk. XI, §§ 155, 160; Peck, *Desiderata Curiosa* (1779 edn.), pp. 390, 396; Whitelocke, *Memorials*, ii. 414. Sources as far apart as the Army pamphleteers and the royalist M.P. Thomas Coke, who was with the King at Newport, agree on the dis-tribution of offices. Among other posts assigned, Nathaniel Fiennes was to be Secretary of State and Samuel Browne Solicitor-General: *Merc. Milit.*, no. 5 (14-21 Nov. 1648: [B.M.] E. 473, 8); H.M.C., *Portland*, i. 593.

[13] Warwick, *Memoirs* (1813), p. 359; Airy, ed., *Burnet*, i. 74-6; Laurence Echard, *History of England*, 3rd edn. (London, 1720), pp. 647-50.

all suggest that he would have preferred an agreement of some sort, though on very different terms from those so nearly concluded at Newport. Army opinion in October was that he had again defected to the middle group, had joined 'sweet tongued' Pierrepont, Evelyn, and the Fiennes gang, and would 'betray the Army and people'.[14]

Had Vane and Pierrepont known positively, as their radical friends had long since insisted and as they themselves must also have suspected, that Charles's concessions were insincere and mere time-wasting, their attitude to the negotiations would doubtless have been closer to that afterwards attributed to them. The King's scepticism about the 'Mock-Treaty' had not been lessened by the glacial progress of its opening sessions. Even as he conceded the militia he told one of the conspirators plotting his escape: 'The great concession I made this day, was merely in order to my escape, . . . for my only hope is, that now they believe I dare deny them nothing, and so be less careful of their guards.'[15] But though clear to posterity, Charles's duplicity could only be suspected by his contemporaries from their knowledge of his record. The moderates could not afford to believe that it was impossible to bind him by a settlement that he would not afterwards repudiate. Being realistic men, they had their doubts; as early as 21 September, St. John's client John Dillingham had heard from the Isle of Wight that 'they expect no more but a spinning out of time'.[16] They had their doubts, but they had nowhere else to turn.

While some were negotiating at Newport, other middle-group leaders were improving the Treaty's prospects at Westminster. They were, it is clear, intent upon a *general* settlement, a complete

[14] *Merc. Milit.*, no. 1 (10–17 Oct. 1648: [B.M.] E. 468, 35). In no. 5 of the same (14–21 Nov. 1648: [B.M.] E. 473, 1) there is another attack on 'the Grandees of the Junto that use to rule the Army'. It seems to me inconceivable that Vane could have been chosen as a commissioner unless it was known that he wanted agreement with the King. Possibly he changed his mind at Newport. But it seems more likely that he hoped to persuade Charles to accept a settlement close to the *Heads of the Proposals*; this would not be inconsistent with Cromwell's language in the letter to Hammond on 6 Nov. (Abbott, *Cromwell*, i. 677). None of the published biographies of Vane provides an adequate account of his behaviour in 1648; John Willcock, *Life of Sir Henry Vane the Younger* (London, 1913), pp. 167–75, is perhaps the best. The most impressive study of Vane, Dr. Violet Rowe's London Ph.D. thesis, 1966, accepts Clarendon's view that Vane was insincere in the negotiations. This must be treated with respect; nevertheless I am not convinced. I am grateful to Dr. Rowe for explaining her views to me.

[15] Charles I to W. Hopkins, 9 Oct. 1648: Firebrace, *Honest Harry*, p. 344. Cf. also ibid., pp. 345–6, and Charles I to Ormonde, 28 Oct.: Thomas Carte, ed., *Collection of Original Letters and Papers* (London, 1739), i. 185.

[16] Dillingham to Lord Montague, 21 Sept. 1648: H.M.C., *Montagu of Beaulieu*, pp. 163–4.

resumption of normal government. The King would be restored, hedged in by legal restrictions and guided by safe, reliable council-lors like Say and the others rumoured for office. As a first step towards the return of stability in the counties, the militia would be remodelled, taken out of the hands of the Committees and restored to gentry control. Finally, the judiciary would be reconstructed, with the middle group's own lawyers at the summit; St. John as Chief Justice of Common Pleas, Samuel Browne as Chief Baron of the Exchequer.[17] Meanwhile they guided the Treaty through the Commons with their usual tactical skill, confirming Charles I's opinion of the 'great influence as to resolutions of the Houses' which some of the commissioners possessed.[18] When the three radical petitions were presented on 10 October, it was Sir John Evelyn who had them laid aside. When the King's answer to the proposi-tion concerning delinquents was debated ten days later, it was Evelyn and Nathaniel Fiennes who joined the Presbyterians and crypto-Royalists in trying to reduce the number excepted from pardon. On the 26th, when the King's rejection of the permanent abolition of episcopacy was debated, it was Fiennes again who argued that the difference between moderate episcopacy and Presbyterianism was a mere form of words. And when the Newport talks were adjourned for a few days early in November, Say him-self came to London and lobbied busily for the Treaty, assuring St. John at a 'private Junto' that 'if they did not now agree with his Majesty . . . they were the bloodiest men alive, and for his part he would be for his Majesty'.[19]

The incessant chorus of hostility to the Treaty from the radicals was to be expected, and could be surmounted by the voting strength of the middle group and the political Presbyterians. A more serious obstacle was the split in the moderate ranks between the religious Presbyterians and those willing to compromise on reli-gion for the sake of settlement. 'We do not like of your church work', Sir William Lewis grumbled, and when the agreed term of forty

[17] In the end the radicals were placated by the appointment of Wylde as Chief Baron, Browne becoming a Justice of King's Bench. For the original plan see newsletter, 9 Oct. 1648: Carte, *Original Letters*, i. 175–6. The new judges were confirmed at the end of October and sworn in on 22 Nov.: *L.J.* x. 566, 570; Whitelocke, *Memorials*, ii. 459. For the settle-ment of the militia, see below, p. 127.

[18] Charles I to W. Hopkins, 16 Oct. 1648: Firebrace, *Honest Harry*, p. 345.

[19] *Old Parl. Hist.* xviii. 35; *Merc. Milit.*, no. 1 (10–17 Oct. 1648: [B.M.] E. 468, 35); no. 5 (14–21 Nov.: [B.M.] E. 473, 8); *The True Informer or Monthly Mercury* (14 Nov.: [B.M.] E. 526, 28), p. 16. Say did not return to Newport: *L.J.* x. 584–610.

days for the Treaty expired on 27 October, conclusion seemed as far off as ever. The Treaty was extended, but the Presbyterians, though anxious for agreement on every other ground, made it impossible by their rigidity. If the King would not abandon episcopacy, Swynfen thought, all the earlier discussions were 'but a fight off the shore, which makes the ensuing rough ocean the more terrible'. Swynfen was among the leaders of those who combined moderate politics with extreme Presbyterian opinions, and all Crewe's urgent messages from Newport failed to make him more flexible. The Presbyterians would be adamant, Evelyn warned Potts, 'if you work not his majesty to a better understanding'.[20] There was plenty of non-Presbyterian sentiment to which the compromisers could appeal. That acid old anti-clerical John Selden and his pious fellow antiquarian Sir Simonds D'Ewes both opposed forcing the King's conscience, William Jesson and other members spoke openly for episcopacy, and even the outwardly Presbyterian Lionel Copley moved 'to pare off some of the excretions of the Covenant'.[21] But the combination of radicals intent on wrecking the Treaty and Presbyterians intent on using it to establish their own ecclesiastical polity, made the outlook bleak indeed. The middle groupers recognized as much, as Say's dramatic appeal to Charles showed. Their favoured divine, Ussher, whose appointment to attend the King at Newport was no coincidence, claimed to have persuaded Charles to accept moderate episcopacy, but the proposal was apparently not even discussed in Parliament. It was indeed Nathanial Fiennes who insisted, in a conference with the Lords on 30 October, that the King must consent to the sale of bishops' lands, to make a revival of episcopacy impossible.[22]

In spite of the Presbyterian barrier, progress was made at Newport in the first six weeks of the Treaty. This, and the obvious determination of the moderates at Westminster to reach a settlement at all costs, convinced the Army leaders that no further time must be lost. As early as 26 September, Marchamont Nedham observed, the heavy turnout at the call of the House made the radicals 'gnash the teeth for mere vexation', and mutter menacingly

---

[20] Lewis to Potts, 12 Oct. 1648; Evelyn to Potts, 18 Oct.: Cary, *Memorials*, ii. 34, 37 (in Evelyn's letter the passage printed as 'your old brother Price' reads in the MS. 'your old brother Presb.'); Swynfen to Crewe, 13 Oct.: *Cal. S.P. Dom.*, *1648-9*, pp. 302-3. See also J. S. [pelman?] to Potts, 24 Oct.: Bodl. MS., Tanner 57, fol. 385.
[21] *Old Parl. Hist.* xviii. 102-3, 112-13; *Merc. Milit.*, no. 1 (10-17 Oct. 1648: [B.M.] E. 468, 35); no. (3) (24-31 Oct.: [B.M.] E. 469, 10).          [22] *Rel. Baxt.* i. 62; *L.J.* x. 570.

about a purge. The most important convert to this new spirit of urgency was Henry Ireton, who resumed his place in the Commons on the 30th. It was, he now thought, 'high time, considering how the members of Belial flocked this day about the righteous'.[23]

*     *     *

That the Treaty would be broken off did not seem unlikely. A mood of violence was abroad. 'It was dangerous for any member of the House or of the army to walk without company, for fear of being assassinated', Whitelocke recalls. Derby House was told of a plot to murder eighty leading radicals, and rumour soon expanded the number to 120. Miles Corbet was set on by royalist thugs while on his way to the House; two officers were murdered in London; Col. Rainsborough, prophetically, was attacked by marauding Cavaliers near St. Albans; and stories of assaults on M.P.s and officers were widespread. All seemed confirmed when the news that Rainsborough had been murdered near Pontefract reached London on 1 November. In such an atmosphere the probability of a coup was recognized on all sides. 'I hear of things abroad', Sir John Evelyn warned Potts on 18 October, and on the 30th Sir Dudley North was expecting 'some interruptions'.[24]

The interruptions would be delayed, however, until the Army had hammered out its line of action. Of the desires of the politically conscious minority among the rank-and-file there could be little doubt. Fired with sectarian enthusiasm, inspired by Leveller visions of freedom, and enraged by the summer's useless bloodshed, they were all for drastic action. But the officers, despite their Biblical exaltation of the previous spring, were still not of one mind. Fairfax, in his slow, inarticulate way, opposed anything resembling a coup, and although the Army Council was by now in the habit of acting in his name without much regard to his feelings, his influence had not been completely extinguished. More important, Cromwell remained tormented by indecision, deliberately choosing

[23] *Merc. Prag.*, no. 27 (26 Sept.-3 Oct. 1648: [B.M.] E. 465, 19); *Perfect Occurrences*, no. 92 (29 Sept.-6 Oct.: [B.M.] E. 526, 13).

[24] Evelyn to Potts, 18 Oct. 1648; North to Potts, 30 Oct.: Cary, *Memorials*, ii. 37, 48; Whitelocke, *Memorials*, ii. 413, 433; *Perfect Diurnall*, no. 270 (25 Sept.-2 Oct.: [B.M.] E. 526, 11); *The Declaration of the Armie Concerning the City of London* (8 Oct.: [B.M.] E. 465, 38); *A New Discovery of a Great and Bloody Plot* (28 Oct.: [B.M.] E. 469, 8); *A Full and Exact Relation of the Horrid Murder . . . of Col. Rainsborough* (4 Nov. [B.M.] E. 470, 4). There are several versions of the assault on Corbet; see newspapers for week of 28 Sept.-5 Oct.: [B.M.] E. 465, 29-39.

to stay in the north, far from the centre of action.[25] In his absence the direction of Army policy devolved inevitably on the willing shoulders of Henry Ireton, the one man with the determination, the intellectual honesty, the dialectical skill, and the unshakable conviction of the God-given rightness of his conduct to drive through the hesitations of his more politic colleagues. Ireton, far more than Cromwell, could accept the appalling risks that the use of the Army against Parliament entailed; the risks of Leveller revolution, of uniting the rest of the nation in armed resistance to a militant minority, of being left with a government with no more legitimacy than the sword. The obstacles were formidable. Even Ireton was able to bring the officers to his solution only after weeks of argument and manœuvre; and he could impose it on Ludlow and his other civilian allies only in a seriously modified form.

Ireton's difficulties were clear enough. His reappearance in the Commons prompted reports early in October that he was threatening to resign his commission. Then, after a public disagreement with Fairfax, he retired to seclusion to draft the document which later appeared as the Army's *Remonstrance*.[26] An attempt was made to silence his regiment by dispersing it through the counties of Surrey, Sussex, and Hampshire. At Farnham on the 16th the officers and men announced their refusal to comply. They also adopted a petition to Fairfax which confirms that Ireton had by now been converted to Ludlow's arguments for disrupting the Treaty.[27]

Whitelocke later ascribed to this petition 'the beginning of the design against the King's person'.[28] If not the beginning, it was an important stage in the mobilization of Army opinion. After a disarming assurance that the regiment, like everyone else, desired 'a safe and well-grounded peace', the petition complained that justice had not been done against the 'contrivers or abettors' of the second Civil War, declared that the King had betrayed his trust,

[25] See below, pp. 119, 121, 148-50.

[26] Letters of intelligence, 9 Oct. and 6 Nov. 1648: Carte, *Original Letters*, i. 175, 193; John Lilburne, *The Legal Fundamental Liberties of the People of England*, 2nd edn. (1649: [B.M.] E. 567, 1), p. 35. See also [George Bate], *Short Narrative of the Late Troubles in England*, ed. E. Almack (London, 1902), p. 101. Both Brailsford, *The Levellers*, p. 358, and R. W. Ramsey, *Henry Ireton* (London, 1949), p. 111, place Ireton's attempted resignation after 27 Sept. Rumours about Ireton's intentions were still circulating a month later: see Fitzjames Letter-book, ii, fol. 34ᵛ (Northumberland MSS.).

[27] *The Moderate*, no. 15 (17-24 Oct. 1648: [B.M.] E. 468, 24); *The True Copy of a Petition Promoted in the Army* (16 Oct.: [B.M.] E. 468, 18); summary in *Old Parl. Hist.* xviii. 77-8.

[28] Whitelocke, *Memorials*, ii. 424.

and pronounced him 'guilty of all the bloodshed in these intestine wars'. There was, the soldiers asserted, 'a prevalent party of his creatures, who in Parliament, and elsewhere, act his design, and endeavour to re-inthrone him'. There followed a demand for 'impartial and speedy justice . . . upon all criminal persons', and a clear indication of their intentions towards Charles I: 'that the same fault may have the same punishment, in the person of King or Lord, as in the person of the poorest commoner'. Those who continued to 'act or speak in the King's behalf' should be proceeded against as traitors. It is inconceivable that this petition can have been presented without Ireton's encouragement, likely indeed that he was himself its author; it therefore marks the beginning of his campaign to make Fairfax and his fellow officers accept the risks of purposeful action. One further step remained before the officers could present a united front, the convening of a General Council of the Army, a step which was among the demands made by Ingoldsby's regiment at Oxford in a petition to the General sometime before the end of the month.[29]

The General Council began its sessions in the choir of St. Albans Abbey on 7 November. Officers only attended; there was to be no repetition of Putney democracy. After prayers and a sermon, 'certain papers' submitted by the regiments were briefly discussed, among them presumably the petition of Ireton's men. But many officers had not arrived, and it was not until the 8th that the Council got down to details. Ireton's tactics are plain. In its early sessions the Council was allowed to discuss relatively uncontroversial grievances—pay, quartering, provisions for widows and orphans, justice against Rainsborough's murderers (news of the Pontefract affray had just reached them). On the 9th Ireton introduced proposals dealing with the old chestnuts of barrack-room agitation, arrears and indemnity. Then, on the 10th, when more officers had arrived and had been suitably prepared by the Commissary-General's persuasive appeals, Ireton introduced his version of the general programme on which he intended to unite the Army: the draft of the Army *Remonstrance*. A lengthy and complicated document, it was considerably amended during the discussions at St. Albans. But it already included as its main provisions two crucial

[29] *The Moderate*, no. 17 (31 Oct.–7 Nov. 1648: [B.M.] E. 472, 15); *Kingdomes Weekly Intelligencer*, no. 284 (31 Oct.–7 Nov.: [B.M.] E. 470, 10); Whitelocke, *Memorials*, ii. 432. Fairfax refused to answer the petition, and referred it to a Council of War: *Merc. Milit.*, no. 1 (10–17 Oct.: [B.M.] E. 468, 35).

points: a purge of Parliament, and the trial of the King and other leading delinquents. In spite of Ireton's preparations, however, there was immediate opposition. Supported by several others, Fairfax is said to have announced that he would do nothing 'tending to overthrow the government of the kingdom', and that he looked forward to a 'just, long-desired agreement' between King and Parliament. Only six votes were cast against a motion that the Army 'acquiesce to the result of the Treaty'. News of these divisions soon reached London, convincing Marchamont Nedham that the radicals in the Commons were merely playing for time, until it was possible for Cromwell and Ireton 'to unite the whole Army upon one interest against the Treaty'.[30]

After this discouraging episode Ireton could only wait while the gathering momentum of the petitioning campaign stiffened the officers' resolution. More petitions arrived in the first few days at St. Albans. Col. Pride's men denounced the Treaty, called for justice against the King and for a purge of the 'contrary minded, false, royal, and neutral party', urging the Council not 'to attend forms and customs in this extremity'. The regiments of Fleetwood, Whalley, Barkstead, and Rich passed on from the now familiar call for 'impartial justice', to a demand for the immediate dissolution of Parliament and a new constitutional settlement in which 'the supreme power may be declared and determined', and 'rules may be set down between the people and their representatives'.[31] Both demands and rhetoric were reminiscent of 1647, and Ireton must have known that it would be even harder than it was then to maintain Army unity if the more conservative officers did not allow the General Council to take the lead.

---

[30] There is no record of the St. Albans debates corresponding to that of the Putney or Whitehall debates. *Representations and Consultations of the Generall Councell of the Armie at S. Albans* (14 Nov. 1648: [B.M.] E. 472, 3), provides the fullest account of the early proceedings, supplemented by *Packets of Letters*, no. 35 (14 Nov.: [B.M.] E. 472, 9); *A Remonstrance from the Army to the Citizens of London* (15 Nov.: [B.M.] E. 472, 13); *The Declaration of Lieutenant-Generall Cromwel* (17 Nov.: [B.M.] E. 472, 20); and *Merc. Prag.*, no. 34 (14–21 Nov.: [B.M.] E. 473, 7). Nedham's account, while generally valuable, is mistaken in expecting Cromwell's imminent appearance at headquarters. I suspect that all the pamphlets exaggerate the strength of opposition to the *Remonstrance*. Attendance lists for 7, 16, 25, and 28 Nov. are given in *Clarke Papers*, ii, App. D. See also Gardiner, *Civil War*, iii. 498–9, and Brailsford, *The Levellers*, pp. 358–9.

[31] *Moderate Intelligencer*, no. 195 (7–14 Dec. 1648: [B.M.] E. 476, 24); from the reference to the recent 14-day extension of the Treaty, Pride's petition must be dated early November. *A Petition from Several Regiments* (13 Nov.: [B.M.] E. 470, 32); *Representations and Consultations* ([B.M.] E. 472, 3).

While Ireton was working for united action in the south, the same pressure of the radical rank-and-file was being applied to the officers in the north, where Cromwell had returned from Scotland to command the siege of Pontefract. Radical feeling is well illustrated by a letter from Cromwell's secretary Robert Spavin to his friend William Clarke at St. Albans on 2 November. Welcoming the news that action was imminent, Spavin continued:

> I verily think God will break that great idol the Parliament, and that old job-trot form of government of King, Lords, and Commons. It is no matter how nor by whom, sure I am it cannot be worse if honest men have the managing of it—and no matter whether they be great or no. . . . The Lord is about a great work, and such as will stumble many mean-principled men, and such as I think but few great ones shall be honoured withall.[32]

On 10 November there was a meeting near York of representatives from all the northern regiments which confirmed Spavin's suspicions of Cromwell and other 'great ones'. The agents unanimously endorsed the petitions of the southern regiments, resolved to 'live and die' with the General Council, and chose spokesmen to go to St. Albans to support the demand for 'justice upon all persons whatsoever'. The officers, however, agreed to this only after bitter argument, which Cromwell ended with a compromise proposal that the move should be accompanied by a last appeal to Charles I to accept the Newport propositions in full, thus making military intervention unnecessary. That Cromwell, while profoundly distrusting both King and Treaty, was still prepared to acquiesce if Charles accepted a permanent Presbyterian establishment, is clear from his letter to Robert Hammond on 6 November. He preferred Presbyterianism to episcopacy, was ready to co-operate with the Presbyterians if they insisted on severe restrictions on the King's power, and regarded a forcible dissolution followed by new elections as preferable to a purge; the letter contains no echo of the radicals' demand that the King should be tried. Cromwell was still a man of the middle group.[33]

It appears that Fairfax and the moderate officers at St. Albans at this time adopted the same expedient, a final appeal to the King.

[32] H.M.C., *Leybourne-Popham*, pp. 8–9.

[33] Cromwell to Hammond, 6 Nov. 1648: Abbott, *Cromwell*, i. 676–8 (see also Gardiner, *Civil War*, iii. 512–15); *Declaration of the Army* (14 Nov. 1648: [B.M.] E. 472, 6); *Declaration of Lieutenant-Generall Cromwel* (17 Nov.: [B.M.] E. 472, 20). The soldiers' suspicions of Cromwell are mentioned in a newsletter of 2 Nov.: Carte, *Original Letters*, i. 194.

Though he certainly did not encourage it, Ireton may have accepted
it to manœuvre the moderate officers into accepting the *Remonstrance* when it failed, as it was bound to do.[34] Even if a serious
approach was made, however, its failure had nothing to do with
Ireton's success in getting the Council to adopt the *Remonstrance*,
for the opposition had collapsed before the final reply from Newport
was received. As late as 15 November there was a meeting at the
*Bull's Head* in St. Albans at which the dissident officers declared
'their most pious and unanimous resolutions for peace'. The same
day some of the soldiers' agents wrote to their friends in London
denying that they intended to subvert monarchical government,
and promising not to obstruct the Treaty providing the Army's
reasonable demands were met.[35] Yet the very next day the Council
approved the *Remonstrance* in principle, and a committee was
appointed to revise and 'fit it for to be tendered to the Parliament'.[36]
Flushed with victory, Ireton and his allies drew up a letter to
Hammond, the King's guardian in the Isle of Wight, to enlist his
support. Though it was sent after a delay of several days, and was
to be delivered only if Hammond seemed likely to abandon his
scruples against military intervention, the fact that it was written
on the 17th confirms the date of Ireton's own consciousness of

[34] Gardiner's account of this admittedly obscure episode (*Civil War*, iii. 499–505) is
misleading. He says that the decision to intervene in the Treaty by an approach to Charles I
was made after Fairfax had opposed Ireton's draft *Remonstrance* on 11 Nov. For this Gardiner
cites *Packets of Letters*, no. 35, and the dispatch to Joachimi dated 17/27 Nov., in B.M.
Add. MS. 17677T (Dutch Transcripts), fol. 283. In fact, *Packets of Letters* says just the
opposite: that the Army 'will not meddle in the Treaty' and will 'acquiesce to the result'.
The letter to Joachimi is inaccurate in detail (for example, repeating the unfounded rumour
that Cromwell was at St. Albans on the 16th), and in any case says nothing definite about an
approach to the King, noting that the Council has not yet reached an agreed policy (I am
grateful to George Hilton Jones for his help in translating this dispatch). However, it is
possible that some overture was made privately by Fairfax and the moderate officers, though
certainly not with Ireton's and the Council's official approval. Reports from the Isle of Wight
on the 15th said that Charles had replied to a letter from Fairfax: *Remonstrance from the Army
to the Citizens* ([B.M.] E. 472, 13); *Declaration of Lieut.-Gen. Cromwel* ([B.M.] E. 472, 20).
The King's terms as listed in *His Majesties Declaration Novemb. 17* ([B.M.] E. 473, 5), and
followed by Gardiner, may indeed have been based on this letter. Although the pamphlet
cited appears more reliable than some others that appeared at this time, e.g. the obviously
spurious *His Majesties Message to the Lord Generall Fairfax* (16 Nov.: [B.M.] E. 472, 15*),
its title is misleading, for if Charles had made a formal declaration in reply to the Army,
other observers at Newport would have noted it. He may, however, have sent Fairfax a private
letter, which was perhaps leaked to the press by some interested party. If, as alleged, it was
dated 17 Nov., it cannot have been responsible for the changed atmosphere at St. Albans,
which had occurred before it can possibly have arrived.

[35] *Remonstrance from the Army to the Citizens* ([B.M.] E. 472, 13).

[36] *Clarke Papers*, ii. 54; *Ludlow's Memoirs*, i. 205; *Old Parl. Hist.* xviii. 159.

victory. 'It hath pleased God', the officers told Hammond, '. . . miraculously to dispose the hearts of your friends in the Army, as one man (together with the concurrence of the godly from all parts) to interpose in this treaty'. The intervention would not only 'refresh the bowels of the Saints', they went on, but also satisfy 'every honest Member of Parliament when tendered to them, and made public; which will be within a very few days'. By the 18th news had reached London that there had been a sharp swing of opinion in the General Council towards Ireton and against the Treaty.[37]

A similar hardening of opinion occurred in the northern army at precisely the same time. It may well have been inspired by arguments from St. Albans. On the 18th it was reported from Cromwell's headquarters at Knottingley: 'Capt. Joyce was here from the Council at St. Albans, and has away with him a very honest letter, signed by all sorts of honest commanders here, who petition for justice upon all delinquents from the King to the beggar; and favour the settlement of the Kingdom upon the London Petition of the 11 of September.'[38] Radical pressure, Leveller pressure, was being applied to bring the northern army into line. Perhaps Joyce also brought messages from Ireton to Cromwell; certainly Cromwell's own letters immediately reflect a striking sense of urgency. Forwarding the petitions to Fairfax on the 20th, he added, 'I do in all, from my heart, concur with them.' Cromwell's own doubts about acting before the conclusion of the Newport negotiations were not quite stilled: 'We could perhaps have wished the stay of [the *Remonstrance*] till after the treaty', he admitted to Hammond a few days later. But he wisely kept in step with the opinion of his officers. 'I know God teaches you', he concluded his letter to Fairfax: God through the mouth of Henry Ireton, a modern transcription might read.[39]

What then produced this remarkable transformation, in which within a few days Ireton forged the unity so obviously lacking on 15 November, and compelled the final adoption of his *Remonstrance*

[37] *Merc. Prag.*, no. 34 (14-21 Nov. 1648: [B.M.] E. 473, 7); *Letters between Col. Robert Hammond . . . and the Committee of Lords and Commons at Derby-House* (London, 1764), pp. 87-8. Although written on the 17th, the letter was not sent until the 22nd: *Clarke Papers*, ii. 54, n. The delay may have been caused by an attempt to get Fairfax's agreement: the 17 Nov. letter assures Hammond that he will receive a duplicate from the General within a few days.

[38] *Moderate Intelligencer*, no. 192 (16-23 Nov. 1648: [B.M.] E. 473, 15).

[39] Abbott, *Cromwell*, i. 690-1, 698; Nathan Drake, *Journal of the . . . sieges of Pontefract Castle*, ed. W. H. D. Longstaffe (Surtees Soc., xxxvii, Pt. II, 1861), App., p. 102.

as agreed policy on the 18th? The explanation can be found at Westminster. By now it was clear that the moderate majority of the Commons were determined to reach agreement with the King, to circumvent the Army and the radicals, at any cost.[40] Logic might teach that the deadlock on the ecclesiastical settlement was complete; but the moderates could not afford to be logical. Thus on the 15th, after debating the King's latest answers, the Commons voted to accept his often repeated request to come to London 'in honour, freedom and safety', and have his lands and legal revenues restored. It was a decisive step, as Henry Ireton was soon to warn them: 'that great and dangerous evil' of the King's return to London in effect meant unconditional restoration. The Commons added that the King's return should be only as soon as the Treaty was completed, but this vital qualification tended to be overlooked in the immediate flash of optimism. 'There is like to be peace if the soldiery interpose not', Sir John Gell wrote on the day before this vote, 'and whether they will or not, I can say nothing.' The radical press quickly answered him. From the Leveller *Moderate* came the call:

> The Treaty's now effected, all's agreed;
> Draw, draw for Freedom, or we're slaves indeed.

Communicated to the Army, both at St. Albans and Pontefract, the expectation of an imminent conclusion of the Treaty thus enabled Ireton to secure the united front for which he had long been working.[41]

Only one essential remained: to prevent the Levellers from getting out of hand. It was apparently Cromwell who first suggested working out an agreed line with them; 1647 was sufficient proof that they were less dangerous if brought under control, even at the price of concessions. In the latter part of October he wrote from Pontefract to some of the 'Independents' in the City to this effect,

[40] I cannot accept Gardiner's contention (*Civil War*, iii. 481-2) that after 27 Oct. agreement was impossible. Neither the commissioners nor the majority in Parliament thought so; nor indeed the Army leaders, for if the Treaty was doomed to fail their interposition would have been pointless.

[41] *C.J.* vi. 76-7; [Sir John Gell] to John Gell, 14 Nov. 1648: Chandos-Pole MSS. (Newnham Hall), 56/14; *The Moderate*, no. 18 (7-14 Nov.: [B.M.] E. 472, 4). See also *Merc. Elen.*, no. 51 (8-15 Nov.: [B.M.] E. 472, 8), and *Merc. Prag.*, no. 34 (14-21 Nov.: [B.M.] E. 473, 7). On the 17th the Scots Commissioners in London were expecting swift agreement: A. F. Mitchell and J. Christie, eds., *Records of the Commissions of the General Assemblies*, ii (Scot. Hist. Soc., xxv, 1896), 113.

and at his suggestion meetings began in the first week of November. The first session was a stormy one. Lilburne vehemently opposed the Army proposals to purge or dissolve Parliament and execute the King without a constitutional programme well beyond anything so far discussed. For the time being, Lilburne argued, it was necessary 'to keep up one tyrant to balance another': the alternative was rule by the sword. After some further bickering a committee which included Lilburne and Wildman for the Levellers, Robert Tichbourne and John White for the Independents, was appointed to draft a new *Agreement of the People*, which would be combined with the rest of the Army's programme.[42] On 15 November the committee met at the *Nag's Head*, near Blackwell Hall, and agreed to recommend the summoning of a constitutional convention to revise the *Agreement*. Thus improved, the *Agreement* would be endorsed by Parliament, which would then be dissolved and a new one elected on the proposed reformed franchise. These suggestions were promptly sent down to St. Albans, and were responsible for some important last-minute alterations to the *Remonstrance*.

On the 18th the General Council completed the work of the more decisive session two days earlier. Convinced by Ireton's persuasive tongue, united by the apparently imminent restoration of the King's powers, and assured of rank-and-file support, the Council made the amendments necessary to pacify the Levellers. Some of the earlier meetings had been open, but the Council 'sat close' on that Saturday. Only two negative votes were cast when the final draft of the *Remonstrance* was carried to a division. The Army was ready.[43]

\*     \*     \*

The Army *Remonstrance* took four hours to read when it was presented to the Commons by a delegation of officers on Monday, 20 November.[44] It is the nearest thing we have to a manifesto of the revolution which the Army was about to begin, and therefore demands close analysis. Implicit in it are two fundamental beliefs, on which Ireton and the Levellers could agree in principle, how-

[42] Lilburne, *Legal Fundamental Liberties*, pp. 33–4; Gardiner, *Civil War*, iii. 500–1; Brailsford, *The Levellers*, pp. 361–2.

[43] *Merc. Milit.*, no. 5 (14–21 Nov. 1648: [B.M.] E. 473, 8); *A New Remonstrance and Declaration from the Army* (18 Nov.: [B.M.] E. 472, 23); Gardiner, *Civil War*, iii. 507–8.

[44] *Merc. Prag.*, no. 35 (21–8 Nov. 1648: [B.M.] E. 472, 35); Text of *Remonstrance* in *Old Parl. Hist.* xviii. 161–238.

ever they might differ about their application: first, the sovereignty
of the people, buttressed by representative government and a contract between ruler and ruled, and secondly the use of divine providence as proof of the godliness or otherwise of any given course of
action. This second, theological, assumption, is used in the *Remonstrance* to provide a moral basis for both the Army's recent behaviour
and its current proposals. Thus the King's defeat in the second
Civil War showed that 'God would thereby declare his designing
of that person to justice'. But it is also used to buttress the doctrine
of the sovereignty of the people. Ireton admits that the maxim
*Salus Populi Suprema Lex* can be used improperly to defend un-
justified rebellion against 'law and magistracy'. But God will show
whether the principle is being used legitimately: if so, the cause
will be successful, if not, He will make it fail.[45]

   *Salus Populi*: the refrain runs through the *Remonstrance*, and is
repeatedly echoed in Army and Leveller propaganda in the autumn
of 1648.[46] In the *Remonstrance* it is used both negatively, to argue
that the Treaty is against the public interest, and positively, to
justify a thorough-going programme of constitutional reform. The
arguments against the Treaty rest on the contention that Charles I
has broken the original contract, under which he had 'a limited
power to rule according to laws . . . with express covenant and oath
also, obliged to preserve and protect the rights and liberties of the
people'. Repeated breaches of faith have shown that the King cannot be trusted. There is no sign of remorse for past misconduct,
his principles are irreconcilable with those of Parliament (there can
be no reconciliation 'of light with darkness, of good with evil'), and
experience shows that princes never observe agreements limiting
their powers. Although Ireton is weak on supporting historical
examples, he is much stronger in his identification of Charles I's
'Court Maxims' by which the repudiation of royal promises
extracted under force could always be justified. Noting how successful the King's friends had been in making the Parliament appear
responsible for military government (Charles was in fact himself
to blame, as the Army was needed to protect the people against
him), Ireton repeated Ludlow's argument that even a conditional
restoration would enable the King to put himself at the head of

   [45] *Old Parl Hist.* xviii. 161-2, 179.
   [46] See, for example, *The Moderate, passim*; and *Salus Populi Solus Rex* (17 Oct. 1648:
[B.M.] E. 467, 39).

a popular movement against high taxes, and overturn the settlement with public support. Punishment of the King would not only be an act of just retribution, it would provide a final refutation of contentions that the King was above the law. As an example it would be 'of more terror and avail than the execution of his whole party', and would 'let his successors see what themselves may expect, if they attempt the like'. The conclusion was obvious: to break off this 'evil and most dangerous treaty', and bring 'the capital and grand author of our troubles' to justice.[47]

It is in the proposals for constitutional reform that the hand of the Levellers can be seen, and which represent the compromise worked out in the last days at St. Albans. Again starting from the *Salus Populi* principle, the *Remonstrance* demands a reformed, more representative government. Not necessarily a republic: the door was left open for the enthronement of Charles's second son, York, if he could give satisfaction for past behaviour. The 'costly pomp' of monarchy was only to be 'suspended' for a number of years to provide compensation for poor people who had suffered in the wars, and an elective monarchy was proposed, with the elected king disclaiming his veto powers. Parliament was to set a date for its own dissolution (on this Ireton and the Levellers could agree), with annual or biennial parliaments elected in the future on a reformed franchise to destroy the electoral influence of King and Lords. On this, as far as it goes, Ireton and the Levellers could agree too; but Ireton, as he had shown at Putney, would be content with redistribution and a franchise limited to substantial property-owners, while the Levellers wanted something more. For the time being, however, this was left unsaid. There would also be a written constitution, with a declaration of parliamentary sovereignty, and certain reserved powers. In particular, Parliament was not to 'censure or question any man . . . for any thing said or done in reference to the late wars', Royalists excepted; and, more sweepingly, 'they may not render up, or give, or take away, any the foundations of common right, liberty, or safety contained in this settlement and agreement'. These constitutional fundamentals would be established by 'a general contract or Agreement of the People', to which all office-holders, kings included, would subscribe. Here again, the Leveller influence is obvious, as it is in the *Remonstrance*'s final suggestions that Parliament should

[47] *Old Parl. Hist.* xviii. 187, 194, 212, 214, 226-8.

consider law reform and other proposals in the London petition of 11 September.[48] Essentially, Ireton had given the Levellers some vague promises for the future, in return for their acquiescence in the more limited revolution that he envisaged. Ireton's programme was limited to a dissolution of Parliament and justice against the King, followed by either a very limited monarchy or a republic, and a more rational parliamentary system, which by redistribution would put power firmly in the hands of the gentry and the middling sort, and make the country safe for the Saints. Based as it was on a theory of contract and natural law, it would be a far cry from the traditional government by the three estates and the supremacy of the antiquated common law for which even progressive reformers in the middle group still stood. Even if Ireton could circumvent the Levellers, it would still be a revolution.

The *Remonstrance* brought home to the silent members the probably imminent end of their existence as a Parliament. During its reading, one observer noted, the Army's friends carefully watched the reactions of their enemies. As soon as it was finished, Sir Peter Wentworth, Thomas Scot, and Cornelius Holland moved for an expression of thanks to the Army for their 'so seasonable Remonstrance'. The opposition was not quite silenced. First on his feet was the garrulous, irrepressible William Prynne, new to the House (he had taken his seat for Newport, Cornwall, only on the 7th), but impossible to silence in any circumstances. 'So far from being seasonable', Prynne declared, the *Remonstrance* 'was subversive of the law of the land', leading only to 'desolation and confusion'. Prynne was followed by Sir Ralph Assheton, who demanded that the doors be locked and that everyone present solemnly deny his complicity in the *Remonstrance*. A gang of 'sectaries in arms' were trying to dictate to Parliament, one member thought, while another saw in the *Remonstrance* an argument for immediate agreement with the King. After these wild explosions the debate petered out, and consideration of the *Remonstrance* was postponed for a week, by which time the Treaty would be completed in one way or another. This rebuff to the Army may even have been supported by some of the radicals, who were said to have wanted to delay matters until the Army's preparations for the march to London were completed. But the military delegation was above such tactical niceties,

[48] *Old. Parl. Hist.* xviii. 229, 233-4.

pursuing the members downstairs after the debate with muttered warnings.[49]

There followed a few days' lull, while the Army readied itself, and the Commons awaited the King's final replies. The fortnight's extension of the Treaty expired on the 21st, and the commissioners were already at Cowes, at the waterside, when Parliament's reprieve until the 25th sent them scurrying back to Newport. 'All the propositions are now sent to the King', Sir John Gell told his son, 'and if he condescends quickly there may be yet had a peace.'[50] Quickly, before the Army marched: this was the essential. The King did not condescend quickly, stonewalling to the end in defence of the last shreds of episcopacy, encouraged perhaps by Ussher's flattering sermon on his birthday, the 19th. But even after debating Charles's latest answers the Commons still could not swallow the radical Mildmay's demand for the immediate recall of the commissioners, and voted one last extension of the Treaty until Monday night, the 27th.[51] The House also continued the work that intermittently occupied it for more than a month: disbanding the supernumerary forces raised during the second Civil War, which the radicals and their friends in the County Committees wished to keep in being, and preparing a new Militia Ordinance that would return the local forces to the safe hands of the gentry. The ordinance was passed on 2 December, an essential stage in the restoration of the old structure of government, but once more too late to be effective.[52] All now turned on what the Army would do to implement the *Remonstrance*.

Early in November there had been troop movements threatening an imminent move on London, with detachments quartered in

[49] *C.J.* vi. 81; Whitelocke, *Memorials*, ii. 457. For the debate see *Old Parl. Hist.* xviii. 238-9 (from *Merc. Prag.*); *Merc. Elen.*, no. 53 (22-9 Nov. 1648: [B.M.] E. 473, 39); and Letter of intelligence, 20 Nov.: Bodl. MS., Clarendon 31, fol. 312. Zouch Tate and John Maynard were among others who spoke against the *Remonstrance*.

[50] Peck, *Desiderata Curiosa* (1779 edn.), p. 406; [Sir John Gell] to John Gell, 21 Nov. 1648: H.M.C., *Ninth Report*, App. II (Chandos-Pole MSS.), p. 394.

[51] Wedgwood, *Trial of Charles I*, p. 14; *C.J.* vi. 86; *Merc. Prag.*, no. 35 (21-8 Nov. 1648: [B.M.] E. 473, 35).

[52] Firth and Rait, *A. and O.* i. 1233-51. The nature of the conflict over the local forces can be seen in two rival papers submitted to the Derby House Committee from Somerset in October. The Committee radicals wished to keep the supernumeraries on foot; four local M.P.s, including the moderate John Harington and the more radical (but middle group?) James Ashe as well as the violently anti-military Clement Walker and William Strode, wished to disband them: Bodl. MS. Dep. C. 168 (Nalson Papers, xv), fols. 251, 254. See also H.M.C., *Portland*, i. 499-500; and *Cal. S.P. Dom.*, 1648-9, pp. 297, 300.

villages to the west, some as close as Parson's Green and Knights-
bridge.[53] On the 22nd the Army headquarters was transferred from
St. Albans to Windsor; the move was completed within two days,
and on the 24th the officers 'sat very close in Council' at the Castle.
On the 25th each regiment was directed to send an officer to attend
the General Council, while units which had not yet spoken were
invited to declare their public approval of the *Remonstrance*. And
a committee, which as usual included Ireton, Constable, Harrison,
and Whalley, was appointed to chart the Army's next step.[54] On
Sunday the 26th, in cold, windy weather, there was one of those
great prayer-meetings which always preceded decisive action by
the Army, as the officers sought God 'to direct them in the great
business now in hand'. The preaching, from Hugh Peter and other
celebrities, lasted from nine until five. Inspired reports said that
the officers were united 'as one man', but there was still some argument about 'the opposing of a visible authority', ended by a ruling
that the business of the day was 'only to wait upon God'. Meanwhile the hesitant Robert Hammond, deaf to appeals from Ireton
to support the *Remonstrance*, had been recalled from the Isle of
Wight, and Col. Ewer had been sent to take charge of the King in
his place.[55]

With the adoption of the *Remonstrance*, Ireton was ready to act.
Yet even at this stage the plan to purge Parliament had still not
reached final form. The best evidence for Ireton's intentions at this
time comes from Lilburne, who was at Windsor for several days
immediately before the Army's march on London. Although the
Levellers had persuaded Ireton to accept their amendments at
St. Albans, they were still not satisfied. On 25 November Lilburne
and Wildman went to Windsor armed with proposals to bring the
*Remonstrance* closer to the *Agreement of the People*. Followed by
a train of officers, Ireton came to Lilburne's inn, and a 'large and

[53] Burgoyne to Verney, 8 Nov. 1648: Verney MSS., B.M. Film 636, 9; Letter of intelligence, 9 Nov.: Carte, *Original Letters*, i. 193.

[54] Letter of intelligence, 23 Nov. 1648: Bodl. MS., Clarendon 31, fol. 313; *Perfect Weekly
Account*, 22–9 Nov. 1648 ([B.M.] E. 474, 1); *Clarke Papers*, ii. 55–6. A draft of the circular
to the regiments is in Worcester College, Clarke MS. cxiv, fol. 104. Identical letters to
naval commanders were sent on the 28th: *Clarke Papers*, ii. 62.

[55] Gardiner, *Civil War*, iii. 519–21. Reports of the prayer-meeting in *Clarke Papers*, ii.
58–9, and Rushworth, *Historical Collections*, vii. 1338, minimize the division of opinion.
But see the newsletter in Worcester Coll., Clarke MS. cxiv, fol. 111. Evidence about the
weather from this point is taken from Sir Humphrey Mildmay's diary: B.M. Harl. MS. 454,
fols. 93–4. Mildmay was at Danbury, Essex, which is close enough for a reasonable assumption that London and Windsor experienced similar conditions.

sharp discourse' resulted. Two points of disagreement emerged: toleration, and the judicial powers of Parliament. On the first, Ireton would meet Lilburne only half-way. He would deny the magistrate coercive powers to compel conformity, but would allow restrictive powers to prevent religious practices tending to public disorder. On the second, Ireton wished to make Parliament virtually omnipotent even when no positive law had been infringed, which Lilburne recognized as an invitation to tyranny.[56]

The Levellers were about to leave in disgust, but Harrison, who had sided with Lilburne on the first point, argued for compromise. It is at this point that Ireton's intentions emerge. His plan was for the Army to *dissolve* rather than merely purge Parliament, and to 'invite so many Members to come to them as would join with them, to manage businesses, till a new and equal Representative could by an Agreement be settled'. Lilburne again objected that with King and Parliament uprooted there would be nothing to prevent the Army from ignoring the *Agreement* and ruling by the sword: formal enactment of the *Agreement* must come first. Harrison agreed. 'But, saith he, we cannot stay so long from going to London with the Army as to perfect an Agreement; and without our speedy going, we are unavoidably destroyed: For . . . the Treaty . . . is almost concluded upon.' Lilburne countered by proposing a committee of sixteen to formulate the *Agreement*, whose decisions would be binding on all parties: four Levellers, four London Independents, four officers, and four radical M.P.s. Harrison consulted Cornelius Holland, and the next day they obtained Ireton's approval. Lilburne then returned to London, to set up the committee of sixteen. Returning again to Windsor, he found that the officers had chosen Ireton, Constable, and four others of whom two would attend in rotation. This decision is recorded in the General Council minutes for 28 November, the committee being instructed to join 'such as are sent from London, about the preparing of an Agreement'.[57]

On 26 November, then, Ireton's plan was to dissolve Parliament rather than purge it, and to invite the radical minority to act in an advisory capacity until new elections could be held. There was violent opposition from the radicals in the Commons, who

[56] Lilburne, *Legal Fundamental Liberties*, pp. 35-7; Brailsford, *The Levellers*, pp. 367-8. I cannot accept Gardiner's chronology (*Civil War*, iii. 527), which places Lilburne's first appearance at Windsor only on the 28th; see below, n. 57.

[57] *Clarke Papers*, ii. 61. It is on this last point that my chronology rests; Lilburne's first appearance at Windsor must have been several days earlier.

continued to argue for a purge, not a dissolution. As members of a purged Parliament they could still claim to be the legal source of government; as advisers to an Army after Parliament was dissolved they would be nothing. The argument continued even as the Army began its march to London. The M.P.s stuck to their guns, Lilburne says, though Ireton and Harrison contemptuously dismissed them as belonging only to a 'mock-Parliament' which had forfeited its trust. Only a dissolution, Ireton declared, could guarantee a 'new and free Representative'.[58]

Who were the recalcitrant allies of the Army in the House? Their identity is important, for if Ireton was responsible for the Army's move against Parliament, they were responsible for the precise form it took, as he eventually, against his own inclinations, bowed to their pressure for a purge. One may have been the former courtier-monopolist Cornelius Holland, who was at Windsor with his son-in-law Henry Smith on 26 November, took part in the talks that produced the committee of sixteen, and was according to Lilburne 'the chief stickler for those they called honest men in the House of Commons'.[59] Another was certainly Ludlow, who confirms the fact that Ireton was overruled in the last days of November. Some time before the 28th, Ludlow tells us, some of the officers conferred with the leading civilian radicals, 'to invite them down to the Army, after they should in a public manner have expressed their dissatisfaction to the proceedings of those who had betrayed the trust reposed in them'. Ludlow's friends argued that there were enough sympathetic members to make this course unnecessary, and that it would indeed invite bloodshed, by enabling their enemies to claim the civil authority in opposition to the Army. Better, they thought, 'for the army to relieve them from those who rendered them useless to the public service, thereby preserving the name and place of the Parliament.'[60] No decision was taken at the meeting, but if Ireton was not present himself, he must soon have received the message.

On Tuesday 28 November, in session at Windsor Castle, the General Council passed three important resolutions. One of these, the nomination of members of Lilburne's committee of sixteen, has already been mentioned. The second was 'that the Army should be forthwith drawn up to London to quarter in or about the City',

---

[58] Lilburne, *Legal Fundamental Liberties*, pp. 38, 43; Lilburne *et al.*, *The Picture of the Councel of State* (4 Apr. 1649: [B.M.] E. 550, 14), p. 16.

[59] Lilburne, *Legal Fundamental Liberties*, p. 37.          [60] *Ludlow's Memoirs*, i. 206.

and the third that a Declaration to justify the move should be drafted by Ireton, Constable, Harrison, Whalley, and Hewson.[61] An informal decision to march must have been taken at least a day earlier, for on the night of the 27th men of Fairfax's regiment of horse were at Ockham, Surrey, 'to fetch in provision for three days march to London'.[62] The decision to march destroyed any prospect of serious work on the *Agreement of the People*. The committee of sixteen met at Windsor on the 28th, with all present except the M.P.s, of whom only Henry Marten appeared, and a discussion of general principles took place. The four Levellers then retired to their inn with Marten to redraft the *Agreement*. 'But much was not done in it there', Lilburne records, 'because of their haste to London, to force and break up the Parliament.'[63]

In London there was an abrupt change of mood from the elation of a few nights earlier, when a false rumour that agreement had been reached at Newport produced bonfires in the streets. Reports of the march were already circulating on the 28th, and it was known that the Army would arrive by the end of the week.[64] On the same day it was unsuccessfully moved in the Commons, 'a great part of the Army being on their march towards London', that they should be ordered to desist. On the 29th, when a letter nominally from Fairfax was delivered, warning the Speaker that the Army's patience was exhausted, there was a ripple of alarm from even such stalwart anti-militarists as Prynne and Major-General Browne. London, Whitelocke noted, was 'full of fears of the Army', and there was a growing exodus of frightened Royalists. Christopher Guise could remember how his family 'pawned our plate, buried our money, and so removed'.[65] And still the petitions calling for 'impartial justice' flooded in: from the northern army, from the regiments of Wauton, Scroop, and Saunders, from Sir Hardress Waller's brigade in the

[61] *Clarke Papers*, ii. 61.

[62] Other detachments of this and Ireton's regiments were at West Horsley on that and the following nights, no doubt on the same errand: P.R.O., S.P. 28/57 (Army Committee Papers), fols. 40-2.

[63] Lilburne, *Legal Fundamental Liberties*, p. 38. Prynne later accused the committee of sixteen of having drawn up the list of members to be purged: *Conscientious, Serious, Theological and Legal Quaeres*, 2nd edn. (1660), p. 3.

[64] *Perfect Occurrences*, no. 100 (24 Nov.-1 Dec. 1648: [B.M.] E. 526, 35); Mitchell and Christie, eds., *Commissions of the General Assemblies*, ii. 140; F. R. Raines and C. W. Sutton, eds., *Life of Humphrey Chetham* (Chetham Soc., N.S. xlix-l, 1903), i. 159.

[65] *Kingdomes Weekly Intelligencer*, no. 288 (28 Nov.-5 Dec. 1648: [B.M.] E. 475, 14); *The Moderate*, no. 21 (28 Nov.-5 Dec.: [B.M.] E. 475, 8); *The Declaration of Major-Generall Browne* (6 Dec.: [B.M.] E. 475, 18); Whitelocke, *Memorials*, ii. 463; *Guise Memoirs*, p. 129.

west, from the 'well affected' in Devon, Cornwall, and Berkshire.
Many included ominously far-reaching Leveller demands. The
Commons themselves had to sit through a violent sermon by the
radical Independent George Cokayne, calling for justice against
those guilty of 'shedding innocent blood', at their monthly Fast
Day on the 29th.[66]

On the 30th, the *Declaration* justifying the march appeared.
Protesting at Parliament's refusal to discuss the *Remonstrance*, the
Army appealed over their heads to 'the common judgements of
indifferent and uncorrupted men'. The Army's aim was 'a more
orderly and equal judicature of men in a just Representative'. They
would try to preserve as much 'of the present parliamentary
authority . . . as can be safe, or will be useful to those ends', and gave
the House a last chance to exclude 'corrupt and apostatized members'. Failing this, the Army called on the 'upright' ones to withdraw; they would be regarded as 'having materially the chief trust
of the Kingdom remaining in them', until 'a more full and formal
power in a just Representative' could be settled. 'For all these ends',
they grimly concluded, 'we are now drawing up with the Army to
London, there to follow Providence as God shall clear our way.'[67]

When the *Declaration* went to press, then, Ireton's plan was
unchanged: withdrawal of the 'upright' members and dissolution,
not a purge. It was believed in the Army that their friends in the
House had accepted this programme. As late as the 30th, a newsletter from Windsor reported that since the Commons had refused
to debate the *Remonstrance*, 'the members of the House who were
for it do intend this day to declare and protest against the rest and
come to the Army, and the Army marches tomorrow to the
rendezvous on Hounslow Heath and so on to secure those members
who declare with the Army'.[68] The plan was changed, therefore,
on 30 November. The 'honest members' did not issue their
expected declaration of secession, and it must have been Ireton's
knowledge of their obstinacy which forced the reversal. On
Ludlow's evidence it was only during the march that Ireton gave
way to the civilians and accepted the alternative of a purge. From
Colnbrook he sent word 'that now he hoped they should please

[66] Trevor-Roper, *Religion, the Reformation and Social Change*, pp. 330-1. For the petitions see newspapers and pamphlets in [B.M.] E. 475.

[67] *The Declaration of His Excellency the Lord General Fairfax* (30 Nov. 1648: [B.M.]
E. 474, 13); *Old Parl. Hist.* xviii. 266-72; Rushworth, *Historical Collections*, vii, 1341-3.

[68] Worcester Coll., Clarke MS. cxiv, fol. 116.

me, which I must acknowledge', Ludlow observes, 'they did by
the way which they were taking'.[69]

As the Army marched through the mist of a grey November day,
they were trying to reassure moderate members of the House, for
that evening Whitelocke received a friendly message from Fairfax.[70]
On the same day officers were seizing Charles I at Carisbrooke, and
Fairfax's letter accompanying the *Declaration* had scarcely been
read to the Commons, before word arrived from Robert Hammond
that he too had been arrested. The members at last addressed themselves to the *Remonstrance*, but bravely decided, by a vote of 125
to 58, to reject it. During the evening another letter from Fairfax
reached the Lord Mayor demanding the City's immediate payment
of £40,000 arrears to avert the catastrophe of quartering. Finally,
some of the commissioners reached London from Newport. Hearing that the Army intended to intercept them they had 'dispersed
themselves into several companies', and had travelled by night
along the byways. 'It is generally reported that the King hath
granted all', Sir Roger Burgoyne wrote, 'I pray God it prove so.'[71]

*       *       *

The debate on the King's answers to the propositions of Newport
lasted for more than three days, occupying much of Friday and
Saturday, 1 and 2 December, and the marathon sitting of Monday
the 4th, which ended only in mid morning on the 5th. When the
Commons assembled on a rainy Friday morning, Holles presented
the latest papers relating to the Treaty, and the motion was made
to take the King's answers into consideration. The day's most
notable speech came from Nathaniel Fiennes, who echoed the
arguments of his father, old Say and Sele, that it was time for settlement. It was a remarkable oration, the final testimony of the middle
group. The King's concessions over the militia, the appointment of
officers of state, and the Church, said the man who had drafted the
Declaration of No Addresses less than a year earlier, were 'enough
to secure religion, laws, and liberties'. Since these were the 'only

---

[69] *Ludlow's Memoirs*, i. 206.

[70] B.M. Add. MS. 37344 (Whitelocke's Annals), fol. 231 (significantly omitted from the
printed *Memorials*).

[71] *C.J.* vi. 91-2; *Old Parl. Hist.* xviii. 264-5, 288-9; Cary, *Memorials*, ii. 69-72; *Kingdomes
Weekly Intelligencer*, no. 288 (28 Nov.-5 Dec. 1648: [B.M.] E. 475, 14); Whitelocke,
*Memorials*, ii. 465; 'Lawrans' [Nedham] to Nicholas, 4 Dec.: Bodl. MS., Clarendon 34,
fol. 7[v]; Burgoyne to Verney, [30 Nov.]: Verney MSS., B.M. Film 636, 9.

K

things which the Parliament had so often declared to be the ground
of their quarrel', nothing further was necessary. The King's agreement to a suspension of episcopacy, even its permanent suspension
unless Parliament ruled otherwise, amounted in effect to its permanent abolition. To refuse 'so fair an offer', Fiennes thought,
'were to betray the weakness of the Presbyterian cause . . . as if it
would not endure the test of a three years trial'. The only recorded
answer (though there must have been others) came from the newly
rich silkman Edmund Harvey, worried as always about his security
of tenure in the unaccustomed magnificence of Fulham Palace: 'the
purchasers and contractors would not be contented with leases for
ninety-nine years'. Eventually the radicals attempted to put the
question, but were beaten by 133 to 102, and the debate was
adjourned.[72]

The afternoon was devoted to the more pressing matter of the
Army. Fairfax's letter to the Lord Mayor was read, and the City
was advised to placate him by paying the £40,000. Prynne, who had
recovered his courage, was against even this, moving that the Army
be declared 'rebels and traitors', but saner counsels prevailed. When
the Speaker was directed to order Fairfax to stop the advance on
London, a provocative clause, that the Army's march was 'dero-
gatory to the freedom of Parliament', was deleted by a vote of 44
to 33. The small numbers in the division indicate the lateness of the
hour, and the House rose some time after seven o'clock.[73]

By now the Army was only a mile away. The main force had
rendezvoused that morning on Hounslow Heath: two full regiments
and seventeen troops of horse, five full regiments and ten companies
of foot. Fairfax issued a proclamation ordering the soldiers to maintain the strictest discipline; officers were not to be absent from their
commands without written leave. By evening the rain-drenched
force had reached Kensington and was encamped in Hyde Park.
Whitelocke, who supped at the Earl of Clare's, found the company
there, like everyone else in London, 'full of trouble' at the Army's
approach.[74]

[72] C.J. vi. 92; Old Parl. Hist. xviii. 286-7; Merc. Prag., nos. 36-7 (5-12 Dec. 1648:
[B.M.] E. 476, 2); Whitelocke, Memorials, ii. 465.

[73] C.J. vi. 92; Old Parl. Hist. xviii. 289; [Nedham] to Nicholas, 4 Dec. 1648: Bodl.
MS., Clarendon 34, fol. 8. The Speaker's letter to Fairfax is printed in The Moderate,
no. 21 (28 Nov.-5 Dec.: [B.M.] E. 475, 8).

[74] Old Parl. Hist. xviii. 289-90; Clarke Papers, ii. 65; The Moderate, no. 21 (28 Nov.-
5 Dec. 1648: [B.M.] E. 475, 8); B.M. Add. MS. 37344 (Whitelocke's Annals), fol. 231.

Before the troops began to move off next morning (on another wet day), two deputations arrived. One was from the Speaker, commanding the Army to halt. Alas, replied Fairfax, the orders to march had already been issued, and it was too late to countermand them. He sent Sir Hardress Waller to explain this to the Commons, and to suggest that it might help if, even yet, they would consider the *Remonstrance*. But the House, Waller found, was 'intent upon other matters', and he was not admitted. The other deputation came from the Common Council. The citizens said that they were attempting to raise the £40,000 as quickly as possible; collectors with money in hand had been ordered to pay it in within two days. If the Army entered the City, they pleaded, it 'would make provision grow dear, and decay trade'. The officers greeted this with derision; Fairfax merely said that he expected the money by Monday the 4th.[75]

At about noon the final advance to Westminster began. When Fairfax arrived at Whitehall the Army's friends were there to welcome him. Lord Grey of Groby obsequiously held his stirrup when he alighted, other M.P.s attended him 'bare-headed to his lodging, which he entered with great magnificence'. Fairfax may not have been entirely happy about the policy which he was implementing, but he was obviously enjoying himself.[76] The common soldiers found less comfortable quarters. Many lay on 'bare boards' for lack of bedding; the foot at Whitehall, York House, and St. James, the horse at the Mews, with smaller parties in Durham House and other empty mansions, some as far afield as Southwark. Even the houses of M.P.s were not spared, though Sir Robert Harley was allowed to pay a contribution in lieu of quartering. In Covent Garden the men tied their horses 'to the doors of noblemen, knights and gentlemen's houses'. Thanks to Fairfax's orders and the efforts of zealous colonels like Hewson, only a few minor incidents of misbehaviour, such as soldiers jeering at passers-by as they marched, were reported. There was little direct obstruction from the terrified City, though on Saturday night a chain set up at one of the gates by an over-zealous official had to be blown up

[75] Cary, *Memorials*, ii. 73-4; *Moderate Intelligencer*, no. 194 (30 Nov.–7 Dec. 1648: [B.M.] E. 475, 26). The Lord Mayor's order to collectors of assessment is in B.M., 669 f. 13 (52). Common Council decisions and exchanges with the Army are in Guildhall, Common Council Journal, xl (1641–9), fols. 304ᵛ-6.

[76] *The Moderate*, no. 21 (28 Nov.–5 Dec. 1648: [B.M.] E. 475, 8); *Merc. Elen.*, no. 54 (29 Nov.–6 Dec.: [B.M.] E. 475, 22).

with gunpowder.[77] Opinion of the soldiers' deportment varied with
the observer. Whitelocke thought they 'behaved themselves with
unusual civility', but a Royalist was enraged as they 'swaggered
about the streets'. The occupation evidently persuaded more visiting gentlemen to leave and spend the New Year with their tenants,
and the exodus was swollen by an Army proclamation ordering
Royalists out of London. Whatever may have been the truth about
the soldiers' behaviour, on 4 December Fairfax thought it necessary to issue another order commanding them not to 'straggle about
the City'. The abusive carriage alleged against some of the men
was indirectly admitted, but blamed on imposters, 'divers loose
persons . . . in the garb of soldiers', against whom dire threats of
court-martial were uttered, and later implemented.[78]

Shutting its ears to these martial noises, the House continued its
debates. On Saturday, 2 December, the King's answers at Newport
were again taken up. Whereas Fiennes had dominated the previous
day's debate, it was now the turn of an opponent of the Treaty.
Young Sir Harry Vane could speak not only as a friend, albeit a
recently wavering one, of the Army, but also as one who knew all
about the Newport negotiations from the inside. Yet his attitude
remains puzzling. His conduct during the spring, and the fact that
he had been at Newport at all, shows that he wanted *some* sort of
agreement with the King; and he showed his dislike of the Purge
by staying away for six weeks afterwards. Yet his conclusions as to
the worthlessness of the agreement so narrowly missed at Newport
are not in doubt. By this debate, he began ominously, 'we shall soon
guess who are our friends, and who our enemies'. Looking back to
the happy days after the Vote of No Addresses, when 'the Kingdom
had been governed in great peace', Vane recalled how peace had
been shattered by the malignant combination between the Scots
and the City. The Treaty, he decided, had been a mistake from the
beginning; the King, even monarchy itself, could not be trusted.

[77] *Clarke Papers*, ii. 68; [Nedham] to Nicholas, 4 Dec. 1648: Bodl. MS., Clarendon 34,
fol. 7; Diary of Isabella Twysden, *Archae. Cant.* li. 127; Assheton to Driver, 5 Dec.:
Chetham's Library, MS. A3, 90; H.M.C., *Portland*, iii. 165. Further details from newspapers, 28 Nov.–6 Dec.: [B.M.] E. 475, 14–22. See also *Old Parl. Hist.* xviii. 293; and Rushworth, *Historical Collections*, vii. 1350.

[78] Whitelocke, *Memorials*, ii. 467; *Kingdomes Weekly Intelligencer*, no. 288 (28 Nov.–
5 Dec. 1648: [B.M.] E. 475, 14]; *Three Proclamations by his Excellency the Lord General
Fairfax* (5 Dec.: [B.M.] E. 475, 9). Recent recruits seem to have been responsible for some
of the incidents: *Perfect Occurrences*, nos. 103 (15–22 Dec.), 104 (22–30 Dec.): [B.M.]
E. 526, 42, 45).

Let them therefore 'return to their former resolution of making no more addresses to the King; but proceed to the settling the government without him, and to the severe punishment of those who had disturbed their peace and quiet'. Thus, Sir Harry concluded, they would conciliate the Army, and fulfil the programme of the *Remonstrance*. His flirtation with the middle group was over.[79]

No other speech on the Saturday approached Vane's in importance. The moderates seem to have felt that further delay would be to their advantage, to allow people to recover from the shock of the Army's approach. Prynne therefore moved for an adjournment 'till they were a free Parliament', released from military intimidation. The radicals Prideaux, Wroth, and Wentworth all pressed for a quick vote for exactly opposite reasons. Cromwell's friend Richard Norton reproved Prynne: 'take heed what you say against the Army, for they are resolved to have a free Parliament to debate the King's answer, if we refuse'. He moved for candles so that the debate could be concluded that night, but this was denounced as an attempt to get a vote when the more pacific elderly members had gone to bed, and the House adjourned until Monday morning.[80]

The session of Monday, 4 December, broke all records, lasting without a break until, at the earliest estimate, eight o'clock on Tuesday morning, and concluding with the crucial vote on the King's answers.[81] Before the main debate could be begun, letters from the Isle of Wight reported the King's removal to Hurst Castle. This produced some further delay, and a vote that the Army's action was 'without the knowledge or consent of this House'.[82] Two rival motions then held the attention of the House for almost twenty-four hours. The one preferred by the radicals

[79] *Old Parl. Hist.* xviii. 290–1; Clarendon, *History*, Bk. XI, § 200. See also *Ludlow's Memoirs*, i. 208, for the impact of Vane's speech.

[80] *C.J.* vi. 93; *Old Parl. Hist.* xviii. 291–2. Norton's hard line is difficult to reconcile with the fact that he was Lord Say's son-in-law, and a clear middle-group man.

[81] Gardiner, *Civil War*, iii. 532–3, is mistaken in describing two separate sessions on the 4th and 5th. According to his account, the House rose on Tuesday morning after rejecting the motion to put the question by 144 to 93, and reassembled later in the day for the main debate. Although the *Journal* prints the proceedings separately under the two dates, the newspapers and all other contemporary accounts make it clear that it was one continuous session. There was strictly speaking no session of Tuesday, 5 Dec. at all. Cf. *Old Parl. Hist.* xviii. 302, 447, and newspapers in [B.M.] E. 475, 20, 27; E. 476, 2–14; E. 526, 38. That the session ended at about 8 a.m. is confirmed by a letter to Lord Wharton, written immediately afterwards: Bodl. MS., Carte 80, fol. 740. Although assigned by Gardiner's MS. Calendar to Arthur Annesley, the mutilated signature looks to me more like that of the younger Vane.

[82] A radical attempt to delete the word 'consent' was defeated, 136 to 102: *C.J.* vi. 93; *Old Parl. Hist.* xviii. 293–5.

was framed, 'Whether the King's answers to the Propositions of both Houses be satisfactory'. As only a committed Royalist could vote for this, it was bound to be defeated. A 'close committee' of moderates therefore decided to withdraw it, and when the radicals moved to put the question they were voted down by 144 to 93. In its place appeared the motion, which the Lords placidly passed the same day without division, 'That the answers of the King to the Propositions of both Houses are a ground for the House to proceed upon for the settlement of the peace of the Kingdom'.[83] It was vaguely, even ambiguously drafted, and could thus attract the support of all who wanted any kind of settlement with the King.

No satisfactory record survives of this great debate. No diary, no letters from excited listeners; apart from one long speech all we have are a few scattered references in the newspapers, with Nedham's audacious *Mercurius Pragmaticus* as usual in the van. Nevertheless some impression of its progress can be reconstructed. A motion for candles was narrowly carried by 124 to 113, and the members settled down to make a night of it. As the debate meandered on through the early dusk and into the darkness of a blustery December evening, most of the accustomed spokesmen for the extreme factions managed to have their say. For accepting the King's concessions were the men who had long been marked down as partisans of the peace party, the Presbyterians, the 'moderate party': old men like Sir Robert Harley and Sir Benjamin Rudyard, prudent men like Sir Simonds D'Ewes and Sir Harbottle Grimston, bitter men like Clement Walker. On the other side stood ranged the former war party, the Independents, the 'violent party', the friends of the Army: from out-and-out republicans like John Blakiston and Thomas Scot, through all the shades of radicalism represented by the two Vanes, Prideaux, Sir Henry Mildmay, John Hutchinson, and Alderman Thomas Hoyle, to the time-serving profiteer Edmund Harvey. It may be significant that after Fiennes's speech on the 1st, there is no record of any major intervention in the debate by the middle group, unless Edward Stephens, who was John Crewe's brother-in-law, can be so regarded. Perhaps the diurnalists forgot to record their speeches; more likely they had given up. The time for speech-making was over.

[83] *C.J.* vi. 93; *L.J.* x. 624; *Old Parl. Hist.* xviii. 302; William Prynne, *Case of the old Secured, Secluded, and now Excluded Members* (1660), in *Somers Tracts*, vi. 545; *The Moderate*, no. 22 (5-12 Dec. 1648: [B.M.] E. 476, 5).

The arguments of both sides had been so often rehearsed that the newspapers, understandably, give only general summaries. They can be reduced to the moderates' contention that the King could be relied on to keep his agreements, and the radicals' equally strong conviction that he could not. He was, Mildmay said, 'no more to be trusted than a lion that had been caged, and let loose again at his liberty'.[84] If Nathaniel Fiennes and Sir Henry Vane had dominated the two previous days' debates, the palm for the third day must go equally surely to William Prynne. Seizing what might be the last opportunity of his short parliamentary career, Prynne (never a man for brevity) went to work in a speech of over three hours' duration. As usual, Prynne is original only in his wearisome comprehensiveness, rehearsing every possible argument for the Treaty, demolishing every conceivable argument against it, and impugning in every imaginable way the motives and integrity of its opponents. Those who regarded the King's refusal to grant Presbyterianism for more than three years as the crucial issue, Prynne contended, in fact wanted no ecclesiastical settlement at all, but only to hang on to Church lands picked up at bargain prices. Let the Army do its worst, Prynne concluded defiantly, the House should respect only its conscience and integrity. When he at last sat down, Prynne recalls, Speaker Lenthall was so overcome that he had to go out 'to refresh himself': well he might.[85]

Gradually, as the night wore on, the members drifted away. At one time there were over 340 present, but by Tuesday morning the number had fallen to 214. At last the motion to put the question was carried by 129 to 83; the main question passed without further division. Ostensibly the Commons had voted that the partial agreement reached at Newport provided a basis for further negotiations; they had in fact voted for a restoration, eleven years too early. It was a moment of high passion, and there were angry scenes. According to a royalist pamphleteer, Lenthall warned the members that adhering to their vote would inevitably mean their own destruction. Ludlow and several others tried to enter a formal

---

[84] *Old Parl. Hist.* xviii. 301-2 (as usual, the main source of this account is *Merc. Prag.*). Lucy Hutchinson gives a version of her husband's speech in *Hutchinson*, p. 267.

[85] *The Substance of a Speech Made in the House of Commons by Wil. Prynne* (25 Jan. 1648/9: [B.M.] E. 539, 11*); also in *Old Parl. Hist.* xviii. 303-445. The speech was to the motion that the King's answers were satisfactory, and must therefore have been given at an early stage of the debate. *The Moderate*, no. 22 (5-12 Dec.: [B.M.] E. 476, 5) gives the estimate of three hours' duration. See also Lamont, *Marginal Prynne*, pp. 182-3.

protestation against the vote, on the lines of House of Lords procedures, but were told that this was against the rules of the House.[86]

All hope of restraining the Army had vanished. Nevertheless the
House made a last effort to avert the inevitable, appointing a
committee to go to headquarters 'for the keeping and preserving
a good correspondence between the Parliament and the Army'.[87] It
was heavily dominated by men of the middle group: Evelyn of
Wiltshire, Pierrepont, Ashhurst, Whitelocke's friend and fellow
commissioner of the Great Seal, Sir Thomas Widdrington, with the
addition of two Presbyterians, John Maynard and John Birch, and
the radical Prideaux, who had many friends in the Army. When
the committee assembled later in the day they found that the
Council was not in session, and they were kept waiting for several
hours. At last Fairfax was permitted to tell them that 'the officers
not being then with him, he desired them to come tomorrow morning'.[88] Like the Commons, the Council had been in session throughout the night, 'debating upon high matters'.

The last preparations could now be made. As soon as the House
rose, Ireton, Harrison, Ludlow, and some other leading officers
and M.P.s met 'in a chamber near the Long Gallery' in Whitehall.[89]
Ludlow recalls 'a full and free debate', which according to one of
Lilburne's informants was bitterly acrimonious, marked by the old
disagreement between the Army advocates of dissolution and the
M.P.s who wanted only a purge. A purged Commons, Ireton

[86] [Bate], *Short Narrative*, ed. Almack, p. 104; *Ludlow's Memoirs*, i. 208-9. Lucy Hutchinson incorrectly says that her husband and four others did in fact enter their immediate
dissent: *Hutchinson*, p. 268. John Bulkeley later asserted that the majority would have been
more than two to one if old members had been able to survive the all-night sitting: *Burton's
Diary*, iii. 106. It was generally accepted that the vote on putting the question corresponded
with opinion on the question itself, though at least one contemporary observer doubted this:
*Moderate Intelligencer*, no. 194 (30 Nov.-7 Dec. 1648: [B.M.] E. 475, 26).

[87] *C.J.* vi. 93.

[88] This is what Pierrepont reported to the Commons on the 6th: *C.J.* vi. 94. The pamphlets
give a different version, but can, I think, be disregarded. Prynne says that Fairfax was ready
to listen, but was overruled by his officers, who insulted the committee: *Vindication of the
Imprisoned and Secluded Members* (23 Jan. 1648/9: [B.M.] E. 539, 5), pp. 28-9. See also
*Merc. Prag.*, nos. 35-6 (5-12 Dec.: [B.M.] E. 476, 2), and *Perfect Weekly Account*, 29 Nov.-
6 Dec. ([B.M.] E. 475, 20).

[89] There are two accounts of the meeting: by Ludlow, who was there, and Lilburne, who
was told about it by one of the participants 'immediately after it happened': *Ludlow's
Memoirs*, i. 209; Lilburne, *Legal Fundamental Liberties*, p. 38. Ludlow says that there were
others present besides officers and M.P.s, but I can think of no one important enough to have
been admitted, except perhaps Hugh Peter. It is tempting to suppose that Lilburne's
informant was his ally Henry Marten, but I know of no corroborative evidence for his
presence.

insisted, would be 'a mock-power, and a mock-parliament'. In the end, however, he bowed to the inevitable, accepting an immediate purge on the understanding that the House would then dissolve itself, and 'procure a new and free Representative'. The continuation of the division is important, for it demonstrates the officers' stubborn adherence to a programme of thoroughgoing parliamentary reform, and foreshadows the eventual dissolution of the Rump in 1653 after its repeated failures to undertake it. The conference also determined the qualifications necessary to put a member on the list to be purged: a vote for the crucial motion that morning, and/or one against the August motion declaring those who assisted the Scots invaders rebels and traitors.[90] Finally, a subcommittee of six, three officers and three civilian M.P.s, withdrew into a private room to make the detailed arrangements. It was agreed that the Army should be mustered in the morning, guards posted in and around Westminster Hall, and that only members 'faithful to the public interest' should be permitted to enter. 'To this end', says Ludlow, 'we went over the names of all the members one by one, giving the truest characters we could of their inclinations.' Armed with these decisions, Ireton went off to give the necessary orders to the regiments, and to acquaint the wretched Fairfax of what was being done in his name.[91]

The question remains: who were the six members of this subcommittee? Of the three officers, Ireton was undoubtedly one, Harrison almost certainly another. Pride himself may have been the third, though there is no conclusive evidence to establish him as anything more than the obedient instrument of a policy dictated by others. If not Pride, it might have been any one of half a dozen colonels then in London: Sir William Constable and Sir Hardress Waller seem the most likely. Of the three non-military M.P.s, Ludlow was one, on his own statement. Lord Grey of Groby, who stood at Pride's elbow the next morning to identify the members, may have been another, though it is possible that he took on the job on his own initiative to gratify his sense of importance. For the third, the most likely candidate is Cornelius Holland, who had been prominent in the discussions at Windsor, and whom

[90] This decision is recorded in a letter of intelligence written during the day by someone in the Army: Worcester Coll., Clarke MS. cxiv, fol. 128.

[91] *Ludlow's Memoirs*, i. 209-10. It is possible that a further meeting of the General Council was held to ratify these decisions: *The Staffe set at the Parliaments owne Doore* (8 Dec. 1648: [B.M.] E. 475, 29).

Prynne later accused of having helped to draw up Pride's list.[92] Whatever the exact composition of the subcommittee, it is clear that its decisions represented a last-minute compromise between the views of Ireton and Ludlow. Ireton had committed the Army to decisive action to frustrate the Treaty, and had united the officers behind his programme. But he wanted a withdrawal of the radical members, a dissolution, and a future settlement guaranteeing regular parliaments on a more equitable (though not democratic) franchise. Ludlow wished to preserve the name of Parliament, but to place power in the hands of the select minority who would survive the Purge. Ireton wished to use Parliament to implement the Army's reform programme; Ludlow to use the Army to expel his political opponents and leave power in civilian hands. In these two contrasting policies much of the future history of the Rump is implied. In the meantime, however, the centre of the stage was occupied by Colonel Thomas Pride.

[92] However, Prynne confuses the committee which planned the Purge with Lilburne's committee of sixteen, which it obviously was not. See above, n. 63.

# VI

## THE PURGE

UNTIL Cromwell's return to London, everything went according to plan. The fateful Wednesday, 6 December, was a dry, blustery day. The regiments duly paraded at seven o'clock, and in the cold light of dawn the noise of marching men and shouted orders echoed through the otherwise empty streets; Sir Dudley North remembered hearing the soldiers as they passed 'with great cries'. Parliament's normal guards, the innocuous City trained bands, came marching down to Westminster to perform their daily service. In Whitehall they found their way blocked by a thousand men of the New Model. While the officers conferred there were ribald shouts from the troopers, urging the citizens to 'go home and look to their shops, and . . . their wives'. There might have been trouble, but the right man was on the scene; Major-General Skippon, the Londoners' beloved old commander, appeared and persuaded them to return to the City.[1] By eight o'clock, when the members began to assemble, the dispositions were complete: Rich's horse and Pride's foot were stationed in Palace Yard, Westminster Hall, the Court of Requests, and on the stairs and lobby outside the House of Commons. Two other regiments patrolled the neighbouring streets.[2]

The worried M.P.s must have guessed what was afoot by the

---

[1] North, *A Narrative of some Passages in . . . the Long Parliament*, in *Somers Tracts*, vi. 587; *C.J.* vi. 95; *The Staffe set at the Parliaments owne Doore* (3 Dec. 1648: [B.M.] E. 475, 29). Wedgwood, *Trial of Charles I*, p. 41, assigns the encounter with the trained bands to the previous evening, but it clearly occurred on the morning of the 6th. Their orders were to guard the City during the night, and to march to Westminster in the morning. Guildhall, C.C. Journal, xl (1641-9), fol. 301ᵛ

[2] Whitelocke, *Memorials*, ii. 468; *Merc. Elen.*, no. 55 (5-12 Dec. 1648: [B.M.] E. 476, 4). Except where otherwise stated, the remaining events of 6 Dec. are derived from the chief narratives of the Purge: *Staffe set at the Parliaments owne Doore* ([B.M.] E. 475, 29); *The Parliament Under the Power of the Sword* (7 Dec.: B.M. 669 f. 13, 54); *The Second Part of the Narrative Concerning the Armies Force and Violence upon the Commons House* (23 Dec.: [B.M.] E. 477, 19); [Prynne], *A True and Ful Relation of the Armies forcible seising of divers Eminent Members of the Commons House* (13 Dec.: [B.M.] E. 476, 14); [Prynne], *A Full Declaration of the true State of the Secluded Members Case* (30 Jan. 1659/60: [B.M.] E. 1013, 22); and the summary in *Old Parl. Hist.* xviii. 449-61.

time they reached Palace Yard. On the stairs leading to the House
they encountered Col. Pride, flourishing his list of the members
to be secured. Pride knew only a few of them by sight, but an
obliging door-keeper helped him out until Lord Grey arrived to
provide more reliable identification. 'This is the person', John
Bulkeley heard one of them tell Pride as he came apprehensively
up the stairs. At first it was all very polite. To each member Pride,
hat in hand, gave 'a courteous salutation', and told them that he
had orders to arrest them, before handing them over to his waiting
officers. Some of the intended victims must either have entered the
House before Pride arrived, or have slipped through without being
recognized, but this was soon rectified. Messages were sent in to
Edward Stephens and John Birch and they were 'pulled out . . .
as they looked out at the door'. Defiantly Birch shouted into the
chamber to know 'Whether they would suffer their Members to be
pulled out thus violently before their faces, and yet sat still?'[3]

It was the irrepressible member for Newport who made the
longest, if not the loudest, protest. As he went up the stairs, he tells
us, Pride barred his way: 'Mr. Prynne, You must not go into the
House, but must go along with me.' Prynne indignantly replied
'that he was a member of the House, and was going into it to discharge his duty'. With that he 'thrust up a step or two more', but
was overpowered by Pride, Sir Hardress Waller, and some other
soldiers, who dragged him down to the entrance to the Court of
Requests. Prynne exploded: 'it was an high breach of the privileges
of Parliament, and an affront to the House.' Calling on the bystanders
to take notice, Prynne declared 'that they, being more and stronger
than he, and all armed, and he unarmed, they might forcibly carry
him whither they pleased; but stir he would not thence of his own
accord'. It was yet another contest between law and force, and not
for the first time was Prynne in the short run the loser. He was
hustled away to join the other arrested members, who by now were
under guard in the near-by Queen's Court.[4]

Meanwhile, according to Ludlow, about 120 members had
entered the House of Commons. They can scarcely have needed
to be told what was taking place outside, but a message was brought
in by John Doddridge, who had been with Prynne on the stairs;

---

[3] *Kingdomes Weekly Intelligencer*, no. 289 (5–12 Dec. 1648: [B.M.] E. 476, 9); Whitelocke,
*Memorials*, ii. 468; *Ludlow's Memoirs*, i. 210; *Burton's Diary*, iii. 106.
[4] *Old Parl. Hist.* xviii. 449.

the House promptly ordered the Serjeant-at-Arms to go to the
Queen's Court and invite the members there to come and take their
seats. The Serjeant returned with the not surprising information
that the victims 'seemed willing to consent', but that an officer had
said that he could not release them without orders.[5] There was talk
of suspending the session in protest, but a majority felt it more
important to prevent, as Ludlow put it, 'such inconveniences as
might otherwise fall upon the nation, if the whole power should be
left in the hands of an army'. They therefore sat tight, sent Skippon
to the City to continue his work of conciliation, and ordered Pierrepont's committee to negotiate for the members' release. Sir John
Evelyn went to fetch Widdrington, who with Whitelocke was holding court in Chancery, to join them.[6] While the committee was
absent on its unpromising errand, the House received its first formal
communication from its new masters. Lt.-Col. Axtell appeared,
and after some discussion was permitted to announce that the
General and Council of War had some proposals to present; after
further discussion these were delivered by Col. Whalley. Briefly,
they amounted to demands that the Eleven Members of 1647, with
the addition of Major-General Browne, should be brought to
justice; that the ninety-odd members who had voted for their
readmission or against declaring the Scots and their confederates
rebels and traitors, should be permanently excluded; that others
who had voted against the Army at various times, above all on the
previous day, should be suspended; that members innocent of
complicity in these 'treacherous, corrupt, and divided councils'
should make public declaration to this effect; and that the House
should fix a date for its own dissolution, and for 'a speedy succession
of equal representatives'. As the two final points show, Ireton had
not abandoned his programme, even though he had given way to
Ludlow on the tactics of the Purge.[7]

While Axtell and Whalley were at the House, Pierrepont's committee were encountering an icy reception at headquarters. Fairfax

---

[5] *Ludlow's Memoirs*, i. 211; *C.J.* vi. 93. There is no record of it in the *Journals*, but the
other accounts agree that the House again ordered the Serjeant to go with his mace to fetch
the members, and that he was forcibly prevented from leaving the lobby.

[6] *Ludlow's Memoirs*, i. 211; *C.J.* vi. 93; Whitelocke, *Memorials*, ii. 470.

[7] That there was opposition to hearing Axtell's message is shown by the fact that he was
called in twice before being allowed to deliver it: *C.J.* vi. 93-4. The Army's demands are
given in *The Humble Proposals and Desires of His Excellency the Lord Fairfax* (17 Dec. 1648:
[B.M.] E. 475, 25).

first offered them a verbal answer to the Commons' message, but
kept them waiting when they asked for it in writing, and a second
visit was no more fruitful. The General Council obstinately refused
to see in their demands that the prisoners be released the 'positive
pleasure' of the House, though they hinted that their eyesight might
improve if the Commons responded to Whalley's proposals. The
Army, in other words, would desist from purging if the House
would purge itself. It is not surprising that the committee disintegrated in the face of this stonewalling. Birch had already been
arrested; Evelyn and Widdrington left during the day.[8]

The Purge threatened to disrupt other bodies besides the House
of Commons. The Lords managed to hold a desultory session
attended by their Speaker Manchester and six other peers. But
after hearing prayers by the Presbyterian Stanley Gower, they made
one order on a law case, voted six weeks' leave for the Earl of
Stamford, and hastily adjourned.[9] When Whitelocke and his colleagues of the Great Seal arrived at Westminster Hall to hold their
Chancery session they were stopped by two soldiers and allowed to
enter only after Whitelocke had expostulated to an officer. The
commissioners were uncertain whether they ought to sit, but
allowed themselves to be persuaded by the ubiquitous Lord Grey.
Even after Widdrington's temporary departure with Pierrepont
and Evelyn, the court heard some cases, until Nicholas Love, who
was a Six Clerk as well as a radical M.P., told them that the Commons thought they ought to adjourn, because 'clients and counsel
could not with freedom attend'. It was agreed that Whitelocke
should go into the House to consult about this, 'which service
I undertook, and the more willingly', that inveterate time-server
recalls, 'to try what countenance I might have from the soldiers
then at the door'. Somewhat to his surprise, Whitelocke got
past Pride without being questioned, and managed to convince
the Speaker that the Chancery business was too important to be
interrupted. On the way back Whitelocke was comforted to note
that he was greeted by Pride 'with more than ordinary civility'.
When Widdrington rejoined them, the commissioners were able
to resume their session, and the managers of the Purge had won

---

[8] *C.J.* vi. 94; *Moderate Intelligencer*, no. 194 (30 Nov.–7 Dec. 1648: [B.M.] E. 475, 26).
The disappearance of Evelyn and Widdrington is established by the absence of their signatures from the committee's later messages. The signatures are not printed in *C.J.*, but are in
the copy in Worcester Coll., Clarke MS. cxiv, fol. 122ᵛ.

[9] *L.J.* x. 624.

another victory in their effort to avoid a total disruption of public business.[10]

Throughout this long and crowded day, the principal targets of the Purge were waiting in the Queen's Court. Accounts differ as to the exact number of those arrested; but the best estimate is forty-one for this Wednesday, 6 December; a few more were added on the 7th. The forty-one included four of the recently returned commissioners from the Isle of Wight (Wenman, Grimston, Crewe, and Bulkeley), but not the even more vulnerable Holles and Glyn; presumably they had fled after the vote on the previous day. Five others of the old Eleven Members were there, however (Clotworthy, Edward Harley, Sir William Lewis, Massey, and Sir William Waller), as well as others who had been targets of the Army's wrath, men like John Birch, Lionel Copley, old Sir Robert Harley, and Henry Pelham, a marked man for having accepted the Speakership when Lenthall defected to the Army in July 1647. There were men who had helped to smooth the path of the Treaty in the Commons (Francis Drake, John Swynfen), who had been tellers in important votes for it (Sir Walter Erle, Francis Gerard, Sir Samuel Luke, Sir Robert Pye); or who had spoken for it in debate (D'Ewes, Nathaniel Fiennes, Sir Thomas Soame, Edward Stephens). And there were those two vehement anti-militarists Prynne and Clement Walker, with their equally passionate Somerset colleague William Strode.[11]

As they waited the unfortunate forty-one were frequently reminded of their guards' bitter feelings, the officers having passed the word that these were the culprits responsible for withholding their pay, the natural inference being that they had pocketed it themselves. The hours passed slowly. At about three o'clock Hugh Peter, 'with a sword by his side, like a boisterous soldier', came bustling in to take a list of the prisoners for the General's use. He then disappeared, to return soon afterwards with Fairfax's order to release Fiennes and Sir Benjamin Rudyard. Lord Say's influence must have been at work in the one case, while Rudyard was too old and decrepit to be dangerous, and had powerful friends

---

[10] Whitelocke, *Memorials*, ii. 470-1. The passage about Pride's greeting is omitted, for the usual reasons, from the printed version, but is in B.M. Add. MS. 37344 (Annals), fol. 233[v].

[11] The possibility that others were arrested is discussed below, pp. 211-12. Glyn's last recorded appearance at Common Council was on the 5th: Guildhall, C.C. Repertories, lix (Court of Aldermen Proceedings, 1647-9), fol. 321.

like his patron Pembroke, whose support might yet be secured.[12] As darkness began to fall, Peter again returned with a group of officers to tell the prisoners that they were to be taken to Wallingford House. Coaches were waiting at the Lords' stairs, and the grumbling members were herded into them. Instead of to Wallingford House, however, the coaches took them only a few yards to the back door of 'a common victualling-house' kept by a certain Mr. Duke, who did a good business with lawyers attending the Court of Exchequer and their clients. The house was 'dark and low', and was appropriately named *Hell*.[13] The prisoners were marched into the dining-room, and spent an uncomfortable night in two upstairs chambers. Six of them with houses near by, including Sir Robert Pye and Sir Robert Harley, who was sneezing with a cold, were offered release on parole to appear before the General in the morning, but would promise only to appear in the House instead, so they had to stay with the rest. By six o'clock, when the Commissioners of the Great Seal ended their Chancery session, all was quiet around Westminster Hall; both prisoners and soldiers had gone.[14]

One other event of 6 December deserves mention. During the evening Oliver Cromwell made his belated appearance in Whitehall, after riding down from the north. His late arrival, indeed his behaviour during the entire month before the Purge, suggests that he was a reluctant accomplice of the revolution, however fully he had been kept informed of Ireton's intentions. Cromwell had spent the early autumn on the northern border and in Scotland, settling the government in friendly hands, and it was widely believed that when this was finished, by the middle of October, he would return to London.[15] He did not do so. Instead he stayed to command at the siege of Pontefract, a stronghold of no more than nuisance value now that the second Civil War was over. He could have been with the officers at St. Albans and Windsor if he had wished, but he

---

[12] *Merc. Elen.*, no. 55 (5–12 Dec. 1648: [B.M.] E. 476, 4); H.M.C., *Seventh Report*, Appendix (House of Lords MSS.), p. 116.

[13] Henry Marten, as always, was ready with the appropriate jest: 'Since Tophet was prepared for Kings, it was fitting their friends should go to Hell.' The Yorkshire radical Sir John Bourchier is said to have been a regular patron of *Hell*: *Mystery of the Good Old Cause*, p. 30. Two other alehouses adjoining Westminster Hall were *Heaven* and *Purgatory*: Pepys *Diary*, 28 Jan. 1660 and n.

[14] Welbeck MSS., Edward Harley, Misc. (B.M. Loan, 29/88), no. 73; Whitelocke, *Memorials*, ii. 471.

[15] See, for example, Letter of Intelligence, 14 Oct. 1648: Bodl. MS., Clarendon 31, fol. 277ᵛ. For Cromwell's movements see Abbott, *Cromwell*, i. 645–708. His attitude to the Purge is discussed with great insight by Wedgwood, *Trial of Charles I*, pp. 25–6, 31–2, 37, 43.

chose to stay away from the scene of decision; obviously he had not made up his mind. By 20 November it was thought at Pontefract that Cromwell would leave for London in about a fortnight, and in the meantime he made it clear that he supported the petitions from his Army against the Treaty. But he said nothing explicit about a purge, or about his own intentions, and at the same time was assuring Robert Hammond that he would have preferred the *Remonstrance* to be delayed until after conclusion of the Treaty.[16] News of the publication of the *Remonstrance* reached his headquarters at Knottingley on the 22nd, and three days later it was still thought that Cromwell intended to wait another week before moving south with the main body of his forces.[17]

On 28 November Cromwell was still before Pontefract. On that same day an urgent summons was sent him from Fairfax and the officers at Windsor ordering him to headquarters 'with all convenient speed possible'.[18] Confronted with a positive order, Cromwell still took his time. A fast-riding courier could have brought the order to Pontefract within forty-eight hours. Cromwell could therefore have left by the 30th, and have been in London by Saturday, 2 December: this, indeed, is what people at Windsor expected.[19] Cromwell certainly received the order by the evening of the 30th, because on the following day a report from Mansfield stated that he was at last moving south, and that he expected to reach Nottingham that night. But he then took five days to cover roughly 135 miles from Nottingham to London. Even allowing for bad roads in winter, this is scarcely 'all convenient speed'. If he had wished,

[16] See above, p. 121. Rumours that Cromwell was at St. Albans for a few days shortly before the *Remonstrance* was adopted (e.g. in *Merc. Prag.*, no. 34: 14-21 Nov. [B.M.] E. 473, 7) can be disregarded.

[17] Letter from Knottingley, 25 Nov. 1648: Worcester Coll., Clarke MS. cxiv, fol. 101. By this time Cromwell was assuring Fairfax that he intended to leave on the following Tuesday, the 28th: Abbott, *Cromwell*, i. 707. Abbott assigns this letter to 29 Nov., assuming that Cromwell left on Tuesday, 5 Dec., and is here telling Fairfax of this intention. As he had in fact left by the 1st (see below), this reasoning is unsound. The letter refers to the *Remonstrance* as though it had only just been received. As the text reached Knottingley on the 22nd, and as Cromwell is unlikely to have waited a week before commenting on it to Fairfax, some earlier date must be preferred. I think it should be dated between the 23rd and the 25th.

[18] Charles Fairfax to Col. John Morris, 28 Nov. 1648: B.M. Add. MS. 36996 (Pontefract Transcripts), fol. 137; *Clarke Papers*, ii. 62-3.

[19] A Letter of intelligence from Windsor, 30 Nov. 1648: Worcester Coll., Clarke MS. cxiv, fol. 116, says 'the Lieut. General will be here on Saturday'. John Rushworth used to take only twenty-four hours between London and York in 1642 (*D.N.B.*: 'Rushworth'). But that was in summer, when roads were better.

L

Cromwell could have left the regiments behind, and have been in London well before the Purge; but he chose to stay with them as far as Dunstable, and as the Mansfield report put it, to 'come no faster than they march'.[20] Either Cromwell did not expect the crisis to come to a head so quickly, unlikely in view of the order from Windsor on the 28th, or he preferred to arrive after the moment of decision. His self-imposed absence during November, his preference for delaying the *Remonstrance*, and his dilatory journey from Pontefract, make the latter conclusion inescapable. Intelligent contemporaries were quick to note that Cromwell had deliberately stayed away. He 'never vouchsafed his presence when the *Remonstrance* was hatching', says Marchamont Nedham; '. . . observe farther, that Oliver forbore coming to London, till after the force acted upon the House of Commons'. Ludlow records that when Cromwell at last arrived on the evening of the 6th, he said 'that he had not been acquainted with this design; yet since it was done, he was glad of it, and would endeavour to maintain it'.[21] It is of course inconceivable that Cromwell was unacquainted with the design. Perhaps he shared Ireton's objections to a purge and would have preferred a dissolution. But even this is unlikely, in view of his later objections to proposals that the Army should impose on the purged Parliament a deadline for dissolution; in January 1649 he still thought it 'more honourable and convenient for them to put a period to themselves'.[22] The most likely solution is that he balked at the use of force against constitutional authority, but could suggest no alternative which would avoid splitting the Army. Not for the last time was Oliver torn between the two conflicting principles of Puritan idealism and constitutional propriety. Like most of his military colleagues, he was still following the more decisive leadership of Henry Ireton.

\*      \*      \*

Cromwell's appearance in the Commons the next morning gave the House a useful pretext for opening the day's proceedings without facing awkward questions about the legality of acting in the absence of the imprisoned members. There is a certain appropriateness in Cromwell's entry accompanied by another prominent

[20] *Moderate Intelligencer*, no. 194 (30 Nov.–7 Dec. 1648: [B.M.] E. 475, 26); *Merc. Elen.*, no. 55 (5–12 Dec.: [B.M.] E. 476, 4).
[21] *Merc. Prag.*, no. 39 (19–26 Dec. 1648: [B.M.] E. 477, 30); *Ludlow's Memoirs*, i. 211–12.                                    [22] *Clarke Papers*, ii. 170.

recent absentee, Henry Marten. When someone raised the question of their missing colleagues, Marten proposed that instead of bothering about them, they should first 'consider the deserts' of the Lieutenant-General: without dissent the House voted their thanks for Cromwell's great services. They also thanked Skippon for his action in turning back the guards from the City, and voted to dispense with the citizens' services in the future.[23] The crucial question was whether the eighty or so members attending would adhere to the informal decision taken the previous day not to conduct any more business until the prisoners had been released. With interruptions caused by the delivery of further protests from other members who were being kept out (Pride's men were still at the door), debate on this question occupied most of the day. In the end there was a compromise: it was decided to 'proceed with the proposals of the Army', but the debate was put off until the following Saturday. According to Prynne, this still left an angry minority who promptly left the House, 'resolving to come no more till the House and members were righted'.[24] But there were persuasive arguments for those who stayed, even if they disliked the Army's actions. As usual, the cause of prudence is well stated by Whitelocke:

Many of these, upon debate and advice of friends, and considerations that they were chosen by their country to serve for them in this parliament, and that the violence was not offered to these, but to other members, whereof these were not made the judge, nor was it left in their power to desert the parliament and their trust, whilst they might have liberty to continue in that service. These reasons persuaded many to continue.[25]

While the debate proceeded, the Purge was continuing outside. As on the Wednesday, the place was surrounded by soldiers; this time men of the regiments of Deane and Hewson. When John Doddridge and his father-in-law, Sir Thomas Dacres, arrived at half past nine they were turned back on the stairs. A servant of the Serjeant-at-Arms identified them to an officer, who noted that their names were in a list he carried. After another unavailing effort

---

[23] *C.J.* vi. 94-5; *Merc. Prag.*, nos. 36-7 (5-12 Dec. 1648: [B.M.] E. 476, 2).

[24] [Prynne], *True and Ful Relation*, p. 9. The vote was 50-28 (*C.J.* vi. 95), but it is impossible to determine how many of the twenty-eight did in fact withdraw. Of the two tellers, Prynne seems to have been right about Sir John Trevor, who did not return until the following 28 June, but not about Lislebone Long, who was certainly present on and after 18 Dec.

[25] *Memorials*, ii. 472, and cf. also p. 494. As usual in the printed version, the impersonal replaces the first person singular of the MS.: B.M. Add. MS. 37344, fol. 234.

to enter, Dacres and Doddridge withdrew to write an indignant protest to the Speaker. Sir Edward Partheriche wrote a separate letter reporting similar treatment, and George Booth, the robust member for Cheshire, added his signature to yet another prepared by several fellow members whom he met angrily pacing up and down in Westminster Hall. Altogether about fifty members were kept out on the Thursday, many apparently because they had 'stickled for the privilege of Parliament, and restoration of their members, then in hold, the day before'.[26] Three others were arrested: the Cornishman Thomas Gewen, who had been in trouble with the Army for his part in the events of July–August 1647, the Devonian Charles Vaughan, and Sir William Lytton, one of the Barrington clan, and perhaps for this reason quickly released by order of Sir William Constable later in the day. Gewen and Vaughan were taken to the Queen's Court, and from there sent to join the others arrested on Wednesday.[27]

Altogether, something approaching 100 members were either arrested or secluded on the first two days of the Purge. In spite of the preparations made by Ludlow and his colleagues, it looks as if there was still a good deal of uncertainty among the officers about who was to be kept out now that the ringleaders had been secured. When Sir Roger Burgoyne wrote to his exiled friend Sir Ralph Verney on the 7th, he was still not sure about his status. Burgoyne attended the House that day in spite of the soldiers, and was not 'meddled with', while expecting 'very suddenly to be repelled, though not imprisoned'. Yet Burgoyne's letters show his firm opposition to the Army and support for the Treaty, and it is hardly likely that he had confined these opinions to his private correspondence.[28] Many more than 100 effectively removed themselves, without waiting for the Army. Some, like Sir Ralph Assheton, stayed quietly at home; 'no great security', he admitted. Others followed the presumed example of Holles and Glyn and fled before the soldiers could lay hands on them. Francis Chettel had left in a hackney coach with Sir Anthony Ashley Cooper on

[26] *Moderate Intelligencer*, no. 195 (7-14 Dec. 1648: [B.M.] E. 476, 24); *Kingdomes Weekly Intelligencer*, no. 289 (5-12 Dec.: [B.M.] E. 476, 9); *C.J.* vi. 94; Cary, *Memorials*, ii. 74-5; *Clarke Papers*, ii. 137-8. The figure of fifty is a rough average drawn from a number of contemporary estimates.

[27] *Old Parl. Hist.* xviii. 453. [Prynne], *True and Ful Relation*, p. 11, identifies the Vaughan as Charles, member for Honiton, thus removing the possibility of confusion with Edward Vaughan, who had been arrested the previous day.

[28] Burgoyne to Verney, 7 Dec. 1648: Verney MSS., B.M. Film 636, 9. Burgoyne did not attend after the 7th.

the 4th, and retired to Dorset.[29] Young Capel Luckyn, son-in-law of the imprisoned Sir Harbottle Grimston, seems to have gone down to Essex on the day of the Purge.[30] The Army must therefore have removed far more than 100 members by the evening of 7 December; and even then they were not finished.

Throughout this misty, drizzly day, the original victims had awaited the Army's decision on what to do with them. They had spent an uncomfortable Wednesday night in *Hell*. There were no beds, Prynne recollected, and those who tried to sleep did so on the floor or on benches. Most of them, however, passed the long night reading or walking up and down, talking and piously singing psalms. When morning came, there was no breakfast, and the Provost-Marshal, who was in charge, was persuaded to go to head-quarters to request some. He returned at about eleven o'clock, with news that the General Council intended to interview them at Whitehall. Once more the hungry and exhausted members were herded into coaches, and taken under strong guard to the King's Lodgings in Whitehall, where they arrived at about noon, and where Gewen and Charles Vaughan joined them. Here they were kept 'in a very cold room without fire' for several hours, while the General Council insolently debated more pressing business. They were at last provided with 'some burnt wine and biscuits'. It was dark before the officers at last condescended even to tell them that they were too busy to see them, but that they would receive the Army's terms tomorrow. The members were then marched off on foot to two inns in the Strand, the *Swan* near Charing Cross, and the *King's Head*. A strong force of soldiers surrounded them, with each member's arm firmly held by a musketeer. Half a dozen of the more aged and infirm were taken to the inns by coach, but the rest had to submit to more 'opprobrious speeches' from the marching soldiers. At the inns there were more guards outside and 'at every chamber door'. Even on Friday morning there was no opportunity for the members to state their case to the General Council. All that

---

[29] Assheton to Driver, 12 Dec. 1648: Chetham's Library, MS. A 3, 90; Sir Anthony Ashley Cooper, Autobiographical Fragment, in W. D. Christie, *Life of Anthony Ashley Cooper, First Earl of Shaftesbury* (London, 1871), i, App., p. l. The printed version is ambiguous about the date of Chettel's departure, but the MS. in the Shaftesbury papers (P.R.O., S.P. 30/24/8, 1) confirms that he left London on 4 Dec.

[30] C. Luckyn to Mary Luckyn, 15 Dec. 1648: J. H. Round, ed., 'Some Essex Family Correspondence in the Seventeenth Century', *Essex Arch. Soc. Trans.* N.S. vi (1898), 210. Luckyn does not say that he left London on the 6th, but it is clear that he arrived at Waltham on the 7th, having come directly from London.

came was another offer from Fairfax to Sir Robert Harley and Sir John Meyrick (and perhaps some of the others), that they could go home if they would give parole not to oppose the Army. Again they refused, and prisoners they remained.[31]

The 'affairs of great concernment' which occupied the General Council all through Thursday involved the City of London. The Army had occupied Westminster and some of the suburbs, but they had not yet entered the City itself. The objections to doing so were obvious. Nothing could be more unpopular than quartering; in London, already disaffected, it might provoke resistance. There were people in the City whom the Army preferred not to offend. Besides, the threat of quartering was a valuable bargaining card: once used, it could not be played again. Yet the Army needed money— even though the Army Committee had assigned £5,500 on the 5th (it was paid on the 8th), the City had still not produced their £40,000. They also needed accommodation. If the secluded members had slept on the floor during their night in *Hell*, so too had the soldiers in their billets for almost a week. The Lord Mayor and Common Council were invited to procure supplies of bedding, but did nothing about it. To be sure, at a cost of £100, they sent a hundred barrels of 'good strong beer' and two cartloads of bread, butter, and cheese, 'the best could be found in all London'.[32] Bread and cheese and beer were very welcome, but they were no substitute for hard cash.

On the first day of the Purge the Army had received what the officers regarded as an evasive answer from the City about the £40,000 arrears; the Treasurers at War had assigned all recently collected assessments to other purposes.[33] It was, no doubt, discussion of the response to this which gave the officers their excuse not to talk to the imprisoned members. At all events, on Friday the 8th, Fairfax issued a proclamation justifying the forcible collection of bedding, with quartering as an alternative, and at about two o'clock troops under Col. Deane moved into the

---

[31] This paragraph is based on the sources listed in n. 2 above, also Prynne, *Case of the old Secured . . . Members*, in *Somers Tracts*, vi. 546; and *Merc. Prag.*, nos. 36–7 (5–12 Dec. 1648: [B.M.] E. 476, 2). Some of the members accepted the parole offer, according to *The Moderate*, no. 22 (5–12 Dec.: [B.M.] E. 476, 5), and *Perfect Weekly Account*, 6–13 Dec. ([B.M.] E. 476, 14), but there is no reliable corroborative evidence for this.

[32] *Staffe set at the Parliaments owne Doore* ([B.M.] E. 475, 29); Guildhall, C.C. Repertories, lix (Court of Aldermen Proceedings), fol. 321; P.R.O., S.P. 28/57 (Army Committee Warrants), fol. 369.

[33] *The Moderate*, no. 22 (5–12 Dec. 1648: [B.M.] E. 476, 5); Guildhall, C.C. Journal, xl, fol. 306v.

City.[34] Artillery was soon conspicuously displayed at Blackfriars, large forces quartered in St. Paul's and St. Martin's Ludgate, and other detachments distributed around Paternoster Row, Cheapside, Lombard Street, 'and all the heart of the City'. One party marched to Old Bailey to look for the sheriff, their old enemy Major-General Browne. The Lord Mayor managed to satisfy them that Browne would eventually surrender himself, though he was still attending the Court of Aldermen two days later.[35] But it was money the Army needed. A force drawn mainly from Hewson's regiment went to secure the Parliament's main treasuries: those of the Committee for Advance of Money at Haberdashers' Hall, one of its subcommittees at Weavers' Hall, and the Committee for Compounding at Goldsmiths' Hall. Others went by mistake to the Excise Office in Broad Street, but were recalled with apologies. Guards were left at Haberdashers' and Goldsmiths' Halls, but at Weavers' Hall the door was battered down, £27,000 seized, loaded into carts, and taken to Whitehall. Fairfax justified all this to the Lord Mayor as necessary to provide money for quartering allowances until the City paid up its £40,000, pointing out that there were precedents for the seizure of local treasuries to collect arrears in other places.[36]

To all this the only visible resistance was the vain protest of an official at Weavers' Hall. A few angry butchers congregated around Newgate Market, threatening trouble, but were quickly dispersed by a party of horse. For the second time within little more than a year the Army enjoyed its triumphant occupation of the malignant City. At Guildhall, the troopers looked up at the giant statues of Corineus and Gog-Magog, and 'remembering', in the enthusiastic words of one ambitious journalist, 'what Giant-words were spoken before their coming to the City, they compared the vain confidence and rhodomontadoes of the living to the statues of the dead'.[37] Inside the Guildhall, the Common Council the next day,

---

[34] *A Declaration of . . . the Lord Generall Fairfax* (11 Dec. 1648: [B.M.] E. 475, 40); *Moderate Intelligencer*, no. 195 (7–14 Dec.: [B.M.] E. 476, 24).

[35] *The Demands and Desires of His Excellency the Lord General Fairfax* (11 Dec. 1648: [B.M.] E. 475, 36); *Letter from the Lord Mayor* (11 Dec.: [B.M.] E. 475, 39); Guildhall, C.C. Repertories, lix, fol. 322.

[36] *Clarke Papers*, ii. 68–9; Rushworth, *Historical Collections*, vii. 1356; *Letter of His Excellency Thomas Lord Fairfax, To the . . . Lord Mayor* (8 Dec. 1648: [B.M.] E. 475, 32); *Letter from the Lord Mayor* (11 Dec.: [B.M.] E. 475, 39); *Merc. Elen.*, no. 55 (5–12 Dec.: [B.M.] E. 476, 4); *Perfect Occurrences*, no. 102 (8–15 Dec.: [B.M.] E. 526, 40*).

[37] *Kingdomes Weekly Intelligencer*, no. 289 (5–12 Dec. 1648: [B.M.] E. 476, 9); *Perfect Occurrences*, no. 102 (8–15 Dec.: [B.M.] E. 526, 40*).

the 9th, appointed a committee to discuss with Fairfax the disposition of the money taken from Weavers' Hall, offering security for
the £40,000 if the Army withdrew. Fairfax promptly replied that
he would do so only if all assessments payable up to the following
25 March were handed over within a fortnight. In the meantime,
he sarcastically assured the citizens, the continued quartering of
the Army would 'facilitate your work' in collecting the money.[38]
To reinforce this argument another regiment was sent into the
City, and was quartered at inns and private houses. By now there
were guards at all the gates, and at St. Paul's the soldiers made
bonfires of the seats to warm themselves; the aldermen protested,
but could offer no more than 'a chaldron or two of sea-coals'
instead. A supercilious Royalist was soon commending 'the power
of reformation, which had now to the amazement of the world
brought not only men, but horses also to church', and observing
'what goodly stables we had in London'.[39]

On Friday, 8 December, the Commons were also enjoying the
power of reformation, having appointed it a day of Fasting and
Humiliation. There were sermons by the great Stephen Marshall,
who belied his Presbyterian past by loudly praising the Army, by
the Independent Joseph Caryl, who called for 'love and union',
and by Hugh Peter, who hinted mysteriously that the Army 'would
not be so unreasonable as men imagined', and advised the members
to adjourn until the following Tuesday, to give time for compromise efforts to materialize. Whitelocke was present at the
sermons, and recalled that 'divers seemed to marvel that I was not
secured'.[40] Whitelocke's friends must have been very naïve. The
sermons over, the Commons took a collection for poor and maimed

[38] Guildhall, C.C. Journal, xl, fols. 307-8ᵛ; C.C. Repertories, lix, fols. 322-5; Whitelocke, Memorials, ii. 473; Letter from the Lord Mayor (11 Dec. 1648: [B.M.] E. 475, 39);
The Moderate, no. 22 (5-12 Dec.: [B.M.] E. 476, 5); Kingdomes Weekly Intelligencer, no. 289
(5-12 Dec.: [B.M.] E. 476, 9).

[39] R. W[iddrington] to Mr. S[heldon], 29 Dec. 1648: B.M. Add. MS. 4162 (Birch
Transcripts), fol. 205; Guildhall, C.C. Repertories, lix, fols. 322ᵛ, 326. However, the
cathedral was still available for a sermon to the soldiers on Sunday, the 11th: Evelyn to
Browne, 18 Dec.: Evelyn (Bohn edn.), iii. 33. Whitelocke, Memorials, ii. 473, says that two
regiments marched in on the 9th. Perfect Occurrences, no. 102 (8-15 Dec.: [B.M.] E. 526,
40*), contains a list of the regiments and the places where they were quartered. See also
Merc. Elen., no. 55 (5-12 Dec.: [B.M.] E. 476, 4), and Kingdomes Weekly Intelligencer,
no. 289 (5-12 Dec.: [B.M.] E. 476, 9).

[40] B.M. Add. MS. 37344 (Whitelocke's Annals), fol. 234. The sermons are summarized
in Merc. Prag., nos. 36-7 (5-12 Dec. 1648: [B.M.] E. 476, 2); see also Trevor-Roper,
Religion, the Reformation and Social Change, pp. 331-2.

soldiers and widows, and followed Peter's advice by adjourning until the 12th.[41] The first phase of Pride's Purge was over.

\*       \*       \*

Government, judiciary, commerce had all been disrupted, even though the revolution was still far from having run its course. Sir Ralph Assheton noticed the growing paralysis a week earlier, before the Purge. 'The confusion doth retard almost all things', Sir John Gell grumbled. Political instability, as usual, was reflected in financial nervousness, and there was that familiar modern phenomenon, a flight from the pound. Sir Roger Burgoyne anticipated it as soon as the *Remonstrance* came out on 20 November, and a month later he noted a decline of about seven per cent in the pound's exchange value since the beginning of the Purge.[42]

In spite of efforts by the managers of the Purge to preserve continuity, the House of Commons was not the only branch of government to be interrupted. The Lords sat even more briefly on the 7th than they had done on Wednesday, hearing prayers and then hastily adjourning until the 12th.[43] The Derby House Committee was unable to meet until the 18th, and although another meeting was held the next day, that seems to have been the end of it, though a few letters went out in the committee's name on the 22nd, and it was not formally abolished until February.[44] The Commissioners of the Great Seal met at Westminster on the morning of the 7th, but went home without hearing any cases. On Saturday, at Whitelocke's suggestion, they met in the seclusion of the Middle Temple. On Monday they sat again, but found little business to be done. Lord Grey of Groby, obviously enjoying himself as one of the ruling junto, tried to persuade them not to sit the next day, because of important business in Parliament for which their attendance was required, but the commissioners decided to ignore his advice, 'to prevent any failure of justice'. By sitting all day on the 12th (Whitelocke came home so tired that he had to rest all the next day), the commissioners had gained another useful respite from their parliamentary duties.[45]

---

[41] *C.J.* vi. 95. They thus ignored their earlier decision to debate the Army's proposals on the 9th.

[42] Assheton to Driver, 5 Dec. 1648: Chetham's Library, MS. A3, 90; Sir John Gell to John Gell, 12 Dec.: Chandos-Pole MSS. (Newnham Hall), 56/14; Burgoyne to Sir R. Verney, 20 Nov. and 21 Dec.: Verney MSS., B.M. Film 636, 9.

[43] *L.J.* x. 625.                    [44] *Cal. S.P. Dom.*, *1648-9*, pp. 337, 340, 342-3.

[45] Whitelocke, *Memorials*, ii. 472-4; B.M. Add. MS. 37344 (Whitelocke's Annals), fol. 235.

Although the Commons had ordered their committees to continue
to sit during the adjournment after the 8th, these too were seriously
affected. When the Committee for Compounding met on the 11th
there was no quorum, and this happened again on the 14th, though
on both occasions some routine business was done. The Committee
for Advance of Money managed to round up five members on the
11th, but on the 15th only three could be found. The Army Committee held no meetings for more than a fortnight, routine warrants
being signed by single individuals. The Navy Committee seems to
have been similarly interrupted. An occasional secluded member
still took part in committee business—Robert Jenner, for example,
was at Goldsmiths' Hall on the 14th, and Scawen (who had not
been secluded but had withdrawn from the Commons) continued
to sign Army Committee warrants until the 26th.[46] But the Army
had done its work too well. By locking out the members they had
made it almost impossible to govern the country.

In these circumstances, talk of a compromise that would enable
some of the secluded members to resume their places is understandable. Another argument for it was the continuing possibility
of a Leveller explosion at a time when Ireton and Lilburne were
still arguing bitterly about the terms of the revised *Agreement of
the People*. By the time the *Agreement* was presented to the General
Council on the 12th, the indignant Lilburne had once more decided
that the officers were 'a pack of dissembling, juggling knaves', the
worst being that 'cunningest of Machiavellians', Henry Ireton.[47]
Cromwell's return to London was followed by several hints of
moderation. Hugh Peter's restraint in the Fast Day sermon on the
8th was widely noted, and was connected by well-informed
observers with 'the many fawning overtures and offers of accord'
made to the imprisoned members over the week-end. Rumours
were being spread of the possibility, even now, of a last-minute
settlement in which the King would be retained with minimal
powers.[48] On the 12th a few of the imprisoned members were
allowed to go home, without making any of the entangling promises

[46] P.R.O., S.P. 23/5 (C. for Compounding Order-book), fols. 35ᵛ, 36ᵛ; S.P. 19/6 (C. for
Advance of Money Order-book), pp. 133, 135; S.P. 28/57 (Army Committee Warrants),
fols. 290–369; B.M. Add. MS. 35332 (Ordnance Office Register), fols. 116ᵛ–17. The first
Navy Committee order since the 6th is dated 13 Dec.: Add. MS. 22546 (Navy Papers), fol. 19.
[47] Lilburne, *Legal Fundamental Liberties*, pp. 38–9.
[48] *Merc. Prag.*, nos. 36–7 (5–12 Dec. 1648: [B.M.] E. 476, 2), 39 (19–26 Dec.: [B.M.]
E. 477, 30).

that had previously been demanded, merely giving their word to
appear when called by the Commons. The lawyers Thomas Lane,
Henry Pelham, and Charles Vaughan were the first to profit from
this leniency, the two former at the request of Whitelocke's friend
(and Fairfax's brother-in-law) Sir Thomas Widdrington. Sir
Simonds D'Ewes got out on the 14th, and Sir Harbottle Grimston
at least by the 15th, when he received a protection order from
Fairfax.[49]

Any immediate possibility of compromise was destroyed, however, by the Army's unshaken determination to see that its enemies
in the Commons, old and new, were effectively silenced. When the
House reassembled on the morning of the 12th, the members again
encountered the familiar sight of a strong force of soldiers, the
officers flourishing yet another list of enemies to be purged. At
least nine more members were excluded that day, including the
wealthy Somerset clothing magnate John Ashe, the two Kentish
members, John Boys and Sir Humphrey Tufton, and Sir Nicholas
Martyn of Devon. Two more, the opportunist courtier Sir John
Hippisley and Edward Stephens's son-in-law, Robert Packer, were
kept out on Wednesday the 13th.[50] The interesting cases here are
Ashe and Boys. The former was a man of great influence through
his chairmanship of the Committee for Compounding; he had
a consistently middle-group or war-party record, and as recently
as 4 December had been teller in a vote intended to conciliate the
Army. Boys, too, had been regarded as a radical by the moderates,
as a moderate by the radicals, ever since his election in 1645; he
too was one of the middle group, though not one of the Fiennes–
Pierrepont connection. He had been sceptical about the Treaty at
the beginning, and in December was still regarded as 'a great friend
of the Army'.[51] That men like Ashe and Boys were now victims of the

---

[49] *Old Parl. Hist.* xviii. 467; *Merc. Elen.*, no. 55 (5–12 Dec. 1648: [B.M.] E. 476, 4);
Note by D'Ewes to letter dated 14 Dec.: B.M. Harl. MS. 382 (D'Ewes Corr.), fol. 153;
Fairfax order, 15 Dec.: B.M. Sloane MS. 1519, fol. 190. Grimston was reported to have
escaped as early as the 7th, and to have reported his whereabouts to Fairfax by letter:
*The Moderate*, no. 22 (5–12 Dec.: [B.M.] E. 476, 5). But there is no corroborative evidence
for this.

[50] *Second Part of the Narrative*, pp. 4, 7. Ashe is here given only as 'Mr. Ashe', but
John was the only one of the three Ashes to be secluded: [Prynne], *Vindication of the Imprisoned and Secluded Members* (20 Jan. 1648/9: [B.M.] E. 539, 5).

[51] *C.J.* vi. 93. For Ashe's past record see Underdown, 'Party management', *E.H.R.*
lxxxiii (1968), 249–50. For Boys's see Underdown, ed., 'Parliamentary Diary of John Boys',
*B.I.H.R.* xxxix (1966), 143–4.

Purge shows how far the Army's resort to force had alienated many of their former friends.

These continued reminders of military power produced more indignation in the House. Ashe's exclusion was reported by Nathaniel Stephens, another man with radical connections, who had attended meetings with John Lisle and Cornelius Holland in the autumn, and may have voted with them against the crucial motion on 5 December.[52] If the House did not vindicate its privileges, Stephens threatened, he would withdraw. The debates of 12 to 14 December were vital to the Long Parliament's future. If some way could be found to keep men like Stephens in the House, at least some prospect of preserving constitutional government remained; if they were forced out there was none. The radicals, however, had the bit between their teeth. On the 12th they at last began to debate the Army *Remonstrance*, and repealed the summer's votes which had readmitted the Eleven Members and had annulled the Vote of No Addresses. The next day they also repealed the famous vote of 5 December. A committee was then appointed to draw up a protestation 'in detestation of those former votes'; the germ, in fact, of the declaration of dissent to the vote of 5 December, which soon became the test for membership.[53]

There were many who shared Nathaniel Stephens's indignation. Pierrepont and the middle-group leaders were thought to be preparing a formal protest against the Purge. Nothing came of this, but the grandees who had not been forcibly secluded continued to absent themselves. When 'wise William' visited Whitelocke on the 19th, he was still fuming with rage at the members who continued to sit. But there was a continuing procession of withdrawals. When the Commons met on the 14th, indeed, there was no quorum, and the soldiers were still detaining half a dozen suspected moderates in the lobby. Lenthall sent the Serjeant-at-Arms to tell the soldiers that the House would have to adjourn unless they were admitted, and they were reluctantly allowed

---

[52] *Second Part of the Narrative*, pp. 4–5; *Merc. Prag.*, no. 27 (26 Sept.–3 Oct. 1648: [B.M.] E. 465, 27). In the vote of 5 Dec. 'Mr. Stephens' was one of the tellers for the Noes: *C.J.* vi. 93. This could not have been Edward Stephens, who was arrested next day. In terms of both age and status as a county member, Nathaniel was so obviously senior to both the other two Stephens, John and William, that I am almost certain he is the one intended when no Christian name is given.

[53] *C.J.* vi. 95–6; *Old Parl. Hist.* xviii. 464–5, 471–2; *Merc. Prag.*, no. 38 (12–19 Dec. 1648: [B.M.] E. 476, 35); *Merc. Elen.*, no. 55 (5–12 Dec.: [B.M.] E. 476, 4).

in.[54] The rapidly shrinking House now made one last feeble gesture towards legality. By a vote of 35 to 18 it was agreed that a new committee should be sent to the General to discover 'upon what grounds the Members of the House are restrained', now that the Commons had begun to debate the *Remonstrance*. The smallness of the vote, and the difficulties of getting a quorum, show that many must have followed the unheroic reasoning of Whitelocke and Widdrington and stayed away.[55]

If the Army and its friends in the Commons were doing nothing to further the cause of compromise, neither were the imprisoned members. They had been fortified by a sermon on a snowy Sunday, the 10th, in which the preacher compared them with the Jews in the fiery furnace and exhorted them to 'faith and constancy'. On Monday they were visited by Robert Packer's parents; 'we found them very cheerful', Mrs. Packer reported.[56] On the same day they completed a *Solemn Protestation* which was published on the 12th. In language which suggests Prynne's authorship, they complained of 'the highest and most detestable force and breach of privilege and freedom ever offered to any Parliament of England', and called for proceedings against the Army and its supporters as 'disturbers of the peace and settlement of the Kingdom'. When this was presented to Parliament on the 15th, the enraged radicals appointed a committee to inquire into its publication, and after angry speeches from Mildmay, Blakiston, and Sir James Harrington passed an ordinance disabling all who had a hand in it from sitting in Parliament or holding public office again. The pathetic handful of Lords who were also sitting that day duly endorsed this ordinance.[57]

The imprisoned members were still enduring their now moderately comfortable captivity at the *Swan* and the *King's Head*.

[54] *Merc. Elen.*, nos. 55 (5–12 Dec. 1648: [B.M.] E. 476, 4); 56 (12–19 Dec.: [B.M.] E. 476, 36); *Merc. Prag.*, no. 38 (12–19 Dec.: [B.M.] E. 476, 35); Whitelocke, *Memorials*, ii. 477; R. Johnson to H. Chetham, 12 Dec.: Raines and Sutton, eds., *Life of Humphrey Chetham*, i. 166.

[55] Prideaux was the only survivor from Pierrepont's committee. The new committee reported on the 20th that the officers still refused to answer: *C.J.* vi. 97, 101. Whitelocke records the conventional arguments for abstention: *Memorials*, ii. 475 (as usual in the first person in the Annals: B.M. Add. MS. 37344, fol. 235). There is a list of seventy-one members sitting on the 12th and 13th in *Merc. Prag.*, no. 38 (12–19 Dec. 1648: [B.M.] E. 476, 35). See below, p. 219.

[56] *Perfect Weekly Account*, 6–13 Dec. 1648 ([B.M.] E. 476, 15); Philippa Packer to John Gell, 12 Dec.: Chandos-Pole MSS. (Newnham Hall), 31/10.

[57] *A Solemn Protestation of the Imprisoned and Secluded Members* (12 Dec. 1648: B.M. 669 f. 13, 55); *C.J.* vi. 97–8; *L.J.* x. 631; *Old Parl. Hist.* xviii. 473–4.

Another victim was secured on the 12th, when Major-General Browne was at last arrested. The Court of Aldermen sent a deputation to ask for his release, but as it included the two radical M.P.s, Atkin and Penington, its arguments may have been less than persuasive. Taken before the Council at Whitehall, Browne defiantly accused his captors of trying to set up 'a monstrous conception of a military anarchy, with a Parliament of the meanest of the Commons'. Finding this sort of language, as Col. Hewson put it, 'too peremptory', the officers consigned the obstinate sheriff to prison at St. James's, where he was left in a bare room 'without hangings or bedding'.[58]

Perhaps as a result of the Major-General's provocative line, the officers now decided to remove several of his colleagues from the inns in the Strand to closer confinement; more severe proceedings were apparently contemplated against them than against the rest. In the late afternoon the Marshal, Capt. Lawrence, brought a verbal order from the Council to take Waller, Massey, Copley, and Clotworthy from the *King's Head* to St. James's. Following the usual rules of the game, they protested and demanded the order in writing. While the Marshal went to get it, the four Presbyterian officers drew up a formal protest. When Lawrence returned at about six o'clock, Waller, calling on the other prisoners and bystanders to listen, and in 'a distinct and audible voice', read his paper, the *Protestation at the King's Head*. Although it repeats a slender, familiar stock of arguments, it is a well-penned document which conveniently summarizes the case of the secluded members:

We whose names are hereunto subscribed, being Members of the House of Commons, and free men of England, do hereby declare and protest before God, angels, and men, that the General and officers of the Army, being raised by the authority of Parliament, and for defence and maintenance of the privileges thereof, have not, or ought to have any power or jurisdiction to apprehend, secure, detain, imprison, or remove our persons from place to place by any colour or authority whatsoever. . . . And that the present imprisonment and removal of our persons is a high violation of the rights and privileges of Parliament, and of the fundamental laws of the land, and a higher usurpation and exercise of an arbitrary and

[58] Rushworth, *Historical Collections*, vii. 1361; *Old Parl. Hist.* xviii. 465 (which gives a different version of Browne's remarks); *Second Part of the Narrative*, p. 5; *Kingdomes Weekly Intelligencer*, no. 290 (12–19 Dec. 1648: [B.M.] E. 476, 39); *Merc. Prag.*, no. 38 (12–19 Dec.: [B.M.] E. 476, 35); *His Majesties Declaration and Remonstrance* (14 Dec.: [B.M.] E. 476, 23); Guildhall, C.C. Repertories, lix, fol. 325.

unlawful power, than hath been heretofore pretended to, or attempted by this, or any King or other power whatsoever within this realm; notwithstanding which, we and every of us do declare our readiness to submit ourselves to the legal trial of a free Parliament, for any crime or misdemeanour that can or shall be objected against us.[59]

As Waller's ringing tones died away, there was a chorus of added protest from the other prisoners, that the Army's rule was 'worse than that of the Grand Turk or Janizaries', worse than anything devised by the King's evil councillors. But the unfortunate four were unceremoniously bustled into coaches, and guarded by musketeers, carried off through the darkness to St. James's. Like Browne, they found themselves in bleak surroundings, in 'a foul room where the soldiers had lain some nights before', without curtains or bedding; good enough for common soldiers, they felt, but scarcely for retired generals. As for the *Protestation*, Capt. Lawrence did his duty by presenting it to the General Council. They refused to look at it, and it was left lying on the table.[60]

*     *     *

The Army was in control; Parliament was reduced to submission, London firmly in their grip. But could the Purge be undone, could moderate opinion be mobilized, even at this late hour, against the revolution? The Presbyterian ministers were willing to try, controlling as they did most of the London pulpits, still a major force in influencing public opinion. On 17 December they preached so fiercely against the Purge that the Army Council sent them a stern warning. Undeterred, at a meeting during the following week they resolved 'to drive on furiously' whatever the cost. At another ministerial meeting on the 22nd they prayed heartily for the imprisoned members: 'we bear testimony to God's cause with you', Stanley Gower told his patron, Sir Robert Harley.[61]

Not all the preaching and praying, however, was against the Purge. For the Puritan Saints, the extreme Independents, sectaries and millenarians of various hues, this was the dawn of a new day, a last chance of completing the Godly Reformation, the rule of the

---

[59] *A Declaration of the taking away of Sir William Waller . . . from the Kings head in the Strand, to St. James* (12 Dec. 1648: B.M. 669 f. 13, 57). See also *Old Parl. Hist.* xviii. 465-6; Rushworth, *Historical Collections*, vii. 1361.

[60] *Second Part of the Narrative*, pp. 5-6.

[61] [Nedham] to Nicholas, 21 Dec. 1648: Bodl. MS., Clarendon 34, fol. 12; Gower to Harley, 22 Dec.: Welbeck MSS., Harley Papers (B.M. Loan, 29/119).

Saints, perhaps even the Fifth Monarchy itself. Their only fear was that the leaders might once more draw back, might again prove too politic to allow religious enthusiasm to overcome constitutional hesitations. When Hugh Peter preached in the courtyard at White-hall on Sunday, 17 December, people flocked to hear him, and 'were amazed at the wonderful things they heard from him, and the great appearances they saw of God among the soldiery'. There would have been no shortage of texts for the lively Hugh: perhaps he chose the one on which he preached to a handful of Parliament-men on the following Friday, in St. Margaret's, when he compared Moses leading the Israelites out of Egypt with the Army's leading the people of England out of bondage, by 'rooting up monarchy'.[62] Among his military hearers there would be little sympathy for the plight of a few secluded or imprisoned members, or much lamenta-tion over a constitution that had denied them representation. One observer shortly after the Purge could find no one 'from one end of London to the other', who had any tears for the victims.[63]

Some supporters of the Purge were less confident than Hugh Peter and his friends that all was now set fair for Godly Reforma-tion. In the northern army under Lambert's command the back-sliding of Cromwell and Ireton in 1647 was vividly remembered, as it was by John Lilburne and the suspicious London Levellers. 'It is the great fear of the well-affected, that the Army through some temptation or other may fall off, and not act vigorously', Thomas Margetts wrote after the officers before Pontefract had adopted a declaration welcoming the Purge.[64] Obviously much depended upon the Army's next moves. There was in fact both in the Army and among the radical remnant in Parliament a division of opinion between advocates of a hard and a soft line, the latter including no less a figure than Oliver Cromwell. If the doves were successful, the possibility existed that even yet the work of the Purge might be undone, the secluded members restored, the King not brought to the scaffold, and the Godly Reformation frustrated by the preserva-tion of the main outlines of the old constitution and social order.

On some aspects of policy, of course, hawks and doves were in full agreement. It was easy to repeal the malignant Militia Ordinance

---

[62] *A Declaration collected out of the Journalls of Parliament*, no. 3 (13-20 Dec. 1648: [B.M.] E. 477, 7); *Old Parl. Hist.* xviii. 477. See also Trevor-Roper, *Religion, the Reformation and Social Change*, pp. 332-3.

[63] *Staffe set at the Parliaments owne Doore* ([B.M.] E. 475, 29).

[64] Margetts to William Clarke, 13 Dec. 1648: *Clarke Papers*, ii. 70.

of 2 December, and to pass ordinances remodelling the Corporation of London—a pressing matter in view of the imminence of the Common Council elections on the 21st.[65] But the crucial question was the disposition of the King. On Tuesday, 12 December, the General Council of the Army began a new series of discussions on the revised *Agreement of the People*. After an interminable debate on the coercive powers of magistrates in matters of religion, on the 15th the Council turned to the future of the King. It was agreed that he should be brought 'speedily to justice', and a committee was appointed to consider the best way of doing it. Significantly, it included neither Ireton nor Cromwell, though the latter was making one of his rare appearances at the Council. It looks as if there were doubts (which would have been well founded) about the generals' willingness to do anything more than depose Charles, if that, and that the hard-line policy of bringing him to trial was being pushed on by more radical officers of lower rank. The officers then resumed their discussions of the *Agreement*, and a shocked John Evelyn heard 'horrid villainies' propounded when he managed to eavesdrop at a disorderly debate presided over by Ireton on Monday the 18th.[66] It was now the turn of the Commons, but it was not until the 23rd that they appointed a committee to consider how to proceed against the King and other capital offenders.

The House had in fact been preoccupied by the question of their own membership, which had to be settled before anything effective could be done about the King. It will be recalled that on the 13th a committee had been appointed to draw up a protestation against the votes to which the Army objected. The committee does not seem to have been very active, and on the 18th a number of additions to it were made, with instructions to draw up a declaration of dissent to the vote of 5 December; Thomas Scot took over the chairmanship. Even though it was already difficult enough to persuade members to attend (on the 19th, according to Nedham, it took them two hours to get a quorum, which was obtained only by summoning several members from their

[65] *C.J.* vi. 97-101; Firth and Rait, *A. and O.* i. 1251-3. For the debates on these matters see *Merc. Prag.*, nos. 38 (12-19 Dec. 1648: [B.M.] E. 476, 35); 39 (19-26 Dec.: [B.M.] E. 477, 30). John Evelyn thought that the main purpose of the Army's occupation of London was to control the elections: Evelyn to Browne, 18 Dec.: *Evelyn* (Bohn edn.), iii. 33.

[66] *Moderate Intelligencer*, no. 195 (7-14 Dec. 1648: [B.M.] E. 476, 24); *Clarke Papers*, ii. 73-132; De Beer, ed., *Evelyn*, ii. 546. See also Evelyn to Browne, 18 Dec.: *Evelyn* (Bohn edn.), iii. 34-5. The Army committee (*Clarke Papers*, ii. 132) contained no officer above the rank of Lt.-Col.

M

lodgings)[67] Scot's committee went ahead. All members would have to declare their dissent to the 5 December vote before their right to sit was established; there was to be no compromise with the secluded members unless they abandoned their principles. Thirty-four members duly rose in their places on Wednesday, 20 December, and made their dissent, three more following suit on the 21st, and another seven on Christmas Day.[68] The new test drove away still more of the remaining handful of members, some perhaps upset by the General Council's insulting reply to the House's renewed request for information about the imprisoned members: Fairfax responded by asking them not to 'trouble themselves to send any more to him concerning this business'. By a vote of 32 to 19 the depleted House decided to renew their application in spite of this rebuff, but there was obviously no chance of a satisfactory answer. At all events, there was a further exodus of members, some of them leaving for only a few days, some for longer.[69] The hard-liners were determined to show that those who were not for them were against them.

But, even among the survivors, there were still people who were not hard-liners, and who were still desperately seeking compromise. Among them were men of middle-group attitudes, some of them prominent in the Army; one was Oliver Cromwell. It is striking how markedly the conduct of Army policy had changed since the Lieutenant-General's arrival in London. Before the Purge Ireton had made the running, in alliance (though sometimes in conflict over details) with Ludlow and the radical M.P.s, but always providing firm and decisive leadership for the more militant colonels and junior officers. Once Cromwell was in London, however, the clarity and directness of Army policy disappeared; there were hesitations, changes of line. Cromwell's whole career made it inevitable

[67] *Merc. Prag.*, no. 39 (19–26 Dec. 1648: [B.M.] E. 477, 30).

[68] All entries relating to the dissent were erased from the *C.J.* in Feb. 1660, but the sequence of events can be reconstructed from the manuscript Journal (House of Lords R.O.); Rushworth, *Historical Collections*, vii. 1366; H.M.C., *Portland*, i. 506; Prynne, *Case of the old Secured . . . Members*, in *Somers Tracts*, vi. 546; and Bodl. MS. Dep. C. 168 (Nalson Papers, xv), fol. 279. See also below, p. 214, n. 13.

[69] *C.J.* vi. 101; Rushworth, *Historical Collections*, vii. 1369; *Merc. Prag.*, no. 39 (19–26 Dec. 1648: [B.M.] E. 477, 30); *Old Parl. Hist.* xviii. 484. This last names 'William Carew' among the defectors: Carent must be intended, not Carew, who certainly took the dissent on 20 Dec. Of those who had been sitting on the 12th and 13th, at least twelve (perhaps more) seem to have been absent after the 20th: Ashhurst, Carent, Robert Goodwin, Herbert Hay, Rous, Algernon Sidney, Skinner, Philip Smith, Snelling, Brian Stapleton, Wayte, White, and Wilson.

that sooner or later the native conservatism, the backward-looking
Elizabethan nostalgia of the Huntingdon country gentleman, would
regain the mastery over the Puritan idealism, the zealous hankering
for Godly Reformation of the New Model officer. Even in the Vote
of No Addresses debate in the previous January, Cromwell had
held fast to the principle of monarchy: only 'necessity' could
'enforce an alteration'.[70] If the King could be forced to accept
chains more unbreakable than those so nearly agreed on at Newport,
the Purge would be superfluous and could be undone, apart perhaps
for proceedings against a malignant handful only slightly larger than
the Eleven Members. The compromise for which Cromwell seems
to have been working in the dark December days before Christmas,
therefore, had three parts: release of all but the most irreconcilable
of the imprisoned members, negotiations to restore the remainder
to the House of Commons, and a final effort to seek agreement with
the King.

  Release of the imprisoned members was the easiest. On the 20th,
while the enthusiastic radicals were falling over themselves to take
the dissent, Fairfax sent for sixteen of the prisoners to be brought
to his lodging in Whitehall. As usual they were kept waiting for
a few hours to show who was the master. Eventually, however,
Ireton, Whalley, and Nathaniel Rich came out with the news that
Fairfax was ill, but that he and the other officers had agreed that
the sixteen should be released unconditionally. It was even hinted
that they were free to take their seats in the House (which the
House was of course on that very day making impossible). The
harmony of this pleasing scene was somewhat marred by a comic-
opera interlude between Ireton and Prynne. Although not one of
the sixteen invited, Prynne had somehow managed to accompany
them. When Ireton discovered Prynne's presence, he angrily
ordered the Marshal to remove him. Prynne refused to budge.
'He should be thrust out by the head and shoulders', Ireton
warned. Prynne promptly launched into one of his easily triggered
tirades: 'that the Army endeavoured utterly to subvert the fundamental laws . . .' and much more in the same vein. Still talking
volubly, the member for Newport was taken back to the *King's
Head*. Only twenty now remained in the Army's custody, and
of these Sir Richard Onslow and William Priestley appear to
have been released by the 25th, and Sir Robert and Edward Harley

---

[70] Boys's Diary, *B.I.H.R.* xxxix (1966), 156.

on that day.[71] Even Cromwell must have felt that against the remaining sixteen the Army would have to take measures more effective than those against the Eleven Members in the previous year.

Releasing prisoners who were under the Army's exclusive control was one thing: the other parts of the Cromwellian compromise were more difficult. For the approach to the King, the chosen intermediary was the Earl of Denbigh, one of the feet-dragging aristocratic generals of the first Civil War. On the 19th, accompanied by three other peers (Pembroke, Salisbury, and North), Denbigh visited Fairfax at headquarters. Marchamont Nedham gives an unlikely version of their conversation as including an offer by the Lords to renounce their peerage, followed by some scornful replies by the officers. It is more likely, however, that the real topic of conversation was Denbigh's forthcoming visit to Windsor, ostensibly to see his brother-in-law Hamilton, but actually to carry the final ultimatum to the King. The terms appear to have been three: Charles was to abandon his negative voice, consent to the perpetual alienation of bishops' lands (and thus the perpetual abolition of episcopacy), and 'abjure the Scots'.[72] Meanwhile other means were being used to humour the peers, for on the same day the Commons passed, and Pembroke's secretary Oldisworth carried to the Lords, an ordinance appointing the Earl Constable of Windsor.[73]

By this time Whitelocke was engaged, at Cromwell's suggestion, in a delicate series of negotiations aimed at fulfilling the third part of the programme: resolution of the parliamentary crisis. Even on the disposition of the King, Cromwell and his son-in-law were seriously at odds. Ireton wanted to have him tried first, before the others, such as Hamilton, against whom proceedings were intended: Cromwell wanted to take Hamilton first, presumably to allow

---

[71] *Old Parl. Hist.* xviii. 476–7; Rushworth, *Historical Collections*, vii. 1369; *Second Part of the Narrative*, p. 8; *Merc. Prag.*, no. 39 (19–26 Dec. 1648: [B.M.] E. 477, 30); *Moderate Intelligencer*, no. 197 (21–28 Dec.: [B.M.] E. 536, 18); H.M.C., *Portland*, iii. 165; [Nedham] to Nicholas, 21, 25, and 26 Dec.: Bodl. MS., Clarendon 34, fols. 12, 17, 19ᵛ. The sixteen released on the 20th were Boughton, Bulkeley, Buller, Crewe, Erle, the two Gerards, Irby, Knightley, Lister, Luke, Meyrick, Pye, Soame, Edward Vaughan, and Wenman. Francis Drake appears to have been released before this date. The sixteen prisoners remaining on the 26th were Birch, Browne, Clotworthy, Copley, Gewen, Green, Leigh, Lewis, Massey, Prynne, Edward Stephens, Strode, Swynfen, Walker, Sir William Waller, and Wheeler.

[72] [Nedham] to Nicholas, 21 Dec. 1648: Bodl. MS. Clarendon 34, fol. 12. See also Gardiner, *Civil War*, iii. 555–6 and n.

[73] *C.J.* vi. 100–1. Pembroke promptly appointed a kindred spirit, Whitelocke, as his deputy: B.M. Add. MS. 37344 (Whitelocke's Annals), fol. 236ᵛ.

more time to bring the King to reason.[74] Through Whitelocke and
his friend Widdrington, Cromwell proposed to restore respectability to the regime: to restore a House of Commons that would
bear some resemblance to its former self, would be content to preserve the title of king without the power, and would provide the
officers with the moderate backing necessary to frustrate the
Levellers. The moves had to be kept highly secret. If revealed they
would bear out the suspicions expressed by men like Spavin and
Margetts, would convict Cromwell of losing touch with his soldiers,
as he had done in 1647. Cromwell had to keep outwardly in step
with his revolutionary friends, but he could still make a last effort,
with the help of Denbigh and Whitelocke, to circumvent them
before it was too late. It was a typical middle-group manœuvre.
Only one thing was lacking: the middle group.

On Monday, 18 December, therefore, as soon as the Chancery
rose, Whitelocke and Widdrington went 'by appointment' to the
office of the Master of the Rolls, who also happened to be William
Lenthall, Speaker of the House of Commons. Lenthall was there,
and Cromwell soon arrived with one of his colonels, Richard
Deane. 'We had a long discourse together about the present affairs',
Whitelocke says, 'and then another time was appointed by the
Lieutenant-General for us to meet again.' It may not have been
coincidental that before the talks resumed Whitelocke was visited
by Pierrepont, though if an effort was made to bring him into the
discussions it was unavailing. On the 19th, Whitelocke went to visit
Cromwell, 'who lay in one of the King's rich beds in Whitehall'.
It was the beginning of a ripening friendship. On this occasion
Cromwell, says Whitelocke, 'was very courteous to me, and desired
my company as often as I could'. The Commissioners of the Great
Seal were busy in Chancery matters for the next two days, but on
the 21st Whitelocke and Widdrington again met Lenthall and
Cromwell 'and discoursed freely together'. At the end of it, the two
commissioners were asked to draw up a paper summarizing the discussions; at the 'earnest desire' of Lenthall and Cromwell they spent
the next day (a public Fast) in Whitelocke's study hard at work on it.
The object of the exercise is summarized by Whitelocke:

> To endeavour to bring the army into some fitter temper. We were
> likewise to frame somewhat in order to the restitution of the secluded
> members, for an answer for the army to the messages of the house . . .,

[74] Grignon to Brienne, 21 Dec. 1648: quoted in Gardiner, *Civil War*, iii. 551, n.

and heads for a declaration, what the parliament intendeth for the settlement of the kingdom, to be considered of, and offered to the parliament
and council of the army. . . . Both the members of the house, and chief
officers of the army, having engaged and trusted us only therein, we
prayed to God to direct us in it, and that neither of us might receive any
prejudice, but the kingdom might receive good by this our employment,
and the courses of the army be moderated (as it was in some measure at
this time,) though it brake out again into violence afterwards.[75]

Between Saturday, 23 December, and Monday, the 25th, the
attempted compromise broke down. On Saturday the Commons
appointed their committee to consider how to proceed in justice
against the King, thus satisfying republican sentiment in the Army,
further inflamed by outbursts like that of Hugh Peter at the Fast
Day sermon on the 22nd. But many thought that there was an
element of sham about it, and that the names of such known
moderates as Whitelocke and Widdrington on the committee
demonstrated that it need not be taken too seriously. Nicholas Love
told one of Nedham's informants that the charge 'would be nothing,
but what he knew the King could clearly acquit himself of'. But
there was menace in it for the King, too, for in fact Cromwell was
keeping his options open. On the Saturday night Lenthall said 'that
if the King came not off roundly now in point of concession, he
would be utterly lost'.[76] During the day there had been a sharp
debate in the Commons on the question of trying the King, and
even in the purged House strong opposition was expressed. Whitelocke and Widdrington put in brief appearances, before going on to
another secret conclave at the Speaker's chamber. Various solutions
were advanced, from outright republicanism to deposition and
a regency in the name of Charles's youngest son, the Duke of
Gloucester. No agreement was reached, but another meeting was
arranged for the Monday, Christmas Day.[77]

Over the week-end, even before Denbigh's failure at Windsor
was known, the atmosphere changed. When Monday came, the
Commons spent the day in a long and fruitless debate over the

[75] *Memorials*, ii. 477–9. Some of the details are omitted from the printed version, and are
taken from B.M. Add. MS. 37344 (Whitelocke's Annals), fols. 236ᵛ–7.

[76] [Nedham] to Nicholas, 25 Dec. 1648: Bodl. MS., Clarendon 34, fol. 17. For Peter's
sermon see Trevor-Roper, *Religion, the Reformation and Social Change*, pp. 332–3.

[77] Whitelocke, *Memorials*, ii. 479–81. This omits Whitelocke's statement that he and
Widdrington attended the House on the 23rd: B.M. Add. MS. 37344 (Annals), fol. 238.
The scheme to instal the Duke of Gloucester as King is discussed below, p. 183.

readmission of the secluded members. This, one would have
thought, was the crucial moment for the forces of restraint to speak
out. Yet Whitelocke and Widdrington, who were in the Queen's
Court on Chancery business, did not respond even when asked to
attend 'to make up a House', but 'came home at noon'.[78] As they
cannot yet have known of Denbigh's failure, something else must
have convinced them that the compromise was doomed. The most
likely explanation is that the discussions on Saturday night, and
perhaps further unrecorded conversations on Sunday, made it
quite clear that nothing would induce the soldiers to spare Charles I,
or the radicals to abandon the barrier against the secluded members
represented by the declaration of dissent. The private meeting
arranged for Monday did not occur: there was nothing left to talk
about. Cromwell, clinging to hopes from Denbigh, still tried to
stave off the inevitable. When the Army Council discussed the trial
on Christmas Day, he and Ireton again aired their differences in
public. Ireton still held out for bringing the King to 'speedy
justice'; if he meant execution, he must have changed his mind
about it again a few days later. Cromwell, on the other hand, argued
that 'there was no policy in taking away his life'. Only six officers
supported Ireton's demand for extreme measures, but it was
decided to press on with the trial, leaving the question of the
sentence open. On the same day Denbigh went to Windsor with
Cromwell's last offer: the King either refused to see him or rejected
it.[79] It was now clear even to Cromwell that the reign of Charles I,
though not necessarily the monarchy, had ended.

One more door had been slammed. Rather than face the pressure
to join in the preparations for the trial to which they were immediately subjected, Whitelocke and Widdrington quietly left London.
They got away by coach on the morning of the 26th, spent the
night at Maidenhead, and reached Phillis Court, Whitelocke's
house near Wallingford, on the following day. A relieved Lord
Commissioner of the Great Seal was soon able to ride 'abroad in
the fresh air . . . to view my woods, and took some partridges with

---

[78] Whitelocke, *Memorials*, ii. 481; B.M. Add. MS. 37344 (Annals), fol. 239; *The Moderate*,
no. 24 (19-26 Dec. 1648: [B.M.] E. 536, 2).

[79] *Mercurius Melancholicus*, 25 Dec. 1648-1 Jan. 1648/9, quoted in Firth, ed., *Clarke
Papers*, ii, Pref., p. xxx, cf. also p. 146 n.; Gardiner, *Civil War*, iii. 556-7. Wedgwood,
*Trial of Charles I*, p. 77 and n. 30, has understandable doubts about the Denbigh mission.
But it accords too well with the rest of the known facts about the compromise scheme to
be disregarded.

a setting dog. . . . Both Sir Thomas Widdrington and myself were
well contented to be absent.' The King would be tried, and the
secluded members would not be restored. Cromwell still admitted
his indecision. He would 'pray God to bless their counsels', he told
the Commons on the 26th, 'though he were not provided on the
sudden to give them counsel'. But the trial of the King could no
longer be avoided: 'Providence and necessity had cast them
upon it.'[80]

[80] Whitelocke, *Memorials*, ii. 484-5; B.M. Add. MS. 37344 (Annals), fols. 239ᵛ-41;
Abbott, *Cromwell*, i. 719; quoted in Wedgwood, *Trial of Charles I*, p. 80.

# VII

## THE COMMONWEALTH ESTABLISHED

THE failure of Cromwell's conciliation scheme enabled the revolution to regain some of its lost momentum. On 4 January the Commons passed the ordinance setting up the High Court of Justice to try the King. When the Lords refused to co-operate, the Commons invested their own acts with the force of law, and defiantly proclaimed that 'the people are, under God, the original of all just power'.[1] On the 8th the High Court began its sessions; the King was sentenced on the 27th and executed in Whitehall on the 30th. The House of Lords was abolished by resolution of the Commons on 6 February, the monarchy the next day, though it was another month before the necessary legislation was completed. On 14 February the republic created its own executive body in the form of a Council of State. With *Salus Populi* echoing from their lips, the revolutionaries began the unprecedented transformation of a kingdom into a commonwealth. God's people, Capt. George Joyce told the Army Council, were about 'such things as were never yet done by men on earth'.[2]

There was plenty of revolutionary rhetoric, yet it could not disguise the fact that the new order was being created by men who really shared few common objectives. Pride's Purge had been inspired by agreement to disrupt the Treaty of Newport, but by agreement on little else. In the weeks after the Purge there was continuing friction between the single-minded handful who saw clearly the path to the promised land, and the prudent majority whose vision was not blinding enough to penetrate the thorns and briars of the wilderness. The men who by February 1649 had established themselves in power included dedicated radicals like Ireton and Ludlow, but also half-hearted pragmatists of Bulstrode Whitelocke's type. Even among those who promptly proclaimed themselves, either as regicides or as dissenters to the 5 December vote, were many who did so only because 'Providence and necessity had

[1] *C.J.* vi. 111.     [2] Woodhouse, *Puritanism and Liberty*, p. 176.

cast them upon it', not because they looked beyond the constitutional revolution to a total reconstruction of society. The activists were split too, between the civilians and the military; we have seen the division already in Ireton's policy of immediate dissolution and sweeping parliamentary reform, confronting Ludlow's insistence on preserving what residue of legal authority remained in the attenuated House of Commons. The military themselves were divided between political reformers like Ireton and exuberant Saints like Harrison, who cared little for constitutions and looked only for a Puritan millennium in the name of the Fifth Monarchy.

Revolutions in the end are always disappointing to revolutionary idealists. There are many reasons why the Puritan Revolution failed to live up to the expectations of its more fanatical promoters. One is that few indeed of the leaders in the Rump really shared the radical aspirations of their followers in the regiments and gathered churches. They purged Parliament and executed Charles I because they saw that nothing less would satisfy the Army. But almost as much as their secluded opponents, they feared the dangerous combination of intense political passion and religious militancy that coincided with conditions of depression and near-famine during the winter of revolution. Perhaps the wild Ranters and Diggers could be discounted as the inevitable lunatic fringe of revolution. But the Levellers could not, nor could the Baptists and other sectaries who stopped short of political democracy, but called loudly for other parts of the Leveller programme: law reform and the abolition of tithes, for instance. Like the leaders in the Rump, the Levellers and sectaries were a vocal minority—but successful revolutions are made by minorities.

The immediate response of the political nation to the great events at Westminster shows both the vigour of these revolutionary forces and their minority position. For the seventeenth century the modern term 'public opinion' obviously has little meaning. Nevertheless, in a vague and indefinite way, public opinion existed and could not be ignored. It could be artificially stimulated, as had been shown by earlier petitioning campaigns. Both sides recognized its importance, and the chorus of pamphlets and sermons reached a climax in the weeks between the Purge and 30 January. There was no shortage of argument or information in London, as the rival presses thundered forth their angry rhetoric. The radicals had no difficulty about getting their newsbooks and pamphlets distributed outside of London, through their various information-networks in the Army, the County Committees, and the congregations. The moderates, on the other hand, had always been reluctant to appeal to the people. Sir Ralph Assheton had once asked his steward if there were in Clitheroe and the other little Lancashire towns any book-sellers who might be induced to distribute Presbyterian propaganda—and then showed his lack of concern by forgetting the answer. On the day of the King's execution he remembered the matter again, noting that there might be profit as well as politics in it: 'nothing more coveted or vendable than news.' Too late, he sent down a few dozen useful pamphlets by the Preston carrier.[3]

Assheton was right, the country hungered for news. Far away in Dorset, John Fitzjames had asked a London friend just before the Purge for 'a perfect account, beyond that of the mercuries, of the next week's transactions'. Fitzjames liked to read the papers on both sides, the lively *Pragmaticus* as well as the duller parliamentarian newsbooks, and had a healthy scepticism for journalists of all kinds, asking for 'news in writing, as well as lies in print'. But his appetite for both was voracious. 'Pray send me some news,' he cried during the crisis, 'you do not imagine how hungry we are here.'[4] When it came, the news was often confusing or contradictory. Humphrey Chetham was told by one correspondent that all the Lancashire members were either arrested or secluded, by another the next day that all except William Langton were in flight or hiding. Soon he heard that only Ashhurst and Rigby were still sitting, a week later that they had all gone down to Lancashire, and finally that John Moore was the only survivor of the Purge. Poor Chetham, who wanted to know who could pull strings to help him escape being appointed sheriff, was not surprisingly reduced to bafflement.[5]

But although the news might be late or misleading, it was still possible for the minority of Englishmen who were politically conscious to form an opinion. The seclusion of the local member, John Barker, provoked riots at Coventry; a militia regiment had

[3] Assheton to Driver, 30 Jan. and 16 Feb. 1648/9: Chetham's Library, MS. A 3, 90.

[4] John Fitzjames to C. Levitt, 24 Sept. 1648; to J. Maniford, 2 Dec.; to H. Fitzjames, 30 Dec.; to C. Levitt, 7 Apr. 1649: Fitzjames Letter-book (Northumberland MSS., B.M. Film 330), ii, fols. 27, 40, 44ᵛ, 57ᵛ.

[5] J. Rogerson and R. Johnson to H. Chetham, 11, 12, 19, and 26 Dec. 1648, 2 Jan. 1648/9: Raines and Sutton, eds., *Life of Humphrey Chetham*, i. 161-71.

to be sent to restore order. Sir Anthony Irby got a letter from
the corporation of Boston expressing confidence in his loyalty,
and looking forward to the 'further public service which your
place and trust calls for'. But few of his colleagues were as
fortunate. Sir Ralph Assheton hinted that he would like a testi-
monial similar to Irby's from the bailiffs of Clitheroe, but none
was forthcoming. George Booth angrily reported his seclusion
to his Cheshire constituents, but he too waited in vain for a reply.[6]
To the torrent of manifestos and vindications, to the deluge of
words churned out by Prynne in these weeks, there was no visible
response.

More successful than the secluded members were the Presbyterian ministers. Safe in their pulpits, they could reach a wider
audience than the pamphleteers, and they were less easily dismissed
as corrupt and self-interested than the politicians. The London
clergy's opposition to the coup, already demonstrated in December, became steadily less restrained. At the regular monthly fast
on 27 December, for which the preachers had been appointed
before the Purge, Thomas Watson had the temerity to tell the
Commons that they flew in the face of God by acting against 'that
order and government which He hath set up in his Church',
observing further that this sacred polity included monarchy. When
the House refused to authorize publication of his sermon, Watson
defiantly had it printed himself.[7] On 11 January the London
ministers relented slightly from their previous refusal to negotiate
with the officers, and sent Marshall, Calamy, and some of the others
to see Fairfax. All they did, however, was repeat their already known
distaste for the Army's proceedings. When further meetings were
proposed, they said that they were willing to come back and casti-
gate the officers' sins, but not to compromise with them. On Sunday,
the 14th, some of them (Calamy and Cornelius Burges, among
others) were thought to have hinted that they might even be
willing to swallow the King's conviction, provided that it was
not followed by execution. But as Burges was already at work

---

[6] T. W. Whitley, *Parliamentary Representation of the City of Coventry* (Coventry,
1894), p. 90; *A Letter Written to an Honourable Member of the House of Commons* (20 Dec.
1648: B.M. 669 f. 13, 60); Assheton to Driver, 12 Dec. 1648, 2 Jan. 1648/9: Chetham's
Library, MS. A 3, 80; Booth to gentlemen of Cheshire, 19 Dec. 1648: *Clarke Papers*, ii.
137-8.

[7] Thomas Watson, *Gods Anatomy upon Mans Heart* (27 Dec. 1648: [B.M.] E. 536, 7). See
also Trevor-Roper, *Religion, the Reformation and Social Change*, pp. 334-5.

on the ministers' *Vindication*, which appeared on the 20th and denounced the whole trial in the most uncompromising terms, this seems unlikely.[8] More than one Independent cleric joined in the chorus of opposition: the mystical William Sedgwick and Fairfax's old chaplain, Joshua Sprigge, were the best known.[9]

The Presbyterian clergy outside of London were no less vocal. In Somerset they were preaching hard in December 'to incense the people against this Reformation . . . both in Church and State', a local radical complained. It was the same story in Devon, where at least two ministers were arrested by the Army a few weeks later for reading the *Vindication* of their London brethren from the pulpits.[10] Lancashire, of all counties the one where the Presbyterian establishment was being most systematically imposed, was the scene of a particularly violent campaign. 'The pulpits in these parts ring against the Army', it was reported from Warrington on 22 December. The situation was the more serious because the supernumerary forces raised during the second Civil War by Col. Ralph Assheton of Middleton, a strong Presbyterian like his kinsman and namesake Sir Ralph of Whalley, were still on foot. In November Assheton's men had been 'very insolent' against the Army, and they publicly declared their opposition to the *Remonstrance*. Efforts to disband them met with no success, even after Ireton had the ordinance authorizing Assheton's command repealed. Preaching at Lancaster on 4 January, Thomas Smith described them as 'the honestest army in the kingdom, for they would stand for the Presbyterian government'. In a violent sermon against heretics, Anabaptists, and Independents, Smith declared that 'there would be no peace till the Scots came into the kingdom to suppress the Independents' and sectaries' army'. At about the

---

[8] *Clarke Papers*, ii. 182 and n.; Calamy, *Continuation*, p. 737; *Moderate Intelligencer*, no. 200 (11–18 Jan. 1648/9: [B.M.] E. 538, 21); *The Moderate*, no. 27 (9–16 Jan.: [B.M.] E. 538, 15); R. H. K. Hinton, ed., *A Serious and Faithful Representation of . . . Ministers of the Gospel within the Province of London* (18 Jan. 1648/9; reprinted, Reading, 1949), esp. pp. 2–3. The *Vindication of the Ministers of the Gospel in . . . London* (20 Jan.) is printed in Calamy, *Continuation*, pp. 737–43, and in *Somers Tracts*, v. 258–62.

[9] Sedgwick, *Letter to his Excellency Thomas Lord Fairfax* (28 Dec. 1648: [B.M.] E. 536, 16); Sprigge, *Certain weighty Considerations Humbly tendered and submitted to the . . . High Court of Justice* (28 Jan. 1648/9: [B.M.] E. 540, 13). See also Wedgwood, *Trial of Charles I*, pp. 55, 134.

[10] Letter from Somerton, 24 Dec. 1648: Rushworth, *Historical Collections*, vii. 1381–2; Letter from Ottery St. Mary, 10 Feb. 1648/9: *The Moderate*, no. 31 (6–13 Feb.: [B.M.] E. 542, 11).

same time a meeting of ministers at Preston considered petitioning Assheton not to disband until he had firmly settled 'the Presbyterian government within this county'.[11]

Opposition from the Presbyterians was to be expected. Almost equally dangerous to the new government was the aroused enthusiasm of its own supporters, the now expectant Saints. As in the previous autumn, there was a flood of petitions, spontaneous or inspired, calling on the Army to complete the righteous work it had begun. After the Restoration everyone conveniently remembered sabotaging them; the regicide Thomas Wayte claimed to have opposed two, one in Leicestershire and another in Rutland.[12] Whatever people thought in 1660, not all of them were stopped. Vavasor Powell and John Jones promoted one in North Wales, William Kenwricke and men of the old Weldon clique another in Kent.[13] In Somerset radical opinion was mobilized, as usual, by Colonel John Pyne. He had been sent a prompt account of the Purge by his friend Rushworth, and it received his enthusiastic endorsement. Pyne would have preferred an inside job, the House purging itself, but action by the Army was the best alternative. The Purge had been necessary, he told Rushworth, because 'the corruptness of man's unsancti[fi]ed nature' had caused the degeneration of the Long Parliament. 'Inevitable ruin must have befallen honest men without a Purge', Pyne went on; for more than a year he and his friends had wished for one.[14] His henchmen were soon dutifully at work on a petition. The fiery Baptist preacher, Thomas Collier, once an Army chaplain, was apparently its author, and people were 'persuaded and threatened' into signing by Pyne himself. Presented to the Commons on 21 December, the Somerset petition contained the usual formula: reformation 'according to

[11] *Moderate Intelligence*, nos. 192, 197 (16–23 Nov. and 21–8 Dec. 1648: [B.M.] E. 473, 15 and E. 536, 18); *Merc. Prag.*, nos. 36–7 (5–12 Dec.: [B.M.] E. 476, 2); *Merc. Elen.*, no. 55 (5–12 Dec.: [B.M.] E. 476, 4); *The Moderate*, no. 37 (20–7 Mar. 1648/9: [B.M.] E. 414, 20); [Nedham] to Nicholas, 21 Dec. 1648 and 26 Jan. 1648/9; Bodl. MS., Clarendon 34, fols. 12, 88ᵛ; *Clarke Papers*, ii. 160–2.

[12] *Cobbett's State Trials*, v. 1218. See also above, p. 93, n. 57, for the possibility of an Essex petition, obstructed by Carew Mildmay, at about this time.

[13] *Colls. Hist. and Arch. Relating to Montgomeryshire*, xxi (1887), 346; Kent petition; Bodl. MS., Tanner 57, fols. 476–87. I am not entirely convinced by the argument of A. M. Everitt, *Community of Kent*, pp. 271–2, that the presence of signatures of dubious validity discredits the Kent petition altogether. Some are certainly transcribed (from other copies of the petition?), but a careful analysis of the signatures might still be rewarding.

[14] Pyne to Rushworth, 16 Dec. 1648; B.M. Sloane MS. 1519 (Civil War Letters), fol. 188.

God's word', justice against 'great offenders', and encouragement for the soldiers by payment of their arrears.[15] Talk of a second petition to bring charges against leading Presbyterians such as Prynne and Walker does not seem to have been followed by action. Nevertheless, there was exultation in the ranks of the godly. Pyne's Committee took advantage of it to form an association with the activists of the adjacent counties, raising volunteers to defend the revolution. 'The Lord hath raised up the spirits of all the honest party', a Somerton radical announced early in January, claiming, no doubt with much exaggeration, that over 12,000 men had been listed for the dual programme of the Army *Remonstrance* and the Levellers' September petition. Later in the month there was a great meeting near Taunton at which the well-affected declared themselves ready to live and die for Parliament and Army. A worried local lawyer was soon fearing that almost any day they might wake up to find the *Agreement of the People* 'sent into every parish for subscriptions'.[16]

All over England a militant minority of Puritan Saints rejoiced at the Purge, called for stern measures against Charles I, and often took spontaneous local action in pursuit of the same ends, with the assistance of their friends in the Army. Forces from Chepstow marched to Monmouth and other small towns, confiscating stores of weapons which they thought would 'serve very well for arming the voluntary auxiliaries in the county'.[17] In Herefordshire a group of malcontents seized their opportunity to overthrow the Harleys, and with the aid of mutinous supernumeraries being mustered for disbanding to arrest young Robert Harley and some of his cronies. Wroth Rogers, the local Army commander (and a fervent radical Puritan), was soon raising a force of 500 volunteers to supplement his own regulars. From them came the usual endorsement of

[15] *The Humble Petition of divers Gentlemen, Ministers, and well-affected Inhabitants in the County of Somerset* (21 Dec. 1648: B.M. 669 f. 13, 68). See also *C.J.* vi. 102; Rushworth, *Historical Collections*, vii. 1369; 1381-2; *Perfect Occurrences*, no. 103 (15-22 Dec.: [B.M.] E. 526, 42); H.M.C., *Seventh Report*, Appendix (House of Lords MSS.), p. 113; and information of Joshua Garment: P.R.O., S.P. 29/1 (S.P. Charles II), fol. 94. The original petition, with signatures, still existed in 1660, 'in the chamber over the Duchy Court': H.M.C., loc. cit.

[16] *C.J.* vi. 104; Rushworth, *Historical Collections*, vii. 1371, 1381-2; *Kingdomes Weekly Intelligencer*, no. 291 (19-26 Dec. 1648: [B.M.] E. 536, 5); *The Moderate*, no. 26 (2-9 Jan. 1648/9: [B.M.] E. 537, 26); *A Declaration of the Cornish-men Concerning the Prince of Wales* (9 Feb.: [B.M.] E. 542, 4); J. Turberville to J. Willoughby, 23 Jan.: *Somerset & Dorset N. & Q.* xix (1929), 168.

[17] *The Armies Modest Intelligencer*, no. 2 (25 Jan.-1 Feb. 1648/9: [B.M.] E. 541, 2).

the revolution in London.[18] Petitions and declarations congratulat-
ing the Army and calling for 'justice and freedom' came in from
every side—from Glamorgan, from Livesey's officers in Kent, from
Newport Pagnell, from a hundred other places.[19]

Most important, they included one from London. A marked
shift of power in the City had been a significant, and intentional,
by-product of the Purge. The Common Council elections on
21 December had been carefully rigged, parliamentary ordinances
being rushed through during the previous three days to prevent the
election of Royalists or of people who had subscribed the June 1648
engagement for a personal treaty. The move was remarkably effective, only a third of the old Presbyterian-dominated Council being
re-elected. The newcomers were in many cases committed Independents, often that 'middling sort' of Londoner who had been the
radicals' main support in recent months. The Presbyterian Lord
Mayor, Abraham Reynardson, attempted to enforce the oath of
allegiance on the new members, but was forbidden to do so by the
House of Commons. When a radical petition for impartial justice
was presented on 13 January, the Common Council was well prepared. The Lord Mayor arrived late, refused to permit the minutes
to be read, and when the radicals insisted on proceeding with the
next business, the petition, he and his supporters among the aldermen walked out. Owen Rowe and Robert Tichbourne, the opposition leaders, took charge of the meeting, had the petition adopted,
and presented it to Parliament. The radicals were half-way to taking
over the City; equally important, the capital's support for the
revolution had been impressively displayed.[20]

These demonstrations of popular support, which continued for
some weeks after the King's execution, were no doubt welcome
to the men at Westminster. But popular enthusiasm could all too
easily get out of hand, and even the regicides must have taken note
of the appeals to the September petition and other hints of Leveller
sentiment which the declarations often contained. Some of the

[18] *Merc. Elen.*, no. 58 (26 Dec. 1648–2 Jan. 1648/9: [B.M.] E. 536, 31); *Moderate Intel-
ligencer*, no. 197 (21–8 Dec. 1648: [B.M.] E. 536, 18); Petition of Thomas Blayney: P.R.O.,
S.P. 28/49 (Army Co. Papers), fol. 261. See also Robert Harley's account in H.M.C.,
*Portland*, viii. 9.

[19] See newspapers for Dec. 1648 in [B.M.] E. 536. 'Near a hundred have been printed':
*Moderate Intelligencer*, no. 197 (21–8 Dec.: [B.M.] E. 536, 18).

[20] Sharpe, *London*, ii. 297–9; James E. Farnell, 'The Usurpation of Honest London
Householders: Barebone's Parliament', *E.H.R.* lxxxii (1967), 24–6.

petitions went beyond the standard demands for impartial justice and Godly Reformation to include proposals which might well frighten off the pragmatic moderates whose passive support, at least, the Rump needed to retain. The Kent petition, for example, suggested that authority over all militia forces should be vested in the Army, and commissions given only to 'such as adhere to the Parliament and Army in their present proceedings'; this was repeated in another petition from the same county a few weeks later. A Surrey petition presented on 1 February wanted a purge of the militia, to exclude neutrals and those who might be charged with even 'a probable suspicion of evil'. The Surrey radicals wanted J.P.s and other officials 'chosen by the well-affected' of the county, which would either have involved an unprecedented degree of grass-roots democracy, or more likely a form of local dictatorship by the Saints of the gathered churches. They also called for the abolition of tithes, while a petition from Norfolk went further in demanding an outright congregational theocracy in the name of the Fifth Monarchy. A petition from Rye wanted to maintain the revolutionary momentum by purging the County Committees and creating better channels for circulating information, to 'animate the soldiery and well-affected'. In Herefordshire the radicals were too weak to demand anything more controversial than greater emphasis on the propagation of the gospel; the county was notoriously one of the 'dark corners of the land'. To appeal to such moderates as had not shared the fate of the Harleys they placed greater emphasis on the standard items of gentry discontent—the ending of free quarter, reduction of taxation, and greater concern for bringing dishonest officials to account. But though some were more broadly based, most of the petitions of early 1649 proclaimed yet again the intense ferment among the radical Puritans.[21]

The Army, the City, the counties: all had spoken. Yet the support demonstrated for the revolution was more impressive for its intensity than its volume. Even in the Army the activists were few and scattered, striving to radicalize the apathetic majority. Their emphasis on the material benefits that would follow prompt endorsement of their leaders' actions shows that they knew it.

[21] Whitelocke, *Memorials*, ii. 518-19; *The Moderate*, nos. 30, 31 (30 Jan.-6 Feb., and 6-13 Feb. 1648/9: [B.M.] E. 541, 15 and 542, 11); *Kingdomes Weekly Intelligencer*, no. 297 (30 Jan.-6 Feb.: [B.M.] E. 541, 17); S. R. Gardiner, *History of the Commonwealth and Protectorate*, new edn. (London, 1903), i. 29-30; Thomas-Stanford, *Sussex in the Civil War*, pp. 214-16.

N

Thomas Margetts and other firebrands in Lambert's northern army had been instrumental in setting up a 'standing council of officers' to meet every Friday, and had sent Adam Baynes and another captain to maintain liaison with the forces in London. 'Take all opportunities to make us in the north to be as forward for the future as others', Margetts urged Baynes, 'that our esteem may be as great, for I fear in our Declaration we come a little after the fair. If we come last in acting, I doubt we shall come last in pay too as heretofore.' Yet in spite of this cogently mundane argument, Margetts was still unable to keep up the pitch of revolutionary fervour among the officers. 'We never had a council of public affairs since you went,' he told Baynes on 13 January, 'we have so few actors.'[22]

\*     \*     \*

Minority or no minority, this vocal body of radicals was of crucial political importance. On the one hand it confirmed the willingness of moderates like Whitelocke to stay in power and strive to stem the tide so that even more threatening changes might be averted. On the other it persuaded their more courageous colleagues to proceed with the trial of the King and thus avoid a fatal split in the Army. Some of them needed little urging. Men like Thomas Scot and the exuberant Colonel Harrison went to their deaths in 1660 rejoicing, as Harrison put it, that the 'presence of God was with his servants in those days'. Scot composed his own epitaph: 'I would be content it should be set upon my monument— if it were my last act I own it—I was one of the King's judges.' For those with less conviction, there were the radical preachers and the soldiers to remind them of the need for action. Some of the Leveller leaders, Lilburne most notably, had already defected, seeing in the officers' new-found republicanism a trick to siphon off the pressure for more far-reaching change. But among the soldiers and junior officers enthusiasm still ran high. The Army, Captain Joyce proclaimed, was called to 'the greatest work of righteousness that ever was amongst men', and should not be restrained by the 'spirit of fear' which he detected in Fairfax and other principal officers.[23]

In spite of such militant outbursts, the course of the King's trial continued to demonstrate the hesitant and divided counsels that

[22] Margetts to Baynes, 13 and 16 Dec. 1648: B.M. Add. MS. 21417 (Baynes Corr.), fols. 18-19; Same to same, 13 Jan. 1648/9: Nathan Drake, *Journal*, App., p. 104.
[23] Wedgwood, *Trial of Charles I*, pp. 93, 223; Scot, speech, 14 Feb. 1658/9: *Burton's Diary*, iii. 275; Trevor-Roper, *Religion, the Reformation and Social Change*, pp. 333-4; Woodhouse, *Puritanism and Liberty*, p. 175.

beset the revolutionary leaders. Down to the very opening of the trial it remained uncertain whether it was intended to end with a sentence of execution or merely of deposition, and in either case whether this would be followed by a republic or a regency in the name of the young Duke of Gloucester. Even Ireton, who was busy with the Army Council debates on the *Agreement of the People* in the last days of December, began to waver as he listened to Cromwell's politic doubts. Speculation and wishful thinking about the two generals' intentions abounded; both of them did in fact still harbour fleeting hopes of being able to call a halt to the trial at some point short of actual regicide. Oliver's appearances at the Council were infrequent, but he was there on 29 December to hear the curious visions recounted by Elizabeth Poole, the obscure widow from Abingdon, in whom the officers had found a new prophetess. Cromwell may have detected in her some possible political value. At all events the clairvoyant lady was again permitted to edify the Council on 5 January, when she concluded her performance by handing in a paper denouncing the scheme to execute the King. She was closely questioned about it, Ireton in particular trying to commit her to being against the execution but not the trial itself.[24]

Even when the court began its preliminary sessions on the 8th the generals were still vacillating. The proposal to enthrone the Duke of Gloucester was still in the air, and was apparently being pressed by some of the middle-group leaders who had withdrawn from Parliament after the Purge.[25] Almost to the very eve of the trial, arguments about 'drinking to Harry the Ninth' were continuing among members of the High Court of Justice, and Whitelocke heard that some of them still wished to try Hamilton first, instead of the King.[26] Col. Barkstead told one of Nedham's

---

[24] *Clarke Papers*, ii. 150–4, 163–5. For examples of speculation about Cromwell's and Ireton's intentions see *Merc. Prag.*, nos. 40–1 (26 Dec. 1648–9 Jan. 1648/9: [B.M.] E. 537, 20); and copy of a letter, 8 Jan.: Carte, *Original Letters*, i. 202.

[25] *The Queens Majesties Letter to the Parliament of England* (5 Jan. 1648/9: [B.M.] E. 537, 9); [Nedham] to [Nicholas], 8 Jan.: Bodl. MS., Clarendon 34, fol. 72ᵛ. Nedham notes the City Independents' rejection of a proposal to enthrone Gloucester made by 'divers of that faction that have forborne sitting in the House since the force committed'.

[26] When Whitelocke left London just after Christmas, he had arranged to be supplied with secret intelligence by Ralph Darnell, one of the clerks of the House of Commons. Not realizing that his patron was back in town and lying low, on 6 Jan. Darnell reported as follows: 'It was this day ordered that the Commissioners . . . do meet on Monday . . . in the Painted Chamber. Some desired that they should meet in the Exchequer Chamber, but because there had been a quarrel about drinking to Harry the Ninth in the Painted Chamber (Duke Hamilton being then meant), it was appointed in the Painted Chamber. I know not the

informants that 'for aught he knew their next councils might overthrow their former resolutions'. The disputes were public knowledge, as Sir John Gell told his son on the 8th: 'There hath been
old daubing to cement the divisions mentioned in my last.'[27]

By this time enough daubing had been done for the High Court
to begin its work, though it was not until the 20th that the trial
opened in earnest. There can be no doubt that the situation was
transformed by the belated conversion of Oliver Cromwell to whole-
hearted support for the revolution. Providence and necessity—the
unyielding determination of the Army radicals and the congregated
Saints—had cast Cromwell upon the trial; now the same two
intangibles dictated that the King must die. Once his mind was
made up, once God had spoken and there was no alternative,
Cromwell's doubts were forgotten; not only the King, but monarchy
itself would be destroyed. 'We will cut off his head with the crown
upon it', he answered Algernon Sidney's legalistic objections. It
was Cromwell who kept his head when John Downes unnerved
some of the other commissioners and succeeded in temporarily
adjourning the court. And it was Cromwell who ruthlessly hounded
the waverers into putting their signatures to the death warrant.
When all allowance is made for the interested testimony of frightened
men in 1660, there can be no doubt that in the end Oliver Cromwell
took the lead in the execution of Charles I. But it was only in the
end, and there were good reasons why many were unwilling to
believe it. The court's decision to spend the 24th examining witnesses in committee seemed another sign of uncertainty, the result
of the doubts openly expressed by Fairfax and Skippon. And as
late as Sunday, the 28th, it was said, some of the Army grandees
offered the King life 'and some shadow of regality' if he would
accept their very stringent terms. But these were groundless

weight of that argument, you may perhaps conceive the meaning of it': Whitelocke Papers
(Longleat), x, fol. 1. The passage is tantalizingly obscure, and the significance of the choice
of the Painted rather than the Exchequer chamber escapes me, as it escaped Darnell. However, it is worth recalling that Cromwell at one time wished to try Hamilton first (see above,
p. 168). Possibly this proposal ('Hamilton being then meant') may have led to incautious
expressions of support for the Gloucester project by some members of the High Court of
Justice.
    [27] [Nedham] to [Nicholas], 8 Jan. 1648/9: Bodl. MS., Clarendon 34, fol. 72$^v$; [Sir John
Gell] to [John Gell], 8 Jan.: H.M.C., *Ninth Report*, App. II (Chandos-Pole MSS.), p. 394.
Gell's earlier letters are at Newnham Hall, but those after 25 Dec. 1648 have disappeared.
The extracts printed in the H.M.C. report suggest that they might contain valuable informa-
tion on the background to the trial.

rumours, mere wishful thinking. By the time the trial opened Cromwell had burned his boats.[28]

Cromwell was not the only belated convert to the revolution. Some of the regicides signed the death warrant only through fear and weakness, a human inability to withstand Cromwell's brutal threats. There was poor John Downes, who made the awkward scene on the 27th, though he had hitherto shown no qualms about the course of events. He had regularly attended the Commons since the Purge, and had been one of the first to take the dissent to the 5 December vote. It is not surprising that after the scene in court Downes's friends concluded that he had 'turned madman or Cavalier'.[29] Thomas Wayte made less noise at the trial (though he may have supported Downes's move to adjourn) but his arguments that he was lukewarm about the revolution carry somewhat more conviction. He seems to have withdrawn from the Commons on 12 or 13 December and to have gone home to Leicestershire; he later claimed to have suppressed republican petitions there and in Rutland. He returned to London around 25 January, and according to his own story signed the death warrant only when forced into it by Cromwell and Ireton, who were collecting signatures at the House of Commons. He certainly avoided taking the dissent until 1 February.[30] Then there is the case of Richard Ingoldsby, who was absent from both the Commons and the court on military duty, and attended only the final session to sign the death warrant. It suited the Restoration authorities not to question his amusing but unlikely story, that Cromwell forced his wrist and guided the pen. Yet his total absence from the earlier proceedings, coupled with his later reputation as one who could 'neither

---

[28] Letter of intelligence, 25 Jan. 1648/9: Carte, *Original Letters*, i. 210; Walker, *Independency*, ii. 109. The argument in Wedgwood, *Trial of Charles I*, pp. 76–80, that Cromwell was determined to bring Charles I to justice in December must be respected, but on all the evidence presented in this and the previous chapter I am bound to disagree. For the whole trial, however, hers is outstandingly the best account.

[29] H.M.C., *Seventh Report*, Appendix (House of Lords MSS.), pp. 158–9; *Cobbett's State Trials*, v. 1210–14. See also Wedgwood, *Trial of Charles I*, pp. 157–8.

[30] H.M.C., *Seventh Report*, Appendix (House of Lords MSS.), pp. 156–7; *Cobbett's State Trials*, v. 1218–19; Wedgwood, *Trial of Charles I*, pp. 173–6. The absence of Wayte's name from the *C.J.* after 13 Dec. gives his story some credibility. He was added to the Goldsmiths' Hall committee early in January, but this does not prove that he was in the Commons then, and he did not attend the committee during January: P.R.O., S.P. 23/5 (C. for Compounding Order-book). Wayte claims to have been tricked into attending the court by a message allegedly from Lord Grey. He had served under Grey in the Civil War, and although they had then quarrelled he and Grey were apparently again on good terms in 1648: *D.N.B.* ('Wayte').

preach nor pray', suggests that he was hardly one of the revolutionary enthusiasts.[31]

Downes in the end signed the death warrant. But his hesitations are a valuable reminder that there were many M.P.s who accepted the first stage of the revolution, the Purge, without regarding the King's execution as its inevitable sequel. This may well explain some of the curious omissions from the original list of members of the court, as well as the defections of some who were named. The men who drew up the list naturally wanted to give it a respectable appearance, to include as many men of recognizable prestige as they could. There was some feeling in the Army that as many different regiments as possible ought to be represented. 'Is it not a little disobligement'? Thomas Margetts asked when he found none of the officers of his brigade listed.[32] Similarly, some effort at regional distribution of the civilian members of the court seems to have been made. This was not always possible: Yorkshire had more than twice as many members as any other county, while there were only a few from the south-west. But even if Yorkshire was over-represented, it is still strange that that long-winded, zealous Puritan Luke Robinson was omitted. And given the lack of members from the western counties, where was the Army's 'dear friend and true patriot', William Eyre, who had been Charles I's guardian at Hurst Castle and had recently been elected for Chippenham?[33] Where, most remarkably, was the leader of the Somerset radicals, John Pyne? He had been promoting the petition for justice against the King in December, and his presence in the county to keep order may have been thought desirable.[34] But this need not have prevented his being named to the court, as the inclusion of Haselrig, who was in a similar position, shows. Perhaps his friend Prideaux kept him off the list, wishing not to expose him to such dangerous eminence for the same reasons that led him to resign his

[31] D.N.B. ('Ingoldsby'); Wedgwood, Trial of Charles I, pp. 174-5.

[32] Margetts to [Adam Baynes?], 6 Jan. 1648/9: Nathan Drake, Journal, App., p. 103.

[33] Robinson came to London only at the end of the trial. He was named to a committee on 27 Jan., and took the dissent on the 29th: C.J. vi. 124. His later speeches show his zeal for the 'Good Old Cause': Burton's Diary, i, passim. Eyre was elected on 29 Nov., but some 'scruples of conscience' over the oaths of supremacy and allegiance delayed his taking his seat until 15 Jan.: C.J. vi. 117; Clarke Papers, ii. 66 n.; Ludlow's Memoires, ii. 53; Burton's Diary, iii. 76.

[34] Pyne was in Somerset at least until 18 Jan., and cannot be traced in the Commons until the 31st. P.R.O., S.P. 23/102 (C. for Compounding), p. 309; S.P. 19/108 (C. for Advance of Money), fol. 187; Bates Harbin, ed., Somerset Quarter Sessions Records, iii. 76; C.J. vi. 126-7.

own office as Solicitor-General rather than have anything to do with the trial.

Further proof that there was no absolute correspondence between support for the revolution and actual regicide is clear from the defection of some of those who were named to the court. A good many men supported the Purge, took the dissent promptly, and attended the court on one or more occasions, but then disappeared from its sessions. Some of course were faint-hearted timeservers, dishonest racketeers like Edmund Harvey and Cornelius Holland. But more dedicated radicals like Isaac Penington, Sir James Harrington, and Sir Thomas Wroth also took the cautious line. Others who had committed themselves by taking the dissent in December and were thereupon named to the court did not attend at all: Thomas Atkin, Denis Bond, and Alexander Rigby are striking examples. Obviously it was possible to accept the Purge, and even take part in the preliminary proceedings against the King, in the expectation that the outcome would merely be deposition. It was possible to draw the line at execution, as many did and Downes would have liked to do, and yet support other parts of the Army's design.[35]

On the whole, it was the men of solidly established rank and status who drew back. It is true, as the most recent, and best, account of the trial points out, that the court as originally named represented 'the most respectable and substantial elements in the country'.[36] Yet the impression of solid repute is sustained only when all the original members of the court are taken together, without distinguishing between the regicides and those who either did not attend, or did so only briefly. The court named in the ordinance included a Scottish peer, an Irish peer, four sons of English peers, a Knight of the Bath, and eleven baronets. But the Scottish peer (Fairfax) attended only one preliminary session, and his wife shouted some famous interruptions during the trial. The Irish peer (Mounson) attended only until 26 January and did not sign the death warrant. Of the four sons of English peers, two (Lord Lisle

[35] Not all the promoters of the Purge would have agreed. Francis Buller was told that he and the other victims were secluded because they 'had not hearts to that eminent and most high piece of justice which was to be done on the King'. [John Moyle] to Buller, 22 Sept. 1649: *Buller Papers*, p. 110.

[36] Wedgwood, *Trial of Charles I*, pp. 96–7. My analysis of the court in the following paragraph is based on the lists of members and attendances in *Cobbett's State Trials*, iv, 1050–1135.

and Benjamin Weston) never attended, while Lisle's brother Algernon Sidney came only to three preliminary sessions and left after
making a scornful protest. Only one, Lord Grey of Groby, was a regicide. The K.B. (Wentworth) stayed away altogether, a conveniently
sprained ankle keeping him out of London during the time of
danger.[37] Only four of the eleven baronets were regular attenders and
signed the death warrant. Of these four, Sir William Constable's
family, though distinguished, might serve as a classic example of
the notorious declining gentry; both Sir Michael Livesey and Sir
Gregory Norton (an Irish baronet anyway), were upstarts without
deep roots in their counties; only Sir Thomas Mauleverer was a man
of really secure position. The baronets who declined the summons
to the court, on the other hand, were nearly all men of solid wealth
and status: Sir William Armine, Sir John Barrington and his
brother-in-law Sir William Masham, Sir William Brereton, Sir
Arthur Haselrig, and Sir Gilbert Pickering. Only Sir Peter Temple,
whose indebtedness was of disastrous proportions, can be put in
the same dubious category as Constable, Livesey, and Norton.

Several of these defecting baronets had notably radical records.
Haselrig had been a determined leader of the war party and of the
radical wing of the Independents; he was to be equally prominent
in the Rump and to give unqualified approval to the principle of the
sovereignty of the people. Yet he stayed away, ruling the North,
later made much of the fact that he had 'naught to do with Pride's
Purge', came to London only after the execution, and then refused
the original engagement to the Council of State rather than endorse
the Army's proceedings.[38] Brereton's conduct is puzzling; he was
in London during the trial, and was close to several of its managers,
yet still managed to avoid open participation. Bradshawe, the president of the court, was both his kinsman and political client, and Sir
William was also on friendly terms with Hugh Peter. There were
those in 1660 who remembered seeing Brereton in the Painted
Chamber several times during the trial, deep in conversation with
Bradshawe and Peter, and Cromwell was said to have identified him

[37] Algernon Sidney to Leicester, 12 Oct. 1660: Blencowe, ed., *Sydney Papers*, p. 237;
Wentworth to Speaker, [24 Feb. 1648/9]: Cary, *Memorials*, ii. 123.

[38] Haselrig, speeches, 7 Feb. and 8 Mar. 1658/9: *Burton's Diary*, iii. 99; iv. 78; Peck,
*Desiderata Curiosa* (1779), p. 413. Haselrig's signature appears on an Army Committee
warrant dated 2 Jan.: P.R.O., S.P. 28/58, fol. 58. However, in the absence of other references
to Haselrig's presence in London, I conclude that the warrant must be misdated, or that
Haselrig signed it retrospectively.

as one of the group that made the final decisions. Yet for all that he attended none of the court's sessions, and avoided formal commitment until the deed was done, taking the dissent only on 5 February.[39] The absence of such men as Haselrig and Brereton meant that although the court as originally nominated was indeed representatively respectable, the court which actually tried and sentenced Charles I was drawn, proportionally, from less impressive social groups. It was not, as the Royalists sneered, a court of brewers and draymen. But it was not a court of the gentlemen of England.

There remains one supremely important absentee whose inactivity provides a clue to the revolution almost as crucial as Oliver Cromwell's belated conversion: Thomas, Lord Fairfax, the Lord General himself. Had Fairfax vigorously supported both the Purge and the trial he might have been the most powerful man in the kingdom; had he effectively opposed both he might have prevented them or have plunged the country into renewed civil war. Fairfax was not a politician. Like most of the parliamentarian gentry, in so far as he had any constitutional ideas they were entirely conventional, the product of instinct and prejudice rather than theory. Magna Carta, he announced in 1647 when he was shown the blessed document, was what the Army had been fighting for all along— hardly the fervent slogan of a revolutionary. But he was a sincere and dedicated believer in the Army's cause, the cause of Godly Reformation. His behaviour in 1648 and 1649 is an important illustration of one common response to the dilemma that faced political conservatives who were also Puritan reformers. Cromwell resolved it in one way, by action; Fairfax in another, by inaction. His apparent paralysis in January 1649 helps us to understand the inability of the moderates in and outside the Army to withstand the militant minority.

Fairfax was a Puritan reformer. Yet he was certainly not a radical Independent. Sir Philip Warwick thought him a man of 'a rational temper, not fanatical', incapable of Cromwell's occasional bursts of

---

[39] *Cobbett's State Trials*, v. 1126-7, 1201; *C.J.* vi. 132. Bradshawe denied being a client of Brereton's in a letter to Rushworth, 30 Aug. 1647: John Rylands Library, English MS. 745 (John Watson, 'Memoirs of the Bradshawe Family'). But their relationship is clear from Brereton's correspondence: B.M. Add. MSS. 11331-11333, *passim*. Brereton attended a sermon by Peter in Rotterdam many years before, and received a complimentary letter from him in 1645: E. Hawkins, ed., *Travels in Holland . . . by Sir William Brereton* (Chetham Soc., i. 1845), p. 6; B.M. Add. MS. 11331, fols. 79-80. It might be noted that Brereton had been beaten up by the Earl of Northampton a few weeks before the trial. Perhaps he had not fully recovered: Wedgwood, *Trial of Charles I*, p. 52.

righteous enthusiasm.[40] Like so many of his type, he was a sincere
but undifferentiated Puritan, certainly not hostile to Independents
in the Army (otherwise he could scarcely have been its general),
and equally happy with chaplains of all varieties ranging from the
radical William Dell to the moderates Joshua Sprigge and Edward
Bowles, and the Presbyterians Richard Stretton and Cornelius
Todd.[41] But in spite of his tolerant temper, Fairfax, as an impressive
body of opinion including Clarendon, Whitelocke, and Thomas
Hobbes agrees, either 'thought himself' or 'was truly what he pretended to be, a Presbyterian'.[42] His wife and mother-in-law, the
formidable old matriarch Lady Vere, were both Presbyterians of
a far more partisan hue. In 1647 Lady Fairfax developed, Lucy
Hutchinson says, 'a bitter aversion' to her husband's Independent
chaplains, and became so abrasive that she drove away many of his
Independent friends. Her influence over the General, people noted,
was particularly strong when Cromwell was out of the way, and she
became intensely unpopular in the Army, especially after it was
discovered in 1647 that she was relaying to Charles I inside information about discussions in the Army Council.[43] Matters cannot have
been helped by her notorious outbursts at the King's trial. Shortly
after the trial one of Fairfax's female relatives reported an unnerving
experience in Yorkshire: 'As I passed Doncaster I was in danger of
my life by the soldiers that took me to be your General's lady, but
God be thanked I escaped with much fear, for they held a pistol to
my breast.'[44]

Under the influence of his wife and her mother, Fairfax was
inclining towards religious Presbyterianism in 1648. But he still
showed no sign of being seriously out of sympathy with the aims
of the more militant officers. Loyal to his men, he sympathized

[40] Warwick, *Memoirs* (1813), p. 281.
[41] Bowles, Dell, and Sprigge are all in *D.N.B.* For Stretton and Todd see Matthews,
*Calamy Revised*, pp. 467, 487.
[42] Thomas Hobbes, *Behemoth*, in Maseres, *Tracts*, ii. 587, 615; Clarendon, *History*,
Bk. IX, § 168; X, §§ 88, 140; Whitelocke, *Memorials*, iii. 206. That Fairfax sometimes used
his influence to support the appointment of Independent clergy proves nothing. Many such
recomendations, like that of John Oxenbridge to Berwick, were made at the request of the
inhabitants: H.M.C., *Various Collections*, i (Berwick-on-Tweed MSS.), 17. Such an appointment can be balanced by Fairfax's installation of a most intolerant Presbyterian at Nottingham: *Hutchinson*, p. 242.
[43] Gardiner, *Civil War*, iii. 203; *Hutchinson*, pp. 241–2; *Ludlow's Memoirs*, i. 242; Lisle
to Leicester, 23 Oct. 1649: B.M. Add. MS. 18737 (Misc. Autograph Letters), fol. 82.
[44] Elizabeth Fairfax to Col. Charles Fairfax, [Jan. 1648/9?]: B.M. Add. MS. 36996
(Pontefract Transcripts), fol. 143.

with their grievances over pay and disbandment, and could justify the use of the Army against Parliament in 1647 on the unassailable grounds that at that time it was the Presbyterians who were attempting to 'raise a new war'. On his own statements, he always opposed revolutionary political action, whether purging parliaments or executing kings—but neither of these were real issues until the autumn of 1648.[45] When they became real issues, Fairfax began to hang back, as Ludlow discovered in September and Ireton soon afterwards. Although he could not prevent either the adoption of the *Remonstrance* or its presentation to Parliament, it was known that he had opposed Ireton's first draft in the Council, and that he had 'absolutely refused to concur' in the final version.[46] By this time he was already under attack by Army radicals, who noted the malign influence of his civilian adviser, Dr. William Staines, and his efforts to by-pass or reject the soldiers' petitions; on one occasion he threatened the authors with court martial. In December he was thought to be still trying to suppress extremist opinions. When Lambert's men sent up their declaration calling for justice, their agent was advised to present it only when the Council was in session, 'and not to his Excellency alone'. A Leveller journalist warned Fairfax to pay more attention to the soldiers' demands, lest they 'follow the example of those in Poland, who . . . have cut their landlords' throats because they would not regard their groans'. Invective of this kind was not confined to professional radicals in the left-wing weeklies: some of it came from the Army's own ranks. If an anonymous address to the soldiers, circulated early in January, can be regarded as an authentic expression of their feelings, they were bitterly disappointed at the outcome of the occupation of London. Instead of being rewarded for their services, they were 'thrust into empty houses whilst our officers drive a bargain with the City and endeavour to enrich themselves'. Let them take literally Parliament's declarations that power resided in the people, the manifesto ended: 'We the private soldiers represent the people and our officers the magistrate, whom we may as properly call to an account and

[45] Fairfax, *Short Memorials*, in Maseres, *Tracts*, ii. 446, and Firth, *Stuart Tracts*, p. 358. Fairfax claims to have frustrated an earlier attempt to purge Parliament by delaying the order for the Army to march until it was too late. He couples this with the events of the spring of 1648, but I agree with Gardiner, *Civil War*, iii. 182 n., that Aug. 1647 is a more likely date—if, indeed, the whole incident is not a figment of Fairfax's imperfect memory. But see above, p. 85 and n. 30.

[46] Letter of intelligence, 20 Nov. 1648: Bodl. MS., Clarendon 31, fol. 312. See also above, p. 118.

alter and change them . . . as the people do their superiors and governors.'[47] It is not difficult to imagine Fairfax's reaction to such outbursts: willing to condone radical action by his officers, he feared it from the men, as tantamount to mutiny and social revolution.

Fairfax's later justification of his conduct at the time of the Purge rests on his belief that he ought to all costs to retain his command to prevent its falling into more dangerous hands. Like Whitelocke, in other words, he still hoped to act as a restraining force from within.[48] Decisions were already being taken in his name and his signature added retrospectively. He was not consulted about the final arrangements for the Purge, but merely informed of them by Ireton. Quite possibly Fairfax regarded the whole operation as an elaborate bluff, to persuade Parliament to debate the *Remonstrance*, and to collect the assessments due from the City. His apparent preoccupation with technical, administrative details during the occupation of London suggests that he was content to proceed with the second aim even when he discovered that his officers had different views about the first. In his statements to various committees sent to negotiate the release of the imprisoned members he was obviously merely the mouthpiece of the General Council, and when Prynne sent him an angry letter from the *King's Head* on 26 December he professed to be unaware that Prynne was still a prisoner.[49] True or untrue, it was a pitiable admission.

As long as there was any remote possibility of compromise, Fairfax continued to preside over the Army Council. Perhaps deliberately, he missed the session of 15 December, when the first decisions about the King's trial were made, and he rarely attended during the following weeks. He was still involved in compromise discussions with the London Presbyterian ministers, and it was to him that Denbigh and the other peers came on the 19th when they set in motion the final mission to the King at Windsor.[50] Like everyone else, he was probably uncertain about the intentions of

[47] *Merc. Milit.*, nos. 1, 5 (10-17 Oct. and 14-21 Nov. 1648: [B.M.] E. 468, 35; E. 473, 8); Margetts to Adam Baynes, 13 Dec.: B.M. Add. MS. 21417 (Baynes Corr.), fol. 18; MS. Address to soldiers (4 Jan. 1648/9: [B.M.] E. 537, 8).

[48] Fairfax, *Short Memorials*, in Maseres, *Tracts*, ii. 441-51, also in Firth, *Stuart Tracts*, pp. 352-64.

[49] *Mr. Prynnes Demand of his Liberty to the Generall* (26 Dec. 1648: B.M. 669 f. 13, 65), also in *Old Parl. Hist.* xviii. 484-8; *Mr. Prynnes Letter to the Generall* (3 Jan. 1648/9: B.M. 669 f. 13, 67), also in *Somers Tracts*, v. 184-6.

[50] See above, p. 168. For the Council debates see *Clarke Papers*, ii, 71-135, 182, and App. D. I am grateful to Charles Hoover for further information, from Clarke MSS.

Cromwell and Ireton, and may have believed, right down to the opening session of the court, which he attended, that they were not in earnest about the execution. If so, he was right.[51]

Fairfax's hesitations up to this moment are easily explicable. After the trial opened he was clearly the only person who could stop it, and was the target of a stream of advice from the Prince, the Dutch ambassadors, the secluded members, and others to do so. Why did he not act? There are several answers. In the first place, in politics he was psychologically incapable of acting decisively.[52] Secondly, as he later pointed out, to have done so might have split the Army and led to renewed bloodshed, from which the Cavaliers alone would profit. Finally, the case for trying to divert Cromwell and Ireton by private argument was overwhelming. His wife's reckless outbursts in Westminster Hall were certainly made without his knowledge, but they must have made his task as a possible conciliator more difficult. He was reported to be under tremendous pressure to join in the trial—'baited with fresh dogs' as Nedham put it—and even to have been under partial restraint before it was over. But such extreme measures were unnecessary: the officers simply kept him talking until it was too late. In the end he seems to have been surprised when told that the King was dead.[53]

Fairfax's dilemma was a common one in the crisis of 1648-9. Like others who had supported the Army's moves in the past, he could see no practical way of opposing them in the present. He had no party of his own, being isolated by his position from the moderates, and by his convictions from the radicals. He too shared in the paralysis which afflicted the political nation, apart from the militant Saints, as day succeeded terrifying day. The gamble that by acquiescing in the *Remonstrance* and the Purge the Levellers might be headed off and the predominance of the gentry preserved, in the end succeeded. But the price was Charles I's head and the proclamation of the republic.

\* \* \*

While the handful of more or less committed revolutionaries

[51] See Wedgwood, *Trial of Charles I*, pp. 27-9, 71-4, 89-90, 104-7, for sensible discussion of Fairfax's position.

[52] Contemporaries agree about his indecisiveness: Clarendon, *History*, Bk. X, § 140; XI, § 235. Writing to Hyde in Feb. 1658, the Royalist Daniel O'Neill describes him as 'a slow beast and inconstant': Bodl. MS., Clarendon 57, fol. 129. For the 1649 appeals to Fairfax see Wedgwood, *Trial of Charles I*, pp. 171, 187-8.

[53] Gardiner, *Civil War*, iii. 577, n., 579-80; Wedgwood, *Trial of Charles I*, pp. 187-8, 194-5.

were bringing Charles I to the block, they had also to deal with two particularly obstinate groups of political enemies: the Levellers and the secluded members. The latter were perhaps the less dangerous. Naturally they continued their ineffective protests. Edward Stephens publicly called on Fairfax to save the King's life. Prynne twice wrote demanding his liberty, with some choice comments on the Army's pursuit of 'the designs and projects of Jesuits, Popish priests, and recusants', and threatening an action for unlawful imprisonment.[54] On New Year's Day he published a vitriolic *Brief Memento* to the whole 'unparliamentary Junto', once again accusing them of connivance in a Jesuit plot to destroy king and constitution. The enraged Commons promptly ordered the Army to suppress it, and sent two of their members, Humphrey Edwards and John Fry, to question its author. Prynne followed his usual tactics of refusing to answer unless ordered to do so by 'a lawful authority', and denounced the effrontery of his two inquisitors for sitting in the Commons at all (both had been involved in disputed elections); 'whereupon', says Prynne complacently, 'they departed somewhat discontented'. On 10 January, when Edwards and Fry reported all this to the House, it was voted that Prynne should be sent for by the Serjeant-at-Arms; another blunder, as it enabled him to reply that he was still in the Army's custody, and thus could not have obeyed even if it had been a legal command. On the same day three distinguished lawyer-M.P.s—William Ellis, John Maynard, and Thomas Waller—moved in Chancery on Prynne's behalf for a writ of habeas corpus. This was a tricky one for the Commissioners of the Great Seal, but Whitelocke managed to persuade Lenthall that there were no legal grounds on which habeas corpus could be denied, so the writ was granted. The decision to release so articulate an opponent is a striking demonstration of the revolutionaries' continuing respect for legal formalities, even at the height of their revolution.[55] Not that such leniency was likely to placate Prynne or his friends. On 16 January he and eleven other secluded members wrote to the Presbyterian licenser James Cranford, asking him to authorize publication of a formal

[54] E.S., *Letter of Advice, from a Secluded Member . . . To his Excellency, Thomas Lord Fairfax* (30 Dec. 1648: [B.M.] E. 536, 38). For the two Prynne broadsides see n. 49 above.
[55] *C.J.* vi. 111-12, 115-16; Whitelocke, *Memorials*, ii. 493. Dr. Denton to Sir R. Verney, 11 Jan. 1648/9: Verney MSS., B.M. Film 636, 9. Prynne's *Briefe Memento to the present Unparliamentary Junto* is printed in *Somers Tracts*, v. 174-83. His answers to Edwards and Fry are in *Vindication of William Prynne* (10 Jan.: B.M. 669 f. 13, 69).

*Vindication* against the Army's charges. It duly appeared on the 20th, answering the accusations point by point, and providing a forthright justification of their conduct during the Treaty of Newport.[56] But the time for argument was over.

Prynne's success in Chancery seems to have led to the prompt release of most of the remaining imprisoned members. Birch and Clement Walker were apparently released in January; the house arrest to which the two Harleys and Edward Vaughan had been confined after their release from full imprisonment came to an end by 12 February, and on the same day Thomas Gewen got out. Edward Leigh was still under restraint on 17 January, but the absence of further references to him, and to Edward Stephens, Green, Swynfen, and Wheeler as imprisoned shows that they must soon have been released. William Strode, however, had to wait until April.[57] Meanwhile, Massey audaciously accomplished the first of the exploits which soon gave him a great reputation as an escape artist. On 19 January, while attention was directed to the King's journey from Windsor, Massey's servant came to St. James's disguised as a woman. The two men changed clothes, and both left unmolested. Soon Massey was in Holland, and from this time on he was a Royalist.[58] This left only Clotworthy, Lewis, and the other three military men—Browne, Copley, and Sir William Waller. They were moved from St. James's to Windsor on 26 January, and all had long spells of imprisonment ahead of them.

Legality may have been belatedly observed in Prynne's case; but it was certainly ignored in the seclusion of the members who had not been imprisoned. On 3 January the General Council at last condescended to provide the Commons with information about them. The officers restated their case against the hard-core minority, accusing them of having led a faction of crypto-Royalists and 'real Presbyterians', recapitulated their numerous instances of attempted

[56] *Vindication of the Imprisoned and Secluded Members of the House of Commons* (23 Jan. 1648/9: [B.M.] E. 539, 5).

[57] R. Parkinson, ed., *Autobiography of Henry Newcome* (Chetham Soc., xxvi–xxvii, 1852), ii. 199; *D.N.B.* ('Walker'); H.M.C., *Portland*, iii. 167; Leigh to D'Ewes, 17 Jan. 1648/9: B.M. Harl. MS. 383 (D'Ewes Corr.), fol. 215. Strode was imprisoned for seventeen weeks: E. Green, 'Col. William Strode', *Somerset Arch. & Nat. Hist. Soc. Proceedings*, xxx, Pt. ii (1884), 61.

[58] [Nedham] to [Nicholas], 26 Jan. 1648/9: Bodl. MS., Clarendon 34, fol. 86; *A Short Declaration by Colonel Edward Massie* (19 Jan.: [B.M.] E. 451, 7). For Massey's later escapes, see David Underdown, *Royalist Conspiracy in England, 1649–1660* (New Haven, Conn., 1960), pp. 55, 263.

betrayal since 1645, and declared that if they had not been frustrated in December 1648 they would have established 'a lasting dominion shared betwixt the King and themselves in a perpetual Parliament'. The members still under restraint were those previously impeached and never acquitted, or close allies of theirs against whom new evidence would be produced. The other secluded members, the officers blandly suggested, were entirely free to resume their seats, the House having established satisfactory procedures by enabling them to dissent to the 5 December vote. Francis Thorpe, now heading the committee dealing with the officers, reported this ludicrous answer on the 4th. A week later the House voted it satisfactory and appointed a committee to consider whether any further steps should be taken.[59]

So far from being an invitation to the victims of the Purge to return, the dissent was of course an insuperable barrier. There seem to have been undercover efforts, presumably by people like Cromwell, to get some of them back, approaches which upset Army radicals like Captain Joyce. On 12 January Nedham noted that certain secluded members had been 'wrought upon by fair words and threats', and were likely to relent in their opposition.[60] But such moves, if they really were made, had no visible results. Once the preliminary sessions of the High Court of Justice began, to be sure, a few of those who had merely withdrawn began to reappear, now that they could no longer be accused of having initiated the proceedings. Whitelocke and Widdrington, who had secretly returned to London four days earlier, took their seats on the 8th, the day the court assembled. As usual, Whitelocke had no difficulty in extracting comforting support from like-minded men of prudence: Chief Justice Rolle, for instance, who thought that those not actually excluded 'could not dispense with their attendance and performance of their duty'; or Lenthall, who was afraid that the Army intended to put him out of the Speaker's chair, and 'claim all by conquest'.[61] The younger Vane may have resumed his seat on

[59] *The Humble Answer of the General Council of Officers of the Army* (3 Jan. 1648/9: [B.M.] E. 537, 14); *C.J.* vi. 111; Whitelocke, *Memorials*, ii. 494; Rushworth, *Historical Collections*, vii. 1390.

[60] *Clarke Papers*, ii. 182; [Nedham] to Nicholas, 12 Jan. 1648/9: Bodl. MS., Clarendon 34, fol. 73ᵛ.

[61] Whitelocke, *Memorials*, ii. 491, 494-5. The printed version, however, is wrong in giving the 9th as the date on which Whitelocke took his seat: B.M. Add. MS. 37344 (Whitelocke's Annals), fol. 243.

20 January, though he did not take the dissent until 1 February.[62] But only a handful of members took the dissent during January; most, if not all of them, were obviously committed to the revolution from the beginning. When one of the secluded members wandered into the House on the 29th, he was promptly put out again, and it was ordered that nobody who voted for the 5 December motion should be readmitted.[63]

Even after the King's execution, when Cromwell was said to be making approaches to the secluded members through friendly clergy like Stephen Marshall and Philip Nye, only a tiny handful complied. Henry Oxinden, who had not been secluded, came to London in February and was immediately invited to sit, but could find, he said, 'no persuasions or arguments from any to convince or prevail with me in honour or conscience'.[64] The only secluded members who certainly took the dissent in February were John Ashe, for whom the chairmanship of the Goldsmiths' Hall committee evidently meant more than political consistency, Sir John Hippisley, the elder Vane, and the lawyer Erasmus Earle.[65] Some members continued to attend important committees even though they abstained or were secluded from the House. Sir Anthony Irby, Sir Thomas Soame, John Stephens, and Robert Jenner were all occasionally at Goldsmiths' Hall in January, but gradually they dropped out, and after 24 February committees were restricted to active Rumpers. Jenner and Stephens attended for the last time that day, and the indefatigable Prynne, who had put in a couple of appearances at the Committee of Accounts on the 17th and the 22nd, also came no more.[66] None of this shows any real break in the unity of the secluded members. During the King's trial it was noted that their leaders 'have their private Juntoes daily'. This may have been true of a few of the more determined ones who

[62] Leicester's Journal: H.M.C., *De L'Isle*, vi. 580; Prynne, *A Full Declaration* (30 Jan. 1659/60: [B.M.] E. 1013, 22), p. 23. Dr. Rowe thinks that Vane did not sit before he took the dissent on 1 Feb., but Leicester and Prynne concur that he did.

[63] *The Moderate*, no. 29 (23–30 Jan. 1648/9: [B.M.] E. 540, 20); Rushworth, *Historical Collections*, vii. 1427. For the January dissenters, see below, p. 215.

[64] Henry Oxinden to Henry Oxinden of Barham, 15 Feb. 1648/9: B.M. Add. MS. 28002 (Oxinden MSS.), fol. 117. For the overtures by Marshall and Nye see Anthony Wood, *Athenae Oxonienses*, ed., P. P. Bliss (London, 1813–20), iii. 964; cited by Trevor-Roper, *Religion, the Reformation and Social Change*, p. 338.

[65] Samuel Gardner may also have returned in February: see below, p. 216, n. 19.

[66] H.M.C., *Portland*, i. 506; P.R.O., S.P. 23/5 (C. for Compounding Order-book), fols. 48–65; S.P. 28/252 (C. of Accounts Order-book), pp. 216–18: the committee was in process of being wound up.

O

remained in London, but most retired to their estates to brood
over their misfortunes. Many no doubt shared the fears of Sir
Ralph Assheton, who told his steward that he was 'exceedingly
threatened if they caught me'. Lord Say showed his opinion of
the situation by retiring to his remote fastness of Lundy in the
Bristol Channel.[67]

The secluded members might not be very dangerous; the
Levellers certainly were. They still had plenty of support in the
Army, and they had to be contained. It will be recalled that in
November Ireton had accepted Lilburne's proposal of a committee
of sixteen to revise the *Agreement of the People*, but that little had
been done by the time of the march on London.[68] Early in December
the committee again went to work and produced a version of the
*Agreement* which included redistribution of constituencies, household suffrage (servants and beggars excluded), a summary of necessary social reforms, and a guarantee of a broadly defined religious
toleration. When this was presented to the Army Council on
12 December, Lilburne found to his surprise that it was still to be
subjected to further revision by the generally unfriendly officers.
He and several others therefore withdrew from the sessions in disgust, and in the ensuing debates the Levellers were deprived of
their most effective spokesmen. This time they had no agitators
from the regiments to support them, and they were further weakened
by the tendency of millenarian zealots such as Harrison and the
preacher William Erbury to adopt an attitude of indifference to constitutional provisions, on the grounds that the dictatorship of the
Saints, the Fifth Monarchy itself, was at hand.[69] Nevertheless, a few
sympathetic officers put the Leveller point of view, Ireton made
some concessions, and consideration of the *Agreement* continued
at Whitehall, with occasional digressions to discuss the King's trial.
It appears from the imperfect record of the sessions that the only
subject treated at length was religious toleration, which was
explored in great detail with the help of Independent divines like
Nye and Goodwin, as well as Collier, Hugh Peter, and other radical
Army chaplains. There is no need to revise the traditional conclusion that Ireton and his officers kept the Army Levellers talking

[67] *The Moderate*, no. 27 (9–16 Jan. 1648/9: [B.M.] E. 538, 15); Assheton to Driver,
2 Jan.: Chetham's Library, MS. A 3, 90; C. H. Firth, *The House of Lords during the Civil
War* (London, 1910), p. 231.
[68] Above, pp. 129, 131.
[69] Brailsford, *The Levellers*, pp. 381, 384–5. See also above, pp. 158, 165.

while they went ahead with their own more limited revolution.[70]

Ireton, to be sure, made a few concessions. He could afford to, to gain time, knowing that the document was unlikely to be implemented. And even with the concessions, the *Agreement* that was finally adopted by the Army Council on 15 January was still a long way from the more liberal version that had come out of the committee of sixteen. Parliament was to be dissolved not later than 30 April 1649, and biennial parliaments thereafter elected by a sweepingly redistributed system of constituencies. But this was Ireton's policy as much as the Levellers, clearly derived from the *Heads of the Proposals* and the whole thrust of his policy in the autumn of 1648. The franchise would be vested in persons assessed for the poor rate—and here Ireton had gone a long way to meet the Levellers, for though not quite household suffrage, this was much wider than the traditional forty shilling freeholder franchise of the counties.[71] A strict division of executive and legislature was to be enforced, with members of the Council of State, Army officers, and receivers of public money all declared ineligible for election to the representative. Certain reserved powers were withheld from the legislature, dealing with impressment, indemnity, debts on the public faith, equality before the law, and the judicial powers of Parliament; the representative was also forbidden to 'level men's estates, destroy property, or make all things common'. But this was not the written constitution, with clear-cut guarantees against executive or legislative tyranny, for which the Levellers had argued in the autumn. Nor were they pleased by the ambiguous provision on religious toleration.[72]

In any case the precise terms of the revised *Agreement* were in large measure academic. What is important is that its discussion preoccupied many of the Army Levellers, and made it more difficult for Lilburne to divide the soldiers after his walkout. Furthermore, it was presented to the Commons on 20 January, the very day

---

[70] The only adequately recorded sessions of the Council are those of 14 Dec. and 13 Jan.: Woodhouse, *Puritanism and Liberty*, pp. 125-78. See also Brailsford, *The Levellers*, pp. 384-90.

[71] For a comparison of this with other Leveller proposals, see Macpherson, *Possessive Individualism*, pp. 114-15.

[72] Text of *Agreement* in Gardiner, *Constitutional Documents*, pp. 359-71. Lilburne's criticisms are in *Englands New Chains Discovered* (26 Feb. 1648/9), in Haller and Davies, eds., *Leveller Tracts*, pp. 157-60. And see Brailsford, *The Levellers*, pp. 389-90.

that public sessions of the High Court of Justice began. In such circumstances there was little prospect of its even being discussed by the House. It was received, there was no motion to debate it, and it was quickly forgotten. In contrast to the officers' behaviour when Parliament had ignored the November *Remonstrance*, there was no audible protest from the Army.

*     *     *

By the time the King was dead and the Levellers thus circum-vented, the men at Westminster had taken several critical steps that foreshadowed the nature of their new regime. In spite of their divisions they had to govern the country. They had therefore to provide some sort of public justification for their actions, to define, however roughly, the legal and philosophical basis on which their government rested; and to remodel the institutions of the country so that their revolution could not be undone, either by counter-revolutionary Presbyterians and Royalists, or by still dissatisfied Levellers. But the men who made the revolution were still legalists and practical politicians as well as enthusiastic idealogues. While they framed further revolutionary measures, while they abolished the monarchy and the House of Lords, they defiantly proclaimed their aims in the rhetoric of revolution. But they also worked hard to broaden the base of the new regime, to make it appeal to the realistic pragmatists for whom any government, even this one, was better than anarchy. They were pursuing two incompatible aims, revolution and conciliation, and in doing so they ensured from the first that their revolution would be abortive.

So much might almost have been guessed from the new regime's first official apology, which was published as a *Declaration of the Commons of England* on 15 January. It contained no ringing call to the millennium, no trumpet-blast ushering in a new Puritan Zion. It was indeed a curiously negative document, confining itself to a justification for the Purge and its aftermath. There was the usual historical introduction. Victorious in the war, Parliament had been about to achieve a settlement that would have made England 'the happiest nation in the world', when its work had been sabotaged by a malignant group of crypto-Royalists, 'carried away by base avarice and wicked ambition'. The *Declaration* recounted the conventional arguments against the Treaty of Newport, stressing that no agree-ment made with Charles I could ever have been permanently binding. At one point in its denunciation of the Isle of Wight terms it came close to a theory of popular sovereignty, arguing that the retention of the King's legislative veto would leave 'still in his power a check to any just desire of the people'. But this was buried in a text that appealed more strongly to material, or if not material then Presbyterian, aspirations. The religious clauses of the Newport Treaty (which, the *Declaration* forgot to mention, had not been finally concluded) would have left the purchasers of bishops' lands without ultimate security of tenure, and they would thus be 'defrauded of their bargains'. For the Presbyterians there was even an appeal to the Covenant; if the Newport terms had gone through, then 'episcopacy itself, which they had covenanted to extirpate, should yet remain in the root'.[73]

The same mixture of conventional and theoretical arguments, with the former more strongly emphasized than the latter, is regularly repeated in the Rump's official propaganda in January 1649. The revolutionaries might appeal to the law of nature and the sovereignty of the people; but they appealed even more to English law and the sovereignty of Parliament. Bradshawe's final oration at the sentencing of Charles I is a good example: there are occasional bows to the contract and the origins of law in the people, but far more to historical precedents and to the King's crimes in violation of the laws of England. Some of the leaders might feel, as did their emergency Solicitor-General John Cook, that they were acting 'not only against one tyrant, but against tyranny itself'.[74] On the principle of *Salus Populi* the Commons might proclaim the sovereignty of the people, as they did in the resolutions of 4 January. But having done so, in the same resolutions they quickly appropriated it to themselves: 'That the Commons of England, in Parliament assembled, being chosen by, and representing the people, have the supreme power in this nation.'[75]

It is entirely in character that, having proclaimed their own sovereignty, the revolutionaries should still have hesitated about permanently altering the constitution. When the Lords resumed their sessions after a week's interval on 9 January, they sent

[73] *A Declaration of the Commons of England . . . expressing their Reasons for the Adnulling and Vacating of these Ensuing Votes* (15 Jan. 1648/9), in *Somers Tracts*, v. 167-73; also printed in *Old Parl. Hist.* xviii. 503-13.

[74] John Cook, *King Charles, his Case* (Feb. 1648/9), quoted in Wedgwood, *Trial of Charles I*, p. 10. See also ibid., pp. 159-61.

[75] *C.J.* vi. 109-11; *L.J.* x. 641-2, for the events surrounding the 4 Jan. resolutions.

messengers to the Commons to communicate some routine business. Their appearance provoked a lively debate about the propriety of recognizing the Lords' existence, and they were kept waiting while it proceeded. Someone proposed that the two Houses should be combined, but this received little support, Whitelocke pointing out that the peers could easily dominate a single chamber: 'one might carry a dozen or twenty of [the Commons] to vote as they list.' When one of the radicals suggested that they should abolish the House of Lords outright Cromwell asked 'if they were all mad . . . to incense all the peers of the whole kingdom against them, at such a time when they had more need to study a near union with them'. Cornelius Holland, Marten, Ludlow, and Ireton all wanted to ignore the Lords' messages, but were twice outvoted. On the 18th the matter was raised again, when it was proposed that the Lords should be asked to concur in the votes of 4 January. This time the radicals had more success, and the suggestion was rejected.[76]

Until after the King's execution the matter was left in abeyance, a pathetic handful of peers continuing their desultory sessions, able only to 'sit and tell tales by the fireside', as a contemptuous observer described their meetings. On 1 February, however, the Lords took the initiative, proposing a joint committee 'to consider the settlement of the government'. This time their messengers were not admitted, and on the 6th, after a 'long and smart' debate lasting for two days, the Commons voted to put an end to the Upper House altogether. Once again Cromwell argued against it. But by 44 to 29 the Lords went down, and the protesting Whitelocke was directed to frame the Act of abolition. On the same day Denbigh and five other peers assembled for their last session. They heard prayers, disposed of a rectory, and adjourned—for another eleven years, as it turned out.[77]

Only after disposing of the Lords did the Commons turn to the final extirpation of monarchy. They had already prohibited the proclamation of another king on pain of treason, but the formal abolition of the institution had to wait until 7 February. On that day it was voted 'that the office of a king in this nation, and to have the power thereof in any single person, is unnecessary, burdensome,

[76] *C.J.* vi. 115, 121; [Nedham] to Nicholas, ? Jan. 1648/9: Bodl. MS., Clarendon 34, fol. 73ᵛ. See also Gardiner, *Civil War*, iii. 566.
[77] Firth, *House of Lords*, pp. 209–13; *L.J.* x. 649–50; *C.J.* vi. 129, 132; *Ludlow's Memoirs*, i. 220; Whitelocke, *Memorials*, ii. 519–21.

and dangerous to the liberty, safety, and public interest of the people of this nation; and therefore ought to be abolished'. The same committee charged with preparing the Act to abolish the Lords was directed to prepare another one implementing the resolution against monarchy. Not until 19 March were the two Acts passed, but the effective abolition was accomplished by the votes of 6 and 7 February.[78]

Besides these changes in the legislative power, the revolution necessitated a corresponding remodelling of the judiciary. Once again its accomplishment demonstrates how many of the revolutionaries hesitated to make a final break with legality, and their anxiety to commit wavering moderates like Whitelocke and Widdrington to the new regime. The willingness of the two Commissioners of the Great Seal to be used in this way had already been evident in mid January. Their two noble colleagues, the Earl of Kent and Lord Grey of Wark, made difficulties about issuing writs adjourning the law term, on the grounds that they could not legally do this without the Lords' consent. Whitelocke and Widdrington duly got authority from the Commons to act alone. Widdrington, however, was again wrestling with his conscience, and although he prudently retained his Commons seat by taking the dissent on 1 February, a week later he resigned from the Seal to pursue his legal practice. But Whitelocke went blandly on. With Prideaux and Lisle he was involved in altering the style of writs and making other necessary changes of court procedure, helping to draft the Act which implemented these important technicalities. The judges also needed new commissions. Six of them, including the M.P.s Samuel Browne and Cresheld, refused to serve in any circumstances. The other six, including St. John and Wylde, were willing to continue, though St. John at least was hostile to the new regime. But they needed a suitable replacement for the old oath of allegiance, and assurances that the government would not violate the 'fundamental laws'. Once more Whitelocke played the part of manager, getting the judges to draw up the necessary declaration and having it rushed through the Commons in time for the delayed opening of the term on 9 February.[79]

[78] *C.J.* vi. 133; Firth and Rait, *A. and O.* ii. 18–20, 24; *Old Parl. Hist.* xviii. 554; Whitelocke, *Memorials*, ii. 522.

[79] *C.J.* vi. 119, 123–4, 128, 133–5; Firth and Rait, *A. and O.* i. 1262–3; *Old Parl. Hist.* xviii. 544; xix. 8; Whitelocke, *Memorials*, ii. 497–501, 509, 522–3, 528–9; Prynne, *A Full Declaration* (30 Jan. 1659/60), p. 23.

Whitelocke's own position as Lord Commissioner had already been confirmed. On the 8th, he and Widdrington took the old Great Seal to the House of Commons, where it was ceremonially smashed to pieces; the two commissioners were awarded the fragments as souvenirs. John Lisle and Richard Keeble were appointed to replace Widdrington and the two peers, and Whitelocke made a long speech full of half-hearted protestations of his own wish to retire. But he was, he knew, 'very deeply engaged with this party', and was no doubt sincere in his belief that in these revolutionary times there was an 'absolute necessity' of preserving what was left of the legal system. Resignation would mean, as St. John said in justifying his own decision to remain as Chief Justice, an interruption of 'public justice between party and party', with unthinkable consequences. Conceding, as he told the House, that 'a strict formal pursuance of the ordinary rules of law' had scarcely been conspicuous in recent weeks, Whitelocke was also sure that his continued membership of the Commons was 'according to the known laws of England'. Once again, his arguments expressed the feelings of many who had had no part in either the Purge or the King's trial. 'Unavoidable necessity hath put us upon those courses', he declared, in words which echo only half of Cromwell's appeal to 'Providence and necessity'. If Providence decreed a revolution, it would surely evoke greater enthusiasm than if it was required by necessity alone. 'My obedience', Whitelocke concluded, 'is only due to you, and there is no other visible authority in being but yourselves.'[80]

So Whitelocke announced his decision to serve the republic. The tepid ambiguity of his language was in striking contrast to the proud republicanism of the new Great Seal with which he was entrusted. Designed with the assistance of Henry Marten, it bore on one side the arms of England and Ireland, and on the reverse a representation of the House of Commons in session. Beneath this pleasing scene appeared the legend: 'In the first year of Freedom, by God's blessing restored.'[81]

The adherence of moderates like Whitelocke ensured that the first year of freedom would not offer many more blessings to the revolutionary groups who had brought the new regime to power.

[80] Whitelocke, *Memorials*, ii. 524-7; *The Case of Oliver St. Iohn, Esq. Concerning his Actions During the late Troubles* (30 July 1660: [B.M.] E. 1035, 5), p. 10.
[81] *Old Parl. Hist.* xviii. 502; Whitelocke, *Memorials*, ii. 492.

The leaders, Ludlow says, were determined to exclude 'those who were likely to undo what they had done'. Yet, he adds, they were also 'unwilling to lose the assistance of many honest men, who had been in the country during the late transactions'.[82] Having voted on 29 January that no one who had voted for the 5 December motion should be admitted, three days later they set up a committee to receive the dissents of others who had not yet come forward. Thirty members quickly took the dissent that same day. By no means all of them had been in the country 'during the late transactions', and several of them were regicides who for one reason or another had only just found time to fulfil the formalities. But the speed with which these, and numerous other dissenters who came forward during the next few days and weeks, were accepted into the House, made the Commons a very different body from the one which had pushed righteously on towards revolution from mid December to the end of January.[83]

The readiness of the leadership to accept in positions of authority people who were not wholehearted supporters of the recent changes is further evident in the establishment of the Commonwealth's new executive body, the Council of State. On 7 February a committee was appointed to draw up a list of nominees. It was composed of five dedicated revolutionaries: Ludlow, John Lisle, Cornelius Holland, Robinson, and Thomas Scot. Yet of the forty-one councillors they proposed, barely half had demonstrated that they were really committed to the revolution either by signing the King's death warrant or by taking the declaration of dissent before the execution. Among the remaining twenty were such well-known moderates as Fairfax, the peers Denbigh, Mulgrave, and Grey of Wark, and the judges Henry Rolle and Oliver St. John. They also included the Earls of Pembroke and Salisbury, neither of them enthusiastic radicals, to say the least; the younger Vane, whose general opposition to both Purge and trial had been made plain; and Whitelocke. Once again it is evident that Ludlow and his friends were anxious to enlist as many moderates as could reasonably be expected to accept the *fait accompli*. In this some of their radical friends obviously thought they were going too far, for both Pembroke and Salisbury were elected only after the House had been divided against them. The names of Ireton and Harrison, the

---

[82] *Ludlow's Memoirs*, i. 223.
[83] For the February dissenters, see below, pp. 215-17.

principal architects of the military coup, provoked hostility from the opposite side. Both were rejected without a division, and Holland and Robinson took their places.[84]

If the nominating committee wanted a Council of State composed of resolute men who would drive the revolution on to its logical conclusions, they erred on the side of moderation. Of the peers named, Grey of Wark and Mulgrave both refused to serve, while the other three all had serious reservations when asked to subscribe an engagement giving retrospective approval to the events of the past two months, including an endorsement of the proceedings of the High Court of Justice. Fairfax, Skippon, Sir Gilbert Pickering, and Rowland Wilson also refused to subscribe. Difficulties over the High Court of Justice might have been expected from such people as Whitelocke and Alexander Popham, but they came also from such apparently consistent radicals as Haselrig, Sir James Harrington, and Denis Bond. Cromwell in the end produced a characteristic compromise, by which the councillors were allowed to subscribe one of several variants of the engagement, drawn up by the Council itself. They were permitted to 'approve of what shall be done by the Commons in Parliament, the supreme authority of this nation, but nothing of confirming what was past'.[85] Ireton, it is worth noting, was the chief author of the engagement, obviously hoping to restrict the new executive to the real revolutionaries. Once again he found it impossible to overcome the residual constitutionalism still lurking in the minds of his civilian allies.

When the Council of State was elected, then, there were already signs that the men who had established the Commonwealth had no intention of allowing the revolution to get out of control. Even stout republicans like Ludlow and Thomas Scot were also politicians who wanted to stay in power, and could appreciate the benefits of moderate support. Even more important were the reservations of men like Cromwell, converted to regicide by the dictates of Providence, but never quite allowing Puritan zeal to overcome their ingrained attachment to Common Law and Parliament. They needed moderate allies like Whitelocke, and having acquired them were inevitably restrained by them. And they needed them not only

[84] C.J. vi. 133, 140-1, 143; Ludlow's Memoirs, i. 222-3.
[85] Cal. S.P. Dom., 1649-50, p. 9; Peck, Desiderata Curiosa (1779 ed.), p. 413; C.J. vi. 147; Whitelocke, Memorials, ii. 537-8. See also Gardiner, Commonwealth, i. 4 and n., 6-7; Perez Zagorin, 'The Social Interpretation of the English Revolution', Journal of Economic History, xix (1959), 384 n.

because of the danger of counter-revolution from the right, but also because they feared a social revolution from the left. Early in January, when the *Agreement* was still under consideration, Sir Ralph Assheton had expressed a common view when he observed that the revolutionaries were out not only to 'destroy both King, Parliament and kingdom', but also to 'model some strange way of tyranny over the people'.[86] For Presbyterians of his type, this was shorthand for constitutional and social reform tending to democracy. His expectations were not fulfilled.

[86] Assheton to Driver, 2 Jan. 1648/9: Chetham's Library, MS. A 3, 90.

# VIII

## THE PURGERS AND THE PURGED

THE revolution of 1648-9 was over. But what actually had happened? In a general way, of course, we already know. We know that Parliament was purged, roughly who was purged, by whom, and for what ostensible reasons. Nevertheless, there are many questions that narrative history cannot answer, that are still worth asking of a historical situation such as Pride's Purge. Were there, for instance, significant differences between supporters and opponents of the revolution in such things as age, education, religion, and social status? A sociologist would wish to ask these questions of a sample of the entire 'political nation'. We cannot do that, but we can at least make some effort to do so of the only large group at our disposal, the Members of Parliament. We need not expect that quantification will magically provide exact answers to all questions; history is not an exact science. The vexing difficulties of definition and classification, the imprecision, for example, of such terms as Presbyterian and Independent, help to undermine the most carefully compiled statistics. The evidence about individual M.P.s varies enormously in both quality and quantity. We know a great deal about the behaviour of leaders like Cromwell and Ludlow, Holles and Glyn. But at the other extreme, can we even guess the political motives of such a man as Robert Andrews, member for Weobley, who sat on only one committee before the Purge and few afterwards, was never a teller, and whose sole recorded contribution to debate (in Richard Cromwell's Parliament) was the memorable utterance, 'a good motion, but not seasonably offered'?[1]

Lack of evidence is not our only problem. The M.P.s form a convenient and clearly defined group, but they are not a sample of the political nation. However unimpressive sometimes as individuals, M.P.s were by definition exceptions, leaders, not part of the common herd. With all their limitations, we might expect them to

[1] *Burton's Diary*, iii. 233.

have distinctive qualities which had taken them to the top. We should therefore refrain from assuming that conclusions based on the behaviour of M.P.s are necessarily valid for the nation as a whole. Our survey is therefore bound to have only a limited value. Yet it is still a worthwhile exercise, even if it merely confirms, or gives greater precision to what we think we already know.

The nominal membership of the House of Commons in 1648 was 507. When the Purge began, however, twenty seats were vacant. One member, William Eyre, had been returned at Chippenham as recently as 29 November and had not taken his seat; but he was entitled to sit, and did so on 15 January.[2] The analysis in this chapter deals with the behaviour of M.P.s between the Purge and the execution of the King. It is therefore legitimate to include Eyre and two others elected even later than he was: George Wylde and Edward Nevill, returned at Droitwich and East Retford on 7 and 21 December respectively. Wylde was first admitted to the House on 15 December, but a petition contested his election, and he was not confirmed in the seat until 29 January.[3] Nevill entered only on 5 May, but he could have been seated by early January if he had wished. The return of these two reduces the vacancies to eighteen, and leaves us with 489 M.P.s to be studied.[4]

Another eighteen members, however, must be removed from consideration because they were more or less permanently absent from the House for reasons unconnected with the Purge. We may be fairly sure of what some of them thought about it, but there is no objective way of assessing their responses. Five (Walter Strickland, Sir John Coke, Sir William Drake, Sir John Holland, and Walter

---

[2] Dates of returns, unless otherwise stated, are from *Return of the Names of Every Member returned to serve in each Parliament* (1878), i; dates of admission from *C.J.* For places for which writs had been issued but no returns made see W. D. Pink, 'Three Unknown Members of the Long Parliament', *N. & Q.* 9th Ser. x (1902), 383. For Eyre's admission, see above, p. 186 and n. 33.

[3] *Perfect Occurrences*, no. 103 (15-22 Dec. 1648: [B.M.] E. 526, 42); *C.J.* vi. 124.

[4] Several of the vacant seats were empty because of long deadlocked election disputes like those involving Sir Anthony Ashley Cooper at Downton, Fairfax and Nathaniel Rich at Cirencester. There are no convincing candidates for inclusion among the vacant seats. Alexander Pym has sometimes been accepted as an M.P., returned with Prynne for Newport, Cornwall, in the autumn of 1648: Brunton and Pennington, *Members of the Long Parliament*, pp. 29, 136. But this rests on a single entry in one of Prynne's pamphlets, and as Prynne did not include Pym in any of his other lists, he was obviously not very confident of his membership. There is no sign that Pym ever appeared in the House, yet there would have been no political obstacle to his doing so, for he was a consistent adherent of the radical faction in his county: see my forthcoming study of Civil War Somerset. He was sheriff in 1650-1, a further indication that he was not an M.P.

Long) were out of the country.[5] Nine others were in England, but too old or ill to attend Parliament. They had all been regularly excused whenever the House was called in 1648; most of them had been absent for years.[6] Four more (St. John, Cresheld, Samuel Browne, and John Wylde) had been made judges of the common law courts in November, and so by convention did not attend the House, though they did not resign their seats. The first three of these undoubtedly opposed the Purge: St. John's attitude is well known, while Browne and Cresheld immediately resigned rather than serve the Commonwealth. Wylde, equally certainly, approved of it. Nevertheless, it would be unsound to include them as active members during the Purge. They could not have been secluded: they were not there. Deducting these eighteen absentees, we have then 471 whose behaviour during the period of revolution must be examined.

\*       \*       \*

The 471 M.P.s can be divided into five groups: the active revolutionaries who openly committed themselves to the revolution while it was in progress during December and January; the conformists who avoided formal commitment at that time, but accepted the *fait accompli* in February, when they could no longer be incriminated in the execution of the King; the abstainers, who were not actually secluded, but showed their opposition by staying away from Parliament at least until the spring of 1649; the victims of the Purge who were secluded; and the hard core of the Army's enemies, who

---

[5] *D.N.B.* ('Strickland'); *C.J.* v. 235, 329, 349, 459; vi. 34; H.M.C., *Seventh Report*, Appendix (Verney MSS.), p. 457; H.M.C., *Hodgkin*, p. 119; Bodl. MS., Tanner 321 (Holland's Speeches), fol. 8ᵛ; Keeler, *Long Parliament*, pp. 137, 159-60, 256-7. There is no evidence to support Dean Keeler's statement that Long actually took his seat in 1648.

[6] The old or ill were Richard Browne (New Romney), John Cowcher, Sir Charles Le Gros, John Moyle, Jr., and Edward Owner: Keeler, *Long Parliament*, pp. 119, 144, 248-9, 282-3, 292. A mistaken report of Moyle's death in 1646 led to the issue of a writ to replace him; he actually died in Jan. 1651: Rylands Library, Pink MS. 307/263. Richard Shuttleworth, Jr., died in Jan. 1649, George Abbot, Michael Noble, and Richard Barwis in February: J. Harland, ed., *House and Farm Accounts of the Shuttleworths* (Chetham Soc., xxxv-xlvi, 1856-8), ii. 274 (which corrects Keeler, op. cit., p. 339); *D.N.B.* ('Abbot'); Josiah C. Wedgwood, *Staffordshire Parliamentary History* (London, 1919-34), ii. 84; Keeler, op. cit., pp. 99-100. Barwis was active in the North in December, but died before his attitude to the Purge became clear: C. R. Hudleston, ed., *Naworth Estate and Household Accounts* (Surtees Soc., clxviii, 1953), pp. 41, 45-6, 52. I suspect that he would have supported it. Not all M.P.s who died early in 1649 are omitted: John Alford died on 5 Jan., but was already known to have been secluded.

suffered imprisonment as well as seclusion. Only by separating these categories is it possible to make the distinctions which are obscured by treating all subsequent members of the Rump, whether early enthusiasts or belated conformists, as part of the same group.

Unfortunately the evidence on which the analysis must be based is distressingly imperfect. The Journals of the Commons tell us who were named to committees during the crucial period, but only rarely (as when they made reports or acted as tellers) who were actually present.[7] No political diaries record these passionate months, and very little private correspondence; letters are the first victims of revolution. Newspapers and pamphlets are uncertain guides, while the Whitelockes and Ludlows, in memoirs written years afterwards, speak only in general terms. Nevertheless, if we look carefully at what evidence remains, nearly all the 471 M.P.s can be assigned to one or other of the categories with a fair degree of confidence. It is, however, vital to adopt some objective method for placing them, and to avoid mere guesswork based on their earlier or later behaviour, the charges of their enemies, and above all their own statements made in subsequent self-justification.

The imprisoned members are easily identified. Several lists of them were published within a few days of the Purge, and they coincide almost exactly. There is no doubt that forty-one members were arrested on the 6th (two of them, Rudyard and Nathaniel Fiennes, being released the same day); three more (of whom Sir William Lytton was immediately released) on the 7th; and one more, Major-General Browne, on the 12th. The only possible additions to these are the younger Robert Harley, whose name is in several lists, but whose arrest in Herefordshire was only indirectly connected with the Purge, and Sir Henry Cholmley.[8] According to

---

[7] Nomination to a committee is no proof of actual presence in the House. Whitelocke was absent until 8 Jan., but was named to a committee on the 6th: *C.J.* vi. 112.

[8] The earliest lists are in *Parliament Under the Power of the Sword* (B.M. 669 f. 13, 54), and in several newspapers in B.M. (pressmarks E. 476 and E. 526), some of which omit the members arrested on the 7th. For Browne's arrest, see above, p. 162. *Merc. Elen.*, no. 55 (5-12 Dec.: [B.M.] E. 476, 4), lists Denzil Holles as imprisoned, but is not corroborated by the others. There are several incomplete lists, as in *The Articles and Charge of the Army* (8 Dec.: [B.M.] E. 475, 30), and some very inaccurate ones, e.g. *A Perfect List of forty eight Members of Parliament Seized on by the Army* (Dec. 1648). The list in Rushworth, *Historical Collections*, vii. 1355, is an accurate collation of several earlier ones, that in *Old Parl. Hist.* xviii. 467-8, less critically compiled. For Harley's arrest see above, p. 179. Prynne lists Cholmley as imprisoned in *True and Ful Relation*, p. 11, and in *Vindication of the Imprisoned and Secluded Members*. But cf. Letter of intelligence, 23 Nov. 1648: Bodl. MS., Clarendon 31, fol. 313; and *Merc. Elen.*, no. 55. For names see below, App. A.

Prynne, Cholmley was 'seized at his lodging and sent prisoner to the *Crown*', but in fact he seems to have been in Yorkshire, possibly still in confinement after his quarrels with the Army commanders at the siege of Pontefract. Young Harley and Cholmley were certainly secluded, but they were not among those arrested in London at the time of the Purge. We are left then with forty-five imprisoned members.

The secluded members are somewhat more difficult; there are plenty of later lists, but they do not inspire much confidence. Two lists, however, were published within seven weeks of the Purge, and can be used as a starting-point. One of them, in Prynne's *Vindication of the Imprisoned and Secluded Members*, looks authoritative, and gives the names of ninety-eight members. However, it is not exhaustive, as it omits at least another dozen who on quite solid evidence were certainly secluded. A much longer list containing 214 names had been published somewhat earlier, on 26 December.[9] This anonymous production was obviously hastily compiled. It makes no distinction between the imprisoned and the secluded, contains several confusing mis-spellings and duplications, and includes one man (Herbert Board) who had been dead for months. At a time so close to the Purge the author, whoever he was, must have been working to some extent from guesswork, and could not possibly have known whether members absent in the country had been actually secluded or were merely abstaining voluntarily. Nevertheless, the guesswork of an observer in December 1648 is likely to be better informed guesswork than is possible for anyone three centuries later. It therefore seems legitimate to collate the anonymous *List* with Prynne's, excluding the obvious errors and adding a few names which do not appear in either—young Robert Harley, for instance, and Samuel Gott.[10] When this is done we arrive at a total of 186 M.P.s who were secluded but not imprisoned at Westminster. This is higher than some contemporary estimates, but not much higher than others, including that of the Scots

[9] *A List of the Imprisoned and Secluded Members* (26 Dec. 1648: B.M. 669 f. 13, 64). The list in Prynne's *Vindication* is followed almost exactly by *Old Parl. Hist.* xviii, 468-71. There are several later lists in Prynne's pamphlets in 1659-60, but as they include members who had refused to sit in the restored Rump without having been secluded in 1648, they are irrelevant to our purposes.

[10] Gott signed a request to license the *Vindication* on 16 Jan.: H.M.C., *Portland*, iii. 166. A letter from him to John Swynfen in 1650 clearly implies that he was secluded: William Salt Library, Salt MS. 454 (Swynfen MSS.).

Commissioners in London, who reported on 26 December that over 200 had been either secluded or imprisoned.[11]

At the other extreme, the revolutionaries also present some difficulties of identification. There is in their case no reliable contemporary list to guide us, though there are plenty of unreliable ones based on individual opinion, usually hostile, about the members' behaviour. Whether or not a man is imprisoned is a clear matter of fact; whether he is actively supporting, or merely acquiescing in, a revolution is much harder to decide objectively. Still, it is possible to separate the active revolutionaries from the conformists. The crucial factor, surely, must be the date of the individual's public commitment to the revolution. Anyone committing himself at a time when by doing so he was exposing himself to possible future reprisals if the revolution failed, must be regarded as a genuine supporter. Anyone who postponed his commitment until it was safe to do so without fear of unpleasant consequences was equally certainly a mere conformist. Now there are two clear signs of revolutionary commitment: signature of Charles I's death warrant, and/or an early declaration of dissent to the vote of 5 December. Although some of the regicides suffered long and agonizing indecision before they signed, their signatures are hard facts which cannot be explained away. Whatever their private reservations, when confronted with the final choice they burned their boats behind them. We have then forty-three M.P.s who were regicides and therefore revolutionaries.

There is also no doubt that the early dissenters should be numbered among the hard core. The abstention of many supporters of the Purge from the High Court of Justice shows that it was quite possible to be a revolutionary without accepting the execution of the King as the necessary outcome. But by publicly declaring

---

[11] Mitchell and Christie, eds., *Commissions of the General Assemblies*, ii. 144. On the same day the Commissioners sent the Committee of Estates a marked list: *Acts of the Parliament of Scotland*, vi, Pt. ii (1872), 692–3. If it was the list published that day and referred to in n. 9 above, this would of course destroy the Scots' value as independent witnesses. However, *Moderate Intelligencer*, no. 197 (21–8 Dec. 1648: [B.M.] E. 536, 18) says that 'about 150 that were never in prison' were secluded by the 13th. *Second Part of the Narrative* (23 Dec.: [B.M.] E. 477, 19) gives a figure of nearly 200, presumably including the imprisoned members. In his letter to Fairfax, 3 Jan. 1648/9 (*Somers Tracts*, v. 186), Prynne suggests 150, in addition to those imprisoned; and the *Declaration and Protestation* which he and Walker published on 19 Jan. (B.M. 669 f. 13, 74), goes as high as 160. I think many lower estimates in other pamphlets relate to the events of 6 and 7 Dec. only, though I am unable to account for the low figure in the 19 Jan. *Vindication*.

P

abhorrence of the Newport motion, the early dissenters were pro-claiming their support for the Army's recent actions and for the sweeping political and constitutional changes that were bound to follow, even if the King was merely deposed and left alive. And by doing this before the King had been disposed of, they were laying themselves open to later charges of complicity. We need to look, then, for the early dissenters. Identifying them is not an entirely simple matter, because many of their names were erased from the Journals of the Commons early in 1660. Until then they were available to people in the know, but they were not given wide publicity. Nedham proclaimed their infamy in *Pragmaticus*, but his list of their names was mere guesswork. Government papers were more reticent, for reasons suggested by *The Moderate* when the dis-senting process first began. Their names, the Leveller journalist remarked, 'should have been inserted, if wise men had not thought it might have proved very inconvenient to them'.[12] Prynne, however, managed to get hold of their names, and a reasonably accurate list of early dissenters can thus be compiled. By the end of December 1648 at least forty-four, perhaps as many as fifty, members had sub-scribed.[13] Thirty of these were regicides, but the other twenty can be added to the forty-three regicides already defined as revolutionaries.

[12] *The Moderate*, no. 24 (19–26 Dec. 1648: [B.M.] E. 536, 2). It is worth noting that on 13 Jan. the Commons gave explicit orders that no one should be allowed to copy entries from the Journals: *C.J.* vi. 117.

[13] See above, p. 166. Identification of the early dissenters (see below, App. A), is based on a list of the first day's subscribers in an anonymous letter to Fairfax, 22 Dec.: Worcester Coll., Clarke MS. cxiv, fol. 131. This establishes the authenticity of Prynne's list in *A Full Declaration* (30 Jan. 1659/60), p. 21, which follows the Clarke MS. list for 20 Dec. with only one exception. Prynne is also confirmed by what can be read through the deletions in the MS. Commons Journal, and for 21 Dec. by *C.J.* vi. 102. I have therefore accepted him as authoritative for days on which dissents were erased. The list in *Merc. Prag.*, no. 39 (19–26 Dec.: [B.M.] E. 477, 30), is totally inaccurate. Walker, *Independency*, ii. 48–9, follows the Clarke MS. and Prynne lists, with a few additions. Some of these—Denis Bond and Sir Thomas Wroth, for instance, given by Walker as dissenting on 20 Dec.—I have accepted, provided that there is no contradictory evidence from other sources. Some dissents must have been made without being recorded in the Journal. Careful inspection of the MS. reveals no trace of Henry Marten, for one, yet it seems inconceivable that he can have omitted to subscribe (*Merc. Prag.*, loc. cit., says he did so on 20 Dec.). However, Walker cannot be accepted uncritically. He lists John Gurdon, Roger Hill, Luke Hodges, Edmund Prideaux, and Benjamin Valentine as December dissenters, whereas the Journal shows that they all subscribed in February. Francis Allen is given as an early dissenter in *Old Parl. Hist.* xviii. 482. I know of no earlier authority for this, but accept it in view of Allen's obvious importance in the Commons throughout the revolutionary period, and in the absence of any other date for him. Although he failed to sign the death warrant, Allen took the hard line in the High Court of Justice. See depositions of W. Watton and R. Downes, 27 Oct. and 3 Nov. 1660: H.M.C., *Seventh Report*, Appendix (House of Lords MSS.), pp. 158–9.

There is no difficulty about adding to the December dissenters the names of William Eyre, the new member admitted on 15 January, and the eleven M.P.s (six of them regicides) who dissented on the 29th.[14] The problem is to know where to draw the line between the revolutionaries and the adjacent group, the conformists who merely acquiesced in a *fait accompli*. No dissents were recorded between 29 January and 1 February. A difference of only three days may seem insignificant, yet the conclusion is irresistible that this is the point of distinction. Only three days, but they were momentous ones, for on one of them Charles I went to the block. Anyone taking the dissent before 30 January could be accused of openly condoning the execution; by 1 February the deed was done, and all the plausible arguments for conformity repeated by Whitelocke and his like could come into play. 'Divers members [have] since the death of the King, intimated a desire to come in', a newspaper noted on the 1st.[15] The names of the men involved confirm the journalist's hint that by that time men of a different character were ready to dissent. Among the eleven dissenters on the 29th were Cromwell and Ireton as well as four other regicides. Those on 1 February, on the other hand, included Whitelocke, Widdrington, and the younger Vane, all known opponents of both the Purge and the King's trial. True, five of the 1 February dissenters were also regicides and thus qualify as revolutionaries. Presumably they had been too busy with the trial to attend the House at times when dissenting was the order of business; Cromwell and Ireton, after all, had only found time for it three days earlier. Most of the remainder can, however, be placed in the second, conforming group.[16]

We have then sixty-nine revolutionaries who were regicides or early dissenters, or both. Two others can be added on the evidence of their behaviour or public statements at the time, even though they dissented a day or two too late. Major-General Skippon, who dissented on 2 February, was evidently unhappy about the trial and seems to have attended the Commons only occasionally during

---

[14] *C.J.* vi. 117, 124.

[15] *Moderate Intelligencer*, no. 203 (1–8 Feb. 1648/9). I am indebted to Blair Worden for this reference.

[16] *C.J.* vi. 124, for 29 Jan. dissenters; Prynne, *A Full Declaration*, p. 23, for those on 1 Feb. In fact no dissents at all were recorded between 25 Dec. and 29 Jan. The Journal contains no deletions between these dates according to the order of 22 Feb. 1659/60, which is the one under which dissents were struck out. Deletions occur during this period under orders of 21 Feb. 1659/60, but these did not concern the names of dissenters: see *C.J.* vii. 846, 848.

January. Yet he had ensured that 6 December would be bloodless by turning back the trained bands, had continued to use his influence over the militia to keep the City quiet during the following weeks, and had proposed the disqualification of Royalists and Presbyterians in the Common Council elections.[17] John Pyne, the Somerset dictator, was one of the 1 February dissenters. But he can be categorized as a revolutionary by the opinions expressed in his letter to Rushworth on 16 December, as well as by his promotion of the petition for justice in his county. With the addition of these two special cases, we arrive at a figure of seventy-one revolutionaries.[18]

All that remains is to distinguish the conformists from the abstainers. Once more the crucial factor is the date of dissent to the 5 December vote, and once more this is not as arbitrary a distinction as it may appear. With only a few exceptions, anyone who subscribed during February can be assigned to the conformist category. The exceptions are the handful of late-dissenting regicides, and also a few people who had been secluded in December but recanted and dissented in February.[19] As in the case of the earlier ones, erasures from the Journals make it difficult to get a complete list of the February dissenters, especially as the newspapers were less interested in them. But the names of some are recorded, and most of the others can be recovered by careful search.[20] The problem, as before, is to establish a convincing terminal date to distinguish conformity from genuine abstention. Actually this is not very

[17] See above, pp. 143, 151. Wedgwood, *Trial of Charles I*, p. 76.

[18] For Pyne, see above, pp. 178, 186, and n. 34. It will be observed that my identification of seventy-one revolutionaries is markedly lower than the 121 suggested in my article 'The Independents Reconsidered', *J.B.S.* iii (1964), 81, 83-4. That figure, as I stressed at the time, was only tentative and provisional, based on what I can now see was an insufficiently precise definition of 'revolutionary'.

[19] John Ashe, Erasmus Earle, Sir John Hippisley, the elder Vane, and possibly Samuel Gardner are in one or both of the lists of secluded members, and there is independent evidence for the seclusion of Ashe, Hippisley, and Gardner. Ashe dissented on 3 Feb. (*C.J.* vi. 130), Vane on the 10th, Hippisley on the 12th, and Earle on the 17th (House of Lords R.O., MS. Commons Journal). The date of Gardner's dissent is unknown. He first appears on a committee on 26 Apr., his only appearance during the entire Rump period, and thus possibly a clerical error. If he dissented it must have been, for reasons given below, in February. John Baker, who dissented on 1 Feb., is given as secluded in the 26 Dec. *List*, but I think this is almost certainly an error for Barker.

[20] Prynne, *A Full Declaration*, p. 24; *Cal. S.P. Dom.*, *1649-50*, p. 1; Walker, *Independency*, ii. 115. There are deletions under the order of 22 Feb. 1659/60 on fourteen days between 1 and 19 Feb. 1648/9: *C.J.* vi. 128-45. I have deciphered almost all the names through the deletions in the MS.

difficult. By the end of February the Rump's Members began to feel that time was running out for those still sitting on the fence, and that almost all of those who had in truth opposed the vote of 5 December had returned. On the 22nd they voted that no one else should be admitted to the House or to committees, except those who had been unable to dissent because of absence on military employment.[21] Some exceptions were allowed on the 28th, when Aldworth, Andrews, Barrington, Charles Fleetwood, Hoyle, Stockdale, and Wentworth were given permission for a later dissent; on the same day two other members, Burrell and Skinner, subscribed and were admitted. William Carent was also allowed to dissent on 5 March under the old rule, but he was the only member admitted during the whole of March.[22] Also, on the 5th, a new and smaller committee was appointed to consider further applications, and was directed to take into account the applicants' past record and their behaviour 'during the late transactions'. Composed of five hardheaded revolutionaries—Lisle, Holland, Ludlow, Robinson, and Scot—it was obviously designed to make entry into the Rump more difficult.[23] Indeed, after Carent's return, no more recommendations for admission were made until 6 April, which indicates that by then we are dealing with men of a different category.

The conformists can therefore be defined as those who took the dissent between 1 February and 5 March (except those already in other categories as regicides or secluded members), with the addition of those who were given special permission for a later dissent on 28 February and afterwards availed themselves of it: that is to say, all the seven named except Barrington. This gives us seventy-three conformists, to whom must be added Speaker Lenthall, and nine others for whom no date of dissent can be found. Lenthall was apparently never required to take the dissent; but he was obviously a conformist, not a revolutionary. Some of the other nine had occasionally been present in the House before 29 January without having dissented. But in view of the fact that the early dissenters have been already identified with reasonable certainty, and that there is no evidence of erasures from the Journal after 5 March, it seems clear

---

[21] H.M.C., *Portland*, i. 506 (dated 23 Feb.); *Cal. S.P. Dom., 1649-50*, p. 10; *Perfect Diurnall*, no. 291 (19-26 Feb. 1648/9: [B.M.] E. 527, 25); Whitelocke, *Memorials*, ii. 539.

[22] *C.J.* vi. 152-3, 155. No more dissents are recorded in March, and there are no erasures under the 22 Feb. 1659/60 order.

[23] *C.J.* vi. 157; *Ludlow's Memoirs*, i. 223. John Hutchinson was added to the committee in June: *C.J.* vi. 237.

that they all must have dissented during February.[24] Altogether, then, we have eighty-three M.P.s in the conformist category.

By process of elimination, eighty-six members remain who were neither revolutionaries, conformists, secluded, or imprisoned. A good many of them (at least thirty-one) were afterwards admitted to the Rump, on dates ranging from Christopher Martyn's arrival on 16 April 1649 to Sir John Dryden's belated reappearance three years later. They had not been the targets of the Army's wrath, but all of them, by their long absences, had shown that they were not supporters of the revolution. In some cases there is something better than negative evidence for their abstention. William Ashhurst was said to be 'again accepted into the House' on 19 December, but to have quickly withdrawn when the Army refused to compromise. Sir John Barrington, as we have seen, was given permission to return but did not do so, even though he was often in London.[25] William White was one of many members whose health mysteriously failed them in January and February 1649. He told the Speaker on 1 March that he was 'sick of a fever at York', but although he claimed to be willing to dissent, he did not in fact return until 14 May.[26] The middle-group leaders William Pierrepont and Evelyn of Wiltshire were among the abstainers, as were Nathaniel Stephens and John Harington.[27] No doubt a majority of those who abstained during the early months of the republic would have shared the obviously centre position represented by these few examples.

I am acutely aware of the objections that can be raised to this

[24] At least three, perhaps more, totally undecipherable dissenters can be detected under the erasures in the MS. Journal. The nine whose dissent dates remain unknown are John Browne, Feilder, Hallowes, William Hay, Lechmere, Rous, Humphrey Salway, Algernon Sidney, and Wallop. All except Browne were named to committees or actually present in the House during February. Browne might possibly be one of the missing December dissenters (see above, n. 13), as his name appears frequently in the *Journals* in December and January; he also attended the High Court of Justice fairly often almost to the end. However, he is not named as an early dissenter by any of the pamphleteers, and I think it more probable that, like his brother-in-law John Trenchard, he subscribed early in February. His subsequent disappearance from the Journals until July may have been the result of absence in Dorset: Mayo, ed., *Dorset Committee Minute Book*, pp. 494, 506.

[25] R. Johnson to H. Chetham, 19 Dec. 1648: Raines and Sutton, eds., *Life of Humphrey Chetham*, i. 168; Prynne, *A Full Declaration*, p. 18. Barrington went to London on 27 Feb., 16 Apr., and 4 June: Essex R.O., D/DBa/A3 (Barrington Accounts, 1645-51), fols. 51-3.

[26] White to Speaker, 1 Mar. 1648/9: Bodl. MS., Tanner 57, fol. 544; *C.J.* vi. 208.

[27] See above, p. 160. The repeated efforts made in 1651 and 1652 to persuade Harington to return to the House show that the only obstacle was his own abstention: see below, p. 291 and n. 97.

method of classifying members by the date of their dissents. Among other things I find it hard to explain the late dissents of several men of generally radical record who at first seemed to be supporting the revolution. There was a good deal of coming and going in December and January by members who attended the House for a few days without subscribing. Some of them undoubtedly took fright at the proceedings against the King. Richard Salway is one such case. He was active in the Commons intermittently until 17 January, and even helped to draft the famous resolutions proclaiming the sovereignty of the people; yet he delayed his dissent until 14 May. Henry Marten's friend Sir Peter Wentworth is another. He was sitting at least until 14 December, perhaps later, but then retired to the country for his health, political as well as physical; a series of 'sprains and bruises, by falls and other mischances', he told Lenthall, kept him there until the danger was over.[28] Brian Stapleton, Thomas Westrow, and George Snelling were also thought to be supporting the Army in December, yet withdrew and either took the dissent late or not at all.[29] William Sydenham was in Dorset during January, came to London early in February and voted against the abolition of the House of Lords. But he then withdrew again, and was not formally admitted to the Rump until 3 August.[30]

These are not the only difficulties. There are the simple problems of identification caused by clerks and journalists who did not always distinguish between three Hodges (two of them named Thomas). four Stephenses, five Temples, and many other multiplications of surnames. Yet there is no satisfactory alternative to the dissent as

[28] Wentworth to Speaker, [24 Feb. 1648/9]: Cary, *Memorials*, ii. 123. For reports of his presence in the Commons in December and early January, see *Merc. Elen.*, nos. 55, 56 (5–12 and 12–19 Dec. 1648: [B.M.] E. 476, 4, 36); *Merc. Prag.*, nos. 38, 40–1 (12–19 Dec. and 26 Dec.–9 Jan. 1648/9: [B.M.] E. 476, 35; E. 537, 20); and *C.J.* vi. 96.

[29] *A Remonstrance and Declaration of Severall Counties, Cities, and Burroughs* (1 Jan. 1648/9: [B.M.] E. 536, 23). The list of radicals in this pamphlet is obviously based on informed opinion about those still sitting after the Purge. But although Thomason acquired his copy on 1 Jan., it is dated 23 Dec., too early to take account of the dissent procedure. Apart from William Edwards, apparently included in error, all those listed had dissented by 5 Mar., except Salway, Stapleton, Westrow, and Snelling. The list, with an incomplete summary of the rest of the pamphlet, is printed by Yule, *The Independents*, pp. 131–2.

[30] Mayo, ed., *Dorset Committee Minute Book*, pp. 488–94; Ashley Cooper, Autobiographical Fragment, in Christie, *Shaftesbury*, i, App., p. li; *C.J.* vi. 132, 274. According to G. F. Sydenham, *History of the Sydenham Family* (East Molesey, Surrey, 1928), pp. 234, 703, he went abroad during the interval and was admitted to the University of Leyden on 10 May.

the objective test for determining the categories. Any other method involves the use of subjective criteria, which are even more open to question. Richard Salway perhaps ought logically to have supported the revolution, and until the King's trial appeared to be doing so, but the fact remains that he delayed proclaiming his commitment for another four months. If we were to say that occasional presence in the House during December and January, coupled with even an early February dissent, were indications of revolutionary behaviour, we should have to label Whitelocke and Widdrington as revolutionaries, which they emphatically were not. With such imperfectly recorded events no method can claim absolutely final accuracy. A few members may be misplaced in one category or another, but by adhering as honestly as possible to the objective tests at least those errors are avoided that stem from the historian's own presuppositions.

At the end of this tedious methodological exercise, we have then 471 M.P.s divided into the following categories, which will for convenience in future be referred to by initials.

| Revolutionaries (R) | 71 (15%) |
| Conformists (C) | 83 (18%) |
| Abstainers (A) | 86 (18%) |
| Secluded (S) | 186 (40%) |
| Imprisoned (I) | 45 (9%) |

*       *       *

There are many possible questions we might ask of these statistics. Not all of them, alas, are susceptible to statistical answer. One wonders, for example, whether the members of the five groups display any significant psychological differences. Did the Rs perhaps contain a noticeably higher proportion than other groups of men with recognizably rebellious traits, the result of parental conflict or other forms of disturbance? At first sight there are some very promising examples. The Puritan Blakiston, we might suppose, was acting out his hostility to his father, the Laudian canon of Durham, when he signed the King's death warrant. John Lisle came of a broken home; his mother neglected him (Sir John Oglander says that she 'looked not to anything'), and his father became a slovenly alcoholic. Eventually John got the old man's estate away from him, allowing him only £150 a year and the 'nasty chamber' in which he died. Sir John Bourchier's violent rages in his conflict with Wentworth in 1633 made his enemies conclude that he was going the way of his father, who died insane. Augustine Garland was sane enough, but had a disorderly history. With another future regicide, Adrian Scroop, he had led a student riot at Lincoln's Inn in 1635, and had been imprisoned and suspended for it.[31]

Before we conclude that the revolutionaries were characteristically abnormal, a collection of psychotics and madmen, sons killing their fathers when they killed their king, overgrown adolescents re-enacting the student protests of the 1630s, it is unfortunately necessary to point out that there are some equally striking examples of disturbed behaviour in the other groups. Lord Lisle (C) quarrelled with his father, the Earl of Leicester, almost incessantly—in December 1652 they came to blows—and Lisle was obviously jealous of the parental preference for his younger brother Algernon. Sir Peter Temple (A), like Lisle, was jealous of a younger brother, constantly bickered with his father over money, and engaged him in bitter Chancery lawsuits. Robert Harley (S) was another who had been a rebellious son, neglected by his mother in favour of his compliant older brother Edward; invariably thought 'stubborn', irresponsible, and 'discontented', and suffering from frequent 'fits of ague' which may have been psychosomatic in origin.[32] Nor were members of other groups any less prone than the Rs to other kinds of disturbed behaviour. Thomas Hoyle (C) sank into deep melancholia after the King's death, was haunted by headless phantoms, and after at least one unsuccessful attempt, committed suicide on the first anniversary of the execution.[33] William Edwards and Sir Humphrey Tufton (both S) seem to have been almost as violently quarrelsome as Bourchier, even if there is no evidence of mental

[31] Roger Howell, 'Newcastle Regicide: the Parliamentary Career of John Blakiston', *Archae. Aeliana*, 4th Ser. xlii (1964), 208-9. For Lisle, see Bamford, ed., *Oglander*, pp. 123-5. For Bourchier, *V.C.H.*, *Yorks.*, *N. Riding*, ii. 162, and J. T. Cliffe, *The Yorkshire Gentry from the Reformation to the Civil War* (London, 1969), p. 350. For Garland, *Records of the Honorable Society of Lincoln's Inn: the Black Books*, ii (1898), 327-30.

[32] Leicester's Journal, 16 Dec. 1652: H.M.C., *De L'Isle*, vi. 614 (cf. also Lisle to Leicester, 17 June 1656: Blencowe, ed., *Sydney Papers*, pp. 270-1); E. F. Gay, 'The Temples of Stowe and their Debts', *H.L.Q.* ii (1938-9), 419; Keeler, *Long Parliament*, p. 358; T. T. Lewis, ed., *Letters of the Lady Brilliana Harley* (Camden Soc., lviii, 1854), pp. 8-148, *passim*; Notestein, *English Folk*, p. 285.

[33] *Autobiography of Mrs. Alice Thornton* (Surtees Soc., lxvii, 1873), pp. 210, 212; *Life of Master John Shaw*, in *Yorkshire Diaries and Autobiographies* (Surtees Soc., lxv, 1875), p. 146. Hoyle's earlier attempt is noted in *Merc. Prag.* for 17-24 July 1649 (I am indebted to Blair Worden for this information).

instability in their families. George Horner (S) did not go as far as Garland in leading a riot, but as a student he had assaulted so august a dignitary as the chief butler of Lincoln's Inn, and during the Civil War was one of several members to show a propensity for duelling. Sir Henry Cholmley (S) was another who had been expelled from an Inn, in this case the Inner Temple, for bad behaviour.[34] Perhaps these instances reflect no more than a normal degree of youthful passion, but what are we to make of the case of Lionel Copley (I)? At the mature age of fifty-seven he was accused of assaulting a neighbour, Richard Firth, and of having 'put a bridle into his mouth, got on his back, and ridden him about for half an hour, kicking him to make him move'.[35] A sadistic-authoritarian behaviour-pattern, or (with the implied addition of a saddle on poor Firth's back) the enact-ment of a defiant rebuttal of the well-known Leveller cliché?

The truth is that such isolated examples tell us something about the psychology of individuals, but in the absence of statistical sup-port nothing about the psychology of the groups to which they belong. In the same way it is unsafe to argue that the Rs were more sexually emancipated because they included that 'legislative Priapus' Henry Marten; Gregory Clement, expelled from Parlia-ment in 1652 for 'lying with his maid'; Gilbert Millington, who if Lucy Hutchinson is to be believed frequented brothels and eventu-ally had to marry an 'alehouse wench . . . a flirtish girl of sixteen'; and Humphrey Edwards, whose tastes extended, according to Clement Walker, to incest with his aunt.[36] For such details we have to rely on their enemies, as we do for assertions that some of them were more than moderately addicted to the bottle: Thomas Chaloner, for example, who liked to go 'potting' with his witty friends Tom May and Henry Nevill, or John Pyne, whom Walker accuses of being 'often inspired with sack'.[37]

[34] M. J. Groombridge, ed., *Chester City Council Minutes, 1603–1642* (Record Soc., Lancs. and Cheshire, cvi, 1956), pp. 83–4; Keeler, *Long Parliament*, pp. 134, 366; *Lincoln's Inn, Black Books*, ii. 319; *C.J.* iii. 351–5.

[35] *Depositions from the Castle of York* (Surtees Soc., xl, 1861), p. 125.

[36] Brunton and Pennington, *Members of the Long Parliament*, p. 60; *Hutchinson*, p. 211; *The Case between Clement Walker Esq. and Humphrey Edwards, truely stated* (June 1650: B.M. 669 f. 15, 38).

[37] W. Rowe to Cromwell, 28 Dec. 1650: John Nickolls, ed., *Original Letters and Papers of State . . . among the Political Collections of Mr. John Milton* (London, 1743), p. 43—hence-forth cited as *Milton State Papers*. Arthur Annesley ironically describes Chaloner as 'temperate': [Annesley], *England's Confusion* (1659), in *Somers Tracts*, vi. 520. Walker's comment on Pyne is in *Independency*, i. 91.

Any temptation to equate radicalism with free living can be countered by producing similar instances from the other side. Sir Edward Baynton (C) not only had a violent temper which often got him into duels, but also spawned several illegitimate children, and dispensed a hospitality so liberal that it frequently led to his guests' servants being unable to get them home safely.[38] John Selden (S) openly lived in sin with the Countess of Kent, while Sir William Playters (S) had a reputation for sexual prowess second only to Henry Marten's. Nothing is known of the adult habits of Thomas Grantham (A), but as a schoolboy he seems to have been precociously vicious, trying to corrupt his younger school-fellow John Hutchinson; unsuccessfully, Lucy of course assures us.[39] Lord Carr (S) was one of the drunken party at the *White Horse* tavern at Christmas 1648 that was broken up by soldiers after the carousers had emptied a chamber-pot on them from an upstairs window. Finally there is William Wray (S), the 'mad captain' who accompanied John Evelyn on his travels for a time in 1646, 'little minding anything save drinking and folly', the diarist records, and finding even Geneva a place for amorous adventure rather than Calvinist repentance.[40] All these diverting anecdotes are valuable reminders that Long Parliament M.P.s were men with human frailties, but of no more value for the study of group behaviour than the discovery that Thomas Boone (C) had only one eye, and George Thomson (C) only one leg.[41]

Lack of evidence for all but a handful of the members makes a statistical investigation of these psychological questions impossible. But there are other matters in which counting heads is possible: age, for example. Were any of the groups significantly older or younger than the others? In our own day we know all about the importance of the generation-gap, so this is a logical starting-point. The House of Commons in 1648 naturally contained men of several quite different generations; young men with hopes and

[38] John Evelyn had a narrow escape after a visit to Baynton in 1654: de Beer, ed., *Evelyn*, iii. 112. See also Keeler, *Long Parliament*, pp. 101-2.

[39] Ibid., p. 306; *Hutchinson*, p. 41. Aubrey's well-known gibe about Selden will be remembered.

[40] *The Moderate*, no. 26 (2-9 Jan. 1648/9: [B.M.] E. 537, 26); De Beer, ed., *Evelyn*, ii. 480-534.

[41] J. J. Alexander, 'Dartmouth as a Parliamentary Borough', *Devonshire Assoc. Transactions*, xliii (1911), 353. Thomson's wooden leg was the result of a war wound, but both Annesley and Holles make sneering references to it: Annesley in *Somers Tracts*, vi. 524; Holles in Maseres, ed., *Tracts*, i. 269.

expectations, old men with experience and memories. There were venerable members like Sir Thomas Cheeke and Sir Benjamin Rudyard who would have vividly remembered the Spanish Armada; one, Sir Oliver Luke, had served in Parliament in the sixteenth century; another, Sir William Constable, had taken a youthful part in the Essex conspiracy; many more would have remembered Fawkes and Catesby. There were also men in the House—Fagge, Lechmere, John Pelham—who were to live on into the eighteenth century. The importance of the highly ideologically committed generation of the 1620s has already been mentioned. Its existence is the most likely explanation for the fact that when the Long Parliament divided at the outbreak of the Civil War the Parliamentarian M.P.s had a remarkably higher average age than the Royalists.[42] Were the revolutionaries of 1648-9 also drawn to any significant extent from this generation, or were they perhaps young activists not yet tamed by experience?

The ages, within a few years either way, of 439 out of the 471 members under study are known. Rough estimates for almost all the rest can be made, and averaging them in is unlikely to distort the statistics materially.[43] On the whole the figures bear out the '1620s generation' hypothesis. Men under thirty were only half as likely to be Rs as men in their forties. The Rs, to be sure, were not the only group to be somewhat older than the average: the Is were strikingly so, containing an even larger percentage of the men of the 1620s than the Rs, and also by far the highest percentage of the old, the over-sixties. This might suggest a tendency on the part of the men of the 1620s to be more strongly committed on either side, and it is certainly true that the As contained a smaller percentage of them than any of the other groups. But we should also remember that men in their forties might naturally be expected to be among the leaders and the most strongly committed. Some of the older members were relapsing into senescent caution or inactivity, younger ones had not had time to be marked down as leaders; thus fewer of them were imprisoned, many more merely secluded. It is indeed striking that four-fifths of the Is and over two-thirds of the Rs were over forty, whereas none of the other groups contained such a preponderance of older men. The other interesting fact is

[42] Brunton and Pennington, *Members of the Long Parliament*, pp. 15-16, 188. And see above, p. 8.
[43] Below, App. B, Table I.

the high percentage of the young members, those under thirty, who were secluded. The young men seem to have been the most typically opposed to the Purge, more so even than the over-sixties if the S and I categories are taken together.

If a man's age may influence his political conduct, so may his family status—whether he is an eldest or a younger son, a married man or a bachelor. The younger son was a familiar phenomenon, having to make his own way in the world, often by office-holding, a legal or military career, or in trade. One might expect the politics of younger sons to be affected by the personal challenges they faced, the greater self-reliance demanded of them; equally, they might well be influenced by the financial consequences of their situation.[44] Evidence exists for the position in family of more than nine-tenths of the M.P.s, and for roughly the same proportion of each group. Some interesting differences emerge when they are divided into the owners of estates (eldest sons who had inherited), heirs whose fathers were still living, and younger sons.[45] The inheritors of estates represent about six-tenths of every group except the As, of which they form almost three-quarters: abstention might well be the position most attractive to men of property. The As, correspondingly, contain the lowest percentage of younger sons, who with less to lose might be more likely to take firm positions on one side or the other. The statistics bear out to a slight, but not a dramatic, degree the expectation that younger sons might be more radical than their elder brothers, a markedly higher percentage of them being Rs or Cs than is the case with the inheritors or heirs to estates. The Rs contain the highest proportion of younger sons, almost a third of them being in that category, but the Cs and Is include almost as many; it would be absurd to describe the Rs as a party of younger sons. Perhaps the most interesting feature is the marked conservatism of heirs whose fathers were still alive. In proportion to their numbers (which being smaller, introduce a greater possibility of statistical error) far more of them were Ss, far fewer

---

[44] Aylmer, *King's Servants*, p. 259, finds the presence of younger sons in the Caroline bureaucracy less common than one might expect. However, among active royalist plotters in the 1650s younger sons predominated, the owners of or heirs to estates generally keeping out of trouble: Underdown, *Royalist Conspiracy*, pp. 323-4.

[45] Below, App. B, Table II. Some younger sons had, of course, established themselves as the heads of independent families, others had not; but it seems a needless complication to separate them. In a few cases the heirs were to estates owned by their grandfathers, their own fathers having died: George Booth, for example.

were Rs, than either their 'fathers' or 'younger brothers'. This could be explained on either psychological or economic grounds. The typical heir might have been more conservative because of psychological dependence on his father, a reluctance to act out the symbolic destruction of parental authority. Or he may simply have been unwilling to risk the paternal wrath if he took the radical line, to court the danger of being cut off without a penny.

Analysis of the members' marital status is more difficult because of the imperfections of the record. It is relatively easy to discover whether or not a man married at some time during his life, but dates of marriage are not always available, and the absence of information about the date of a wife's death and of the husband's remarriage often makes it impossible to decide whether or not a man was a widower. Speculation about the psychological results of widowerhood and its possible reflection in political behaviour is therefore beyond us. The evidence, such as it is, suggests that there were forty-nine bachelors in this much-married House of Commons, and that bachelors, like younger sons, were more likely to take clearcut political stances. The Cs and As, both of which groups might appeal to the politically cautious, contain barely half the percentage of bachelors in the other groups.[46]

When we come to education we are on firmer ground, at least if we are content with university and professional education. No doubt some interesting conclusions could be drawn about the influence of different kinds of elementary and grammar schools, but the names of the schools or tutors of so few of the members can be discovered that statistical investigation is not worth while. The universities and Inns of Court, on the other hand, provide very full records of admission, even though they do not tell us what, if anything, the student did after he was admitted. Still, the personal contacts made with other undergraduates might be important for an individual; so might the intellectual or spiritual influence of a tutor or chaplain. Once more it should be stressed that we are dealing with M.P.s, men of a governing class, most of whom shared a common educational experience. It would therefore be wrong to expect any dramatic variations in the educational background of the various groups. Still, some important differences do emerge.

After all the expulsions and recruitings, it is suprising to find

[46] Below, App. B, Table III.

that the proportion of members sitting in December 1648 who had attended a university or an Inn was at least as high as it had been for the members who sat before the Civil War.[47] This disposes of contentions that the Recruiters were a crowd of uneducated soldiers and tradesmen. As between the groups, the most obvious differences are those at the two extremes, the Rs and the Is. The Rs contained a slightly lower percentage of men who had been entered at an Inn, and a markedly lower one of university men, than the House as a whole: a reflection, as we shall see, of the fact that the Rs contained more men of lower social status than did the other groups.[48] The Is, on the other hand, include by far the highest proportion both of university men and those who had attended an Inn. As between the two universities, a substantial majority of the members went to Oxford. Cambridge is somewhat more heavily represented among the Rs, but so it is among the As, and it is noticeably under-represented among the Cs, the second-line radicals, who were much more likely to be Oxford men. If it is assumed that the revolution was the work of radical Puritans, and that Cambridge was more likely to produce such attitudes than Oxford, the statistics do not really bear out the supposition.[49]

When the four Inns of Court are compared the differences are clearer. Gray's Inn and the much smaller Inner Temple were the radical ones, Lincoln's Inn and Middle Temple more conservative. Gray's Inn men comprise less than thirty per cent of the M.P.s who had attended an Inn, but forty per cent of the Rs with such experience. Gray's Inn and Inner Temple tend to be more strongly represented in groups R and C; Lincoln's Inn and Middle Temple in groups S and I. The radicalism of Gray's Inn was nothing new. Its members had tended in 1640-2 to be more parliamentarian and less royalist than those of other Inns; at that time the Inner

---

[47] Below, App. B, Table IV. For the 1640-2 members, see Brunton and Pennington, *Members of the Long Parliament*, pp. 6-7. Keeler, *Long Parliament*, p. 27, gives a rather higher estimate for both categories. See also Lawrence Stone, 'The Educational Revolution in England', *Past and Present*, no. 28 (July 1964), 63.

[48] See below, p. 238.

[49] Only four Oxford and five Cambridge colleges provide as many as ten M.P.s, and such small numbers make generalization hazardous. For what it is worth, it may be noted that at Oxford Magdalen, and at Cambridge Christ's, seem to have produced a higher proportion of radicals than the other colleges. It may be frivolous to note that Sidney Sussex men tended to share the middle-group position of their most distinguished colleague, Oliver Cromwell.

Templars had also been a good deal more royalist.[50] As the Inns, like the universities, still had some regional affiliations, it might be asked whether the apparent differences in the political complexions of the Inns can be explained on regional grounds, or whether the political atmosphere of an Inn influenced its students, regardless of their region. Gray's Inn, for example, drew heavily on the North, the Midlands, and East Anglia. If the members from these areas who were not university or Inn-educated show the same political variations as those who were, education as an explanation of behaviour in 1648–9 can be discounted.

When the regional origins of the members are examined, this indeed proves to be the case. Apart from the M.P.s from the sparsely populated north-west, Wales and the border counties, whose representatives display a markedly, and perhaps expectedly conservative tone, only one of the regions departs significantly from the norm: the north-east.[51] The members from Yorkshire and the counties beyond the Tees included a strikingly high proportion of radicals. The safest procedure when dealing with such small numbers is to combine groups R and C and to compare them with the two conservative groups, S and I. When this is done the north-eastern members are radical by almost three to one; in no other region do the radicals even approach parity with the S and I groups. The question remains: were these men from beyond the Humber more radical because of their regional origins, or because of their education? The answer is that it was quite clearly the region rather than the university or Inn that was decisive. Only four north-easterners went to Oxford (two of these were Rs, one an A, and the other an S), but those who went to Cambridge divide six to one, and those who were at Gray's Inn nine to one as between the R/C and S/I groups. Both Cambridge and Gray's Inn men from other regions show a clear majority on the other side, even those from the east and south-east, the next most radical regions. If the north-easterners are left out, Gray's Inn men are only slightly more radical than those from other Inns, less so indeed than those from Inner Temple. While if Gray's Inn men are left out, the north-east is still on the radical side by almost two to one. The experience of living in 'those poor, rude and ignorant parts', as Cromwell described them, of being part of a beleaguered Puritan minority

[50] Brunton and Pennington, *Members of the Long Parliament*, p. 6.
[51] Below, App. B, Table V.

in a sea of popery and apathy, and perhaps (as was the case with several of them) of having suffered from the long arm of Wentworth and the Council of the North, made members from the north-east particularly inclined to support or acquiesce in a revolution.[52]

Age, position in family, education, and regional origins have been examined, but what of the members' occupations? The overwhelming majority of Long Parliament M.P.s were of course country gentlemen. The only other occupations providing more than a tiny handful of men were trade, office, and the law. There were a few members who might be classed as professional soldiers (almost all of them Rs or Cs), and a sprinkling from other professions, like the physician John Palmer, and noblemen's secretaries such as Hugh Potter and Edward Thomas. But the merchants, bureaucrats, and lawyers are the only groups large enough to be statistically significant. The first two will be considered at a later stage, but as we have just been discussing legal education, it seems logical to proceed by examining the lawyers.[53]

There were eighty-eight lawyers in the House at the time of the Purge. They divided politically in about the same proportions as the House as a whole. The only variations are the rather higher percentage of them in the C group, and the correspondingly lower one among the As. Not more than a fifth of any other group were lawyers, whereas almost a quarter of the Cs were, against barely an eighth of the As. Lawyers, one might suppose, were somewhat more likely to be conformists than men of other occupations. If he lacked the strong convictions that would lead to his being secluded or imprisoned, the lawyer might well see no point in absenting himself from Parliament, when by attending he could perhaps improve his practice, and protect the legal system (and his fees) from the threatened assaults of idealistic reformers. The legal mind's typical concern for practical results and distaste for empty idealistic gestures might reinforce such arguments. The tendency to conformity, the avoidance of abstention, is even more striking when it is noted that of the eleven

---

[52] Cromwell to Speaker, 11 Mar. 1650/1: Abbott, *Cromwell*, ii. 397. For the general point, see Howell, *Newcastle*, pp. 63-5, 72-7.

[53] Below, App. B, Table VI. I have regarded as lawyers all M.P.s who had been called to the Bar, with the addition of a few provincial attorneys below this status who were engaged partly or mainly in legal practice, e.g. Thomas Pury, Sr., and Thomas Scot. Not all the barristers were still practising lawyers (D'Ewes, for instance), but there is no reliable way of distinguishing them. For the merchants and office-holders see below, pp. 238, 252-3.

Q

A lawyers, no less than six belatedly adhered to the Rump after March 1649.[54]

\*     \*     \*

From these preliminary characteristics, we move to matters of opinion: the political and religious affiliations of the men of 1648-9. As might be expected, the Is had the greatest parliamentary experience, both in the Long Parliament and as members of earlier parliaments.[55] Over half the members sitting in 1648 were Recruiters elected after the resumption of by-elections in August 1645, but not much more than a third of the Is come into this category. The percentage of Is who had sat in the Short Parliament, and whose parliamentary memories went back to the passions of the 1620s, was also markedly higher than for any other group. This is not surprising: they were older, and they were leaders, marked men. The Ss follow the norm both in respect of election to the Long Parliament and of experience of earlier parliaments. The Cs, however, while having a normal experience of earlier parliaments, contain a higher percentage of original Long Parliament members, and a correspondingly lower one of Recruiters. The Rs, though only just below average in their earlier parliamentary experience, include a markedly higher percentage of Recruiters than the House as a whole. This may lend support to the charges of Prynne and other Presbyterian propagandists that the Recruiter elections were carefully managed in order to strengthen the radicals in the House.[56] But of all the groups the As, the men in the middle, had the least experience. They included nearly as high a proportion of Recruiters as the Rs, and easily the lowest percentage of members who had sat in earlier parliaments. The As do not appear to have been significantly younger than the other groups, so some other explanation for this must be sought. One possible solution is that although the As included a number of highly active politicians, such as William Pierrepont and the Wiltshire Evelyn, who abstained out of conviction, they also included many others who had never been politically active and abstained out of apathy.

Parliamentary experience is one thing: political behaviour is quite another. There are reasonably reliable indications of the earlier political conduct of barely half the 471 members. In some cases it amounts only to accusations, more or less well founded, of

---

[54] Richard Edwards, Fell, John Lenthall, John Stephens, Wastell, and White.
[55] Below, App. B, Table VII.     [56] Underdown, *E.H.R.* lxxxiii (1968), 248 and n.

royalist sympathies, and as the alleged Royalists are naturally to be found almost exclusively within the ranks of the As, Ss, and Is, it does not tell us much that is new about the men of 1648-9. With the Royalists disposed of, we are left with just under half of the active membership of the House who can be associated with the earlier political factions. The proportions of the different groups who can be so categorized, however, vary considerably. We know something about almost all the Is, more than half of the Rs and Cs, but only two-fifths of the As, and barely a third of the Ss. Many back-benchers appear occasionally as tellers in divisions, or in other ways give some indication of their opinions, but without sufficient regularity or consistency for us to be able to associate them with one of the parties. Although some of them may have been party men, it is reasonable to suppose that most were not, but were simply independent gentry of the familiar type. Nevertheless, in spite of the variations in the completeness of our knowledge of the groups, some obvious conclusions are possible.

Ninety-two members can be associated with one or more of the war-time parties before the recruiting of the House began in August 1645.[57] Not surprisingly, at the two extremes there proves to be an almost total correspondence between political sympathies during the war and in 1648-9. Old peace-party members divide overwhelmingly against the revolution; old war-party men almost equally strongly in favour of it. Even when wavering members of the two parties are included, the proportions are still five to one, or a little less in the case of the war-party men. The behaviour of the old middle group that had been led by Pym and St. John is less predictable, but all the more significant. No member of the R group came of a consistently middle-group background, and only one member of the Cs (Sir William Masham), though two other Cs, Reynolds and Whitelocke, had been on the peace-party fringe of the middle group. Even when those who had been on the war-party fringe are added—men like Cromwell, Mildmay, and Purefoy (all Rs), the elder Armine, Brereton, and Robert Goodwin (all Cs) —a large majority of the old middle group can still be found among the S and I groups.

[57] Below, App. B, Table VIII. In assigning Members to parties I have relied on Hexter, *Reign of King Pym*, and the articles by Valerie Pearl and Lottie Glow cited above, Intro., p. 2, and p. 62 n. 52. A few members are assigned to more than one party, because of the common habit of drifting between the middle group and the two other parties. The total for all three parties therefore exceeds ninety-two.

Much the same conclusions follow an examination of members of the post-war parties. Altogether, 146 members can be fairly clearly categorized as Presbyterian, middle-group, or Independent, once again with a few duplications. At the extremes, the correlation between earlier behaviour and action in 1648-9 is even more striking than in the case of the earlier parties. Not one of the Rs or Cs shows any evidence of consistent Presbyterianism in politics, nor even one of the As. Without exception, known Presbyterians were either imprisoned or secluded. Ludlow and the others who drew up Pride's list had done their work well. The total absence of Presbyterians from the Rs and Cs is balanced by the Independents' almost equally complete absence from the S and I groups. Only two possible Independents were secluded, but of these John Ashe probably belongs more properly to the middle-group, while the evidence for Nathaniel Bacon's radicalism dates from the very early days after his election late in 1645.[58] The Independents, however, were somewhat more likely than the Presbyterians to abstain, almost a tenth of them doing so, and their support for the revolution was thus slightly less than unanimous. But once again, it is the behaviour of the middle-group members that is most interesting. More than twice as many of them were victims of the Purge than were its supporters, and precisely a third of them abstained. Of those members of the S and I groups whose politics in 1645-8 can be determined, almost a quarter were men of the middle group—more than a quarter if John Ashe and Nathaniel Bacon are included.

Besides the construction of lists of more or less consistent party men, there is one other way in which light on earlier political opinions can be obtained. The men who seceded from Parliament after the Presbyterian-inspired riot at the end of July 1647 included members of both radical Independent and middle-group inclinations. But those who fled to the Army or signed the engagement in support of that action were not necessarily party men, not necessarily Independents of either type. Also among them were probably a number of non-party men, honestly upset by the use of force against the House. Whatever they were, however, on this important occasion they took their stand on the Independent side. Those who stayed at Westminster during the Speaker's absence were not necessarily Presbyterians either—they included John Venn and a number of other consistent radicals. Nevertheless, the names of

[58] Pearl, *E.H.R.* lxxxi (1966), 491 n.

those who stayed, or who in other ways supported the Eleven
Members, include most of the known opponents of the Army at
that time. The two groups based on these events in 1647 are roughly
equal in size. When their behaviour at Pride's Purge is compared,
the expected conclusions emerge. The Presbyterians of 1647 were
secluded or imprisoned in 1648, but only three of those who had
supported the Army suffered the same fate. Yet once again, almost
a quarter of the Army's old friends abstained after the Purge.

The middle-group can legitimately be regarded as part of the
Independent party during the years 1645-8. On this definition of
the Independents, the split in the party by the time of the Purge
can be statistically demonstrated. Out of the hundred consistent
Independents, not much over a third were Rs, barely a quarter were
Cs. More than another third—outnumbering the Rs—were either
As, Ss, or Is, all of which groups were opposed to the Purge. If the
lists of consistent party men are combined with those based on
behaviour in July and August 1647, the same result is reached.
Although the Presbyterians are almost solidly against the revolution, the Independents again divide into three. Almost exactly
a third are Rs, another third are Cs, just over another third are As,
Ss, or Is. Once again it becomes clear that the revolution of 1648-9
can no longer be regarded as a move by the Independent party
against the Presbyterians.

It was in fact a move by one section of the Independent party, the
radical wing, against moderates of all political colours: Presbyterians, former middle-group Independents, and non-party men.
That such men as Nathaniel Fiennes, Crewe, and Knightley were
marked down for imprisonment in December 1648 confirms how
much the Purge was directed almost as much against the middle-
group leadership as it was against the Presbyterians. The former
radical Independents either supported the Purge or gave belated
acquiescence as Cs; but most of the middle-group Independents
who had taken the lead in the Newport negotiations went into
opposition.

So much for politics, but what of religion? The difficulties of
classifying M.P.s according to their religious preferences have
already been alluded to.[59] To do so without introducing repeated
qualifications is indeed misleading: most members were Puritans
in a general sort of way, but not as completely absorbed by the finer

[59] Above, pp. 15-23.

shades of controversy as the clergy. Many of them enjoyed a theo-
logical argument, but as Nathaniel Fiennes reminds us, they could
still be tolerant of godly men whose opinions differed from theirs.
The Presbyterian Harington could dine with the Independent
Cromwell one April day in 1652, and cheerfully swap scriptural
texts with him.[60] Opinions, too, often changed with the times.
Whitelocke, with his apparent Independency while courting
Rowland Wilson's widow, is a good example. The goldsmith
Francis Allen is another. According to Baillie he was originally
a 'professed Presbyterian', who by February 1646 had become an
Independent in politics. Like other M.P.s he was named a Presbyterian elder, but his parish minister at St. Dunstan's in the West
was an Independent, and may have influenced him. After the revolution Allen apparently moved even closer to the Independents, for
as patron of the livings of Acton and Ealing he presented prominent
Independent ministers (Thomas Elford and Thomas Gilbert) to
each. Yet he was no radical, voting with the Presbyterian Purefoy
in favour of tithes on 18 May 1649.[61] The contradictions of such
men as Allen can perhaps be reconciled by noting Clement Walker's
distinction between classical and congregational Presbytery: the
latter, he observed, 'differs little or nothing from Independency'.
It is in this sense that the term 'Presbyterian Independent' is used
in this study.[62]

Some estimate of the religious position of rather more than half
the 471 M.P.s can be made.[63] In some cases the evidence is strong,
in others it is based on inference. The members' own statements
have been used whenever possible, supplemented by second-hand
information when it appears reliable, by the evidence of voting in
the Commons, and by the implications of presentations to livings
in the gift of individual M.P.s. This last form of evidence is

[60] B.M. Add. MS. 10114 (Harington's Diary), fol. 31.

[61] *Baillie*, ii. 353 (Baillie here uses Presbyterian as a religious term, Independent as a
political one). Amon Wilbee, *Comparatis Comparandis*, Pt. 2 (Oxford, 6 Nov. 1647: [B.M.]
E. 413, 1), p. 17, describes Allen as a 'pretending Independent'. Lambeth Palace, MS.
Comm. III/3 (Admission Book, 1654–5), Pt. ii, p. 154; MS. Comm. III/4 (Adm. Book,
1655–6), p. 526; Yule, *The Independents*, pp. 85, 143; Matthews, *Calamy Revised*, pp. 182,
221, 369. Before Elford went to Acton both Philip Nye and his son John were ministers
there, but there is no evidence that Allen presented them.

[62] Walker, *Independency*, ii. 11. See also above, p. 18. I have adopted the term 'Presbyterian Independent' to describe people who seem to have supported this kind of congregational presbytery, but also those who moved from Presbyterian to Independent without
clearly demonstrating that they were either. I thus retain Hexter's term, but with a very
different meaning.                                    [63] Below, App. B, Table IX.

particularly hazardous, as patrons were often influenced by other factors than the minister's theological complexion. They might present a man because they wished to do him a good turn as an old friend of the family; because the parishioners wanted him; because they thought him a godly man of sound learning whatever his views; or simply because they could not find anybody else. Patrons certainly often presented ministers whose views they did not share. Sir Richard Onslow presented the radical Nehemiah Beaton to his living at Merrow, Surrey, but it would be absurd to deduce from this that Onslow, the leading Presbyterian in his county, was a religious radical. The evidence of presentations is useful, therefore, if it displays a very clear pattern, or corroborates other information.[64]

In spite of these difficulties, the statistics include substantially more than half of all except the S group. And as the Ss whose opinions are known show absolute unanimity on the Presbyterian side (many Presbyterians were of course really moderate episcopalians for whom Presbytery was the only option open), it seems unlikely that the shortage of information about the others causes much distortion. As we might expect, there is a marked correlation between religion and politics in the two extreme groups, but much less correlation for the groups in the middle. With only one known exception (Nathaniel Fiennes), the men in the S and I groups were unanimously Presbyterians or covert supporters of moderate episcopacy. The Rs, on the other hand, were heavily Independent, with a significant infusion of sectaries.[65] Even so, of the Rs whose religious persuasions are clear, a fifth were Presbyterians, and it is entirely probable that the proportion would be higher if we knew more about the others: Independents, being a minority, tended to be better known. The combination of revolutionary politics with Presbyterian religious views is evident in men like Purefoy, and was sufficiently common to make it unsafe to regard religious Independency and political radicalism as necessarily cause and effect. Finally, it is interesting to note the high percentage of religious Presbyterians among the Cs. Of those whose views are known the Presbyterians form a clear majority, and again it seems likely that if we had information about the others the majority would be even

---

[64] Lambeth Palace, MS. Comm. III/4 (Admission Book, 1655-6), p. 553; Yule, *The Independents*, p. 148; Matthews, *Calamy Revised*, pp. 42-3.

[65] I use the term very broadly, to include Baptists like Carew and Hutchinson, but also Deists and freethinkers like Marten and Thomas Chaloner.

greater. Bearing in mind the fact that all the Cs were in the Rump by the end of February 1649, it is obvious that the prospects for a radical religious settlement after the revolution were dim indeed.

\* \* \*

To define political and religious categories may be difficult; to agree on acceptable definitions for an analysis of the members' social status is no less so. Obviously we are dealing with status-groups, not social classes in the modern sense, and equally obviously we cannot use income as a measure of status. True, in the seventeenth century as at other times there was a rough correlation between rank and income. People at the top of the status hierarchy tended also to be near the top of the income hierarchy, and vice versa. But it is still unsound to argue from one to the other. There were wide variations between the average wealth of members of the same status group in different regions: the poverty of the northern gentry was well known. Furthermore a man could be rich, and still not have been rich for long enough to pass through the needle's eye of social acceptance. John Ashe of Freshford was regarded as 'the greatest clothier in England' before the Civil War. His personal estate was worth £15,000, and he employed over a thousand workers. After the war he became even richer, expanding his estates and attaining an annual income of £3,000 by 1656.[66] Yet in the status hierarchy no one would have ranked the Ashes anywhere near as high as their neighbours the Pophams and Haringtons.

What categories, then, are we to adopt? It would be logical to use the customary seventeenth-century ones—peers, baronets, knights, esquires, gentlemen, yeomen, and so on. However, almost all the M.P.s would fit into the second, third, and fourth of these categories, and this would not produce much real enlightenment. It seems preferable to construct a system of classification which has more to tell us in the light of recent historical controversy. Five categories have therefore been adopted: greater gentry; county gentry; lesser gentry; merchant/gentry; and merchants. The greater gentry include the sons of peers, baronets and their sons, and members of families which had provided knights of the shire in the century before 1640, thus demonstrating their roles as leaders of their counties. The county gentry are the men slightly below this

[66] Keeler, *Long Parliament*, p. 91; *V.C.H., Wiltshire*, iv. 153; *Burton's Diary*, i. 127.

level: knights and their sons, members of families which had provided M.P.s for borough seats, or had filled such county offices as
high sheriff or deputy lieutenant. The lesser gentry are those at the
next level, whose families had aspired to nothing higher than producing an occasional J.P.; this definition, it should be stressed, is
somewhat broader, and includes men of somewhat higher status
than that which equates the lesser gentry only with the very small
parochial gentry. Merchant/gentry are the men whose main occupation was trade, but who were of recent gentry origins: Anthony
Bedingfield and Peregrine Pelham are good examples. Finally, the
term merchant is used here in a very broad sense, and includes all
the M.P.s who were not of recent gentry origin. Some of them were
not technically merchants, as for instance the brewer Matthew
Allin and the shipwright Edward Boate. Others were men whose
origins are impenetrably obscure, like those of Benjamin Valentine,
and are classed with the merchants on the grounds that wherever
they came from, it must have been from outside the landed establishment.[67]

Obviously no scheme of classification can be followed absolutely
rigidly. Some members—Nutt, Hill, and Alured, for example—
belonged to families which had occasionally provided M.P.s for
near-by boroughs during the previous century, but which in every
other way look like lesser gentry.[68] None of these can be regarded
as county gentry in the same sense as families like the Oxfordshire
Doyleys, the Dorset Erles, or the Isle of Wight Leighs. Charles
Vaughan's father sat for several Devon boroughs in Elizabeth's
reign, but this was the result of his employment by the Earl of
Bedford, not of his own county status; Charles Vaughan has therefore also been classed as lesser gentry. A few members have thus
been moved down. A few others have been moved up, though only
on the advice of experts who know far more than I do about the
status hierarchies of their counties.[69]

With the categories established and the members tabulated, the

---

[67] For a convenient summary of the seventeenth-century status hierarchy see Lawrence
Stone, 'Social Mobility in England, 1500–1700', *Past and Present*, no. 33 (Apr. 1966),
18. My own categories are slightly different because of the particular needs of this study.

[68] Brunton and Pennington, *Members of the Long Parliament*, pp. 50, 165. For a comment
implying that Alured was not one of the Yorkshire 'great ones' see T. Tindall Wildridge,
ed., *The Hull Letters* (Hull, [1887?]), p. 17.

[69] Henry Oxinden, for example, who is classed as greater gentry on the advice of Professor Everitt, to whom I am grateful for resolving many doubts.

resulting statistics show what we should perhaps expect: a rough, but not absolute correlation between status and politics.[70] One way of approaching the question is to compare the county with the borough members. Although a few lesser gentry had been elected for their counties in the unusual circumstances of 1640 and in the recruiter elections, on the whole we should expect the knights of the shire still to be men of higher status than the borough members. Compared with their borough colleagues, slightly fewer county members do indeed turn out to be Rs or Cs, slightly more are Ss or Is. The correlation becomes clearer when we examine the more detailed statistics. Barely half the Rs and considerably less than half the Cs were greater or county gentry; on the other hand two-thirds of the Ss and Is were men of this solid status. Fewer than a tenth of the greater gentry were Rs, compared with almost double that proportion of the lesser gentry, and exactly double of the merchants. Less than a quarter of the greater gentry, and less than a third of the county gentry were either immediate or conforming supporters of the revolution; considerably more than half of both categories were secluded or imprisoned. In both the lesser gentry and merchant categories, however, the Rs and Cs outnumber the combined S and I groups. But there is an interesting difference between the greater and the county gentry. Although the Rs contained very few greater gentry, they included a very substantial number of county gentry, more indeed than any other group except the Is. The county gentry in fact seem most likely to have had strong opinions, a much smaller percentage of them being either As or Cs than is the case for any of the other categories.

So far our analysis has been based on the members' status in the 1640s, treating it as a fixed quantity. Obviously there were stable families, but there were also others on the way up or the way down. There were members of well-known declining families like the Constables and Temples. There was the less familiar case of Nicholas Lechmere (C), who was making a modest recovery through the law, but whose family during the previous two centuries had gone through a typical cycle of rise and fall. Yeoman origins; slow rise in the fifteenth century; marriage to an heiress and profitable leases of Church lands about 1540. Then disaster in the time of Lechmere's recusant grandparents. 'In their days the estate of our family received much diminution,' Nicholas tells us, 'occasioned

[70] Below, App. B, Table X.

(partly) by their religion, (partly) by tedious suits in law . . . but chiefly by their superfluous housekeeping.'[71] It is worth asking whether this kind of mobility influenced behaviour during the crisis. Were men of old and stable families less likely to be Rs than those whose families were declining or had only recently arrived? It has been found that in some counties the old, indigenous families tended more to Royalism or hostility to parliamentarian and committee centralization than those of more recent origins.[72] This does not seem to have been the case with the M.P.s. Men from Tudor families may have been slightly more conservative than those from either older or newer families, but the variations are too small to permit confident assertions. However, when the members from families evidently in decline by 1640 are included a different result emerges. Secure, established families can be defined as those of the greater and county gentry of Tudor or earlier origin, not in decline by 1640. Insecure or unestablished families can be defined as those of the lesser gentry, the new gentry (established since 1603) and the declining gentry, with the addition of the merchants. When these two broad and roughly defined categories are compared, the conclusions suggested by the comparison of status become clearer.[73] The A and I groups divide between the secure and insecure in approximately the same ratio as the House as a whole: forty-five to fifty-five. Nearly two-thirds of the Rs and considerably more than two-thirds of the Cs, on the other hand, came from insecure or unestablished families. The S group, however, is noticeably more stable, with a clear fifty-five to forty-five majority on the other side.

There was then a definite connection between status and political behaviour in the revolution of 1648-9. This rough-and-ready analysis does not prove that the Rs were a party of *nouveaux riches*, declining or lesser gentry and merchants. But it does suggest that the revolution had more appeal to men of such descriptions than it had to the greater and county gentry. Status was not the only factor influencing men's conduct: education, region, past politics, religious views, and perhaps directly financial interests (which remain to be discussed), may also have helped to determine the actions of any single M.P. As between the groups acquiescing in the

---

[71] Lechmere, in E. P. Shirley, *Hanley and the House of Lechmere* (London, 1883), p. 16. See also *V.C.H., Worcs.*, iv. 97-8.

[72] Kent, for example: Everitt, *Community of Kent*, pp. 36-41, 118-20, 191, 324.

[73] Below, App. B, Table X A.

revolution, the Rs were undoubtedly more ideologically motivated than the Cs. Far more of them were religious Independents or sectaries, and at the same time more of them were greater or county gentry. It is arguable, in other words, that the Cs included distinctly more men who had no strong political or religious commitment to the revolution, but conformed to the new regime in the hope of improving their positions, or arresting their families' decline. Men of established rank and status were less inclined to be revolutionaries. This is not particularly surprising: people with a lot to lose are not usually inclined to rock the boat. But it seems, worth insisting on this point once again, because there has been in recent years a tendency to question the importance of social factors in the Puritan Revolution, and to argue that the revolutionaries included a rough cross-section of the political nation.[74] It is of course dangerous to argue that because M.P.s divided as they did therefore the nation as a whole must have done so; we have to look outside Parliament before we can really decide whether or not the revolution was the work of the declining and lesser gentry and the 'middling sort'. Indeed, the statistics suggest that however determined the leaders may have been in executing Charles I and setting up a republic, there were still important restraints on their radicalism. Even if rather a large number of them came from insecure families, more than half the Rs were still drawn from the traditional governors of the kingdom. Though the rank and file might wish to push further into revolution, it is unlikely that the greater and county gentry who formed a majority of the Rs would permit it.

After status, it is natural to consider the question of financial motivation. We are dealing with human beings, so it is not surprising to find many men in all the groups for whom monetary considerations were all-important. The Is included such as Lionel Copley and Sir John Clotworthy, whose dishonesty was monumental, and John Birch, who as Ludlow rightly observed, 'used to neglect no opportunity of providing for himself'. Among the Ss was Sir Thomas Pelham, incredibly rich, but still 'a man that never thinks himself sure enough of money', as the Earl of Leicester ruefully concluded after experiencing Pelham's rough tactics in 1647. Many no doubt would have agreed with Sir William Uvedale (another S) that 'it is the rule that we ought to look to ourselves

[74] See above, p. 4, and n. 6.

in the first place'.[75] The enormously acquisitive Haselrig was a C, and so was the cowardly Sir Peter Wentworth, who vindictively hounded the aged Royalist, George Warner, to get his estate.[76] As for the Rs, even if we make some allowance for political bias in the charges repeatedly levelled at such men as Harvey, Blagrave, and Gregory Clement, the size of their appetites is still pretty plain. There can be no disputing the fact that Harvey eventually went to gaol for embezzling over £50,000 as a commissioner of customs.[77]

All this is very true, though it is also true that among all five groups we can find many contrasting examples of men who put ideals and convictions above self-interest. Indeed, not all the men involved in even these regrettable examples were inspired *solely* by greed. Copley and Clotworthy, after all, were imprisoned for their politics, not their racketeering. But a statistical analysis may help us to decide whether some of the groups were possibly more strongly motivated financially than the others. It is of course difficult to estimate the income of even the best documented seventeenth-century family. Rentals record only income from land, omitting that from other sources such as office; tax assessments, as always, are misleading if not downright dishonest; and estates often horribly entangled in marriage settlements and burdened with complicated and elusive annual charges.[78] It is doubtful if years of hard labour could produce accurate figures for the incomes of more than a minority of Long Parliament M.P.s. It therefore seems sensible to abandon the hopeless quest for total accuracy from which reliable medians and averages could be calculated, and to be content with estimates which, however unsatisfactory for the economic historian, can still help to answer the sort of questions we are concerned with.

The M.P.s for whom rough estimates can be made have been

---

[75] *Ludlow's Memoirs*, i. 393; Leicester to Salisbury, 13 Jan. 1647/8: H.M.C., *De L'Isle*, vi. 442. Uvedale is quoted by Keeler, *Long Parliament*, p. 370.

[76] *L.J.* ix. 477-9; *C.J.* v. 453; *Cal. C. Comp.*, pp. 1454-6; H.M.C., *Seventh Report*, Appendix (House of Lords MSS.), pp. 35-6, 99; Cary, *Memorials*, ii. 123; Holles, *Memoirs*, in Maseres, *Tracts*, i. 268; *V.C.H.*, *Warwickshire*, vi. 275, 280. Wentworth was spreading damaging stories about Warner as early as 1646 and trying to keep his authorship of them a secret. Wentworth to Brereton, 13 Mar. 1646: Birmingham Public Library, Brereton's Letter-book, Apr.-May 1646. The whole affair puts Wentworth in a very ugly light.

[77] *D.N.B.* ('Harvey'). See also Sir W. Dugdale to [J. Langley?], 26 Jan. 1655/6: H.M.C., *Fifth Report*, Appendix (Sutherland MSS.), p. 175.

[78] For discussion of the difficulties see Lawrence Stone, *Crisis of the Aristocracy* (Oxford, 1965), pp. 129-37.

divided into three classes: the rich, with incomes before 1642 of
over £1,000 a year; the comfortably well-to-do, with between £500
and £1,000; and those of lower income, with less than £500 a year.
Pre-war income, it should be stressed, is the criterion; men whose
fortunes were altered by the war will be considered in due time.[79]
A fairly confident estimate of income is sometimes possible even
without positive evidence. Benjamin Valentine left no record of his,
but was obviously a poor man, dependent on Parliament's handouts.[80] Even when we have reasonable evidence, it is sometimes
difficult to know how to divide income between a father and a son.
In a few cases we know what the son was getting: John Pelham, for
example, had an allowance of £600 a year from his father Sir
Thomas in 1648, though he generally spent it several months
ahead.[81] Sir John Burgoyne had settled property on his son when
Sir Roger married in 1642, though the young man still complained
five years later that his average annual income since the settlement
had been less than £200.[82] But there are other cases of settlements,
such as that of Walter Yonge and his son Sir John, which are not so
clear, and yet others, such as that of Sir Dudley North, in which
a son with a substantial income of his own was still required to contribute to his father's household expenses.[83] To escape from these
difficulties, eldest sons who could expect to inherit are regarded as

[79] The goldsmith Francis Allen, for example, was obviously very rich by the end of the
Civil War, but it is impossible to determine how much of his wealth was acquired during
the war: he and other similar cases are therefore excluded from the statistics. Estimates of
pre-war income only have been used, except for a few cases in which later estimates exist
and it appears probable that the owners' estates did not alter significantly in value during
the troubles.

[80] Valentine was voted £5,000 for his sufferings with Eliot in and after 1629, but had
received only half of this when he died; lands worth £300 a year were then settled on his son:
*C.J.* v. 56; vii. 172. In 1644 he was granted £100 to relieve his poverty: ibid. iii. 656. During
the war Parliament granted weekly stipends to many members as compensation for loss of
income. The grants were usually of £4 per week, more in a few cases. Valentine got only £3
per week, presumably a reflection of his modest circumstances: Bodl. MS. Dep. C. 166
(Nalson Papers, xiv), fol. 223. John Fry is another whose obvious lack of means makes it
possible to put him into the under-£500-a-year category without direct evidence of his
income. His family's property in 1660 was no more than three small farms: *Somerset and
Dorset N. & Q.* iv (1875), 208.

[81] B.M. Add. MS. 33145 (Pelham MSS.), fol. 207ᵛ et seq.

[82] Keeler, *Long Parliament*, pp. 122-3; J. W. Ryland, *Records of Wroxhall Abbey* (London,
1903), Intro., pp. xxxvii-xxxviii, and pp. 128-9, 191; Sir R. Burgoyne to Sir R. Verney,
1 July 1647, 8 Nov. 1648; Verney to Burgoyne, 3/13 Dec. 1648: Verney MSS., B.M. Film
636, 7, 9. Keeler is wrong in saying that Sir Roger was unmarried during the Long Parliament. By 1647 he had four children.

[83] Keeler, *Long Parliament*, pp. 286, 404; *D.N.B.* ('Dudley, fourth Baron North').

possessing the income in reversion, and have been arbitrarily awarded the same incomes as their fathers.

Estimates of income, of the level of approximation here permitted, are available for rather less than three-quarters of the M.P.s.[84] The men for whom no estimates are possible were presumably for the most part of middle or lower income, but there is no reason to suppose that their absence seriously distorts the statistics, except perhaps to cause a slight exaggeration of the wealth of the As, who are somewhat under-represented. With this reservation, the income figures suggest much the same conclusions as those of status: there is a distinct correlation between income and political behaviour when a large enough group is being studied, even though there may not necessarily be for any single individual. There is, first of all, a clear upward gradient (apart from a slight surplus of As) in the percentages of the rich to the known members of each group as we travel in a conservative direction from the Rs to the Is. They make up only a quarter of the known Rs, more than two-fifths of the Cs, more than half the As, Ss, and Is. For those with incomes of less than £500 a year, the gradient is reversed. Almost half the Rs whose incomes are known were comparatively poor men, and the proportion of poor men in each group falls off steadily to less than a fifth of the Is. To put it another way, less than a tenth of the rich men were Rs, compared with twice as high a proportion of the moderately wealthy, and almost a quarter of the poorer men.

Income, however, does not tell the whole story. A man might have a large income, and yet be disastrously encumbered with debts; if so, he might be tempted to try to recover his fortunes in a revolution. It was not unknown for men to enter Parliament to protect themselves from creditors: 'Many got shelter in the House . . . against their debts', Lucy Hutchinson observes.[85] Samuel Terrick (S) was one such case; eventually, in 1658, he went spectacularly bankrupt. James Temple (R) and Sir Thomas Walsingham (C) were both arrested for debt before many years passed, while that classic bankrupt, Sir Peter Temple (A), was rumoured to have gone into hiding during his abstention from the Commons in 1649. Not long before he had assaulted a corn chandler who came with a bill, telling him that 'he was a rogue to ask money of a

84 Below, App. B, Table XI.
85 *Hutchinson*, p. 256.

Parliament-man'.[86] At first sight, the Rs seem to contain a rather large number of men who were in serious trouble, even if not quite bankrupt. Among them were Sir William Constable; Sir John Bourchier, who had suffered badly at the hands of the Court of Wards, had been heavily fined by Wentworth for inclosure, and was still claiming £6,000 compensation in 1651; and the notorious Henry Marten. True, the worst of Marten's debts were the result of his wartime losses and contributions, but it is also true that he inherited some very large debts from his father.[87] There are, to be sure, plenty of debtors in the other groups. In 1639 Sir Thomas Jervoise (C) was having to hide from his creditors, while a few years earlier Sir Poynings More (S) fled abroad to escape his debts. Alexander Popham (C) had a large income—almost £3,000 in 1650 from his Hunstrete estates alone—but he and his brother Edward had incurred debts to the tune of £38,000 on the death of an older brother.[88] The problem is of course complicated by the war. Many was the landowner who, like Sir Neville Poole (S), had to sell property 'by reason of debts, etc. heightened in the recent unhappy troubles'.[89] But a member had a better chance of being

---

[86] For Terrick see John Terrick to Brereton, 3 [Nov.] 1645: B.M. Add. MS. 11332 (Brereton Letter-book, 1645), fols. 44ᵛ, 50ᵛ—the letter contains several direct admissions of his son's need to seek election to escape his creditors. Also S. Charlton and E. Gower to Sir R. Leveson, 3 and 29 June 1658: H.M.C., *Fifth Report*, Appendix (Sutherland MSS.), pp. 167, 199. For James Temple see *C.J.* v. 572, 649; vi. 574; vii. 249–61. Also H.M.C., *Seventh Report*, Appendix (House of Lords MSS.), p. 27; and *D.N.B.* ('James Temple'). For Walsingham, *C.J.* vii. 273–4; and Everitt, *Community of Kent*, pp. 28, 45, 117, 181, 310. For Sir Peter Temple see Dr. Denton to Sir R. Verney, 26 Apr. 1649: Verney MSS., B.M. Film 636, 9. Also Wilbee, *Comparatis Comparandis*, Pt. 2 ([B.M.] E. 413, 1), p. 36; and *C.J.* vi. 219. For the whole family and their debts see the articles by E. F. Gay in *H.L.Q.* i (1937–8), 367–90; ii (1938–9), 391–425; vi (1942–3), 258–9.

[87] Constable was selling extensively in the 1630s. His income in 1642 was £1,500 a year, but his debts were enough to justify Fairfax's subsequent description of his 'now narrowed fortune': *D.N.B.* ('Constable'); Sir Charles Firth and Godfrey Davies, *Regimental History of Cromwell's Army* (Oxford, 1940), p. 400; Cliffe, *Yorkshire Gentry*, pp. 123, 280, 351, 353. I am indebted to Dr. Cliffe for information about Constable's finances, and those of other Yorkshire members. For Bourchier see *D.N.B.* ('Bourchier'); Cliffe, *Yorkshire Gentry*, pp. 302–3, 350; Yule, *The Independents*, p. 90; *V.C.H.*, *Yorks.*, *N. Riding*, ii. 160; and *C.J.* vi. 612–13. Marten's finances are discussed with admirable judgement by C. M. Williams, 'Political Career of Henry Marten' (Oxford D.Phil. thesis, 1954), ch. ix.

[88] Keeler, *Long Parliament*, pp. 237, 278, 310. For further light on More's finances see Folger Library, Washington, MS. Lb. 702 (Loseley MSS.). The total received by Popham's receiver at Hunstrete for the year ending July 1650 was £4,042, but this included £1,123 from the sale of land to Richard Aldworth of Bristol. 'Hunstrete Audit', 1649–50: Somerset R.O., Popham MS. DD/PO/32.

[89] W. B. Crouch, 'Parliamentary History', in T. R. Thomson, ed., *Materials for a History of Cricklade*, rev. edn. (Oxford, 1961), p. 146. See also Keeler, *Long Parliament*, pp. 309–10.

compensated for wartime losses, and cases of indebtedness caused primarily by the war ought more properly to be left for later discussion.

In tabulating the pre-war debtors, no effort has been made to distinguish between cases of really disastrous and of merely serious debt.[90] The first category includes only families who, like the Temples, appear to have been on the brink of ruin. The second category includes those like the Pophams who had suffered but were in no danger of complete collapse. Even granted the small numbers involved, and the limitations of the evidence, it is clear that of all the groups the Rs were indeed the most embarrassed. Out of fourteen very rich Rs, five were in serious or disastrous trouble before the war. Five of the twenty-seven rich Cs had also been in trouble, against only three As, and only one S of similar wealth. The cumulative impression of the Rs as men who, far more than their enemies, tended to be of lower rank, lower incomes, and more unstable fortunes, becomes ever clearer.

It becomes clearer still when we look at other possible sources of financial motivation. Besides poverty or debt, many material considerations might lead an M.P. to throw in his lot with the revolution. He might have large claims on the state, which would be less likely to be repaid if he went into the political wilderness. Even in 1648, many members had still not received all the arrears of pay or other sums due to them for war services. Many held public faith bills for loans to the State. Some had submitted, or were about to submit, requests for compensation for loss of office or damage to their estates during the wars; not quite the same thing as public debts, but still putting them in a similar category to that of the State's creditors, for both wanted to be repaid out of public funds. It is not always clear whether an earlier claim was still outstanding in whole or in part in 1648. Parliament often made votes of money, but they were not always promptly paid. Still, members who were not getting their money were quick to protest about it, so the absence of complaint can usually be taken as indicating that they were satisfied.[91] All outstanding claims, together with a few special

[90] Below, App. B, Table XII.

[91] Sir Richard Darley, father of the M.P.s Henry and Richard, was voted £5,000 for his losses in Sept. 1648: *C.J.* v. 693; *L.J.* x. 493. He obviously could not have collected all this by December, but there is no sign of any later protest by the Darleys, so this case had been regarded as closed by the time of the Purge, and their claim is omitted from the Table. Purefoy was still collecting from an earlier grant in 1649, but he got another vote of £1,000

R

cases of members demanding other forms of compensation for their
services, have been tabulated after being translated (sometimes
approximately) into monetary terms.[92]

It is arguable, and indeed likely, that the statistics under-estimate
the claims of the A, S, and I groups. Apart from the minority who
returned to the Rump they were out of favour after 1648, and their
petitions were more likely to disappear, if they were indeed presented, before being recorded by the Commons or one of the great
committees. On the other hand, as a disgruntled member of the
Committee of Accounts complained, 'if a Parliament-man, a grand
officer, or a kinsman had anything to pass, it was . . . put on with all
vigour'.[93] Yet even if some allowance is made for this, it is still
obvious that the Rs and Cs both included a high proportion of men
who were creditors of the State, or had other claims which could
only be satisfied by the action of Parliament. Many members of all
groups had subscribed as Adventurers for Ireland in 1642, but so
many, and usually in such relatively small amounts, that it seems
appropriate to separate them from members with other claims.[94]
The statistics show very clearly that the Rs were more likely than
any other group to obtain financial benefit from the revolution,
almost half of them having claims other than in Ireland—in the case
of two-fifths, very large ones. Almost a third of the Is had similar
claims: like the Rs, most of them were men who had been very active
and had dipped deep into their pockets during the war. Their

in September for his losses. Only the latter grant has been counted as involving an outstanding claim: *C.J.* v. 8; vi. 294; *Cal. C. Comp.*, pp. 51, 1316. On the other hand there are
many cases of earlier grants which had certainly not been fully paid by 1649. Sir William
Lister still had £500 owing in Apr. 1649, Constable £1,750 in Jan. 1650, both from grants
made long before the Purge: *C.J.* v. 108; vi. 343; *L.J.* viii. 306; ix. 95; Firth and Rait,
*A. and O.* ii. 100.

[92] Below, App. B, Table XIII. The special cases include that of Sir John Danvers, who
had ruined himself by his architectural and horticultural extravagance. In 1648–9 he was
trying to recover his fortunes by overthrowing the will of his royalist brother, the Earl of
Danby, who had left all his property to a sister, Lady Gargrave. As Sir John's case rested
largely on his service to Parliament, it seems reasonable to regard this claim as being of the
same nature as a State debt. O. L. Dick, ed., *Aubrey's Brief Lives* (London, 1949), p. 81;
*C.J.* iv. 403; vi. 232, 304; H.M.C., *Sixth Report*, Appendix (House of Lords MSS.), pp. 93,
113; *Cal. C. Comp.*, p. 1638. For more on Danvers's debts see *Cal. of Comm. for Advance of
Money*, pp. 459–65; and J. J. Slade, 'The Yorkshire Estates of the Danvers of Dauntsey',
*Wilts. Arch. & Nat. Hist. Magazine*, l (1942–4), 214–18.

[93] John Ufflet, *A Caution to the Parliament, Councel of State, and Army* (25 Aug. 1653:
[B.M.] E. 712, 6), p. 4.

[94] Subscriptions of Irish Adventurers are taken from J. R. MacCormack, 'The Irish
Adventurers and the English Civil War', *Irish Historical Studies*, x (1956–7), 21–58.

chances of being paid were rather slim, even if they escaped the
hostile examination of their finances which was to be the fate of
Clotworthy and Copley. Major-General Browne, for example, not
only stayed in prison, but also suffered the cancellation of the
State's debt of £9,000 to him in September 1650.[95] But apart from
the Is, as might be expected, the enemies of the revolution had less
to gain or lose. Fewer than a sixth of the S group had claims outside of Ireland, and little more than a tenth had large ones. The Cs,
on the other hand, included in their number over a quarter with
non-Irish claims, many of them, for example those of the two
heavily indebted Hampshire gentlemen, Jervoise and Wallop, very
large ones indeed.[96]

This does not prove that the Rs and Cs were motivated solely by
hopes of recovering public debts. Alexander Popham, who could
claim over £5,000, may have had financial motives for supporting
the Rump. But it would be absurd to put Edmund Ludlow, who was
obviously ideologically committed, in the same company, even
though he had over £2,000 arrears owing him, and the chance of
getting confirmation of his ownership of the £1,200 worth of buried
treasure which he had unearthed at Wardour Castle after the siege.[97]
The members of the S and I groups with claims against the State
obviously put principle above profit. Some of them doubtless had
no alternative. It would have been unthinkable for Browne or Sir
Robert Harley (who was liable for £6,000 in debts of the Herefordshire Committee) to have made spectacular recantations. Yet a less
prominent man like Henry Peck, who claimed over £4,000 for
losses to his Forest of Dean ironworks, might more easily have come
to terms.[98] He did not do so, and there is no reason to suppose
that some of the Rs were any less principled. Indeed, the large
sums owing to many of the Is suggest that the statistics tell us as
much about the proportions of the groups active in the Civil War
as they do about the motives of the men in 1648 and 1649. The
charges of greed and self-interest cannot be dismissed entirely,
but they ought to be assessed individually, a task beyond the reach
of quantification. Much would depend on the size of the debt
compared with the man's total wealth. Arrears of £779 would

[95] C.J. vi. 462.
[96] Cal. C. Comp., pp. 348, 439, 479, 542, 2372, 2533, 2631; Cal. of Comm. for Advance
of Money, pp. 461–3; C.J. vi. 290, 296; vii. 177, 182, 190.
[97] C.J. vi. 196, 508–9; MacCormack, Irish Hist. Studies, x. 54.
[98] Firth and Rait, A. and O. ii. 101; C.J. v. 484; vi. 78–9, 102; L.J. x. 557, 594.

be insignificant for the very rich Sir Richard Hoghton, whereas
losses of £300 might be crucial for the Cambridge chandler John
Lowry.[99]

The question of State debts is closely related to that of the
purchase of confiscated lands. The sales of Church lands in progress since 1647, and those of Crown and royalist lands which
followed the revolution, were largely necessitated by the great
volume of debt which Parliament had no other way of paying off.
Except in the case of the fee-farm rents, payment was by doubled
bills or debentures; only small balances were paid in cash. Purchasers of confiscated lands were in fact creditors collecting debts
on terms, none too favourable to them, set by the government.[100]
It would therefore be rash to assume that purchase implies a particular political stance on the part of the buyer. It might, to be sure,
as people at the time were well aware. Edmund Harvey observed
in August 1648 that the most backward London citizens 'were such
of the Presbyterian party as have no engagement upon Bishops'
lands'. Harvey should have known; his own purchases at Fulham
turned him, says Clement Walker, 'from a furious Presbyter to
a Bedlam Independent'. When Lord Paget bought £6,000 worth
of fee-farm rents in 1650, Lord Lisle concluded that 'his Lordship
is made a good Commonwealthsman'.[101] If there was a connection
between purchase and politics, it was likely to be a two-way process.
A creditor might buy because he expected, and wanted, the new
regime to survive, preferring to collect his debt in lands rather than
gamble on the return of the King, which in effect was what the
creditor who refused to purchase was doing. But once having
bought, the purchaser had a stake in the regime's survival, and would
be more inclined to support it. Reluctance to purchase might also
imply the belief in certain political values, a rejection of any infringe-
ment of the rights of property. D'Ewes felt from the first that they
would 'live to repent' the day when Parliament began to debate 'the

[99] Firth and Rait, *A. and O.* ii. 100; *C.J.* vi. 263; Cromwell to Speaker, 10 July 1649:
Abbott, *Cromwell*, ii. 91. Hoghton was very rich. His father had been worth almost £3,000
a year in 1632, and the estate still brought in nearly £2,000 a year after the Restoration, in
spite of war damage and the father's composition: J. H. Lumby, ed., *Cal. of the Deeds and
Papers in the Possession of Sir James de Hoghton, Bart.* (Record Soc., Lancs. and Cheshire,
lxxxviii, 1936), pp. 18, 20.

[100] H. J. Habakkuk, 'Public Finance and the Sale of Confiscated Property during the
Interregnum', *Econ. H.R.* 2nd Ser. xv (1962-3); see esp. pp. 73, 75, 82-3, and Table I, p. 87.

[101] *Merc. Prag.*, no. 22 (22-9 Aug. 1648 [B.M.] E. 461, 17); Walker, *Independency*, ii. 13;
Lisle to Leicester, 3 Aug. 1650: H.M.C., *De L'Isle*, vi. 482.

fatal ordinance for selling men's estates'.[102] But the fact that most sales merely involved the cancellation of old debt makes it impossible to infer that the purchasers were necessarily supporters of the revolution. All that can be said is that they were men who were owed money by the State.

The subject, however, is still worth investigating. An M.P. might buy confiscated land because he could see no other way of recovering his debts. But the purchase might still be a profitable transaction, adding immensely to his income. Not all the doubled bills and debentures that paid for the purchases were offered by their original owners. Clement Walker accuses several members, including Sir Gregory Norton and his special enemy Humphrey Edwards, of speculating in debentures, using their privileged positions to buy them at more than the usual discount, and then using them to pay for their lands. William Heveningham was certainly engaged in a transaction of this kind in 1651.[103] Complaints that members abused their positions to get land at bargain prices are too common to be disregarded. A 1653 pamphlet describes how M.P.s were allowed to jump the queue at Gurney Hall, often using 'friends at table' to get such favourable contracts that they could 'pay for the manor out of the mansion-house or the woods'.[104] Several Rumpers who made large purchases, including Garland and Haselrig, were members of the Committee for Removing Obstructions or other committees that would have given them profitable inside information about the sales.

There are some difficulties about discovering the names of the real purchasers in some of the sales, and this may lead to an underestimate of the extent to which members of the S and I groups were purchasers. Yet with this reservation, it is still clear that the Rs and Cs were much more likely to be purchasers than members of the other groups.[105] Almost two-thirds of the Rs and well over half the

---

[102] B.M. Harl. MS. 166 (D'Ewes Journal, 1644-5), fol. 255ᵛ.

[103] Walker, *Independency*, ii. 207-8; Heveningham to John Hobart, 21 Jan. 1650/1: Bodl. MS., Tanner 56, fol. 249.

[104] [John Hall], *A Letter written To a Gentleman in the Country, touching the Dissolution of the late Parliament* (3 May 1653: [B.M.] E. 697, 2), p. 7.

[105] Below, App. B, Table XIV. Printed lists of purchases, e.g. in *Collectanea Topographica et Genealogica*, i (1834), and the notices of discharge from sequestration issued by the Committee for Compounding, give the original purchaser, who in many cases was only an agent: Joan Thirsk, 'The Sales of Royalist Land during the Interregnum', *Econ. H.R.* 2nd Ser. v (1952-3), 190-1. If some M.P.s bought through agents, others in effect *were* agents. Some were Army officers buying for their regiments, others trustees for payment of the debts of

Cs bought lands, against only a fifth of the As and just over a tenth of the Ss and Is. Once again, these differences partly reflect the fact that a larger proportion of the R and C groups had been strongly committed to the cause during the war, and were now recovering their debts. Still, the statistics on land purchase confirm the earlier ones: the Rs had more to gain than the other groups by staying in power. The extent to which members of the different groups bought Church lands is interesting. Crown and royalist lands came on the market only after the revolution, when its victims had less opportunity as well as perhaps less desire to take advantage of them. The sales of Church lands were already in full swing before the Purge, yet even so, few indeed of the S or I members made any effort to acquire them. Some who did, then or later, were religious Presbyterians, for whom profit and principle coincided: John Birch is a conspicuous example.[106] There were a few other opponents of the revolution who also made extensive purchases: Thomas Hussey (A), obviously a new man on the make, was one of them.[107]

The Rs and Cs were not the only members to be influenced by material considerations. Not all even of them were, yet more must have been than in any of the other groups. The point is further reinforced by a consideration of the vexed subject of office-holding. The relationship of place to politics is as complicated as other aspects of human behaviour. Human beings rarely move absolutely predictably according to their immediate self-interest.[108] The place-man, like anyone else, might be affected by a number of conflicting

local committees, e.g. William Heveningham's purchase, 1 June 1650: *Coll. Top. et Gen.* i. 290. See Thos. Atkin to Mayor of Norwich, 28 Feb. 1649/50: B.M. Add. MS. 22620 (Collections re Norwich), fol. 127. Purchases of this type have been excluded from the Table. On the other hand, those involving men apparently buying the lands of royalist relatives as trustees have been included, as there is no reliable way of distinguishing them from other purchasers. Careful search of the Close Rolls, in which all conveyances are recorded, would of course resolve many of these problems. The author's remoteness from London has prevented him from undertaking so formidable a task. Thus although some of the 'concealed' purchases have been identified in the Table, I make no claim that these figures are anything more than provisional, and subject to correction.

[106] For Birch's purchases see Webb, ed., *Military Memoir of Col. Birch*, pp. 153–5; and John and T. W. Webb, *Memorials of the Civil War . . . as it affected Herefordshire and the adjacent counties* (London, 1879), ii. 310. Some additional Birch purchases not noted by Webb are recorded in Bodl. MS. Rawl. B. 239 (Register of Sales of Bishops' Lands), pp. 55–8. This MS. has additional entries not given in *Coll. Top. et Gen.* i, which is printed from a copy of the register with no entries after 19 Mar. 1651/2.

[107] *V.C.H., Hampshire*, iii. 305, 334, 340, 349; iv. 213. Hussey, to be sure, adhered to the Rump in June 1649.

[108] For an excellent discussion of place and politics see Aylmer, *King's Servants*, ch. vi.

motives—the subtle influences of background and education, the explicit ones of politics and religion, the practical ones of loyalty to a patron or a constituency. But there is no doubt that in 1648 as at other times, men valued their places, and that many M.P.s who did not possess an office would have been glad to get one. When Sir Walter Erle (I) was removed from his post as Lieutenant of the Ordnance in January 1649, the place was immediately 'snapped at', Whitelocke records, with his usual interest in the game he played so well. When in October John Lisle was thought to be on his death-bed, gossip was already appointing a new Commissioner of the Great Seal while it awaited further medical bulletins. And when the Earl of Pembroke died early in 1650 there was an ugly rush for his numerous places. The Earl of Leicester wanted his son, Lord Lisle, to secure one of them. Lisle was not enthusiastic. 'It cannot be obtained without making of friends, which is a high price', he told his father, 'much more, in my opinion, than it is worth.' Lisle had never asked for any place or gift, he added later, and if he was going to start now it was absurd to 'begin with a thing of so little value'.[109]

The table of office-holders assimilates placemen of many different kinds: professional bureaucrats like Humphrey Salway and Richard Edwards, legal dignitaries like Whitelocke and Widdrington, military men, politicians who had climbed into office to add to their income, like the two York members, Allanson and Hoyle; and country gentlemen such as Sir John Curzon, for whom office was probably only of marginal importance.[110] There were also members who were not placemen themselves but had close relatives who were, and might have been affected by this. Denis Bond, for example, was said to have got offices for a dozen of his kinsmen, while Thomas Toll in 1648 was busy protecting his son's claim to a customs post at King's Lynn.[111] But to include them would open

[109] Whitelocke, *Memorials*, ii. 498; Lisle to Leicester, 11 Oct. 1649, 1 Feb. 1649/50, 26 and 30 Mar. 1650: H.M.C., *De L'Isle*, vi. 461, 472, 477; Collins, *Sydney Papers*, ii. 678.

[110] Below, App. B, Table XV. There are as usual some technical problems. Military governorships were often honorary posts, but some were clearly places of profit, like those held by James Temple at Tilbury and Haselrig at Newcastle; only the latter kind are included. Some M.P.s had been compensated for loss of earlier office, but cannot be regarded as office-holders in 1648: Charles Fleetwood, Nathaniel Bacon, and Rudyard, for example. Fleetwood, however, is included as a soldier, and Bacon gets into the second part of the Table through his appointment as an Admiralty judge in Aug. 1649.

[111] *Mystery of the Good Old Cause*, pp. 11, 43; *Merc. Prag.*, no. 23 (29 Aug.–5 Sept. 1648: [B.M.] E. 462, 8); *C.J.* vi. 54; *L.J.* x. 521, 542, 600; H.M.C., *Seventh Report*, Appendix (House of Lords MSS.), p. 64.

up an infinite vista of problems, and the best procedure is to limit ourselves to those who themselves held offices of profit, and in the first instance to those in office in December 1648.

As usual, the statistics only partly confirm previous hypotheses. The common Royalist-Presbyterian argument that the Rs and Cs were a gang of ruthless adventurers, feathering their nests behind a smokescreen of ideology, is not refuted, but neither is it completely confirmed. True, the proportion of placemen is distinctly higher in the R and C groups than the others, but even so it amounts to only just over a quarter of the Cs, and not much more of the Rs. Many office-holders were no doubt influenced by their desire to stay in power: well over half of them were either Rs or Cs, less than a third Ss or Is. Not all even of the office-holding Is lost their posts: Sir Robert Pye and William Wheeler were still comfortably ensconced in the Exchequer more than three years after the Purge.[112] However, dismissal was at least a probable consequence of opposition, and in fact half the placemen in the I group and almost half of those in the S group were removed within a year or two. The prospect did not deter men like Sir Robert Harley and Clement Walker, and Harley duly lost his Mastership of the Mint, Walker his post in the Exchequer. If office was a strong motive for some of the Rs—Blagrave and Holland, for example—so it was for some of the Cs, whom Whitelocke typifies so well. Yet the C was no more likely than the R to be an office-holder, which again should make us pause before we ascribe self-seeking motives to all of them. It is also worth noting that almost half of the As who had held places in 1648 afterwards entered the Rump, but that even so, the proportion of 1648 office-holders among the Rump's later adherents is no higher than among the early ones.

Some slightly different results are obtained if we tabulate all office-holders during the years 1649–53, those who acquired posts after the coup as well as those already in possession. The man who obtained office later can be regarded as at least a potential placeman in 1648. A fair number of Rumpers who had not previously held places were rewarded after the Purge: Humphrey Edwards, for example, got Clement Walker's job. By 1653 the proportion of office-holders in the Rump was consequently much higher, a fact of some importance when the allegations of corruption and self-seeking

---

[112] R. J. Fletcher, ed., *Pension Book of Gray's Inn* (London, 1901-10), i. 390. And see above, p. 50.

levelled against the Rumpers in later years are remembered. But as with the pre-war Caroline bureaucrats, gain, retention, or loss of office were as likely to be the results of political allegiance as the cause. Just as there were actual placemen who lost their jobs, so there were potential placemen who were secluded and made no effort to win their way to favour by later conformity. Thomas Povey (S) already had all the attributes of the placeman he became under the Protectorate as Martin Noel's henchman and secretary to the Council for the West Indies. Such a man might have been tempted to repudiate his past and recover his declining fortunes. But Povey was a man of strong conservatism, author of a neutralist pamphlet in earlier days, and his opinions counted for more than his hopes of advancement.[113] The desire for power, profit, and place was certainly stronger among the Rs than in any other group: the conclusion is inescapable. But no more than the other members were the Rs totally inspired by self-interest.

\*       \*       \*

The statistics have spoken. They have not worked miracles; they have not answered unanswerable questions. They have shown that there were indeed significant differences between the purgers and the purged in some respects, but in others only marginal ones. They have not shown that the revolution was *essentially* about either politics or religion; or that it was essentially either a class struggle or a mere *coup d'état* by a crowd of backwoods outsiders trying to get in. They do perhaps suggest that it was a mixture of all of these things. But final conclusions about its meaning ought to be deferred until we have observed the revolution's further consequences both in Parliament and outside. When the time comes, we can relate what the statistics tell us about the M.P.s to the other evidence. To make this easier, let us end the chapter by constructing brief profiles of the 'typical' members of each parliamentary group.[114]

---

[113] The son of an Auditor of the Exchequer, Povey was the chief support of several brothers and other members of what he described as his 'broken family'. The outlook of the professional office-holder is evident in his Letter-book: B.M. Add. MS. 11411. His earlier pamphlet was *The Moderator, expecting Sudden Peace, or Certaine Ruine* (16 Feb. 1642/3: [B.M.] E. 89, 21). The conservative tone of the pamphlet is echoed in several asides in the Letter-book. See esp. fol. 91ᵛ.

[114] Some of the characteristics suggested by the statistics have been put into sharper focus in the profiles.

The typical R was a married man in his mid forties. He had prob-ably inherited an estate, but was quite possibly a younger son. He had gone to one of the Inns of Court, most likely Gray's Inn, and was less likely to have attended a university. He may possibly have come from the north-east of England. He had no previous parlia-mentary experience, entered the Long Parliament in a by-election after August 1645, and attached himself to the radical wing of the Independents; he joined the Speakers in seceding to the Army at the end of July 1647. In religion he probably, but not necessarily, tended to Independency. Of county gentry status, he came of a rather insecure family, and was probably not a rich man, having a pre-war income of less than £500 a year; if richer he may well have been in serious debt. He was likely to have large financial claims against the State, and to recover some of these debts in the form of Church, royalist or Crown lands, in that order of pre-ference. He may have been an office-holder, and if not was quite likely to become one after the revolution.

The typical C was also a married man, and also in his mid forties. He too had inherited an estate. He was educated at Oxford or at an Inn; if the latter probably Middle Temple or Gray's, and may well have been a lawyer by profession. He came from either the south-east or the south-west. He too had not previously been an M.P., but had been elected to the Long Parliament in 1640, tended to support the war party and later the radical Independents, and pos-sibly seceded to the Army in 1647. He was probably a religious Presbyterian. Of lesser gentry status, his family was likely to be either relatively new or declining, but with the help of his income from the law and perhaps from office he was tolerably rich, with an income of over £1,000 a year. Like his R colleague, he probably had claims against the State, but not such large ones, and they may have been confined to his subscription as an Irish Adventurer. If they amounted to more than this, he probably bought con-fiscated lands, more likely Church or royalist lands than Crown property. He too may have been a placeman or have been about to become one.

The typical A was younger, possibly in his thirties, but also married and with an inherited estate. He may have gone to either Oxford or Cambridge or an Inn, and if the latter would have pre-ferred Lincoln's or Gray's Inn; he was, however, most unlikely to be a professional lawyer. He too came either from the south-east or the western counties. Like the R, he was a Recruiter with no previous parliamentary experience, and if he showed any political consistency in the Long Parliament it was as a supporter of the middle group; he may possibly, like so many of that group, have seceded to the Army in 1647. In religion he was Presbyterian, with only a slight tendency towards Independency. Of greater gentry status, but possibly rather insecure family, he was a rich man, with an income of over £1,000 a year. He was not likely to have claims against the State, and consequently did not acquire confiscated lands. Nor was he an office-holder in 1648, though he had a slight chance of becoming one by 1653.

The typical S was a married man in his mid-forties, and had probably inherited an estate, though he might possibly be the heir to one with a father still living. He had gone to Oxford or an Inn of Court, preferring Lincoln's Inn or Middle Temple before the others. He too came either from the south-east or the south-west. Another Recruiter without previous experience in Parliament, he may have been under suspicion of having flirted with the Royalists, and if he adopted a recognizable political stance in the Long Parliament it was as a Presbyterian; he probably stayed at Westminster during the Speaker's absence in July and August 1647. His religious views were outwardly Presbyterian, though secretly he may have preferred moderate episcopacy. Of greater gentry status, stable family, and large income (over £1,000 a year), he had no claims against the State, was therefore very unlikely to have bought or to be contemplating buying confiscated lands, and was not an office-holder. He was in fact a very solid and representative country gentleman.

The typical I was older, nearly fifty, probably married, and with an inherited estate. He had been educated at both Oxford and an Inn, most likely Middle Temple, and came from either the south-east or the Midlands. A man of experience, he was an original member of the Long Parliament, who may well have sat in the Short Parliament and even in those of the 1620s. During the war he had been attached to either the peace party or the middle group, and was more probably Presbyterian (though still just possibly middle group) between 1645 and 1648. Even if not one of the Eleven Members or their immediate supporters, he had stayed at Westminster in July and August 1647. Like his S colleague, he was a Presbyterian in religion, perhaps at heart preferring moderate episcopacy. One of the county gentry, of possibly insecure family, he was nevertheless a rich man, with an income of over £1,000 a year. He was likely to have claims against the State, possibly large ones, but did not recover these debts in the form of confiscated lands. He may have been an office-holder in 1648, but if so probably lost his place after the Purge.

# Part Three · Epilogue

## IX

### THE RUMP

THE ambiguities of the revolution of 1648-9 determined the ambiguities of the Rump. The disappointment of idealistic expectations, it has already been remarked, is a common feature of revolutions. We all know what happened to the high hopes of 1789, of 1917, of a dozen other revolutions. But most of these later upheavals accomplished at least some of their initial aims: in none is the gap between ideals and performance as striking as in the England of 1649. In France the revolution decelerated into stagnation after a dramatic *coup d'état*, when the cold draught of Thermidor extinguished the passionate reformist violence of the Convention. But the English Commonwealth never approached the fervour of the Convention. The Rump silently and imperceptibly achieved its own Thermidor.

Yet we have seen that there was plenty of revolutionary rhetoric at the outset, encouraging the confident expectation of the militant minority that the day of justice and freedom, the completion of Godly Reformation, was about to dawn. 'The powers of this world shall be given into the hands of the Lord and his Saints', Thomas Harrison exulted. '. . . This is the day, God's own day, wherein he is coming forth in glory in the world.'[1] All around him stood men uplifted by the conviction that the Lord was with them. 'We have seen God', George Wither proclaimed after the miraculous victory of Rathmines in the summer of 1649, 'On the Heights, and in the Deep/We have seen thy steps O God.'[2]

[1] Woodhouse, *Puritanism and Liberty*, p. 178.
[2] Wither, *Carmen Eucharisticon* (1649), quoted in C. V. Wedgwood, *Poetry and Politics under the Stuarts* (Cambridge, 1960), p. 115.

But the Lord's work was not being done for the benefit of the godly party alone. 'What we seek is not for ourselves, but for all men', Harrison told the Army Council. All Europe was in turmoil, and the English militants sensed wild, exciting opportunities. The Civil War had once been seen as the first stage of a great religious crusade: the Scottish general Leslie wanted to march on to Paris and burn Rome itself after they had won the war in Britain. Now it became something else, a crusade against monarchy in the name of the sovereignty of the people. The idealism of reformers like Samuel Hartlib, who aimed at 'the reformation of the whole world', was replaced by a strident republicanism. 'This Army', proclaimed Hugh Peter, 'must root up monarchy, not only here but in France and other kingdoms round about.' After England they must liberate French Huguenots, German peasants: 'Monarchy must down all the world over.' Even in 1649 there were stories of agents in France, 'who under colour of merchandise, vent antimonarchical and anarchical tenets, and sow seeds of popular liberty'. Andrew Marvell, a man of sensible moderation, could see Cromwell as the architect of European liberation: 'A Caesar he ere long to Gaul,/To Italy an Hannibal,/And to all states not free/Shall climacteric be.' And even so phlegmatic a soul as Admiral Robert Blake was carried away by the enthusiasm. In 1651 he sailed into Cadiz, and in the main square proclaimed the imminent end of tyranny, the forthcoming destruction of monarchy throughout all Europe.[3]

The doctrine of world revolution was not the only sign that men felt themselves to be at the dawn of a new day. There was the characteristic revolutionary contempt for custom and tradition. All things would be reformed by the clear light of natural reason. Hugh Peter wanted to burn the old records in the Tower as 'monuments of tyranny'.[4] The Puritans never went as far as the French in constructing a new calendar, but Henry Marten's 'In the first year of Freedom' was a beginning, later documents under the Great Seal showing that 1650 was the second year of freedom, 1651 the third, and so on.[5] And there was discussion of going on to more sweeping

[3] For all this see Hill, *Puritanism and Revolution*, pp. 123–32; Trevor-Roper, *Religion, the Reformation and Social Change*, pp. 332–3. Also Woodhouse, *Puritanism and Liberty*, p. 178; and Walker, *Independency*, ii. 149–50. The Marvell verse is from the 'Horatian Ode', lines 97–104.                [4] Hill, *Puritanism and Revolution*, pp. 77–8.

[5] This was, of course, a substitute for the old method of dating by regnal year. For an example see F. A. Inderwick, 'Rye Under the Commonwealth', *Sussex Archae. Collections*, xxxix (1894), 3.

calendar reform. The talk at Whitehall, Thomas Margetts noted in 1650, was of 'reformation of names of months and days, as that instead of January, February, etc., Sunday, Monday, etc., we shall only say the first, second, etc., month or day'.[6] Other relics of a superstitious past would be ruthlessly swept away. The law would be in English instead of Norman-French. Cathedrals, useless monuments of popery and episcopacy, would be demolished and the proceeds used for relief of the poor.[7] As in 1793 and 1794 there was a new interest in enlightened reform; in education, in humanitarian projects like hospitals and the treatment of sick and maimed soldiers as a national rather than a local problem. The Rump adopted the practice of sending the wounded to convalesce in the genteel luxury of Bath—to the disgust of the hotel lobby, which dominated the corporation, it might be noted.[8] The radical Puritan Samuel Chidley looked forward to the day when 'all trades should flourish, and no poor starve in the streets . . . no more people should be put to death for trifles, but their precious lives saved according to the word of God'.[9]

Out of the multiplicity of sects, out of the excited chorus of political debate, voices were heard calling for absolute freedom. The Diggers repudiated the tyranny of private property, the Ranters the restraints of conventional morality. Zionism, vegatarianism, a dozen other modern isms were in the air. The mad hatter of Chesham, Roger Crab, reached the irreducible dietary minimum of dock leaves and grass at about the time he gave away all his worldly goods to the poor. During a sermon by Peter Sterry in the austere surroundings of Whitehall chapel in 1652 a woman in the congregation stripped naked, with joyful cries of 'Welcome the Resurrection!' All things were possible, the world was to be made new, the reign of King Jesus was just round the corner.[10]

Yet the humanitarianism was peripheral, most of the militant language mere rhetoric, the exciting experiments confined to the furthest fringe of revolution. For those with more rational

---

[6] Margetts to W. Clarke, 12 Nov. 1650: H.M.C., *Leybourne-Popham*, pp. 77-8.

[7] Gardiner, *Commonwealth*, ii. 22-3.

[8] *C.J.* vii. 128; *Cal. S.P. Dom., 1651-2*, p. 600; *1652-3*, pp. 320-55; Whitelocke, *Memorials*, iii. 193; A. J. King and B. H. Watts, *Cavaliers and Roundheads: a chapter in the history of Bath* (Bath, 1887), p. 39.

[9] Chidley to Cromwell, 3 Feb. 1650/1: *Milton State Papers*, p. 58, quoted in Margaret James, *Social Problems and Policy during the Puritan Revolution* (London, 1930), p. 303.

[10] Hill, *Puritanism and Revolution*, pp. 141-2, 314-16; Gardiner, *Commonwealth*, ii. 95.

expectations the actual record of the Commonwealth was a grievous disappointment. The Levellers were without illusions from the start; Lilburne set the tone of their attack in *England's New Chains Discovered*.[11] It made no difference to him, a soldier facing court martial declared, whether he suffered under a king or under the 'Keepers of the Liberties of England'. Both stood for the same 'corrupt administrations in the law, treble damage for tithes, persecution for matter of conscience, and oppression of the poor'.[12] But even men with higher hopes were quickly disappointed. Robert Bennet, the Rump's ruler of Cornwall, was complaining as early as February 1650 about the 'loss of liberty amongst the poor people'. The government, he thought, was totally deaf to popular grievances, 'a sad omen . . . in these days of pretended reformation'. John Pyne, his counterpart in Somerset, agreed that the Rump had failed to advance 'the privileges and freedom of the people', and denounced such oppressions as 'the taking away the right of the poor in their commons'. Young Isaac Penington, son of the London alderman and M.P., first thought of the Commonwealth as a doctor, but soon discovered that 'most men are grown sick of both the physician and the cure'. Even Hugh Peter was in low spirits during the early months of the republic, though admittedly he had a personal tragedy to contend with, the mental disturbance of his wife.[13]

The Rump's leaders were worried and baffled by their unpopularity. Hoyle's sensational suicide was both a warning and a symptom of the tensions under which they lived. Many feared sharing the fate of their murdered diplomats abroad. At Rowland Wilson's funeral in March 1650 (another suicide, it was rumoured), there were demonstrations against Lord President Bradshawe, and the unfortunate Whitelocke, who had to walk with him in the procession, was frightened almost out of his wits. In the end he and Bradshawe slipped quietly away and got into the church privately.[14]

The morale of the republic was collapsing, dedication to Godly

[11] 26 Feb. 1648/9. Printed in Haller and Davies, *Leveller Tracts*, pp. 157-70.

[12] *The Hunting of the Foxes* (21 Mar. 1648/9), in *Somers Tracts*, vi. 55; also in D. M. Wolfe, ed., *Leveller Manifestoes of the Puritan Revolution* (New York, 1944), p. 376.

[13] Bennet to Sir H. Waller, 16 Feb. 1649/50: Folger Library, Washington, MS. Add. 494 (Bennet MSS.), p. 195; Case of John Pyne, 1660: H.M.C., *Ninth Report*, App. II (Pyne MSS.), p. 494; Isaac Penington, Jr., *A Word for the Common Weale* (15 Feb. 1649/50: [B.M.] E. 593, 10); *Winthrop Papers*, v. 319-20, 337, 357. Bennet added prophetically that the country needed 'a righteous lawgiver to rule in judgement'.

[14] B.M. Add. MS. 37345 (Whitelocke's Annals), fol. 54. The incident is omitted from the printed *Memorials*.

S

Reformation being replaced by corruption and self-seeking. Every-one knew of the scandalous conduct of Henry Marten and his like, though Gregory Clement was the only Rumper to be expelled for it. The ostentation of such men as Sir Arthur Haselrig was equally notorious. His magnificent coach became a standing joke, and by 1652 his page was going about in velvet livery, with 'silver sword and silver buckles upon his shoes, and silk stockings'. It was only half in jest that a visiting New Englander greeted Hugh Peter as 'Archbishop of Canterbury' after seeing the size of his retinue at Whitehall.[15] On 1 January 1649 the Army set up its own committee to investigate charges of corruption against M.P.s; in July it went so far as to deliver to the Judge-Advocate depositions against Speaker Lenthall himself. There, needless to say, the matter rested.[16] The Scots colours taken at Dunbar hung proudly in Westminster Hall; the Commonwealth had triumphed over its enemies at home and abroad. But the sacrifice of ideals to expediency was plain to all. The first time the demolition of cathedrals was pro-posed, in February 1651, the proceeds were to be used for the relief of the poor. When the scheme was raised again in the summer of 1652, the purpose was to get money for the Navy.[17]

\*     \*     \*

The point, of course, is that in only a very limited sense was the Rump a revolutionary regime. The crucial decision was taken immediately after the King's execution. By encouraging as many M.P.s as possible to align themselves with the Commonwealth, even if in their hearts they did not believe in it, the original Rumpers themselves helped to destroy what impetus the revolution pos-sessed. If they would but go through the motions of dissenting to the 5 December vote, and later would take the Engagement to be 'true and faithful to the Commonwealth of England', the Rump did not inquire too closely into their inward motives. Much of the Commonwealth's own propaganda was indeed directed to securing the support of the conformists, of those whom it could not afford

[15] Dr. Denton to Sir R. Verney, 9 Sept. 1652: H.M.C., *Seventh Report*, Appendix (Verney MSS.), p. 459; W. Coddrington to John Winthrop, Jr., 19 Feb. 1651/2: *Massa-chusetts Hist. Soc. Collections*, 4th Ser. vii (1865), 281.

[16] Edward Jenkes, *Ten Articles Already proved upon Oath against An Evil Member now in the Parliament* (3 July 1649: B.M. 669 f. 14, 52); Jenkes, *To all the People of England . . . The humble Remonstrance of Edward Jenkes* (4 Aug.: B.M. 669 f. 14, 62).

[17] Gardiner, *Commonwealth*, ii. 22–3, 187.

to alienate. The acquiescence of the half-hearted was necessary to keep the wheels of government turning, and the revolutionaries were determined that they should turn, rather than be totally replaced. The Commons had proclaimed the sovereignty of the people in the 4 January resolutions, but by declaring themselves the repositories of that sovereignty they had at once sought to escape from the dangerous logic of their own principles.

In the spring of 1649, through press, pulpit, and magistracy, the republic strove to educate public opinion in both the meaning and the limits of the new doctrine. At York Assizes, on 20 March, Serjeant Francis Thorpe took the usual line: *Salus Populi Suprema Lex*. 'The people (under God) is the original of all just power', he told the Grand Jury. But Thorpe quickly added that government was accountable to the people only 'in their politic constitution, lawfully assembled by their representative'.[18] More directly aimed at moderate opinion were the words of Thomas Edgar, a Suffolk J.P. addressing his colleagues a month later. There might be various opinions about the best form of government, Edgar told his fellow justices; but 'those in public employment in a Commonwealth must not desert government because the way or form doth not like them. Though one kind of government be better than another, yet take that is next rather than none.'[19]

The early months of the Commonwealth were full of such pragmatic appeals. The Presbyterian Francis Rous repeatedly urged others of his opinion to join him in active support for the Rump. The sub-title of one of his tracts sufficiently indicates his general line: 'A vindication of our lawful submission to the present government, or to a government supposed unlawful, but commanding lawful things.' Passive obedience was not enough, said Rous, for the distinction between this and active obedience was illogical. If the former, paying taxes for instance, was permissible, then so must be the latter, for example serving as a magistrate or an M.P.[20] 'Let every soul be subject to the higher powers', he began on another occasion, pointing out the many historical precedents for legitimate obedience to *de facto* governments. And even an unlawful regime

---

[18] *Sergeant Thorpe Judge of Assize . . . His Charge as it was delivered to the Grand-Jury at Yorke Assizes* (1649), in *Harleian Miscellany*, ii. 1-19. See esp. pp. 2-3.

[19] *Two Charges, As they were delivered by T. E[dgar] Esquire* (1650), quoted by Underdown, *J.B.S.* iii (1964), 70.

[20] Rous, *The Bounds and Bonds of Publique Obedience* (27 Aug. 1649: [B.M.] E. 571, 26), esp. p. 66.

was better than anarchy: if the natural governors refused to govern the inevitable result would be social collapse. 'When no man may act to give justice, may not every man take freely from his neighbour what he list, and so level the rich with the poor?'[21] Such practical, Hobbesian arguments for conformity had wide appeal. They were repeated, for instance, by Marchamont Nedham when he turned his coat again and announced his support for the Commonwealth in May 1650. Ever since the previous autumn he had been willing to make his peace 'upon rational terms'.[22]

A similar propaganda campaign followed the imposition of the new loyalty oath, the Engagement to the Commonwealth, which was required of all office-holders and ministers early in 1650. Even so apparently whole-hearted a supporter of the republic as William Heveningham had his doubts about it, and had to be reassured by the Independent Dr. John Goodwin. Earlier oaths to preserve monarchy, which worried Heveningham, were summarily brushed aside; anyone who refused the Engagement, Goodwin thought, must have 'a conscience most ridiculously boggling'.[23] The Engagement naturally created more serious difficulties for those less committed than Heveningham. In February 1650 Lord Lisle advised his father Leicester and his uncle Northumberland to take it: 'if things should break now, we which are the engagers should carry a very ill character upon us, but if it grow general it will grow nothing'. Northumberland soon subscribed, as did several other peers, and Leicester was able to follow suit without feeling that he was betraying his order. For the secluded members, the penalties of not subscribing, particularly the exclusion from the benefit of legal process, caused much heart searching. Samuel Gott was 'in a cloud not knowing what to do or say', when he exchanged views on the subject with John Swynfen early in 1650. If such determined enemies of the Commonwealth as Gott and Swynfen were perplexed and tempted to subscribe, those whose pasts raised fewer obstacles and whose consciences were more elastic had no such

---

[21] Rous, *The Lawfulnes of obeying the Present Government, and Acting under it*, 3rd edn. (1650), pp. 1–9, 16.

[22] Nedham, *The Case of the Commonwealth of England Stated* (8 May 1650: [B.M.] E. 600, 7); Nedham to H. Oxinden, 8 Nov. 1649: Dorothy Gardiner, ed., *The Oxinden and Peyton Letters, 1642–1670* (London, 1937), p. 160. See also Gardiner, *Commonwealth*, i. 253–5.

[23] J. G[oodwin] to Heveningham, 2 Jan. 1649/50: Holkham MS. 684, no. 41: noted in H.M.C., *Ninth Report*, App. II (E. of Leicester MSS.), p. 370.

problems. For the most part, only the most rigid of the Presbyterians refused.[24]

The appeal to the moderates, beginning in the spring of 1649,
was aimed at encouraging stability and obedience throughout the
country. Within the House the conformists were of course already
installed by the end of February. However it is regarded, the Rump
cannot be seen as a body dominated by a single party, whether we
call that party Independent or anything else. There was no single
revolutionary party, but instead a collection of different groups who
could co-operate on some issues, not on others. Within the Rump
were committed Commonwealthsmen like Ludlow, Marten, and
the Chaloners—but they were a minority. Alongside them sat men
who were not involved with any of the factions, independent country
gentry in the true sense. Such men are, of course, naturally elusive.
Many of them, like Sir Roger Burgoyne, never came back after the
Purge. But on Lucy Hutchinson's evidence some did: 'the gentlemen who were of the other faction, or of none at all, . . . forsook not
their seats'.[25] Among the members active and prominent in the
Rump, the two Dorset men, John Browne and John Trenchard, the
Sussex member Herbert Morley and his faithful brother-in-law
John Fagge, and the two Hampshire men, Sir Thomas Jervoise and
Henry Wallop, all seem convincing candidates for inclusion in the
independent category—though the independence of the two last-
named may have been compromised by their desperate insolvency.
Many members who played only an imperceptible part in the
Rump's proceedings were of a similar type, turning up only when
they thought that important interests (their own as well as the
public's) were involved. Some possible examples are the two
Nottinghamshire men, Gervase Pigot and Edward Nevill; Peter
Brooke; Sir Edward Baynton; Sir Roger North; and those three
very belated adherents, Hugh Rogers, Sir Thomas Wodehouse, and
Sir John Dryden. When to these are added the conforming office-
holders like Whitelocke, whose enthusiasm for reform was tepid at
best, it is clear that the convinced radicals in the Rump were a distinct minority.

They were a minority, and they knew it. Even Thomas Scot was

[24] H.M.C., *De L'Isle*, vi. 472–6; [Gott] to Swynfen, [1650]: William Salt Library, Salt
MS. 454 (Swynfen MSS.), no. [6A]. For a useful summary of the arguments used in the
Engagement controversy see John M. Wallace, *Destiny His Choice: the Loyalism of Andrew
Marvell* (Cambridge, 1968), pp. 45–64.
[25] *Hutchinson*, p. 268.

realistic enough to admit that there was insufficient support for
them in the country for them to be able to risk alienating what little
they had. Two deductions could be drawn from this. First, the
Commonwealthsmen would have to go slowly on reform, convince
the nation that they were responsible men who could be trusted,
and by reducing taxes work for a more favourable climate of opinion
before embarking on new experiments. 'England is not as France',
Scot reminded Cromwell in November 1650, 'a meadow to be
mowed as often as the governors please; our interest is to do our
work with as little grievance to our new people, scarce yet proselyted,
as possible.'[26] Secondly, recognizing that new elections, in the existing state of gentry opinion, would mean the undoing of what little
they had achieved already, they would have to prolong their own
power, rejecting the Army's demand for new elections. Even Henry
Marten accepted this. In 1650 he told the Rump that the Commonwealth 'was yet an infant, of a weak growth and a very tender constitution; . . . nobody would be so fit to nurse it as the mother who
brought it forth, and . . . they should not think of putting it under
any other hands until it had obtained more years and vigour'.[27]

The leaders of the Commonwealth believed in liberty, but they
also believed in defining it themselves. Not long before the Purge
a pamphleteer had expressed a common view when he recognized
that left to themselves, a majority of Englishmen would be for the
King. But 'it is not *vox*, but *salus populi* that is the supreme law', he
went on. '. . . If the common vote of the giddy multitude must rule
the whole, how quickly would their own interest, peace and safety
be dashed and broken?' Their appointed leaders would decide how
to liberate them, working from 'common, plain, general and universal
reason, and moral principles'.[28] Like the Jacobins a century and a
half later, Ireton's friends had discovered that men might have to be
forced to be free, and that it was the privilege of a revolutionary élite
to determine the general will. Harrison and the Fifth Monarchy Men
went even further, seeing themselves as appointed by God to lead
the people out of bondage, against their wills if necessary. Cromwell,
too, could operate on the same principles, especially in his more
elevated moments of enthusiasm. 'Who can tell how soon God may

---

[26] Scot to Cromwell, 2 Nov. 1650: *Milton State Papers*, p. 28.
[27] Clarendon, *History*, Bk. XIV, § 6. See also Gardiner, *Commonwealth*, i. 243-4.
[28] *Salus Populi Solus Rex* (17 Oct. 1648: [B.M.] E. 467, 39), esp. pp. 17-19. Brailsford,
*The Levellers*, p. 345, n. 8, suggests Hugh Peter as the author.

fit the people for such a thing [as free elections]?' he asked the Barebones Parliament in July 1653; Cromwell had always preferred
'what's for their good, not what pleases them'. The Welsh radical
John Jones agreed with him. 'I had rather do a people good though
against their wills, than please them in show only, to the hazard-
ing of their peace and well being', he said in 1651.[29]

Arguments like this could, of course, be used as well against the
radical left as against the conservative gentry right. They were
particularly relevant during the early months of the Commonwealth when the Leveller threat was still undiminished. So far from
being diminished, indeed, in the late winter and spring of 1649 it
appeared to be reviving in a new and more virulent form. Lilburne
led the way with new pamphlets and petitions, and in the Army, in
London, and among the discontented peasantry of the Home
Counties there were renewed stirrings. At Hitchin in March
soldiers led a demonstration, posting up copies of *England's New
Chains Discovered*, and assuring the local radicals that they would
'live and die with them in their deliverance . . . from this new
tyranny'. Protests against high prices, depression, quartering, and
excise mingled with denunciations of the Norman Yoke and appeals
for democracy. Lilburne and the other leaders were arrested at the
end of March, but still the ferment continued. Winstanley and his
Diggers appeared menacingly on St. George's Hill, and in the
months that followed echoes of his communist experiments were
heard as far afield as the counties of Buckingham, Northampton, and
Gloucester. At the end of April there were Army mutinies over the
old issues of pay and service in Ireland. A Leveller soldier, Robert
Lockyer, was singled out as the ringleader and shot, providing his
cause with another martyr and his friends with an opportunity for
a great green-ribboned demonstration at the funeral. The Army
Levellers exploded in renewed mutiny, and there was alarm in
London until Fairfax and Cromwell cut them down at Burford.[30]

The reaction was inevitable. During the previous summer Henry

[29] Abbott, *Cromwell*, iii. 64; Jones to Dr. W. Staines, 19 Nov. 1651: Joseph Mayer, ed.,
'Inedited letters of Cromwell, Colonel Jones, Bradshaw and other Regicides', *Trans. Hist.
Soc., Lancs. and Cheshire*, N.S. i (1861), 191. The paradoxes in Cromwell's view of liberty
are nowhere better discussed than in Christopher Hill, *Oliver Cromwell, 1658–1958* (Hist.
Assoc., G.S. 38, 1958).

[30] For this paragraph, see Brailsford, *The Levellers*, pp. 472–9, and chs. xxiv–xxvi;
W. Schenk, *The Concern for Social Justice in the Puritan Revolution* (London, 1948), pp. 64–9.
For a recent estimate of the spread of Digger influence see K. Thomas, 'Another Digger
Broadside', *Past and Present*, no. 42 (Feb. 1969), 57–60.

Marten, intoxicated with visions of liberty, had raised a regiment of volunteers 'for the People's Freedom against all tyrants whatsoever'. There were complaints about his highhanded requisitioning of horses, panic-stricken protests from people of property. But 'the rustics of Berkshire' and other counties had flocked to him, it was noted. Now, however, Marten's private army was effectively neutralized, incorporated in the Army and silenced.[31] All over England the men of property were closing ranks. Cromwell pounded the table and exhorted the Council of State to crush the Levellers: 'if you do not break them, they will break you'. The Earl of Leicester thought that *The Moderate* was out to 'invite the people to overthrow all property as the original cause of sin, and by that to destroy all government, magistracy, honesty, civility and humanity', and that the paper should be suppressed. It was, a month later.[32] Nedham, after his conversion to the Commonwealth, could dismiss the Levellers as 'only the rude multitude, who understand no more of the business than that it may prove a hopeful way to mend their own out of other men's fortunes', and interpreted their political ideas as Ireton had done in 1647 as leading inevitably to communism. Deserted by the London Baptists, by their few allies in Parliament such as Marten, and crushed in the Army, the Levellers were still useful ammunition for official propagandists.[33]

\*    \*    \*

It is therefore hardly surprising that the Rump failed to live up to the more extravagant expectations of its original creators. In all four of the main areas of policy in which the men of 1648-9 had had high hopes of achieving major changes—religion, the law, social reform and parliamentary reform—a similar pattern can be seen. Initial effort is followed by a relapse into inertia, which is broken by three flickerings of reformist energy, each the result of pressure from the Army. The first of these came after Cromwell's famous letter from Dunbar. 'Curb the proud and the insolent . . . Relieve

---

[31] *Clarke Papers*, ii. 56 and n. Army committee for forces and garrisons, order 16 Feb. 1648/9: Worcester Coll., Clarke MS. lxxii. See also Brailsford, *The Levellers*, pp. 342-3. But see also below, p. 298.

[32] Leicester's Journal, Aug. 1649: H.M.C., *De L'Isle*, vi. 590-1; Frank, *Beginnings of the English Newspaper*, p. 198.

[33] Nedham, *Case of the Commonwealth*, pp. 71, 78-9. For the desertion of the Baptists see Brailsford, *The Levellers*, pp. 487-8, 541-2; and Haller and Davies, *Leveller Tracts*, pp. 21-2, 213, 228-9.

the oppressed', he told the Commons as he contemplated the fruits
of victory. The second followed the even more sweeping victory at
Worcester. Let not 'the fatness of these continued mercies . . .
occasion pride and wantonness', he warned them. The third was
stimulated by the Army petition of August 1652, which demanded
a wide range of reforms including the abolition of tithes, swift
action on law reform, and more 'speedy consideration' of new
elections.[34] A brief survey of the Rump's accomplishments in each
of the four fields will confirm the argument already advanced that
the failure of the Commonwealth as a reformist regime was inherent
in the very nature of the revolution.

The Rump's inability to achieve a clear-cut religious settlement
was largely the result of its internal divisions. That the Commons
still contained a large proportion of Presbyterians was obvious to
contemporaries, many of whom were less inclined than later historians to blanket all Rumpers under the name Independent. The
Purge, a pamphleteer declared in March 1649, had not been one of
Presbyterians by Independents: 'there are as sound and godly
remaining in the House, and that Presbyterians also, if not far better
than any that were impeached'. The Army, he pointed out, did not
'in the least intend either Presbyterian or Independent as such, but
as they were men acting against the glory of God, and the good of
the kingdom'.[35] Clement Walker also noted the importance of the
Presbyterian survivors of the Purge in the spring of 1649. Confronted with Leveller mutinies and the threat of worse disorders,
Cromwell, he argued, attempted a 'fraudulent reconciliation and
uniting of interests', with conciliatory gestures towards both religious and erstwhile political Presbyterians in the House. To please
the former Oliver was said to have moved 'that the Presbyterian
government might be settled'; though as Walker points out he did
not explain whether he meant classical or congregational Presbytery.
To please the latter, he proposed 'that the secured and secluded
members might again be invited into the House'.[36] Clarendon, like
other Royalists, was not always very discriminating in his descriptions of his enemies; which makes it all the more striking that both
then and later he recognized the survival in the Rump of 'many who

---

[34] Abbott, *Cromwell*, ii. 325, 463; Gardiner, *Commonwealth*, ii. 224-6.

[35] Franciscus Leinsula, *The Kingdoms Divisions Anatomized* (4 Mar. 1648/9: [B.M.]
E. 545, 25). See Underdown, *J.B.S.* iii (1964), 65, for the reluctance of even William Prynne
to describe his enemies as Independents.

[36] Walker, *Independency*, ii. 157, and cf. also ibid. iii. 11.

pretended to be, and in truth were, as great Presbyterians as any in the houses'.[37] Disgruntled religious radicals often had good reason to complain about the strength of the Rump Presbyterians. One of Cromwell's correspondents complained bitterly about their influence in March 1651, instancing two recent outbursts of intolerance: the expulsion of the Unitarian John Fry, and the refusal of the House to thank the Antinomian Sidrach Simpson for a sermon in favour of laymen's preaching. Those who had proposed Simpson as preacher, Cromwell was told, were 'exceedingly reflected upon'.[38]

The wide variety of opinion represented by these four observers is a good reason for taking them seriously. They are, in any case, corroborated both by the statistics in the previous chapter and by the actual course of events in the Rump. It will be recalled that a high percentage of the original revolutionaries were Independents or more radical Puritans, who would have been in favour of sweeping changes. Even so, a fifth of the revolutionaries were Presbyterians, and almost another fifth Presbyterian-Independents, in other words supporters of congregational Presbytery. But a majority of the February 1649 conformists (who it will also be remembered outnumbered the revolutionaries) were Presbyterians, and of those whose views are known only a third were of Independent or sectarian sympathies.[39] When the later adherents to the Rump are added—newly elected members and former abstainers who were admitted after April 1649—the strength of the Presbyterians becomes even more evident. To consolidate all Rumpers into a single statistical line is admittedly a crude procedure. The Rump was not a completely stable body; besides gaining members by election or readmission, it lost others by expulsion (Fry, Clement, Lord Howard) and more often by death. But a complete analysis of the members at a series of points in time would be hopelessly cumbersome. Even a crude consolidated figure shows how evenly balanced the Rump became in its later years: forty-three per cent Independents or sectaries, fourteen per cent Presbyterian-Independents, forty-three per cent Presbyterians.[40] The Rump's lack of

[37] Hyde memorandum, 30 Sept. 1649: *Nicholas Papers*, i. 141; Clarendon, *History*, Bk. XII, § 71; Bk. XIV, §§ 1-2.
[38] — to Cromwell, 15 Mar. [1651]: *Milton State Papers*, pp. 82-3.
[39] Above, p. 235.
[40] Below, App. B, Table IX (b). Once again I think this may even be an underestimate of the strength of Erastian Presbyterianism in the Rump. I suspect that a large proportion of the unknowns would be in this category if we knew more about them.

action to satisfy the radicals' urgent cries for the completion of
Godly Reformation is clearly explained by the close balance of
opinion. And that close balance was the result of the revolutionaries'
decision to admit the conformists.

The Rump's legislative record was not quite barren, of course.
Its effective achievements were confined to provisions for the better
maintenance of ministers, the promotion of evangelical campaigns
in the 'dark corners of the land', and some slight extensions of
religious toleration. The 'lame Erastian Presbytery' painfully established in previous years by Assembly and Parliament was not dis-
mantled, but circumstances obviously now made its effectiveness
a matter of local choice. In June 1649 the members of the Taunton
classis were uncertain even 'whether there be any course warranted
by the Word wherein ministers may proceed to the administration
of the sacrament as the case now stands'.[41] The Rump was not
inclined to press on further with the strengthening of Presbytery,
but it had no coherent alternative. Such legislation as was enacted
occurred only during the first phase of the Rump's existence, concluding with the repeal of the Elizabethan church-attendance laws
on 27 September 1650. After that date there was much talk, but
no action.

The Rump's first vote on religion may have given some encouragement to the radicals. On 18 May 1649, by a single vote, they defeated
a proposal to refer the question of tithes to what they must have supposed would be an unsympathetic committee.[42] But the Bill for the
maintenance of ministers which was passed into law less than
a month later made no concessions to radical demands for abolition. The Bill, which had been given two readings as long ago as
November 1646, vested impropriated tithes owned by the now
defunct bishops, deans, and chapters, together with revenues from
First-Fruits, in a board of trustees. These were to pay augmentations to ministers and schoolmasters when so ordered by Parliament, acting on the advice of the Committee for Plundered Ministers.
An annual revenue of £20,000 out of Crown lands was guaranteed
for this purpose until impropriations should produce this amount.[43]

[41] Elders and ministers to H. Jeanes, 13 June 1649: Shaw, *Church under the Commonwealth*, ii. 422.

[42] *C.J.* vi. 211; Whitelocke, *Memorials*, iii. 36.

[43] A second Act in the spring of 1650 made a few technical changes in the system: Firth
and Rait, *A. and O.* ii. 142-8, 369-78, 391; Shaw, *Church under the Commonwealth*, ii.
214-21.

The provision of more equitably distributed endowments was
valuable, of course, though it merely extended the existing practice
of paying augmentations out of sequestered tithes, which had long
been done by the County Committees and the Committee for
Plundered Ministers. It can scarcely be regarded as a measure of
dramatic innovation, and in some respects indeed it strengthened
the system of an established ministry supported by tithes.

On this matter the Council of State was more advanced than the
Commons. On 20 June the Council included the abolition of tithes
in a list of reform measures proposed for consideration in the
Rump's next session.[44] In August the House was at work on a
general declaration on Church government, and a Presbyterian
attempt to write into it a specific endorsement of the legality of
tithes was beaten in a small House. Nevertheless, the draft of the
declaration still contained a promise not to change 'the present
maintenance by tithes' until an adequate alternative was 'visibly
provided and firmly settled'.[45] But the Rump could never agree on
any such alternative. On 29 April 1652 they were still discussing it,
referring it to a new committee for the propagation of the gospel,
and ordering the continued payment of tithes in the meantime.[46]

The most important result of the 1649 Act for ministers' maintenance was the authorization of a new survey of parish livings.
This was undertaken by commissioners operating under the authority
of the Great Seal. By the summer of 1650 they were hard at work in
the counties, holding inquests by local juries, and collecting much
useful information about the nature of ministerial endowments, as
well as making recommendations for the union or division of parishes
for the better preaching of the word. Had the Rump shown real
energy in pursuing the often proposed scheme for a national 'propagation of the gospel', the commissioners' returns would have been
immensely productive. But in fact the usual inertia prevailed, and
most of them were left to moulder in Chancery, with action being taken
only in a few individual cases as long as the Rump was in power.[47]

Only in Wales and the northern counties did the revolution lead

---

[44] *Cal. S.P. Dom.*, 1649–50, p. 199; *C.J.* vi. 240; Whitelocke, *Memorials*, iii. 57.
[45] *C.J.* vi. 275; H.M.C., *Portland*, i. 515.                        [46] *C.J.* vii. 128.
[47] *C.J.* vi. 354, 359, 365; Whitelocke, *Memorials*, iii. 151; Shaw, *Church under the Commonwealth*, ii. 249–51, 603–4. The active commissioners included religious Presbyterians as well
as Independents. John Harington, for example, was an active member of the Somerset commission: Lambeth Palace, MS. Comm. XIIa/15 (Parliamentary Surveys), fols. 348–62,
401–21, 451.

to dramatic progress for the cause of Godly Reformation. These were of course areas which had long been of serious concern to Puritans, for their continued languishing in the grip of popery. The Committee for the Propagation of the Gospel in Wales, it has been rightly said, was 'the culmination of two or three generations of puritan aspiration and effort'.[48] But in spite of spontaneous missionary work after the Civil War by Vavasor Powell, Walter Cradock, and other Welsh preachers, no official attack on the problem was made until Pride's Purge had removed most of the Welsh Presbyterians from the Commons. Myddeltons, Owens, and Wynns were unlikely to look with favour on such dangerous experiments as Hugh Peter's call for itinerant preachers and the pooling of tithes. But when, after a petition from Wales, the propagation scheme came before the Rump in January 1650, the principality was represented mainly by aristocrats whose major interests lay elsewhere, like Algernon Sidney and Lord Herbert (soon to succeed as fifth Earl of Pembroke), and radical enthusiasts like the Merioneth Baptist John Jones, and Philip Jones of Swansea, who arrived as a new member early in February, in time to help see the Bill through the House.[49] The Bill for the northern counties could also be passed because it dealt with a region whose special problems were notorious. The members from the north-east, it will be remembered, tended strongly to political radicalism; they also included a good many who were Independent in religion. Of those with interests in the counties immediately affected, Haselrig (the bill's promoter), his son-in-law George Fenwick, and the younger Vane were all strong Independents. So were the two members for Appleby, Ireton and Richard Salway, whose connection with the area was, however, solely the result of their having enjoyed Lord Wharton's patronage.[50]

Uncontroversial measures for the propagation of the gospel in

[48] Christopher Hill, 'Propagating the Gospel', in Bell and Ollard, eds., *Historical Essays*, p. 47. For the whole subject, besides this essay, see also Hill, 'Puritanism and "the dark corners of the land" ', *T.R.H.S.* 5th Ser. xiii (1963), 77–102; and Nuttall, *Welsh Saints*, esp. ch. iii.

[49] Hill, in Bell and Ollard, eds., *Historical Essays*, pp. 40–1. The only other Welsh Rumpers were Thomas Wogan and Henry Herbert, neither of whom demonstrate clear religious sympathies, and Sir John Trevor, who has been described as an 'advanced Puritan': Dodd, *Stuart Wales*, p. 126. However, Trevor's patronage of Stephen Marshall suggests that he was more probably a moderate: Marshall, *The Sinne of Hardnesse of Heart* (26 July 1648: [B.M.] E. 455, 3), Dedication.

[50] The surviving member for Cockermouth was Francis Allen, whose religious position is discussed above, p. 234. I have no evidence for the religious preferences of Sir Thomas Widdrington, Lord Howard (the new member for Carlisle), and the younger William

New England and Ireland were also passed in 1649 and 1650.
A general propagation Act for the whole of England had been discussed intermittently ever since 1646. It was revived early in 1650,
as an alternative to the passage of further special Acts similar to
those for Wales and the North, for which some counties were
petitioning. But the Rump's failure to settle the tithes question,
and the passage of the·interim measures for ministers' maintenance,
combined to take the steam out of the agitation. The propagation
Bill was occasionally discussed in committee during the next two
years, but by February 1652 it had gone completely to sleep. At
this time a new committee was appointed to consider the proposals
of Dr. John Owen and other divines for a general settlement that
would include some definition of the fundamentals of doctrine.
The new committee at first met regularly, receiving plenty of advice
from the ministers, but it too seems to have been stalemated by the
Rump's divisions. For a long time after May 1652 it held no meetings, and it eventually reported only during the final flurry of
activity that preceded the dissolution. By this time pressure from
the sects, from millenarians in Parliament like Harrison, was
seriously arousing expectations of radical reform, and there was
a corresponding rallying of opinion on the other side to preserve a
'settled ministry'. But Cromwell's dissolution put an end to it all.[51]

The Rump's religious radicals had more success in the matter of
toleration, though even here progress was slow and halting. The
established Presbyterian system had no teeth, and although both
Prayer Book and Mass remained proscribed, for other tender consciences the Commonwealth fulfilled some of the hopes engendered
by the revolution. The Presbyterians tried hard to prevent it. On
7 August 1649 a motion to include in the proposed declaration on
religion a clause endorsing Presbyterian government and the use
of the Directory was carried to a vote; the result was a tie, which
Lenthall settled by giving his casting vote for the Independents.

Armine. But the last-named's father, Sir William, joined the Presbyterians in voting against
the Bill, though some other evidence suggests that he was a moderate Independent: *C.J.* vi.
374. See also Shaw, *Church under the Commonwealth*, ii. 226.
    [51] Herefordshire petition, 23 Mar. 1649/50: B.M. Add. MS. 11053 (Scudamore MSS.),
fols. 110-11; *Rel. Baxt.* i. 69-70; Thomas Braman and others to R. Major, 27 Feb., also
Hampshire petitions, Feb. and Mar. 1652/3: B.M. Add. MS. 24861 (Major MSS.), fols. 67,
71-2. For Owen's proposals see Gardiner, *Commonwealth*, ii. 96-102. For the propagation
Bill, Shaw, *Church under the Commonwealth*, ii. 80-4. Shaw's conclusion (p. 84) that the
Rump 'accomplished absolutely nothing towards the announcement of a Church government scheme' is only slightly too severe.

A committee was thereupon appointed to review the Directory and the acts establishing Presbyterianism, and to draft a new declaration that would satisfy tender consciences. The Presbyterians were well represented by such zealots as Purefoy, John Gurdon, and Sir William Strickland, which may explain why the declaration never materialized. On 16 August the Army Council petitioned for repeal of the penal laws, though carefully exempting popery and prelacy from any form of toleration. A Bill was duly introduced a month later; it received two readings, went into committee, and again nothing was done. Another Bill that had been introduced on 29 June to repeal the compulsory church attendance laws had no more success. Indeed, the Rump soon declared that it had no intention of allowing a 'universal toleration'. Only after Cromwell's Dunbar letter a year later was the Bill repealing compulsory church-going revived. Its passage on 27 September 1650 was the Rump's last effective effort in the field of religious reform.[52]

Most Rumpers obviously put the enforcement of a Puritan code of morality ahead of religious liberty. Several repressive Acts were passed during the summer of 1650, including a strict sabbath-observance law, the famous measure imposing the death penalty for adultery, and an Act against unlawful swearing. More important, as it might be used to undermine religious toleration, was the Act against blasphemy. Although milder than the Presbyterian measure of 1648, it was effective enough to deal with the Ranters' disturbing excesses, which were shocking to Presbyterians and Independents alike. The radicals succeeded in carrying minor amendments to the blasphemy and adultery Bills. But these were small successes, and scarcely affected the general trend towards repression in the summer of 1650. And the change of direction after Dunbar was short-lived. During the remainder of its life, the Rump made only one more gesture towards toleration; in June 1652 it voted that even recusants could not be forced to attend Protestant worship against their consciences.[53]

* * *

Law reform and social reform were pursued no more energetically. Much of the pressure for law reform came from the Levellers

[52] *C.J.* vi. 275; H.M.C., *Portland*, i. 515; Whitelocke, *Memorials*, iii. 87-8; Gardiner, *Commonwealth*, i. 173; ii. 3; Shaw, *Church under the Commonwealth*, ii. 77-8; Firth and Rait, *A. and O.* ii. 423-5.

[53] *C.J.* vi. 404, 453; vii. 138; Firth and Rait, *A. and O.* ii. 383-9, 393-6, 409-12; Gardiner, *Commonwealth*, i. 255-6; ii. 2-3; Shaw, *Church under the Commonwealth*, ii. 78.

and the lower ranks of the Army.[54] But not all of it. Col. Thomas
Pride looked forward to the day when the lawyers' gowns would be
hung alongside the Scots colours in Westminster Hall. Less rhetorically, Commonwealthsmen like Ludlow, Ireton, and Marten always
saw a rationalized legal system as an integral part of their reform
programme. Even Cromwell was for it. 'The sons of Zeruiah are
yet too strong for us', he complained to Ludlow in 1650, 'and we
cannot mention the reformation of the law, but they presently cry
out, we design to destroy property; whereas the law . . . serves only
to maintain the lawyers, and to encourage the rich to oppress the
poor.'[55] But as in the case of religion, the broadening of the Rump's
membership in and after February 1649 introduced many men who
had no interest in reform, and regarded discussion of it as dangerous
to the social order. There were the usual sporadic efforts in the early
days of the Commonwealth, signs of renewed activity after Dunbar,
and much more serious consideration of the matter after Worcester.
Yet the results were relatively minor.

The opposition to law reform was naturally led by the lawyers.
Among the original revolutionaries there were only fourteen
lawyers. By the end of February 1649 another twenty had been
admitted, among them those two reliable defenders of the *status quo*
Whitelocke and Widdrington. Two of the original lawyers, George
Wylde and Alexander Rigby, died in 1650, but their places were
taken by a number of late admissions (among them the judges
Oliver St. John and John Wylde). By the end of 1651 there were
forty-four lawyers in the Rump. Not all of them attended regularly
—Thomas Atkin was always complaining of the absence of his
fellow member for Norwich, Erasmus Earle, who preferred to spend
his time in Westminster Hall, 'to his great advantage'.[56] But
although the typical lawyer may have devoted more time to practice
than to Parliament, he might be expected to attend the House when
his interests were threatened. The proportion of lawyers to the

---

[54] See Brailsford, *The Levellers, passim*; James, *Social Problems*, pp. 326–7; and Stuart
E. Prall, *The Agitation for Law Reform during the Puritan Revolution* (The Hague, 1966),
pp. 23–5.

[55] *D.N.B.* ('Pride'); *Ludlow's Memoirs*, i. 246–7. Ireton's attendance at the Middle
Temple gave him, says Whitelocke, 'a little knowledge of the law, which led him into the
more errors': *Memorials*, ii. 163, 473.

[56] Atkin to Mayor of Norwich, 23 May 1650: B.M. Add. MS. 22620 (Collections re
Norwich), fol. 162. See also Atkin's letters of 31 Jan., 7 Feb., and 7 Mar. 1649/50, and
22 Nov. 1649: ibid., fols. 119, 121, 129, 137. It might be noted that Earle's brother-in-law
was the royalist judge John Fountaine.

rest of the House did not increase significantly; but it is obvious
that in a body which was rarely attended by more than a hundred
members, the lawyers could form a knowledgeable and determined
interest group, working against all but the most innocuous reforms.[57]

For more than four years the lawyers conducted an astute and
on the whole successful delaying campaign. Whitelocke, from his
vantage-point at the summit of the legal hierarchy, was always
ready, and at great length, to 'vindicate the honour' of his profession. In November 1649 the Commonwealthsmen, with their
usual 'great picque' against the lawyers, proposed to exclude them
from the House. Whitelocke answered in a long speech, denying
the alleged historical precedents for such exclusion, and pointing
out the great services lawyers had rendered the republic both as
soldiers and M.P.s. On another occasion Whitelocke attributed the
whole agitation against lawyers and the law to the dangerous
machinations of 'some military persons' outside Parliament. He
was partly right, for at the time of this second speech, in November
1650, there was indeed talk in the Army of a petition asking again
that lawyers be expelled from the House.[58]

In spite of Whitelocke's stonewalling, the Rump did complete
some positive legal reforms, though not enough to satisfy the
reformers. Between September 1649 and April 1650 three Acts for
relief of prisoners for debt were passed, and another to redress
delays to litigants arising out of the cumbersome procedure of
appeals by writ of error.[59] Sometimes reform was held up by disagreement between radicals and reform-minded lawyers, as when
a Bill to establish courts for probate, marriage, and divorce cases,
which at least some lawyers accepted, was rejected on 18 May
1649.[60] Leveller criticism of unnecessary legal offices produced
a committee in June 1650 to consider 'what offices in this Commonwealth are burdensome to the people', and to make suggestions for
their abolition or regulation; but again nothing came of it.[61]

By this time the Rump had set up its own committee to consider
law reform. It displayed little energy at first, but received a powerful

---

[57] See above, pp. 229-30 and n.

[58] Whitelocke, *Memorials*, iii. 118-24, 273; Rushworth to W. Clarke, 30 Nov. 1650:
H.M.C., *Leybourne-Popham*, p. 78.

[59] Firth and Rait, *A. and O.* ii. 240-1, 321-4, 357-8, 378-9.

[60] Roger Hill was a teller in its favour. Another Bill on the same subject received a second
reading on 4 Aug., but made no further progress: *C.J.* vi. 211, 274-5.

[61] *C.J.* vi. 432.

T

stimulus when Cromwell's letter after Dunbar echoed the strong feeling in the Army. 'Reform the abuses of all professions', Cromwell admonished the Parliament, adding a clear thrust at the lawyers: 'if there be any one that makes many poor to make a few rich, that suits not a Commonwealth.' The only effective result of this was the Act for holding court proceedings in English, passed on 22 November 1650. This produced another long speech from Whitelocke in defence of the Common Law, though in the end he supported the Bill.[62] Whitelocke's willingness to accept moderate change shows that the lawyers realized that the pressure was too strong for them to be able to rely on total and obstinate opposition: concessions would have to be made as the price of preserving the main citadel. Already, some months earlier, in May 1650, there had been meetings between lawyers and Army officers at which it was agreed to draw up proposals for shortening suits and reducing costs. In October, when the Bill for holding court proceedings in English was under consideration, other measures were referred to the Rump's committee. They were to consider how to redress unnecessary legal delays, to examine the law officers' salaries and fees, and to consider how to procure a more impartial selection of juries; another committee was set up to look into the question of prison reform.[63] But as usual a period of activity under pressure from the Army was followed by a relapse. The committees produced no concrete results, and as 1651 wore on it became clear that stronger language from outside would be required to spur the Rump into action.

The pressure was renewed after Worcester. The military threat to the Commonwealth had been removed, and the soldiers were coming home to demand the reforms for which they had been fighting. Equally important, officers like Cromwell and Harrison (though not Ireton, who went to his grave in Ireland in November 1651) were returning to their seats in the Rump. By December law reform had again become a live issue. On the day after Christmas the Rump decided to supplement the work of its own moribund committee with a new, special commission, made up of men who were not M.P.s, to consider the whole field of law reform. The new commission, it has recently been shown, was very far from being

---

[62] Abbott, *Cromwell*, ii. 325; Whitelocke, *Memorials*, iii. 260–73; Firth and Rait, *A. and O.* ii. 455–6.
[63] Whitelocke, *Memorials*, iii. 194, 253–4; *C.J.* vi. 487–8.

a radical, reformist body. With the distinguished Matthew Hale as its head, it included the royalist lawyer John Fountaine, and a strong contingent of political moderates and trimmers of the type of Alderman Fowke and Sir Anthony Ashley Cooper. Among the twenty-one members of the commission there were only five radicals: the Baptists Josiah Berners, Samuel Moyer, and William Packer, the Kent firebrand Thomas Blount, and the real mouthpiece of reform, Hugh Peter. Their inclusion was doubtless necessary to make the commission fully representative, but it is also likely that they were put there to keep the reformers outside Parliament quiet. That tactical considerations of this kind were present in the minds of some members of the Rump is clear from a letter written by Sir John Danvers during the selection of the commission. Colonel Robert Overton, Danvers advised Whitelocke, ought to be one, being 'both rational and learned, and of good estate in land of inheritance, whose forward zeal to justice and right made the Levellers assume to own him as a pillar of theirs'. But, Danvers pointed out, Overton was quite harmless. He had remained 'trusty to the public interest', and his inclusion would be 'for the better tempering of any remaining party of the said Levellers'.[64]

If such were the Rump's tactics, they were successful. The commission co-operated at all times with the Rump's own committee, which in turn usually accepted the commission's quite moderate proposals; Whitelocke, as usual, was always at hand if a compromise was needed. Hugh Peter talked a good deal in his 'very opinionative' way, making much of his knowledge of Dutch law, 'wherein', says Whitelocke, 'he was altogether mistaken'.[65] The radicals could talk, but they were out-manœuvred. Even so, the Hale commission's achievements were not entirely negligible. In 1652 it produced schemes for the establishment of county courts (though not the elective ones demanded by the Levellers), for the complete abolition of imprisonment for debt, for the abolition of fines on original writs, and a number of other useful reforms. Like

---

[64] Danvers to Whitelocke, 26 Dec. 1651: Whitelocke Papers (Longleat), xi, fol. 159 (I am indebted to Blair Worden for this quotation). In the end Overton was not nominated. For the membership of the commission see Mary Cotterell, 'Interregnum Law Reform: the Hale Commission of 1652', *E.H.R.* lxxxiii (1968), 691–3. It would be interesting to know why ten of the original nominees were not chosen, and why Rushworth, Sir Henry Blount, and Fountaine were added. There was visible opposition both to the radical Thomas Blount and the royalist Fountaine: *C.J.* vii. 67–74.

[65] Whitelocke, *Memorials*, iii. 388.

Whitelocke, the commission's lawyers were willing to contemplate procedural improvements, especially if the vested interests they represented stood to gain by them.[66]

Yet once again, all this promising spadework was buried in the quagmire of inertia. In March 1652 the Rump committee sent up, in Whitelocke's care, several of the Hale commission's proposals. Three Bills reached the committee stage, but that was the last that was heard of them; other measures did not get even that far. Willing to make gestures to reform, even to permit the more progressive lawyers to submit positive proposals, the Rump was still unable to overcome its own habits of evasion and delay. Ludlow and Cromwell were both impressed by the lawyers' tactical skill. When a Bill for registering deeds was in committee, it was 'so managed by the lawyers' that the mere definition of the term 'encumbrances' occupied a full three months. When the Rump was dismissed in April 1653 the Hale commission's scheme for reform of the whole legal system was about to be discussed; 300 copies had been printed for the members' use. But only one measure reached the statute book. On 8 April the Rump at last set up the probate court which they had been desultorily discussing ever since 1649. It was left for the Barebones Parliament to make real progress.[67]

Social reform also produced much talk but little action. The payment of augmentations to schoolmasters out of sequestered tithes, coupled with the general climate of Puritan resolve during the early 1650s, gave some stimulus to education, but it would be an exaggeration to say that the Rump had a distinctive educational policy. It was, of course, anxious to control the ideological content of the curriculum, voting on 29 July 1651 that 'former primers used in the late king's time be suppressed, and new ones used'. When in 1650 a Durham petition revived the project of a northern university, it was supported by Cromwell and Haselrig; a committee was appointed, but nothing positive was done.[68] Nor was anything

---

[66] As they were, for example, by the abolition of fines on original writs. For the commission's achievements see Cotterell, *E.H.R.* lxxxiii (1968), 697–702.

[67] *Ludlow's Memoirs*, i. 333–4; Cromwell, speeches 4 July 1653, 21 Apr. 1657: Abbott, *Cromwell*, iii. 58; iv. 493; *C.J.* vii. 249–53; Firth and Rait, *A. and O.* ii. 702; James, *Social Problems*, pp. 332–3. See also Prall, *Agitation for Law Reform*, pp. 52–67; Prall's account suffers from his failure to use the commission's Minute-book in B.M. Add. MS. 35863, which, however, is used extensively by Cotterell.

[68] James, *Social Problems*, pp. 324–5; Whitelocke, *Memorials*, iii. 324. For the whole subject of education see W. A. L. Vincent, *The State and School Education, 1640–1660* (London, 1950). The Rump, as Vincent shows (pp. 48–51) continued the Long Parliament's

striking achieved in the treatment of the poor. Projects for relieving poverty were advanced on all sides, ranging from John Cook's ambitious, idealistic programme of reform, to Hartlib's scheme for a nationally endowed workhouse system, and Peter Chamberlen's tempting proposal of a joint-stock company which would make a profit out of employing the poor. Hartlib also proposed an Office of Addresses 'for the relief of human necessities', which would include a labour exchange among its other services.[69]

In the desperate circumstances of 1649 both need and opportunity for reform were clear. The war had disrupted local government, but although the J.P.s quickly regained their powers after it was over, they were still less subjected to detailed supervision from Whitehall than they had been in pre-war days. The depressed condition of trade and the disastrous harvests from 1646 to 1649 produced an unprecedented concentration of poverty, underlining the revolutionary situation of 1648-9. Clubmen began to appear menacingly once more, plundering for corn in the Severn valley. The number of vagrants increased, while facilities for dealing with them had still not recovered from the war. Coal prices were especially high in the late winter, partly because of the reimposition of the wartime levy at Newcastle in 1648, and there was serious shortage in London, with people dying of cold and hunger if Clement Walker is to be believed. Food prices continued to rise in 1649, and were even closer to famine levels.[70] Although trade slowly recovered after 1649 and food prices fell, the need for more effective poor relief was still an urgent matter.

The Rump did what any government would have done; they tried to bring prices down. In February 1649 they appointed a committee to make recommendations, and a month later they ordered the J.P.s to enforce the laws against engrossing. The London fuel shortage produced an order to the Lord Mayor to find out why normal supplies were not arriving, and another Rump committee to consider 'all the charges and impositions laid upon coal'. Not until

earlier policies by protecting school endowments. But it did little more than this. The Commonwealth innovations were the result of *local* action, by bodies like the propagators: below, p. 329.

[69] For these and other schemes see James, *Social Problems*, pp. 273-83, 311-14. James's identification of Cook as a Royalist-Anglican because of his conservative economic philosophy is, of course, incorrect, but reveals a good deal about her own assumptions.

[70] *Perfect Occurrences*, no. 105 (29 Dec. 1648-5 Jan. 1648/9: [B.M.] E. 527, 3); Walker, *Independency*, ii. 151; James, *Social Problems*, pp. 35-66, 243-54; Thirsk, ed., *Agrarian History*, iv, App., Tables vi, vii; Hoskins, *Agr. Hist. Rev.* xvi (1968), 20, 29.

September, however, was the levy taken off, and fiscal necessity
soon led to its restoration, though at a lower rate.[71] More general
measures of price control did not get very far. A Bill 'abating the
price of victuals' was read twice in April 1649 but died in committee, as did a similar Bill a year later. An Act regulating the price
of beer was passed in September 1649, but for the most part the
Rump relied on the variable efforts of local authorities to control
prices by restricting malting and brewing and thus make larger
supplies of grain available. In April 1649 a general order was sent
to J.P.s reminding them of their duty in setting wage rates. The
Rump was doing what any government would have done. A revolutionary government might have been expected to do more.[72]

One popular scapegoat for high prices was the excise. The excise
was a serious burden to trade, a pamphleteer declared in 1650, and
greatly disheartened 'the most ingenious and industrious party'—
the Commonwealth's urban supporters, in other words. In a demonstration at Frome in January 1649 the rioters had been described
as 'not the scum and malignants of the town, but such as have faith-
fully served the Parliament'. Another disturbance at Ormskirk
a year later, however, was said to have been the work of 'the meaner
sort', who attacked the excise commissioners at an inn and were
kept off at pistol-point until troops arrived. Troops also had to be
called at Shaftesbury in March 1650, and there were outbreaks
near by, at Poole. But the Rump was desperately short of money,
and the general excise had to remain, a serious burden on the poor.
There were indeed men in the House who thought, as John Moyle
did, that the excise was 'the easiest and equallest tax that possibly
can be', the only rational substitute for monopolies.[73]

In its approach to poor relief, the Rump showed little more concern for the interests of the lower orders. There was a good deal of
discussion during the months of depression and mutiny early in
1649, though when a petition on behalf of the poor was presented
in March the Commons answered vaguely that this was only one
of many important matters under consideration. In the circular

[71] *C.J.* vi. 187, 293; James, *Social Problems*, p. 265. For the coal question see Howell,
*Newcastle*, pp. 276-7.

[72] James, *Social Problems*, pp. 265-9; Gardiner, *Commonwealth*, i. 39; Firth and Rait,
*A. and O.* ii. 244-5.

[73] James, *Social Problems*, p. 38; *The Moderate*, no. 29 (23-30 Jan. 1648/9: [B.M.]
E. 540, 20); Whitelocke, *Memorials*, iii. 156, 162; Moyle to Bennet, 13 Nov. 1649: H.M.C.,
*Hodgkin*, p. 46.

ordering J.P.s to enforce the poor law with special energy the Rump claimed to be 'very sensible and compassionate' of the condition of the poor.[74] But good intentions were not translated into action. Nothing came of a Bill on the subject that was in committee at this time. In May an Act for relieving and employing paupers and for punishing vagrants was passed, the only such legislation during the Rump's entire history. But the Act was confined to London, and although a committee was told to prepare a Bill for the whole country it did not materialize. During the Army's reform campaign in the autumn of 1650 a committee was appointed to review all existing laws relating to the poor. It was this committee which proposed that cathedrals should be demolished to relieve poverty (a beginning was made at Lichfield, at least), and also suggested an investigation of poor funds by the commissioners for charitable uses. In 1652 there were more committees but no legislation. Another Bill was given a second reading in October, but had not reached the statute book by the time of the Rump's downfall.[75] Recent investigation suggests that earlier descriptions of the Rump's poverty programme as one of 'harshness coupled with failure' may be unfair. Although the Commonwealth was naturally interested in suppressing vagrancy, this was not its sole concern. Once local government recovered from the war, the poor law was more efficiently, perhaps even more benignly, administered than it had ever been. But this was the result of local initiative, the energy and public spirit of Puritan J.P.s, not of any concrete action by the Rump. Hugh Peter presented a 'model about the poor' to the Hale commission, but it made no progress.[76]

The well-publicized grievances of copyholders and smallholders were similarly neglected. The Levellers had long been campaigning on their behalf against the whole 'Norman' system of primogeniture and 'base tenures'. And there had been the customary complaints about enclosure and the destruction of common rights by acquisitive landlords; the Digger outbreaks were only the most spectacular incidents in a widespread protest movement. In 1649 the Council of State talked of legislative action, and in the following

[74] Speaker to Wilts. J.P.s, 19 Mar. 1648/9: H.M.C., *Various Collections*, i (Wilts. Q.S. MSS.), 118.

[75] *C.J.* vii. 127, 190, 255-60; Firth and Rait, *A. and O.* ii. 104-10; James, *Social Problems*, pp. 284-6, 295-8; Gardiner, *Commonwealth*, ii. 23, 227.

[76] B.M. Add. MS. 35863 (Hale Commission Minute-book), fol. 76ᵛ. See James, *Social Problems*, ch. vi, esp. pp. 299-302, for the older view. A recent corrective is in A. L. Beier, 'Poor Relief in Warwickshire, 1630-1660', *Past and Present*, no. 35 (Dec. 1966), 77-100.

year the circuit judges were told to announce that a Bill was under consideration; but it never reached fruition. In March 1652 a Bill dealing with arbitrary fines and the alienation of copyholds was approved by both the Hale commission and the Rump's law reform committee, but it too was stillborn.[77]

It is difficult to resist the conclusion that the Rump was more protective of the rich and powerful than of the poor and oppressed. Acts for fen drainage in Lincolnshire and Yorkshire (against which Lilburne led some violent protests), for reducing the costs of lords of manors in Exchequer proceedings, and against the poaching of deer, encountered far less difficulty than the abortive series of poor laws.[78] John Cook's old-fashioned attacks on the evils of a competitive economy were drowned by the growing chorus from the improvers. Enclosure, Walter Blyth proclaimed, would have benefits for all, far exceeding any that could come from a levelling of estates. Former soldier, sequestration agent, and surveyor, Blyth was a good spokesman for those profiting from a fluid land market and the new interest in progressive farming. The Rump could satisfy the improvers by doing nothing. For the encouragement of commerce action was needed. It is unnecessary here to explore in detail the Rump's commercial policy; sufficient to note that it owed far more to the plans of men like Hartlib and Henry Robinson for the promotion of trade than to their projects for genuine social reform. The Council of Trade, the Navigation Act, the policy of maritime aggression leading to the Dutch war, all anticipate the course of English policy for the rest of the century. The Council was directed to consider the question of monopolies versus free trade, but in practice the privileges of great corporations like the East India and Levant companies were invariably upheld. There is no sign that the Rump ever seriously contemplated a general loosening of trade in the interests of the small traders, the provincial clothiers, or the outports.[79]

*       *       *

The first three topics of reform were all important. The fourth, parliamentary reform, was crucial to the Rump's survival, and the

[77] *C.J.* vi. 240; James, *Social Problems*, pp. 94-8, 333; Schenk, *Concern for Social Justice*, pp. 66-71; Hill, *Puritanism and Revolution*, pp. 189-93; Brailsford, *The Levellers*, pp. 443-50.

[78] Firth and Rait, *A. and O.* ii. 130-9, 447-9, 548. For the fen riots see James, *Social Problems*, pp. 125-8; Pauline Gregg, *Free-Born John* (London, 1961), pp. 308-9; and Maurice Ashley, *John Wildman* (London, 1947), pp. 77-80.

[79] James, *Social Problems*, pp. 106-15, 151-74.

failure to grapple with it led in the end to the regime's destruction. A fatal division of opinion can be traced back to the weeks before December 1648, when Ireton had recommended an immediate dissolution and new elections, and Ludlow had insisted on a purge that would leave the civilian radicals in power. In essence the conflict between these two positions continued throughout the Commonwealth. The Army continued to demand a dissolution and new elections under a reformed franchise and a redistribution of constituencies. The civilian Rumpers clung tenaciously to power, proposing that their own seats should be guaranteed in the next Parliament, and elections held only in constituencies that were vacant because of the Purge or for other reasons. Had he been at Westminster, Ireton would undoubtedly have taken the lead in the campaign for thoroughgoing reform. After the King's execution, according to Lenthall, he showed his desire to make a clean break with the past by proposing that the very name of Parliament should be changed to 'the representative of the people'. Whether he would have been successful is another matter. As his ability to unite the Army in the autumn of 1648 shows, he had considerable political skill. But he was lacking in tact, and his unpopularity in the Rump is demonstrated by his failure to gain election to the original Council of State. 'Few men', says John Cook, 'knew more of the art of policy and self interested prudentials, but never man so little practised them.'[80] In any case Ireton was in Ireland from the summer of 1649 until his death two years later. The other generals were similarly engaged, and it was only after Worcester that Cromwell returned to press for action. The Rump was thus left to its own devices, and the course of parliamentary reform was consequently an erratic one.

The Rump's first important move, it will be recalled, had been the admission of the conformists, who still further strengthened the forces of conservatism. Dissolution and redistribution were discussed on 16 and 17 March in a debate on a new declaration justifying the recent revolution; but the declaration in the end contained only vague promises. Something more was needed to placate the Army, especially during the days when the Leveller mutineers were in arms. Reviewing the troops in Hyde Park on 9 May before

---

[80] Lenthall, in *Monarchy Asserted to be the Best, Most Ancient, and Legal Form of Government* (1660), *Somers Tracts*, vi. 357; John Cooke, *Monarchy No Creature of Gods Making* (Waterford, 26 Feb. 1651/2: [B.M.] E. 1238, 1), Preface.

marching against the Levellers, Cromwell promised that Parliament would soon agree to a swift dissolution and a new representative. The Council of State added its voice, and six days later, after a long debate, the Commons appointed a committee under the younger Vane to consider the 'succession of future Parliaments and the regulating of their elections'.[81]

But the Rump was more interested in the nature of its own membership in the present than in discussion of hypothetical future parliaments. On 31 May the five-man committee under Cornelius Holland which for nearly two months had been considering applications for admission was directed to draw up a list of all absent members, and to advise the House which ought to be admitted and which permanently expelled. They reported on 9 June, proposing that only those members who would endorse the trial of the King should be admitted, but this was rejected and the House fell back on the old test of dissent to the 5 December vote. However, no more applications would be considered after 30 June, and those who did not give satisfaction by then would be expelled and their places filled by new elections.[82] If this decision was adhered to and the House recruited again, the prospects for Ireton's 'new representative' were bleak indeed. Cromwell took the point at once and denounced the whole scheme, suggesting instead that the House should adjourn for the summer. The Council of State thereupon drew up a list of Bills on which action should be taken before the adjournment, adding that the new representative ought to have high priority in the next session, and recommending that Vane's committee continue its work during the recess. In fact the Rump did not adjourn, but presumably through Cromwell's opposition the final report from Holland's committee was repeatedly delayed; in July it was noted that the Commons were 'still at a stand about readmitting the excluded members'. Eventually, on 23 July, the report was made, and led to the return of eleven abstainers; three other cases were referred back to the committee.[83]

[81] C.J. vi. 208-10; Whitelocke, Memorials, ii. 555-6; iii. 33; Gardiner, Commonwealth, i. 50, 57.

[82] On the 19th Hutchinson was added to the committee, and they were ordered to meet daily until the 30th: C.J. vi. 221, 228, 237. The erased entries of 9 June are in Whitelocke, Memorials, iii. 47; Walker, Independency, ii. 210; and printed in B.M. 669 f. 14, 39.

[83] Letter of intelligence, [July 1649]: Carte, Original Letters, i. 299; Whitelocke, Memorials, iii. 57; Gardiner, Commonwealth, i. 86. The three cases referred back were those of the two Barnardistons and Thomas Cholmley: C.J. vi. 268. They were never in fact admitted. For the abortive adjournment scheme see below, p. 295, n. 103.

At this point the Rump's membership was stabilized, for no more
secluded members or abstainers were admitted until November
1650; during this time the only additions were Walter Strickland,
who returned from Holland, and four newly elected members.[84] In
September 1649 opinion was moving strongly towards the recruiting
scheme. John Moyle thought that if the absent Cornish members
did not immediately return the county should petition for new
writs to replace them, and Lord Lisle (whose brother Algernon was
on Vane's committee) told his father that new elections would
shortly be ordered, under careful regulations to see that only
persons loyal to the Commonwealth got in.[85] This was made easier
by a vote on 11 October that all members should take the Engagement; on the same day Vane's committee was ordered to make a
swift report. Early in December it was voted that all those who had
not met the 30 June deadline were to be disabled, Major-General
Browne being singled out for immediate expulsion.[86]

On 9 January 1650 the Vane committee at last produced its
report.[87] In so far as it was complete, it was a compromise between
the views of the Army and of the politicians; but it was not complete, for the committee had reached an impasse on several important
matters. The Army had always argued for a redistribution based on
rational, equitable principles. In 1647, in the *Heads of the Proposals*,
they had urged a distribution of constituencies 'proportionable to
the respective rates they bear in the common charges and burdens
of the kingdom'. In the November 1648 *Remonstrance* they had
called more generally for the Commons to be made 'an equal
representative of the whole people electing'. In the revised *Agreement of the People* of January 1649 they had accepted some features
of the Levellers' earlier redistribution scheme, limiting the membership of the House to 400, and allocating seats to the counties and
boroughs in detail. Vane's committee accepted the 1647 principle

---

[84] The Earl of Salisbury, Henry Nevill, Thomas Birch, and Philip Jones.

[85] Moyle to Bennet, 1 Sept. 1649: Folger Lib., MS. Add. 494, p. 165; Lisle to Leicester,
26 Sept.: H.M.C., *De L'Isle*, vi. 456. However, Moyle told Francis Buller on the 22nd that
he thought there might still be no obstacle to the readmission of any secluded member who
would 'cordially own' the Commonwealth: *Buller Papers*, p. 110.

[86] *C.J.* vi. 305-6, 328-9; Gardiner, *Commonwealth*, i. 176; Moyle to Buller, 18 Dec.
1649: *Buller Papers*, p. 111.

[87] *C.J.* vi. 344-5. According to Moyle, there had been an earlier report in November;
this had been referred back to the committee, which had at the same time been enlarged:
Moyle to Bennet, 13 Nov. 1649: H.M.C., *Hodgkin*, p. 47. There is no reference in the *C.J.*
to this, though four additions to the committee were made on 2 Nov.: vi. 318.

that representation should be based on taxation. According to John Moyle, 'the rule by which they went . . . is the Army's monthly rate [the assessment], that is one representative for every £200; so Cornwall, being £2,000 per mensem, is to have ten representatives'. As in the revised *Agreement* the House was to contain 400 members, and the committee also generally followed the *Agreement* in the allocation of seats among the counties.[88]

But Vane and his colleagues had been unable to agree on the status of the boroughs, or on the qualifications for either voters or M.P.s. The January 1649 *Agreement* had granted the vast majority of seats to the counties, but had retained separate representation for some of the larger towns. As Moyle put it, the committee could not decide 'whether they shall be chosen by boroughs (if it shall be thought fit to have burgesses) or else by all the freeholders of the respective counties as the knights of the shire are'. The report made no attempt to settle the problem; the counties' quotas were drawn up with no suggestions whether or how they should be divided among the boroughs. Other crucial questions were left to the House to decide, including the duration of future parliaments, the nature of the franchise, and of the members' qualifications. And in the report's final paragraph the hardening of opinion against the Army, the determination of the Rumpers to hold on to their seats as firmly as they had in the Purge, was made plain. 'Those members now sitting in Parliament' were to retain their seats and be counted as part of the quota of each county.

There was an obvious connection between the discussions of the Rump's own membership and the scheme for the new representative. The more secluded members and abstainers that were restored, the less meaningful future elections as proposed in the Vane report would be; the stronger the barrier against genuine parliamentary reform. The Rump's internal divisions, to be sure, made progress even on this limited basis very slow. For several months the House considered the report every Wednesday in committee of the whole, but gradually the discussion petered out as the war with Scotland became a more pressing concern.[89] After Dunbar there was a revival of interest, and the House began systematically

---

[88] Moyle to Bennet, 13 Nov. 1649: H.M.C., *Hodgkin*, p. 47. See Vernon F. Snow, 'Parliamentary Reapportionment Proposals in the Puritan Revolution', *E.H.R.* lxxiv (1959), 409–42, for a not very illuminating comparison of these and other redistribution schemes.

[89] *C.J.* vi. 345–455, *passim*; Whitelocke, *Memorials*, iii. 141, 143, 155.

working through the list of absent members to decide which ought
to be protected from the new elections and which expelled. In
November the Army's friends revived the proposal that an endorsement of the King's execution should be made an additional test for
membership; few even of the existing Rumpers would have been
able to subscribe this, and the overwhelming majority of constituencies would have been open for the elections. But as usual the
Rump was disinclined to do anything so drastic, and was content
with a belated, general congratulation to the members of the High
Court of Justice for their courageous discharge of their duty.[90]

No official record exists of the Rump's proceedings in committee.
Two letters written in January 1651, however, provide a few clues
about what was happening. Lord Lisle told his father that they were
engaged in 'the exclusions of the separated members', noting that
William Pierrepont was one of those recently voted out. A more
detailed account in a letter from John Trevor to Swynfen is worth
quoting at length:[91]

The new representative goes on slowly. Once a week the Grand Committee of the House sit about, and in the rooms of such as are now absent,
they proceed to vote new elections, but according to the new proportion.
To some that are received in favour they forbear to vote new elections,
but refer the consideration of them to the House: some of these are Mr.
Selden, Sir B. Rudyard, Mr. Westrow, Col. Norton, Mr. Hollis the
younger, Sir Richard Onslow, Mr. Bacon. They are not come to you yet,
the alphabet being in S.

The scheme for the new representative, in other words, had become
one for the permanent expulsion of Pride's victims, followed by
another recruiting of the House. But once again the Rump's usual
inertia took over. There were occasional discussions in committee
until 21 May 1651, but no real movement until the autumn.

When reform again became a live issue after Worcester it was in
an entirely new political climate. The republic had been saved, the

[90] *C.J.* vi. 486–576, *passim*; Gardiner, *Commonwealth*, ii. 4; Rushworth and Margetts to
Clarke, 30 Nov. 1650: H.M.C., *Leybourne-Popham*, pp. 78–9.
[91] Lisle to Leicester, 7 Jan. 1650/1: H.M.C., *De L'Isle*, vi. 486; Trevor to Swynfen,
9 Jan.: William Salt Lib., Salt MS. 454 (Swynfen MSS.), no. 6. Trevor was a secluded
member, but was presumably kept informed by his father, Sir John, who was an active
Rumper. The inclusion of Bacon's name in this list is puzzling. Both Francis and Nathaniel
Bacon had been secluded, but both were admitted to the Rump on 6 June 1649: *C.J.* vi. 225.
However, there are no more references to Francis in the Rump after that date, so perhaps
he had never availed himself of his right to sit, and had therefore been disqualified again.

wars were over, and it was time for a general settlement. So at least
thought Oliver Cromwell, and so did some of his old friends. There
followed a temporary resurrection of something indeed very like
the old middle group. The friendship between Cromwell and
Oliver St. John had been broken by the Purge, and although St.
John had agreed to serve the Commonwealth as Chief Justice, his
relations with Cromwell remained distant.[92] But when the victorious
general returned to London in triumph after Worcester, St. John
was one of the official delegation which went out to Aylesbury to
receive him. They had 'much discourse' with Cromwell over dinner,
Whitelocke noted, 'my Lord Chief Justice St. John more than all
the rest'. Cromwell's stately behaviour at this time aroused radical
suspicions of his intentions. They also noted that he chose 'new
friends'; in fact they were not new, merely a resumption of the old.[93]
From subsequent events it can be deduced that his new policy
involved moderate reform, a swift dissolution and new elections to
satisfy the Army, and a concentration on settlement through an
Act of oblivion to satisfy moderates like St. John. The chief
casualties would be the civilian Rumpers, who would have to give
up their intended perpetuation of their own power.

On 16 September Cromwell took his seat in the House of
Commons. On the same day new reform measures were introduced,
'for satisfaction of soldiery and the ease of the people', as Whitelocke describes them (among them was the Act of oblivion), and
debate was resumed on the new representative. On the 25th it was
agreed that a completely new Bill should be brought in, which would
set an explicit date for dissolution and establish the rules for a complete, general election: the Vane report and the recruiting scheme
had been abandoned.[94] The new elections Bill was given a second
reading on 10 October, and was frequently discussed in grand
committee for the next month. On 14 November, after a six-day
debate, Cromwell and St. John at last persuaded the House to set
a definite dissolution date. They won the day by the narrow margin

---

[92] St. John served with Cromwell on the committee that in June 1650 tried to persuade
Fairfax not to resign his command: Whitelocke, *Memorials*, iii. 207-11. On 22 Sept. 1650
he wrote Cromwell a friendly letter; but Cromwell evidently did not reply, and in December
his wife was anxiously urging him to answer St. John's letters: *Milton State Papers*,
pp. 24-6, 40.

[93] Whitelocke, *Memorials*, iii. 351; *Ludlow's Memoirs*, i. 282, 344.

[94] Whitelocke, *Memorials*, iii. 353; *C.J.* vii. 18-20. New alignments among the civilian
radicals seem to be indicated by Thomas Scot's support for Cromwell against the opposition of Mildmay and Sir James Harrington.

of only two votes, and some arm-twisting seems to have been necessary to achieve even this. A few days earlier, Daniel Blagrave had
received a mysterious message from Cromwell about 'whether he
should be ch[osen?] again in a new Parliament', presumably a warning that he would not be if he did not support the motion. The outcome is said to have caused consternation among Rumpers with
'large accounts or unworthy actions to answer': Blagrave may have
been one of them. The date selected was something of an anti-
climax: 3 November 1654, still almost three years away.[95]

Cromwell and St. John, meanwhile, were actively improving the
climate in the House for their other proposals. On 10 October the
committee on admissions was revived, and within a few weeks four
old members had been admitted. Three of them, it is worth noting,
were former middle-group supporters—Westrow, John Stephens,
and Say's son-in-law Richard Norton—and the fourth, Sir Thomas
Wodehouse, a country gentleman of impeccable moderation.[96]
At the same time pressure was being put on at least one other
abstaining moderate to return and strengthen this new middle
group in the House. On 14 October John Harington, who was still
on close terms with St. John, received from the Chief Justice the
first of several suggestions that he should come back to Parliament.
Six weeks later St. John moved in Harington's favour in the House
itself, though the Somerset member's evident lack of interest prevented any action being taken.[97] If other abstainers had kept diaries
it is quite likely that we should find that Harington was not the only
member to receive such suggestions at this time.

Although the 1651 Bill for a new representative was soon frozen
in the same procedural ice that always imprisoned reform proposals
in the Rump, other aspects of the settlement scheme made some
progress. The Hale commission, Owen's proposals for a Church
settlement, and in February 1652 the passage of the Act of oblivion
(which the radicals managed to make more severe than was originally
intended), were all part of the same programme. Cromwell and St.
John were out to reunite the 'godly party' on lines similar to those
proposed by the middle group before 1648, and in a way that
strikingly anticipates much of the Protectorate. The next step was

---

[95] *C.J.* vii. 27-37; Whitelocke, *Memorials*, iii. 358, 360; Newsletters, 15 and 16 Nov.
1651: *Clarke Papers*, ii. 233; Josten, ed., *Ashmole*, ii. 591.

[96] *C.J.* vii. 27, 29, 44.

[97] B.M. Add. MS. 10114 (Harington's Diary), fols. 29ᵛ, 30ᵛ. The pressure on Harington
continued at least until May 1652: ibid., fol. 31.

a cautious political reconnaissance to see how much of the old constitution might be restored. In December 1651 Cromwell called
a private meeting of leading Army officers and M.P.s (mostly
lawyers) to discuss the prospects for settlement. The idealistic
Harrison wanted to begin with 'civil and spiritual liberties', but
Whitelocke, as Cromwell must have guessed he might do, proposed
as the first business the choice between monarchy and a republic.
Cromwell jumped at the suggestion. All the other officers were
firmly for a republic; the lawyers all hankered after monarchy.
Widdrington, as usual, was for the Duke of Gloucester. Whitelocke
suggested setting a date at which the exiled Charles II or his brother
York would be allowed to surrender and make a settlement. St.
John said nothing about the Stuarts, but agreed that 'something of
monarchical power' was necessary to preserve 'the foundation of
our laws and the liberties of the people'. Cromwell echoed his
words: the Stuarts were politically impossible, but a definitive
settlement 'with monarchical power in it' was indeed the best
solution. The broad outline of the Protectorate was already taking
shape in his mind.[98]

The officers' opposition meant that for the present Cromwell and
St. John would have to wait. And very soon they lost control of the
Commons, as the Army's reform campaign made the Rumpers
inclined to dig their heels in and resist a dissolution as a concession
to military pressure. In February 1652 Blagrave was already
wondering 'whether the soldier shall overcome the Parliament or
the Parliament the soldier'. In May the Cromwell-St. John scheme
was being challenged. The Commons resumed discussion of how
to be 'supplied with members', and there was support both for
restoring the secluded members and for holding a new series of
recruiter elections to replace them; however, the previous autumn's
Bill was also occasionally debated in committee for a few weeks.[99]
Nothing more was done until after the Army petition of 13 August
1652. In its original form this demanded immediate dissolution,
but Cromwell used his moderating influence, and in the end the
petition asked only for 'speedy consideration' of new elections,
restricted to 'such as are pious and faithful'. Radical officers were
already muttering about a forcible dissolution, to frustrate the

---

[98] Whitelocke, *Memorials*, iii. 372-4.
[99] Josten, ed., *Ashmole*, ii. 605; *C.J.* vii. 123, 130-6; Whitelocke, *Memorials*, iii. 420, 422;
Gardiner, *Commonwealth*, ii. 173-4, 223.

Rump's evident resolve 'to sit to perpetuity'. The Rump therefore
wisely decided to make some gesture towards reform, and on
14 September they sent the Bill for the new representative to a committee headed by John Carew, abandoning the grand committee
procedure in the interests of the Bill's 'more speedy' passage. This
may have pleased the Army, but at the same time the formerly
agreed dissolution date was dropped, so the whole matter was in
the air again.[100]

At the end of 1652 Carew's committee had still not reported.
Both Parliament and Army were now completely fragmented. The
Rump had come a long way since 1649, and in the course of time
new alignments had inevitably been made, new issues had arisen.
By 1652 the great one was the Dutch war, on which the divisions
had little to do with earlier struggles. The Army too was hopelessly
split. Harrison and the Fifth Monarchy enthusiasts were again
imbibing intoxicating draughts of millenarianism: after dissolving
the Rump they would put government in the hands of the Saints in
a carefully rigged election based on a religious qualification.
Lambert, on the other hand, was the leader of those who wanted
a dissolution followed by elections based on the 1649 *Agreement's*
redistribution scheme and a redefined property qualification.
Cromwell was vacillating. He too wanted a dissolution, but was
torn between Harrison's Puritan authoritarianism and the moderate
constitutionalism which Lambert now represented.

Pressure from the Army and the sects was resumed early in 1653.
When the Bill for the new representative was put in Harrison's
charge it looked for a time as if the Saints had won. On 13 January
the Council of State agreed with a committee of the officers that
immediate dissolution was essential. Harrison's hostility to free
elections had much support in the Army, and a circular letter to the
regiments defined the new policy as one calling for successive parliaments of 'men of truth, fearing God and hating covetousness'.
Unexpectedly Cromwell swung over to Harrison. Either he was
swept away by the Army's infectious passion, or his suspicions of
Lambert, who was believed to be intriguing with his opponents in
the Rump, clouded his judgement. At the last minute, after the Bill
for the new representative had been piloted through the House by
Haselrig (Harrison did not co-operate) Cromwell withdrew his

---

[100] *Ludlow's Memoirs*, i. 348; E. Chillenden to Clarke, 28 Aug. 1652: H.M.C., *Leybourne-Popham*, p. 104; *C.J.* vii. 164, 178; Gardiner, *Commonwealth*, ii. 224-6.

U

support, even though it was not far from the solution for which he and St. John had previously been working. Haselrig's Bill seems to have been based on Lambert's proposals, including dissolution, redistribution (over whose details there was some haggling in the House in March), and a £200 property qualification for voters; the scheme was later incorporated almost intact in the *Instrument of Government*. The Bill also evidently included a clause exempting Rumpers from having to face the first elections, which would be held on 3 November: the old recruiting scheme in modified form. However, when on 20 April Cromwell expelled the Rump, he did so primarily not because of the recruiting scheme (though this was a convenient pretext), but because they proposed the very electoral system that he had himself espoused not long before, and which now seemed to offer insufficient guarantees for the rule of the Saints. Another eight months would have to pass before the logical outcome of his association with St. John could be implemented.[101] Once more the Rump's procrastination had obstructed the completion of a rational settlement before it was too late.

\*     \*     \*

There are many reasons why the Rump achieved so little. Part of the explanation involves something common to all reformist regimes. Members of the Rump might or might not be religious idealists and reformers; they were also practical men who had to govern the country. Like all governments then and now, they found the routine, day-to-day burden of administration too complicated to leave much time for discussion of long-range planning. Defence against the Commonwealth's enemies, internal and external, was necessarily their first priority; this meant dealing with Ireland, Scotland, the French, Royalists in and outside the country, and finally, overwhelmingly, the Dutch war. It meant the militia, the

---

[101] It is still impossible to be certain exactly what happened during the crisis. There are serious contradictions between the evidence of observers in Apr. 1653 and later accounts, including Cromwell's. The traditional argument that dissolution was necessary to frustrate the Rumpers' intention to perpetuate themselves is puzzling, in view of the Commons' recent proceedings, which imply that Haselrig's Bill would have ensured pretty complete electoral reform. See *C.J.* vii. 244, 261–78; C. H. Firth, 'Cromwell and the Expulsion of the Long Parliament in 1653', *E.H.R.* viii (1893), 526–34; and Abbott, *Cromwell*, ii, ch. xvi. Gardiner's account (*Commonwealth*, ii. 232–65) obviously requires considerable modification. My own brief summary, I am well aware, grievously oversimplifies a very complicated situation. I owe much to Blair Worden for his stimulating comments and advice on this and other problems of the Rump.

navy, and foreign policy. Reform invariably, and naturally, took second place. Prominent reformers like Ireton and Ludlow were absent for long periods in Ireland, others who remained were swamped in administrative detail. Like many idealists who find themselves in power, they obviously enjoyed it. Sir Harry Vane made naval affairs his main job; only secondarily was he concerned with Godly Reformation. Thomas Scot became head of the regime's intelligence operations. Without displaying the genius of a Walsingham or a Thurloe he was still very competent, and must have devoted a good deal of time to it.[102] Large defence expenditures raised corresponding fiscal problems, made all the greater by the burden of debt inherited from the war, which threatened to swamp the Commonwealth in bankruptcy. Excise and assessment Bills and complicated measures putting confiscated lands up for sale all took up far more time than idealists in the country thought proper. Law reform, tithes, and the new representative would have to wait their turn.

Part of the trouble was lack of efficient parliamentary management. The Council of State was effective enough as an executive, but it showed little skill in getting the necessary business done in the House with sufficient speed. Especially in its first year, the Council contained a higher proportion of radicals than the Commons, and often urged more serious attention to reform, but without following it up.[103] This meant interminable argument and procedural delay, stonewalling in committees, three months debate over encumbrances, long lectures from Whitelocke and the lawyers.

Yet even if the Rump had managed its business more efficiently

---

[102] C. H. Firth, ed., 'Thomas Scot's Account of his Actions as Intelligencer during the Commonwealth', *E.H.R.* xii (1897), 116-26; Underdown, *Royalist Conspiracy*, pp. 20-1, 61-3.

[103] The abortive adjournment scheme of June 1649 is a good example. On 11 June the House accepted Cromwell's suggestion that they should adjourn in the near future, and asked the Council to draw up a list of high-priority Bills. A Council committee headed by Henry Marten did so, and had it presented to the Commons on the 22nd. The Rump dealt effectively enough with some of them: money Bills, a new treason law, Bills for the sale of Crown lands, relief of debtors, and the suppression of unlicensed books and pamphlets. But both the Act of oblivion and the Bill for repealing the church-attendance laws got no further than second readings. There was no progress at all on the more general topics of reform on which the Council wanted a beginning, so that action could be completed after the recess: law reform, the abolition of tithes, and the new representative. And the adjournment itself came to nothing. *C.J.* vi. 229-45, 250, 255; *Cal. S.P. Dom., 1649-50*, pp. 180, 185, 199; Firth and Rait, *A. and O.* ii. 158-254; Whitelocke, *Memorials*, iii. 57.

and had found more time for long-term reconstruction, it still would not have fulfilled the hopes of the righteous. There were distinct limits to the radicalism of even its original members, the architects of the revolution. Most of them, like Oliver Cromwell, were dedicated Puritans, but they were also country gentlemen who had no thought of changing the social order. Disturbed by the breach in the godly party, worried by their isolation, and fearful of the Levellers to their left and the Royalists to their right, they held out an immediate olive branch to the conformists, to men who were even less interested in making further changes than they were themselves. The Rump's frustrations were of its own making, and followed logically from the nature of the revolution. In the end the typical Rumper was not the determined Commonwealthsman, not Edmund Ludlow or Henry Ireton. It was not even Oliver Cromwell. It was Bulstrode Whitelocke.

# X

## THE REVOLUTION AND THE COMMUNITIES

THE revolution in Parliament stopped in its tracks. So did the revolution outside, and for much the same reasons. The revolutionaries were a divided minority confronting a social and political system of immense strength, much of which they themselves accepted. In many places the revolutionary minority barely existed. Where it did exist, it was usually composed of small cells of Puritan Saints, deliberately separating themselves from the reprobate majority whose welfare they were determined to direct. Sometimes—in counties like Cornwall, Hereford, and Somerset, towns like Bedford and Colchester—these minorities took advantage of the Purge to seize or consolidate power. As the traditional governing families were everywhere overwhelmingly hostile to the revolution, power tended to drift further into the hands of new men, often from outside the old county or borough establishments.

Such changes were not the Rump's intention. The government's first preoccupation was stability. It had to govern the country and to take whatever local allies it could find. The Rump indeed willingly embraced the conforming moderates, if only they would take the Engagement. If they were men of stature in their localities, so much the better; if not, the Rump would make do with lesser men. In either case they would have to be carefully supervised. Possibly the lesser parochial gentry, now coming to power in so many places, shared the same attachment to the independence and integrity of their county communities that was so passionately held by the traditional local governors. But circumstances drove the Rump inexorably down the path of centralization. The Commonwealth had little *committed* support among the old governing families—its local officials tended to be either not committed, or not from the governing families. At the same time the Rumpers were determined to avoid revolutionary changes which might bring the lower orders to power. To some extent they could rely on the common acquiescence in even an unpopular government as a shield against anarchy; but for the positive implementation of policy they were bound to insist on even greater direction from Whitehall. The Commonwealth was far from being the paradise of local independence of which the country gentry had dreamed in 1640. As in other areas of policy, the Rump's attitude to the local communities was the product of circumstance; and circumstance dictated centralization.

The need for strong government was obvious. High prices, shortages, near famine in some places; depression and unemployment; smouldering opposition by the poor and 'middling sort' to the excise: all intensified the fear of Leveller or Digger explosions. The gentry were no less restive. Complaints about taxation and quartering were as common early in 1649 as ever. There had been a county meeting at Worcester just before Christmas to oppose the latest charges. In Lancashire, Assheton's Presbyterian levies could be blamed for the quartering, but everywhere else the culprit was the Army. In spite of their reduction to discipline, Henry Marten's men were still causing 'insufferable violences and oppressions' in April 1649, this time in Hampshire. At about the same time, men of Harrison's regiment were exacting quartering money at Bath, threatening to imprison an obstructive mayor, and telling the local gentry that 'their lands and the whole kingdom was theirs'. They invaded Prynne's house at Swainswick, did a lot of damage and extorted food and money before drinking themselves under the table. Even members of the Rump were not spared. Col. Stubber's men came to Sir James Harrington's house and threatened to break into his pregnant lady's room if they were not given all they wanted; reminded of the law, they replied that 'they esteemed it not so much as a straw'. Outrages of this kind were still continuing a year later, when John Ashe complained of abusive behaviour by soldiers at his house at Freshford. Any delay in the collection of assessments brought swift retaliation from the Army. Lambert's and Rokeby's regiments sent agents into Bedfordshire to bully the local authorities, warning that they would immediately resort to quartering if the money was not forthcoming. Prynne's threat to raise the county against his persecutors was ineffective, but one of the abstaining members, Robert Clive, was more successful in Shropshire a few weeks later. Troops on the way to Ireland were attacked by a tumultuous mob under Clive's leadership, denounced as traitors and rebels, and their horses seized and sold.[1]

The threat of disorder was compounded by the danger that large numbers of officials might withdraw after the revolution and create an anarchic situation in the counties. Some J.P.s and sheriffs regarded their commissions as invalid after the death of the King. The Rump tried to reassure them, quickly approving a new oath for J.P.s, and passing an Act enabling local officials to perform their duties until new commissions were issued. But widespread reluctance to serve the Commonwealth was still evident a month later, when the Commons sent out a circular letter to the sheriffs. Recalcitrant J.P.s were to be told to take the oath at the next sessions; those who refused were to be immediately reported to Westminster.[2] Still there were complaints about the unwillingness of magistrates to act or take the oath. Judges and chairmen of Quarter Sessions desperately called on J.P.s not to desert their posts. Francis Thorpe defended the revolution at York on 20 March, Robert Bennet at Truro a few weeks later, and Thomas Edgar urged the Suffolk J.P.s not to defect even if they disliked the government. Some of these appeals may have been effective, but at Exeter on 17 March, when Chief Baron Wylde made a 'gallant speech' to vindicate Parliament's recent proceedings, only seven of the forty Devonshire J.P.s came to hear him.[3]

Anxious as it was to secure the adherence of the local magistrates, the Rump was at the same time contemplating a purge of unreliable J.P.s. On 8 February they appointed a committee to 'view the commissioners of the peace' and make recommendations to the Commissioners of the Great Seal. It was soon reported that the committee had voted to put all secluded M.P.s out of their local commissions; if they did, the decision was never ratified by the House, and was not universally followed.[4] However, the committee may have been

---

[1] John R. Burton, *History of Bewdley* (London, 1883), App., p. xxxiii; *Cal. S.P. Dom., 1649–50*, pp. 113, 162–3, 282; *1650*, pp. 126, 206; *Cal. C. Comp.*, pp. 226–7; [Hants] Committee to Mildmay, 19 Apr. 1649: *Clarke Papers*, ii. 212–13 (wrongly attributed to Wilts. by Firth); William Prynne, *Legall Vindication of the Liberties of England* (July 1649: [B.M.] E. 565, 3), pp. 36–40; T. Margetts to Adam Baynes, 20 May 1649: B.M. Add. MS. 21417 (Baynes Corr.), fol. 141; *A Perfect Summary of an Exact Dyarie*, no. 23 (18–25 June 1649: [B.M.] E. 531, 4).

[2] Cary, *Memorials*, ii. 110–14; *C.J.* vi. 142, 163–4; Firth and Rait, *A. and O.* ii. 5–6.

[3] *Perfect Occurrences*, no. 116 (16–23 Mar. 1648/9: [B.M.] E. 527, 39). For the speeches by Thorpe and Edgar see above, p. 263; for Bennet's, below, p. 308.

[4] *C.J.* vi. 134; *The Moderate*, no. 31 (6–13 Feb. 1648/9: [B.M.] E. 542, 11).

thought too vindictive to please the moderate Rumpers now returning to the House in increasing numbers. In April the committee
procedure was abandoned, and the duty of selecting J.P.s was
restored directly to the Commissioners of the Great Seal. Their
review took months to complete. In August the Council of State
found it necessary to remind the circuit clerks to send in the names
of J.P.s absent from the last assizes. But eventually it was finished,
assisted by the Engagement's weeding-out process, and there
were extensive purges of J.P.s in many counties in the summer
of 1650.[5]

If energetically enforced, the Engagement would have been a
most effective means of driving the revolution forward to the reign
of the Saints. The Act of 2 January 1650, by which subscription
was required of the whole population, with forfeiture of legal rights
as the penalty for refusal, would have created a state something like
that envisaged in the *Agreement of the People*. The franchise and all
other attributes of citizenship would have been restricted to a privileged revolutionary élite.[6] But as usual the Rump moved slowly.
A good many non-subscribing officials were removed, and government newspapers in 1650 are full of accounts of enthusiastic mass
compliance. But ejecting the refusers, whether J.P.s or the more
articulate clergy, was a slow process. In Herefordshire many
ministers took the Engagement with reservations which were
accepted by the J.P.s; the Council had to demand unqualified subscription. In November 1650 Parliament was still urging J.P.s to
see that non-subscribing ministers were promptly removed, a sure
sign that often they had not been.[7] If the Rump had been intent on
a massive purge of local officials and ministers it could have insisted
on immediate enforcement of the Engagement in the early months
of 1650. That it did not is one more sign of the leaders' desire for as
broad a base of support as possible. Pressure was applied gradually
to make the moderates conform in the end, but in a way that permitted the outward acquiescence of men who paid only lip-service
to the principles of the revolution. Only where the local governors
refused to comply was there room for the promotion of more than
a handful of new radicals.

   [5] *C.J.* vi. 187, 306–7; *Cal. S.P. Dom., 1649–50*, p. 262; Whitelocke, *Memorials*, iii. 14.
See below, p. 311, for the resulting purges.
   [6] The point is made by Gardiner, *Commonwealth*, i. 176, 193–4.
   [7] *Cal. S.P. Dom., 1650*, p. 150; Rushworth to W. Clarke, 30 Nov. 1650: H.M.C.,
*Leybourne-Popham*, p. 78; Gardiner, *Commonwealth*, i. 246.

Eventually the Rump obtained a corps of local officials on whom it could depend. As we shall see, they were a miscellaneous lot, ranging from acquiescent survivors of the old oligarchies to militant republican arrivals. But they were not left to run their counties on their own. Many of the most important functions of county government were controlled not by the J.P.s but by separate bodies such as the County Committees and their successors. Nor were these other institutions left to their own devices.

The Rump's centralizing tendencies are strikingly shown in the reorganization of the sequestration system in the winter of 1649-50. If radicals like Pyne expected that the revolution would leave them with virtually uncontrolled power in their counties, they were swiftly disillusioned. Until this time the County Committees had enjoyed almost complete control over sequestration money, using it to pay their own expenses and those of their local forces, only small balances being returned to Goldsmiths' Hall. Although by 1649 most of the county levies had been disbanded, their arrears and debts often remained unpaid. But in 1649 fiscal pressure persuaded the government to tap sequestration funds more fully; the Rump was saying that it needed the money for the New Model's arrears, and that the local forces were simply out of luck. In August the county solicitors were ordered to pay *all* sequestration money to Goldsmiths' Hall. There were loud protests from the Committees, and in many places the sequestrators refused to hand over the money; the Rump countered by relieving them of their duties. It soon became clear that the Rump needed the sequestration money not just to pay the Army's arrears, but to make up the general deficit. On 25 January 1650 the new system was therefore made permanent by statute. In future, sequestrations would be handled by three commissioners in each county, who would be appointed by Goldsmiths' Hall, and responsible to them alone.[8]

It was the end of the old County Committees. What the moderates of 1646-7 had failed to achieve had been forced on the Rump by fiscal necessity. There were bitter complaints from the activists. Deprived of his handouts to supporters, Pyne argued, the soldiers would now turn Leveller; only 'the old deceitful interest', the

---

[8] *Cal. C. Comp.*, pp. 146-69; Firth and Rait, *A. and O.* ii. 329-35. In April the Goldsmiths' Hall committee was itself replaced by a body of commissioners from which M.P.s were excluded: ibid. ii. 382-3.

Presbyterians, would rejoice.[9] Not that he and others like him were
going to abandon the struggle. The appointment of the new commissioners provided another opportunity for the exercise of power
and patronage. They were nominated by the M.P.s from the
county concerned; only if there were no active M.P.s did Goldsmiths' Hall actually make the choice. The hand of Sir Henry
Mildmay can be seen in the selection of the Colchester Puritans
John Maidstone and Abraham Barrington for Essex; of Allanson,
and the other Yorkshire members, in that of Matthew Alured,
Ralph Rymer, and two York aldermen for their county. In Somerset
there was a glorious row between Pyne and John Ashe, the retiring
chairman of Goldsmiths' Hall, before a compromise was reached.
Many of the new appointees had been agents of the old Committees,
but they were now working for the central government, not for
their counties. Not surprisingly there was widespread obstruction
by the men they displaced.[10]

If no further action was taken, the Rump would now have to rely
on the J.P.s for the police and military functions previously performed by the County Committees. But too many of the J.P.s were
men of equivocal loyalty, members of the old governing class who
took the Engagement only to protect their local interests. Not that
the Rump intended to get rid of them; on the contrary, the regime
depended on the acquiescence of the moderates. But for duties that
were more directly political, men of less doubtful principles were
essential. The Assessment Committees needed purging, but were
not very important. Far more crucial to the survival of a Commonwealth beset by internal and external enemies was the militia.

The Rump at first showed less enthusiasm than the Council of
State for a new militia Act. A Bill was before the House in April
1649, but it received a second reading only on 25 September, and its
passage was not completed until July 1650. By then the new militia
was already in existence, county commissioners having been

    [9] Pyne to W. Clarke, 17 Nov. 1649: H.M.C., *Leybourne-Popham*, p. 51. In a letter to
Col. E. Ceely on 30 Nov. Fitzjames comments (ironically?) on the recent generosity of
Pyne's Committee: Fitzjames Letter-book (Northumberland MSS., B.M. Film 331),
iii, fol. 5ᵛ.
    [10] Most of the commissioners were approved in Feb. 1650: *Cal. C. Comp.*, pp. 171–4.
For Maidstone and Barrington see J. H. Round, 'Colchester during the Commonwealth',
*E.H.R.* xv (1900), 648–59; and Gardiner, *Commonwealth*, iii. 177. For the Kent com-
missioners, Everitt, *Community of Kent*, p. 289. The Somerset argument can be followed
in *Cal. C. Comp.*, pp. 173–358, *passim*; and see my forthcoming study of Civil War
Somerset.

appointed by the Council of State, and ordered to proceed on the basis of the draft Bill of September 1649. Besides their directly military functions, the commissioners were authorized to investigate conspiracies and suspicious meetings, and to disarm papists and ill-affected persons. After some delay, they were also given the power to assess property-owners worth £10 a year, or with £200 in personal estate, for horses and arms. The character of the men who took charge of the new militia ensured that it would involve one more stage in the undermining of the county communities in favour of Whitehall.[11]

As in the counties, so in the towns. In most places the old course of borough government went on unchanged in the 1650s, except in so far as the State intervened to put it into reliable hands. Such intervention was common enough, but limited in scope. The Rump might remove mayors and aldermen, but as long as their successors would take the Engagement they did not have to be deeply ideologically committed. Urban politics after the Purge illustrate once again how much the revolutionaries were a minority movement, and how little the Rump relied on them.

The country had to be governed. At first the Rump dealt with borough problems pragmatically. There were people to be reassured, like the Barnstaple authorities, who sought legal advice at Exeter immediately after the King's death, 'to be informed how to proceed'. There were people to be corrected, like the Recorder of Launceston, the secluded M.P. Thomas Gewen. Refusing to issue orders of the borough court in the name of the 'Keepers of the Liberties of England', the old Presbyterian had composed his own formula: 'in the name of Thomas Gewen, Esquire, Recorder of Launceston'. There were people to be punished, like the authorities of Exeter. The mayor refused to attend the spring assizes or to proclaim the Commonwealth, contemptuously throwing the proclamation in the gutter. Chief Baron Wylde fined him £200, and temporarily paralysed the city courts by questioning the validity of the charter.[12] And there were people to be weeded

---

[11] Firth and Rait, *A. and O.* ii. 397–402; *C.J.* vi. 299; *Cal. S.P. Dom., 1649–50,* pp. 80, 256, 414, 521. There is a copy of the draft Bill of Sept. 1649 in Folger Lib., MS. Add. 494 (Bennet MSS.), p. 188.

[12] J. R. Chanter and T. Wainwright, eds., *Reprint of the Barnstaple Records* (Barnstaple, 1900), ii. 158; Coate, *Cornwall in the Civil War,* p. 250; H.M.C., *Exeter,* p. 206; W. Cotton and H. Woollcoombe, *Gleanings from the Municipal and Cathedral Records . . . of the City of Exeter* (Exeter, 1877), p. 141. Yule, *The Independents,* p. 24, is sadly in error in thinking the Exeter corporation a hot bed of Independency. See also below, p. 319.

out, like the mayors and aldermen who were refusing the Engagement.

Some corporations had already been dealt with long before the
imposition of the Engagement by the Act of 5 September 1649.
The revolution in London had been completed by the abolition of
the veto powers of the Lord Mayor and aldermen: in future they
would sit in a unicameral Common Council, with only single votes.
On 2 April the royalist Lord Mayor, Reynardson, was dismissed
and sent to the Tower for refusing to proclaim the Act against
monarchy; his replacement was the Independent Thomas Andrewes.
Other dissident aldermen were forced to resign, and Glyn soon gave
up the recordership in favour of the radical lawyer William Steele.[13]
At Winchester the corporation was similarly remodelled in September, by an Act that must have been in preparation long before the
Engagement was passed. A new mayor, three aldermen, and seven
benchers were all named by the Rump.[14]

Once the Engagement was required, drastic intervention by the
Rump became common. Few of the old town oligarchs were enthusiastic about the new test. When it was presented to the corporation
of Nottingham in February 1650 they all, with one exception, asked
for time to consider it: 'only Mr. Huthwait subscribed now'.[15]
Towns of particular strategic importance were carefully watched.
Even so, local resistance was evident in the number of places that
had to be reprimanded for permitting reservations or unauthorized
forms of the oath. This happened at Exeter, and at Southampton
the military governor had to certify who had actually complied.[16]
At these and numerous other towns, mayors who refused the
Engagement were quickly ejected by the Rump. Other boroughs
acted themselves without waiting for the government to intervene.
At Bridgwater the mayor and three other members of the corporation were replaced. For the most part, towns in which officers were
removed elected their own replacements, or, as at Yarmouth,

[13] Sharpe, *London*, ii. 304-16; Gardiner, *Commonwealth*, i. 39. For Andrewes see Pearl,
*London and the Puritan Revolution*, pp. 309-11.

[14] *C.J.* vi. 294; H.M.C., *Seventh Report*, Appendix (House of Lords MSS.), p. 100.
Among the new benchers were three obvious Commonwealth supporters (Muspratt,
Hooker, and Champion), who were appointed sequestration commissioners for Hampshire
in 1650: *Cal. C. Comp.*, p. 173.

[15] W. H. Stevenson *et al.*, eds., *Records of the Borough of Nottingham* (London, 1882-
1956), v. 256.

[16] *Cal. S.P. Dom.*, *1649-50*, pp. 312, 323-4, 337, 366, 387; J. Silvester Davies, *History of
Southampton* (Southampton, 1883), p. 488.

received nominations from the Council or Parliament that had originally been proposed by the well-affected of the town. But in some cases the government forcibly imposed its own nominees. Once again, strategic places were singled out for this kind of treatment. Two aldermen were nominated for Hull early in 1651, and during the Worcester campaign the Rump replaced both an alderman of Chester and the town's Recorder, the M.P. John Ratcliffe.[17] Yet even after this partial purge radicals continued to complain about corporations which still included men unsympathetic to the Rump. 'Corrupt and dangerous', some of them described the corporation of Radnor in 1652, 'a grievance and burden to all the godly and well-affected in these parts'.[18]

The relationship between the Rump and the boroughs was not, of course, a one-way process. Many towns, as we shall see, used the revolution to achieve goals previously denied them. At first the Rump treated proposals from the towns on their merits. On 22 November 1649, in response to a petition asking for revision of Northampton's charter, a committee for corporations was established under the chairmanship of Augustine Garland, to which petitions from other places were subsequently referred. The committee was told to deal with these requests so as to bring the charters concerned into line with the government of the Commonwealth. During the next three years a good many petitions were presented, often by parties to local struggles in which the petitioners were trying to gain the advantage with the help of the central government.[19] In a few cases Garland's committee decided in favour of greater local self-government and a wider franchise, but there is not enough evidence to prove that this was a consistent policy. More likely the Rump, as usual, was merely responding to events, and was content with any kind of local government run by men faithful to the Commonwealth.

Only in September 1652 did the Rump show any sign of

---

[17] *Cal. S.P. Dom.*, *1650*, p. 137; *1651*, pp. 22, 31, 71, 329; *1651–2*, pp. 6, 168; *C.J.* vi. 407, 619; vii. 1, 12; Mayor and others of Bridgwater to Speaker, 26 Apr. 1650: H.M.C., *Portland*, i. 523; original in Bodl. MS. Dep. C. 159 (Nalson Papers, viii), fol. 17; John Tickell, *History of the Town and County of Kingston Upon Hull* (Hull, 1796), pp. 495–7.

[18] *Cal. C. Comp.*, p. 578.

[19] Bedford, Arundel, Stamford, Rye, and Reading were among many other places petitioning: *C.J.* vi. 324, 326–7, 351, 384, 507. I am indebted to John Libby's seminar paper at Brown University, 1969, for much enlightenment on the Rump's policy towards the boroughs. The article by B. L. K. Henderson, 'The Commonwealth Charters', *T.R.H.S.* 3rd Ser. vi (1912), 129–62, is in fact almost entirely concerned with the Protectorate.

developing a coherent policy towards the boroughs. On the 14th of
that month Garland's committee was directed to call in all borough
charters and amend them after deciding 'how corporations may be
settled as may be suitable to . . . the government of a commonwealth'.[20] In part this was a move to complete the institutional base
of the Commonwealth, to root out the last reminders of royal
authority. But 14 September was also the day on which Carew's
committee was told to proceed with the Bill for the new representative: with parliamentary elections now a real possibility, the
status of the boroughs had immediate political importance. The
calling-in of the charters produced a buzz of alarm in the boroughs.
Liskeard took legal advice about it. So did Chard, where a box was
bought for the precious document's conveyance to London. At
Beccles the portreeve took delaying action, and managed to have
the date of surrender repeatedly postponed until the Rump was
ousted. But most of the charters were obediently submitted.[21]
Like the Rump's other projects, the scheme for revising the charters
was never completed. But although evidence for the activities of
Garland's committee is scarce, there can be no doubt that the Rump
intended to impose its view of the national interest over the local
interests of the counties and boroughs. And the political implications suggest that it was anticipating the efforts of Cromwell,
Charles II, and other later governments which remodelled the
corporations for their own purposes.

*        *        *

What was the nature of the local regimes which the Rump thus
helped to install after the revolution? Let us first consider the
counties. The transformation of their power structures had already
gone a long way by 1648. In many places even the great parliamentarian families had lost their influence, and where the bulk of

---

[20] *C.J.* vii. 178.

[21] John Allen, *History of the Borough of Liskeard* (London, 1856), p. 243; Somerset R.O.,
Chard Borough MS. D/B/CH, Box 1; *Report of Commissioners on Municipal Corporations*
App. IV (1835), 2133. Sandwich, Chester, Canterbury, Leicester, Bath, and Boston are
among other places recording the demand or presentation of charters: H.M.C., *Fifth Report*,
Appendix (Sandwich MSS.), p. 571; *Eighth Report*, App. I (Chester MSS.), p. 385; *Ninth
Report*, App. I (Canterbury MSS.), p. 164; Helen Stocks and W. H. Stevenson, eds.,
*Records of the Borough of Leicester . . ., 1603-1688* (Cambridge, 1923), p. 417; C. W. Shickle,
ed., 'Copy of the Chamberlain's Accounts of the City of Bath' (typescripts at B.M.); Gladys M.
Hipkin, 'Social and Economic Conditions in the Holland Division of Lincolnshire, from
1640 to 1660', *Reports and Papers of Assoc. Archit. Socs.* xl, Pt. ii (1931), 192; *C.J.* vii. 257.

the old establishment had been royalist or localist in sentiment, as in Weldon's Kent or Pyne's Somerset, the process was almost complete. Minorities from outside the normal governing circle had entrenched themselves in the County Committees, and were beginning to do so in the Commissions of the Peace. Socially this meant a displacement of county families by outsiders, upstarts, and lesser gentry; in political and religious terms it brought to power men whose active support came mainly from the radical Puritan congregations. And it also involved the undermining of the quasi-independence of the county communities by government from Westminster. The revolt of the communities in 1648 had failed, first in the defeat of localism in the second Civil War, and then again at Pride's Purge, when a Militia Ordinance that would have restored much of the gentry's power was one of the first legislative casualties. Although in some counties men of the old type were still in charge— Barnardistons in Suffolk, Onslows in Surrey—the writing was on the wall.

The country had to be governed. But within the political nation the Rump was a minority regime, and its supporters in the counties, as even Pyne admitted, 'a very small remnant'.[22] The Commonwealth depended heavily on individual local leaders, informal counterparts of the French *Intendants*, or on small groups where no single dominant figure emerged. In many respects they took over the old role of the aristocracy and the courtiers, ensuring that the policies of the central government were effectively enforced. Their circumstances were much more difficult, for they could not command the deference customarily enjoyed by their peacetime predecessors. They could, however, rely on three things: the power of Parliament, the help of the Army, and the passive obedience of the acquiescent majority, who still preferred peace to disorder.

Some of the local bosses are already familiar to us. In Somerset the Purge merely confirmed Pyne's power by getting rid of such noisy enemies as Prynne, Strode, and Clement Walker. The Kent dictator, Sir Anthony Weldon, died in October 1648, but his place was immediately taken by Sir Michael Livesey, who governed the county just as ruthlessly. In Buckinghamshire, though Thomas Scot's busy prominence in the Rump can have left him little time for county affairs, the leadership was still firmly in the hands of his and Simon Mayne's faction. The Dorset Committee lost such secluded

²² Pyne to Clarke, 17 Nov. 1649: H.M.C., *Leybourne-Popham*, p. 51.

members as Sir Thomas Trenchard and the Erles. This reduced
the size of the oligarchy but did not alter its nature. It was very much
a family affair: John Trenchard, his sons-in-law Bingham and
Sydenham (the latter soon left to become Governor of the Isle of
Wight), and his brother-in-law John Browne. In Sussex there was
a similar network of M.P.s led by Herbert Morley, and yet another
in Yorkshire, composed of most of the local members who had survived the Purge.[23]

In many counties the supreme power was in the hands of military
men, who might or might not be members of the Rump. Sir Arthur
Haselrig ruled the northern counties with a strong hand. Major-
General Harrison enjoyed equal power in Wales after the propagation Act. In Herefordshire the rule of the Harleys was replaced by
that of Col. Wroth Rogers. The dominant figure in the south-west
was another military man, Sir Hardress Waller. He had commanded
the western forces during the previous year; the general disinclina-
tion of the local J.P.s to act after the King's death, and the virtual
collapse of the Devon Committee, increased his responsibilities.
Early in 1650, however, he went to Ireland, and his place was taken
by Cromwell's brother-in-law, John Disbrowe.[24]

Not all the Rump's 'Intendants' were M.P.s or Army officers. In
a few places local men emerged from relative obscurity to grasp the
leadership. Two striking examples are Robert Bennet in Cornwall
and Thomas Birch in Lancashire. Bennet's chance came when most
of the M.P.s who had dominated the Cornish Committee were
ejected by the Purge. Of lesser gentry stock, Bennet had been a
colonel under Lord Robartes during the war, and later treasurer to
Massey's brigade; but he took charge of the county only after the
revolution. In 1649 he worked closely with Waller, with whom he
was on very friendly terms, to keep Cornwall obedient, and to
remodel the local committees and the Commission of the Peace.
Addressing the J.P.s at Truro Sessions in April, Bennet justified
the Purge and the execution of the King as acts of righteousness
and justice, necessary for the preservation of liberty. He was also
an ardent Anabaptist, and his regime gave ample scope for the

[23] Everitt, *Community of Kent*, pp. 273, 276-7; A. M. Johnson, 'Buckinghamshire',
ch. iii; Mayo, ed., *Dorset Committee Minute Book*, pp. 472-572, *passim*. The local activity
of the Sussex and Yorkshire members is evident from *C.J.*, *Cal. S.P. Dom.*, and *Cal. C.
Comp.*

[24] For the influence of Rogers and Waller see *C.J.*, *Cal. S.P. Dom.*, and *Cal. C. Comp.*,
*passim*. For Harrison see Dodd, *Stuart Wales*, pp. 147-51.

promotion of men of like opinions. 'It seems that Providence hath placed you there for such a time as this', Sir Hardress commended him.[25] Thomas Birch's rise to power in Lancashire was not very different. After the Purge the old leaders—Asshetons, Shuttleworths, and Hoghtons—all disappeared. Of the remaining Lancashire M.P.s, Rigby and Fell were absorbed in their legal careers, and John Moore's interests were as much in Ireland as in his county. Birch, one of a widespread lesser gentry clan near Manchester, had like Bennet been a colonel in the Civil War. In 1649 he moved into the power-vacuum in the county and became the Commonwealth's most active and energetic agent. He too was a fervent Puritan.[26]

The Rump depended heavily on men like these. They in turn relied even more on the lesser or parochial gentry to make their administrations effective. The continued retreat of the traditional governors into opposition or inactivity can be observed in all the main centres of county authority: the Commissions of the Peace as well as the County Committees and their successors. Yet the Rump was careful not to make unnecessary enemies. While the revolution was in progress there had been talk of sweeping purges of J.P.s. Pyne hinted at it when he said that he would be delighted to frustrate the Presbyterian design to keep 'honest men' off the Commission of the Peace. In fact his implementation of this implied threat was relatively mild, though notorious firebrands like Prynne and Strode were naturally removed. Instead of creating trouble for himself by dismissing unreliable moderates, Pyne tried to swamp them by the addition of new men, and the promotion of others to the Quorum.[27] Until the Commissioners of the Great Seal completed their review, it was much the same story in other counties. Active enemies of the

---

[25] Folger Lib., MS. Add. 494 (Bennet MSS.), pp. 121–95; Bennet, *King Charle's Trial Justified . . . Being the sum of a Charge given at the last Sessions held at Trewroe . . . Aprill 4, 1649* (9 May 1649: [B.M.] E. 554, 21). For Bennet see also *D.N.B.*; M. Coate, ed., 'An Original Diary of Colonel Robert Bennett of Hexworthy (1642–3)', *Devon and Cornwall N. & Q.* xviii (1934–5), 251–9; and Coate, *Cornwall in the Civil War*, pp. 252–4. Bennet was not admitted to the Rump until Oct. 1651, but he was already angling for a seat at West Looe, with Waller's help, in May 1649.

[26] W. D. Pink and A. B. Beaven, *Parliamentary Representation of Lancashire* (London, 1889), p. 189; Yule, *The Independents*, p. 88. According to Blackwood, 'Lancashire, 1635–1655', pp. 46–7, the Birches were among only four gentry families in the county who were religious Independents. For Birch's prominence in 1649 see *Cal. S.P. Dom., 1649–50, passim*. He was elected to the Rump in Oct. 1649.

[27] Pyne to Rushworth, 16 Dec. 1648: B.M. Sloane MS. 1519, fol. 188. Pyne explained his intention of promoting many J.P.s to the Quorum in a letter to John Preston, 16 Apr. 1649: Somerset R.O., Hippisley MS. DD/HI/10.

X

Rump were dismissed, but the less vehement of the secluded members remained as J.P.s until 1650, in some cases longer. Sir William Spring, Sir Dudley North, and Sir Philip Parker were all in the Suffolk commission in 1650, as were Lord Fitzwilliam, George Mountagu, Zouch Tate, and Sir Christopher Yelverton in Northamptonshire. John Boys and Sir Thomas Trenchard went off their commissions in March 1650, but even such prominent men as Glyn and Bulkeley were still unmolested. Some secluded members were actually added to their commissions in the two years after the Purge. Jenner and Thistlethwaite became J.P.s in Wiltshire in June 1649, Kyrle and Hoskins in Herefordshire a month later. Even more remarkably, Denzil Holles's son Francis became a Dorset J.P. in March 1650, as did a number of other secluded members in other counties.[28]

By this time the Engagement had revealed those who could least be relied on. Colonel Pyne had welcomed the loyalty oath with delighted approval. It would make 'a notable discovery and indeed rout amongst all professions and callings', he cheerfully reflected as he went busily about swearing the J.P.s, constables, and tithing-men.[29] John Fitzjames, on the other hand, approached it with distaste. He had been restored to the Dorset commission in November 1649—'crowded' in, as he put it without enthusiasm—but for several months he refused to take the oath or attend Quarter Sessions. This reluctance, he said, was not caused by 'any unwillingness in me to serve my country', but by a general dislike of political tests. 'The more slow the more sure, says the proverb', he added, '. . . Such oaths as are over hastily swallowed, are the most easily vomited up again.' In the end Fitzjames complied, but there were many who did not. Even so previously loyal a member of Pyne's radical clique as John Preston hesitated a long time, taking the Engagement only in January 1651.[30]

The fact that people like Preston could delay their subscription to the Engagement and still remain J.P.s shows how cautiously the

[28] Information about changes in the Commissions of the Peace in this and the following paragraphs comes from P.R.O., C 193/13/3 (*Liber Pacis*, 1650), and from the files of the History of Parliament Trust. I am grateful to Duke Henning and Thomas G. Barnes for making this material so easily available to me by beginning their list of J.P.s at an earlier date than originally intended.

[29] Pyne to Clarke, 17 Nov. 1649: H.M.C., *Leybourne-Popham*, p. 51.

[30] Fitzjames letters, 24 Nov. 1649 (2), 12 Jan. 1649/50: Letter-book (Northumberland MSS., B.M. Film 331), iii, fols. 3ᵛ-4, 22. Certificate of Preston's subscription to Engagement, 15 Jan. 1650/1: Somerset R.O., Hippisley MS. DD/HI/10.

Rump was moving. Nevertheless, in the summer of 1650, after the review by Whitelocke and his colleagues of the Great Seal, there were widespread dismissals. The extent of the purge varied considerably from place to place. It was particularly sweeping in Lincolnshire, where forty-seven J.P.s were removed, over half of them in Lindsey. Twelve went out in Bedfordshire and thirteen in Cheshire, more than a third of the commission in each case, and there were changes in some of the Welsh counties as Harrison's propagators established their grip. But in other counties there were few dismissals: only four out of forty-five J.P.s in Gloucestershire, for example, though in this case nineteen new magistrates were added. In Leicestershire, however, where only three J.P.s were removed, there appears to have been only one addition.[31]

Magistrates were still being replaced at a brisk pace in 1651, and there was another acceleration in the spring and summer of 1652, which affected a dozen or more counties. But these developments scarcely suggest a major purge, rather that J.P.s were removed only when they refused the Engagement or resigned for other reasons. But the defection of the old governing families had gone a good deal further than the official lists might suggest. After the dismissal of the secluded members, only eight Somerset J.P.s were removed between 1649 and the end of 1652; the commission still included Horners, Haringtons, and other famous names. But apart from Pyne and Alexander Popham, the great ones rarely attended Quarter Sessions. The active J.P.s were lesser men: minor gentry like John Buckland and Richard Jones; rising lawyers like Thomas Syderfin and John Turberville; and the usual bevy of Pyne henchmen like the Ceelys and Robert Morgan. Even former stalwarts of the Pyne machine were beginning to fall away. Richard Trevillian was removed from the commission in 1650, Henry Henley in the following year, and John Preston at his own request early in 1652.[32]

The Commonwealth, Clarendon afterwards declared, brought into local power 'a more inferior sort of the common people . . . who were not above the condition of ordinary inferior constables six or seven years before'.[33] After making the usual allowance for the

[31] In many counties there were no changes at all during the summer, though in some of these (e.g. Somerset, Worcestershire, Kent, Herefordshire), there had been a few earlier in the year.

[32] Alexander Pym to Preston, 20 July 1651, Francis Swanton to Preston, 27 Mar. 1652: Somerset R.O., Hippisley MS. DD/HI/10.

[33] Clarendon, *History*, Bk. X, § 151. Quoted in Hill, *Puritanism and Revolution*, p. 208.

natural exaggeration of the embittered emigré, there is still some truth in Clarendon's statement, though the most dramatic changes came only in the last months of the Rump and even more spectacularly during the Barebones period. Early in 1653 there appeared on the Somerset commission such men as Richard Bovett of Taunton, George Sampson of Kingsbury, and John Barker of High Ham, all of whom had risen from obscurity as officers of the County Committee. Another new J.P., John Gay of Englishcombe, had indeed been constable of his hundred as recently as 1642, while James Cottington of Frome, another Pyne client, who had been added in 1651, had been only a collector of assessments. In Norfolk, Thomas Pedder of Hunstanton, who became a J.P. in March 1653, was another recent constable. In Herefordshire, Warwickshire, and many other counties, the same advance of the lesser gentry into the Commissions of the Peace occurred. But it was a gradual process; only in 1653 did the trickle of new men become a torrent.[34]

The same continuing displacement of the greater families can be observed in the County Committees. In the year between the revolution and their disappearance, the secluded members were removed, but otherwise there were only minor changes in their composition. The most sweeping were in Herefordshire, where the Harley faction was replaced by seven new members, most of them allies of Wroth Rogers.[35] In Kent the last moderates, John Boys among them, left the Committee, and Livesey's support came even more than Weldon's had done from the lesser gentry and the handful of radicals of the stamp of Thomas Blount and William Kenwricke. In Essex radicals like Sir Henry Holcroft, Sir Thomas Honywood, and such lesser men as Joachim Matthews continued their

[34] For documentation of the Somerset changes see my forthcoming study of Civil War Somerset. For Pedder see D. E. Howell James, ed., *Norfolk Quarter Sessions Order Book*, *1650-1657* (Norfolk R.S., xxvi, 1955), Intro., pp. 4-5. For Warwickshire see Beier, *Past and Present*, no. 35 (1966), 93 and n., 94. Selected Commissions of the Peace since 1558 are given for six counties in J. H. Gleason, *Justices of the Peace in England, 1558 to 1640* (Oxford, 1969). My impression of the new arrivals after 1645, compared with these earlier commissions, is that there was a slight increase in the number of J.P.s from new families between the end of the war and 1652, followed by a much more marked one in 1653. I am confident of this in Somerset, but for other counties it is only an impression, which I should like to see tested quantitatively. See also below, pp. 340-1.

[35] *C.J.* vi. 290. John Pateshall did not sign the Saints' letter of 7 May 1653 (*Milton State Papers*, p. 92), but was a Baptist deacon: B. R. White, 'The Organization of the Particular Baptists', *Journ. Eccl. Hist.* xvii (1966), 224 n. Four of the others either signed radical petitions or can be otherwise associated with the Rogers faction.

domination of the county; more moderate leaders were either, like Sir William Masham, absorbed by their duties at Westminster, or like the Earl of Warwick and Sir John Barrington, out of politics altogether.[36] Although a few Dorset moderates continued to attend the Committee, their hearts were not in it, and power drifted further into the hands of the Trenchard-Browne group. Fitzjames, to be sure, returned briefly in September 1649, but only to get his arrears approved, so that he could buy the Church lands of which he had been tenant. 'Now if ever, kissing goes by favour', he wisely observed.[37]

More important than the decaying Committees were their successors, the Militia commissions, which must have included all the really prominent men in the counties who were actively committed to the Rump. Unfortunately no full list of the commissioners has survived, but enough can be pieced together for some counties to show that they, even more than the J.P.s, included a large number of recent upstarts. This was conspicuously the case in Somerset. Besides the obvious leaders—Disbrowe, Pyne, Alexander Popham, and Sir Thomas Wroth—they included one other M.P., the unimpressive Carent, and one other man of stature, Alexander Pym of Brymore, eldest son of the great John Pym. All the remainder came from the radical faction on the old Committee or in other ways owed their elevation to Pyne or Popham; one was not even a freeholder. None of them had been in the gentry-dominated commission of December 1648, nor would they have had any chance of such eminence until Pyne promoted them. They were, as John Ashe contemptuously dismissed them, Pyne's very 'slaves and vassals'.[38] And the officers they appointed reflected even more strikingly the Commonwealth's lack of appeal to men of the old governing class. Most were minor gentry, some not even that: among the captains were a South Petherton innkeeper, the postmaster at Crewkerne,

[36] Quintrell, 'Committee for Southern Essex', pp. 143-4, 152, 160-80. See also above, p. 34. Attendances at the main Essex Committee between 29 June and 7 Dec. 1649 have been extracted from B.M. Harl. MS. 6244 (Essex Co. Co. Order-book).

[37] Fitzjames to R. Stephens, 5 Sept. 1649: Letter-book (Northumberland MSS., B.M. Film 330), ii, fol. 70ᵛ. See also fols. 48-82, *passim*.

[38] Ashe to Denis Bond, 17 May 1650: *Cal. C. Comp.*, p. 226; and P.R.O., S.P. 23/118 (C. for Compounding Papers), p. 893. The signatures of twenty commissioners can be found on Somerset militia documents in 1650-1; the maximum number for each county was twenty-one. The other commissioner was presumably Sir John Horner, who received a copy of the commission: Mells MSS., no. 247. George Sampson was not a freeholder in 1648: Somerset R.O., Hippisley MS. DD/HI/9.

and a Sutton Mallet yeoman who could not sign his name. In spite
of the demise of the old Committee Pyne was more clearly in control
than ever. But the men who responded to his call in 1650, mustered
with apparent enthusiasm early in 1651, and eagerly turned out to
march towards Worcester in September, represented a further stage
in the erosion of the county community.[39]

The other Somerset commissions were less important, and no
more impressively manned. When the Assessment Commissioners
met at Somerton in July 1649, only eleven out of the forty-one
turned up. Prominent men like the Horners and Strodes had been
replaced by another cohort of obscure Pyne or Popham clients, like
John Locke of Pensford, the philosopher's father, new men working their way up the county ladder such as the lawyers Turberville
and Thomas Gorges, and townsmen like Stephen Hasket and
Thomas Mead of Wells, Edward Sealey of Bridgwater, and Thomas
Wrentmore, whose family were Axbridge drapers.[40] Men of the
same type did most of the work in the 1650 Church survey, although
John Harington also showed his continuing concern for Godly
Reformation by his willingness to serve. The lesser men would
always have been employed in the minor commissions of local
government; it is their presence as J.P.s and Militia Commissioners
that marks the real change in the balance of power.

The commissions of other counties tell the same story. The
Herefordshire militia was run by Wroth Rogers, the radical Independent John James, old enemies of the Harleys such as Miles Hill and
Robert Higgins, lesser men whose only claim to prominence was
their involvement in radical petitions, and outsiders like Major
Stephen Winthrop, one of Harrison's officers. As for the assessment, the 1649 commissions included only two former Harley supporters (Thomas Rawlins and the younger Ambrose Elton); of the
other survivors from before the Purge at least half were to sign
radical petitions. A few men of stature reappeared: Sir John Bridges
and Sir Richard Hopton, for instance, no doubt because of their

---

[39] For activities of the Somerset militia see *Cal. S.P. Dom.*, *1650*, and *1651*, *passim*;
P.R.O., S.P. 28/242 (Somerset Militia Papers). The Sutton Mallet yeoman, William
Gapper, was sometimes described as 'Gent.' by 1650, but was only a yeoman in the 1648
Freeholders' Book: Somerset R.O., Hippisley MS., DD/HI/9. He signed a receipt for pay
(in the Militia Papers) with a mark. He was able to sign his name by 1659. Somerset Militia
Cmrs. to Whitelocke, 11 Aug. 1659: Bodl. MS., Clarendon 63, fol. 185.

[40] For the Assessment commissions, see Firth and Rait, *A. and O.* ii, *passim*. There are
some documents illustrating the work of the commissioners in B.M. Add. MS. 28273
(Memo-book of John Locke, Sr.), fols. 87–123.

long-standing hostility to the Harleys. Even John Birch retained his place; again previous enmity to the Harleys may have helped. But these were exceptions. Most of Wroth Rogers's allies were new men.[41] Yorkshire was too big to be run by a military outsider like Rogers. A handful of the old families—Boyntons, Saviles, and St. Quintens—were still active in local government after the Purge. But other important men like Sir Richard Hawkesworth, Sir Thomas Remington, and Darcy Wentworth, all active in earlier years, were seen no more. In the new militia the leaders were the Rump M.P.s and their relatives (Peregrine Lascelles and Matthew Alured, for instance), the penniless peer Lord Eure, and the usual flock of lesser gentry. Many men unknown before their promotion under the old County Committee now made further advances. Ralph Rymer, the former treasurer, became a sequestration commissioner; others became J.P.s for the first time. From Westmorland to Wiltshire, from Kent to Caernarvonshire, the same influx of soldiers, strangers, and social upstarts continued.[42]

But even among the lesser gentry the Rump's committed supporters were a small remnant. In most counties there were enough conformists to give the Commissions of the Peace a respectable appearance, but many J.P.s were as unenthusiastic as Fitzjames. For more politically sensitive positions such as the militia it was difficult to find enough suitable men who were willing to serve. Where there was an already well-entrenched local regime, as in Kent or Somerset, the difficulty could be overcome. But where, as in Devon, there was no such organization, the Rump was in trouble. Even before the Purge the Devon Committee had been at the point of collapse, relying on a handful of M.P.s to keep it going. Few of

---

[41] *Cal. S.P. Dom., 1650*, p. 509. James and others to Speaker, 17 Mar. 1650/1: H.M.C., *Portland*, i. 561, with signatures and additions in Bodl. MS. Dep. C. 159 (Nalson Papers, viii), fol. 114. Besides those named above, John Herring, Walter Merrick, and John Woodyate were commissioners who signed radical petitions, as did several of the militia officers. For the Assessment commissions, see Firth and Rait, *A. and O.* ii, *passim*.

[42] I am grateful to John Thelin for his assistance in analysing the Yorkshire commissions in Firth and Rait, *A. and O.* For militia and sequestration affairs, see *Cal. S.P. Dom., 1648-9-1651, passim*; also *Cal. C. Comp.*, pp. 171, 243, 379–80, 615–16; and *Cal. of the Comm. for Advance of Money*, pp. 86, 105. For Lord Eure see A. Gooder, *Parliamentary Representation of the County of York, 1258-1832*, ii (Yorks. Arch. Soc., Record Series, xcvi, 1937), pp. 55–6. Officials and committeemen who became Yorkshire J.P.s in this period include Christopher Ridley, John Clayton, Richard Etherington, Richard Robinson, and William Thornton. For examples of the trend in other regions see Everitt, *Community of Kent*, p. 296; and Dodd, *Stuart Wales*, pp. 143–51. But cf. Everitt, ed., *Suffolk and the Great Rebellion*, Intro., pp. 25–6, 36.

the other committeemen attended, and there was a complete lack
of authority in the remote Exmoor parishes. In 1649 things went
from bad to worse. Almost all the M.P.s were removed by the Purge,
and the only Devonians in the Rump were the obscure Christopher
Martyn, and the Dartmouth merchant Thomas Boone. Influenced
by a determined preaching campaign by the Presbyterian clergy,
the local gentry dragged their feet even more heavily. Sir Hardress
Waller did his best, but only five or six men attended the Committee, it was reported in August, 'and they but seldom'. When
Waller's successor, Disbrowe, came to settle the new militia in
February 1650 he was greatly discouraged. 'Few of the gentry
appears in it', he told Robert Bennet.[43]

The absence of a sufficient number of committed Commonwealth supporters had several consequences. In Kent it meant
a bewildering turnover in the Assessment commissions, as parochial
gentry were hopefully named in one commission only to be dropped
from the next when they were found reluctant, unreliable, or incompetent.[44] In many places a small number of men were hopelessly overburdened by a multiplication of responsibilities, or
forced to take on jobs they did not want. John Moyle complained
of the lethargy of most of the J.P.s: two or three conscientious ones
were made 'pack horses for all the rest, and . . . laught at for their
pains'. The Cornish sequestrators were certainly among the pack-
horses. They were, they pointed out, commissioners for sequestrations, for administration of the Engagement, for assessments, for
the Church survey, and for the militia, as well as being J.P.s. In all
these duties, they told their Goldsmiths' Hall employers, 'we are
obliged to give constant attendance, because of the paucity of those
that appear for the public'.[45]

This was the problem of the revolution. After 1648 local government was in the hands, theoretically, of the godly, the 'honest

---

[43] Justinian Peard to Richard Hill, 17 Nov. 1648; Robert Spry to Comm. for Sequestrations, 15 Dec.: B.M. Add. MS. 5494 (Seq. Comm. Papers), fols. 99-100; Spry to Comm.
for Compounding, 2 Mar. 1649/50: *Cal. C. Comp.*, p. 180; Letter from Exeter, 17 Mar.
1649/50: *Perfect Occurrences*, no. 116 (16-23 Mar.: [B.M.] E. 527, 39); Alex. Rigby to
Speaker, 7 Aug. 1649: Bodl. MS., Tanner 56, fol. 89; Disbrowe to Bennet, 9 Feb. 1649/50:
Folger Lib., MS. Add. 494 (Bennet MSS.), p. 191.

[44] Everitt, *Community of Kent*, pp. 296-7.

[45] Moyle to Robert Bennet and Anthony Rous, 1 Sept. 1649: Folger Lib., MS. Add. 494
(Bennet MSS.), p. 165; Cornish commissioners to Goldsmiths' Hall, 17 Oct. 1650: *Cal.
C. Comp.*, p. 335. Cf. similar complaints by officials in Cumberland and Devon: ibid.,
pp. 232, 293, 304.

party', the 'well affected'. But the godly were not a single party. They included, to be sure, many who hoped to build a new republican Zion. But they also included men whose careers and material prosperity depended on the survival of the Commonwealth, and many more who were only acquiescing survivors of the old governing class, staying in office to prevent worse disasters. Conservatives like Clement Walker feared the Commonwealthsmen as 'a party of antimonarchists, schismatics and Anabaptists'.[46] The description does indeed fit some of the new men: in nearly every county an occasional J.P. or commissioner reminds us of their existence. Lilburne's old ally Samuel Highland became a J.P. in Surrey in April 1649; removed two years later, he was back again under Barebones. Martin Pyke, who became a J.P. in Kent in July 1651, signed a letter recommending nominees to the Barebones Parliament as one of the 'friends to the [gathered] churches'. Of the newcomers in Somerset, John Barker was a violent Commonwealthsman; like most of Pyne's other henchmen, he was later notably tolerant of radical Puritans and Quakers. The Herefordshire leaders also, for the most part, shared Wroth Rogers's zeal. In Wales an occasional yeoman or draper, members of Morgan Llwyd's or other radical congregations, moved up the ladder in these years. Such men provided much of the pressure for reform, and looked forward, in the words of one of their declarations, to 'the great and long desired Reformation'.[47] In April 1653 they were still looking forward to it. They were a minority, even among the Rump's local governors.

Because of a few spectacular examples it is easy to exaggerate the number and importance of these radical zealots. Being the most energetic and enthusiastic of the regime's agents, some of them, to be sure, did well out of it. Even the godly expected, and sometimes received, their earthly reward. In March 1652 the eminent Welsh divine Walter Cradock wrote to Cromwell commending a 'renowned ancient saint' named Rice Williams, who had been 'pitched upon by the Saints here' for a post in the bureaucracy. Williams was admittedly incompetent in 'clerkship', but Cradock suggested that

---

[46] Walker, *Independency*, iii. 7.
[47] Herefordshire Saints to Cromwell, 7 May 1653: *Milton State Papers*, p. 92. Many of the signatories are identifiable as members of the Rogers faction. For the others mentioned in this paragraph see Gregg, *Free-Born John*, pp. 325, 338 (Highland); *Milton State Papers*, p. 97 (Pyke); above, p. 37 (Barker); Dodd, *Stuart Wales*, p. 144 (Llwyd's congregation, etc.).

he might be able to do the job jointly with a man of greater skill.[48]
More efficient and more ambitious was the Yorkshireman Captain
Adam Baynes. He was an Assessment commissioner in 1649—his
first entrance into county government. He had done well in the
Army, and under the Commonwealth he did even better, getting
a job in London as an excise commissioner, speculating in debentures, and making large purchases of confiscated lands. Pyne's client
Richard Bovett was another who profited, getting a good slice of
the estates of the royalist Sir John Stawell. Few, however, went so
far so fast as Anthony Pearson in Durham. As a young man he
became Haselrig's secretary and helped to manage Sir Arthur's vast
new Durham estates. With his patron's help he was appointed to
several lucrative local offices, and was put on most of the northern
Commissions of the Peace. He moved quickly to extreme Puritan
opinions, 'nursed up', he said after the Restoration, 'with the
chimerical notions of those giddy times', and eventually became
a Quaker. Though going further than his employer in religion, he
did no more than copy Haselrig in acquisitiveness, picking up
several forfeited estates at good prices. The combination of high-
flown Puritan zeal with a careful eye to the main chance was a
common feature of the 1650s.[49]

*       *       *

The nature of the new regimes in the boroughs was equally
mixed. In a few scattered places there was pressure for revolutionary change. Even more than their counterparts in the counties,
the urban oligarchies were composed of men of limited horizons,
often little concerned by national issues, and regarding their first
loyalty as being to their town. They would make what minimum
adjustment was necessary to protect the town's interests; they
might absorb some of the radical Puritans into the corporation if
they were vocal and determined enough. But the demand for serious
change usually came only from a minority and was easily resisted.
    Except for the partial purge achieved by the Engagement, most

[48] Cradock to Cromwell, 29 Mar. 1652: *Milton State Papers*, pp. 85-6. The man proposed as Williams's helper was an officer and former servant of Major-General Harrison.
For Williams see Dodd, *Stuart Wales*, p. 125.

[49] *D.N.B.* ('Baynes'); J. Y. Akerman, ed., *Letters from Roundhead Officers . . . chiefly
addressed to Captain Adam Baynes* (Bannatyne Club, ci, Edinburgh, 1856), esp. Pref.,
p. xiii; *Cal. C. Comp.*, pp. 1428, 1430, 2064; *Cal. S.P. Dom.*, *1655-6*, p. 312; Penney, ed.,
*Extracts from State Papers Relating to Friends*, pp. 137-41.

of the changes in borough governments after the revolution were the product of local circumstance. Often nothing much happened. Towns like Newcastle, Bristol, and York, whose government had already been remodelled by the expulsion of Royalists after the Civil War, experienced no second revolution. These broadenings of the oligarchy to include men from just outside the old 'inner ring' deprived any potential opposition of its natural leaders, while ensuring that there would be no dangerous experiments, for the new leadership differed only marginally in quality from the old. Henry Dawson's friends, who took over Newcastle in 1645, included fewer of the Hostmen and mercers who had monopolized Tyneside government before the war, but were still men of substance.[50] Lesser places were even more placid. The corporation of Boston quietly ignored the revolution, remaining on good terms with their M.P., Sir Anthony Irby, in spite of his seclusion. Even at Weymouth, where there was a sweeping purge in January 1649, this seems to have been the climax of a long struggle to root out disqualified Royalists, and would have occurred even without a revolution in London.[51]

When changes occurred, they were often for negative reasons, as corporation members were frightened into retirement by the Engagement or the general dangers of the times. Many towns had difficulty in finding replacements. At disaffected Exeter in September 1649 two mayors-elect refused to serve, and for a year there was no mayor; several other members of the corporation withdrew. Although the city was more co-operative after Dunbar, in 1651 it was still sometimes hard to get a quorum for council meetings. There had always been people reluctant to accept the tiresome and expensive burdens of local office, but the tendency to escape by paying a fine increased markedly after 1648, even in so Puritan a city as York. The Southampton Court Leet complained in 1652 that so many people were defaulting that they could not assemble a jury. In 1650 Barnstaple had a mayor who was illiterate, which might suggest an eruption of the lower orders, but was more

[50] Howell, *Newcastle*, pp. 173-5; Latimer, *Annals of Bristol in the Seventeenth Century*, pp. 207-14; G. C. F. Forster, 'York in the Seventeenth Century', *V.C.H., City of York*, pp. 176-9; Claire Cross, 'Achieving the Millennium: the Church in York during the Commonwealth', in G. J. Cuming, ed., *Studies in Church History*, iv (Leiden, 1967), 134-5.

[51] Hipkin, *Reports of Assoc. Archit. Socs.* xl, Pt. iii (1931), 191-2 (and see also above, p. 176); M. Weinstock, ed., *Weymouth and Melcombe Regis Minute Book* (Dorset Record Soc. i, 1964), pp. 73-6.

probably the result of an absence of alternatives. At Orford several
mayors and other officers were elected in quick succession while
still under twenty-one. We may conclude, in the absence of any
evidence of a nation-wide generational rebellion, that the young men
governed at Orford because older and wiser ones would not.[52]

Although many towns were little affected by the revolution, there
were a few which swung significantly leftward. Sometimes this was
no more than a change of personnel at the top. Rumpers themselves
occasionally held borough offices. Peregrine Pelham and George
Serle were mayors of Hull and Taunton respectively in 1649, James
Nelthorpe of Beverley in 1652. Unfriendly recorders were removed
either by the Rump or by local action at Abingdon, Maidstone,
Southampton, and other places.[53] In a few boroughs new men made
spectacular advances because of their connections with the Commonwealth regime. Richard Bovett moved from Wellington to Taunton
only after the Civil War, but was mayor of his adopted town by 1651.
William Whiting and Thomas Mead were elected to the corporation of Wells only in 1647 or later; Whiting was mayor in 1650,
Mead in 1653. Both were republicans, and Mead had long been one
of Pyne's allies; a person 'very powerful in those times', his enemies
long remembered. Even in stable places like Newcastle there were
some remarkably rapid promotions: William Johnson joined the
corporation (as an alderman) only in 1652, but was mayor a year
later.[54]

Were these newcomers generally religious as well as political
radicals? There is no simple answer. The usual problems of
categorizing the obscure are compounded by the convenient destruction that overtook so many boroughs' recent records in 1660.
Clergy or laity, many people had no definable religious position, or
changed with the times. George Scortwreth, preacher at Lincoln

[52] Cotton and Woollcoombe, *Exeter Records*, pp. 143–54; Forster, *V.C.H.*, *York*,
pp. 176–7; E. R. Aubrey, ed., *History and Antiquities of Southampton . . . by John Speed*
(Southampton Record Soc., 1909), p. 55 n.; Chanter and Wainwright, eds., *Barnstaple
Records*, ii. 247; H.M.C., *Var. Coll.* iv (Orford MSS.), 268.

[53] *C.J.* vi. 293, 328; J. Dennett, ed., *Beverley Borough Records, 1575–1821* (Yorks. Arch.
Soc., Record Series, lxxxiv, 1932), p. 103; Bromley Challenor, ed., *Selections from the
Municipal Chronicles of the Borough of Abingdon* (Abingdon, 1898), p. 144; Sir J. R. Twisden
and C. H. Dudley Ward, *The Family of Twysden and Twisden* (London, 1939), pp. 343–4;
Davies, *Southampton*, pp. 184–5.

[54] P.R.O., Asz. 24/21 (W. Circuit Order-book), fol. 192ᵛ; David Underdown, 'A Case
Concerning Bishops' Lands: Cornelius Burges and the Corporation of Wells', *E.H.R.*
lxxviii (1963), 30–1; Howell, *Newcastle*, p. 176.

Cathedral in 1649, flirted with Independency, but later, according to hostile Quakers, found the Presbyterians richer and more numerous.[55] There was certainly no universal promotion of radical Puritans. Much depended on the strength of the local sects and the calibre of the established ministers. When a moderate Puritan preacher dominated the religious life of a town the sects were less likely to flourish. During his ministry at Kidderminster, Baxter complacently recalled, there was 'not a Separatist, Anabaptist, Antinomian, etc., in the town'. There were Baptists among the poorer inhabitants of York, but they made no headway against the men of solid position and opinions who ran the city.[56] Often the radical sects had close ties with the Army garrisons. At Poole the townsmen stood firm against a handful of 'exorbitant Levellers and Ranters', allies of the Baptist, Leveller-inclined governor, Lt.-Col. John Rede. Among Rede's alleged misdeeds was the intrusion of a Baptist soldier as lecturer in one of the churches, in opposition to the 'orthodox and well-affected' clergy favoured by the magistrates. After a running conflict in which Rede disarmed the militia officers and arrested the mayor, the secluded M.P. George Skutt intervened and had the militant governor removed.[57] At Rye in 1652 John Evelyn heard 'one of the canters' preaching to the garrison; the corporation complained that the officers encouraged the men 'to despise and contemn all government and ministers thereof'.[58]

Many towns were divided, though few as violently as Poole or Rye. The magistrates of Leicester, including the Rumper Peter Temple, vigorously repressed the Baptists, but in the end the corporation itself split on religious lines and was unable to appoint to a vacant lectureship. Southampton was equally divided, and so too was Reading, where the 'godly-pretending party' in 1650 petitioned against the corporation's 'malevolent practices'.[59]

But although we should not exaggerate the immediate political consequences, there is no doubt that radical Puritanism did advance

---

[55] J. W. F. Hill, *Tudor and Stuart Lincoln* (Cambridge, 1956), pp. 167–8.

[56] *Rel. Baxt.* i. 87; Forster, *V.C.H., York*, p. 204; Cross, in *Studies in Church History*, iv. 122, 141.

[57] B.M. Stowe MS. 189 (Civil War and Commonwealth Papers), fols. 43–4, 52–5; *Cal. S.P. Dom., 1651*, pp. 149, 171, 173, 220; *1651–2*, p. 18. See also Bayley, *Civil War in Dorset*, pp. 343–8.

[58] Inderwick, *Sussex Archae. Coll.* xxxix (1894), 8; Mayor and Jurats to Morley and others, 20 Nov. 1651: H.M.C., *Thirteenth Report*, App. IV (Rye MSS.), p. 217.

[59] Stocks and Stevenson, eds., *Leicester Records*, pp. 385–7, 400; Aubrey, ed., *Speed's Southampton*, pp. 171, 175–7; H.M.C., *Eleventh Report*, App. VII (Reading MSS.), p. 218.

in the towns during the Commonwealth, with new congregations appearing in many places. In Bristol, the Broadmead Baptists long remembered 'those halcyon days of prosperity, liberty, and peace'. Denis Hollister, who was one of them, was already becoming a citizen of great influence. At Wells the Baptists had formed a congregation by the spring of 1653; for months before they had been disturbing Cornelius Burges's sermons in the cathedral. Their leader, the passionate shoemaker David Barret, was elected to the corporation at about this time. One of Robert Bennet's Baptist friends, Hunt Greenwood, was mayor of Liskeard in 1649; his enemies alleged that he had never even been elected a burgess. Greenwood became steward in 1652, was mayor on several later occasions, and was altogether the most powerful man in the little town.[60]

In most of these places the handful of radicals, whether religious or political, were quietly absorbed. In a very few cases the Commonwealth led to changes that resulted in striking, though temporary, experiments in democracy. The gaps in so many boroughs' records may conceal other instances, but two at least are well documented: at Bedford and High Wycombe. There were two kinds of citizens under the old constitution at Bedford: some sixty wealthy burgesses, who were automatically members of the Common Council, and a much larger number of freemen, who elected only thirteen representatives to that body. In 1647 the freemen began a long struggle for a more popular form of government. The burgesses counterattacked by taking the election of the thirteen away from the freemen altogether, vesting it in the mayor and Common Council. After a compromise had momentarily patched things up, in 1649 the freemen again took the offensive. Their leader was Samuel Gibbs the younger, who had served in the Army, and now, full of Leveller idealism, had come home to demand his rights. That he was prevented from following his trade by a strict enforcement of apprenticeship regulations cannot have made him any better-disposed towards the old men who ran the town. Supported by his brother Thomas,

---

[60] Edward B. Underhill, ed., *Records of a Church of Christ, Meeting in Broadmead, Bristol, 1640–1687* (Hanserd Knollys Soc., London, 1847), pp. 17–18, 28, 39, 43; Latimer, *Annals of Bristol in the Seventeenth Century*, p. 239; Underdown, *E.H.R.* lxxviii (1963), 31–3; Allen, *Liskeard*, pp. 242–6, 259, 281, 468. Bennet, it might be noted, was Recorder of Liskeard. There are many references to Greenwood's connection with him in Folger Lib., MS. Add. 494 (Bennet MSS.); esp. pp. 121, 507. See also Coate, *Cornwall in the Civil War*, pp. 272–4.

John Easton (son of a Baptist alderman), and a number of other radicals, on 28 November 1649 Gibbs petitioned the Rump for revision of the Bedford charter. The committee on corporations took the popular side. In January 1650 Bedford was given what the old guard later called the 'Levelling constitution'. The distinction between burgess and freeman was abolished, and a Common Council of eighteen was elected, as were the mayor and aldermen, by all enfranchised citizens. The oligarchy was quickly overthrown. In the first elections in March 1650 only four old councillors were returned. Several of the newcomers had signed the November petition, and at least eight were members of the Baptist congregation to which John Bunyan also belonged. Aided by the elder Easton and another Baptist alderman, John Grewe, and with occasional help from the central government, Gibbs's friends ran Bedford on more democratic lines until the Restoration.[61]

High Wycombe, even more than Bedford, had been governed by a self-perpetuating clique of leading burgesses, many of them brewers or inn-keepers. There had been an unsuccessful attempt to challenge them at the 1640 elections, but the real conflict arose after the war. The issue was the disposition of poor relief funds. The corporation was chronically short of money, and had been in the habit of raiding charitable bequests. The Overseers of the Poor received £20 a year out of the cornmarket tolls, but in the conditions of depression at the end of the war this was sadly insufficient. In 1647, after efforts to increase the sum had failed, the Overseers brought suit against the corporation in Chancery. This got nowhere, and in September 1649 the retiring mayor withheld the corn tolls completely to pay the corporation's debts. There was a serious riot, and troops had to be brought in. The Council of State duly intervened, ordering the new mayor, the conservative Nicholas Bradshawe, to restore the corn tolls to the Overseers. The struggle soon took on both political and religious colouring. Bradshawe's party denounced their enemies as Levellers, and the Recorder, the secluded M.P. Thomas Lane, moved to indict them for non-attendance at church. The leader of the Overseers, Samuel Guy, was in fact a separating Independent. In October 1650 Thomas

---

[61] Guy Parsloe, ed., *Minute Book of Bedford Corporation, 1647–1664* (Beds. Hist. Record Soc. xxvi, 1949), Intro., pp. viii–xi, xxxii–xxxiv, and pp. 9–35; *C.J.* vi. 326; Letter from Bedfordshire, 13 May 1653: *Milton State Papers*, pp. 92–3. See also C. G. Parsloe, 'The Corporation of Bedford, 1647–1664', *T.R.H.S.* 4th Ser. xxix (1947), 151–65.

Scot, who had replaced Lane as Recorder, stepped in to help the radicals. Bradshawe's successor as mayor was replaced by one of Guy's allies, Stephen Bates, 'a discreet religious person, nominated by the well-affected', who was not yet an alderman. For a time the revolution brought better treatment for the poor of High Wycombe. However, the town's constitution was not altered, and the struggle was renewed during the Protectorate. Even so, a closed corporation had been shaken by a rebellion supported by the underprivileged. It could have happened only during a revolution.[62]

Although in Bedford and High Wycombe the Commonwealth had democratic implications, in most places power still went with property. Unless they had a material grievance such as aroused them at High Wycombe, the poor were apathetic, and even among the 'middling sort' the Commonwealthsmen were a minority. Where the radicals came to power they often therefore simply replaced one kind of oligarchy by another. Colchester is a good example.

Before the Civil War Colchester had been an unusually turbulent place; the townsmen, Laud was told in 1636, were 'like those of Ephesus, their Diana is their liberty'. During and after the war a conservative oligarchy of the wealthier citizens was opposed by a militant Puritan minority, which had some support from the disenfranchised.[63] In 1648 Colchester went through the fire. Through conviction or necessity, all but a handful of the leading citizens found themselves, like the moderates in Kent and other counties, defending the local community against the New Model Army. When the town fell to Fairfax there was an immediate purge. Out went the mayor and another dozen corporation members, in came a new mayor, the radical leader Henry Barrington, and some twenty others, most of them Barrington supporters. Among the newcomers were men of radical Puritan inclinations, Baptists or future Quakers. Barrington, who was accused of favouring sectaries in the distribution of poor relief, was at least a sympathizer. At the

[62] There is an excellent account of the struggle in L. J. Ashford, *History of the Borough of High Wycombe . . . to 1880* (London, 1960), pp. 122–44. However, Ashford does not seem to have used the documents in G. Eland, ed., *Papers from an Iron Chest at Doddershall, Bucks.* (Aylesbury, 1937), which throw some further light on the political and religious implications of the dispute. See also *C.J.* vi. 480; R. W. Greaves, ed., *First Ledger Book of High Wycombe* (Bucks. Record Soc. xi, 1956), pp. 132–58; and W. H. Summers, 'Cromwell's Charter, High Wycombe', *Records of Bucks.* vii (the parts were published 1891–7), 511–28.

[63] Rickword, *Essex Review*, v (1896), 197–204. See also above, p. 42.

outset of the Commonwealth all seemed set fair for Barrington and his party. With the help of Sir Henry Mildmay, he and his son were picking up lucrative appointments in Colchester and the county,[64] and their power in the town would have been secure if they had had any substantial local support. But in fact it began to slip away. Aldermen were elected by all the propertied citizens, or burgesses at large. Between 1649 and 1654, only one out of seven new aldermen was a Barrington supporter; the others included a principal enemy, the draper Thomas Reynolds. In 1656 Barrington's party petitioned for a new charter, complaining that the old one gave 'too great a power ... to the people to slight the magistracy of the place'. The outcome was a closed corporation, by which the rule of the godly minority was guaranteed. In Colchester at least the revolution was not a movement for popular liberty.[65]

Of all the urban centres, London was overwhelmingly the most important. By the summer of 1649 the capital had been made safe for the revolution. For four years the Rump strove to keep the government of London in reliable hands. The men to whom the Rump looked in the City included the aldermen-M.P.s Allen, Atkin, and Penington, and such staunch republicans as Tichbourne, Rowe, and Stephen Estwick. Many of the new leaders, like Rowe and Tichbourne, were members of Independent congregations; a few were wealthy Baptists, like Samuel Moyer of the Levant Company, a man prominent in many of the Rump's agencies. Such men might be advanced Puritans, but they were not revolutionaries, and with the aid of trimmers like Alderman John Fowke they kept London in step with the generally moderate policies of the Rump. They might be willing to undertake a limited, rational reform of City government—to abolish, for instance, the private sale of offices, to replace fees and perquisites with salaries. But they had no intention of tinkering with the system of election to Common Hall by the liveries, undermining the monopoly rights of the great companies, or permitting the democratization of the companies themselves.[66]

---

[64] Henry was appointed Master of King James' Hospital, Colchester; his son Abraham Barrington was treasurer and later commissioner for sequestrations in Essex: B.M. Add. MS. 36792 (Presentations under the Great Seal), fol. 5ᵛ; *Cal. C. Comp.*, pp. 171, 173.

[65] The Colchester conflict was debated at length by Round, *E.H.R.* xv (1900), 641-64; and Gardiner, *Commonwealth*, iii. 177; iv. 57-77. For the most part I have followed Round's analysis.

[66] My account of London politics is based mainly on Farnell, *E.H.R.* lxxxii (1967), 24-46. See also above, p. 180.

Y

Yet in London, far more than the rest of the country, there were many people who wanted to go further. Londoners tended to be more politically conscious than provincials. The strength of Leveller and radical Puritan feeling among the craftsmen and journeymen was repeatedly shown in Common Council elections. John Lilburne, fresh from his triumphant acquittal, was one of those elected in December 1649. The Rump promptly had him excluded, but there were plenty of other new councillors who even if not Levellers were still of advanced opinions, like John Fenton and the Baptist Praise-God Barbone. Until the latter part of 1651 the radicals held their own, with some set-backs. In Dowgate ward in the December 1650 elections the victors were men who had signed the engagement for the personal treaty in 1648, and were thus technically disqualified. Yet the Rump, led by Allen and Atkin, upheld the election against Harrison's opposition. During the crisis before Worcester the radicals obtained an emergency Militia Committee, in which they were well represented. But Fenton was accepted only after the Rump Presbyterians had unsuccessfully divided the House against him.[67] After Worcester, when Cromwell and St. John were promoting a moderate settlement, the tide turned completely. Fowke was Lord Mayor in 1652, and promptly ruled that only freemen paying scot and lot were eligible for election to Common Council; with the Rump's encouragement, the wealthy citizens were reversing the enlargement of political rights begun during the revolution. In December 1652, not surprisingly, Barbone and Fenton lost their seats. The breach between the moderate City Independents and the radicals paralleled that in the nation as a whole, and was an important reason for the downfall of the Rump.

During their years of influence, the radicals pressed strongly for further reform. In the autumn of 1649 Fenton and his friends began a campaign to make Common Hall directly representative of the citizens rather than of the livery companies, and thus democratize the election of the Lord Mayor and sheriffs. Fenton was soon censured and expelled from the Common Council, and the twelve leading companies petitioned against such dangerous proposals. On 14 December 1650 Common Council heard arguments at the Guildhall, with those weighty lawyers John Maynard, Matthew Hale, and John Wylde representing the companies, and Wildman and John Price the reformers. Maynard, as usual, was firmly

[67] *C.J.* vi. 619.

against popular government, stressing the pernicious consequences that would follow if London set an example to lesser corporations. Wildman responded by appealing to the phrase on which the Commonwealth itself was founded: 'The original of all just power under God proceeds from the people.' Wildman won the argument, but the proposed reform was never implemented.[68]

Efforts to democratize the livery companies were no more successful. In some cases campaigns to give more power to the commonalty had begun before 1648, but the pressure increased markedly after the revolution. In December 1648 the rank and file of the Clothworkers demanded a general meeting of the company to elect the master and wardens. They did not get it, and although they returned to the attack with a petition to Parliament in 1650, the masters beat them off with a few minor concessions. When the commonalty of the Goldsmiths' Company demanded a share in electing their officers, the masters walked out of the meeting; the rebels elected a rival slate, but after petitions from both sides the Rump, as usual, upheld the oligarchs. In the Merchant Taylors' Company there was a struggle between the small employers and the working tailors; the governors divided the opposition by siding with the workers and giving them the regulating committee they wanted, rightly calculating that it would be ineffective. The agitation varied from company to company, but taken altogether there can be no doubt that it was intensified by the revolution. A Saddlers' petition in 1652 spoke the authentic language of radical rhetoric. England having been freed from the Norman Yoke, it ought now to be freed from oppression by corporations set up by 'the late tyrannical king and his progenitors'.[69]

\* \* \*

The Commonwealth's local regimes were so varied that generalization about them is difficult. The new rulers, in Parliament or outside, were far from being universally reformers, radical Puritans, and republicans. The nature of the revolution precluded any clean sweep of either personnel or policies. The radicals might press for further reforms, and given the presence of powerful sympathizers like Pyne, Haselrig, and Harrison, and the promotion of many less

---

[68] Farnell, *E.H.R.* lxxxii. 32-4, 36-7; Ashley, *Wildman*, pp. 73-6; James, *Social Problems*, pp. 230-1.

[69] For all this see James, *Social Problems*, pp. 193-223.

eminent ones, they were likely to get some of them. But the survival
of the moderates prevented really revolutionary changes. Furthermore, not all the new rulers were men of high principle; they were
interested in power and the perquisites it brought. And in the
unstable circumstances of the times, with royalist land on the market
and many other tempting opportunities for profit, the perquisites
were many.

Complaints about the self-interested corruption of the local
officials, like those against the Rumpers themselves, cannot always
be taken at face value. But there is no doubt that many of the new
men were in a hurry to get on, as the careers of Bovett, Pearson, and
their like remind us. It was easy for soldiers or officials to mis-
behave. When the lease of the royalist Sir Philip Musgrave's estate
was put up for auction in Westmorland in 1650 there were several
higher bids, but the property went to Major Arthur Scaife, whose
soldiers threatened and denounced as Levellers all who opposed
him. Sequestration commissioners in many counties had bad
reputations. Those in Berkshire were particularly corrupt. 'They
cry out "The State, the State",' an enemy complained, 'but their
private interest is their Diana.' Officials in Yorkshire made a nice
profit out of selling certificates of subscription to the Engagement
to poor people who did not know the law.[70]

Corruption was widespread, but it was not universal. Even the
moderates who survived in the counties were usually Puritans of
fairly strong convictions, and were willing to accede, verbally at
least, to some of the reformers' demands. A Herefordshire county
petition in March 1650 included several standard items: law reform,
the abolition of base tenures, and the oppression of small traders
and freeholders by such matters as increased iron-workings in the
Forest of Dean and the obstruction by weirs on the Severn and Wye.
The gentry would have liked to add abolition of the assessment and
the funding of the Army on the excise, but this regressive proposal
was resisted by the freeholders.[71]

In spite of the occasional expression of reform sentiment, the
social policies of the Commonwealth's county regimes differed only

---

[70] *Cal. C. Comp.*, pp. 196, 601, 615, 619; H.M.C., *Ninth Report*, App. I (Yorks., N.
Riding MSS.), p. 331. Daniel Blagrave may have had some part in the Berkshire commissioners' rackets; perhaps these were involved in the Army's charges against him in the
last months of the Rump. See Josten, ed., *Ashmole*, ii. 638, 644; *C.J.* vii. 257.

[71] Petition of the J.P.s, Gentlemen, and Grand Jury of Herefordshire, 23 Mar. 1649/50:
B.M. Add. MS. 11053 (Scudamore MSS.), fols. 110-11.

in degree from those of earlier governments. Reformers like Hartlib who wanted the Rump to treat poverty as a national problem, did not, as we have seen, make much headway. The J.P.s of many counties responded, as they had to, to the Speaker's warning letters in the spring of 1649. At Taunton Assizes in July the Grand Jury recognised the need to improve poor relief 'in this time of dearth', and the court ordered the J.P.s to enforce the law accordingly. The evidence from Warwickshire suggests that even without much prodding from Westminster, the J.P.s did a lot to alleviate the plight of the poor, and went further than the mere suppression of vagrancy. Their energy, indeed, strikingly illustrates the typical Puritan concern for both social action and efficiency.[72]

But in spite of the protests of reformers like Robert Bennet, in more controversial matters the new regimes usually sided with the rich and the powerful. Sir Arthur Haselrig got into a bitter conflict with Lilburne over a Durham colliery he had seized, and won hands down. John Pyne might denounce violations of rights of common, but he showed no hesitation about defending law and order. He stood firm against the Levellers, put down anti-excise demonstrations, and was immediately called on when the recurrent disorders in Selwood forest got out of hand and led to the destruction of the fences of a royalist landowner.[73] It is difficult to see that the new county regimes had a distinctive social policy at all. The gentry who still had most of the power were unlikely to espouse new policies, while the newcomers from lower social levels were too few to make much difference.

Nor, outside Wales and the northern counties covered by the propagation Acts, is there any sign that the new regimes were much interested in further religious changes. The contrast between the energy of the propagators and the lethargy in most other places is strikingly evident in the matter of education. In Wales, and to a lesser extent in the North, new schools sprang up like mushrooms. Obviously this was partly because they were more needed there than in more developed regions where the educational revolution of the previous century had already done its work. But the reformist zeal

[72] P.R.O., Asz. 24/21 (W. Circuit Order-book), fols. 144v-5. I am grateful to John Cockburn for letting me use his transcript of the order-book. For the Warwickshire evidence see Beier, *Past and Present*, no. 35 (1966), 77-100.

[73] Gregg, *Free-Born John*, pp. 309-10; Brailsford, *The Levellers*, pp. 610-11; Case of John Pyne, 1660: H.M.C., *Ninth Report*, App. II (Pyne MSS.), p. 494; *C.J.* vi. 221; *Cal. S.P. Dom.*, *1651*, p. 304; *1652-3*, pp. 301, 422-3.

of Vavasor Powell, Morgan Llwyd, and their friends shows what
might have happened if the Rump had passed the general propagation Act desired by the radicals, and had sent itinerant preachers
into the rest of the land. Conservatives feared the proposed itinerants
as the political agents of revolution. Their purpose, said Clement
Walker, was[74]

to preach anti-monarchical seditious doctrine to the people, . . . to raise
the rascal multitude and schismatical rabble against all men of best
quality in the kingdom, to draw them into associations and combina-
tions with one another in every county, . . . that themselves alone may
inhabit the earth, and establish their new tyranny or Kingdom of the
Saints.

It did not happen. Congregations of Baptists and Fifth Monarchy
Men sprang up in many places. There was the proliferation of
extreme opinions that usually occurs during revolution, with
Ranters being succeeded by Quakers as the chief threats to the
social order. By 1652, indeed, the philosopher Robert Boyle was
afraid that among 'the giddy multitude . . . this multiplicity of religions will end in none at all'. The Presbyterian system, the London
clergy complained in November 1649, remained 'weak in power,
and of no repute with many'.[75] But over most of England the
Presbyterians still dominated the pulpits; even in Pyne's Somerset
the clergy preached regularly against the Commonwealth. Robert
Bennet would have liked to root out some of them from the Cornish
parishes, but was reproved by his friend John Moyle. 'I know you
stand for liberty of conscience', Moyle observed when Bennet tried
to remove a Scotch Presbyterian from Duloe, '. . . I trust you will
afford him that latitude that you desire to have yourself.' The handful of Independents who held benefices under the Commonwealth
shows how little the situation in the counties had really changed.[76]
The 1650 Church survey was conducted by eminently moderate

[74] *Independency*, ii. 156-7. For the schools founded by the propagation see Vincent, *The
State and School Education*, pp. 53-4, 135.

[75] Boyle to John Mallet, 2 Mar. 1651/2: B.M. Add. MS. 32093 (Mallet MSS.), fol. 293;
*A Vindication of the Presbyteriall-Government, and Ministry . . . Published, By the Ministers,
and Elders, met together in a Provincial Assembly, Novemb. 2d. 1649* (London, 1650: [B.M.]
E. 582, 3), Intro.

[76] Whitelocke, *Memorials*, iii. 247, 276, 288; Moyle to R. Bennet, 16 Nov. 1650: Folger
Lib., MS. Add. 494 (Bennet MSS.), p. 269; Yule, *The Independents*, pp. 23-6, and App. C.
Yule is, of course, quite right in pointing out that there were many Independent congrega-
tions outside the parish system.

men, more anxious to improve the parish system than to replace it. And when in the last months of the Rump radical reform seemed imminent, the country gentry spoke out against dangerous experiments. A petition from Hampshire in February 1653, for instance, supported by such secluded Presbyterians as Bulkeley and Whitehead, called for the continuation of tithes and the admission only of 'orthodox and fitly qualified' persons to the ministry. All over England moderate men of all denominations or none were closing ranks.[77]

Like the Rump, the local regimes were too preoccupied with keeping order and staying in power to have time for social or religious novelties. The militia commissioners might lack gentility, but for maintaining public order they were effective enough. In some counties, Kent and Somerset especially, they were particularly severe towards the old gentry and aristocracy. Sir Thomas Peyton suffered badly at Livesey's hands, and it may not have been accidental that the Kent militia chose the Earl of Leicester as one of their targets for plundering. George Luttrell, the owner of Dunster Castle, was an active J.P., but this did not save him from the demolition of part of the castle by order of the Council of State. The indignation such things aroused was well expressed by one of the Earl of Northumberland's servants when, just before the Purge, Haselrig proposed to move the county gaol to the Earl's castle at Warksworth. 'I marvelled how any inferior subject durst presume to think to make the principal house of a peer of the realm, a gaol', the Earl's man told the officer who brought the order.[78] Nor were the secluded members exempt from indignities. John Harris complained to Bennet that he and his brother-in-law James Cambell had had their swords taken away—by a mere corporal. Even though not legally required to do so, Francis Buller meekly provided Bennet with a detailed itinerary when he was about to travel to another part of Cornwall. The Harleys were often in trouble. Old Sir Robert was denied permission to live at Shrewsbury in April

77 B.M. Add. MS. 24861 (Major MSS.), fols. 67-72. Baxter promoted a similar petition in Worcestershire: *Rel. Baxt.* i. 69-70; G. F. Nuttall, *Richard Baxter* (London, 1965), p. 77. The Hampshire petition duly produced a counter-petition from the radical Independents.

78 Everitt, *Community of Kent*, pp. 276-7; *Cal. S.P. Dom.*, *1650*, pp. 281, 294; *1651*, pp. 109, 210-11, 220; Prynne, *True and Perfect Narrative of what was done* . . . *7-9 May 1659* (May 1659: [B.M.] E. 767, 1), p. 59; Sir H. C. Maxwell Lyte, *History of Dunster* (London, 1909), i. 196-200; Robert Watson to Hugh Potter, 22 Nov. 1648: Northumberland MSS., Q ii, 153 (B.M. Film 398).

1650, and a few months later all three of his sons were arrested, Edward being subsequently banished from Herefordshire.[79] They were not the only secluded members to suffer during the months of tension that surrounded Worcester and Dunbar.

In the towns even more than the counties local government usually went on in the old way. Mayors and aldermen nearly always preferred the narrow interests of their propertied constituents to visionary schemes of social reform. Although more generous policies triumphed at High Wycombe, in most places there was little awakening to the problem of poverty. London won some gains for its Corporation for the Poor, and in the critical early months of 1649 many towns were temporarily stirred to action. At Nottingham the corporation investigated a serious coal shortage, and voted £20 for supplies to be used for setting the poor to work. The magistrates of Wigan and Ashton-Under-Lyne sponsored a relief fund, with the aid of the local gentry. Plague, unemployment, the astronomical increase in food prices, and the general damage inflicted by the wars made it urgent 'to keep in the infected, hunger-starved poor, whose breaking out jeapordiseth all the neighbourhood'.[80] But this was no more than town governments would have done in any period to alleviate desperate suffering and preserve law and order. In March 1651 the corporation of Leicester discussed depopulation and inclosure, always a pressing local issue, and during the following year they supported a petition to Parliament on the subject. But the times were unpropitious, and Leicester seems to have been the only town to join the lonely traditionalist voices in opposition to Walter Blyth's improvers.[81] In what borough records survive there are few signs of concern with education, though it is true that the still unreconstructed Bedford corporation in March 1649 discussed remedying the decay of the local grammar school.[82]

[79] Harris to Bennet, 18 June 1649; Buller to Bennet, 10 Feb. 1650/1: Folger Lib., MS. Add. 494 (Bennet MSS.), pp. 151, 305; H.M.C., *Portland*, iii. 172, 187-9; viii. 9; *Brilliana Harley Letters*, pp. 233-6; *Cal. S.P. Dom., 1650*, pp. 75, 290, 306, 387, 523.

[80] *Nottingham Records*, v. 259-60; *A True Representation of the present sad and lamentable condition of the County of Lancaster* (24 May 1649), in G. Ormerod, ed., *Tracts Relating to Military Proceedings in Lancashire during the Great Civil War* (Chetham Soc. ii, 1844), pp. 277-8.

[81] Stocks and Stevenson, eds., *Leicester Records*, pp. 396, 412, 414.

[82] Parsloe, ed., *Bedford Corporation Minute Book*, pp. 9-10. Local initiative sometimes led to attempts to reform schools by commissioners for charitable uses: Vincent, *The State and School Education*, pp. 51-2. But I see no evidence that these were the result of action by corporations.

The urban oligarchies had more practical concerns. The revolution presented dangers; it also presented opportunities. Many was the town which saw the chance of picking up confiscated property or rents, or which tried to improve its position at the expense of local rivals. As always, special economic interests were carefully pursued. Newcastle ruthlessly defended its monopoly of the coal carrying-trade against the interloper Ralph Gardiner; and lacking a representative in the Rump after Blakiston's death they cultivated other M.P.s for special favours. Stamford got £1,500 out of delinquents' estates for improving the navigation of the Welland. Bath was unwilling to contribute to the upkeep of wounded soldiers, but had no objection to spending money on entertaining M.P.s who would promote a scheme to improve the Avon; one of them, William Eyre, was made a freeman and the usual fee remitted, 'in respect he may do us a greater favour'.[83] Everywhere towns continued to insist on the exclusion of 'strangers' from local trades, all the more so in view of the lapse of the apprenticeship laws and the greater mobility of population after the wars. At Rye in 1651 severe restrictions were imposed on the employment of disbanded soldiers who were not previous residents, provoking disorderly protests by the garrison.[84]

There was nothing new about such policies. Peculiar to the Interregnum were the frequent purchases of Crown and ecclesiastical lands and fee-farm rents. Most corporations bought whatever they could lay their hands on, stretching their resources to the limit, or borrowing from wealthy members.[85] Cathedral cities were especially well placed to buy up Church property, both for financial purposes and to take over the jurisdictions of now defunct rivals. Sometimes there was a cover of religious intent, sometimes not. Salisbury bought houses in the cathedral close and earmarked them 'for the ministers'; but Exeter used one of theirs for a workhouse, turned the bishop's palace over to the Hospital of St. John, and

---

[83] Howell, *Newcastle*, pp. 290, 302 *et seq.*; *C.J.* vi. 507; King and Watts, *Cavaliers and Roundheads in Bath*, p. 39; C. W. Shickle, ed., 'The First Book of Minutes of the Council' (Typescript, Bath Reference Lib.), ii. 17-18, 20.

[84] Mayor and Jurats to Morley and others, 20 Nov. 1651: H.M.C., *Thirteenth Report*, App. IV (Rye MSS.), pp. 217-18. The Army petition of 13 Aug. 1652 complained about the restrictions imposed by corporate towns on the employment of ex-soldiers: Gardiner, *Commonwealth*, ii. 224.

[85] Latimer, *Annals of Bristol in the Seventeenth Century*, p. 234; Stocks and Stevenson, eds., *Leicester Records*, p. 397; *Nottingham Records*, v. 269-72; J. M. Guilding, ed., *Reading Records* (London, 1892-6), iv. 363-4.

built a new sergemarket in the cloisters. At Wells the corporation
converted a newly purchased canonical house into a hall for
Quarter Sessions, and sold others to their own members or their
friends. To retain their property, the corporation brilliantly contested a long legal battle with the Presbyterian Burges, who was
installed in both the cathedral and the deanery. In the end they
emerged with much of the property and also with a large part of the
episcopal tolls and judicial rights that Burges thought were included
in his purchase. Apart from the lawsuits, it was the same story elsewhere: Lincoln, York, and other cities expanded their jurisdictions
by taking over former cathedral liberties.[86]

There were other possible gains. Rival towns could be challenged:
Reading, for instance, tried to get the Assizes and Quarter Sessions
away from Abingdon.[87] For Oxford this was an obvious time to
settle old scores with a university already being reconstructed by
parliamentary visitation. When in the autumn of 1648 the Vice-
Chancellor reminded the mayor of his duty to come to St. Mary's
to swear fidelity to the University, he met with blank refusal. In
February 1649 the summons was unwisely repeated, with a demand
for the traditional St. Scholastica's day fine and submission. This
time the city not only refused to comply, but proceeded to petition
Parliament against the University's arbitrary powers.[88] Finally,
there were lords of manors to be dealt with. Not all towns regarded
these archaic survivals with dislike: little Bishop's Castle, for
example, was still quietly entertaining its royalist lord, Sir Robert
Howard, in October 1649.[89] But where, as at Aylesbury, there was
a Thomas Scot to give a lead, it was a different matter. In May 1649
the Aylesbury burgesses demanded restoration of the rights of
common in Heydon Hill of which their lord, Sir John Packington,
had allegedly deprived them. A Rump committee considered the
case, and early in 1650 Packington gave way. Forced into it, he said
after the Restoration, by 'terrors and extremities', but actually at

---

[86] H.M.C., *Various Collections*, iv (Salisbury MSS.), 241; H.M.C., *Exeter*, p. 214; Cotton
and Woollcoombe, *Exeter Records*, pp. 174-5; Underdown, *E.H.R.* lxxviii (1963), 18-48;
Hill, *Tudor and Stuart Lincoln*, pp. 163-4; Forster, *V.C.H., York*, p. 182; Cross, in *Studies
in Church Hist.* iv. 139.

[87] Guilding, ed., *Reading Records*, iv. 470.

[88] Andrew Clark, ed., *Life and Times of Anthony Wood* (Oxford Hist. Soc., 1891-1900),
i. 150; *The Humble Petition of the Mayor, Aldermen . . . of the City of Oxon.* (6 Apr. 1649).

[89] H. C. Maxwell Lyte, 'Manuscripts of the Corporation of Bishop's Castle', *Shropshire
Arch. and Nat. Hist. Soc., Trans.* x (1887), 131; H.M.C., *Tenth Report*, App. IV (Bishop's
Castle MSS.), p. 405.

the price of a substantial reduction of his composition fine, he signed the necessary agreement. A body of local trustees now became in effect the government of the town. Here is a clear case in which the revolution led directly to a grant of urban self-government; only after 1660 did the Packingtons get their feudal rights back.[90]

But with a few exceptions like Aylesbury and Bedford, the Commonwealth did little to satisfy revolutionary hopes of liberty and reformation. The attitude of the majority, who were not revolutionaries, was one of reluctant acquiescence. There was an exception to this in the late summer of 1651, when national feeling produced an impressive turnout against the Scots, in which men of all classes shared. Even the secluded Sir Richard Onslow took up arms, though, old fox that he was, he took care to reach Worcester too late for the battle. But in normal times the majority of Englishmen viewed the Commonwealth apathetically. The Rumpers themselves encouraged a reduction in the political temperature. Some were beginning to sound very like the men they had supplanted. All that ministers should do, said Thomas Atkin, was 'preach Christ, and cry down sin'; they should stay out of politics, and not 'stir up the people to disobedience'. Many people, even among the clergy, had always agreed with him: Ralph Josselin, for instance, who even in 1649 questioned the right of ministers 'to intermeddle thus in all difficulties of state'.[91] If the preachers were unwilling to meddle, it is unlikely that the less politically conscious laity would be more inclined to risk their necks on either side.

[90] *C.J.* vi. 206, 326-7, 331; *Cal. C. Comp.*, p. 1195; *V.C.H.*, *Bucks.* iii. 10. Scot (who according to some accounts married Packington's daughter as his second wife) kept his part of the bargain by later helping to defeat a proposal to include Packington in one of the Acts of Sale: *C.J.* vii. 209.

[91] Speaker Onslow's Account: H.M.C., *Fourteenth Report*, App. IX (Onslow MSS.), pp. 477-8; *Cal. S.P. Dom.*, *1651*, p. 531; Atkin to M. Linsey, 5 July 1650: B.M. Add. MS. 22620 (Collections re Norwich), fol. 172; *Josselin's Diary*, p. 63.

# XI

## CONCLUSION

PRIDE'S Purge was both a symptom and a cause of the failure of
the Puritan Revolution. The circumstances which produced it, and
the way in which it was conducted, demonstrate the revolutionaries'
fatal divisions, their inability to agree on a common programme.
The real pressure for revolution came from the Army, the Levellers,
and the sects, but the leaders who made policy both then and in the
weeks that followed, shared only a few of the desires of their supporters. Ireton, Burnet rightly says, was the Cassius of the revolution, the man who 'stuck at nothing that might have turned England
into a commonwealth'.[1] But even Ireton went only a little way with
the Levellers in their demand for a total reconstruction of the State.
He wanted a dissolution of Parliament, a redistribution of constituencies, and regular elections for a new representative, but he
did not want them badly enough to break with his allies in the
House. Ludlow and the civilian radicals wanted some reforms, too,
but they wanted first to preserve an appearance of constitutional
respectability, and to avoid outright rule by the Army. They feared
immediate elections as entailing the risk of either a Leveller advance
from the left, or more likely a royalist counter-revolution from the
right. Their refusal to secede and form an emergency government
with the help of the Army forced Ireton to abandon his dissolution
scheme and to accept the Purge, which left them, not the more
militant Army, in power.

Besides being a symptom of division, the Purge was a prime cause
of the revolution's decline into stagnation once King and Lords had
been disposed of. By retaining the fiction of constitutional continuity, even more by preserving the power of Ludlow, Scot, and
their friends, the Purge prevented the clean break with the past
that the Levellers, and even Ireton to some extent, wanted. Cromwell's unsuccessful effort to obtain the return of the secluded
members just before Christmas 1648 anticipates the immediate

[1] Airy, ed., *Burnet*, i. 79.

broadening of the Rump's membership once the King was safely dead. There were half-hearted men even among the revolutionaries —timeservers like Harvey as well as genuinely puzzled men like Cromwell, impaled between the dictates of Providence and gentry constitutionalism. But although the leaders in Parliament were not universally radical Independents and sectaries, enough of them were to offer the 'godly party' in the country some hope of action. When under pressure from Cromwell and others like him, the Rump opened the door to the conformists in February 1649, the prospects for reform at once began to decline. And the return of the moderates meant that outside Parliament as well as in it there would be no total purge of the political nation. The Leveller scheme for the restriction of political rights to those who would subscribe the *Agreement of the People* dwindled into the imposition of the Engagement to be true and faithful to the Commonwealth—and even this was gently and hesitantly enforced. Both in Parliament and in the local communities the revolutionaries were a minority. They might hang on to power, but they were surrounded by moderate conformists of Whitelocke's type who lacked positive revolutionary convictions.

Behind the immediate circumstances and consequences of the Purge lurks a larger and more fundamental ambiguity in the nature of the parliamentarian cause itself. What after all, as Prynne often asked, was the Good Old Cause? The moderate constitutionalism of 1642 and of the majority of the gentry throughout the Civil War; or the radical Puritanism of 1648-9 and 1653, of the plebeian New Model Army and the sects?[2] Prynne was not the only one who thought he knew the answer. His identification of the issues was accepted, more temperately, not only by the political Presbyterians, but by many Independents as well. The war, said Nathaniel Fiennes, was fought to preserve 'our ancient English Government of the Kingdom . . . our Judicatories fundamental to this government, . . . our Laws and Liberties in and by them preserved'. It was not fought to establish Presbyterian Church government, certainly not for Independency; Fiennes indeed disliked seeing 'the multitude stirred up, by the pulpit and the press, to rise against lawful authority', whether by Scots Presbyterians or English

---

[2] [Prynne], *The Good Old Cause Rightly Stated, and the False Un-cased* (13 May 1659: [B.M.] E. 983, 6*); Prynne, *The Re-publicans and Others Spurious Good Old Cause, Briefly and Truly Anatomized* (13 May 1659: [B.M.] E. 983, 6).

sectaries.[3] But the fierce tempering of religious zeal during the wars, the flourishing of Puritan variety when censorship and ecclesiastical discipline were both removed, meant that the moderates were overtaken by events. The Good Old Cause of 1642 was challenged by another one, the cause of *Salus Populi* and of the Saints. And so in December 1648 the middle-group Independents were shouldered aside along with the Presbyterians, the non-party country gentry, and all those who wished for settlement on the old, traditional lines.

They were shouldered aside, but not for long. Cromwell had embraced the revolution only through the logic of Providence and necessity. Soon he and many like him were moving the Rump back to the old ways. Whitelocke was there from the first; after Worcester, with Cromwell's return from the wars and St. John's from the wilderness there could be another attempt to restore the fractured unity of the godly party. Settlement, oblivion, moderate reform of the Church, the law, the electoral system: the new programme was a realistic adjustment to the new circumstances, for both King and lords were water under the bridge. In this practical restatement of old middle-group policies Cromwell, the reluctant accomplice of the Purge, and St. John, the unrepentant opponent, were preparing the way for a genuine reunion of the political nation. In the discussions of 1651 and 1652 the hopes of conservatives like Whitelocke and the suspicions of radicals like Ludlow found a basis of reality. But Ludlow was wrong when, in his famous panegyric on the Rump he put the blame for its destruction on Cromwell, on 'the ambition of one man' alone.[4] In the first place Cromwell was but one leading advocate of a policy of settlement which had wide support among the moderate gentry in and outside the Rump. In the second, the radical cause itself was hopelessly split, and its own divisions precipitated the Rump's downfall.

Radicals of all persuasions might pay lip-service to *Salus Populi*, but they were very far from being of one mind on how it would be determined. Puritanism always contained an inherent contradiction: the impulse for liberty, the free right of conscience, constantly struggled with the impulse for reform, the duty of the elect to improve the unregenerate. In the Rump, in the Army, in the radical congregations, in the souls of the revolutionaries themselves, the two principles competed. The architects of the Purge saw it as

[3] [Fiennes], *Vindiciae Veritatis*, pp. 6–7, 24.
[4] *Ludlow's Memoirs*, i. 343–4.

the only way for a godly minority to frustrate an evil settlement negotiated by the corrupt majority. Thomas Scot was always for government by the people: 'what was fought for', he asked rhetorically, 'but to arrive at that capacity to make your own laws?' But he knew well enough that the people were not sufficiently radicalized or enlightened to recognize their true interest. 'I am for trusting the people with their liberties as soon as any,' he observed, 'but when they come to irregularities, and the major part grow corrupt, they must be regulated.'[5] It was the dilemma of revolutionary minorities in all ages, made more acute by the Calvinist frame of reference: in the name of liberty, a godly élite would have to govern. The radical Puritans were more honest about it. Even in the Whitehall debates of December 1648, it will be remembered, the Fifth Monarchy Men had been less than enthusiastic about liberal constitutions. Operating, as Harrison claimed to do, 'upon higher principles than those of civil liberty', they were determined to rule, by the sword if necessary, and fulfil the Biblical prophecy 'that the Saints shall take the kingdom and possess it'. It was easy for the more secularly minded Ludlow to expose the fallacies in Harrison's argument when the two old comrades mournfully discussed the collapse of the cause in 1656. Most of their friends, he rightly observed, had engaged for nothing higher than civil liberty, and even on Harrison's showing there was no proof that the Saints were justified in imposing their authority on them. Yet even more than Harrison, Ludlow was himself the victim of the contradiction inherent in the claim of a minority to define the nation's freedom. Civil and spiritual liberty, General Charles Fleetwood told Thurloe in 1654, 'are so intermixed in this day that we cannot sever them'.[6] The statement was logically true, but in the light of the behaviour of Fleetwood's own friends it was also historically false.

\*　　\*　　\*

It was Cromwell, as usual, who temporarily resolved the Rump's contradictions, by swinging over to Harrison and expelling it. 'Who shall govern us by land, astrology knows not', Edward Harley commented.[7] Actually it would not have needed an Ashmole or a Lilly

---

[5] Scot, speech, 29 Jan. 1657/8: *Burton's Diary*, ii. 385, 390-1.
[6] *Ludlow's Memoirs*, ii. 6-8; Fleetwood to Thurloe, 27 July 1654: B.M. Add. MS. 4156 (Birch MSS.), fol. 71.
[7] Edward Harley to Sir Robert Harley, 31 May 1653: H.M.C., *Portland*, iii. 202.

to tell him. The Barebones Parliament was chosen by Cromwell and his officers. Sometimes they accepted the recommendations made by Harrison and the gathered churches, more often they did not. The new assembly contained the same conflicting elements that had struggled for supremacy ever since 1642: the radical Puritans and the moderate constitutional reformers. The Welsh Fifth Monarchists were there, and the Baptists like Samuel Highland, Denis Hollister, and Praise-God Barbone himself. But so were trimming country 'gentlemen like Sir Anthony Ashley Cooper, old middle-group men like Richard Norton, and aristocratic former radicals now turning to moderation, like Edward Mountagu.[8] The threatening attacks on tithes and the law by men of the first type soon led Cromwell to charge them with endangering 'liberty and property' under the watchword 'Overturn! Overturn!' Yet even in Parliament the radicals were not in full control, and in the end they were circumvented by a *coup d'état* by the moderates.

The reform aspirations of the Barebones radicals, it has been observed, were those 'of the London Baptist householders and artisans'.[9] This they were, true enough. But they were the policies of the provincial as well as the metropolitan Saints; in the shires as much as at Westminster in 1653 there was a further marked swing to the left. For the Barebones regime produced even more disruption of local government than the Rump; wholesale changes in the Commissions of the Peace which made the earlier years of the Commonwealth seem like a paradise of stability. Between July and October county after county was purged, as the Saints sought out their enemies to destroy them. In Buckinghamshire there was virtually a clean sweep. The governing clique of Rumpers—Scot, Mayne, West, the Chaloners—went out. So did their lesser allies from the various committees. So did what was left of the old gentry after earlier crises and civil wars—Cheyneys, Dormers, Tyrells, Probys, Drakes. A few of these were restored later in the year and were joined by new J.P.s of such impeccably respectable antecedents as those of Richard Hampden, son of the great parliamentarian. But the replacements also included many who were impenetrably obscure, and others of visibly radical associations such as the

---

[8] Austin Woolrych, 'The Calling of Barebone's Parliament', *E.H.R.* lxxx (1965), 492–513. For Mountagu's change see Underdown, *J.B.S.* iii (1964), 78–9.

[9] Farnell, *E.H.R.* lxxxii (1967), 44.

sequestration commissioner Henry Phillips and the leader of the Wycombe radicals, Samuel Guy.[10]

None of the other county purges equalled that of Buckinghamshire, but many were striking enough. There were more upheavals in Wales, and sweeping changes in Surrey, Devon, the East and North Ridings of Yorkshire, and several other counties. In Herefordshire a score of J.P.s were removed, including the only three remaining titled magistrates (Sir John Bridges, Sir Gilbert Cornwall, and Sir Richard Hopton), and members of such solid families as Eltons, Kyrles, and Baskervilles. In their place appeared a further consignment of Wroth Rogers's allies among the lesser gentry.[11] But besides the new radicals, Baptists like Guy, John Easton of Bedford, and Hollister of Bristol, the newcomers also included men whose only recommendation was that they had been at odds with the Rump, men who had little in common with the Barebones millenarians. A good many J.P.s who had been removed by the Rump now returned: Sir Roger Burgoyne in Warwickshire, John Boys and Henry Oxinden in Kent. Like the Rump, the Barebones Parliament had to govern the country and take its allies where it could find them. No more than the Barebones M.P.s were the J.P.s universally radical Puritans.

Nevertheless, enough of them were to give the moderate gentry a severe case of fright. Society needed to be saved, and Cromwell as the good constable of the parish set out to save it. With the important interruption of the Major-Generals era, the Protectorate was a conservative regime, searching, as Cromwell so often put it, for 'healing and settlement'. In many respects it can indeed be seen as an essentially middle-group regime, the logical adaptation of the ideas of St. John, Fiennes, and their friends, to the conditions of the 1650s. A government with 'somewhat of monarchical power' in it, as Cromwell had agreed was necessary when St. John advocated it after Worcester; a strong executive council; moderate parliamentary reform and redistribution on the lines of Haselrig's Bill of early 1653; a broadly based Church settlement not far removed from that proposed by Owen in 1652, combining toleration with stability; an olive branch to the Presbyterian and even the royalist

[10] Information from J.P. file, History of Parliament Trust. For the men and their families see Johnson, 'Buckinghamshire'. For Guy, above, p. 323.

[11] Herefordshire J.P.s added in 1653 who signed radical petitions and addresses included Robert Weaver, Richard Walsham, Benjamin Mason, John Woodyate, Morgan Watkins, Richard Nicholetts.

z

gentry: all the essentials of their programme were there. It is not surprising that Nathaniel Fiennes could support it and accept high office, that John Glyn could become Chief Justice, or that St. John could be regarded, for all his reluctance to act as an official councillor, as the 'dark lantern' behind the Protectorate.[12]

The tide had turned, and the moderates were drifting back into both politics and administration. At the Wiltshire election in July 1654, Ludlow observed how he and his Commonwealth friends were opposed by the 'Cavaliers' (Ludlow's shorthand for the moderate gentry), 'the imposing clergy, the lawyers and court interest'. At the head of this coalition of would-be saviours of society was that man 'of a healing and reconciling spirit, of all interests that agree in the greatening of himself', Sir Anthony Ashley Cooper.[13] Hopefully the gentry awaited the reduction of the Army and the lessening of taxation. 'If my Lord Protector live but seven years', Thomas Crompton thought in September 1654, 'I am confident we shall be a happy people and see great part of the taxes taken off.' Outside the Army there would have been few to disagree. 'We have laid long enough under a land tax', complained another old Rump moderate, Sir William Strickland.[14] Already country gentlemen like John Fitzjames were looking hopefully to Richard Cromwell as a possible heir, rightly seeing him, for all his weakness, as one of themselves.[15]

The Protectorate's appeal to the moderates was drastically lessened after Penruddock's rebellion, when Cromwell reverted to Puritan authoritarianism and installed the Major-Generals. In the 1656 elections the slogan 'No Swordsman! No Decimator!' resounded in constituencies throughout the land. In Herefordshire the county elected Edward Harley in spite of a combined effort by the sheriff and the Major-General to rig the election.[16] In Dorset, dislike of the Major-Generals and their 'tickets' threw moderates like Ashley Cooper and Fitzjames back into opposition.[17] But even

[12] St. John denied it in 1660: *Case of Oliver St. John*. But the evidence is strong, especially for the latter part of the Protectorate. See, for example, St. John to Thurloe, 3 Sept. 1658: *Thurloe's S.P.* vii. 370.          [13] *Ludlow's Memoirs*, i. 388-9, 545-8.

[14] Crompton to M. Worsewicke, 23 Sept. [1654]: B.M. Add. MS. 4159 (Birch MSS.), fol. 123; Strickland, speech, 24 Apr. 1657: *Burton's Diary*, ii. 24.

[15] Fitzjames to Richard Cromwell, 31 May 1655; to C. Levitt, 4 Aug. 1655: Fitzjames Letter-book (Northumberland MSS., B.M. Film 331), v, fols. 21ᵛ, 27ᵛ.

[16] H.M.C., *Portland*, iii. 208.

[17] Fitzjames's correspondence between 5 and 19 Aug. 1656 contains much information about the Dorset election: Letter-book, v, fols. 89ᵛ-95ᵛ.

under the Major-Generals, the gentry's disaffection was not unanimous. In Cheshire some of the old families—Egertons, Leghs, Wilbrahams—were willing to work with the republican Bradshawe against the official candidates; but others, Marburys and Mainwarings among them, stood by the Protectorate, and the influential Brookes were divided.[18] All over England there were curious alliances of moderates and former Presbyterians with radical Commonwealthsmen against the Protectorate's court candidates: Lionel Copley, for instance, worked with Sir Henry Vane and the republicans in Yorkshire.[19] And when Parliament met in September and was promptly purged by Cromwell, among those excluded were old Presbyterians like John Birch, Sir Harbottle Grimston, Sir Anthony Irby, and Edward Harley, old middle-group men like Bulkeley and Boys, as well as republicans like Haselrig, Scot, and John Weaver.[20]

But Cromwell turned his back on the Major-Generals and in 1657 the Protectorate's appeal to the moderates became less equivocal. In January that old middle-group stalwart, John Ashe, proposed that Oliver should take the crown: only a 'government according to the ancient constitution' could establish 'both our liberties and peace . . . upon an old and sure foundation'.[21] The *Humble Petition and Advice*, and Oliver's increasing tendency to listen to moderates like Broghil and break with the Good Old Cause militants, were both symptoms of this growing preference for conservative settlement over military Puritanism. The latter part of the Protectorate was a better time for both aristocracy and gentry. Cromwell himself strengthened his ties with the old peerage by marrying one daughter to a Fauconberg, another to a Rich. Although Wharton and Say both refused Cromwell's invitation to the Upper House, men of their order were really much happier with the Protectorate than with any government since 1648. By March 1658 Northumberland's lawyers were assuring the Earl that 'of late the courts of law have allowed the peerage the privilege of their persons as formerly hath been used'.[22] Meanwhile gentry families long

---

[18] Paul J. Pinckney, 'The Cheshire Election of 1656', *John Rylands Library Bulletin*, xlix (1967), 398–406.

[19] R. Lilburne to Thurloe, 9 Aug. 1656: *Thurloe's S.P.* v. 296.

[20] Remonstrance of excluded Members, 17 Sept. 1656: B.M. Stowe MS. 361, fols. 103–4.

[21] Ashe, speech, 19 Jan. 1656/7: *Burton's Diary*, i. 362–3.

[22] Scawen to Earl, 2 Mar. 1657/8: Letters and Papers (Northumberland MSS., B.M. Film 287), xviii, fol. 18; Firth, *House of Lords*, pp. 250–2.

excluded from power were reappearing in the assessment commissions and Commissions of the Peace. In Somerset, where Pyne's
dictatorial rule was now a fading memory, even the Decimation
Tax commissioners were less vindictive than the Rump's local
governors. 'The gentlemen of this county act very mildly', the
Marquis of Hertford's bailiff discovered with some surprise. In
1657 the Somerset Commission of the Peace was drastically remodelled. Nineteen J.P.s were removed, among them the Rumpers
Carent, Palmer, and Serle, and such local radicals as Alexander
Pym, Thomas English, and John Gay. In their places appeared
representatives of such solid families as Luttrell, Rolle, Rogers, and
Wyndham, and even a sprinkling of Royalists, such as Hugh Smyth
and George Norton.[23]

Richard Cromwell's accession made the outlook for conciliation
even brighter. From Scotland, Monck immediately advised the new
Protector to appeal to the conservative gentry. He should reduce
the Army in order to purge out the 'insolent spirits' and cut taxes,
encourage the religious Presbyterians so as to still the gentry's fears
of the dangerous consequences of toleration, and rely on the counsel
of such men as Pierrepont, Sir George Booth and Alexander
Popham, as well as the obviously Cromwellian St. John and
Broghil.[24] In spirit if not in letter, this is indeed the policy that the
Cromwellians pursued in the following winter. From all parts loyal
addresses, often subscribed by many of the old gentry, flowed in to
congratulate Richard on his accession. Willing to support whatever would 'settle and consolidate . . . all considerable parties',
Fitzjames took a leading part in preparing one in Dorset, relying
for advice on his friend Marchamont Nedham at court, and serving
as a bridge to still disaffected Presbyterians like Denzil Holles.[25]
Prynne was not far wrong in thinking that Richard was overthrown for his attempted alliance with 'the ancient nobility, gentry,
lawyers, and Presbyterians', and his wish 'to revive the old English

[23] W. Orum to T. Gape, 26 Jan. 1655/6: H.M.C., *Bath*, iv. 281. Information from J.P.
file at History of Parliament Trust. For the return of moderate gentry in other regions see
Dodd, *Stuart Wales*, pp. 154-7; Pinckney, *Rylands Lib. Bull.* xlix (1967), 425-6.

[24] Monck paper [15 Sept. 1658]: *Thurloe's S.P.* vii, 317-18.

[25] Fitzjames letters, 7 Aug.-4 Nov. 1658: Letter-book (Northumberland MSS., B.M.
Film 331), vi, fols. 28-44ᵛ. Fitzjames's more favourable attitude to the Protectorate and
hopes from Richard are shown in earlier letters to Nedham between 11 Mar. and 11 July
1658: ibid., fols. 4-22ᵛ. For the addresses see Godfrey Davies, *Restoration of Charles II*
(San Marino, Calif., 1955), pp. 10-11. Suspicions of Nedham's role in providing official
sponsorship of the petitions are in part supported by the Fitzjames evidence.

militia of Trained-bands by degrees for the people's ease in their taxes'.[26]

Country gentlemen might be secretly convinced that only a return to the legitimate monarchy could guarantee their property and privileges; but the Protectorate could be supported as second best. Anything, after all, was better than the Rump. 'I could tell you current stories of the tyranny of a Commonwealth', said Nathaniel Bacon. 'Look into Carthage, Athens. See Sir Walter Raleigh. Every man had liberty to find out the richest to destroy for himself.' Richard Knightley agreed: 'A Commonwealth was never for the common weal.' If they asked too many questions about the constitution, Edmund Fowell thought, they would be 'melted into a Commonwealth again, or worse, if aught can be worse'.[27] Perhaps Samuel Gott was thinking of something worse when he said that he would not 'look forward to *Oceana's* Platonical Commonwealth, things that are not, and that never shall be'.[28] Even old republicans admitted their former errors when they urged Cromwell to take the crown. 'The whole body of the law is carried upon this wheel', said Speaker Lenthall; monarchy was 'the best government for the people's safety'. His nephew Sir John was even more explicit in Richard Cromwell's Parliament: 'What extravagancies have been, from supposing all power was here!'[29] Recantation also came from radicals of less dubious conviction than the Lenthalls. 'I acknowledge the old constitution, by Lords and Commons, to be the best ... I ever thought it', said Francis Thorpe in a convenient lapse of memory. Even Robert Bennet came round. 'I liked a Commonwealth well,' he told Parliament in February 1659, 'but not at this time, when we are so full of distraction.'[30]

Although many of the gentry could accept the Protectorate as the best government we have, many could not. It was still, after all, a military regime, and Cromwell never quite cut his ties with his Army even if he did dismiss radical officers like Harrison and Packer. The Norfolk members debated long and hard before they agreed to sign the 'Recognition' in September 1654, reluctantly

[26] Prynne, *The Re-publicans and Others Spurious Good Old Cause*, p. 3.

[27] Speeches by Bacon (8 Feb. 1658/9), Knightley (14 Feb.), and Fowell (17 Mar.): *Burton's Diary*, iii. 123, 262; iv. 165.     [28] Gott, speech 8 Feb. 1658/9: ibid. iii. 144.

[29] William Lenthall, in *Monarchy Asserted* (1660), *Somers Tracts*, vi. 356, 372; John Lenthall, speech, 18 Feb. 1658/9: *Burton's Diary*, iii. 338.

[30] Speeches by Thorpe (4 Feb. 1657/8), and Bennet (14 Feb. 1658/9): *Burton's Diary*, ii. 447; iii. 266.

accepting the compulsion of necessity so that they could take their seats, and using reasoning much like that of Whitelocke in 1648. When Alexander Popham arrived he told Cromwell 'that he came to do his country service, and not his Lordship'.[31] Reservations about the Protectorate were not confined to the gentry at election time, although they were particularly evident in the campaign of 1656. Even men close to the Protector's family lacked enthusiasm. 'I am yet out of all employment but country ones', Francis Russell told his son-in-law Henry Cromwell in 1655. The court-country division was recurring in something like the old form. 'I came to bring court and country together', said John Bulkeley in April 1659.[32] Too late, before the new Cromwellian alignment had been consolidated the Army moved again, and threw Richard out.

The Protectorate had some appeal to the moderates, but not as much as it might have had but for the memory of Pride's Purge and the Rump. Cromwell, we now know, had not been the instigator of the revolution of 1648–9. But inevitably he was blamed for it, and too much bad blood remained for many of the secluded members and their friends to support him. The Presbyterians were no longer even the vaguely identifiable party they had been in 1648, and they soon went their separate ways. At first, to be sure, adversity gave their leaders some sense of solidarity. In the autumn of 1651, Browne, Clotworthy, Copley, Sir William Lewis, and Sir William Waller corresponded regularly with each other and with the Harleys about the terms which they could honestly accept to obtain their release. 'As we have suffered together,' said Lewis, 'we might . . . agree of a way to desire our liberties.' Copley was anxious not to be caught 'upon that rock of the Engagement', and wondered if they ought to wait until 'the new representative (if that be a real thing)' was in session.[33] In the end their situation was complicated by accusations of complicity in a recent Presbyterian plot, which prolonged the imprisonment of even the more fortunate ones by several

[31] James Mountagu to Lord Mountagu, 10 Jan. 1654/5: H.M.C., *Buccleuch and Queensberry*, i. 311. For the Norfolk members, *Burton's Diary*, i. xxxvi.

[32] Russell to H. Cromwell, 10 Sept. 1655: B.M. Lansdowne MS. 821 (H. Cromwell Corr.), fol. 14; Bulkeley, speech, 5 Apr. 1659: *Burton's Diary*, iv. 347.

[33] There are brief extracts from the secluded members' correspondence in 1651 in H.M.C., *Portland*, iii. 196–7. For much more detail see the originals of these and other letters in Welbeck MSS., Harley Papers (B.M. Loan 29/73, 29/74, 29/84, and 29/176).

months.[34] But eventually all except Browne were released. Clotworthy became an active Cromwellian, Lewis a more passive one.
Copley and Edward Harley went into retirement until 1656, when
they began to support the country interest against the Protectorate.
Sir Robert Harley died that same year, but his second son, Robert,
drifted steadily into Royalism during the later 1650s, as did Sir
William Waller more hesitantly.[35]

The behaviour of other secluded members was equally varied.
Massey admitted his Royalism immediately after his escape from
prison in January 1649. He joined Charles II in exile, was with him
at Worcester, escaped again, and throughout the decade was a busy
conspirator, in England and abroad. Denzil Holles tinkered with
the Royalists in exile and had his estates temporarily sequestered in
1651. But when he returned to England early in the Protectorate it
was to retire to Dorset; until 1660 he avoided political activity
altogether.[36] Although a few others accepted the logic of their position and worked for Charles II, and others again, like Glyn and
Clotworthy, took service under the Protector, most of the Presbyterians followed Holles into retirement. If they were active at all,
it was as 'country' politicians, willing to give the Protectorate a
chance to provide the much-sought settlement, but holding back
from enthusiastic support because of their memories of ten years
before. 'They seem the only party . . . that consult nothing in
common', one of Charles II's Presbyterian agents complained in
1656. This could be explained, he went on, 'either from a universal
diffidence that they have one of another; or a total abandoning of
all thoughts of farther prosecuting anything of public interest:
. . . or lastly from a satisfaction they generally have in the present
government and a resolution to comply with it'.[37]

The Protectorate might strive for settlement, but it could not
command the broad support that was necessary to complete it.
Part of the trouble was the continued muttering from the Army,

---

[34] *Cal. S.P. Dom.*, *1651*, pp. 474–81, 503, 534; *1651–2*, pp. 1–2, 6, 10, 13, 30, 54, 66,
90–1, 125, 157. For the plot see L. H. Carlson, 'History of the Presbyterian Party from Pride's
Purge to the Dissolution of the Long Parliament', *Church History*, xi (1942), 83–122.

[35] *D.N.B.* ('Clotworthy'). For Lewis see Dodd, *Stuart Wales*, p. 156. For Robert Harley
and Waller, Underdown, *Royalist Conspiracy*, pp. 117, 136, 209, 221–40, 308–9, 330.

[36] *Nicholas Papers*, i. 171, 186; H.M.C., *Portland*, i. 585; *Cal. S.P. Dom.*, *1650*, p. 271;
*1651*, p. 149; *Cal. C. Comp.*, pp. 435, 2772. For Massey see above, p. 195.

[37] Draft paper by S. Titus, [1656?]: B.M. Egerton MS. 1533 (Titus MSS.), fol. 55;
G. R. Abernathy, *The English Presbyterians and the Stuart Restoration, 1648–1663* (American
Phil. Soc. Trans., N.S. lv, Pt. ii, Philadelphia, 1965), pp. 17–25.

which provoked Henry Cromwell to ask in exasperation why ever since 1653 the officers had opposed 'all tendency to settlement of any kind?' The Cromwellians might cut their links with the radicals —Ingoldsby boxed a Baptist's ears for opposing his election to Parliament in 1654, and was soon written off by the Saints as one who could 'neither preach nor pray'.[38] They might encourage the reunion of moderate Independents and Presbyterians against the sects, on the lines of the ministerial associations in Worcestershire and other counties—though Baxter's more ambitious plans for national reconciliation came to nothing.[39] Even tolerant men like Nathaniel Fiennes, though they might try to protect the Quaker Naylor from Presbyterian savagery, were moving to the right. It was dangerous, Fiennes agreed, 'to debar the civil magistrats in matters of religion. . . . That is too much liberty.' But the Cromwellians could satisfy neither Quakers who wanted universal toleration, nor Presbyterians who pressed constantly for greater rigidity. There was, said William Morice, 'in the middle way no firm ground to rest upon'.[40]

Presbyterians like Morice were not the only opponents of the middle way. In April 1659 the Army overthrew the Protectorate because of its moderation, and, not knowing what else to do, recalled the Rump. A few of the old Commonwealthsmen— hardened republicans like Scot and Haselrig, religious zealots like Vane and Salway—came back with enthusiasm. But many others showed a strange reluctance. Even more than in the early months of 1649, the Rumpers were afflicted by a remarkable epidemic of disorders—fevers, 'fits of the stone', and various other infirmities.[41] Some of their colleagues—Alexander Popham, for instance—were already beginning the circuitous process of coming to terms with Charles II.[42] But although some old revolutionaries were reluctant,

---

[38] Henry Cromwell to Thurloe, Feb. 1658: *Thurloe's S.P.* vi. 819; John Percival to Sir Paul Davys, 27 June 1654: H.M.C., *Egmont*, i. 545. And see above, pp. 185-6.

[39] Abernathy, *Presbyterians and the Restoration*, pp. 8-16. For an example of Presbyterian-Independent co-operation against the sects see Howell, *Newcastle*, p. 247.

[40] Fiennes, speech, 27 Dec. 1656: *Burton's Diary*, i. 263; Morice to —, 13 Apr. 1658: Bell, *Memorials*, ii. 142-3.

[41] These and other illnesses are mentioned in letters from Livesey, John Gurdon, Hutchinson, John Weaver, and Lascelles to the Speaker, May 1659: Bodl. MS., Tanner 51, fols. 50-63, 146.

[42] Underdown, *Royalist Conspiracy*, pp. 117, 192, 218, 224, 242, 261. John Dormer was another old Rumper making approaches to the Royalists. In June 1659 he made a loan of £100 to the exiled King: H.M.C., *Eighth Report*, App. III (Ashburnham MSS.), p. 6.

others of a different complexion sensed an opportunity. Prynne and a dozen other secluded members appeared at Westminster on 9 May demanding admission, and even succeeded in forcing the adjournment of the Rump's morning session. In the afternoon, however, they encountered the familiar sight of a troop of horse and two companies of redcoats to show them that the secluded members were still secluded.[43]

No more than in its earlier days was the Rump of 1659 a totally revolutionary regime. It had to govern the country, and in any case many of its members shared little of the godly zeal of a Vane or a Harrison. Yet the summer of 1659 again raised the spectre of social revolution in particularly menacing form. Once more the radical sects were on the march, and this time they were headed by the terrifying Quakers. Prynne summed up the general expectations from this 'fresh combination between the Sectaries, Republican, Anabaptistical, Jesuitical, levelling party'. They were, he said, out to 'extirpate the Church and ministry of England, advowsons, glebes, tithes, and demolish all parish churches as antichristian; to extirpate the law root and branch under pretext of reforming and new-moulding it; to sell all corporation and college lands, and set up a popular anarchy, or tyrannical oligarchy among us'.[44] In different language, this is roughly what the Buckinghamshire radicals asked of the Rump towards the end of May. They petitioned for a continual succession of Parliaments, 'with such restrictions and qualifications in relation to elections as may fully secure the interest of the Commonwealth'; the replacement of corrupt and disloyal officials by faithful ones; and the abolition of tithes and copyholds.[45]

Fears that the Rump would install the plebeian Quakers and other radical sectaries in power stalked the minds of the gentry throughout the summer of 1659 and the following winter. There had been talk of Quaker J.P.s even before Richard's downfall. 'Many Quakers are made justices', John Stephens complained, adding

[43] Prynne, *True and Perfect Narrative of what was done . . . the 7 and 9 of this instant May* (1659: [B.M.] E. 767, 1); [Annesley], *England's Confusion,* in *Somers Tracts,* vi. 522. There was a similar scene when the Rump was again restored on 27 Dec.: [Prynne], *A Brief Narrative of the Manner how divers Members . . . Upon Tuesday the 27th of December 1659 . . . were again forcibly shut out* (1659: [B.M.] E. 1011, 4); Abernathy, *Presbyterians and the Restoration,* pp. 27-8, 36.
[44] *True and Perfect Narrative of . . . 7 and 9 May,* p. 20.
[45] Petition of 'divers assertors of the Good Old Cause' in Bucks., 28 May 1659: B.M. Egerton MS. 1048 (Parl. Papers, 1624-59), fol. 163. Cf. also Davies, *Restoration,* p. 120.

that in Gloucestershire one such person 'could lead out three or four hundred with him at any time'.[46] When the Rump came back such fears were intensified by Vane's desire to give power to 'pious and holy persons'—in other words to the Saints. The Quakers themselves prepared lists of suitable J.P.s, and although opposition from Haselrig and other leading Rumpers averted the danger, the Quaker threat was still the subject of hysterical rumour. At Tiverton in July there was a midnight alarm following reports of imminent massacre plotted by the sectaries. At Oxford a fortnight later there was a similar panic at Carfax Church when part of the tower collapsed during a storm just as trumpets outside were summoning soldiers to parade; again, the immediate conclusion was that the Quakers were in arms. When on 26 July the Rump put their new militia in the hands of radicals from the lower ranks of society, it seemed that genuine revolution was indeed at hand. Sir George Booth's rising, in which Presbyterians and Royalists came together against the Rump and the sects, was preceded by large-scale purchases of arms by gentry who claimed to be preparing to defend hearth and home against the Quakers. And the signal for rebellion in Lancashire was an organized preaching campaign in which the text 'Curse ye Meroz' was directed against the sects. Most of Booth's support came from Presbyterians, among them secluded members like Sir Thomas Myddelton and the Chester member John Ratcliffe. But even a few old Rumpers appeared in arms—Peter Brooke and the Cromwellian Richard Ingoldsby, for example. And there is good reason to think that Admiral Edward Mountagu, another strong Cromwellian, left his post in the Sound with the hope of being home if Booth succeeded.[47]

---

[46] Speech, 5 Apr. 1659: *Burton's Diary*, iv. 337.

[47] Underdown, *Royalist Conspiracy*, pp. 255-75; J. F. Maclear, 'Quakerism and the End of the Interregnum', *Church History*, xix (1950), 240-70. Mountagu's position is discussed by Davies, *Restoration*, pp. 206-7, entirely without reference to the royalist approaches to him, though Davies concedes (p. 140 n.) that the Admiral may have been partly motivated by a wish to return in case Booth succeeded. Both David Ogg, *England in the Reign of Charles II*, 2nd edn. (Oxford, 1955), i. 33, and J. R. Jones, 'Booth's Rising of 1659', *Rylands Library Bull.* xxxix (1956-7), 435, take more seriously the possibility that Mountagu was committing himself to Charles II. To the evidence they cite it might be added that the steward at Hinchingbrooke, Robert Barnwell, received a letter from Mountagu on 19 Aug. (the day of Booth's defeat), ordering him to get in touch with his employer's friends and tenants. This must have been written soon after news reached the Sound that Booth was in arms. Replying on the 24th, Barnwell says, 'According to your command I did remember you to those you writ of and to divers that I did know wished you well': Bodl. MS., Carte 73 (Mountagu Papers), fol. 284.

Booth failed because the Army could still unite against the Cavaliers if against no one else, and because, as the Earl of Manchester put it, the moderates were afraid of 'his Majesty's restoration by tumult'.[48] But soon after Booth's defeat the Army and the Rumpers reached the end of their uneasy alliance. In October the officers expelled the Rump, feebly experimented with a Committee of Safety, and then as anarchy spread returned the keys of the House to the Speaker and allowed the Rump to sit again. The last effort of revolutionary Puritanism had failed. It failed because the Army split and because the rest of the nation united against the radicals. It failed, too, because many even of the godly party had lost their old enthusiasm. A handful of zealots might still dream millenarian dreams, but their day had passed. When Richard Cromwell's Parliament met in January 1659 Ralph Josselin observed how 'a spirit of slumber and remissness' hung over the nation. When a few days later Major Burton moved the Commons for a day of fasting and humiliation, his diarist namesake recorded that 'nobody seconded the motion'. Civilian radicals who had welcomed military intervention in 1648 were now thoroughly disenchanted with a political Army. 'It is said the soldiers have ventured their lives', Sir Thomas Wroth sneered: 'They were well paid for it.'[49] John Pyne's soul still panted for 'the true Good Old Cause', but he could only stand by and lament 'the divisions of Reuben'. Hugh Peter despairingly appealed to Monck to make one last effort to save the Protestant cause, in England and abroad, against 'the popish enemy triumphing everywhere'. But Lambert's last hopeless fling in April 1660 showed that it was too late. It was, said Robert Bennet, 'the grand catastrophe'.[50]

*     *     *

On 21 February 1660 Pride's Purge was at last undone, and there were bells and bonfires throughout the land, for Monck had restored the secluded members. Prynne provided his usual touch of comedy as they entered the House, by accidentally tripping up

[48] Underdown, *Royalist Conspiracy*, p. 284. Cf. also Popham's similar attitude: ibid., p. 224.

[49] *Josselin's Diary*, p. 126; *Burton's Diary*, iii. 6; Wroth, speech, 4 Mar. 1658/9: ibid. iv. 17.

[50] [Pyne to George Sampson?], 14 Nov. 1659: H.M.C., *Ninth Report*, App. II (Pyne MSS.), pp. 493-4; H. Peter to Monck, 24 Apr. 1660: H.M.C., *Leybourne-Popham*, p. 179; Endorsement by R. Bennet on letter from William Bennet, 26 Jan. 1659/60: Folger Lib., MS. Add. 494 (Bennet MSS.), p. 573.

Sir William Waller with his old basket-hilted sword, and indeed the whole scene was an appropriate one for hilarity. The moderate settlement which the members had been secluded for attempting in 1648 could now be accomplished, for there was no united Army to prevent it, the Saints were hopelessly split, and a decade of radical rhetoric and occasional radical experiment had convinced the gentry, even some who ten years earlier had acquiesced in a revolution, that there was no safe alternative to the old constitution. The reunion of the moderates was made plain in the elections for a new Council of State. The middle-group Pierrepont and John Crewe topped the poll, and behind them were Rumpers like Morley, Popham, and Widdrington, conformists rather than revolutionaries in 1649, as well as Holles and other old Presbyterians.[51] A moderate Church policy to defend society against the sects; restoration of gentry rule in the counties by reconstruction of the militia and the Commissions of the Peace; a free Parliament elected on the old franchise; restoration of the House of Lords and the legitimate monarchy: this, rather than radical Puritan reformation, was what the gentry had fought for.

But in fact the settlement of 1660 was not the settlement attempted in 1648. Lord Say and a few other obstinate hardliners still tried to insist on the Newport terms as essential conditions of restoration. But now they had no organized party to support them. Some of the secluded members, with Prynne to the fore, had come together as a group during the last winter to work for their readmission. They showed that they had learnt some tactical lessons from experience by their willingness to organize a campaign of pamphleteering and petitioning in favour of a free Parliament. But many of them had already made or were now making their own private terms with the exiled Charles II, and were not interested in wearisome negotiations. There was no longer an effective Presbyterian party nor was there an effective middle group. Thus although a few still nailed their colours to them, the Newport terms were quickly forgotten in the anxiety of the moderate gentry to save society from anarchy. Such limitations on monarchical power as eventually occurred would be the result of developments after the Restoration, not spelt out as prior conditions.[52]

[51] Davies, *Restoration*, pp. 289–95; *C.J.* vii. 849. Other middle-group men were also well placed—Knightley, Gerard, St. John, and Evelyn among them.

[52] Abernathy, *Presbyterians and the Restoration*, pp. 34–49; D. R. Lacey, *Dissent and Parliamentary Politics in England, 1661–1689* (New Brunswick, N.J., 1969), pp. 6–10.

The gentry had again reunited in defence of liberty and property, but this time against the sects, not the King. Abortively under Booth, and more successfully because less violently in the following winter, men of Presbyterian, neutral, royalist, and even Commonwealth pasts came together to preserve the old hierarchical order of society. The Yorkshire gentry who rallied round Fairfax at the turn of the year did so to preserve the rule of law and their own traditional predominance. Like those in other counties who sent addresses to Monck during his march to London, their preference, spoken or unspoken, was for monarchy, not for any mystical devotion to that form of government, but because it alone could preserve the things they regarded as essential. Though they were religious men, religion no longer determined their political outlook (if it ever had), except in so far as it confirmed the fears they felt for Quakers and other sectaries on political and social grounds.[53] The gentry welcomed the return of the secluded members, the election of a free Parliament, and the invitation to Charles II. They welcomed even more the recovery of their old authority as J.P.s and militia officers. The Militia commission of March 1660 confirmed the return of the moderates to local power. It was the resolution of the Warwickshire gentry, Lord Conway told Edward Harley, to establish 'a very gallant militia to consist wholly of gentry and freeholders'. A safe militia; and also a safe ministry, as young Robert Harley put it when he surveyed the Herefordshire situation: no more of 'those fellows to be ministers which Rogers hath kept in several places these divers years, being persons that professed against ordination, and mechanics'.[54]

*　　*　　*

Pride's Purge, like every other major event of the Interregnum, was the resultant of the two conflicting forces of Puritan idealism and gentry constitutionalism. But was it something more than this? Was there a causal relationship between social rank, religious belief,

[53] A. H. Woolrych, 'Yorkshire and the Restoration', *Yorks. Arch. Journal*, xxxix (1956–8), 506. For the gentry and the Restoration in other regions see Dodd, *Stuart Wales*, pp. 162–76; Everitt, *Community of Kent*, ch. ix.

[54] Conway to Edward Harley, 3 Mar. 1659/60, 31 Mar. 1660: H.M.C., *Portland*, iii. 218–20; Robert Harley to Edward Harley, 6 Apr. [1660]: Welbeck MSS., Harley Papers, vii (B.M. Loan 29/177), fol. 77. Wrongly dated 1656 in H.M.C., *Portland*, iii. 208. The return of the moderates to militia commands is obvious from the lists of commissioners in Firth and Rait, *A. and O.* ii. 1426–48.

and political behaviour? The revolutionaries were likely to be radical Puritans or Independents. They were also likely to be men from outside the traditional establishment. Both generalizations can be made more confidently for the rank-and-file than for their leaders in Parliament. In every crisis of the Interregnum—in the winter of 1648-9, in 1653, and again in 1659—the revolutionary pressure was generated in the Army, in London and a few other towns, and in the congregations of the gathered churches. And in all these crises only a handful of the old governing class were actively involved. The conclusions from our statistical analysis of the M.P.s are less clear, blurred by the fact that we are dealing with men in a special position of leadership, and thus more likely to act in a way that was uncommon in the groups from which they were drawn. The typical revolutionary M.P., it will be remembered, was still a country gentleman. Yet he was somewhat less likely to be from a stable, greater gentry family than from one that was new or declining, or of either lesser gentry or mercantile background. The typical secluded member, on the other hand, was much more likely to be a country gentleman of high rank and stable family.

The explanation of this difference, it might be argued, lies in the realm of social psychology: revolution is more likely to appeal to men with disturbed, volatile personalities, or with financial interests to drive them on, and such people are more likely to be found in unstable families. But the fact remains that there was a connection, though not an absolute one, between radical Puritanism and revolutionary behaviour. Among the upper crust in Parliament there were too many men like Purefoy, who combined intense Presbyterianism with support for the revolution, and too many others whose religious views are simply unknown, for the Independent-revolutionary equation to be accepted without qualification. The differences between Presbyterians and moderate, non-separating Independents were too slight to be an adequate explanation of attitudes in so drastic a crisis. It will be recalled that a majority of the conformists of 1649, so far as their views are known, were Presbyterians. But the separating Independents and sectaries held fundamentally different views about the nature of the church and its relationship to society, and these were bound to put them in a different camp from the rest of the political nation. Thus the equation between radical religious views and radical politics holds good, with only a few exceptions like Henry Lawrence, among the Baptists and other sects.

Radicalism of both kinds, however, was much commoner among the less privileged groups than it was in the upper ranks of English society. But the advance to power of the lesser parochial gentry in so many counties during the revolution does not mean that the lesser gentry were by definition revolutionary. It is quite clear, from the difficulties encountered by so many of the county regimes when they looked for men willing to serve them, that they were not. It may help to clear up this point if we invent an imaginary county by way of example. Let us suppose that in Blankshire there are fifty county gentry families, 500 of the lesser gentry, and that fifty men are needed to fill the major county offices. Let us further suppose that one-tenth of each group support the revolution. In normal times all the major offices will be filled by county gentry, but after the revolution only five of them will be willing to serve, and the remaining forty-five places will go to the lesser gentry. As the commissions of local government are now dominated by new men, we might be tempted to conclude that the lesser gentry are overwhelmingly in favour of the revolution. But we should be wrong, for in fact the lesser gentry are no better disposed to the revolution than the county families. There are simply more of them.

Among the yeomen and middling sort the committed minority must have been somewhat larger, though it is obviously impossible to demonstrate this statistically. But even among these groups the vast majority by 1648 were neither radical Puritans nor political revolutionaries. This is particularly true of the yeomen. There is no reason to doubt the evidence of Baxter, John Corbet, and many others that in 1642 the freeholders rallied to the cause of Parliament, the cause of religion, liberty, and property. But there is equally little doubt that by 1645 such men were war-weary and disillusioned. In many southern counties they became Clubmen, organizing themselves to defend hearth and home against both sides. They were no happier under radical committees than under ship-money sheriffs ten years before. When by 1648 years of high taxes, quartering, and economic depression had brought no relief, only a scattered few became Levellers or militant Saints. Far more showed their disenchantment with the Puritan-parliamentarian cause by supporting the conservative petitions for settlement, or by active involvement on the royalist side in the second Civil War. Only in Puritan East Anglia were the freeholders actively loyal to Parliament through thick and thin. Only in Buckinghamshire and a few other counties within the orbit of London did they consistently go further and press for radical reform—and even in these cases it is impossible to say what proportion of the population their petitions represent.

The revolutionaries were a small minority, but they were widely diffused throughout the country, and no town or county was without some, whether political Levellers or religious Saints. But their strength was greatest among the craftsmen and small traders of London and the towns within reach of the capital—Bedford and High Wycombe, for example. In the more distant provinces there were pockets of strong Commonwealth feeling—in the small Cheshire towns, for instance, which supported Bradshawe and Brereton against the Cromwellian and gentry candidates in the 1656 election.[55] But ideological forces were usually complicated, and often overshadowed by local issues. It is difficult to account in any other way for the remarkably varied political behaviour of the towns during the Commonwealth. The Protectorate displays similarly bewildering variety. At Reading the magistrates were Cromwellian, many of the commonalty supporting Commonwealth republicans in opposition. There was some trouble at the 1654 election, and more in 1656, when Daniel Blagrave stood as the popular candidate against the court nominee Colonel Barkstead. But the bitterest conflict occurred in December 1658. A republican mayor attempted to return Blagrave and Henry Nevill, but was overthrown by a Cromwellian *coup* and expelled after a violent scene in the council chamber. 'They tossed the old mayor like a dog in a blanket', a shocked observer reported. The intruding Cromwellians claimed the right of election for a closed corporation, but the Commonwealthsmen had the town behind them, more than 1,000 householders supporting Blagrave and Nevill. And their rights were upheld by Richard Cromwell's Parliament.[56]

There were other towns besides Reading where Cromwellian oligarchies enlisted the government's aid in restricting the franchise. This happened at King's Lynn, where the commonalty had been permitted to vote in 1649, but where the corporation regained the right of election in 1654 and kept it throughout the Protectorate. Only in 1660, when the tide had turned against Puritanism, was the franchise broadened again. Leominster asked for a reduction in the

55 Pinckney, *Rylands Lib. Bull.* xlix (1967), 406, 419.
56 E. A. Smith, in Aspinall *et al.*, *Parliament Through Seven Centuries*, pp. 57-60.

size of its corporation, 'because there are few well-affected'. But local rulers were not always Cromwellian. At both Lincoln and Southampton corporations disaffected to the Protectorate from the right provoked intervention by Major-Generals; whether the magistrates were supported by the commons of the towns it is difficult to say. And the example of Colchester shows that opposition to Cromwellian oligarchs did not always come from the left, as it did at Reading. The majority of Colchester people, at all levels, seem to have sided with the moderate Reynolds against Henry Barrington's regime, and when the Barringtons called on the Major-General to protect them, it was against a conservative, not a republican majority. The 'honest interest' had the town constitution rigged so that a closed corporation could be run by the Saints.[57] For the most part the corporations, as always, tried to keep out of trouble, and to keep their towns on an even keel against the disruptive Quakers and the sects. At Bristol the radicals, led by Denis Hollister and Scot's old assistant, George Bishop (now both migrating to Quakerism), looked to the military governor for support against the corporation oligarchy. But although the Quakers were strong in the town, opposition to them was even stronger, with royalist slogans being chanted by rioting anti-Quaker apprentices. 'The truth is', said one of Bishop's enemies, 'our malignants and neuters, and all sorts, are now so settled again in their trade since the Act of Oblivion, and by reason of peace and quiet the city increaseth in trade, that so they may get money (which is most sovereign to them) and be in quiet, they will be far from any new plots.' The Quakers, he felt, were much more likely to upset the Protectorate's promised stability.[58]

No respectable body of historical opinion tries any more to interpret complex situations like the Puritan Revolution in terms of exclusive, single-cause explanations. The revolutionaries in Parliament were marginally stronger among the unstable and lesser gentry and the merchants. But they included men of very different motives. Some supported the revolution because they were radical Independents working for Godly Reformation; some because they were politicians intent on a more satisfactory political settlement than

[57] H.M.C., *Eleventh Report*, App. III (King's Lynn MSS.), p. 150; Henderson, *T.R.H.S.* 3rd Ser. vi (1912), 158; Hill, *Tudor and Stuart Lincoln*, p. 165; Davies, *Southampton*, p. 491; Round, *E.H.R.* xv (1900), 649–57 (and above, pp. 324–5).

[58] James Powell to Thurloe, 24 Feb. 1654/5: *Thurloe's S.P.* iii. 169–70. See also Latimer, *Annals of Bristol in the Seventeenth Century*, pp. 250–68.

A a

that threatened by the Treaty of Newport; others because they could see no alternative that would satisfy the Army; yet others because they had personal or pecuniary motives for staying in power. It would be absurd to say that economics, status, or class had everything to do with it. Yet it would be equally absurd to say that they had nothing to do with it. The lower down we look in the political nation, the more men we find who were willing to make a clean break with the past, and who saw advantages (personal or political) in a revolution. At all levels of society, however, they were a militant minority, hedged about with compromisers and conformists. The Army rank and file, the Buckinghamshire yeomen, the commonalty of London, Reading, or Bedford, might be temporarily radicalized by the Levellers or the Saints. But they needed material or local grievances—arrears of pay, high prices and depression, a tyrannical corporation oligarchy—to sustain their zeal. Without such additional arguments they were always likely to relapse into apathy and not meddle with matters of state.

The conflict of Puritan idealism with conservative constitutionalism was also one between two directly opposite conceptions of the political nation. On the one hand was what might be called the horizontal theory of political rights—that rights rested on degree, on status, and that only very unusual circumstances (being caught on the wrong side in a civil war, for instance) could justify even the temporary exclusion of the man qualified by rank from the enjoyment of his privileges, or liberties as the seventeenth century was accustomed to call them. 'A nobleman, a gentleman, a yeoman: that is a good interest of the nation', said Oliver Cromwell.[59] None of the gentry in Parliament would have disagreed with him.

But on the other side appeared a very different, vertical theory of political rights—that they should belong to all free men, regardless of status, who subscribed certain political and religious principles. 'The setting up of the people's power . . . to elect all officers, magistrates whatsoever . . . was the primitive foundation of all our late years' confusion', thought William Prynne in one of his rare moments of freedom from the delusion that his enemies were part of a vast international Jesuit conspiracy.[60] But as Prynne and his friend Clement Walker well knew, the revolutionaries had their own definition of 'the people'. Marchamont Nedham put it as well

[59] Quoted by Hill, *Oliver Cromwell, 1658-1958*, p. 16, from Abbott, *Cromwell*, iii. 435.
[60] Prynne, *Brevia Parliamentaria Rediviva* (1662), p. 324.

as anyone: 'That their own faction (whom alone they call the well-affected, and the honest men, excluding all others) are the People. . . . That themselves are the only competent judges of the people's safety, and so . . . may drive on their design against all powers, and forms of government, and law whatsoever, under pretence of that old aphorism, *Salus Populi Suprema Lex.*'[61] Whether the claim to speak for the people was based on natural reason, as by the Levellers and Commonwealthsmen, or on the 'divine and extraordinary right' used by the Fifth Monarchy Men to justify defining their enemies as 'not fit to govern the nation any longer', the result was the same. Those who would subscribe the *Agreement of the People*, the Engagement, or some other test, would be the people. 'The real members of this Commonwealth', said John Spittlehouse in 1653, 'are included in the congregational churches, and the army, and their well-wishers.'[62] The lesson was clear: radical Puritanism and social hierarchy were incompatible. The gentry long remembered it.

In the end the gentry came round to monarchy again because it alone could complete the reunion of the political nation. Radicals or moderates, they had much in common. 'We live as Parliament men but for a time,' William Sydenham had said in 1656, 'but we live as Englishmen always.' And monarchy alone could guarantee their own kind of liberty: liberty to rule the nation without interference from militant Saints, and the counties without interference from Westminster. 'There is as much tyranny in liberty as otherwise', said John Swynfen: 'I would not stir up that liberty that leaves you no liberty here'—defending, that is to say, the freedom of M.P.s to act without regard to external pressure.[63] The gentry had always preferred monarchy. The royalist Earl of Danby, on his deathbed, had foreseen the outcome: 'The King would have the better, for the gentry would stick by him, but the Parliament had only the common people.' When the sheriff of Gloucestershire, Thomas Stephens, was taken prisoner by the Cavaliers in 1645, he rejected his captors' argument that the King's recovery from earlier

---

[61] 'Mercurius Pragmaticus' [Nedham], *A Plea for the King, and Kingdome* (27 Nov. 1648: [B.M.] E. 474, 2), epistle dedicatory.

[62] *An Answer to a Paper entituled A True Narrative of the Cause and Manner of the Dissolution of the late Parliament, upon the 12 of December 1653* (1653: [B.M.] E. 725, 20), esp. pp. 2–3; Spittlehouse, *The Army Vindicated* (1653), quoted by Woolrych, *E.H.R.* lxxx (1965), 498.

[63] Speeches by Sydenham (30 Dec. 1656), and Swynfen (15 Feb. 1658/9): *Burton's Diary*, i. 274; iii. 290.

disasters proved that God was on his side. ''Twas not so, for (said he) almost all the gentry were ever for the King.'[64]

When the news reached Oxford on 13 February 1660 that Monck had declared for a free Parliament, there were, as in other towns, immediate celebrations. Amid the bells and the bonfires the Warden of All Souls, the old Rumper Dr. John Palmer, lay dying. Outside in the street rumps were being roasted, and one was thrown up at his window.[65] Palmer died a few weeks later, with the Good Old Cause in ruins. Yet perhaps he was lucky. At least he did not have to recant as abjectly as old colleagues like Luke Robinson, John Hutchinson, and Sir Gilbert Pickering found it necessary to do. Nor did he live to see Scot and Carew going to the block, or Ludlow and Dixwell fleeing into ignominious exile at Vevey or New Haven. One of those who did live to see it was Robert Bennet, the Rump's man in Cornwall. Naturally he had to walk warily after the King's return, and make at least a token submission. So no doubt there was an element of politic necessity in the letter he wrote in March 1661 to the royalist sheriff of his county. Yet there is also the ring of sincerity in the words of this old Baptist radical, who was also a Cornish country gentleman. Monarchy as now restored, thought Bennet as he looked back over the events of the previous twenty years, was 'the only way under God to reduce this nation under a right balance of estates and degrees, the only hopeful foundation of a lasting settlement'.[66]

[64] Deposition of Christopher Darrell, 23 Apr. 1646: H.M.C., *Sixth Report*, Appendix (House of Lords MSS.), p. 113; *Mercurius Aulicus*, quoted by Firth, ed., *Ludlow's Memoirs*, i. 469.

[65] Clark, ed., *Wood's Life and Times*, i. 303–6.

[66] Bennet to Piers Edgecumbe, 14 Mar. 1660/1: Folger Lib., MS. Add. 494 (Bennet MSS.), p. 605.

*Appendices*

# APPENDIX A

## MEMBERS OF PARLIAMENT

THIS appendix contains the names of all M.P.s eligible to sit at any time between 6 December 1648 and 31 January 1649, classified according to the system explained in Chapter VIII, pp. 209-20. For the eighteen absentees only the member's name, constituency, and date of election to the House are given. This information is also given for the members in each of the other five categories, but is followed, in very compressed form, by a summary of the evidence about each used in the tables in Appendix B.

To give complete citations for every item of information in this appendix would obviously be impossible without doubling the length of this book. I cheerfully leave so formidable a task to the compilers of the official *History of Parliament* when (or if) it is undertaken for this period. Brief biographical references are given for each member; however, much other miscellaneous information has gone into this appendix, derived from sources such as the genealogical works and local histories described in Brunton and Pennington, *Members of the Long Parliament*, pp. 195-9. Many other sources of detailed points of information are described or cited in Chapter VIII, above, and it would be wearisome to repeat them. When I have been able to identify a previously obscure member (as in the case of Robert Andrews), to correct an earlier erroneous identification (as in the case of John Stephens), or to add important new information not readily available, this is noted in a footnote.

It is now necessary to explain the shorthand in which the following entries are written. The member's name, constituency and date of election are followed, in the case of Rumpers, by the date on which he took the dissent to the 5 December vote or was otherwise readmitted to the House. Dates for which only the day and month are given are between 20 December 1648 and 23 July 1649; for later dissents or admissions the year is given as well. If the member was a regicide, this is indicated by (r).

The key to the remaining columns is as follows:

*Age*   age known or estimated, in December 1648.

*Position in family*

e   eldest, or eldest surviving son, who had inherited.
ys   younger son.
h   heir, with father still living.

*Marital status*

m   married.
s   single.

*Education*

C   Cambridge.
O   Oxford.
U   another university.
G   Gray's Inn.
IT   Inner Temple.
L   Lincoln's Inn.
MT   Middle Temple.
(b)   barrister or practising lawyer.

*Region*

E   East (Cambs., Hunts., Lincs., Norfolk, Rutland, Suffolk).
M   Midlands (Beds., Derbyshire, Leics., Northants., Notts., Oxon., Staffs., Warwickshire).
NE   North-east (Durham, Northumberland, Yorkshire).
NW   North-west (Cumberland, Lancashire, Westmorland).
SE   South-east (Berks., Bucks., Essex, Hants., Herts., Kent, London, Middlesex, Surrey, Sussex).
SI   Scotland or Ireland.
SW   South-west (Cornwall, Devon, Dorset, Somerset, Wilts.).
WB   Wales and border (Cheshire, Glos., Herefordshire, Monmouthshire, Shropshire, Worcs.).

*Parliamentary experience*

S   M.P. in Short Parliament.
20   M.P. in any Parliament 1621-9.
10   M.P. before 1620.

*Religion*

S   Sectary.
I   Independent.
P   Presbyterian or covert episcopalian.
P-I   Presbyterian-Independent.

*Earlier political behaviour*

*1643–5*

W     War party.
M     Middle group.
P     Peace party.

*1647*

FA    Fled to Army, July, or signed 4 Aug. Engagement.
SA    Present during Speaker's absence, July–Aug., or supported Eleven Members.

*1645–8*

I     Independent.
M    Middle group.
P    Presbyterian.

*Status*

GG    Aristocracy or greater gentry.
CG    County gentry.
LG    Lesser gentry.
MG   Merchant gentry.
M     Merchant or obscure.
*      declining or new (post-1603) family.

*Income*

1     £1,000 p.a. or above.
2     £500–£1,000 p.a.
3     below £500 p.a.
x     serious pre-war debt.

*Claims against State*

1     claims of £1,000 or above.
2     claims of below £1,000, but including some form of claim other than the Irish Adventure.
3     Irish Adventure only, below £1,000.

*Land purchases*

C     Church lands.
K     Crown lands.
R     Royalists' lands.

*Office*

1     held office before and after Dec. 1648.
2     obtained office after Dec. 1648.
3     lost office after Dec. 1648.

*Principal sources of information*

| | |
|---|---|
| Alexander | J. J. Alexander, *Devon County Members of Parliament*, reprinted from *Transactions of the Devonshire Association* (1912–25). |
| *Arch. Ael.* | *Archaeologia Aeliana.* |
| *Aubrey* | O. L. Dick, ed., *Aubrey's Brief Lives* (London, 1961). |
| Aylmer | G. E. Aylmer, *The King's Servants* (London, 1961). |
| B & P | D. Brunton and D. H. Pennington, *Members of the Long Parliament* (London, 1954). |
| *Baronetage* | G.E.C., *Complete Baronetage* (Exeter, 1900–9). |
| Bates Harbin | S. W. Bates Harbin, *Members of Parliament for the County of Somerset* (Taunton, 1939). |
| Bean | W. W. Bean, *Parliamentary Representation of the Six Northern Counties of England* (Hull, 1890). |
| *BIHR* | *Bulletin of the Institute of Historical Research.* |
| Cliffe | J. T. Cliffe, *The Yorkshire Gentry From the Reformation to the Civil War* (London, 1969). |
| Courtney | W. P. Courtney, *Parliamentary Representation of Cornwall* (London, 1889). |
| *CT & G* | *Collectanea Topographica et Genealogica.* |
| *DNB* | *Dictionary of National Biography.* |
| Dodd | A. H. Dodd, *Studies in Stuart Wales* (Cardiff, 1952). |
| *EAST* | *Essex Archaeological Society Transactions.* |
| *ER* | *Essex Review.* |
| Evelyn | Helen Evelyn, *History of the Evelyn Family* (London, 1915). |
| *Fam. Min. Gent.* | J. W. Clay, ed., *Familiae Minorium Gentium* (Harl. Soc., xxxvii–xl, 1894–6). |
| Ferguson | R. S. Ferguson, *Cumberland and Westmorland M.P.s* (London, 1871). |
| Foster | Joseph Foster, *Alumni Oxonienses . . . 1500–1714* (Oxford, 1891–2). |
| Gooder | A. Gooder, *Parliamentary Representation of the County of York* (Yorks. Arch. Soc. Record Ser., xci, xcvi, 1935–8). |
| *HLQ* | *Huntington Library Quarterly.* |
| *Hutchinson* | C. H. Firth, ed., *Memoirs of the Life of Colonel Hutchinson* (rev. ed., London, 1906). |
| K | M. F. Keeler, *The Long Parliament 1640–1641* (Philadelphia, 1954). |
| Lacey | D. R. Lacey, *Dissent and Parliamentary Politics in England 1661–1689* (New Brunswick, N.J., 1969). |

| | |
|---|---|
| Muskett | J. J. Muskett, *Suffolk Manorial Families* (Exeter, 1900–10). |
| *N & Q* | *Notes & Queries.* |
| Pearl | Valerie Pearl, *London and the Outbreak of the Puritan Revolution* (Oxford, 1961). |
| *Peerage* | G.E.C., *Complete Peerage* (London, 1910–59). |
| Pink & Beaven | W. D. Pink and A. B. Beaven, *Parliamentary Representation of Lancashire* (London, 1889). |
| Pink MSS. | John Rylands Library, Pink MSS. |
| *RLB* | *Bulletin of the John Rylands Library.* |
| *SASP* | *Somerset Archaeological and Natural History Society Proceedings.* |
| *SAST* | *Shropshire Archaeological Society Transactions.* |
| *Sussex A.C.* | *Sussex Archaeological Collections.* |
| *TDA* | *Transactions of the Devonshire Association.* |
| *TLCAS* | *Transactions of the Lancashire and Cheshire Antiquarian Society.* |
| *VCH* | *Victoria County History.* |
| Venn | John and J. A. Venn, *Alumni Cantabrigienses*, Pt. I (Cambridge, 1922–7). |
| *Vis. Wilts. 1623* | G. W. Marshall, ed., *Visitation of Wiltshire, 1623* (London, 1882). |
| Vivian | J. L. Vivian, *The Visitations of Cornwall . . . 1530, 1573, and 1620* (Exeter, 1887). |
| *WA* | *Western Antiquary.* |
| Wedgwood | Josiah C. Wedgwood, *Staffordshire Parliamentary History* (London, 1919–34). |
| Weyman | H. T. Weyman, *Shropshire Members of Parliament* (1926–8). |
| Williams (*G*) | W. R. Williams, *Parliamentary History of the County of Gloucester* (Hereford, 1898). |
| Williams (*H*) | W. R. Williams, *Parliamentary History of the County of Hereford* (Brecknock, 1896). |
| Williams (*O*) | W. R. Williams, *Parliamentary History of the County of Oxford* (Brecknock, 1899). |
| Williams (*Wales*) | W. R. Williams, *Parliamentary History of the Principality of Wales* (Brecknock, 1895). |
| Williams (*Worcs.*) | W. R. Williams, *Parliamentary History of the County of Worcester* (Hereford, 1897). |
| Wood | A. C. Wood, *Nottinghamshire in the Civil War* (Oxford, 1937). |
| Y | George Yule, *The Independents in the English Civil War* (Cambridge, 1958). |
| *YAJ* | *Yorkshire Archaeological Journal.* |

| Name | Constituency / Date of election | Category | Date of dissent | Age | Position in family | Marital status | Education | | Region | Parliamentary experience | Religion | Earlier political behaviour | | | Status | Income | Claims against State | Land purchases | Office | Principal sources of information |
|---|---|---|---|---|---|---|---|---|---|---|---|---|---|---|---|---|---|---|---|---|
| | | | | | | | University | Inn | | | | 1643–5 | 1647 | 1643–8 | | | | | | |
| ABBOT, George | Tamworth 1645 | X | | | | | | | | | | | | | | | | | | DNB, Wedgwood |
| ALDWORTH, Richard | Bristol 1646 | C | 18 Apr.[1] | 58 | e | m | | | SW | | | | SA | | M | | 1 | K | | Note 2 below |
| ALFORD, John | Shoreham 1640 | S | | 58? | e | m | O | | SE | S, 20 | I? | | SA | I? | CG | 1? | 2 | C | | K |
| ALLANSON, Sir William | York 1640 | C | 5 Feb. | 58? | ys | m | | | NE | | | | | | M | | 3 | C | I | K |
| ALLEN, Francis | Cockermouth 1640 | R | Dec. ? | 65+? | | m | | | SE | | P-I | | FA | I | M | | 1 | CKR | | B & P, Y |
| ALLIN, Matthew | Weymouth 1645 | S | | 50+? | | m | | | SW | | | | | | M | 3? | 1 | | | B & P, Pink MSS. 296/72 |
| ALURED, John | Hedon 1645 | R | 29 Jan. (r) | 41 | e | m | O | G | NE | S | | | | | LG | 3 | | | | K |
| ANDREWS, Robert | Weobley 1640 | C | 27 Apr.[1] | 43 | h | m? | O | MT | MT | | | | | | LG | 3 | | | | Note 3 below |
| ANLABY, John | Scarborough 1646 | R | 29 Jan. | 35? | e | m | | G | NE | | I? | | | | LG | 3 | | | | Gooder, Bean |
| ANNESLEY, Arthur | Radnorshire 1647 | S | | 34 | h | m? | O | L (b) | SI | | P | | | P | GG* | ?x | | | | DNB |
| APSLEY, Edward | Steyning 1645 | R | 29 Jan. | 46? | e | s | C | | SE | | | | | | CG | 2? | | | | Venn, Sussex A.C. 4 |
| ARMINE, Sir William, Bt. | Grantham 1641 | C | 13 Feb. | 55 | e | m | C | G | E | | P-I | W/M | FA | I | GG | 1? | 3 | | | DNB, K |
| ARMINE, William | Cumberland 1646 | C | 2 Feb. | 26 | | s | | | E | 20 | | | | | GG | 1? | | | | B & P |
| ARTHINGTON, Henry | Pontefract 1646 | A | 23 July | 34? | e | m | | | NE | | P? | | | | LG | 2 | | | | Gooder |
| ARUNDELL, John | W. Looe 1647 | S | | 24? | e | s? | | | SW | | | | | | LG | | | C | | Pink MSS. 296/164 |
| ASHE, Edward | Heytesbury 1640 | C | 2 Feb. | 49 | ys | m | | | SW | | | | SA | I | M | 1? | 3 | CR | | K |
| ASHE, James | Bath 1645 | C | 2 Feb. | 26? | ys | m? | | IT (b) | SW | | | | SA | | LG | 1? | 3 | | | Y |

¹ See note 1 below.

(366)

| Name | Seat | St | Date | Age | a | b | U | Inn | Reg | S | P? | W/M | SA | I/M | M | n | n | CR | n | Sources |
|---|---|---|---|---|---|---|---|---|---|---|---|---|---|---|---|---|---|---|---|---|
| ASHE, John | Westbury 1640 | S | 3 Feb. | 51 | e | m | | ?(b) | SW | S | P | W? | SA | M? | LG | 1 | 1 | R | I | K, Bates Harbin |
| ASHHURST, William | Newton 1642 | A | | 41 | e | m | | | NW | S | P | | SA | | GG | 1? | | R | | Bean, Pink & Beaven |
| ASSHETON, Ralph | Lancs. 1640 | S | | 43 | e | m | O | G | NW | | P | | | | | | | | | K |
| ASSHETON, Sir Ralph, Bt. | Clitheroe 1640 | S | 25 Dec. | 52? | e | m | C | G | NW | S, 20 | P | | | P | | 1 | | | | K, Lacey |
| ATKIN, Thomas | Norwich 1645 | R | | 60+? | e | m | | | E | S, 20 | | | SA | 1 | M | 1? | 1 | C | | B & P, Y, Pearl |
| AYSCOUGH, Sir Edward | Lincs. 1640 | S | | 52 | e | m | C | | E | 20 | | | | | CG | 2 | 3 | | | K |
| AYSCOUGH, William | Thirsk 1645 | A | | 28? | e | m | | | NE | | | | | | LG | | | | | Bean, Pink MSS. 296/259 |
| BACON, Francis | Ipswich 1646 | S | 6 June | 48 | ys | s? | C | G (b) | E | | P? | | | | GG | | | | | B & P |
| BACON, Nathaniel | Cambridge U. 1645 | S | 6 June | 55 | ys | m | C | G (b) | E | | P | | | | GG | 1? | 3 | | 2 | *DNB*, B & P |
| BAKER, John | E. Grinstead 1645 | C | 1 Feb. | 60? | e | m | O | IT | SE | | | | | | LG | 1 | | | | Y, Foster |
| BAMPFIELD, Sir John, Bt. | Penryn 1640 | A | | 38 | h | m | O | MT | SW | | P? | | FA | 1? | GG | 2? | | | | K |
| BARKER, John | Coventry 1640 | S | 23 July | 55+? | e | m? | O | | M | | P | | | | M | 1 | 2 | | | K |
| BARNARDISTON, Sir Nathaniel | Suffolk 1640 | A | | 60 | e | m | | | E | S, 20 | P? | | | | GG | 1 | 2 | | | *DNB*, K |
| BARNARDISTON, Sir Thomas | Bury St. E. 1645 | A | | 32? | h | m | | G | E | | P? | | | | GG | 1 | 3 | | | *DNB* |
| BARRINGTON, Sir John, Bt. | Newtown 1646 | A | | 33 | e | m | C | G | SE | | P? | | | | GG | 1 | 1 | | | Lacey |
| BARROWE, Maurice | Eye 1645 | S | | 51 | e | m | C | G | E | | | | | | LG | 2? | 2 | | | B & P, Muskett |
| BARWIS, Richard | Carlisle 1640 | X | | | | | | | | | | | | | | | | | | K |
| BAYNTON, Sir Edward | Chippenham 1640 | C | 1 Feb. | 55 | e | m | O | L | SW | S, 20, 10 | P | W | SA | P | GG | 1 | | | | K |
| BAYNTON, Edward | Devizes 1640 | S | | 30 | h | s | O | | SW | S | P | | | | GG | 1 | | | | K |
| BEDINGFIELD, Anthony | Dunwich 1640 | S | | 46 | ys | s | | | E | S | P? | | | | MG | 1? | | | | K |
| BELL, William | Westminster 1640 | A | | 50+? | e | m | | | SE | S | | | | | M | 3? | 2 | K | | K |
| BELLINGHAM, James | Westmorland 1646 | S | | 25 | h | m? | | | NW | | P? | | | | GG | 1 | | | | K |

| Name | Constituency / Date of election | Category | Date of dissent | Age | Position in family | Marital status | Education University | Education Inn | Region | Parliamentary experience | Religion | 1643-5 | 1647 | 1645-8 | Status | Income | Claims against State | Land purchases | Office | Principal sources of information |
|---|---|---|---|---|---|---|---|---|---|---|---|---|---|---|---|---|---|---|---|---|
| BENCE, Alexander | Aldeburgh 1640 | A | | 53? | ys | m | | | E | | P? | | | | M | 1 | 1 | | | K |
| BIDDULPH, Michael | Lichfield 1646 | S | | 68? | e | m | O | MT | M | | | | | | LG | 3? | | | | Wedgwood |
| BINDLOSSE, Sir Robert, Bt. | Lancaster 1646 | S | | 24 | e | m | C | | NW | | | | | | GG | 1 | | | | Bean, Pink & Beaven |
| BINGHAM, John | Shaftesbury 1645 | C | 2 Feb. | 38? | h | m | O | MT | SW | | I? | | FA | P | CG | | 1 | C | | B & P, Y, Foster |
| BIRCH, John | Leominster 1646 | I | | 32 | h | m | | | WB | | P | | | | MG | 3? | | C | | DNB, Lacey |
| BLAGRAVE, Daniel | Reading 1648 | R | 25 Dec. (r) | 42 | ys | m | O? | IT (b) | SE | | P | | | | CG | 3? | 1 | CKR | 1 | DNB, Above, p. 51, n. |
| BLAKE, Robert | Bridgwater 1646 | C | 5 Feb. | 50 | e | m? | | | SW | S | P | | | | M | 3?x | | | 2 | DNB |
| BLAKISTON, John | Newcastle-u-T. 1641 | R | 20 Dec. (r) | 45 | ys | m | | | NE | | P? | W | FA | | M | | 1 | C | 1 | DNB, K, Arch. Ael., 4th ser. 42 |
| BOATE, Edward | Portsmouth 1646 | A | | 59 | e | m | | | SE | | | | | | M | 3? | | | 1 | Note 4 below |
| BOND, Denis | Dorchester 1640 | R | 25 Dec.? | 60 | e | m | C | | SW | S | | W | | I | MG | 2? | | | | DNB, K |
| BOND, John | Weymouth 1645 | S | 1 Feb. | 36 | h | s? | C | (b) | SW | | | | | I | MG | 2? | 3 | | 1 | Matthews, Note 5 below |
| BOONE, Thomas | Dartmouth 1646 | C | | 39 | e | m | | | SW | S | P | | FA | | M | | 1 | CR | | B & P, TDA 43 |
| BOOTH, George | Cheshire 1646 | S | | 26 | h | m | | IT | WB | | P | | | I | GG | 1? | | | | DNB |
| BOSCAWEN, Hugh | Cornwall 1646 | A | | 23 | e | m? | | | SW | | P | | | | GG | 1 | 1 | | | Courtney, Lacey |
| BOSVILE, Godfrey | Warwick 1641 | R | 20 Dec. | 52 | e | m | | | NE | S | P | P? | FA | I | CG | 2? | | | | K |
| BOUGHTON, Thomas | Warwickshire 1645 | I | | 48? | ys | m | | | M | 10 | | | | | CG | | 1 | | | VCH Warks. 6 |
| BOURCHIER, Sir John | Ripon 1647 | R | 20 Dec. (r) | 57? | e | m | C | G | NE | 10 | I? | | | | GG* | 1x | 1 | | | DNB |
| BOWYER, John | Staffs. 1646 | S | | 25 | e | m | | | M | | P? | | | | GG | | | | | Wedgwood |

(368)

| Name | | Date | Age | | | C | G | SE (b) | S, 20 | P | W/M | SA | M | LG | | 3 | C | | BIHR 39 |
|---|---|---|---|---|---|---|---|---|---|---|---|---|---|---|---|---|---|---|---|
| Boys, John / Kent 1645 | S | | 41 | h | m | C | G | SE | | | | | M | LG | 3? | 3 | C | | BIHR 39 |
| Brereton, Sir William, Bt. / Cheshire 1640 | C | 5 Feb. | 44 | e | m | O | G | WB | S, 20 | P-I | | FA | I | GG* | 1?x | 1 | CR | I | DNB, K, TLCAS 63 |
| Brewster, Robert / Dunwich 1640 | C | 1 Feb. | 49 | e | m | C | | E | | I | | | | LG | 2 | 1 | C | | B & P, Y |
| Briggs, Sir Humphrey / Much Wenlock 1646 | S | | 37 | h | m | | L | WB | | P? | | | | GG | 1 | 1 | | | Baronetage, SAST, 3rd ser. 2 |
| Brooke, Peter / Newton 1646 | S | 23 July | 36 | ys | m | | | WB | | P | | | | LG | 3? | | | | Bean, RLB 49 |
| Browne, Sir Ambrose, Bt. / Surrey 1640 | S | | 57? | e | m | C | G | SE | S, 20 | P? | | | | GG | 1 | | | | K |
| Browne, John / Dorset 1641 | C | ? | 68 | e | m | O | MT | SW | 20 | P? | | | | CG | 1 | | | | K |
| Browne, Richard / New Romney 1641 | X | | | | | | | | | | | | | | | | | | K |
| Browne, Richard / Wycombe 1645 | I | | 45? | | m | | | SE | | P | | | P | M | 1 | | | | DNB, Baronetage |
| Browne, Samuel / Dartmouth 1641 | X | | | | | | | | | | | | | | | | | | DNB, K |
| Bulkeley, John / Newtown 1645 | I | | 34 | e | m? | O | MT | SE | S | P | | | M | LG | 3? | | | | B & P, Foster, VCH Hants. 4 |
| Buller, Francis / E. Looe 1640 | I | | 45? | e | m | C | MT | SW | S, 20 | P | | | | CG | 1 | | | | K |
| Burgoyne, Sir John, Bt. / Warwickshire 1645 | S | | 57 | e | m | C | MT | M | | P? | | SA | | GG | 1 | | | | Baronetage |
| Burgoyne, Sir Roger / Beds. 1641 | A | 28 Feb. | 30 | h | m | C | L | M | | P | | SA | | GG | 1 | | | | K |
| Burrell, Abraham / Huntingdon 1645 | C | | 58? | ys | m | O | | E | | | | | | MG | 2? | | | I | B & P |
| Button, John / Lymington 1640 | S | | 52 | e | m | O | MT | SE | 20 | | | | | LG | 3? | | | | K |
| Bysshe, Edward / Bletchingley 1640 | A | | 33? | h | m | O | L (b) | SE | | P? | | | | CG* | 1? | | | I | DNB, K |
| Cambell, James / Grampound 1640 | S | | 33 | e | m | O | L | SE | | | | | | CG* | 1? | 3 | | | K |
| Campion, Henry / Lymington 1640 | S | | 62? | e | m | | MT | SE | 20 | | | | | LG | 2?x | | | | K |
| Carent, William / Milborne Port 1645 | C | 5 Mar. | 40? | e | m | | L | SW | | | | | | LG | 3? | | C | | B & P, Pink MSS. 299/390 |
| Carew, John / Tregony 1647 | R | 20 Dec. (r) | 26 | ys | s? | O | IT | SW | | S | | | | GG | 1 | | C | | DNB |
| Carr, Charles, Lord / Mitchell 1647 | S | | 25? | h | s | | SI | | | P? | | SA | | GG* | 3? | 1 | R | | Peerage |

| Name | Constituency / Date of election | Category | Date of dissent | Age | Position in family | Marital status | University | Inn | Region | Parliamentary experience | Religion | 1643–5 | 1647 | 1645–8 | Status | Income | Claims against State | Land purchases | Office | Principal sources of information |
|---|---|---|---|---|---|---|---|---|---|---|---|---|---|---|---|---|---|---|---|---|
| CAWLEY, William | Midhurst 1640 | R | 20 Dec. (r) | 46 | e | m | O | G | SE | 20 | I? | | | I | M | 3? | | KR | | *DNB*, K |
| CECIL, Charles, Vsct. CRANBORNE | Herford 1640 | S | (r) | 29 | h | m | C | | SE | S | | | FA | P? | GG | I | | | | K |
| CECIL, Robert | Old Sarum 1640 | S | | 27? | ys | m | C | | SE | | | | | | GG | | | | | K |
| CEELY, Thomas | Bridport 1645 | S | | 46 | e | m | O | | SW | | | | | | M | 3? | | C | | B & P |
| CHALONER, James | Aldborough 1648 | R | 20 Dec. | 45 | ys | m | O | MT | NE | | | | | | GG* | ?x | | K | | *DNB* |
| CHALONER, Thomas | Richmond 1645 | R | 1 Feb. (r) | 53 | ys | m? | O | IT | NE | | S | | | I | GG* | ?x | | C | 2 | *DNB* |
| CHARLTON, Robert | Bridgnorth 1646 | S | | 57 | ys | s? | | G | WB | | P? | | | | CG | | | R | | Foster, *SAST*, 53 |
| CHEEKE, Sir Thomas | Harwich 1640 | S | | 75? | e | m? | C | L | SE | S, 20, 10 P | | | | | CG | 1? | 1 | | | K |
| CHETTEL, Francis | Corfe Castle 1646 | S | | 31? | e | m? | | MT | SW | | P? | P | | | LG | 3? | | | | B & P |
| CHOLMLEY, Sir Henry | New Malton 1641 | S | | 39 | ys | m | | IT | NE | | P? | P | | P | GG* | 2x | | R | | K |
| CHOLMLEY, Thomas | Carlisle 1646 | A | | ? | | m | O | | NW | | P? | | | | M | 3? | 1 | | 2 | Note 6 below |
| CLARKE, Samuel | Exeter 1646 | S | | 31 | ys | m | O | | SW | S | | | | | M | 3? | 1 | | | Foster, *TDA* 61 |
| CLEMENT, Gregory | Fowey 1648 | R | 20 Dec. (r) | ? | h | m | | | SW | | | | | | M | 1? | 1 | CKR | | *DNB*, B & P |
| CLINTON, Edward, Lord | Callington 1646 | S | | 24 | h | m? | | | E | | P? | | | | GG | 1 | 1 | | | B & P, *Peerage* |
| CLIVE, Robert | Bridgnorth 1646 | A | | 34 | e | m | C | L | WB | | P? | | | | LG | | | | | *SAST*, 4th ser. 5 |
| CLOTWORTHY, Sir John | Maldon 1640 | I | | 45? | e | m | | | SI | S | P | P/M | SA | | CG* | 1? | 1 | | | K |
| COKE, Sir John | Derbyshire 1640 | X | | | | | | | | | | | | | | | | | | K |
| CONSTABLE, Sir William, Bt. | Knaresboro' 1642 | R | 29 Jan. (r) | 66? | e | m | | IT? | NE | 20 | I | | FA | I | GG* | 1x | 1 | CK | 1 | *DNB*, K |

| Name | Constituency / Year | Status | Date | Age | Ed. | M. | Rel. | Region | | | W | FA | P | Class | | | | Notes |
|---|---|---|---|---|---|---|---|---|---|---|---|---|---|---|---|---|---|---|
| COPLEY, Lionel | Bossiney 1647 | I | | 41 | ys | m | | NE | P? | | | SA | P | LG | | | I | Gooder |
| CORBET, Sir John, Bt. | Shropshire | S | | 54 | e | m | | L · WB | P? | M | | FA | | GG 1? | | | | DNB, K |
| CORBET, John | Bishop's Castle 1640 | C | Feb.? | 39 | e | m | C | G (b) · WB | P? | | | FA | | LG | C | | | Y, SAST, 2nd ser. 10 |
| CORBET, Miles | Gt. Yarmouth 1646 | R | 1 Feb. (r) | 53? | ys | s? | C | L (b) · E · S, 20 | I | W | | FA | I | CG 2? | 3 | 1 | 3 | DNB, K |
| COWCHER, John | Worcester 1640 | X | | | | | | | | | | | | | | | | K |
| CRESHELD, Richard | Evesham 1640 | X | | | | | | | | | | | | | | | | K |
| CREWE, John | Brackley 1640 | I | | 50 | e | m | ● | G (b) · M · S, 20 | P | M | | M | | CG* 1? | | | | DNB, K |
| CROMPTON, Thomas | Staffs. 1647 | A | 22 May | 42 | e | m | O? | M | | | | | | CG* 3 | | | | Wedgwood |
| CROMWELL, Oliver | Cambridge 1640 | R | 29 Jan. (r) | 49 | e | m | C | E. · WB · S, 20 | I | W/M | | FA | I/M | LG 3x | 3 | CKR | | DNB |
| CROWTHER, William | Weobley 1646 | A | | 50+? | e | m | O | WB | | | | FA | | M | I | | | Williams (H), Pink MSS. 299/678, TDA 41, 42 |
| CRYMES, Elisha | Tavistock 1646 | S | | 32 | e | m | O | L · SW | | | | | | CG* ?x | | | | |
| CURZON, Sir John, Bt. | Derbyshire 1640 | S | | 50 | e | m | O | IT? · M · S, 20 | | M | | | M? | GG 1? | | | 3 | K |
| DACRES, Sir Thomas | Herts. ,1641 | S | | 61 | e | m | C | SE · 20 | P | | | SA | P | GG 1? | I | | | K |
| DACRES, Thomas | Callington 1646 | S | | 39 | h | m | O | SE · L | | | | | | GG 1? | | | | B & P, Foster |
| DANVERS, Sir John | Malmesbury 1645 | R | 20 Dec. (r) | 63 | ys | m | O | SW · L · S, 20, 10 | I? | | | FA | I | GG* 1x | I | C | | DNB |
| DARLEY, Henry | Northallerton 1641 | A | 11 May | 53? | h | m | C | NE · G · 20 | I? | | | FA | | CG 1 | | CR | | K |
| DARLEY, Richard | New Malton 1645 | R | 20 Dec. | 48? | ys | m | | NE · WB | | | | | | CG | | | | Gooder |
| DAVIES, William | Carmarthen 1646 | S | | ? | | | O? | | | | | | | LG? | | | | Note 7 below |
| D'EWES, Sir Simonds, Bt. | Sudbury 1646 | I | | 46 | e | m | C | E · MT (b) | P | P | | SA | P | GG 1 | | | | DNB, K |
| DIXWELL, John | Dover 1640 | R | 20 Jan. (r) | 38? | ys | s | | SE · L (b) | I? | | | | | CG* | | | | DNB |
| DODDRIDGE, John | Barnstaple 1646 | S | | 38 | e | m | | SW · MT (b) | | | | | | MG | | | | Alexander, Williams (G) |
| DORMER, John | Buckingham 1646 | C | 22 Feb. | 37 | e | m | O | SE · L (b) | | | | | | GG 1 | | | | Y, Pink MSS. 300/779 |

| Name | Constituency / Date of election | Category | Date of dissent | Age | Position in family | Marital status | University | Inn | Region | Parliamentary experience | Religion | 1643–5 | 1647 | 1645–8 | Status | Income | Claims against State | Land purchases | Office | Principal sources of information |
|---|---|---|---|---|---|---|---|---|---|---|---|---|---|---|---|---|---|---|---|---|
| DOVE, John | Salisbury 1645 | R | 20 Dec. | 50? | | m | | | SW | | | | | | M | 3? | | CKR | | DNB |
| DOWNES, John | Arundel 1645 | R | 20 Dec. (r) | 36? | | m | | IT (b) | SE | | | | | | M | 2 | 1 | CR | 3 | DNB, K |
| DOYLEY, John | Oxford 1641 | S | | 46 | e | m | O | | M | | | | SA | P | CG* | 2?x | | | | Williams (O) |
| DRAKE, Sir Francis, Bt. | Berealston 1646 | A | | 31 | e | m | | IT | SW | | | | | | GG | | | | | Baronetage, TDA 41, 42 |
| DRAKE, Francis | Amersham 1641 | I | | 38? | ys | m | C | | SE | | P? | | SA | P | CG* | 2? | 2 | | | K |
| DRAKE, Sir William, Bt. | Amersham 1640 | X | | | | | | | | | | | | | | | | | | K |
| DRYDEN, Sir John, Bt. | Northants. 1640 | A | 21 Apr. 1652 | 68 | e | m | O | MT | M | | | | | | GG | 1? | 3 | | | K |
| DUNCH, Edmund | Wallingford 1640 | R | 20 Dec. | 45 | e | m | | G | SE | S, 20 | | | FA | | CG | 1 | | | | K |
| EARLE, Erasmus | Norwich 1647 | S | 17 Feb. | 58 | | m | C | L (b) | E | | | | | | LG | 3 | | | | DNB |
| EDWARDS, Humphrey | Shropshire 1646 | R | 20 Dec. (r) | 34? | ys | m? | | G (b) | WB | | | | FA | I | CG | 2 | | CK | 2 | DNB |
| EDWARDS, Richard | Christchurch 1645 | A | 4 June | 44 | e | m | C | IT (b) | M | | | | SA | | LG | 3? | | | 1 | CT & G 6 |
| EDWARDS, William | Chester 1646 | S | | 53? | ys | m | | | WB | | | | | | MG | 3? | | R | | Note 8 below |
| EGERTON, Sir Charles | Ripon 1646 | S | | 62 | e | m | C? | L | NE | | | | | | CG | | 1 | | 1 | Venn, Pink MSS. 300/27 |
| ELFORD, John | Tiverton 1645 | S | | 45 | e | m | C? | MT (b) | SW | | | | | | LG | 3? | | | | TDA 66, 67 |
| ELLIS, William | Boston 1646 | S | 4 June | 41 | ys | s | C | G (b) | E | S | | | | | CG | 3? | | | | DNB, K |
| ELLISON, Robert | Newcastle-u-T 1640 | S | | 35 | | m | | | NE | | P? | | | | M | | | R | | Arch. Ael., 4th ser. 23 |
| ERISEY, Richard | St. Mawes 1647 | A | | 58 | e | m | U | MT | SW | | | | | | CG | 1? | | | | K |
| ERLE, Thomas | Wareham 1640 | S | | 27? | h | m | O | MT (b) | SW | S | | | | M? | CG | 1? | | | | K |

| Name | Seat | | Date | Age | | | | | | | | | | | | | | | | | Ref |
|---|---|---|---|---|---|---|---|---|---|---|---|---|---|---|---|---|---|---|---|---|---|
| ERLE, Sir Walter | Weymouth 1640 | I | | 62 | e | m | O | MT | SW | S, 20, 10 | P | M | SA | M/P | CG | 1? | 3 | | | 3 | K |
| EVELYN, George | Reigate 1645 | S | | 31 | e | m | O | MT | SE | | P? | | | | CG | 2? | | | | | Evelyn |
| EVELYN, Sir John | Bletchingley 1640 | S | | 57 | ys | m | C | MT | SE | 20 | P? | P | | | CG | 1 | 3 | | | | K |
| EVELYN, Sir John | Ludgershall 1640 | A | | 47 | e | m | C? | MT | SW | S, 20 | I? | M | FA | M | CG* | 1x | | | C | | K |
| EXTON, Edward | Southampton 1640 | A | | 58? | e | m? | | | SE | | | | | | M | 2? | | | C | | K |
| EYRE, William | Chippenham 1648 | R | 15 Jan. | 30 | h | s? | O | | SW | S | P? | | | | CG | | | | C | | Y, Vis. Wilts. 1623 |
| FAGGE, John | Rye 1645 | C | 5 Feb. | 24? | e | m | | G | SE | | | | | | LG | | | | | | DNB, Lacey |
| FEILDER, John | St. Ives 1647 | C | Feb.? | 31? | e | m | | MT | SE | | | | | | LG | 3?x | 1 | | R | | Y, Pink MSS. 301/65 |
| FELL, Thomas | Lancaster 1645 | A | 23 July | 49? | e | m | O | G (b) | NW | | P? | | | | LG | | | | K | 1 | DNB |
| FENWICK, George | Morpeth 1645 | C | 17 Feb. | 45? | e | m | C | G (b) | NE | | I | | FA | | LG | | | | CR | 2 | DNB |
| FENWICK, Sir John, Bt. | Northumber'd 1641 | A | | 71+? | h | m | | | NE | S, 20 | | | | | GG | 1 | | | | 3 | DNB, K |
| FENWICK, William | Northumber'd 1645 | A | | 31? | h | m | C | G | NE | | | | | | GG | 1 | | | | | Baronetage |
| FIENNES, James | Oxfordshire 1640 | S | | 47? | ys | s | C | L | M | S, 20 | | M | FA | | GG | 1 | | | K | | K |
| FIENNES, John | Morpeth 1645 | A | | 38? | ys | m | C | | M | | S | | FA | M | GG | | 2 | | C | | DNB |
| FIENNES, Nathaniel | Banbury 1640 | I | | 40 | e | m | O | MT | M | S | I | M | FA | | GG | | 3 | | | | DNB, K |
| FITZWILLIAM, William, Lord | Peterborough 1640 | S | | 39? | ys | m | C | | M | S | | | | | GG | 2? | | | | | K |
| FLEETWOOD, Charles | Marlborough 1645 | C | 14 May¹ | 28? | e | m | | G | M | | I | | | I | CG* | | 3 | | KR | 1 | DNB |
| FLEETWOOD, George | Bucks. 1645 | R | ? (r) | 27 | ys | m | | | SE | | S | | FA | I? | GG | 2? | | | | | DNB |
| FOWELL, Sir Edmund | Ashburton 1640 | S | | 55 | e | m | | | SW | | | | SA | | CG | 2? | | | K | | K |
| FOWELL, Edmund | Tavistock 1646 | S | | 50? | e | s | O | MT | SW | | | | SA | | MG | | | | | | Foster, TDA 42 |
| FOXWIST, William | Caernarvon 1647 | S | | 38 | e | s | O | L (b) | WB | | | | | | LG | | | | | 1? | Williams (Wales) |

¹ See note 1 below.

Bb

| Name | Constituency / Date of election | Category | Date of dissent | Age | Position in family | Marital status | University | Inn | Region | Parliamentary experience | Religion | 1643–5 | 1647 | 1645–8 | Status | Income | Claims against State | Land purchases | Office | Principal sources of information |
|---|---|---|---|---|---|---|---|---|---|---|---|---|---|---|---|---|---|---|---|---|
| FRY, John | Shaftesbury 1647 | R | 20 Dec. | 39 | e | m | | MT | SW | | S | | | | LG | 3? | | | | DNB, B & P |
| GARDNER, Samuel | Evesham 1646 | S | Feb.? | ? | | m? | | | WB | | | | | | M | | 1 | C | | Williams (Worcs.) |
| GARLAND, Augustine | Queenboro' 1648 | R | 20 Dec. (r) | 47? | e | m | C | L (b) | SE | | | | | | LG | 3? | | CR | | DNB |
| GAWDY, Framlingham | Thetford 1640 | S | | 59 | e | m | | G (b) | E | S, 20, 10 P? | | | | | GG | 1 | | | | DNB, K |
| GELL, Thomas | Derby 1645 | S | | 54 | ys | s | C | IT | M | | | | SA | | CG | 3? | | | 3 | Note 9 below |
| GERARD, Francis | Seaford 1641 | 1 | | 28? | h | s? | | G (b) | SE | | P? | | | P | GG | 1? | | | 1? | K |
| GERARD, Sir Gilbert, Bt. | Middlesex 1640 | 1 | | 61 | e | m | C? | G | SE | 20 | P | M | | M | GG | 1? | 3 | | 1 | K |
| GEWEN, Thomas | Launceston 1647 | 1 | | 64? | | m | O | IT | SW | 20 | P | | SA | P | LG | 3? | | | 3 | W A 6, 7, 10 |
| GLYN, John | Westminster 1640 | S | | 45 | ys | m? | O | L (b) | WB | S | P | M | SA | P | GG | 1? | | R | 1? | DNB, K |
| GODOLPHIN, Francis | St. Ives 1640 | A | | 60? | e | m | O | MT (b) | SW | | | | | | CG | | | C? | | K |
| GOLD, Nicholas | Fowey 1648 | C | 3 Feb. | 50+? | ys | s? | | | SW | | | | | | M | | 1 | | | Y, Baronetage |
| GOLLOP, George | Southampton 1640 | S | | 78? | ys | m | | | SE | 20 | | | | | MG | 3? | | | | K |
| GOODWIN, John | Haslemere 1640 | C | 3 Feb. | 45? | ys | m | | IT (b) | SE | | P? | | | | LG | | 1 | CR | | K |
| GOODWIN, Robert | E. Grinstead 1640 | C | 19 Feb. | 47? | e | m | | IT (b) | SE | S, 20 | P | W/M | FA | M? | LG | | 3 | CR | 1 | K |
| GOTT, Samuel | Winchelsea 1645 | S | | 34 | e | m | C | G (b) | SE | S | P? | | SA | | LG | | | | | Venn, Pink MSS. 303/163 |
| GRANTHAM, Thomas | Lincoln 1640 | A | | 36 | e | m | | | E | S | P? | | | | GG | 2? | | | | K |
| GRATWICK, Roger | Hastings 1645 | C | | 55+? | ys | m | | | SE | | | | | | LG | | | | | Note 10 below |
| GREEN, Giles | Corfe Castle 1640 | 1 | 1 Feb. | 53? | | m | | MT (b) | SW | S, 20 | | M | SA | P? | M | 2? | | | 3 | K |

(374)

| Name | Constituency, year | | Date | Age | | | | G | M | | S? | P | FA | I | GG | | | | | Reference |
|---|---|---|---|---|---|---|---|---|---|---|---|---|---|---|---|---|---|---|---|---|
| GREY, Thomas, Lord | Leicester 1640 | R | 20 Dec. (r) | 25? | h | m | C | L (b) | SE | S, 20 | P | P | SA | I | GG | 1 | | KR | 1 | DNB, K |
| GRIMSTON, Sir Harbottle, Bt. | Colchester 1640 | I | | 45 | e | m? | | L | SW | | P | P | SA | P | GG | 1 | | | | DNB, K |
| GROVE, Thomas | Milborne Port 1640 | S | | 39 | e | m | C? | MT | | | P? | | | P? | CG | | | | | Note 11 below |
| GURDON, Brampton | Sudbury 1645 | A | 4 June | 40 | ys | m | C | IT | E | | P? | | | | CG | | | C | | B & P, Muskett |
| GURDON, John | Ipswich 1640 | C | 21 Feb. | 53 | h | m | C | G | E | | P | W | | I | CG | 1 | | | | DNB, K |
| HALLOWES, Nathaniel | Derby 1640 | C | Feb.? | 66? | e | m | C | | M | | | | FA | | M | 3? | 1 | CKR | 1 | K |
| HARBY, Edward | Higham Ferrers 1645 | A | 23 July | 48 | e | m | C | L | | | P? | | | | LG | 3? | | | | Venn, Y |
| HARINGTON, John | Somerset 1646 | A | | 59 | e | m | O | L (b) | M | | P | | SA | | GG | 1? | | | | Bates Harbin, B & P |
| HARLEY, Edward | Herefordshire 1646 | I | | 24 | h | s | O | L (b) | SW | | P | | SA | P | GG | 3 | | | | DNB |
| HARLEY, Sir Robert | Herefordshire 1640 | I | | 69 | e | m | O | MT | WB | S, 20, 10 | P | W/M | SA | P | GG | 1 | | C | 3 | DNB, K |
| HARLEY, Robert | New Radnor 1647 | S | 21 Dec. | 22 | ys | s | O | | WB | | P? | | | P? | GG | 3? | | | | Note 12 below |
| HARRINGTON, Sir James | Rutland 1645 | R | | 41 | h | m | O | | E | | P-I | | | I | GG | 2?x | 1 | KR | 2 | Baronetage |
| HARRIS, John | Launceston 1641 | S | 25 Dec.? (r) | 62? | e | m | O | L | SW | | P? | | | | CG | 1 | | | | K |
| HARRISON, Thomas | Wendover 1646 | R | 25 Dec. | 32 | h | m | | | M | S, 20 | S | | FA | I | M | 3? | | KR | 1 | DNB |
| HARVEY, Edmund | Gt. Bedwin 1646 | R | 15 Feb. | 45 | e | m | | | SE | | P-I | | SA | M | M | 3? | | CR | 2 | DNB |
| HASELRIG, Sir Arthur, Bt. | Leics. 1640 | C | | 48? | e | m | C | G | M | | I | W | FA | I | GG | 1? | 1 | CR | 1 | DNB, K |
| HATCHER, Thomas | Stamford 1640 | A | | 60? | e | m | C | L | E | S, 20 | P? | | | | CG | | | | | K |
| HAY, Herbert | Arundel 1645 | S | 1 Feb.? (r) | 57 | e | m | G | | SE | | | | | | LG | | | | | Note 13 below |
| HAY, William | Rye 1641 | C | 1 Feb. | 54 | ys | m | C | | SE | | | | | | LG | 3? | | | | K |
| HERBERT, Henry | Monmouthshire 1642 | C | | 31? | e | m | O | MT | WB | | | | | I | GG | 2 | | R | 1 | Williams (Wales) |
| HERBERT, James | Wiltshire 1646 | S | | 25 | ys | m | O | | SW | | | | SA | P? | GG | 1 | | | | Foster, Pink MSS. 303/308 |
| HERBERT, John | Monmouthshire 1646 | S | | 23 | ys | m | O | | SW | | | | SA | | GG | | | | | Foster, Pink MSS. 303/313 |

| Name | Constituency / Date of election | Category | Date of dissent | Age | Position in family | Marital status | Education University | Inn | Region | Parliamentary experience | Religion | 1643–5 | 1647 | 1645–8 | Status | Income | Claims against State | Land purchases | Office | Principal sources of information |
|---|---|---|---|---|---|---|---|---|---|---|---|---|---|---|---|---|---|---|---|---|
| HERBERT, Philip, Lord | Glam. 1640 | S | 23 July | 27 | h | m | O | | SW | S | P? | | | P | GG | 1 | | | | DNB, K |
| HEVENINGHAM, William | Stockbridge 1640 | C | 1 Feb. | 44 | e | m | C | | E | S | P-I | | | | GG | 1? | 3 | CR | 2 | DNB, K |
| HEYMAN, Sir Henry, Bt. | Hythe 1640 | A | 28 June | 38 | e | m | C | G | SE | S | | | | | GG | 1?x | | | | K |
| HILL, Roger | Bridport 1640 | C | 21 Feb. | 43 | e | m | C | IT (b) | SW | S | P | | FA | I | LG | 3? | 3 | CK | | K, B & P |
| HIPPISLEY, Sir John | Cockermouth 1641 | S | 12 Feb. | 60 + ? | ys | m | | | SW | 20 | | | FA | I | LG | ?x | 1 | CK | 3 | K |
| HOBY, Peregrine | Gt. Marlow 1640 | S | | 46 | e | m | | | SE | | | | | | CG | 2? | | | | K |
| HODGES, Luke | Bristol 1646 | C | 2 Feb. | 50 + ? | ys | m | | | SW | S | | | FA? 1? | | MG | 3? | | | 1 | Note 14 below |
| HODGES, Thomas | Cricklade 1640 | S | 4 June | 43? | e | m | | MT | WB | S | | | | | CG | 2? | 3 | C | | K |
| HODGES, Thomas | Ilchester 1646 | S | | 41? | e | s | | L | SW | | | | | | LG | 3? | | | | Note 15 below |
| HOGHTON, Sir Richard, Bt. | Lancs. 1646 | A | | 32 | e | m | | | NW | | P-I? | | | | GG | 1 | 2 | | | Baronetage |
| HOLCROFT, John | Wigan 1646 | S | | ? | e | m | | | NW | S | | | | | LG | ?x | | | | Pink & Beaven, VCH Lancs. 4 |
| HOLLAND, Cornelius | Windsor 1641 | R | 20 Dec. | 49 | | m | C | | SE | | I | W | FA | I | LG | 1?x | 1 | CK | | DNB, K |
| HOLLAND, Sir John, Bt. | Castle Rising 1640 | X | | | | | | | | | | | | | | | | | | K |
| HOLLES, Denzil | Dorchester 1640 | S | | 49 | ys | m | C | G | SW | 20 | P | P | SA | P | GG | 1 | 3 | | | DNB, K |
| HOLLES, Francis | Lostwithiel 1640 | S | | 21 | h | s | C | MT | SW | | | | | | GG | 1 | | | | Peerage |
| HORNER, George | Somerset 1647 | S | | 43 | h | m | O | L | SW | S | P | | SA | P | GG | 1 | | | | Bates Harbin |
| HOSKINS, Bennett | Hereford 1646 | S | | 39 | e | m? | | MT (b) | WB | S | P? | | | | CG* | 1?x | 1 | | | Williams (H) |
| HOYLE, Thomas | York 1640 | C | ?: | 61? | e | m | | | NE | 20 | P | W | SA | I | M | | 3 | | 1 | K |

| Name | Constituency | | Date | Age | | | | | | | | | | | | | | | | Reference |
|---|---|---|---|---|---|---|---|---|---|---|---|---|---|---|---|---|---|---|---|---|
| HUNGERFORD, Henry | Gt. Bedwin 1646 | S | | 36 | ys | s | O | L | SW | | P | | SA | P | GG | 3? | | | | |
| HUNT, Thomas | Shrewsbury 1645 | A | | 49 | e | m | C? | G | WB | | | | | | MG | | | C | 3 | |
| HUSSEY, Thomas | Whitchurch 1645 | A | 2 June | 50? | e | m | | | SE | | | | | | LG | 3 | | | | Pink MSS. 304/674 · 2 |
| HUTCHINSON, John | Notts. | R | 21 Dec. (r) | 33 | e | m | C | L | M | | S | | FA | | GG | 3x | 1 | CR | | DNB |
| INGOLDSBY, Richard | Wendover 1646 | R | ? (r) | 31 | ys | m | O? | G | SE | | I? | | | | CG | 1 | 1 | K | 1 | DNB |
| IRBY, Sir Anthony | Boston 1647 | I | | 43 | e | m | C | L | E | S, 20 | P | P/M | SA | P | CG | 1 | | | | K |
| IRETON, Henry | Appleby 1640 | R | 29 Jan. (r) | 37 | e | m | O | MT | M | | I | | FA | I | LG | 3? | 3 | R | 1 | DNB |
| JENNER, Robert | Cricklade 1645 | S | | 64? | e | m | O | | SW | S, 20 | | | | | M | | | C | | K |
| JENNINGS, Richard | St. Albans 1640 | S | | 29 | e | m | O | IT | SE | S | | M? | SA | M? | CG* | 1x | 1 | R | | K, B & P |
| JEPHSON, William | Stockbridge 1642 | S | | 39? | e | m | O | | SE | S | I? | | FA | | GG | 1? | | | 1 | DNB, K |
| JERVOISE, Sir Thomas | Whitchurch 1640 | C | 1 Feb. | 61 | e | m? | O | | SE | S, 20 | P | | SA | | CG* | 1?x | 1 | R | | K |
| JESSON, William | Coventry 1640 | S | | 50 + ? | ys | m | | | M | | P | | SA | P | M | 1? | 3 | | | K |
| JONES, John | Merioneth 1641 | R | 20 Dec. (r) | ? | e | m | | | WB | S | | | | | LG | 3? | | CK | 2 | DNB, Dodd |
| JONES, William | Beaumaris 1647 | S | | 58? | e | m | | L (b) | WB | | | | | | CG | | | | | Williams (Wakes) |
| KEKEWICH, George | Liskeard 1647 | S | | 34 | e | m | | | SW | S | | | | | CG | | | C | | Note 16 below |
| KEMP, John | Christchurch 1647 | A | | 37 | e | s | | G | SE | S | P | | FA | | LG | 2? | 2 | | | Note 17 below |
| KNATCHBULL, Sir Norton, Bt. | New Romney 1645 | S | | 46 | e | m | C | MT | SE | S | P | P | SA | | GG | 2? | | | | DNB, K |
| KNIGHTLEY, Richard | Northampton 1640 | I | | 38? | h | m | O | G | M | S | P | M | | M | GG | | | R | | DNB, K |
| KYRLE, Walter | Leominster 1640 | S | | 48? | e | m | O | MT (b) | WB | S | | | | | LG | 2? | | | | K |
| LANE, Thomas | Wycombe 1640 | I | | 66? | e | m | C | IT (b) | SE | S, 20 | | | | | LG | 2? | | | | K |
| LANGTON, William | Preston 1640 | S | | 36? | e | m | C | G (b) | NW | | P? | | | | MG | | | | | Venn, Pink & Beaven |
| LASCELLES, Francis | Thirsk 1645 | C | 1 Feb. | 36 | e | m | | G | NE | | | | FA | | LG | 3 | | | | Gooder |

Column reference heading: Foster, Pink MSS. 304/645 · SAST, 4th ser. 12

| Name | Constituency / Date of election | Category | Date of dissent | Age | Position in family | Marital status | University | Inn | Region | Parliamentary experience | Religion | 1643–5 | 1647 | 1645–8 | Status | Income | Claims against State | Land purchases | Office | Principal sources of information |
|---|---|---|---|---|---|---|---|---|---|---|---|---|---|---|---|---|---|---|---|---|
| LAWRENCE, Henry | Westmorland 1646 | A | | 48 | e | m | C | G | E | | S | | FA | | GG | | | | | DNB |
| LECHMERE, Nicholas | Bewdley 1648 | C | Feb. ? | 35 | h | m | O | MT (b) | WB | | | | | | LG | 3?x | | C | | DNB, Williams (Worcs.) |
| LEE, Richard | Rochester 1640 | A | | 57? | e | m | | IT | SE | | | | SA | | LG | 3? | 2 | | | K |
| LE GROS, Sir Charles | Orford 1640 | X | | | | | | | | | | | | | | | | | | K |
| LEIGH, Edward | Stafford 1640 | I | | 46 | e | m | O | MT | M | | P | | | | LG | 2 | | | | DNB, Wedgwood |
| LEIGH, Sir John | Yarmouth, I. of W. 1645 | S | | 50? | e | m | O | | SE | | | | | | CG | 3? | | | | K |
| LEMAN, William | Hertford 1640 | C | 2 Feb. | 55? | ys | m | O | | SE | | | | FA | | M | 1 | 2 | C | 1 | Baronetage, N & Q, 121 ser. 4 |
| LENTHALL, John | Gloucester 1645 | A | 21 June | 23 | h | m? | O | L (b) | M | | | | | I? | CG | 1 | | | | DNB, Williams (G) |
| LENTHALL, William | Woodstock 1640 | C | ? | 57 | ys | m | O | L (b) | M | S, 20 | | | FA | I | LG | 1 | | CKR | 1 | DNB, K |
| LEWIS, William | Brecon 1640 | S | | 22? | h | s | | | WB | | | | | | GG | 2? | | | | Williams (Wales) |
| LEWIS, Sir William, Bt. | Petersfield 1647 | I | | 50 | e | m | O | L | WB | S | P | P | SA | P | GG | 2? | | | | K |
| LISLE, John | Winchester 1640 | R | 20 Dec. | 39? | e | m | O | MT (b) | SE | S | P? | W | FA | I | CG | 2? | 3 | KR | 2 | DNB, K |
| LISTER, Sir Martin | Brackley 1640 | I | | 46? | e | m | O | L (b) | M | S | | | | | CG | | | | | K |
| LISTER, Thomas | Lincoln 1640 | R | 29 Jan. | 51 | e | m | | G | E | | I? | | FA | | LG | 1 | 1 | R | | DNB |
| LISTER, Sir William | E. Retford 1647 | S | | 58? | e | m | | | NE | | | | | | CG | 1 | 2 | | | Cliffe |
| LIVESEY, Sir Michael, Bt. | Queenboro' 1645 | R | 29 Jan. (r) | 37 | e | m | | | SE | | | | FA | I | GG* | | 2 | R | | DNB |
| LLOYD, John | Carmarthenshire 1646 | S | | 32? | e | m | | G | WB | | P? | | | | CG | 2? | | | | Note 18 below |
| LONG, Lislebone | Wells 1646 | C | 22 Feb. | 35 | e | m | O | L (b) | SW | | P | | | | LG | | | CR | | DNB, Bates Harbin |

| Name | Constituency | Elected | | Date | Age | | | O/C | Inn | Region | S | | FA/SA | | Group | | C | | Ref |
|---|---|---|---|---|---|---|---|---|---|---|---|---|---|---|---|---|---|---|---|
| LONG, Walter | Ludgershall | 1641 | X | | 40 | e | s | O | L (b) | SE | | | FA | I | LG | 3 | | | K |
| LOVE, Nicholas | Winchester | 1645 | R | 20 Dec. | 50+? | e | m | | | E | | | | | M | 3? | 2 | CR 1 | DNB |
| LOWRY, John | Cambridge | 1640 | C | 21 Feb. | | e | m | C | | | | | | | LG | 3?x | 2 | | K |
| LUCAS, Henry | Cambridge U. | 1640 | S | | 61? | e | s | C | MT (b) | E | S | | | | GG* | 1? | | | DNB, K |
| LUCKYN, Capel | Harwich | 1648 | S | | 26 | h | m | C | L | SE | S | | | | GG | | 1 | | B & P, *EAST*, n.s. 6 |
| LUCY, Sir Richard, Bt. | Old Sarum | 1647 | A | 23 July | 56 | ys | m | C | L | M | | P? | SA | | CG | | | 1 | DNB |
| LUDLOW, Edmund | Wilts. | 1646 | R | 20 Dec. (r) | 31? | e | s | O | IT | SW | S, 20, 10 | P | FA | I | GG* | 2?x | | CK 2 | *DNB* |
| LUKE, Sir Oliver | Beds. | 1640 | S | | 74 | e | m | C | MT | M | | | | | GG* | 2?x | | | K |
| LUKE, Sir Samuel | Bedford | 1641 | I | | 45 | h | m | | | M | S | P | | P | GG* | 1? | | | *DNB*, K |
| LUMLEY, Sir Martin, Bt. | Essex | 1641 | S | | 52? | e | m | | | SE | | P? | | | GG* | 1? | | | K |
| LYTTON, Sir William | Herts. | 1640 | I | | 62 | e | m | C | | SE | S, 20 | | SA? | | GG | 1? | | | K |
| MACKWORTH, Thomas | Ludlow | 1646 | C | 1 Feb. | 21 | h | s? | C | G | WB | | S | | | LG | | | C | Weyman |
| MARTEN, Henry | Berks. | 1640 | R | Dec.? (r) | 46 | e | m | O | IT | SE | S | W | FA | I | GG* | 1x | | CR | *DNB*, K |
| MARTYN, Henry | Plympton | 1647 | A | 16 Apr. (r) | ? | ys | m | | | SW | | | | | LG | 3? | | C | Alexander, *WA* 8 |
| MARTYN, Christopher | Devon | 1646 | S | | 55 | e | m | O | MT | SW | | | | | CG | | | | Alexander, *WA* 1 |
| MASHAM, Sir William, Bt. | Essex | 1640 | C | 8 Feb. | 56 | e | m | O | IT | SE | S, 20 | P-1 M | | I | GG | 1? | 3 | C | K |
| MASHAM, William | Shrewsbury | 1646 | C | 8 Feb. | 32 | h | m | C | L | SE | | P? | | | GG | 1? | | C | Y, Venn |
| MASSEY, Edward | Wootton Bassett | 1646 | I | | 30? | ys | s | | | WB | | P | SA | P | LG | 3? | 1 | | *DNB* |
| MAULEVERER, Sir Thomas, Bt. | Boroughbridge | 1640 | R | 20 Dec. (r) | 49 | e | m | C | G | NE | | | | | GG | 1 | 1 | | *DNB*, K |
| MAYNARD, Sir John | Lostwithiel | 1647 | S | | 56 | ys | m | C? | IT | SE | | P? | SA | P | CG | | | | *DNB* |
| MAYNARD, John | Totnes | 1640 | S | | 46 | e | m | O | MT | SW | S | P | | P | LG | 3? | | 2 | *DNB*, K |
| MAYNE, Simon | Aylesbury | 1645 | R | 25 Dec. (r) | 36 | e | m | | IT | SE | | I? | FA | I | LG | | | | *DNB* |

| Name | Constituency / Date of election | Category | Date of dissent | Age | Position in family | Marital status | University | Inn | Region | Parliamentary experience | Religion | 1643–5 | 1647 | 1645–8 | Status | Income | Claims against State | Land purchases | Office | Principal sources of information |
|---|---|---|---|---|---|---|---|---|---|---|---|---|---|---|---|---|---|---|---|---|
| MEYRICK, Sir John | Newcastle-u-L. 1640 | I | | 48? | ys | m | | | WB | S | P? | P | | | CG* | | 1 | | | *DNB*, K |
| MIDDLETON, Thomas | Horsham 1640 | S | | 59 | e | m | C | IT | SE | S | | | | | CG* | 2 | 2 | | | K |
| MILDMAY, Sir Henry | Maldon 1640 | R | 21 Dec. | 55? | ys | m | C | G | SE | S, 20 | P-I? | W/M | FA | I | CG | 1 | 1 | CK | I | *DNB*, K, B & P |
| MILLINGTON, Gilbert | Nottingham 1640 | R | 25 Dec. (r) | 53? | e | m | C | L (b) | M | | P-I? | | | | LG | 3 | 1 | R | | *DNB*, K |
| MOORE, John | Liverpool 1640 | R | 25 Dec. (r) | 49? | e | m | C | L | NW | | P | W | | | CG | 1? | 2 | | | K |
| MOORE, Thomas | Heytesbury 1640 | S | | 30 | e | s | | L | SW | S | P | | | | CG* | 1? | 3 | | | K, Lacey |
| MORE, Sir Poynings, Bt. | Haslemere 1640 | S | | 42 | e | m | | IT | SE | 20 | P? | P | | | GG* | 2?x | | | 1? | K |
| MORE, Thomas | Ludlow 1646 | S | | 48? | ys | m | O | | WB | | P? | | | | CG | 3? | | | | B & P, *SAST*, 2nd ser. ? |
| MORGAN, William | Breconshire 1640 | S | | 51? | e | m | | MT (b) | WB | S, 20 | | | | | CG* | 2 | | | | K |
| MORICE, William | Devon 1648 | A | | 46 | e | m | O | | SW | | P | | | | LG | | | | | *DNB*, Lacey |
| MORLEY, Herbert | Lewes 1640 | C | 5 Feb. | 32 | e | m | C | IT | SE | S | P? | W | FA | I | CG | 1? | 3 | | | *DNB*, K |
| MOUNSON, William, Lord | Reigate 1640 | C | 1 Feb. | 46? | ys | m | | G | E | 20 | | | FA | | GG* | 1x | 1 | C | | *DNB*, K |
| MOUNTAGU, Edward | Hunts. 1645 | A | | 23 | e | m | C | MT | E | | I | | | M? | GG | 1? | | | | *DNB* |
| MOUNTAGU, George | Huntingdon 1640 | S | | 25? | ys | m | C | MT | M | | | | SA? | | GG | 2? | | | | K |
| MOYLE, John, Sr. | E. Looe 1648 | A | 6 July | 56? | e | m | O | | SW | | P? | | | | LG | | | | | *DNB* |
| MOYLE, John, Jr. | St. Germans 1641 | X | | | | | | | | | | | | | | | | | | K |
| MYDD.TON, Sir Thomas | Denbighshire 1640 | S | | 62 | e | m | O | G | WB | 20 | | | | | GG* | 1? | | | | *DNB*, K |
| MYDDELTON, Thomas | Flint 1646 | S | | 24 | h | s? | O | | WB | | | | | | GG* | 1? | | | | Williams (*Wales*) |

| Name | Seat / Year | | Date | Age | | | O | G | M | | P | SA | | GG | | | | Reference |
|---|---|---|---|---|---|---|---|---|---|---|---|---|---|---|---|---|---|---|
| NAPIER, Sir Robert, Bt. | Peterborough 1641 | S | | 46 | e | m | | | | | | | | GG | 1? | | | K |
| NASH, John | Worcester 1640 | S | | 58 | ys | | | | WB | S | | | | M | 3? | | | K |
| NEEDHAM, Sir Robert | Haverfordwest 1645? | S | | 47? | e | m | | L | WB | | | | | CG | 2? | | | Williams (Wales) |
| NELTHORPE, James | Beverley 1645 | C | 1 Feb. | 29? | ys | m | | | NE | | | | | M | 3? | CR | | Note 19 below |
| NELTHORPE, John | Beverley 1645 | S | | 34 | ys | s? | C | G (b) | NE | S | P? | SA? | | LG | 3? | C?K? | 1? | Note 20 below |
| NEVILL, Edward | E. Retford 1648 | A | 5 May | 33? | e | m | O | L | M | | | | I | LG | | | 2 | Wood, Fam. Min. Gent. |
| NICHOLAS, Robert | Devizes 1640 | C | 17 Feb. 1640 | 53 | e | m | | MT (b) | SW | S | | | I | LG | | | 3 | DNB, K |
| NICOLL, Anthony | Bodmin 1640 | S | | 37 | e | m | O | | SW | S | P? | SA | P/M | CG | 3? | | | DNB, K |
| NIXON, John | Oxford 1640 | A | | 59 | e | m | | | M | | P | | | M | | | | Williams (O) |
| NOBLE, Michael | Lichfield 1640 | X | | | | | | | | | | | | | | | | K |
| NORTH, Sir Dudley | Cambs. 1640 | S | | 46 | h | m | C | IT | E | S, 20 | P? | | | GG | 1 | | | DNB, K |
| NORTH, Sir Roger | Eye 1640 | S | 23 July | 60 | e | m | | G | E | S, 20 | P? | | | GG | 1 | | | K |
| NORTHCOTE, Sir John, Bt. | Ashburton 1640 | A | | 49 | e | m | O | MT | SW | | P | | | GG | 1 | | 3 | DNB, K |
| NORTON, Sir Gregory, Bt. | Midhurst 1640 | R | 20 Dec. (r) | 50? | e | m | | G | SE | | | FA | | GG* | 3?x | CK | 1 | N & Q, 11th ser. 10 |
| NORTON, Richard | Hants. 1645 | A | 26 Nov. 1651 | 33 | e | m | O | G | SE | S | I | | M | GG | | C | 1 | B & P, Foster, VCH Hants. 3 |
| NUTT, John | Canterbury 1645 | C | 5 Feb. | 44 | e | m | O | MT | SE | S | | | M | LG | 3? | C | | K |
| OLDISWORTH, Michael | Salisbury 1640 | R | 20 Dec. | 57 | ys | m | O | | WB | S, 20 | P | SA | | LG | 3? | | | DNB, K |
| ONSLOW, Arthur | Bramber 1640 | S | | 26 | h | m | O | L | SE | S | P? | | | GG | 1? | | | K, Baronetage |
| ONSLOW, Sir Richard | Surrey 1640 | I | | 47 | e | m | C | L | SE | S, 20 | P | | M | GG | 1? | | 3 | DNB, K |
| OWEN, Arthur | Pembs. 1640 | S | | 41? | ys | m | O | L | WB | | | | | GG | 1 | | | Williams (Wales) |
| OWEN, Sir Hugh, Bt. | Pembroke 1646 | S | | 44 | e | m | | L | WB | S, 20 | | | M? | GG | 1 | | | K, Williams (Wales) |
| OWFIELD, William | Gatton 1645 | S | | 24? | e | m? | C | | SE | | P? | | | CG* | 1? | | 3 | Note 21 below |

(381)

| Name | Constituency / Date of election | Category | Date of dissent | Age | Position in family | Marital status | Education | | Region | Parliamentary experience | Religion | Earlier political behaviour | | | Status | Income | Claims against State | Land purchases | Office | Principal sources of information |
|---|---|---|---|---|---|---|---|---|---|---|---|---|---|---|---|---|---|---|---|---|
| | | | | | | | University | Inn | | | | 1643–5 | 1647 | 1645–8 | | | | | | |
| Owner, Edward | Gt. Yarmouth 1640 | X | | | | | | | | | | | | | | | | | | K |
| Oxinden, Henry | Winchelsea 1645 | | | 34 | e | m | | | SE | | P? | | SA | | GG | | | | | Note 22 below |
| Packer, Robert | Wallingford 1640 | S | | 34? | h | m | O | | SE | | | | | | CG* | 1? | | | | B & P, Foster, VCH Berks. 4 |
| Palgrave, Sir John, Bt. | Norfolk 1646 | S | | 43 | e | m | | IT | E | | | | | | GG | 2? | | | | B & P, Baronetage |
| Palmer, John | Taunton 1647 | C | 5 Feb. | 39 | e | m | O | | SW | | P? | | | | M | 3? | | | I | Foster, Y |
| Parker, Sir Philip | Suffolk 1646 | S | | 46 | e | m | C | IT | E | S | P? | | | | GG | 2? | 2 | | | K |
| Parker, Sir Thomas | Seaford 1640 | S | | 52? | e | m | | G | SE | | | | | | GG | 1? | | | | K |
| Parkhurst, Sir Robert | Guildford 1641 | S | | 45? | e | m | O | IT | SE | S, 20 | | P | | | CG* | 1? | 3 | | | K |
| Partheriche, Sir Edward | Sandwich 1640 | S | | 46 | e | m | O | MT | SE | | P? | P | SA | | CG* | 2? | | | | K |
| Peck, Henry | Chichester 1640 | S | | 51? | e | m | | G | SE | | | | | | LG | 3? | 1 | | | Pink MSS. 322 |
| Pelham, Henry | Grantham 1645? | I | | 51? | ys | s? | C | G (b) | E | S, 20 | I? | W | SA | P | CG | 3? | 1 | | | K |
| Pelham, John | Hastings 1640 | S | | 25? | h | m | C | | SE | S | P? | | | | GG | | | | | Baronetage, Venn |
| Pelham, Peregrine | Hull 1645 | R | 20 Dec. (r) | 46 | e | m | | | NE | | I? | W | | I | MG | 1 | 2 | R | | K |
| Pelham, Sir Thomas, Bt. | Sussex 1641 | S | | 51 | e | m | | | SE | S | | | | | GG | 1 | | | | K |
| Penington, Isaac | London 1640 | R | 25 Dec. | 61? | e | m | C | G | SE | S, 20 | I | W | | I | M | 1? | 1 | R | | DNB, K, Pearl |
| Penrose, John | Helston 1646 | A | | 37 | e | m | | L | SW | | I | | | | LG | 1? | | | | Note 23 below |
| Pickering, Sir Gilbert, Bt. | Northants. 1640 | C | 12 Feb. | 37 | e | m | C | G | M | S | I | | | | GG | 1? | 1 | | | DNB, K |
| Pierrepont, Francis | Nottingham 1645 | A | 7 May | 34? | ys | m | | | M | S | P | | FA | M? | GG | 1? | 1 | | | Wood, Hutchinson |

(382)

| Name | Constituency | | Date | Age | | | C | L | M | S | P | P/M | FA | M | GG | | CR | References |
|---|---|---|---|---|---|---|---|---|---|---|---|---|---|---|---|---|---|---|
| PIERREPONT, William | Much Wenlock 1640 | A | | 41? | ys | m | C | L | M | | | | FA | M | GG | 1? | | *DNB*, K |
| PIGOT, Gervase | Notts. 1646 | A | 23 July | 32 | e | m | C | L | M | | | | FA | | LG | | | Wood, *Hutchinson* |
| PILE, Sir Francis, Bt. | Berks. 1646 | S | | 31? | e | m | O | MT | SE | | | | | M? | GG* | 2? | | B & P, *Baronetage* |
| PLAYTERS, Sir William, Bt. | Orford 1640 | S | | 58 | e | m | | | E | | P? | P | | | GG | 1 | | K, B & P |
| POOLE, Edward | Wootton Bassett 1640 | S | | 31? | h | m | O | L | SW | | | | | | GG | 1 | | K |
| POOLE, Sir Neville | Malmesbury 1640 | S | | 56? | e | m | | G | SW | S, 20, 10 | | M | | | GG | 1 | | K |
| POPHAM, Alexander | Bath 1640 | C | 14 Feb. | 43 | e | m | O | MT | SW | S | P | | | | GG* | 1x | K | K, Bates Harbin |
| POPHAM, Edward | Minehead 1646 | C | 14 Feb. | 35? | ys | m | | MT | SW | | P? | | | 1? | GG* | 3? | 2 | *DNB* |
| POTTER, Hugh | Plympton 1640 | A | | 52 | e | s | | L (b) | SW | S | | P | | | LG | 3? | | K |
| POTTS, Sir John, Bt. | Norfolk 1640 | S | | 55? | e | m | | | E | | P | P | P? | | GG | 3 | | K |
| POVEY, Thomas | Liskeard 1647 | S | | 34? | ys | s | | G (b) | SE | | | | | P | LG | 3?x | | *DNB* |
| PRIDEAUX, Edmund | Lyme Regis 1640 | C | 1 Feb. | 47 | ys | m | | IT (b) | SW | S | P | W | FA | I | GG | 3? | 1 | *DNB*, K |
| PRIESTLEY, William | St. Mawes 1647 | I | | 55? | e | m | C | G (b) | SE | | | | SA | | CG* | 2? | | Courtney, Venn, *VCH Herts.* 3 |
| PRYNNE, William | Newport, Cornwall 1648 | I | | 48 | s | s | O | L (b) | SW | | P | | | P | LG | 3? | | *DNB* |
| PRYSE, Sir Richard, Bt. | Cardiganshire 1646 | S | | 39? | e | m | | G (b) | WB | | | | | | GG | 1? | | Williams (*Wales*) |
| PUREFOY, William | Warwick 1646 | R | 20 Dec. (r) | 68? | e | m | C | G | M | S, 20 | P | W/M | FA | I | CG | | 1 | *DNB*, K |
| PURY, Thomas, Sr. | Gloucester 1640 | C | 1 Feb. | 58? | e | m | | (b) | WB | | | | | I? | M | 3 | | K, Williams (*G*) |
| PURY, Thomas, Jr. | Monmouth 1640 | A | 2 June | 29 | h | m | O | G | WB | | | | | | M | 3 | R | Williams (*G*), (*Wales*) |
| PYE, Sir Robert | Woodstock 1646 | I | | 63 | ys | m | | MT | SE | 20 | P? | P | SA | P | CG* | 1? | 3 | K, Aylmer |
| PYM, Charles | Berealston 1640 | S | | 30? | ys | s | | L (b) | SW | | | M? | | | CG | 3?x | | K |
| PYNE, John | Poole 1641 | R | 1 Feb. | 52? | e | m | O | MT (b) | SW | S, 20 | P-I? | W | | I | CG | 1 | | K, B & P, Bates Harbin |
| RATCLIFFE, John | Chester 1646 | S | | 37 | | m | O | MT (b) | WB | | P? | | SA | | M | | | Foster, Pink MSS. 307/148 |

| Name | Constituency / Date of election | Category | Date of dissent | Age | Position in family | Marital status | University | Inn | Region | Parliamentary experience | Religion | 1643-5 | 1647 | 1645-8 | Status | Income | Claims against State | Land purchases | Office | Principal sources of information |
|---|---|---|---|---|---|---|---|---|---|---|---|---|---|---|---|---|---|---|---|---|
| RAVENSCROFT, Hall | Horsham 1640 | S | | 48? | e | m | O | L | SE | S | | | | | LG | 3? | | | | K |
| REYNOLDS, Robert | Hindon 1640 | C | 13 Feb. 1651 | 47? | e | m | C | MT (b) | E | | P? | P/M | | M | CG* | 1 | 3 | CK | 2 | DNB, K |
| RICH, Charles | Sandwich 1645 | S | 20 Dec. | 32 | ys | m | | IT (b) | SE | | P? | | | P | GG | 1 | | | | DNB, Aubrey |
| RIGBY, Alexander | Wigan 1640 | R | | 54 | e | m | C | G (b) | NW | S | P-I? | W | | | LG | | | | 2 | DNB, K |
| ROBINSON, Luke | Scarborough 1645 | R | 29 Jan. | 38 | e | m? | C | G (b) | NE | | | | | | CG* | 2? | | | 2 | Gooder |
| ROGERS, Hugh | Calne 1640 | S | 20 Nov. 1650 | 26 | e | m? | O | | SW | | | | | | GG | 1? | | | 2 | K |
| ROLLE, John | Truro 1640 | S | | 50 | ys | m | | | SW | S, 20 | | | | | GG | 1? | | R | | DNB, K |
| ROSE, Richard | Lyme Regis 1640 | S | | 45? | e | m | O | MT | SW | S | | | SA | | M | 2? | 3 | | | K |
| ROSSITER, Edward | Grimsby 1646 | A | Feb.? | 28? | e | m? | C | | E | | P? | | | | LG | | | | | Note 24 below |
| ROUS, Francis | Truro 1640 | C | | 69 | ys | m | O/U | MT | SW | S, 20 | P | W | FA | | GG | | | | 1 | DNB, K |
| RUDYARD, Sir Benjamin | Wilton 1640 | I | | 76 | ys | m | O | MT (b) | SE | S, 20 | P | P | FA | | CG* | 1 | | | | DNB, K |
| RUSSELL, Francis | Cambs. 1645 | A | 4 June | 34? | h | m | O | G | E | S, 20 | I? | | FA | | GG* | | 3 | | | B & P, Baronetage |
| ST. JOHN, Sir Beauchamp | Bedford 1640 | A | | 55? | ys | m | C | L | M | S, 20 | | | | | GG* | ?x | | | | K |
| ST. JOHN, Oliver | Totnes 1640 | X | 27 June 1651 | | e | m | | | | | | | | | | | | | | DNB, K |
| SALWAY, Humphrey | Worcs. 1640 | C | Feb.? | 73? | ys | m | O | IT | WB | | | | FA? | | CG | 2? | | | 1 | DNB, K |
| SALWAY, Richard | Appleby 1645 | A | 14 May | 33 | e | m | | | WB | | I | | FA? | I | MG | | | CR | | DNB |
| SANDYS, Thomas | Gatton 1641 | S | | 48 | e | m | O | MT (b) | SE | | P? | | | | LG | 3? | | | | Note 25 below |
| SAY, William | Camelford 1647 | R | 1 Feb. (r) | 44 | ys | m? | O | MT (b) | SE | | | | FA | | LG | 3? | | R | 2 | DNB, Pink MSS. 307/185 |

| Name | Constituency / Year | Status | Date | Age | | | | Region | | | | | | | | | | Reference |
|---|---|---|---|---|---|---|---|---|---|---|---|---|---|---|---|---|---|---|
| SAYER, John | Colchester 1645 | A | | 59? | e | m | | SE | | P? | | FA | | CG | 2? | | | B & P, ER 5 |
| SCAWEN, Robert | 1640 | A | | 46 | ys | m | | SW | | | | | M | LG | 2? | | 3 | K |
| SCOT, Thomas | Aylesbury 1645 | R | 20 Dec. (r) | 43? | | m | C? | SE (b) | | I | | FA | I | LG | 3? | CK | 1 | Note 26 below |
| SERLE, George | Taunton 1640 | R | 20 Dec. | 50? | | | | SW | | P? | | | | M | 3? | C | 1 | K |
| SELDEN, John | Oxford U. 1640 | S | | 64 | s | | O | IT SE 20 | | P | P | SA | P | LG | 1? | | 1 | DNB |
| SEYMOUR, Sir John | Glos. 1646 | S | | 65? | e | m | | MT WB (b) | | | | SA | | CG | 2? | C | | Williams (G) |
| SHAPCOTE, Robert | Tiverton 1646 | S | | 28 | e | m | | L SW (b) | | | | | | LG | 3 | | | Note 27 below |
| SHELLEY, Henry | Lewes 1641 | A | | 49 | e | m | | SE | | | | | | CG | 3? | | | K |
| SHUTTLEWORTH, Richard, Sr. | Preston 1640 | A | | 61 | e | m | O | G NW S | | P? | | SA | | LG | 2? | | 3 | K |
| SHUTTLEWORTH, Richard, Jr. | Clitheroe 1640 | X | | | | | | | | | | | | | | | | Note 28 below |
| SIDNEY, Algernon | Cardiff 1640 | C | Feb. ? | 26 | ys | s | O | G SE | | S? | | FA | I | GG | 1? | C | 1 | DNB |
| SIDNEY, Philip, Lord Lisle | Yarmouth, I. of W. 1640 | C | 1 Feb. | 29 | h | m | O | G SE S | | I | | FA | I | GG | 1 | | 3 | DNB, K |
| SKINNER, Augustine | Kent 1642 | C | 28 Feb. | 55? | e? | m | O | MT SE | | P-I? | | FA | | LG | 3 | CR | 3 | B & P, Foster |
| SKIPPON, Philip | Barnstaple 1646 | R | 2 Feb. | 50 | e? | m | | E | | P-I | | | M | LG | 3? | CK | 1 | DNB, TDA 72 |
| SKUTT, George | Poole 1645 | S | | 50 + ? | | | | SW | | | | | | M | 2 | C | 2 | B & P, Pink MSS. 321 |
| SMITH, Henry | Leics. 1645 | R | 20 Dec. (r) | 28 | e | m | O | L M | | | | FA | | LG | 2 | | 2 | DNB |
| SMITH, Philip | Marlborough 1641 | C | 5 Feb. | 44? | e | m | | IT SW (b) | | | | FA | | LG | 3? | | 2 | K |
| SNELLING, George | Southwark 1645 | A | 22 May | ? | | m | | SE | | P? | | | | M | 3? | | 2 | Note 29 below |
| SNOW, Simon | Exeter 1645 | S | | 58? | ys | m | | SW S | | P? | | | | M | 2? | C | 1 | K |
| SOAME, Sir Thomas | London 1640 | I | | 64? | ys | m | | SE S | | P? | P | SA | | MG | 1? | | | K, Pearl |
| SPELMAN, John | Castle Rising 1646? | S | | 43 | e | m | C | MT E | | | | | | CG | | | | B & P, Venn |

| Name | Constituency / Date of election | Category | Date of dissent | Age | Position in family | Marital status | University | Inn | Region | Parliamentary experience | Religion | 1643–5 | 1647 | 1645–8 | Status | Income | Claims against State | Land purchases | Office | Principal sources of information |
|---|---|---|---|---|---|---|---|---|---|---|---|---|---|---|---|---|---|---|---|---|
| SPENCER, Sir Edward | Middlesex 1648 | S |  | 53 | ys | m | O | L (b) | SE | 20 |  |  |  |  | GG | 2? |  |  |  | Foster, Pink MSS. 308, 321 |
| SPRING, Sir William, Bt. | Bury St. E. 1645 | S |  | 35 | e | m | C | E |  |  | P? |  |  |  | GG | 1? |  |  |  | B & P, *Baronetage* |
| SPRINGETT, Herbert | Shoreham 1646? | S |  | 35 | e | m | C | MT | SE |  |  |  |  |  | CG |  |  |  |  | *Baronetage* |
| STAPLETON, Brian | Aldborough 1645 | A |  | 59? | e | m | O | O | NE |  |  |  |  | I | CG | 2? |  |  | 3 | Bean, *YAJ* 8, 27 |
| STAPLETON, Henry | Boroughbridge 1647 | S |  |  | 32 | h | s | O | IT | NE |  |  |  |  | CG | 2? |  |  |  | *Baronetage*, *YAJ* 27 |
| STAPLEY, Anthony | Sussex 1640 | R | 20 Dec. (r) | 58 | e | m | C | G | SE | S, 20 |  |  |  |  | CG |  |  | C |  | *DNB*, K |
| STEPHENS, Edward | Tewkesbury 1640 | I |  | 51 | e | m | O? | MT | WB |  | P |  | SA |  | CG* |  |  |  |  | K, Williams (G) |
| STEPHENS, John | Tewkesbury 1645 | A | 26 Nov. 1651 | 45 | ys | m |  | MT (b) | WB |  | P? |  | FA? | M? | CG* |  |  | R | 2 | Note 30 below |
| STEPHENS, Nathaniel | Glos. 1640 | A |  | 59 | e | m |  | MT (b) | WB | 20 | P? |  |  | M | CG | 1? |  |  |  | K |
| STEPHENS, William | Newport, I. of W. 1645 | C | 12 Feb. | 32? | ys | m |  | MT (b) | SE |  |  |  | FA? |  | LG | 3? | 2 |  | 2 | B & P, Foster, Pink MSS. 321 |
| STOCKDALE, Thomas | Knaresboro' 1645 | C | 23 July[1] | 55 | e | m |  |  | NE |  | P? |  |  |  | LG | 3 |  |  |  | Cliffe, *YAJ* 23 |
| STRICKLAND, Walter | Minehead 1646 | X | 2 Aug.? 1650 |  |  |  |  |  |  |  |  |  |  |  |  |  |  |  |  | *DNB* |
| STRICKLAND, Sir William, Bt. | Hedon 1640 | A | 22 May | 52? | e | m | C | G | NE |  | P? |  | SA | I | GG | 1 | 3 |  | 3 | *DNB*, K |
| STRODE, William | Ilchester 1646 | I |  | 59 | e | m |  |  | SW |  | P |  |  | P | LG | 2? | 3 |  |  | *SASP* 13, 30, 37 |
| SWYNFEN, John | Stafford 1645 | I |  | 36 | h | m | C | G? | M |  | P |  | SA | M | LG | 1? |  |  |  | *DNB*, Wedgwood |
| SYDENHAM, William | Weymouth 1645 | A | 3 Aug. | 33 | e | m | O? |  | SW |  | P–I |  |  |  | LG |  | 1 |  | 2 | *DNB*, B & P |
| TATE, Zouch | Northampton 1640 | S |  | 42 | e | m | O | MT | M | S | P | W | P |  | GG | 1? |  |  |  | *DNB*, K |

[1] See note 1 below.

| Name | Seat / Year | | Date | Age | | | | | | | | | | | | | | References |
|---|---|---|---|---|---|---|---|---|---|---|---|---|---|---|---|---|---|---|
| TEMPLE, James | Bramber 1645 | R | 20 Dec. (r) | 45? | ys | m | | L | SE | | P? | | FA | CG* | 3?x | R | 1 | *DNB* |
| TEMPLE, Sir John | Chichester 1645? | S | | 48 | e | m | U | | SI | | | | FA? M? | LG | 3?x | | 3 | *DNB* |
| TEMPLE, Sir Peter, Bt. | Buckingham 1640 | A | 23 July | 56 | e | m | | IT? | SE | S | | | FA? | GG* | 1x | | 1 | *DNB*, K, *HLQ* 1, 2, 6 |
| TEMPLE, Peter | Leicester 1645 | R | 20 Dec. (r) | 48 | ys | m | | IT | M | | | | FA | CG* | 3? | | 1 | *DNB* |
| TEMPLE, Thomas | Mitchell 1645 | S | | 34 | ys | s? | | | SE | | | | | CG | 3? | | | *DNB* |
| TERRICK, Samuel | Newcastle-u-L. 1647? | S | | 46 | ys | m | | | M | | | | | MG | 3? | | | Wedgwood |
| THELWALL, Simon | Denbigh 1645 | S | | 30? | h | m | | IT | WB | | | | | GG | | | | K |
| THISTLETHWAITE, Alexander | Downton 1640 | S | | 37 | e? | | O | L | SW | | P? | | | LG | | | | Foster, Pink MSS. 322 |
| THOMAS, Edward | Okehampton 1645 | S | | ? | | | | | SW | 20 | | | | LG? | 3? | | | K |
| THOMAS, Esay | Bishop's Castle 1646 | S | | 53? | | m | | | WB | | P? | | | M | 3? | | | *SAST*, 2nd ser. 10 |
| THOMAS, John | Helston | S | | 51 | e | m | | | SW | | | | | LG | | | | Courtney, Vivian, *WA* 6 |
| THOMSON, George | Southwark 1645 | C | 3 Feb. | 45? | e | m | C | | SE | | S | | SA | M | 1? | C | 2 | *DNB* |
| THORPE, Francis | Richmond 1645 | C | 1 Feb. | 53 | e | m | C | G (b) | NE | | I? | | | LG | 3? | | 1 | *DNB* |
| THYNNE, John | Saltash 1645 | S | | 40 | h? | m | | L (b) | SE | | | | | LG | | | | Pink MSS. 307/289 |
| TOLL, Thomas | King's Lynn 1646 | C | 17 Feb. | 55? | e | m | C | E | | | | | | M | 2? | | | K, B & P |
| TOLSON, Richard | Cumberland 1640 | S | | 25 | h | s | O | L | NW | | | | SA | CG | | | | Bean, Ferguson, Foster |
| TREFUSIS, Nicholas | Cornwall 1646 | S | | 56 | e | m | O | L | SW | S, 20 | | | | CG | | | | Courtney, Vivian, *WA* 8 |
| TRENCHARD, John | Wareham 1640 | C | 1 Feb. | 62 | ys | m | O | MT | SW | S, 20 | | | FA | GG | 2? | KR | 3 | K, B & P |
| TRENCHARD, Sir Thomas | Dorset 1645 | S | | 66 | e | m | O | MT | SW | S, 20 | P? | | | GG | 1? | | | B & P, Foster |
| TREVOR, Sir John | Grampound 1640 | A | 28 June | 53? | e | m | C | IT | WB | 20 | P-I? | P | FA M? | CG | 1 | KR | 1 | *DNB*, K |
| TREVOR, John | Flintshire 1646 | S | | 22 | h | m? | | | WB | | | | | CG | 1 | | | *DNB* |
| TREVOR, Sir Thomas, Bt. | Tregony 1647 | S | | 38? | h | m | | IT (b) | SE | | | | | GG | | | | K, *Baronetage* |

| Name | Constituency / Date of election | Category | Date of dissent | Age | Position in family | Marital status | University | Inn | Region | Parliamentary experience | Religion | 1643–5 | 1647 | 1645–8 | Status | Income | Claims against State | Land purchases | Office | Principal sources of information |
|---|---|---|---|---|---|---|---|---|---|---|---|---|---|---|---|---|---|---|---|---|
| TUFTON, Sir Humphrey, Bt. | Maidstone 1640 | S | | 64 | ys | m | O | IT | SE | | P? | P | | | GG | 2? | | | | K |
| TWISDEN, Thomas | Maidstone 1647 | S | | 46 | ys | m | C | IT (b) | SE | | | | | | GG | 3? | | | | DNB |
| UVEDALE, Sir William | Petersfield 1647 | S | | 61? | e | m | O | MT | SE | S, 20, 10 | | | | | CG | 1? | | | | K |
| VACHELL, Tanfield | Reading 1640 | A | | 47? | e | m? | O | L | SE | | | | FA | | LG | 3? | | | | B & P, Foster |
| VALENTINE, Benjamin | St. Germans 1645 | C | 5 Feb. | 50+? | e | m? | | | WB? 20 | | | | | | M? | 3?x | I | | | DNB, K |
| VANE, Sir Henry, Sr. | Wilton 1640 | S | 10 Feb. | 59 | e | m | O | G | SE | S, 20, 10 P? | | W/M | | M? | GG* | 1? | | CK | I | DNB, K |
| VANE, Sir Henry, Jr. | Hull 1640 | C | 1 Feb. | 35 | h | m | O | G | SE | S | I | W | | I | GG* | 1? | | C | I | DNB, K |
| VASSALL, Samuel | London 1640 | S | | 62 | e | m | | | SE | S | | P | SA | P/M? | M | | I | | | DNB, K |
| VAUGHAN, Charles | Honiton 1640 | I | | 60? | e | m | | IT | SW | | | | SA | | LG | | 3 | | | TDA 66 |
| VAUGHAN, Edward | Montgoms. 1646 | I | | 49? | ys | m? | | IT | WB 20 | | | W | SA | | CG | 1? | I | R | 2 | Williams (Wales), Dodd |
| VENN, John | London 1647 | R | 20 Dec. (r) | 62 | ys | m | | | SE | S | | W | SA | I | M | 2? | I | | 2 | DNB, K |
| WADDON, John | Plymouth 1641 | S | | 58 | e | m | O? | | SW | | | | | | M | 2? | | | | K |
| WALKER, Clement | Wells 1640 | I | | 56? | e | m | O? | MT | SW | | P | | SA | P | LG | | I | | 3 | DNB |
| WALLER, Thomas | Bodmin 1646 | S | | 41? | ys | m | | G (b) | SE | | | | | | LG | | | | 3 | VCH Bucks. 3, Pink MSS. 307/162 |
| WALLER, Sir William | Andover 1648 | I | | 51? | e? | m | O | G | SE | | P | W/M | SA | P | CG* | | I | | I | DNB |
| WALLOP, Robert | Andover 1642 | C | Feb.? | 47 | e | m | O | | SE | S, 20 | | W | | | GG | 1 | I | | | DNB, K |
| WALSINGHAM, Sir Thomas | Rochester 1640 | C | 19 Feb. | 54 | e | m | C | | SE | S, 20, 10 P? | | | | | GG* | 1?x | | R | I | K |
| WASTELL, John | Northallerton 1640 | A | 14 May | 55? | e | m | C | G (b) | NE | | | | | | LG | 3 | | C | | K |

(388)

| Name | Constituency | | | Age | | | | | | | | | | | | | | | | References |
|---|---|---|---|---|---|---|---|---|---|---|---|---|---|---|---|---|---|---|---|---|
| WAUTON, Valentine | Hunts. 1640 | R | ? (r) | 54? | c | m | | | E | | I? | | | | LG | 3 | 1 | K | 1 | DNB, K |
| WAYTE, Thomas | Rutland 1646 | R | 1 Feb. (r) | 33? | e | m | | G, IT | E | | | | | | LG | | 2 | R | 2 | DNB |
| WEAVER, Edmund | Hereford 1646 | A | | 37 | e | m | O | | WB | | P? | | FA | | MG | | | | | Williams (H) |
| WEAVER, John | Stamford 1645. | C | 1 Feb. | 39? | e? | m | O | IT | E | | P? | P | FA | I | LG | 3? | 1 | R | 2 | DNB |
| WENMAN, Thomas, Lord | Oxfordshire 1640 | I | | 52 | e | m | O | IT | M | S, 20 | P-I? | P | | | GG | 1 | | R | 3 | DNB, K |
| WENTWORTH, Sir Peter | Tamworth 1641 | C | 6 Apr.[1] | 56 | e | s | O | L | M | | P-I? | W | | I | CG* | 2?x | 1 | R | 1 | DNB, K |
| WEST, Edmund | Bucks. 1645 | C | 22 Feb. | 40 | e? | m | O | IT | SE | | P-I? | | | | LG | 2 | 2 | R | 1 | Foster, VCH Bucks. 3 |
| WESTON, Benjamin | Dover 1641 | C | 2 Feb. | 35? | ys | m | | G | SE | | P? | | FA | | GG | 1 | | R | 2 | K |
| WESTON, Henry | Guildford 1648 | A | 17 Oct. 1651 | 45 | e | m | O | IT | SE | | I | | | I | LG | 3? | | C | | Y, Foster, Pink MSS. 322 |
| WESTROW, Thomas | Hythe 1645 | A | | 32 | e | m | O | | SE | | P? | | SA | | M | 2? | 3 | C | 3 | B & P, Foster |
| WHEELER, William | Westbury 1640 | I | | 47? | e | m | | | SW | | | | | | M? | 3? | 2 | C | 1 | K |
| WHITAKER, Lawrence | Okehampton 1641 | C | 1 Feb. | 70 | e | m | C | MT | SW | 20 | P | P? | FA | M? | LG | 3 | 2 | C | 1 | K |
| WHITE, William | Pontefract 1645 | A | 14 May[1] | ? | e | m | | IT | NE | S, 20 | P | | | M? | M? | 3? | 2 | C | 1 | Note 31 below |
| WHITEHEAD, Richard | Hants. 1640 | S | | 54? | e | m | O | MT | SE | 20 | P-I? | P/M | M | M | GG | 1? | | | | K |
| WHITELOCKE, Bulstrode | Gt. Marlow 1640 | C | 1 Feb. | 43 | e | m | O | MT | SE | 20 | P-I? | P/M | M | | CG* | 1 | 3 | R | 1 | DNB, K |
| WIDDRINGTON, Sir Thomas | Berwick 1640 | C | 1 Feb. | 48 | e | m | C | G | NE | S | | | | | CG | 2? | | C | 3 | DNB, K |
| WILLS, Henry | Saltash 1646 | S | | 50? | | m | | | SW | | | | | | LG | 3? | | | | Courtney, WA 5, Pink MSS. 307/290 |
| WILSON, Rowland | Calne 1646 | C | 1 Feb. | 35 | h | m | C | G | SE | | I | | | I | M | 1? | 1 | | | DNB |
| WINGATE, Edward | St. Albans 1640 | S | | 42 | h | m | C | | SE | | P? | P | SA | | LG | | | | | K |
| WINWOOD, Richard | Windsor 1641 | S | | 39 | e | m | | L | SE | | P? | | | | CG* | 1 | 2 | | | K, Lacey |
| WODEHOUSE, Sir Thomas, Bt. | Thetford 1640 | A | 17 Oct. 1651 | 63 | e | m | C | | E | S | P? | | | | GG | 1 | | | | K, B & P |

[1] See note 1 below.

| Name | Constituency / Date of election | Category | Date of dissent | Age | Position in family | Marital status | University | Inn | Region | Parliamentary experience | Religion | 1643–5 | 1647 | 1645–8 | Status | Income | Claims against State | Land purchases | Office | Principal sources of information |
|---|---|---|---|---|---|---|---|---|---|---|---|---|---|---|---|---|---|---|---|---|
| WOGAN, Thomas | Cardigan 1646 | R | 1 Feb. (r) | 30? | ys | s? | | | WB | | | | FA | | GG | | 2 | | | DNB |
| WOOD, Richard | Anglesey 1646 | A | | 23? | h | s | C | L | WB | | | | | | LG | 2 | | | | Williams (Wales) |
| WORSLEY, Sir Henry, Bt. | Newport, I. of W. 1640 | A | | 35 | e | m | | | SE | S | | | | | GG | 1 | | | | K |
| WRAY, Sir John, Bt. | Lincs. 1640 | A | | 62 | e | m | C | L | E. | 20, 10 | P | | | | GG | 1 | 3 | | | DNB, K |
| WRAY, William | Grimsby 1645 | S | | 23? | e | s | | | E | | | | | | GG | 1? | | | | Note 32 below |
| WROTH, Sir Thomas | Bridgwater 1646 | R | 20 Dec.? | 64 | e | m | O | IT | SW | 20 | P | | | I | CG | 2? | | | | DNB |
| WYLDE, Edmund | Droitwich 1647 | C | 9 Feb. | 30 | e? | s | O | IT (b) | WB | | | | | | CG | 3? | | C | | Williams (Worcs.), Aubrey |
| WYLDE, George | Droitwich 1648 | R | 29 Jan. | 54 | ys | m | O | IT (b) | WB | 20 | | | | | CG | 3? | | C | 1 | Williams (Worcs.) |
| WYLDE, John | Worcs. 1640 | X | 27 June 1651 | | | | | | WB | S, 20, 10 | P? | | | | GG | | | | | DNB |
| WYNN, Sir Richard, Bt. | Liverpool 1640 | S | | 60 | e | m | | L | WB | | | | | | GG | 1 | | | 1 | DNB, K |
| WYNN, Richard | Caerns. 1647 | A | | 28? | e | m | | | WB | | | | | | GG | 1? | | | | Williams (Wales), Baronetage |
| YELVERTON, Sir Christopher, Bt. | Bossiney 1640 | S | | 46? | c | m | C | G | M | 20 | | M | | | GG | 1 | | | | K |
| YONGE, John | Plymouth 1642 | A | | 47? | h | m | O | MT | SW | | | | | | CG | 2? | | | | Alexander, TDA 66 |
| YONGE, Walter | Honiton 1640 | A | | 69 | e | m | O | MT | SW | | | W/M? | | | LG | 3? | | | 1 | DNB, K |

# NOTES TO TABLE

1. Received special permission for late dissent, 28 Feb.: *C.J.* vi. 153.

2. H. E. Nott, ed., *Deposition Books of Bristol*, i (Bristol R.S., vi, 1935), 243-5. This corrects the erroneous identification in Yule, *The Independents*, p. 84.

3. Robert Andrews the M.P. has never been convincingly identified. Yule, *The Independents*, p. 85, confuses him with Ald. Thomas Andrewes of London. Williams, *Parl. Hist. Hereford*, p. 158, advanced some more likely suggestions, but failed to notice that the M.P. was connected with Northants., in which county he several times recommended ministers to livings: B.M. Add. MS. 36792 (Presentations by Cmrs. of Great Seal, 1649-54), fols. 41ᵛ, 71. Andrews also had some interest in the Earl of Northampton's estate: *C.J.* vi. 458-9. He must therefore have been Robert A. of Harleston, Northants. (1605-67), eldest son of Thomas A. (d. 1650), by his wife Dorothy, daughter of Robert Wilmer of Sywell. Robert was admitted to Lincoln College, Oxford, 1623, and to Middle Temple in the same year. He was again M.P. for Weobley in Richard's Parliament 1659; commissioner for assessments and militia in Northants. 1647-60, and for militia in Herefordshire 1659. His father's will suggests modest, but not impressive wealth. W. C. Metcalfe, ed., *Visitations of Northants., 1564 and 1618-19* (London, 1887), pp. 65-6; Peter Whalley, ed., *History and Antiquities of Northamptonshire, Compiled from the Manuscript Collections of John Bridges* (Oxford, 1791), i. 513-15; George Baker, *History and Antiquities of Northants.* (London, 1822-30), i. 168; Foster, *Al. Oxon.* i. 25; Firth and Rait, *A. and O. passim*; Somerset House, 44 Grey: Will of Thos. Andrewe of Harlestone, pr. 28 Mar. 1651 (*P.C.C. Probates, 1650-1*, p. 164).

4. Boate (1589-1650) was active as a shipwright by 1621. He was Clerk of Out Stores at Chatham 1624; Master Assistant Shipwright 1626; commended for his 'diligent and sincere carriage of things'. Besides Chatham, he worked also at Portsmouth, to which port he moved permanently in 1638, becoming a principal officer of the navy yard; he was elected a burgess of Portsmouth at about the same time as his election to Parliament in 1646. Boate married twice: (1) unknown, but a son born *c.* 1609; (2) 1639, Rebecca Holt, widow, of Portsmouth, who survived him. Brunton and Pennington, *Members of the Long Parliament*, p. 32; Pink MSS. 297/302; Richard J. Murrell and Robert East, eds., *Extracts from Records . . . of the Borough of Portsmouth* (Portsmouth, 1884), pp. 124, 359; H.M.C., *Cowper*, i. 176; *C.S.P., Dom., 1625-35, passim; 1649-50*, p. 248; *1652-3*, pp. 308, 564. I am indebted to John Molyneaux for much of this information.

5. Two John Bonds have often been confused, as in *D.N.B.* Matthews, *Calamy Revised*, p. 63, clarifies them, showing that the M.P. was John Bond, Master of Trinity Hall, Cambridge, and Professor of Law at Gresham College; *not* John Bond, member of the Westminster Assembly and Master of the Savoy.

6. Cholmley appears to have been a Carlisle wool merchant. He owned several houses in the town and was allegedly plundered by Royalists during the war, losing over £1,000. He raised both horse and foot for Parliament, was active

during the siege and again in 1648, during which campaign his eldest son was killed and he taken prisoner by the Scots. However, suspicions that he had connived with the Royalists may explain his failure to gain admission to the Rump in July 1649. He was Collector of Customs at Carlisle (his sons also had customs posts), and in 1650 was appointed Sequestration Commissioner for Cumberland. Mayor of Carlisle 1654-5, he died soon afterwards, leaving a widow, Katherine, four small children, and large debts. Bean, *Northern M.P.s*, p. 50; H.M.C., *Eighth Report*, App. I (Chester MSS.), p. 383; *Cal. S.P. Dom., 1656-7*, p. 211; Abbott, *Cromwell*, i. 671-2; B. Nightingale, *The Ejected of 1662 in Cumberland and Westmorland* (Manchester, 1911), i. 619, 633; *C.J.* v. 245; vi. 268; *Cal. C. Comp.*, p. 312; Pink MSS. 299/481.

7. The difficulty of identifying a Welsh William Davies, or Davids, hardly needs emphasizing. Williams, *Parl. Hist. Wales*, p. 53, thinks the M.P. may have been related to John David, sheriff of Carmarthen borough 1645. Among many others of that name, a William D. of Carmarthenshire, pleb., matriculated at Jesus, Oxford, 1615, aged 16: Foster, *Al. Oxon.* i. 384. A Col. William D. served under Essex in 1644: Firth and Davies, *Regimental History*, Intro., p. xv. Another of the name was an alderman of Haverfordwest: Firth and Rait, *A. and O.* ii. 484, 681.

8. Younger son of Thomas E. of Rhual, Baron of the Exchequer in Chester. William a Chester ironmonger and merchant. Common Council 1623; sheriff 1627; alderman 1631; Mayor 1636 and 1646. Married (1617) Frances Leigh of Chester. Leader of Parliamentarians in Chester 1643, installed as Mayor by Brereton after the city's fall. R. H. Morris, *Siege of Chester* (Chester, 1924), pp. 12-13; Groombridge, ed., *Chester Council Minutes*, pp. 83-4, 123-9, 166; H.M.C., *Fifth Report*, Appendix (Cholmondeley MSS.), p. 344; W. F. Irvine, ed., *Marriage Licences Granted within the Archdeaconry of Chester*, ii (R.S. Lancs. and Cheshire, lvi, 1908), 32.

9. Thomas Gell (1594-1656) was the unmarried younger brother of Sir John Gell, the leading Parliamentarian in Derbyshire. He entered Inner Temple 1611, was a bencher 1620, and built up a large practice at the bar. He was Receiver of the Honour of Tutbury 1633-42. In the Civil War he was Lt.-Col. to his brother, Sir John, and Recorder of Derby 1643. *D.N.B.* ('Sir John Gell'); H.M.C., *Ninth Report*, App. II (Chandos-Pole MSS.), pp. 384-95; *N. & Q.*, 8th ser., xii. 401-2.

10. The Gratwicks were a new Sussex family, rising on the profits of the iron industry. Roger was the third son of Sir William G. of Ulverston, Lancs., and Tortington, Sussex, who was granted arms 1607 and died 1613, by his wife Margaret, daughter of William Lee of South Mimms, Herts. Roger married (1) Elizabeth, daughter of Philip Gratwick of Cowfold, Sussex, (2) [Anne?], daughter of John Selwyn of Friston, Sussex. There were other branches of the family in Sussex in Elizabeth I's reign, but Roger bought the manor of Seaford only in 1642; his nephews inherited Tortington. He was evidently more interested in local than in national affairs, being inactive in Parliament, but Bailiff of Seaford four times between 1639 and 1652, and an active Sussex J.P. after 1646. He died 1655. William Berry, *County Genealogies. Pedigrees of the Families in the County of Sussex* (London, 1830), p. 168; E. H. W. Durkin, ed., *Sussex Manors . . . 1509-1833* (Sussex R.S. xix-xx, 1914-15), pp. 196-7, 387; Thomas W. Hors-

field, *History, Antiquities and Topography of the County of Sussex* (Lewes, 1835), ii. 141; Thomas-Stanford, *Sussex in the Civil War*, p. 9; B. C. Redwood, ed., *Quarter Sessions Order Book, 1642–1649* (Sussex R.S. liv, 1954), pp. xxviii, and *passim*; Pink MSS. 302/384.

11. Thomas Grove (*c.* 1609–91) of Ferne House, Wilts., was the son of Robert G. (d. 1642), by his second wife Honor, daughter of Thomas South of Swallowcliffe, Wilts. Thomas was admitted to Middle Temple 1627. He married (1) 1628, Mary, daughter of John Lowe of Salisbury, widow of his cousin John Grove, (2) Elizabeth, daughter of Edward Lambert of Corston, Wilts., widow of Robert Henley of Leigh, Som. He inherited the manors of Sedgehill and Ferne, other properties at Shaftesbury and on the Dorset–Wilts. border. He was J.P. Dorset 1646, and Wilts. 1652. His speeches in 1659 show his strong Presbyterian views; after 1660 he was a great patron of ejected clergy. Brunton and Pennington, *Members of the Long Parliament*, pp. 30–1; *V.C.H., Wilts.* iii. 106; Matthews, *Calamy Revised*, pp. 288, 452, 564; Pink MSS. 302/473. Information provided by Professor B. D. Henning.

12. Robert Harley (1626–73) was Sir Robert's second son. For his early physical (and psychological?) difficulties see above, p. 221. Less stable than his elder brother Edward, by 1657 he had virtually gone over to the Royalists: Underdown, *Royalist Conspiracy*, pp. 221–5.

13. Herbert Hay (1591–1652) was eldest son of John H. of Hurstmonceaux, Sussex, by his wife Mary, daughter of William Morley of Glynde. After his father's death (1605) he was ward to his uncle, Herbert Morley, uncle also of the M.P. of that name, but *not* (as in Yule, *The Independents*, p. 101) the M.P. himself, who was born only in 1616. Hay was admitted to Gray's Inn 1611, and married (1) Frances, daughter of John Culpeper of Follington, (2) 1645, ——? He inherited Glyndebourne 1618 and lived there, bought other manors between 1622 and 1624. Yule's description of him as a Rumper is as erroneous as his account of the family. Keeler, *Long Parliament*, p. 209; *Sussex Arch. Coll.* xx (1868), 64–5; M. A. Lower, *Worthies of Sussex* (Lewes, 1865), p. 236; Durkin, *Sussex Manors*, pp. 32–3, 161–2, 181; Joseph Foster, *Register of Admissions to Gray's Inn, 1521–1889* (London, 1889), p. 125.

14. Luke Hodges of Bristol was third son of John H. of Shipton Moyne, Glos., who died 1598. His success in trade was apparently not sufficient for him to be elected to the Merchant Venturers' Society, but he was a member of Common Council 1635 and sheriff 1638. He owned land at Clapton, Som., 1623, but he (or a son?) was declared not entitled to bear arms in the Visitation of that year. He was removed from Corporation by Royalists in 1643, but restored 1645, and alderman 1646. By this time he held the post of Customer at Bristol. Although often hard to distinguish from his nephew Thomas H., M.P. for Cricklade, it is clear that Luke was interested in commercial affairs, and often included in committees relating to them. He was named an Excise Commissioner in Jan. 1652, left Bristol at about this time, and died at Westminster in 1656. Yule, *The Independents*, p. 103; *Glos. N. & Q.* i (1881), 362, 455; Latimer, *Annals of Bristol in the Seventeenth Century*, pp. 160, 185, 208, 227, 252, 498; F. T. Colby, ed., *Visitation of the County of Somerset in the year 1623* (Harl. Soc. xi, 1876), pp. 139, 145; Bodl. MS. Dep. C. 166 (Nalson Papers, xiv), fol. 219; *C.J.* vi. 137; vii. 63; *P.C.C. Administrations, 1655–60*, ii (British R.S. lxxii, 1952), 48.

15. Of the two Thomas Hodges, the Cricklade M.P. was quite clearly the one admitted to the Rump on 4 June 1649. Both may have been secluded, but *Old Parl. Hist.* xviii. 483, is wrong in listing the Ilchester M.P. among the dissenters to the 5 December vote. The Ilchester member came of a family settled at Wedmore, Som., by the middle of the sixteenth century. He was the eldest son of George (or Thomas?) H. of Wedmore, who died 1634, by his wife Eleanor, daughter of John Rosse of Shepton Beauchamp. He was born *c.* 1607, was admitted to Lincoln's Inn 1629, and was a J.P. 1646. He died unmarried by 3 July 1649. Colby, *Vis. Somerset, 1623*, p. 53; *Records of the Honorable Society of Lincoln's Inn*, i. (1896), 209; Pink MSS. 304/442.

16. George Kekewich (1614–*c.* 1661) was son of William K. of Catchfrench, Cornwall, who died 1634, by his wife Jane, daughter of William Coode of Morval. The family was well established in Cornwall by the mid sixteenth century, and Carew praises the generosity of the M.P.'s grandfather. George K. married (1) 1634, Alice, daughter of Sir Richard Buller of Shillingham, (2) Mary, daughter of Sir Richard Strode, widow of Edward Stockman of Britford, Wilts., and (3) ——, widow of —— Dowse of Wallop, Wilts. Besides his lands in Cornwall, he acquired property in Wiltshire from his second wife. He was a member of the Cornish County Committee, but his career is difficult to disentangle from that of another George K., who was Captain of St. Mawes Castle 1646. Courtney, *Parl. Rep. Cornwall*, p. 253; Vivian, *Vis. Cornwall*, pp. 252, 254; *Parochial History of Cornwall* (Truro, 1867–72), ii. 54; Davies Gilbert, *Parochial History of Cornwall* (London, 1838), ii. 68; C. S. Gilbert, *Historical Survey of the County of Cornwall* (Plymouth, 1817), ii. 171; Coate, *Cornwall in the Civil War*, p. 224, n.

17. The fullest account is in F. Hitchin-Kemp, *General History of the Kemp and Kempe Families* (London, 1902), Pt. iv, pp. 32–3.

18. I am indebted to Professor Henning and to Mr. L. Naylor, for information supplementing and correcting that in G.E.C., *Baronetage*, iii. 246. The Lloyds were an old Carmarthenshire family of middle rank .(sheriffs in the sixteenth century and in 1627). John was the second, but apparently eldest surviving son of Griffith Ll. of The Forest. G.E.C. is wrong on the identity of his mother, who was in fact Jane, daughter of John Wogan of Stonehall, Pembs. Lloyd's Carmarthenshire estates were evidently small, and he lived at Woking Surrey, where his wife had extensive properties. These, however, reverted to her children by her first marriage when they came of age. Lloyd was a Presbyterian elder in Surrey: Shaw, *Church under the Commonwealth*, ii. 434.

19. The two Nelthorpes produce several puzzles, thanks to the existence of - two James and three John N.s at this time. Two branches of the family descended from John N. of Waghan in Holderness, Yorks., yeoman, who died 1580. He had two sons, Richard N. of Scawby, and Edward N. of Beverley, mercer and draper, who was Mayor of the town 1611, and died 1623. James the M.P. was evidently the sixth and youngest son of this Edward, born *c.* 1619, a mercer and grocer, Mayor 1641 and again 1652. He was perhaps in business at Hull by 1645, and may have been a sub-commissioner of Excise. He does not seem to have been a rich man, and his large purchase of Church lands in Mar. 1648 was presumably the collection of a state debt, or was made as agent for someone else. Bean, *Northern M.P.s*, p. 764, and Mark Noble, *Lives of the English Regicides* (London, 1798), ii. 97, are wrong in saying that he was a nephew of Sir John N., Bt.—this

was a different James N. (of London). G. Poulson, *Beverlac . . . Antiquities and History of the Town of Beverley* (London, 1829), i. 299, 403; A. R. Maddison, ed., *Lincolnshire Pedigrees*, ii (Harl. Soc. li, 1903), 702–3; George Oliver, *History and Antiquities of . . . Beverley* (Beverley, 1829), p. 394; Dennett, ed., *Beverley Borough Records*, p. 103; Wildridge, ed., *Hull Letters*, pp. 52–60; *Coll. Top. & Gen.* i (1834), 7.

20. John Nelthorpe is more difficult to identify. There are two possibilities: John N. of Little Grimsby, elder brother of James the M.P., and his cousin John of Glandford Brigg, Lincs., younger son of Richard N. of Scawby. Both were born 1615, both educated at Glandford Brigg by a Mr. Osgodby, both admitted to St. John's, Cambridge, 30 Apr. 1631, and both admitted to Gray's Inn in Nov. 1634, within a week of each other (Venn, *Al. Cantab.*, Pt. I, iii. 242). The Glandford Brigg J.N. pursued a legal career: called to the bar 1641, Register in Chancery 1647, Ancient of his Inn 1658, created Baronet 1666. He might possibly be identical with the J.N. who was a captain in Rossiter's regiment 1645, and Adjutant-General in the 1650s. However, I think that the lawyer and the soldier were two different men: that J.N. of Glandford Brigg, the lawyer, was the M.P., and his cousin of Little Grimsby the soldier. It seems unlikely (*a*) that a secluded member would have continued to serve as an army officer, and (*b*) that a soldier on active service could have pursued so obviously successful a legal career as the barrister. (The Adjutant-General is described as of Gray's Inn in 1652, but as both cousins attended the Inn this is not conclusive). One or both J.N.s made extensive purchases of Church and Crown lands: I am inclined to think it was the lawyer. To compound the confusion, Professor Caroline Robbins assures me that in the Thompson MSS. at Beverley it is James, not John, who is referred to as Adjutant-General, contrary to *C.J.* vii. 246; *Cal. C. Comp.*, p. 2356; *Cal. S.P. Dom., 1655–6*, p. 175, etc. In addition to refs. above and under James N., see Firth and Davies, *Regimental History*, pp. 159, 164, 194–5; Fletcher, ed., *Pension Book of Gray's Inn*, pp. 342, 423; S. J. Madge, *Domesday of Crown Lands* (London, 1938), pp. 243, 386–95; *Coll. Top. & Gen.* i (1834), 126; and Pink MSS. 322.

21. William Owfield or Oldfield (1624?–64), was son of Sir Samuel O., M.P. for Gatton 1640, who was in turn son of a London fishmonger. Samuel's fortune in 1611 amounted to £22,000, and between 1620 and 1635 he bought manors in Lincs. (Elsham), and Surrey (Chipstead and Upper Gatton). William matriculated at Emmanuel, Cambridge, 1639, and married Mary, daughter of Maurice Thompson. Although apparently not very active as an M.P., he was a member of the Lincs. County Committee 1645, and on other local commissions in both Lincs. and Surrey. He was an elder of the Reigate classis. Keeler, *Long Parliament*, pp. 291–2; *V.C.H., Surrey*, iii. 191, 199; Shaw, *Church under the Commonwealth*, ii. 434; Pink MSS. 322. Information from Professor B. D. Henning.

22. See Dorothy Gardiner, ed., *The Oxinden Letters, 1607–1642* (London, 1933); and *The Oxinden and Peyton Letters, 1642–1670* (London, 1937); also Everitt, *Community of Kent*, pp. 47, 121, 153.

23. John Penrose (1611–52) came of a family long established at Penrose, near Helston, Cornwall. He was eldest son of John P. (died 1617), by his wife Jane, daughter of John Trefusis of Milor. He was admitted to Lincoln's Inn 1632, and

married Amy, daughter of Sir Anthony Baggs. The Penrose estates were estimated as being worth £1,000 p.a. in 1660. In spite of his abstention from Parliament after the Purge he served as a militia captain in 1650, and was still named to
assessment commissions. Courtney, *Parl. Rep. Cornwall*, p. 46; Vivian, *Vis.
Cornwall*, p. 367; Davies Gilbert, *Parochial Hist. Cornwall*, iii. 443-5; R. Pol-
whele, *History of Cornwall* (London, 1816), iv. 102, n.; *Cal. S.P. Dom., 1649-50*,
p. 521; Firth and Rait, *A. and O.* ii, *passim*.

24. For the fullest account see A. C. Wood, 'Colonel Sir Edward Rossiter',
*Repts. and Papers of Assoc. Architectural Socs.*, xli, Pt. ii (1933), 219-35.

25. Mrs. Keeler's preference for Thomas S. of Little Pattensham among the
three possible men of that name (*Long Parliament*, p. 333), is confirmed by a letter
from Thomas S. to his friend Bulstrode Whitelocke, 6 Mar. 1648, dated at Middle
Temple: B.M. Add. MS. 37344 (Whitelocke's Annals), fols. 136-7. Sandys
was admitted to Middle Temple 1617, called to the bar 1625, bencher 1648:
J. B. Williamson, ed., *Middle Temple Bench Book*, 2nd ed. (London, 1937),
p. 117.

26. Scot's later career is well known, but his origins remain obscure. Part of
the trouble seems to stem from the existence of another Thomas S., M.P. for
Aldborough, who died 6 Jan. 1648: see Brunton and Pennington, *Members of the
Long Parliament*, p. 35. The latter was evidently a Yorkshireman, which may
perhaps account for the Mauleverer marriage noted by Yule, *The Independents*,
p. 117. The Aylesbury M.P. was in fact the son of Thomas S. of London, and
Mary, daughter of — Sutton. He attended Westminster School and possibly
Cambridge, and was living at Little Marlow, Bucks., by 1634. He was a local
attorney at Aylesbury (later Recorder), refused to contribute to musters in 1639,
and became Treasurer to the Bucks. County Committee 1644. He married
(1) Alice, daughter of William Allanson of London, and (2) a daughter of Sir John
Packington (?). The family came originally from Essex, but it is interesting to
note that a Thomas Scott was M.P. for Aylesbury in 1596. *D.N.B.*; W. H. Rylands,
ed., *Visitation of Bucks., 1634* (Harl. Soc. lviii, 1909), p. 111; Johnson, 'Buckinghamshire', ch. iii; Venn, *Al. Cantab.* Pt. I, iv. 33; Pink MSS. 307/73.

27. Robert Shapcote (1620-after 1682) was from the junior branch of an old
lesser gentry family, which by the seventeenth century had been reduced to only
small estates. He was the eldest son of Henry S. of Bradninch (died 1632), by his
wife Wilmot, daughter of — Hill. He was admitted to Lincoln's Inn 1638, called
to the bar 1645, Recorder of Tiverton, Bradninch and South Molton 1647.
He served as a colonel 1644-6. He inherited a small estate worth £80 p.a., but
most of his income must have been from his legal practice. He was a member of
the Devon County Committee, J.P. 1647, sheriff 1654. M.P. for Tiverton 1654 and
1656. Alleged to have made Royalist speeches 1654, his denials must have been
convincing, as he became a strong Cromwellian, Solicitor-General and Attorney-
General in Ireland from 1657. E. S. Chalk, 'Notes on the Members for Tiverton',
*Trans. Devon Assoc.* lxvii (1935), 324; *Lincoln's Inn Records*, i. 237; ii. 366-7;
*Cal. S.P. Dom., 1654*, pp. 279-80; H.M.C., *Seventh Report*, Appendix (House of
Lords MSS.), p. 78. I am grateful to Professor Henning and John Ferris for letting
me consult their notes on Shapcote for the History of Parliament.

28. Keeler, *Long Parliament*, p. 339, says that he died in 1650; but the statement in J. Harland, ed., *House and Farm Accounts of the Shuttleworths* (Chetham

Soc. xxxv–xlvi, 1856–8), ii. 274, that he was buried 21 Jan. 1648/9, seems convincing.

29. I can find no evidence to support the two suggestions made rather obscurely by Yule, *The Independents*, p. 118, that George Snelling was either of Chadlewood, Devon (son of John S.), or of Thistleworth, Middlesex (son of George S. of Kingston, Surrey). For these two, see H. A. C. Sturgess, ed., *Register of Admissions to the Honourable Society of the Middle Temple* (London, 1949), i. 120; and W. B. Bannerman, ed., *Visitations of Surrey* (Harl. Soc. xliii, 1899), pp. 161, 167. Instead it seems much more likely the M.P. was a local Southwark man, possibly a brewer. He is described as of St. Olave's, Southwark, at his death 1651: Somerset House, Administrations Acts Book, 1651, fol. 160 (*P.C.C. Admins.* i. 342). There were many other Snellings in Southwark earlier in the century, including a George S. who witnessed the will of Arthur Mott, brewer, 1603: *Index of Wills Proved in the Prerogative Court of Canterbury* (British R.S.), iv. 388; v. 417; vi. 255; *Surrey Wills* (Surrey R.S. iv, 1915–20), pp. 191, 201. Inspection of the originals unfortunately reveals no conclusive trace of the M.P. A George S. was Collector for the Poor in Lambeth 1620–1: C. Drew, ed., *Lambeth Churchwardens' Accounts, 1504–1645* (Surrey R.S. xviii, xx, 1941–50), ii. 13. The M.P. is described as a 'strong-water-man' in *Returne of the People of England* (14 Nov. 1648: [B.M.] E. 472, 7), p. 1. His interest in commercial policy, especially as it affected the brewing trade, is evident. He was named to the Excise committee 5 Jan. 1648, to a committee on the price of ale and beer 5 Sept. 1649, and was made an Excise Commissioner in 1650: *L.J.* ix. 639; *C.J.* vi. 290, 443. He was a Presbyterian elder in his own parish, St. Olave's: Shaw, *Church under the Commonwealth*, ii. 403.

30. John Stephens is wrongly identified in Williams, *Parl. Hist. Glos.*, p. 58, as the son of Edward S., the other Tewkesbury M.P., a suggestion which I mistakenly followed in *J.B.S.* iii (1964), 75. However, Edward's son John was dead by 12 Feb. 1651, and therefore cannot have been the M.P., who was active long after this date: C. H. Hopwood *et al.*, ed., *Middle Temple Records* (London, 1904–5), iii. 1025, 1043. The M.P. was in fact Edward's younger brother, John Stephens (1603–79), of Upper Lypiatt, Glos., second son of Thomas S. (died 1613). He was admitted to Middle Temple 1620, called to the bar 1628, bencher 1650, and Serjeant-at-law 1675: ibid. ii. 650, 733; iii. 1020, 1289. In other respects Williams's account is acceptable.

31. William White was the son of another William W., of Duffield, Derbyshire. He acquired an estate at Bashall, Yorks., by his marriage to Margaret, daughter of Thomas Talbot; the estate was worth £332 p.a. in 1620, but White improved it to £500 p.a. by 1649. In that year he married again, to Francisca, daughter of Sir Edward Barkham of Surrey. White was a clerk in the Court of Wards, was perhaps a lieutenant in the Earl of Stamford's regiment 1642, but was thenceforth a client of the Fairfaxes: agent to Lord Fairfax, Colonel, and Treasurer-at-War for the Northern Army. He was Clerk of Assize in the Oxford circuit 1643–6, and later held the same office in the Northern circuit; his admission to the Inner Temple, however, occurred only after the war, in 1646–7. Apart from his connection with the Fairfaxes, White was not a man of great prominence or influence. Pink MSS. 322; Bodl. MS. Dep. C. 165 (Nalson Papers, xiii), fol. 388; *Holles Memoirs*, in Maseres, *Tracts*, i. 268; *Students Admitted to the Inner*

*Temple* (London, 1877), p. 323; Bell, *Memorials*, i. 41–2, 158, 183, 318–19, 341–2, 376. I am indebted to Donald Pennington and to J. T. Cliffe for further information.

32. The best account of the Wray family is in Charles Dalton, *History of the Wrays of Glentworth* (London and Aberdeen, 1880–1). See vol. ii. 65–82, for William Wray.

# APPENDIX B

## STATISTICAL TABLES

THE tables are based on the information summarized in Appendix A. Actual numbers are given rather than percentages for a number of reasons. A table that gives only percentages can be misleading; one that gives both percentages and actual numbers is likely to be too crowded with detail; while to give both in separate tables would double the length of this appendix. However, the reader will have no difficulty in translating the figures into percentages (as I have often done in Chapter VIII, above), applying the Chi-square test, or doing whatever else his mathematical proficiency permits.

Before approaching the tables, it may be convenient to recall the numbers of M.P.s in each category (p. 220, above):

R: 71.   C: 83.   A: 86.   S: 186.   I: 45.

### TABLE I. AGE

See above, pp. 224–5.

(a) *Median and average ages*

| Group | Median | Average. |
|---|---|---|
| R | 45 | 45·4 |
| C | 47 | 45·8 |
| A | 45/6 | 44·6 |
| S | 46 | 44 |
| I | 48 | 49·1 |
| All M.P.s | 46 | 45·3 |

(b) *Age distribution of the members*

| Group | 21–30 | 31–40 | 41–50 | 51–60 | Over 60 | Unknown |
|---|---|---|---|---|---|---|
| R | 6 | 16 | 25 | 14 | 8 | 2 |
| C | 9 | 21 | 21 | 24 | 8 | 0 |
| A | 9 | 25 | 18 | 24 | 6 | 4 |
| S | 32 | 41 | 45 | 45 | 19 | 4 |
| I | 3 | 6 | 18 | 9 | 9 | 0 |
| All M.P.s | 59 | 109 | 127 | 116 | 50 | 10 |

## TABLE II. POSITION IN FAMILY

See above, pp. 225-6.

| Group | Eldest sons who had inherited | Heirs with fathers living | Younger sons | Unknown |
|---|---|---|---|---|
| R | 40 | 4 | 19 | 8 |
| C | 43 | 10 | 21 | 9 |
| A | 56 | 12 | 10 | 8 |
| S | 99 | 32 | 39 | 16 |
| I | 24 | 6 | 11 | 4 |
| Totals | 262 | 64 | 100 | 45 |

## TABLE III. MARITAL STATUS

See above, p. 226.

| Group | Married | Single | Unknown |
|---|---|---|---|
| R | 60 | 8 | 3 |
| C | 75 | 6 | 2 |
| A | 82 | 4 | 0 |
| S | 153 | 26 | 7 |
| I | 40 | 5 | 0 |
| Totals | 410 | 49 | 12 |

## TABLE IV. EDUCATION

See above, pp. 226-8. A few members attended both Oxford and Cambridge, or were entered at more than one Inn. In such cases only the institution of prior attendance is counted.

(a) *Type of education*

| Group | Attended University | Attended Inn | Both | Neither |
|-------|---------------------|--------------|------|---------|
| R | 34 | 43 | 28 | 22 |
| C | 45 | 52 | 36 | 22 |
| A | 49 | 54 | 43 | 26 |
| S | 103 | 118 | 79 | 44 |
| I | 29 | 32 | 27 | 11 |
| Totals | 260 | 299 | 213 | 125 |

(b) *Institutions compared*

| Group | Oxford | Cambridge | Other[1] Univ. | Gray's | I. Temple | Lincoln's | M. Temple |
|-------|--------|-----------|----------------|--------|-----------|-----------|-----------|
| R | 19 | 15 | 0 | 17 | 10 | 10 | 6 |
| C | 28 | 17 | 0 | 17 | 12 | 6 | 17 |
| A | 24 | 24 | 1 | 16 | 9 | 18 | 11 |
| S | 58 | 44 | 1 | 29 | 21 | 34 | 34 |
| I | 17 | 12 | 0 | 8 | 5 | 7 | 12 |
| Totals | 146 | 112 | 2 | 87 | 57 | 75 | 80 |

[1] Erisey (A) attended Leyden University; Sir John Temple (S) went to Trinity College, Dublin. Rous (C) also attended Leyden, but has been counted under Oxford, the university of prior attendance.

## TABLE V. REGION

See above, pp. 228-9, 362.

| Group | NW | NE | M | E | SE | SI | SW | WB |
|-------|----|----|----|----|----|----|----|----|
| R | 2 | 12 | 8 | 8 | 25 | 0 | 11 | 5 |
| C | 0 | 8 | 7 | 11 | 27 | 0 | 21 | 9 |
| A | 5 | 9 | 14 | 12 | 18 | 0 | 17 | 11 |
| S | 7 | 6 | 16 | 19 | 56 | 3 | 47 | 32 |
| I | 0 | 1 | 9 | 3 | 15 | 1 | 8 | 8 |
| Totals | 14 | 36 | 54 | 53 | 141 | 4 | 104 | 65 |

## TABLE VI. LAWYERS

See above, pp. 229-30.

| Group | Lawyers |
|-------|---------|
| R | 14 |
| C | 20 |
| A | 11 |
| S | 34 |
| I | 9 |
| Total | 88 |

## TABLE VII. PARLIAMENTARY EXPERIENCE

See above, p. 230.

| Group | Original Long Parl. M.P.s | Re-cruiters | Short Parl. | 1621-9 Parls. | Before 1620 | Any pre-Long P. | None |
|-------|------|------|------|------|------|------|------|
| R | 28 | 43 | 18 | 13 | 2 | 23 | 48 |
| C | 45 | 38 | 23 | 17 | 2 | 30 | 53 |
| A | 35 | 51 | 17 | 9 | 1 | 21 | 65 |
| S | 88 | 98 | 53 | 40 | 8 | 69 | 117 |
| I | 29 | 16 | 22 | 17 | 2 | 26 | 19 |
| Totals | 225 | 246 | 133 | 96 | 15 | 169 | 302 |

## TABLE VIII. EARLIER POLITICAL BEHAVIOUR

See above, pp. 230-3.

(a) *Party records of Dec. 1648 M.P.s* (in both the 1643-5 and 1645-8 sections a few members are included in more than one column, because of their tendency to fluctuate between the middle group and one of the other parties).

| Group | 1643-5 | | | 1647 | | 1645-8 | | |
|-------|-------|--------|-----|-----------------------|--------------|--------|--------|------|
|       | Peace | Middle | War | Speaker's Absence | Fled to Army | Presb. | Middle | Ind. |
| R     | 2     | 3      | 15  | 4                     | 30           | 0      | 3      | 32   |
| C     | 3     | 6      | 12  | 6                     | 29           | 0      | 4      | 24   |
| A     | 3     | 3      | 3   | 7                     | 18           | 0      | 12     | 6    |
| S     | 15    | 11     | 4   | 32                    | 2            | 27     | 9      | 2    |
| I     | 10    | 11     | 2   | 25                    | 1            | 24     | 8      | 0    |
| Totals | 33   | 34     | 36  | 74                    | 80           | 51     | 36     | 64   |

(b) *Presbyterians and Independents* (consolidation of 1647 and 1645-8 columns above, regarding 1645-8 middle group and M.P.s who fled to Army as Independents; M.P.s present during Speaker's absence as Presbyterians unless this is contradicted by other evidence).

| Group | Presbyterians | Independents |
|-------|---------------|--------------|
| R     | 1             | 42           |
| C     | 2             | 43           |
| A     | 5             | 27           |
| S     | 42            | 10           |
| I     | 30            | 7            |
| Totals | 80           | 129          |

TABLE IX. RELIGION

See above, pp. 233-6.

(a) *Dec. 1648 M.P.s*

| Group | Sectaries | Inds. | Presb.-Inds. | Presbs. | Unknown |
|-------|-----------|-------|--------------|---------|---------|
| R | 10 | 19 | 8 | 9 | 25 |
| C | 2 | 12 | 7 | 23 | 39 |
| A | 2 | 7 | 3 | 36 | 38 |
| S | 0 | 0 | 0 | 75 | 111 |
| I | 0 | 1 | 0 | 35 | 9 |
| Totals | 14 | 39 | 18 | 178 | 222 |

(b) *Rumpers*

| Group | Sectaries & Inds. | Presb.-Inds. | Presbs. | Unknown |
|-------|-------------------|--------------|---------|---------|
| R | 29 | 8 | 9 | 25 |
| C | 14 | 7 | 24 | 38 |
| Others[1] | 12 | 3 | 22 | 21 |
| Totals | 55 | 18 | 55 | 85 |

[1] This category includes those of the A and S groups who were admitted to the Rump, the three 1648 absentees who were admitted (St. John, Walter Strickland, and John Wylde), and nine new members elected during the Rump period: Robert Bennet; Thomas Birch; William Cecil, Earl of Salisbury; Philip Herbert, fourth Earl of Pembroke; Edward, Lord Howard of Escrick; Philip Jones; Henry Nevill; Carew Raleigh; and Nathaniel Rich.

## TABLE X. STATUS

See above, pp. 236-8.

(a) *County and borough members*

| Group | English county | All county | Others |
|-------|---------------|-----------|--------|
| R | 10 | 11 | 60 |
| C | 10 | 10 | 73 |
| A | 17 | 19 | 67 |
| S | 30 | 38 | 148 |
| I | 7 | 8 | 37 |
| Totals | 74 | 86 | 385 |

(b) *Status distribution of the members*

| Group | Greater gentry | County gentry | Lesser gentry | Merchant gentry | Merchants |
|-------|---------------|--------------|--------------|----------------|-----------|
| R | 15 | 22 | 20 | 2 | 12 |
| C | 23 | 12 | 28 | 2 | 18 |
| A | 30 | 16 | 28 | 3 | 9 |
| S | 76 | 49 | 35 | 9 | 17 |
| I | 13 | 16 | 11 | 2 | 3 |
| Totals | 157 | 115 | 122 | 18 | 59 |

## TABLE XA. SECURE, ESTABLISHED FAMILIES AND OTHERS

See above, pp. 238-9.

| Group | Secure/established | Others |
|-------|-------------------|--------|
| R | 25 | 46 |
| C | 24 | 59 |
| A | 39 | 47 |
| S | 102 | 84 |
| I | 19 | 26 |
| Totals | 209 | 262 |

D d

## TABLE XI. INCOME

See above, pp. 241-3.

| Group | Over £1000 p.a. | £500–1000 p.a. | Under £500 p.a. | Unknown |
|-------|-----------------|-----------------|------------------|---------|
| R | 14 | 13 | 25 | 19 |
| C | 28 | 8 | 26 | 21 |
| A | 30 | 10 | 17 | 29 |
| S | 69 | 32 | 36 | 49 |
| I | 19 | 9 | 6 | 11 |
| Totals | 160 | 72 | 110 | 129 |

## TABLE XII. PRE-WAR DEBT

See above, pp. 243-5.

| Group | Serious pre-war debt | Total in group |
|-------|----------------------|-----------------|
| R | 12 | 71 |
| C | 10 | 83 |
| A | 4 | 86 |
| S | 15 | 186 |
| I | 1 | 45 |
| Totals | 42 | 471 |

### TABLE XIII. CLAIMS AGAINST THE STATE

See above, pp. 245–8.

| Group | Claims of over £1,000 | Below £1,000, other than Irish Adv. | Irish Adv. only | All claims |
|---|---|---|---|---|
| R | 28 | 6 | 3 | 37 |
| C | 19 | 5 | 18 | 42 |
| A | 8 | 9 | 10 | 27 |
| S | 19 | 8 | 14 | 41 |
| I | 12 | 2 | 8 | 22 |
| Totals | 86 | 30 | 53 | 169 |

### TABLE XIV: PURCHASERS OF CONFISCATED LANDS

See above, pp. 248–50.

| Group | Church lands | Crown lands | Royalist lands | All purchasers |
|---|---|---|---|---|
| R | 30 | 22 | 23 | 46 |
| C | 30 | 8 | 26 | 44 |
| A | 11 | 3 | 7 | 17[1] |
| S | 14 | 3 | 9 | 22[2] |
| I | 3 | 0 | 2 | 5 |
| Totals | 88 | 36 | 67 | 134 |

[1] Of the 18 A's who bought lands, 11 were Rumpers.
[2] Of the 21 S's who bought lands, 5 were Rumpers.

## TABLE XV. OFFICE

See above, pp. 250–3.

| Group | Office throughout | Obtained office | Lost office |
|---|---|---|---|
| R | 18 | 12 | 1 |
| C | 21 | 11 | 1 |
| A[1] | 9 | 5 | 3 |
| S[2] | 9 | 1 | 6 |
| I[3] | 5 | 1 | 5 |
| Totals | 62 | 30 | 16 |

[1] Of the 9 A's who kept their offices after December 1648, 5 were Rumpers. Of the 5 who obtained offices after 1648, 4 were Rumpers.

[2] The S who obtained office after 1648 (Nathaniel Bacon) was a Rumper.

[3] The I who obtained office after 1648 was Edward Vaughan (Sequestration Commissioner in Montgomeryshire).

# INDEX

*Note.* The names printed in italics are those of M.P.s in December 1648. For these and all other M.P.s at that time see also Appendix A.